C++ Program Design

An Introduction to Programming and Object-Oriented Design

Third Edition

James P. Cohoon
University of Virginia

Jack W. Davidson
University of Virginia

Boston   Burr Ridge, IL   Dubuque, IA   Madison, WI   New York   San Francisco   St. Louis
Bangkok   Bogotá   Caracas   Kuala Lumpur   Lisbon   London   Madrid   Mexico City
Milan   Montreal   New Delhi   Santiago   Seoul   Singapore   Sydney   Taipei   Toronto

McGraw-Hill Higher Education

*A Division of The **McGraw-Hill** Companies*

C++ PROGRAM DESIGN: AN INTRODUCTION TO PROGRAMMING
AND OBJECT-ORIENTED DESIGN, THIRD EDTION

Published by McGraw-Hill, a business unit of The McGraw-Hill Companies, Inc., 1221 Avenue of the
Americas, New York, NY 10020. Copyright © 2002, 1999, 1997 by The McGraw-Hill Companies, Inc. All
rights reserved. No part of this publication may be reproduced or distributed in any form or by any means, or
stored in a database or retrieval system, without the prior written consent of The McGraw-Hill Companies, Inc.,
including, but not limited to, in any network or other electronic storage or transmission, or broadcast for distance learning.

Some ancillaries, including electronic and print components, may not be available to customers outside the
United States.

This book is printed on acid-free paper.

1 2 3 4 5 6 7 8 9 0 DOC/DOC 0 9 8 7 6 5 4 3 2 1

ISBN 0–07–241163–5
ISBN 0–07–112182–X (ISE)

General manager: *Thomas E. Casson*
Publisher: *Elizabeth A. Jones*
Senior developmental editor: *Kelley Butcher*
Executive marketing manager: *John Wannemacher*
Senior project manager: *Kay J. Brimeyer*
Production supervisor: *Enboge Chong*
Coordinator of freelance design: *David W. Hash*
Cover illustration: *Paul D. Turnbaugh*
Cover design: *Z Graphics*
Senior photo research coordinator: *Lori Hancock*
Supplement producer: *Sandra M. Schnee*
Media technology senior producer: *Phillip Meek*
Compositor: *Interactive Composition Corporation*
Typeface: *10/12 Times Roman*
Printer: *R. R. Donnelley & Sons Company/Crawfordsville, IN*

Library of Congress Cataloging-in-Publication Data

Cohoon, James P.
    C++ program design : an introduction to programming and object-oriented design /
James P. Cohoon, Jack W. Davidson.—3rd ed.
    p.   cm.
    Includes index.
    ISBN 0–07–241163–5
    1. C++ (Computer program language) 2. Object-oriented programming (Computer
science) I. Davidson, Jack W. (Jack Winfred) II. Title.

QA76.73.C153 C653   2002
005.13′3—dc21   2001030617
                                                            CIP

INTERNATIONAL EDITION ISBN 0–07–112182–X
Copyright © 2002. Exclusive rights by The McGraw-Hill Companies, Inc., for manufacture and export. This
book cannot be re-exported from the country to which it is sold by McGraw-Hill.
The International Edition is not available in North America.

www.mhhe.com

Dedicated to:

To Audrey and Joanne, our parents, families, and teachers from whom we have learned so much and owe our gratitude.

Preface

INTRODUCTION

Computers are an inescapable fixture in our lives. They control complex systems such as financial networks, mass transit, telephone systems, and power plants. Tens of millions of people use the Internet to access information, shop, recreate, communicate, and conduct business. Because the computer has become such an intrinsic component of modern life, we believe that everyone should have a basic working knowledge of how computers are programmed.

This textbook is about the fundamentals of programming and software development using C++, a popular high-level programming language developed by Bjarne Stroustrup of AT&T Bell Laboratories. We chose C++ for teaching programming because it supports the development of software using the object-oriented approach. An advantage of object-oriented development is that it lets us build complex software systems employing many of the techniques that have been used for constructing complex physical systems, such as cars, airplanes, or buildings. This book is targeted for a first programming course, and it has been designed to be appropriate for people from all disciplines. We assume no prior programming skills and use mathematics and science at a level appropriate to first-year college students.

Some of this book's important features are

- *The C++ standard is given broad coverage*. Our original naive intent was to offer complete coverage of C++. However, such a presentation would be overwhelming for the beginning student. For example, the language definition describes more than 150 standard classes and libraries. Rather than being encyclopedic, we provide in-depth coverage of all materials that an introductory course would need, introduce much of the remaining material, and give pointers to the rest. We also provide integrated coverage of the important additions and modifications to the C++ language, such as type **bool**, Standard Template Library, namespaces, and exceptions. The breadth of our coverage provides flexibility for the instructor. For example, an instructor may choose not to cover inheritance, but instead to cover templates. For the students, the coverage allows advanced learners to go further in the language, and it makes the book valuable as a reference source.

■ *Classes are introduced early.* Chapter 1 includes a gentle introduction to the object-oriented paradigm. Material is presented there to whet students' appetites. We believe that students must first be client users of objects before they can appreciate the difficulties of designing flexible, usable objects. All proficient designers started as users. The next several chapters introduce and use some standard stream class objects, such as `cout` and `cin`, `string` objects using the Standard Template Library, and a limited number of objects derived from a graphical library developed for the textbook. This experience helps reinforce the concepts of encapsulation, software reuse, and the object-oriented programming paradigm. After this solid introduction to the use of objects, we present approximately 50 classes and ADTs over the final eight chapters.

■ *We present the use of a graphical Application Programmer Interface (API) designed specifically for beginning programmers to develop interesting programs.* We provide a portable, object-oriented graphical library, named EzWindows, for the easy display of simple geometric, bitmap, and text objects. We supply implementations of the API for popular Windows and UNIX compilers. Using the API provides several important experiences for the student. First, students are client users of a software library. As mentioned earlier, using well-designed objects helps novice programmers begin to appreciate good object-oriented design. Their experience as users forms the basis for becoming designers. Second, using the API introduces students to the real-world practice of developing programs using an application-specific library. Third, using EzWindows to perform graphical input and output exposes the student to event-based programming and the dominant mode of input and output used in real applications, and it permits development of exciting and visually interesting programs. This experience motivates the students, and it provides a visually concrete set of objects that help students understand the object-oriented paradigm. EzWindows is simple enough to allow even the first programming assignments to be graphical. Examples using EzWindows are sprinkled throughout the text. However, the presentation is done in a fashion that accommodates instructors who prefer to cover only ANSI materials. For students and instructors who want more advanced graphic capabilities, see Appendix E, which is a complete EzWindows reference. For sample assignments and supplementary materials, visit our Web sites `http://www.mhhe.com/c++programdesign` and `http://www.cplusplus-programdesign.com`.

■ *Software-engineering design concepts are introduced via problem studies and software projects.* Besides containing numerous small examples for introducing C++ and object-oriented design concepts, each chapter considers one or more problems in detail. As appropriate, there are object-oriented analysis and design, algorithm development, and code to realize the design. In addition, two chapters are devoted to the principles of software project development using our EzWindows API (Chapters 10 and 15). These chapters are springboards for software reuse and for projects suitable for individual and group work.

■ *Programming and style tips are presented in boxes that clearly separate this material from the main text.* In addition to explaining C++ and object-oriented programming, we also give advice on how to be a better and more knowledgeable programmer and designer. For example, there are important tips on avoiding common programming errors, writing readable code, and understanding the new directions the standard took, as well as tips on performance and software engineering. Boxes also present one or two pages per chapter of historical information on computing.

■ *Integrated use of the Standard Template Library.* An important component of the C++ language is its Standard Template Library, or as it is more commonly known, the STL. This library provides a rich collection of container classes for representing lists and strings and a set of generic algorithms for important programming tasks such as sorting, searching, and list traversal. Readers first encounter the STL in Chapter 3 when we introduce the string class. In subsequent chapters, additional features are introduced. In particular, Chapter 9 thoroughly explores list representation using the STL's vector container class, and Chapters 11 and 14 give insight on how the STL container classes can be implemented and use their generic algorithms to solve several common programming tasks.

THIRD EDITION HIGHLIGHTS

This third edition incorporates many of the suggestions we have received from both instructors and students. Some of the notable improvements and additions in this edition are:

■ *Self-check questions.* At appropriate points in each chapter there are self-check questions that students can use to check their mastery of the material. The self-check questions are in addition to the exercises at the end of the chapter. The solutions to the self-check questions are available at our Web sites www.mhhe.com/c++programdesign and www.cplusplus-programdesign.com. The self-check questions include both short answer questions as well as programming exercises.

■ *Earlier coverage of classes.* The material on classes is now covered a chapter earlier (Chapter 7). This change reflects the growing consensus that early coverage of classes is possible and the right approach for teaching object-oriented programming using C++.

■ *Coverage of testing and debugging.* An important skill for programmers is how to test and debug the programs they write. Previous editions of the text did not cover this important topic. Chapter 12 provides an introduction to testing and debugging. The chapter discusses various testing techniques such as unit testing, integration testing, and code inspections. The sections on debugging focus on teaching students how to use the scientific method to find bugs. The chapter also discusses common bugs encountered by beginning programmers and how to recognize them.

- *Improved explanations.* The entire text has been reexamined and, based on our own analysis and user feedback, additional examples have been inserted, clarifying figures have been created, and, as appropriate, explanations have been revised and expanded.

CONTEXT

In the early 1990s, with the support of the National Science Foundation, the Department of Computer Science at the University of Virginia began developing a new computer science curriculum. We carefully examined our existing curriculum and those of several other peer schools.

What we found were curricula that emphasized the following:

- Use of a programming language that is rarely used outside of undergraduate courses.
- Construction of small programs, consisting of at most a few hundred lines.
- Development in isolation of text-based programs "from scratch" for each assignment.
- Development in an environment lacking modern tools.
- An informal development with the belief that if a program "works," it is acceptable.

Comparing this situation with the real world, we saw considerable differences. Practicing computer professionals:

- Use programming languages designed for developing large applications that are often thousands or even millions of source lines long.
- Are involved most often in modifying and maintaining such systems rather than in developing them.
- Work in teams, not as single programmers.
- Do system development according to mandated specifications.
- Build systems that use graphical user interfaces to do input and output.
- Use existing libraries and tools to build systems.

To better prepare our students for real-world programming, we developed the first edition of this book. This third edition reflects feedback we have received from both instructors and students as well as our own experience using the book in large introductory programming courses and in a second course on programming and software engineering.

Programming

Most of the important concepts and problems in computer science cannot be appreciated unless one has a good understanding of what a program is and how to write one. Unfortunately, learning to program is difficult. Programming well, like writing well, takes years of practice. In fact, teaching programming and teaching writing are, in some respects, very similar.

Students are taught writing by reading examples of good prose and by writing, writing, writing. In the process, they learn the important skill of how to organize ideas so they can be presented effectively. As students develop their skills, they move from writing and editing a paragraph or several paragraphs to creating larger pieces of prose, such as essays, short stories, and reports.

Our approach to teaching programming is similar to teaching writing but with one very important addition. Throughout the text, we present and discuss many examples of both good and bad programming. Programming exercises give the student the opportunity to practice organizing and writing code. In addition, we offer examples that facilitate learning the practical skill of modifying existing code. This is done through the use of code that is specifically designed to be modified by the student. We have found this mechanism to be effective because it forces the student to read and understand the provided code. In the text, a CD-ROM/World Wide Web icon signals that this code is available on the CD-ROM included with the book and at our Web site.

Why C++?

As we began our new curriculum development, one of the first issues was choosing which programming language to use. Like many departments, we had been using Pascal. Although it was unanimously decided that Pascal should be replaced, the choice of a replacement was the subject of much heated debate. Some of the languages we considered were C, C++, Modula-3, Scheme, and Smalltalk. A deciding factor was that we wanted to use a language that we ourselves use professionally. This decision narrowed the choices to C or C++. Although the decision was not unanimous, we chose C++ based on the belief that the object-oriented paradigm would be the dominant programming paradigm of the future.

In hindsight, we made the correct choice. C++ has continued to grow in popularity, and many companies use it as their development language. Indeed, many of our graduates report that when they interview for a job, a question they are often asked is whether they know C++. We believe that we will see a continuing shift to C++ as the introductory programming language of choice. We have also been pleasantly surprised by the effect on our students. The students in our upper-level courses who have completed our software development sequence can tackle much larger and harder problems than the students who had completed the comparable sequence in our old curriculum. In addition, we have seen substantial migration of other disciplines to C++. For example, all students in the commerce school at our university now take C++, and the engineering disciplines that had previously required Fortran now require C++.

Some of you may be wondering about Java. Java is definitely an interesting language. However, serious software development tools are not yet mature, and the language and its libraries are still undergoing serious revisions. The conventional wisdom of the professionals in our research areas is that Java might be the language for developing graphical user interfaces (GUIs) but that C++ remains the language for application development. If we are to meet our goal of most ably preparing students for computing careers, then C++ is the right educational vehicle.

Introduce objects early

Our experience of teaching C++ over the past 8 years shows that the object-oriented paradigm can be successfully introduced to beginning programmers. In our initial course offerings, we introduced objects near the end of the course and did superficial coverage of objects, classes, overloading, and inheritance. Essentially, we taught C using C++ syntax and input and output mechanisms. This approach failed. It introduced a new concept too late in the course—students were not able to integrate the material. We revised our course to introduce objects earlier and found that this approach worked much better. Students now have time to absorb this material because it is used and reinforced throughout the course rather than just at the end. The objects-early approach is reflected in this text. Students begin using standard objects in Chapter 2. Chapters 3 through 7 introduce the students to the use of graphical objects from the EzWindows API. After this solid introduction to using objects, Chapter 7 introduces classes and the design of objects, and it logically follows the chapters that introduce control structures, functions, and libraries (Chapters 4 through 6). We strongly believe that this is the proper sequencing of the material in an introductory textbook. The students certainly like it! By their second and third assignment they are producing useful software with graphic capabilities.

Software projects

As noted, what we had been teaching in the past was not at all close to what was happening in the real world. To educate future computer scientists in the skills that support the engineering and comprehension of large software systems, reengineering of existing systems, and application of innovative techniques (such as software reuse), our department deemed it necessary to begin introducing this material in the first course. Our software project chapters (Chapters 10 and 15) are vehicles for this introduction. These chapters provide several important experiences for the student. First, both projects use our EzWindows API. Using the API to do event-based programming and graphical input and output exposes students to the programming model typically used in real-world applications, and it permits students to develop more exciting and interesting programs. If desired, the software projects facilitate students' working together in groups of up to four. Again, this practice mirrors the real world, where it is rare for a lone programmer to develop an application. The software projects also illustrate software maintenance. Many of the exercises at the end of the software project chapters call for the student to make major modifications or nontrivial extensions to the project program.

CHAPTER SUMMARY

- *Chapter 1: Computing and the object-oriented design methodology*—basic computing terminology, machine organization, software, software development, software engineering, object-oriented design and programming.

- *Chapter 2: C++: the fundamentals*—program organization, function main(), include statement, comments, definitions, writing readable code, interactive input and output, fundamental types, literals, constants, declarations, expressions, conversions, precedence.

- *Chapter 3: Modifying objects*—assignment statement and conversions, extractions, const objects, increment and decrement, insertion and extractions, string class, Standard Template Library, graphical objects and the EzWindows API.

- *Chapter 4: Control constructs*—logical values and operators, truth tables, bool, relational operators, general precedence, short-circuit evaluation, if statement, if-else statement, sorting, switch statement, enum, while statement, for statement, invariants, do statement, text processing, scientific visualization.

- *Chapter 5: Function usage basics and libraries*—functions, value parameters, formal parameters, actual parameters, invocation, flow of control, activation records, pseudorandom numbers, prototyping, preprocessor, inclusion directives, header files, conditional compilation, software reuse, using libraries, standard streams, manipulators, file streams, file processing, iostream, iomanip, fstream, ctype, string, stdlib, and assert libraries.

- *Chapter 6: Programmer-defined functions*—function definitions, parameters, invocation, flow of control, return statement, scope, local objects, global objects, reference parameters, constant parameters, default parameters, parameter casting, function overloading, initialization, name reuse, top-down design, recursion, in-memory streams, utility functions, Standard Template Library, integrating a quadratic polynomial, financial visualization.

- *Chapter 7: The class construct and object-oriented design*—programmer-defined data types, class construct, information hiding, encapsulation, object-oriented analysis and design, access specification, data members, member functions, constructors, kaleidoscope program, object-oriented factory automation simulator/trainer.

- *Chapter 8: Implementing abstract data types*—data abstraction, object-oriented design, default and copy constructors, inspectors, mutators, facilitators, auxiliary functions, memberwise assignment, const member functions, arithmetic operator overloading, reference return, insertion and extraction overloading, pseudorandom-number generation, ADTs for rational and pseudorandom numbers, and the red-yellow-green game.

■ *Chapter 9: Lists*—one-dimensional arrays, subscripting, parameter passing, initialization, character strings, multidimensional lists, tables, matrices, Standard Template Library, container classes, adapter classes, vector class, vector member functions, sorting, InsertionSort, QuickSort, binary search, two-dimensional search, list representation, initialization lists, iterators, ADTs for maze-traversing robot problem.

■ *Chapter 10: The EzWindows API: a detailed examination*—Application Programmer Interfaces, graphical user interface, event-based programming, window coordinate system, callbacks, mouse and timer events, EzWindows API mechanics, ADTs for simple windows, bitmaps, text labels, and a Simon Says game.

■ *Chapter 11: Pointers and dynamic memory*—lvalues, rvalues, pointer types, addressing, indirection, pointers as parameters, pointers to pointers, constant pointers, equivalence of array and pointer notation, character string processing, command-line parameters, pointers to functions, dynamic objects, free store, new and delete operators, dangling pointers, memory leak, destructors, member assignment, this, ADT for a list of integers.

■ *Chapter 12: Testing and debugging*—black-box testing, white-box testing, inspections, unit testing, integration testing, system testing, statement coverage, equivalence partitioning, regression testing, boundary conditions, code reviews, test harness, path coverage.

■ *Chapter 13: Inheritance*—object-oriented design, reuse, base class, derived class, single inheritance, is-a relationship, has-a relationship, uses-a relationship, shape hierarchy, controlling inheritance, protected members, multiple inheritance, ADTs for rectangles, circles, ellipses, and triangles, an object-oriented kaleidoscope program.

■ *Chapter 14: Templates and polymorphism*—generic actions and types, function template, class template, container class, sequential lists, linked list, iterator class, friends, polymorphism, virtual function, pure virtual function, abstract base class, virtually derived class, virtual multiple inheritance, list ADTs, random-access list, sequential lists, list iterators, singly linked lists, doubly linked lists.

■ *Chapter 15: Software project—bug hunt!*—encapsulation, inheritance, virtual functions, object-oriented design, Bug Hunt game, ADTs for various kinds of bugs and a game controller.

■ *Appendixes* — ASCII character set, general precedence table, iostream, stdlib, time, string and algorithm libraries, vector and other container classes, string class, namespaces, using statements, exceptions, friends, EzWindows API, project and make files.

USING THIS BOOK

This text has more material than can be covered in a single course. The extra coverage was deliberate—it allows instructors to select their choice of topics on programming and software development. The book was also designed for flexibility in teaching. For example, if an instructor desires to move the introduction of classes earlier in the course, he or she can cover iteration after classes and our development of the rational number ADT. If an instructor desires to introduce classes after arrays, then Sections 9.1 to 9.5 and Section 9.12 of Chapter 9 can precede Chapters 7 and 8. Also, the discussion of inheritance in Chapter 13 can precede the coverage of pointers and dynamic objects in Chapter 11. Instructors who do a breadth-first coverage of computer science may choose to omit the software project chapters and substitute material from sources that cover topics such as the social and ethical aspects of computing or elementary formal logic. The testing material of Chapter 12 (Section 12.1) can be covered anytime after the material on classes (Chapter 7) has been introduced. The section on debugging (Section 12.2) relies on array examples, and therefore should be covered after Chapters 9 and 11.

We use the following layout for our course.

Week	Topic	Readings
1	Computing and object-oriented design	Chapter 1
2	Programming fundamentals	Chapter 2
3	Object manipulation	Chapter 3
4	Conditional statements	Chapter 4 (Sections 4.1–4.6)
5	Iteration statements	Chapter 4 (Sections 4.7–4.12)
6	Functions and reuse	Chapter 5, Chapter 6
7	Parameter passing	Chapter 6
8	OO analysis and design	Chapter 7
9–10	ADTs	Chapter 8 (Sections 8.1–8.6)
11	Arrays	Chapter 9 (Sections 9.1–9.4, Section 9.12)
12	Vectors	Chapter 9 (Sections 9.5–9.10)
13	Project—Simon Says, OOA/OOD	Chapter 10
14	Inheritance	Chapter 13

Depending on faculty interests, the material covered in week 13 can vary. In the introductory course at our university, we spend one week every semester on a problem in detail. Generally, this examination contributes to the final project.

SUPPLEMENTARY MATERIALS

In addition to the included CD-ROM, which contains source code and supplementary files for many of our programs and listings, we have developed other materials. For example, there is a set of slide transparencies (approximately 300 slides). The course we teach also has a closed-laboratory component that meets once a week for reinforcing current course topics. For these laboratories, we have developed a student laboratory manual. These materials are available from the publisher. For more detailed information, visit our Web site at `http://www.mhhe.com/c++programdesign`. In particular, we maintain a frequently asked question list (FAQ) and links to helpful C++ and educational sites. Other educational supplements are also available at our class Web site `http://www.cs.virginia.edu/cs101`.

SYMBOLS

The following icons are used in the margins throughout the text.

The World Wide Web (WWW) and CD-ROM icon is associated with some code listings and programs. This icon indicates that the code is available both on the CD-ROM supplied with the book and at our Web site `http://www.mhhe.com/c++programdesign`. When the icon is associated with the label Program, the program consists of a single file. If the icon is associated with the label Listing, a library file or one file in a multifile program is being made available.

The exclamation icon indicates a warning about programming. Often these are tips on how to avoid common programming errors.

The detour icon indicates a set of self-check exercises. The answers to the exercises can be found at our Web site `www.mhhe.com/c++programdesign` or `www.cplusplus-programdesign.com`. The self-check exercises include both short answer questions as well as programming exercises.

The sunglass icon indicates that the associated material is related to programming style. At the current time, a number of conventions are being used. The manner that code is presented in this text generally reflects the dominant convention. (Of course, our variation is the best!)

The book icon indicates that the associated material is concerned with the C++ programming language itself. The two typical uses of this icon are for advanced C++ topics or for describing a recent language extension that can have an impact on software development.

The spotlight icon indicates programming tips or highlights material that presents a more detailed discussion or a sidebar to the current topic.

The abacus icon indicates a discussion on the history of computing. Many people often mistakenly think that computing is simply writing programs. While designing and writing programs is certainly an important part of computing, it is by no means the only thing encompassed by computing. Each chapter contains at least one anecdote regarding triumphs and failures of the pioneers in computing.

THE AUTHORS

Jim Cohoon is a professor in the computer science department at the University of Virginia and is a former member of the technical staff at AT&T Bell Laboratories. He joined the faculty after receiving his Ph.D. from the University of Minnesota. He has been nominated twice by the department for the university's best-teaching award. In 1994, Professor Cohoon was awarded a Fulbright Fellowship to Germany, where he lectured on C++ and software engineering. Professor Cohoon's research interests include algorithms, computer-aided design of electronic systems, optimization strategies, and computer science education. He is the author of more than 60 papers in these fields. He is a member of the Association of Computing Machinery (ACM), the ACM Special Interest Group on Design Automation (SIGDA), the ACM Special Interest Group on Computer Science Education (SIGCSE), the Institute of Electrical and Electronics Engineers (IEEE), and the IEEE Circuits and Systems Society. He is a member of the ACM Publications and SIG Boards and is past chair of SIGDA. He can be reached at cohoon@virginia.edu. His Web homepage is http://www.cs.virginia.edu/~cohoon.

Jack Davidson is also a professor in the computer science department at the University of Virginia. He joined the faculty after receiving his Ph.D. from the University of Arizona. Professor Davidson has received NCR's Faculty Innovation Award for innovation in teaching. Professor Davidson's research interests include compilers, computer architecture, systems software, and computer science education. He is the author of more than 80 papers in these fields. He is a member of the ACM, the ACM Special Interest Group on Programming Languages (SIGPLAN), the ACM Special Interest Group on Computer Architecture (SIGARCH), SIGCSE, the IEEE, and the IEEE Computer Society. He served as an associate editor of *Transactions on Programming Languages and Systems*, ACM's flagship journal on programming languages and systems, from 1994 to 2000. He was chair of the 1998 Programming Language Design and Implementation Conference (PLDI '98) and program co-chair of the 2000 SIGPLAN Workshop on Languages, Compilers, and Tools for Embedded Systems

(LCTES 2000). He can be reached at jwd@virginia.edu. His Web home-page is http://www.cs.virginia.edu/~jwd.

DELVING FURTHER

The following are primary references on the C++ language.

- International Standard for Information Systems—Programming Language C++, ISO/IEC FDIS 14882, Washington, DC: American National Standards Institute, 1998.

- B. Stroustrup, *The C++ Programming Language,* 3rd ed., Reading, MA: Addison-Wesley, 1998.

The following are good sources on libraries and more-advanced object-oriented design, program development, and the Standard Template Library.

- J. Bergin, *Data Abstraction: The Object-Oriented Approach Using C++*, New York: McGraw-Hill, 1994.

- M. D. Carroll and M. A. Ellis, *Designing and Coding Reusable C++*, Reading, MA: Addison-Wesley, 1995.

- M. P. Cline and G. A. Lomow, *C++ FAQs*, Reading, MA: Addison-Wesley, 1995.

- A. Koenig and B. Moo, *Ruminations on C++*, Reading, MA: Addison-Wesley, 1997.

- S. B. Lippman and J. Lajoie, *C++ Primer,* 3rd ed., Reading, MA: Addison-Wesley, 1998.

- S. Maguire, *Writing Solid Code*, Redmond, WA: Microsoft Press, 1993.

- S. Meyers, *Effective C++*, Reading, MA: Addison-Wesley, 1998.

- S. Meyers, *More Effective C++*, Reading, MA: Addison-Wesley, 1996.

- D. R. Musser and A. Saini, *STL Tutorial and Reference Guide*, Reading, MA: Addison-Wesley, 1995.

- P. J. Plauger, A. Stepanov, M. Lee, and D. R. Musser, *The Standard Template Library*, Englewood Cliffs, NJ: Prentice-Hall, 1998.

- B. Stroustrup, *The Design and Evolution of C++*, Reading, MA: Addison-Wesley, 1994.

The following are good sources for learning more about the history and future of computing.

- S. Augarten, *Bit by Bit: An Illustrated History of Computers*, New York: Ticknor & Fields, 1984.

- P. J. Denning and B. Metcalfe (eds.), *Beyond Calculation: The Next Fifty Years of Computing*, New York: Copernicus Press, Springer-Verlag, 1997.

- J. A. N. Lee, *Computer Pioneers*, Piscattaway, NJ: IEEE Press, 1995.

- J. Palfreman and D. Swade, *The Dream Machine: Exploring the Computer Age*, London: BBC Books, 1991.

- H. G. Stine, *The Untold Story of the Computer Revolution*, New York: Arbor House, 1985.

- M. R. Williams, *A History of Computing Technology*, Englewood Cliffs, NJ: Prentice-Hall, 1985.

ACKNOWLEDGMENTS

We thank the University of Virginia for providing an environment that made this book possible. In particular, we thank Jack Stankovic for his tireless efforts in leading the computer science department to national prominence. We also thank Mark Bailey, Alan Batson, Joanne Cohoon, Clark Coleman, John Karro, Sean McCulloch, James Ortega, Jane Prey, Paul Reynolds, and Alfred Weaver for their comments. Thanks also goes to Bruce Childers who helped design and implement the original EzWindows API and Peter Valle who helped revise the EzWindows API for this edition.

We are grateful to Rich Rashid and Amitabh Srivastava of Microsoft Research for providing an environment that allowed the third edition to be completed. Microsoft Research is a great place to think, write, and do research. A very special thanks go to David Hanson, Todd Proebsting, and Chris Fraser of the Programming Language Systems group at Microsoft Research for making us feel welcome and at home. We will miss the interesting and stimulating lunch-time conversations—especially the lunch trips to Hole-in-the-Wall Barbeque for Meatloaf Monday and to Acapalco Fresh for Burrito Thursday.

We thank all of the people at McGraw-Hill for their efforts in making this edition a reality. In particular, we thank Tom Casson, for his support and encouragement; Kay Brimeyer, for her behind-the-scenes product-management skills; John Wannemacher, for his creative marketing ideas; David Hash, for leading the cover-design team; June Waldman, for copyediting the second edition; Jill Barrie for copyediting the third edition; and Janelle Pregler for her careful proofreading of the third edition. Special thanks go again to Elizabeth (Betsy) Jones, our executive editor, for support, direction, and focus throughout this project, and Kelley Butcher, our senior developmental editor, for managing and synthesizing the reviewing process.

We thank the following class testers, readers, and reviewers for their valuable comments and suggestions on the second edition of this text:

Kenneth Bayse, Clark University
Leslie Blackford, Wheaton College
Jacobo Carrasquel, Carnegie Mellon University
John Dailey Jr., University of Illinois
Suzanne Miller Dorney, Grand Valley State University
Gerald Dueck, Brandon University
H. E. Dunsmore, Purdue University
Elizabeth Lee Falta, Louisiana Tech University
William Filter, Sandia National Laboratories
Ann Ford, University of Michigan

Kyle Gillette, George Washington High School of Denver
Robert Holloway, University of Wisconsin
Van Howbert, Colorado State University
Liewen Huang, University of Virginia
Leon Jololian, New Jersey Institute of Technology
Michael Jones, Encyclopedia Brittanica, Inc.
Edward Keefe, Des Moines Area Community College
Andrea Kerslake, Frederick High School
Nancy Kinnersley, University of Kansas
Chih-Fen Koh, State University of New York, Stony Brook
Valeri Kolesnikov, Slippery Rock University
Rhoda Baggs Koss, Florida Institute of Technology
Joel Kraft, Case Western Reserve University
R. Raymond Lang, Xavier University
Jens Lienig, Tanner Research
Rowan Lindley, Westchester Community College
John Lowther, Michigan Technological University
Lewis Lum, University of Portland
Bruce Maxim, University of Michigan at Dearborn
Jin Mazumdar, State University of New York at Fredonia
Michael McCarthy, University of Pittsburgh
Douglas Morris, University of Pittsburgh
Robert O'Neil, Utah State University
Glenn Pavlicek, Bridgewater State College
Howard Pyron, University of Missouri at Rolla
Donna Reese, Mississippi State University
Charles Riedesel, University of Nebraska
Carol Roberts, University of Maine
Paul Schatz, University of Virginia
W. Brent Seales, University of Kentucky
Shashi Shekhar, University of Minnesota
Neelam Soundarajan, Ohio State University
M. A. Sridhar, University of South Carolina
Kirk Stephens, Southwestern Community College
Phil Sweany, Michigan Technological University
Peter Theron, Herzing Community College
Ralph Tomlinson, Iowa State University
Kevin Treu, Furman University
Jane Turk, LaSalle University
Frank Vedro, University of Pittsburgh
David Whalley, Florida State University
Brian Wharry, Elmhurst College

We are also grateful to the following reviewers who provided comments and feedback on the third edition:

Richard Albright, University of Delaware
Ramzi Bualuan, University of Notre Dame

Drue Coles, Boston University
Joseph DeLibero, Arizona State University
Ann Ford, University of Michigan
Juan E. Gilbert, Auburn University
Larry Gordon, University of Alaska, Anchorage
Sherri Harms, University of Nebraska at Lincoln
Robert A. Hovis, Ohio Northern University
Thomas Ibry, University of North Texas
Debbie Keen, University of Kentucky
Andrew Kinley, Rose-Hulman Institute of Technology
Stephen P. Leach, Florida State University
Kelsey Lick, University of California at Riverside
Rose M. Lowe, Clemson University
Robert J. McGlinn, Southern Illinois University
Wayne Miller, University of Kansas
Jay Morris, Old Dominion University
Lawrence J. Osborne, Lamar University
Young Park, Bradley University
Wolfgang Pelz, The University of Akron
Norman Pestaina, Florida International University
Clayton Price, University of Missouri—Rolla
Thomas Scanla, University of Wisconsin
Sung Shin, South Dakota State University
Brenda Sonderegger, Montana State University
Michael Stinson, Central Michigan University
Robert Underwood, Colorado School of Mines
Charles Welty, University of Southern Maine
Rick Zaccone, Bucknell University

We thank our spouses, Audrey and Joanne, and our children for their efforts, cooperation, and sacrifices in making this book happen.

Finally, we thank the users of this book. Many of the changes in this edition were prompted by suggestions we received via electronic mail from users of the text. We welcome your comments, suggestions, and ideas for improving this material. Please write in care of the publisher, McGraw-Hill, or send electronic mail to cohoon@virginia.edu or jwd@virginia.edu.

J. P. C
J. W. D

Contents

Chapter 3

Modifying objects   103

Chapter 4

Control constructs   153

Chapter 5

Chapter 6

Chapter 7

Chapter 8

Chapter 9

Chapter 10

The EzWindows API: a detailed examination   565

Chapter 11

Pointers and dynamic memory   615

Chapter 15

Appendix A

Appendix B

Appendix C

Appendix D

Appendix E

Appendix F

CHAPTER 1

Computing and the object-oriented design methodology

Introduction

Computers are an integral part of life in the new millennium. For example, most of us have surfed the World Wide Web. Computers are also being used in ways that are not as obvious. For example, every time you use your telephone, it likely connects to a computer system. Similarly, on your next plane trip, it may be that the aircraft is landed by a computer system and not the pilot! The term *computer system* is used to emphasize that there are two distinct components: hardware and software. The hardware is the computer itself. The software is the programs that tell the computer what to do. In the telephone system example above, it is the software that provides special features such as call waiting. Designing and building software is especially challenging today, when a piece of software may consist of millions of lines of code. In recent years, the object-oriented programming design methodology has emerged and shown much promise for managing and coping with such complexity. In this chapter, we introduce basic computing terminology and the concepts behind object-oriented design. In successive chapters, we show how to design and write software using the object-oriented programming language C++.

Key Concepts

- CPU
- binary number system
- machine language
- system software
- application software
- operating system
- translation system
- compiler
- abstraction
- information hiding
- encapsulation
- modularization
- hierarchy
- reuse
- object-oriented design
- object-oriented language
- inheritance
- polymorphism

1.1 # BASIC COMPUTING TERMINOLOGY

One of the most daunting aspects of learning a new discipline is mastering the terminology. This situation is particularly true for computer science because computer scientists are fond of using acronyms and abbreviations for almost everything having to do with computers. Sometimes a conversation between two computer scientists can sound like a totally different language if you don't understand the jargon. Indeed, much of the terminology involving computers has become so ubiquitous that it is difficult to discuss computers without using the terminology.

1.1.1   Computing units of measure

Much of the computer terminology computer scientists use involves measures for comparing various aspects of the computer. These measures usually involve the size or capacity of some aspect of the machine or the speed of the machine. In measuring speed, computer scientists sometimes discuss how long it takes to do some operation. In these cases, the units of measures are thousandths, millionths, billionths, and trillionths of a second. Table 1.1 shows the most frequently used measures. As we shall see, current computers do most arithmetic operations in nanoseconds, but computer scientists expect computers to do operations in picoseconds in the near future.

Table 1.1

Common units of measure of computer speed

Fraction of a Second	Value	Abbreviation
10^{-3}	$\dfrac{1}{1,000}$	millisecond or ms
10^{-6}	$\dfrac{1}{1,000,000}$	microsecond or μs
10^{-9}	$\dfrac{1}{1,000,000,000}$	nanosecond or ns
10^{-12}	$\dfrac{1}{1,000,000,000,000}$	picosecond or ps

Rather than use the duration of an operation as a measure of speed, computer scientists sometimes use what is known as the clock rate. The *clock rate* is how many operations the computer can perform in a second and is typically expressed as *cycles per second,* or hertz. For example, a computer with a clock rate of 500,000,000 hertz does something every 2 ns (i.e., $1 \div 500,000,000$). Scientists use the prefixes in Table 1.2, which are from the metric system. For our previous example, we would write 500 MHz (spoken as "500 megahertz"). Clearly, the higher the clock rate, the faster the computer.

In terms of measures of capacity or size, computer scientists prefer to count things using powers of two. This system is convenient because digital

Table 1.2

Commonly used powers of 10 and their abbreviations

Value	Abbreviation
1,000	kilo or K
1,000,000	mega or M
1,000,000,000	giga or G
1,000,000,000,000	tera or T

computers use the binary number system. Table 1.3 shows the powers of 2 that are most often used. As the table shows, the abbreviation for 2^{10} is K, where the K comes from the stem "kilo." The prefix *kilo* is used because 1,024 is closest to 1,000. Similarly, the prefix *mega* is used for 2^{20} because its value (1,048,576) is closest to 1,000,000. When these units are used to specify storage capacity of a machine, we really do mean the exact power of 2. For example, a machine that has 128 megabytes of memory has 128×2^{20} bytes, or 134,217,728 bytes of memory. The use of these prefixes to mean different things can sometimes be confusing. However, the meaning is usually clear from the context. If someone says that he or she got a job offer with a salary of $30K, the person most likely means $30,000, not $30,720 (i.e., $30 \times 1,024$).

Table 1.3

Commonly used powers of 2 and their abbreviations

Power of 2	Value	Abbreviation
2^{10}	1,024	kilo or K
2^{20}	1,048,576	mega or M
2^{30}	1,073,741,824	giga or G
2^{40}	1,099,511,627,776	tera or T

1.1.2   Computer organization

Every computer has four parts (see Figure 1.1). The brain of the computer is the *central processing unit*, or CPU, where computations are performed and decisions are made. *Memory* is where the data and programs are stored while being processed by the CPU. The bidirectional arrow in Figure 1.1 indicates that the CPU can both fetch information from and store information in the memory. Two very important components of a computer are the *input devices* and *output devices* because they are used to communicate information between humans and the computer. The following paragraphs discuss the four components of a computer in more detail.

The CPU is where arithmetic calculations are performed. The arithmetic/logical unit (ALU) of the CPU performs the typical arithmetic operations such as addition, subtraction, multiplication and division. Interestingly, computers use the binary number system, not the decimal number system, to represent numbers. The binary number system has only two digits, 0 and 1. The binary

Figure 1.1

*Computer
organization*

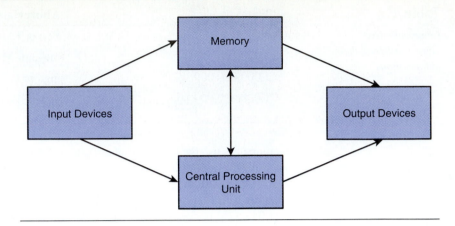

number system is used because the fundamental building block of a computer is a switch, much like the familiar on/off switch for an electric lamp. The state of the switch indicates the value of the digit. In early computers, these switches were built from mechanical relays. The resulting machines were huge. They occupied an entire room, and they required special power and cooling. In today's machines, the switches are made from ultrasmall transistors. Consequently, an entire computer can fit on a single *chip* made of silicon. Because the entire computer fits on a chip, these chips are sometimes referred to as *microprocessors*. Intel's Pentium II® processor contains about 7,500,000 transistors in a package 4.8 inches high and 6.0 inches wide (see Figure 1.2). The successor to the Pentium II, the Pentium III®, has about 28,000,000 transistors.

Figure 1.2

*A Pentium II®
processor*

The principles behind the binary number system are the same as those used in our decimal number system. Both the decimal and binary number systems are *positional number systems*; that is, the position of the digit indicates its relative value. For example, in the decimal number 4,506, the 5 is in the 100's place and thus indicates a value of 500. Reading the number from the right, each digit represents an increasing power of 10. Thus the value of the 4,506 can be expressed as

$$4 \times 10^3 + 5 \times 10^2 + 0 \times 10^1 + 6 \times 10^0$$

The binary number system works exactly the same way except that we use increasing powers of 2. For example, the binary number 1101 represents the value

$$1 \times 2^3 + 1 \times 2^2 + 0 \times 2^1 + 1 \times 2^0$$

which is the decimal value 13 (8 + 4 + 0 + 1). To indicate that a number is in a base other than decimal, the base is written as a subscript at the end of the number. So 100100_2 is the binary representation of the decimal value 36, whereas 1001 represents the decimal value 1,001.

The individual digits of a binary number are referred to as *bits* (from *binary dig*it*). Writing out binary numbers for even moderately large numbers can be tedious, so the bits of a binary number are often grouped together to correspond to a bigger radix (which will be a power of 2, of course). Grouping bits together in threes starting from the right gives a base 8 or octal representation ($2^3 = 8$). Thus the number

01011101_2

can be converted to its octal representation by first grouping the bits in threes. This step yields

$(01)(011)(101)_2$

and the individual groupings can be converted to octal digits. Converting each digit yields

01_2 = 1
011_2 = 3
101_2 = 5

which is the number 135_8. This value can be converted to its decimal value in the same way that a binary number is converted. The difference is that powers of 8 are used. The number 135_8 is

$$1 \times 8^2 + 3 \times 8^1 + 5 \times 8^0$$

which is the decimal value 93.

It's not too hard to convert a decimal representation of a value into its binary or octal representation. To convert a number in the decimal system to its octal equivalent (which is much less work than converting the same value into binary), we can think of the number in octal as …*wxyz*, denoting

$$…w \times 8^3 + x \times 8^2 + y \times 8^1 + z \times 8^0 \text{ or } …w \times 512 + x \times 64 + y \times 8 + z \times 1$$

So the first step is to determine the number of 8s in the number. This value is computed by dividing by 8. The remainder is the value of z. The value of y is computed by dividing the quotient of the previous operation (i.e., the original number divided by 8), which gives the number of 64s in the value. The remainder is the value of y. The process continues until the number we are dividing is less than 8.

To give an example, let's determine the octal and binary representation for the decimal value 458. The computation would proceed as follows:

$$\frac{458}{8} = 57 \text{ with remainder 2}$$

$$\frac{57}{8} = 7 \text{ with remainder 1}$$

$$\frac{7}{8} = 0 \text{ with remainder 7}$$

So the octal representation of 458_{10} is 712. The binary representation is easily obtained by expanding each octal digit to its binary equivalent. The process is

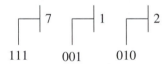

which gives the binary number 111001010.

The standard unit of computer storage on most machines is 8 bits. An 8-bit quantity is known as a *byte*. Because the octal system groups bits in threes and three does not evenly divide eight, base 16 is more commonly used. The base 16 number system is called the *hexadecimal* number system. In the hexadecimal number system, the bits are grouped together in sets of four. Thus there are two hexadecimal digits per byte. Taking the binary representation of 89_{10} and dividing the bits into groups of four starting from the right yields (101) (1001), which is 59_{16}. As a check to see whether we converted the number correctly, we can convert it back to decimal. We use the same process as we did for converting an octal or binary number to decimal except, of course, the base is 16. The number 59_{16} is

$$5 \times 16^1 + 9 \times 16^0 = 80 + 9 = 89$$

which is correct.

Since a hexadecimal digit can take on 16 possible values, extra symbols are required to represent the digits greater than nine. The convention is to use the letters A through F to represent the digits 10 through 15. So the hexadecimal representation of the octal value 712 is $1CA_{16}$, which was obtained by writing the binary equivalent of each octal digit and dividing the bits into groups of four—starting from the right as shown in the following diagram:

$$\begin{array}{ccc} \boxed{}\,1 & \boxed{}\,12 = \text{C} & \boxed{}\,10 = \text{A} \\ 1 & 1100 & 1010 \end{array}$$

Performing arithmetic on positive binary numbers is the same as performing arithmetic on decimal numbers. Both addition and multiplication are illustrated in Figure 1.3. For addition, the binary digits are added starting from the right. When the sum of the two digits is greater than 1, a carry is propagated to the next column. For multiplication, the multiplicand (the top number) is multiplied by the digits of the multiplier starting from the right. For the binary number system, multiplication is particularly simple because we are always multiplying by either a zero or a one. The last step is to sum all the partial products to produce the final product.

Figure 1.3

Binary addition and multiplication

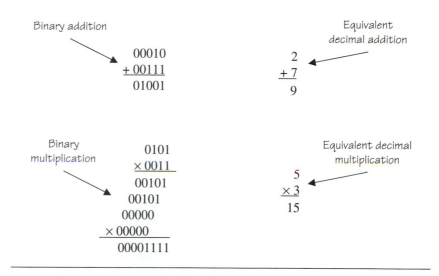

Binary addition

```
  00010
+ 00111
  01001
```

Equivalent decimal addition

```
  2
+ 7
  9
```

Binary multiplication

```
    0101
  × 0011
   00101
   00101
   00000
 × 00000
 00001111
```

Equivalent decimal multiplication

```
   5
 × 3
  15
```

A world consisting of ones and zeros leaves no room for the plus or minus sign, and so we need to adopt some convention for the representation of negative integer values. All computers use a fixed number of binary digits to represent a value. This basic unit of storage is usually called a *word*. To keep things simple, we assume that we are dealing with a computer with an 8-bit word. As previously mentioned, such a quantity is usually called a *byte*.

Based on what we already know, it is clear that the nonnegative integers 0 through 255 ($2^8 - 1$) can be represented in this amount of storage. However, if we want to represent negative values and be able to perform subtraction, then we have to sacrifice the largest positive value.

Most modern computers use a system known as *two's complement* to represent integers. In the two's complement system, nonnegative numbers (i.e., positive numbers and zero) are represented as we described previously. However, negative numbers are represented differently. For a machine with an n-bit word, the two's complement representation of $-N$ is $2^n - N$ represented in binary.

To see this concretely, let's do an example. Again we assume that we are working with a 8-bit word. The two's complement representation of 3 is 00000011. The two's complement representation of -3 is the binary representation of $2^8 - 3$ or 253. The binary representation of 253 is 11111101. Thus the two's complement representation of -3 is 11111101.

The easy way to obtain the two's complement representation of a negative integer is to follow these steps:

Step 1.   Write the two's complement representation of the positive integer.

Step 2.   Complement each bit (replace each 1 by a 0, and each 0 by a 1).

Step 3.   Add 1 to the complemented number.

To give an example, let's choose the value -127_{10}:

Step 1.   01111111   (127_{10} in eight binary digits)

Step 2.   10000000   (its bit-wise complement)

Step 3.   10000001   (add 1 to the bit-wise complement)

So, the two's complement representation of -127_{10} is 10000001.

The acid test is to verify that the addition of the binary representations of 127 and -127 yields 0. The addition is

$$\begin{array}{r} 01111111 \\ +10000001 \\ \hline 100000000 \end{array}$$

Notice the carry out of the most significant bit position. When performing binary arithmetic in which numbers are represented using the two's complement system, the carry out of the most significant bit is discarded. Thus the sum is 0.

From the above examples, we can see that in the two's complement system the most significant bit of the word serves as the sign bit. A one in the most significant bit position indicates a negative value, and a zero indicates a positive value. The range of values that can be represented in an 8-bit word is -128 to 127. In general, the range of values that can be represented in two's complement notation in a word of n bits is -2^{n-1} through $2^{n-1} - 1$.

Two's complement is also important because it gives the computer a way to perform subtraction without having to use a specialized unit. To compute the difference between two binary numbers, x and y, the two's complement of y is produced and then added to x. The result is the difference $x - y$.

Two important characteristics of a CPU are the size of the numbers it handles and how fast it can perform an arithmetic operation. The size of the numbers a CPU can handle is usually given as the number of bits in the largest integer that the CPU can manipulate. A few years ago the largest integer a typical machine could handle was 32 bits. Today, there are CPUs capable of manipulating 64-bit integers. An n-bit integer can represent the decimal values 0 through $2^n - 1$. For example, on a machine with 8-bit integers, the largest number is $2^8 - 1$ or 255. The speed at which a CPU can perform an arithmetic operation is often specified by the time it takes to add two integers. Computers built in the 1940s could add two 31-bit numbers in 150 to 200 microseconds. A typical computer today can add two 32-bit numbers in a nanosecond.

In addition to the ALU, a CPU contains a control unit. The control unit is responsible for fetching instructions from memory and causing the action specified by the instruction (e.g., an add or subtract) to be carried out. Performing the action specified by the instruction is referred to as *executing the instruction*, and the instructions in memory are known as the *program*. The control unit performs these steps of fetching and executing instructions repeatedly. This process, called the *fetch/execute cycle*, is illustrated in Figure 1.4.

Figure 1.4

Fetch/execute cycle of a computer

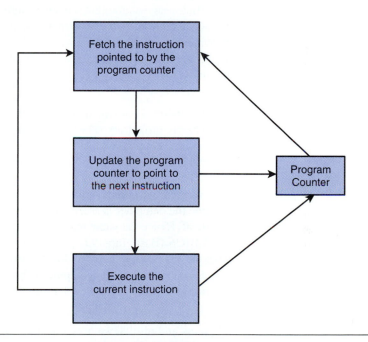

To keep track of which instruction to fetch and execute next, the control unit contains a program counter. The *program counter* holds the memory address of the next instruction to fetch and execute. In most cases, the program counter steps through the program sequentially. That is, instructions are fetched and executed in the order in which they are stored in memory. However, if we could only execute instructions sequentially, the computer would be of limited use. The control unit can test data fetched from memory and can change the program counter based on the outcome of the test. This ability enables the CPU to decide which actions to take based on the data that is being processed. This decision-making is fundamental to all computing devices.

Closely connected to the CPU is *main memory* where data and the instructions that control the operation of the CPU are stored. As we mentioned earlier, for most computers being built today, main memory is organized as a series of locations that each hold 8 bits, or 1 byte, of information. An important property of main memory is that any location or byte can be accessed in a fixed amount of time. For this reason, main memory is sometimes referred to as *random access memory* or RAM. This arrangement is in contrast to storing information on a tape, where to read information in the middle of the tape requires advancing the tape to the proper location. In this case, the time to access information depends on where the information is located. This type of memory is called *sequential access memory*.

Two important characteristics of main memory are its size and its speed. The size of main memory is measured in terms of the number of bytes it contains. In a personal computer, main memory may range from 64 megabytes up to 256 or more megabytes, or MB. So one will often see advertisements for machines saying the machine has 128MB of memory. The speed of main memory is measured in terms of how long it takes to read information from a particular location. Typical speeds on a personal computer range from 10 to 60 nanoseconds.

For most types of random-access memory, the contents are lost when the computer is turned off. This type of memory is called volatile memory. We need some memory that does not lose its contents when the power is turned off. Consequently, in addition to RAM, most computers have *read-only memory* or ROM. This type of memory is nonvolatile; that is, the information stored in it remains there when the computer is turned off. The contents of ROM are set at the time the computer is assembled. After assembly, ROM cannot be written— only read. Hence the name read-only memory. This memory, sometimes called ROM BIOS (Basic Input/Output Subroutines), contains information that identifies the type of computer and instructions that start the computer when it is first turned on. When the computer is turned on and the ROM BIOS program executes, the process is called *booting the machine*.

While a CPU performs computations and main memory is used to store programs and results, we need the ability to get information into the computer for processing and to get the results back out. We also need to be able to store information so that when the computer is turned off we do not lose any results that have been produced. Input devices and output devices handle these two functions. There are hundreds of different types of input devices for transmitting data and instructions to the computer. Some common and familiar devices are a keyboard, a mouse, and a CD-ROM reader. Some not so familiar devices are image scanners, voice input units, joysticks, and light pens. Similarly, there are hundreds of different output devices, each tailored to outputting different kinds of information. Common output devices include laser and inkjet printers (for printed information), display screens and plotters (for graphical type information), and loudspeakers (for sound). Figure 1.5 shows some common input and output devices.

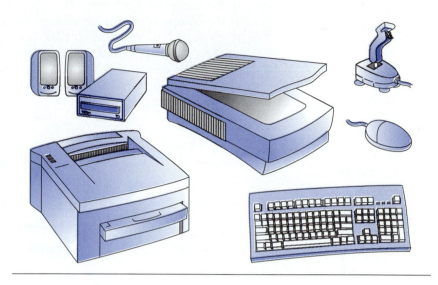

Some devices can handle both input and output, and they are typically referred to as *input/output devices*. Most input/output devices are based on some type of magnetic recording technology. Typical input/output devices are floppy drives, hard or fixed disk drives, and magnetic tape units. Floppy drives write and read small removable disks. Early floppy drives could read and write disks that would hold 360K bytes of information. Current floppy drives hold 1.44 megabytes of data. Many machines now include Zip® disk drives. These removable disks hold 100 to 250 megabytes of information. Fixed or hard disks have a much greater capacity than removable disks such as floppies and Zip® disks. Typical hard disks can hold 30 to 40 gigabytes of information, and disks that hold more than 75 gigabytes of information are becoming available. The disk cannot be removed from a hard disk drive as the disk is held in an airtight container to keep dust and any other foreign particles from interfering with reading and writing information.

A disk must be formatted before use. The formatting operation writes information on the disk so that data can be written and retrieved efficiently. The process of formatting a disk is analogous to the process of drawing lines in a parking lot and numbering the slots. It allows the information to be placed (parked) and retrieved (find your car without wandering through the parking lot) efficiently. This explains why a disk has less space on it after it has been formatted—the lines and numbering take up space.

A very important output device on personal computers is the video display, or monitor (see Figure 1.6). The monitor, sometimes referred to as a *CRT* or *cathode ray tube,* operates much like a television. The monitor is controlled by an output device called a *graphics card*. The graphics card sends the data to be displayed to the monitor in a form that the monitor can handle. Important characteristics of the monitor and graphics card are the refresh rate, resolution, and number of colors supported. The *refresh rate* is how fast the graphics card updates the image on the screen. This process must be done periodically because the phosphors used in the picture tube must be reenergized or they fade. A low refresh rate, such as 60 KHz, can cause eye fatigue because the image flickers imperceptibly. You can often detect the flicker by looking at the screen out of the corner of your eye. Many graphics cards can refresh the screen at rates of 70 to 100 KHz. This rate eliminates the flicker and the accompanying eye fatigue.

Figure 1.6

Video display, or monitor, on a desktop computer

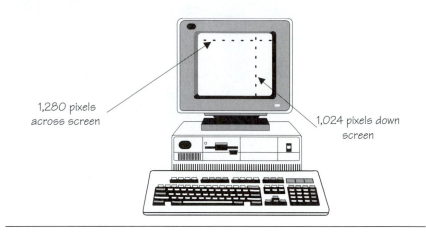

1,280 pixels across screen

1,024 pixels down screen

Flat panel displays are another type of output device that are starting to replace CRTs. Flat panel displays have several advantages over CRTs. First, because they do not use a picture tube, they take up much less space. In computer jargon, flat panel displays have a smaller footprint. Second, because flat panels do not use a picture tube, they consume less energy and emit no electromagnetic radiation. Third, flat panels are exactly that: *flat*. This means the image is not distorted. Currently, flat panel displays are more expensive than CRTs of the same size; however, prices are starting to come down substantially as display manufacturers build more plants.

The other characteristics of the graphics card are the resolution and number of colors displayed. These two characteristics are related. The *resolution* is how many dots per inch can be displayed across and down the screen. A dot in this context is often referred to as a *pixel*, which stands for "picture element." A standard resolution supported by graphics cards that are super video graphics array (SVGA) compatible is 800 by 600: There are 800 pixels across the screen and 600 pixels down the screen. The graphics card stores the information to display at each pixel in its own memory. This way it can constantly refresh the screen without interrupting the operation of the CPU. The CPU and graphics card need to communicate only when the information to display changes. Graphics cards that can display at higher resolutions require more memory. For example, many graphics cards support resolutions running from 1,024 by 768 to 1,920 by 1,440. Such cards require from 16 to 32 megabytes of memory.

Related to the amount of memory and resolution is the number of colors that can be displayed. The graphics card must store the color information to display for each pixel on the screen. To display 256 (i.e, 2^8) colors, we need 1 byte for each pixel. To display "true color," which is defined to be 16.7 million colors, requires 24 bits per pixel. Thus we can see that the number of colors that can be displayed and the resolution are both related to the amount of memory on the graphics card. More memory means a higher resolution or more colors. In most graphics cards, it is possible to trade off more colors and higher resolution. For example, at a resolution of 800 by 600 you can display true color, but at a higher resolution, say 1,024 by 768, you can display only 65,536 colors.

Two very common input devices are the keyboard and mouse. As keys are typed on the keyboard, the software reads the keystrokes and interprets them appropriately. The mouse is also a very useful input device. The typical mouse has one or two buttons and a little ball on the bottom that permits the mouse to be rolled around. As the mouse is rolled, the pointer on the screen moves accordingly. The pointer on the screen is usually referred to as the *sprite*. By moving the mouse so the sprite is pointing to a particular region of the screen (for example, a menu that has been displayed by an application) and clicking a mouse button, we can signal the computer to perform the command indicated by the menu item. Using menus and buttons to give commands to the computer is much simpler than having to type complicated commands that must be memorized.

Self-check Questions

1.   What is $1/10^{12}$ of a second?

2.   What is $1/10^{15}$ of a second? Hint: The answer is not in the book. You will need to look elsewhere for the answer.

3.   A particular disk has a storage capacity of 30 gigabytes. Exactly how many bytes can the disk hold?

4.   What does CPU stand for?

5.   Convert 38 base ten to its binary equivalent.

6.   Convert the binary number 010101 to its decimal equivalent.

7.   What is the octal representation of the base ten number 551?

8.   What is the hexadecimal representation of the base ten number 4,256?

9.   What is the two's complement representation of the integer −101?

10.   What points to the next instruction to fetch and execute?

11.   What does RAM stand for?

1.1.3   Programming

By itself, a computer will not do anything useful. There must be a program that directs the computer to perform some specific task. Indeed, the ability to program a computer to do different tasks is what makes the computer so powerful. A *program* is a sequence of instructions that tells the computer what to do. The instructions are written in a language that is specifically designed for giving commands to a computer. We call these languages *programming languages*. One type of programming language is called *machine language*. A machine-language program is one that a particular computer can understand directly. A machine language consists of instructions that represent the fundamental operations the computer can perform. Consequently, different types of computers use different machine languages. For example, the machine language understood by Intel's Pentium processor is quite different from the machine language understood by IBM's PowerPC® processor.

Part of the design of a computer is determining the fundamental operations the computer can perform and the binary encoding of these instructions. The *binary encoding* is the bit pattern that represents a particular instruction. The operations and their binary encodings are called the machine's *instruction set*. Most machines include instructions for performing arithmetic operations such as add, subtract, multiply, and divide. Another class of instructions is the jump instructions, which can change the program counter.

Even for today's modern computers, machine languages are quite primitive and writing a program directly in machine language is quite tedious. To make matters worse, without some type of assistance, we must directly use the binary encoding of the instructions. To get a first-hand idea of the difficulties of writing machine-language programs, let's write a small program for the hypothetical Pop Machine 100, or PM100 for short.

The PM100 has been designed for use in soda machines. It has a very simple instruction set. A machine instruction on the PM consists of 7 bits. The first 3 bits indicate the operation to perform. These bits are referred to as the *operation code,* or *opcode* for short. The remaining 4 bits are used only by the jump instruction. These 4 bits specify the address of the memory location to fetch the next instruction. Notice that because we have 4 bits for the address, the PM100 can contain up to 16 memory locations. Table 1.4 contains the machine's instruction set.

Let's consider the jump instruction. Its encoding is

110 AAAA

The space between the two parts of the binary instruction separates the opcode from the address. This convention is purely for our convenience. The bit

Table 1.4	Instruction Description	Binary Encoding
PM100 instruction set	Reset machine	000 0000
	Wait for coin	001 0000
	Skip next instruction if coin is not counterfeit	010 0000
	Add coin amount to total	011 0000
	Skip next instruction if total is less than the cost of a can of soda	100 0000
	Take picture and call police	101 0000
	Jump to specified location	110 AAAA
	Dispense a can of soda and give change if any	111 0000

pattern 110 will be interpreted by the machine to mean that it should perform a jump operation. We use the notation AAAA for the next 4 bits to indicate that these bits are an address. When the PM100 executes a jump instruction, the 4 bits that specify the address are moved into the program counter (refer to Figure 1.4). Consequently, the next instruction fetched is from that memory location.

We want to write a program in the machine language of the PM100 that delivers a can of soda and appropriate change when enough money has been deposited. Because there has been a lot of trouble with people putting counterfeit coins in the machine, if a counterfeit coin is detected, the program should direct the PM100 to take a picture of the offender and call the police. It should then reset itself. We hope that the offender will hang around and pound on the machine so that the police will have enough time to make an arrest on the spot. If not, the police have a picture of the offender. The PM100 has a special instruction for detecting bogus coins. It also has an instruction that telephones the police and activates a camera that takes a photograph of the person standing in front of the machine.

The machine-language program for carrying out the desired actions follows.

Memory Location	Instruction	Comments
0000	0000000	Reset the machine
0001	0010000	Wait for a coin
0010	0100000	Skip if coin is not counterfeit
0011	1101000	Jump to location 1000
0100	0110000	Add coin amount to total
0101	1000000	Skip if not enough money received
0110	1101010	Jump to location 1010

0111	1100001	Jump to location 0001
1000	1010000	Take picture and call police
1001	1100000	Jump to location 0000
1010	1110000	Dispense soda and return change
1011	1100000	Jump to location 0000

The instructions are stored sequentially in memory beginning at location 0. The first thing you should do is cover up the comments on the right and examine the program. It is very difficult to determine what the program does. For each instruction, you have to refer to the table that contains the PM100 instruction set and decode the binary instruction. Because we have to use the primitive instructions of the PM100, just getting the logic of the program correct is hard. We have to be concerned with every detail.

How can we tell whether the program does what it is supposed to do? One activity a programmer often does when writing or trying to understand a program is to "hand execute" the code. In this procedure, the programmer acts like the computer and fetches and executes the instructions in the program to determine whether the program will perform properly when executed by the real machine. This process is sometimes called *tracing the execution of the program*. To see how this technique works, let's trace the execution of our simple machine-language program.

We assume that we will begin executing instructions at location 0, and that the cost of a soda is 55 cents. The trace of the execution of the program is shown in Table 1.5.

The first step resets the state of the machine. This action sets the total amount of money received thus far to zero. Next, the instruction at location 0001 is executed. This instruction waits for a coin to be deposited. For the sake of the simulation, we assume that a quarter was deposited. When the coin is deposited, execution continues at location 0010 (step 3). This instruction tests to see whether the coin is counterfeit. It is not, so the instruction at location 0011 is skipped and execution continues at location 0100. This instruction adds the value of the coin to the total. Notice that the total is now 0.25. Next, the program tests to see whether enough money has been deposited to purchase a soda. The total amount is less than 55 cents, so the next instruction is skipped and the instruction at location 0111 is executed. This instruction jumps the program back to location 0001, which waits for the next coin to be deposited. The program continues, and another quarter and then a dime are deposited (steps 7 through 13).

After the dime is deposited and added to the total, execution continues at step 14. This time there is enough money, and the instruction following the skip instruction is executed. This instruction jumps to location 1010. At step 17, a soda is dispensed and a nickel is returned as change. At step 18, the instruction

Table 1.5

Hand execution of the soda machine program

Step	Program Counter	Action	Value of Total
1	0000	Reset the machine	0.00
2	0001	Wait for coin	0.00
		Receive a quarter	
3	0010	Skip if coin not counterfeit	0.00
4	0100	Add coin amount to total	0.25
5	0101	Skip if not enough money	0.25
6	0111	Jump to location 0001	0.25
7	0001	Wait for coin	0.25
		Receive a quarter	0.25
8	0010	Skip if coin not counterfeit	0.25
9	0100	Add coin amount to total	0.50
10	0101	Skip if not enough money	0.50
11	0111	Jump to location 0001	0.50
12	0001	Wait for coin	0.50
		Receive a dime	
13	0010	Skip if coin not counterfeit	0.50
14	0100	Add coin amount to total	0.60
15	0101	Skip if not enough money	0.60
16	0110	Jump to location 1010	0.60
17	1010	Dispense soda; return a nickel	0.60
18	1011	Jump to location 0000	0.60
19	0000	Reset machine	0.00

at location 1011 is executed, so the program jumps back to location 0000 and the machine is reset to await another customer.

Based on our hand execution, it appears the program works correctly when no counterfeit coins are encountered. To ensure that the piece of the program that handles counterfeit coins works, we should also "walk through" that portion of the code.

Such hand executions are extremely valuable in determining what a program is doing. In hindsight, what we did might seem quite tedious. We went into quite a lot of detail to illustrate exactly what was happening. As you develop your programming skills, you will find that you can perform such hand executions on small sections of code with ease. You might need a piece of scratch paper to record values as they change, but generally it is not necessary to write down the steps taken.

Obviously, writing and checking even a medium-size program (500 to 1,000 instructions) in machine language would be quite tedious and error prone. Over the years, programmers have put much effort into developing languages that permit people to write programs in a way that is more natural. At a level slightly above binary machine language is assembly language. Although we still write programs by writing sequences of machine instructions, we no longer write them in binary. Rather we write instructions in a symbolic language called *assembly language*. Then a program called an *assembler* translates the assembly-language instructions into the binary form. Assembly-language programming is a great improvement over machine-language programming because it allows the programmer to focus on solving the problem at hand rather than on the tedious job of encoding instructions in binary.

One of the characteristics of machine- and assembly-language programming is that you need to know the details of the machine being programmed. As we mentioned, each type of machine has its own, unique machine language. The next level of computer languages is high-level programming languages. A distinguishing characteristic of a high-level programming language is that detailed knowledge of the machine being programmed is not required. Another characteristic is that a high-level programming language usually uses a vocabulary and structure that is close to the type of problem being solved. For example, the programming language FORTRAN, which is used to solve scientific and engineering programs, uses a notation that is mathematical. Indeed, the name FORTRAN is derived from the phrase *formula translation*. Because of the close coupling of a programming language to a problem domain, there are literally hundreds of high-level programming languages.

1.2 SOFTWARE

Comparing the use of computers today and as recently as 15 years ago, we have seen an explosion in their use. Certainly part of the reason for this growth is the dramatic decline in the cost of a computer. However, another reason for this explosive growth in the usage of computers has been the development of useful, high-quality software that has made using the computer easy, even for novices. Software can be broadly classified as either application software or system software. The distinction between the two can sometimes be fuzzy, but generally *application software* involves solving a problem or providing a service in a particular problem domain or application area. Obviously, the range of applications is quite large and continues to grow rapidly. This growth is largely because of the increases in computing power at ever lower prices. Indeed, the personal computer revolution fostered the development of several new application areas: spreadsheets, desktop publishing (DTP), personal information managers (PIMs), personal financial managers (PFMs), and presentation managers (PMs).

System software, on the other hand, supports the development and execution of other programs. In some sense, system software bridges the gap between application software and the underlying hardware. The goal is to isolate the programmer from the low-level details of the machine and thus increase productivity. This organizational view of a computer system is illustrated in Figure 1.7.

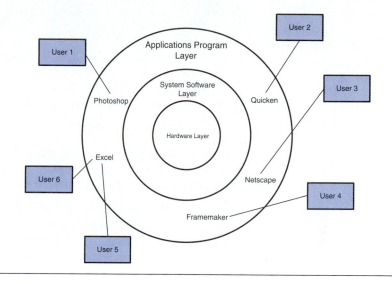

1.2.1   System software

One very important piece of system software is the operating system. An *operating system* is the software that controls and manages the computing resources. These resources include memory, input/output (I/O) devices, and the CPU. The operating system provides services such as allocating memory to a program and handling the control of I/O devices such as the display, the keyboard, and the disk drives. Popular operating systems for personal computers are Windows NT, Windows 2000, and UNIX.

An important service provided by the operating system is the file system. The file system controls how information is organized on a disk so that it can be found and retrieved quickly. The disk has areas where related information is stored together. These areas are analogous to drawers in a file cabinet. One drawer might contain all the files that pertain to first-year students. In the case of a file system, such an area is called a *directory*. Unlike a file cabinet, a directory can contain other directories. Such an organization is called a *hierarchical file system*. Computer scientists like to visualize a file system organized this way as an upside-down treelike structure.

Figure 1.8 contains a tree diagram of the organization of the files on a disk. C: is the *root* of the tree. Below the root are files and directories. For example, cs101 is a directory that contains files and directories that have to do with a course called cs101. In Figure 1.8, cs101 contains two subdirectories, hwk and labs, and one file readme.txt. Filenames should indicate the contents of the

Figure 1.8

*Hierarchical file
system*

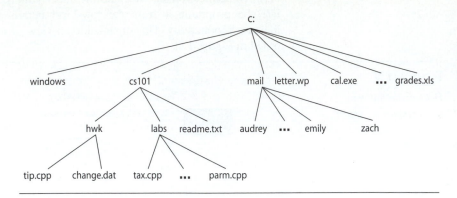

directory. In this example, the name hwk indicates that the files it contains have to do with homework for the course cs101. Similarly, the name labs indicates the directory contains information about the course laboratories.

Similarly, the filename should indicate the type of information contained in a file. A filename has two parts. The part before the period is called the *basename*, and the part after the period is called the *extension*. The extension indicates the format of the file. For example, in the cs101 directory, the file readme.txt has the common extension of txt. This extension indicates that the file contains text that can be read by printing the file to the display or using an editor to read its contents. Another common extension is exe. This extension is used for files that contain an executable program. This type of file cannot be processed by a word processor or text editor.

The basename tells what information the file holds. For example, the readme basename indicates that anyone wishing to understand what the cs101 directory contains should read the contents of this file. As another example, consider the file grades.xls. The xls extension indicates that this file was produced by Excel, a popular spreadsheet application. The grades basename indicates that this file contains a spreadsheet of grades. If you carefully organize files into subdirectories and choose appropriate names, a hierarchical file system provides an effective way to organize information so that it can be found quickly.

Another important part of an operating system is its file management commands. The command names and how to invoke them vary for different operating systems, but their functionality is identical. Most systems have commands for deleting files, renaming files, copying files, and creating directories.

The operating system also provides basic services for performing input and output on a variety of devices. Therefore, a program need not know exactly how to interact with a particular input/output device because the low-level details are handled by the operating system. For example, if a program wants to read a particular file on a disk, rather than access the disk directly, it sends a request to the operating system. The operating system finds the file on the disk, reads the appropriate portions, and then returns the desired information to the program that made the request.

Another operating system service is the management of running programs. Most modern operating systems let multiple programs share the CPU. For example, with the Windows NT operating system you can download a file from a bulletin board to your computer, run a backup program, and run a word processor all at the same time. The operating system's job is to make sure that each program has enough memory to run and is allowed to execute on the CPU when necessary.

Another class of system software is called *translation systems*. A translation system is a set of programs that we use to develop software. A key component of a translation system is a *translator*, or program that reads a program written in one programming language and outputs a new program, possibly in a different programming language. The input to a translator is called the *source program*, and the output is called the *target program*. The language used for the source program is called the *source language*, and correspondingly, the language used for the target program is called the *target language*. Figure 1.9 illustrates the translation process.

Figure 1.9

The translation process

Translators are typically categorized by source and target languages. On page 18, we said that an assembler translates a symbolic machine-language program to a binary machine-language program. A binary machine-language program is sometimes called *object code* or an *object file*. A *compiler* is another type of translator. A compiler processes a program written in a high-level programming language and produces an object file. The process of using a compiler to translate a high-level language program is called *compilation*.

Another type of translator is called a linker. A *linker* combines object files and library files so that they can be executed as a unit. A library contains files of object code for routines that have been developed to perform some particular function or task. Libraries are often supplied by the developer of the compiler or by a company that specializes in providing libraries for a particular purpose. For example, it is common to provide a library that supports input and output operations. Another typical library provides routines to support developing programs that use graphical user interfaces (GUIs). Such a library would contain routines for opening and displaying windows, creating menus, and handling input and output from the mouse.

The output of the linker is a file that can be executed by the computer. This file is sometimes called an *executable*. Using an operating system tool called a *loader*, the executable file can be loaded into the computer's memory and executed.

When doing software development, programmers repeatedly perform the actions of editing a program, compiling it, linking it with already compiled object files and library modules, and then loading and executing it. After viewing how the program behaves, programmers usually must make changes to the program, possibly because the program did not work correctly or because it did work correctly and they must continue developing the program. This process, known as the *edit/compile/execute cycle*, is illustrated in Figure 1.10.

Figure 1.10

Edit/compile/execute software development cycle

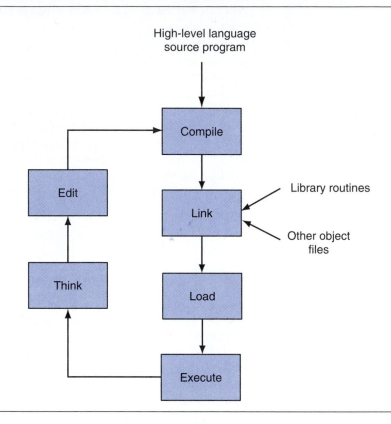

Because this cycle is repeated many times as software is being developed, translation systems have been constructed that assist us with this process. These systems are sometimes referred to as *integrated development environments* (IDEs). The idea is that the editor, compiler, linker, and loader are integrated together and one set of controls is used to invoke them.

Several IDEs support software development using C++. Although they differ in how they look, they essentially offer the same features. The various menu selections enable the programmer to type in code, compile it, link the resulting object file with other object files and libraries to create an executable, and execute the resulting code. Figure 1.11 contains the screen image of the Microsoft Visual C++ IDE. An IDE can be a great time saver because it automates much of the drudgery of developing software.

Figure 1.11

C++ IDE

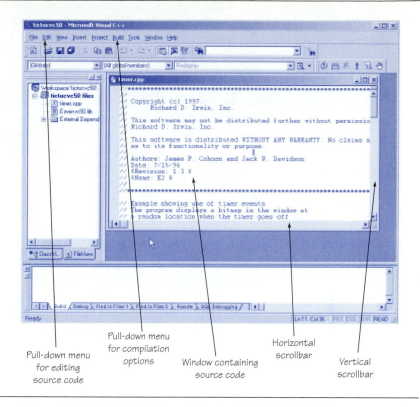

Pull-down menu for editing source code

Pull-down menu for compilation options

Window containing source code

Horizontal scrollbar

Vertical scrollbar

1.2.2 Application software

Although we certainly use the services provided by system software, it is applications programs that make the computer an indispensable tool for most people. Application software can be classified according to the type of application. For example, one category is word processors, which are programs that help produce documents. Some popular word processors are WordPerfect, Microsoft Word, and AmiPro. These programs simplify editing, and they are capable of printing documents on high-resolution printers. Over the years, the power of these word processors has grown tremendously. Early word processors included spelling checkers, but that was about it. Today's versions include grammar checkers, a thesaurus, drawing tools, table creation tools, Web authoring capabilities, and hundreds of other features to facilitate document creation.

Closely related to the word processors, and indeed today there is some overlap, are the desktop publishing (DTP) programs. These programs support the design of documents. For example, they have tools for creating layouts for newsletters and company reports. These application programs support importing text and pictures from other sources. In comparison to word processors, DTP programs have more sophisticated features for handling color, graphics, and large documents such as books.

Another class of application program that has become very popular is the spreadsheet. Indeed, some believe that it was the invention of the electronic spreadsheet that helped initiate the personal computer revolution. Spreadsheets provide a simple and natural way to deal with a wide variety of problems. Accounting operations use spreadsheets extensively because they provide an easy way to do forecasting. For example, simply by changing a few numbers, business people can get an idea of the effect of reduced sales on overall profitability. Most of today's spreadsheets include features for presenting data graphically using several types of line graphs, bar charts, or pie charts. The user selects the data to be graphed and the type of chart to graph it on, and the spreadsheet produces the chart using appropriate colors, keys, and legends.

Another type of application program, personal information managers (PIMs), enables people to organize important personal information. These programs typically include modules for maintaining to-do lists, appointments, and phone directories. On the other hand, personal financial managers (PFMs) enable people to manage personal financial information. Typical packages include modules for maintaining checking account information, monthly budgets, tax estimates, personal net worth, and stock and bond portfolios. One new feature of these programs is the ability to connect to an online service and download a record of charges that have been made on a credit card. This feature eliminates the task of having to manually enter transactions into the program. As the power of the computer continues to grow, we can expect to see both new types of application programs and enhanced features in existing programs.

We now have enough computing terminology under our belts to take a brief look at software development and the object-oriented programming paradigm.

1.3 ENGINEERING SOFTWARE

As computers have become faster, cheaper, and more powerful, they have become indispensable tools for scientists and engineers. Perhaps more importantly though, they have become part of our everyday life. Computers are in common appliances such as televisions, videocassette recorders, and microwave ovens. Furthermore, every time we use the telephone or an automated teller at a bank, we are accessing a network of computers. However, faster, cheaper computers are only one-half of the equation. Recall that previously we used the term *computer system* to indicate that there are two components—hardware and software. While there have been tremendous advances in hardware technology, there have not been commensurate advances in software design. Part of the problem is that the expectations for software have grown considerably. Figure 1.13 illustrates what is known as the *complexity paradox*: the complexity of the system grows as we attempt to make it easier to use.

For example, early systems for graphing data required users to specify in detail how the graph should look by supplying information such as the endpoints of the graph, the scale, and how and where the graph should be labeled.

History of Computing

The beginnings

One way to discuss the history of computing is to discuss the devices that people developed to assist with computing. Most of the early devices were for doing counting and simple arithmetic. One of the earliest devices for computing is still used by small children—fingers. Indeed, early humans developed various systems for counting and doing simple arithmetic such as addition, subtraction, and multiplication using their fingers. These systems were quite complicated and permitted large numbers to be manipulated. Some of these systems are still in use in parts of Asia.

As an aid to counting and calculation, the ancient Chinese used a system of rows of grooves in the sand. Pebbles were placed in the grooves to denote a value. One pebble in the first groove would represent the value one; two pebbles would represent the value two. Each successive groove represented a power of 10. Thus, two pebbles in the second groove and three pebbles in the first represented the value 23.

Later, the system of grooves and pebbles was refined into the form we know as the abacus. An *abacus* consists of beads (the pebbles) strung on parallel wires (the grooves in the sand) (see Figure 1.12). Addition, subtraction, multiplication, and division are performed by moving beads appropriately. In the late 1940s, contests between an experienced user of the abacus and an electromechanical calculator were popular. The contest consisted of performing a set of arithmetic computations. The first to complete the computation won. Interestingly, the person using the abacus almost always won. The abacus, or *soroban* as it is called in Japan, is still in use in isolated parts of Asia and the Middle East.

Figure 1.12

An abacus

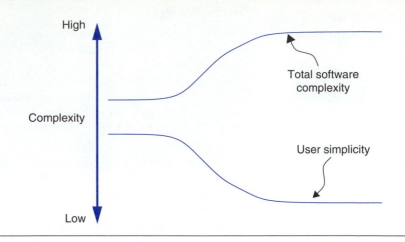

Essentially, the user had to do most of the work. However, new spreadsheet tools contain "experts," which analyze the data and produce a graph automatically. Such automatic graphing systems are much easier to use, but this ease of use comes at a price—increased software complexity.

Several factors account for the increased complexity. First, to do more, the software is larger. It is not unusual for application programs, such as spreadsheets, word processors, and drawing programs, to consist of millions of lines of code. Another factor that increases complexity is the interaction between components. For example, a word processor may contain one component for spell checking and correction and another that provides the services of a thesaurus.

Let's consider the spell-checking component. When a possible spelling error is detected, the spelling checker must report the possible error to the user. Thus the spelling checker must interact with the component of the application that creates a window or a dialog box so that the possible error can be displayed and the user queried about what action, if any, to take. If the user agrees it is a spelling error, the checker can correct the misspelling. To make the correction, the checker must interact with the component of the word processor responsible for replacing text in the document. Obviously, as the number of components grows, the number of interactions between components grows rapidly.

Software engineering is the area of computer science that is concerned with how to build large software systems. The goal of a software engineer is to produce a software system that is

- Reliable
- Understandable
- Cost effective
- Adaptable
- Reusable

Let's examine each of these properties.

A software system should be reliable. That is, it should work correctly and not fail. Imagine that you have spent several hours writing a paper for a course with a word processor and when you are nearly finished, the word processor quits unexpectedly. You lose all your work. Undoubtedly, you would be very upset and rightfully so.

Although the failure of a word processor is annoying, the loss is insignificant compared to the potential loss when a life-critical system fails. A *life-critical system* is one in which a failure could mean the loss of human life. Examples of life-critical systems where software is a major component include commercial and military aircraft, radiation therapy machines, and heart pacemakers. A software failure in one of these systems could have disastrous consequences.

A way to make a software system reliable is to make it understandable; that is, the operation and design of the system should be readily determinable by other software professionals. Being understandable is extremely important because large software systems are constructed by many people working in teams. The construction of the software will go smoother with fewer errors if everyone working on it understands the overall operation of the system and its components.

Understandability is also important because of the long lifetime of software. A software product usually evolves over time, and often software engineers that had nothing to do with the original development of the software make enhancements and fix bugs. This process is sometimes called *software maintenance*. If the next generation of software engineers can understand the operation of the software, modifications to a complex system, although difficult, are doable. On the other hand, it is extremely difficult to make modifications or corrections to a poorly designed system. Indeed, it is often more cost-effective to rebuild the system from scratch. As a measure of the difficulty of maintaining software, experts estimate that 67 percent of the cost of developing software is devoted to maintenance. This cost can be reduced when the design and operation of a system are comprehensible.

From the previous discussion, we can also see that a software system should be cost-effective. That is, the cost to develop and maintain a software system should not exceed the expected profit from selling the system. Many software companies have gone bankrupt because they underestimated the cost of developing a system. A closely related component of cost is the time to design and build the software. Being the first to bring a product to market gives a company a decided advantage over its competitors. Reducing the time to build a software system can reduce costs and can also increase profits.

Because of the long lifetime of software, software should be adaptable. It is often difficult to predict which features and capabilities a client will eventually want in a software product. *Adaptive maintenance* involves changes and additions to the software that improve the effectiveness or competitiveness of the product. By designing software to which additional features and capabilities can be added easily in the future, the software engineer can again reduce overall maintenance costs. Clearly, in terms of adaptive maintenance, under-standability is also a desirable property.

Because of the high development costs, software should be reusable. If many millions of dollars are to be spent to develop a software system, it makes sense to make its components flexible so they can be reused when developing a new system. This strategy is certainly common practice in other businesses. Consider the design and creation of a new car model. The automotive engineer does not design a new car from scratch. Rather, the engineer borrows from the design of existing cars. For example, the engine design from an existing car may be used in a new model. Reuse can improve reliability, reduce develop-ment costs, and improve maintainability. Continuing with our car analogy, if the engine design has been used in a previous model, design problems have likely been resolved. Thus development costs are reduced because a new engine does not need to be designed and tested. Finally, consumer maintenance costs are reduced because mechanics and others who must maintain the car are already familiar with the operation of the engine.

1.3.1   Software engineering principles

Software engineers have developed a number of design principles that help realize the goals in the previous section by managing the inevitable complexity of a large software system.

Abstraction is the process of extracting the relevant properties of an object while ignoring nonessential details. The extracted properties define a view of the object. A car dealer might view a car from the standpoint of its selling fea-tures. Relevant properties include price, color, optional equipment, and length of warranty. On the other hand, a mechanic views the car from the standpoint of the systems that require maintenance. Here relevant properties include the type of oil, the size of the oil filter, and the number and type of spark plug. The relevant properties are defined by how we use or manipulate the object. Clearly, the properties of a car relevant to a car dealer are different from the properties relevant to a mechanic (see Figure 1.14). By focusing on the relevant properties and ignoring irrelevant details, the complexity of dealing with an object is reduced.

Abstraction is essential for managing the complexity of designing and writing software. As an example, let's consider the task of finding a file on a disk and reading its contents. If we had to handle the low-level details of exactly how a particular file is found on a disk and how to read its contents, accomplishing this task would be quite difficult. We would have to understand how data is stored on the disk as well as the low-level commands that control the operation of the disk drive. Fortunately, a file system provides an abstract view of the information on a disk so that we can ignore such low-level details. We can access a file by simply supplying the name of the file. The file system handles the low-level details of reading the data on the disk drive and returning it to the program.

Encapsulation, or *information hiding*, is the process of separating the aspects of an object into external and internal aspects. The external aspects of

Figure 1.14

Two views, or abstractions, of an automobile

an object need to be visible, or known, to other objects in the system. The internal aspects are details that should not affect other parts of the system. Hiding the internal aspects of an object means that they can be changed without affecting other parts of the system. Continuing with our automobile analogy, consider the radio in a car. The external aspects of the radio are the controls and the types of connectors needed to hook the radio to the electrical system, the speakers, and the antenna. The internal aspects of the radio are the details of how the radio works (see Figure 1.15). To install and use a radio in a car, we do not need to know anything about electrical engineering. Essentially, the radio can be viewed as a black box with buttons and cables.

Figure 1.15

Encapsulation of a car radio

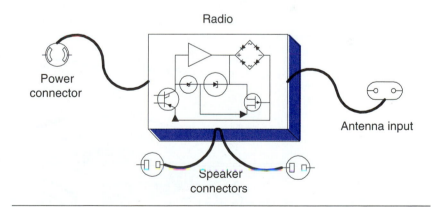

A big benefit of information hiding is that it helps us make changes to complex systems. We can replace the radio in a car with one that includes a CD player without affecting other components of the car. Because the operation of the radio has been encapsulated and the external view of the radio is defined by the controls and connectors, we can simply remove the old radio, insert the new one, and connect it.

When applied to the design of a software system, encapsulation permits the internal operation of a software component to be changed without affecting other aspects of the system. For example, if the principle of encapsulation has been applied correctly to an automated voice-mail system, we should be able to change the component that handles storing the messages without affecting other parts of the system. For example, we might want to increase the number of messages that a user can store. If the message-storing system has been properly hidden and isolated, this change should not affect how users access the system and leave or retrieve messages.

Modularity refers to the process of dividing an object into smaller pieces or modules so that some goal is easier to attain. For example, we might structure a complex object into components so that each component can be tested individually. When an automobile is assembled, the various components, such as the engine, transmission, and radio, have been individually tested already. Modularity reduces both the time to test the completed car and the probability that a car will be assembled with a flaw. Similarly, we might structure an object so that we can easily reuse its components.

Most complex systems are modular. They are constructed by combining simpler working components or packages. Proper modularization of a complex system also helps manage complexity. Breaking things down into smaller, easier to understand pieces makes the larger system easier to understand. For example, an automobile can be decomposed into subsystems (see Figure 1.16). Automobile subsystems include the cooling system (radiator, water pump, thermostat, etc.); the ignition system (battery, starter, spark plugs, etc.); and the exhaust system (catalytic converter, muffler, etc.). By thinking about an automobile in terms of these groups of related abstractions, we can more readily grasp the car's overall structure and operation.

Figure 1.16

Subsystems of an automobile

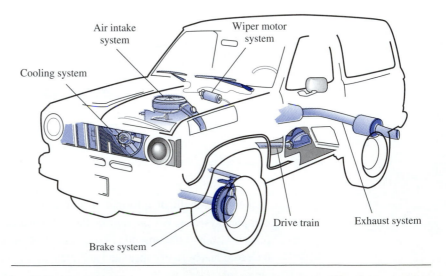

Air intake system

Wiper motor system

Cooling system

Drive train

Exhaust system

Brake system

A ranking or ordering of objects based on some relationship between them is a *hierarchy*. Hierarchies help us understand complex organizations and systems. Figure 1.17 contains an organizational chart of a typical company. The chart shows the hierarchy of the employees based on the relationship of who reports to whom. The company hierarchy helps employees understand the structure of their company and their position in it.

Figure 1.17

An organization chart of a company

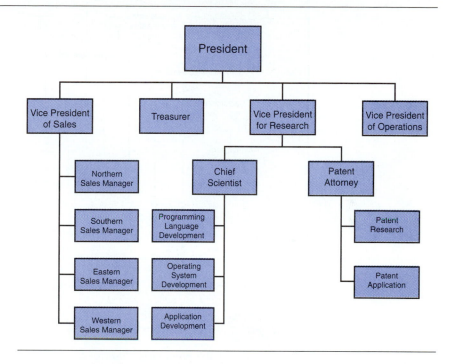

For complex systems composed of abstractions, a very useful way of ordering similar abstractions is from most general to least general. Scientists have long used this technique to identify and classify species of the plant and animal kingdoms. A hierarchical ordering based on natural relationships is called a *taxonomy*. Such a hierarchy makes all the abstractions easier to understand because it exposes the relationship of the characteristics and behaviors they have in common. Figure 1.18 shows the taxonomy of the dinosaurs.

The dinosaurs are divided into two groups depending on their hip structure. The Saurischia (lizard-hipped dinosaurs) group contains the flesh-eating dinosaurs such as the Tyranosaurus and Velociraptor, while the Ornithischia (bird-hipped dinosaurs) group contains the familiar Stegosaur and Triceratops.

Figure 1.18

A taxonomy of dinosaurs

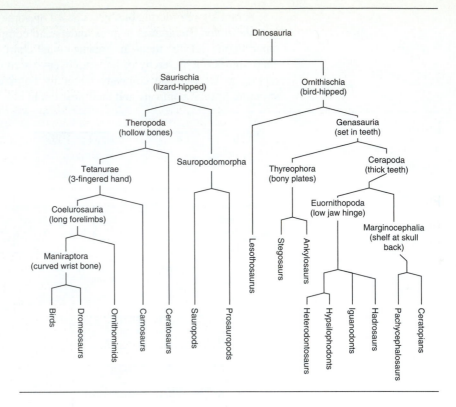

1.4   OBJECT–ORIENTED DESIGN

To support the previously described principles, several design and programming methodologies have been developed. Recently, one approach, object-oriented design and programming, has shown particular promise for helping software developers achieve the goals of reliability, cost-effectiveness, adaptability, understandability, and reusability.

Object-oriented software design promotes thinking about software in a way that more closely models the way we think about and interact with the real world. At an early age, we learn about objects and how to manipulate them. Babies, for example, learn that if they shake a rattle, it will make noise. Later as we develop our cognitive skills, we realize that objects have properties, and we begin to be able to think about them abstractly. For example, a growing baby soon realizes that noise making is a property of all rattles.

To illustrate how viewing the world as objects with properties helps us manage complexity, let's consider an activity that many of us do. You are sitting at home watching television, and you remember that your favorite show will soon be starting on a different channel (see Figure 1.19). You take the remote control, push a button, and the television switches to the proper channel. You settle back and enjoy the show.

Let's analyze this activity. First, you picked up the remote control, which is a physical object. This object has properties like weight and size, and it also can do something. It can send messages to the television. It's not entirely clear how it does this or how the messages are encoded, but you don't need to know that. You only need to know which buttons to push. The buttons are the interface to the remote control. If you understand the interface to an object, you can use it to perform some task without understanding how the object works. Pushing the appropriate buttons caused the remote to send a message to the television. The television is also a physical object with various properties. Upon receipt of the message from the remote, the television changed to the desired channel.

Figure 1.19

Objects interacting via messages

Such interactions are so routine that it is easy to overlook how amazing this activity is. You were able to make two objects interact and perform a complex activity without understanding the internal operation of either object. You were able to do so because you had appropriate abstractions of both objects. Indeed your mental abstractions of the remote control and television mean that you could go to a friend's house and be able to use his or her remote control and television even though your friend has a different brand of television. Similar objects display similar behavior.

This way of dealing with the complex world around us can also be applied to software design and programming. A key step in developing a complex system using object-oriented design is to determine the objects that constitute the system. By carefully creating appropriate abstractions of these objects and separating their internal implementation from their external behavior, we can manage the complexity of a large software system.

So what exactly do we mean by an object? Certainly, physical things are objects. A ball, a file cabinet, an address book, a tree, a computer are all objects. What about things like a number, a word, a bank account, or a musical note? These aren't physical objects, but they are objects because they have properties or attributes and we can perform actions on them. A number has a value, and we can add two numbers together. A word has a length, and if we are talking about a word processor, a word can be inserted or deleted from a document. A musical note has pitch, duration, and loudness. For the most part, something is an object if it has

- A name.
- Properties associated with it.
- Messages that it can understand.

Typically, when an object receives a message, the message either causes the object to take some action or to change one of its properties. In our remote control example, when the television received the "change channel" message from the remote control, it switched channels.

If we are going to take an object-oriented approach to developing software, it makes sense to use a programming language that supports thinking and implementing solutions in terms of objects. A language that has features to support thinking about and implementing solutions in terms of objects is an *object-oriented programming language*. Using an object-oriented programming language to implement an object-oriented design is called *object-oriented programming*. Notice we were very careful to include the phrase "implement an object-oriented design." As you will see later, you can certainly use an object-oriented language, but not think in terms of objects.

Some of the currently popular object-oriented languages are Smalltalk, C++, Eiffel, and Java. The features they have for supporting object-oriented programming are, for the most part, identical. They differ mainly in the terminology they use to talk about objects and the syntax of the language. In the following section, we describe the key features of object-oriented languages for creating and using objects.

1.4.1   Object-oriented programming

To illustrate some of the features of an object-oriented language, let's sketch out the design of a simple computer game called Bug Hunt. The purpose of Bug Hunt, more than anything else, is to help people develop their coordination when using a mouse. The game works like this. A moving bug is displayed in a window on the screen. The bug changes directions randomly (see Figure 1.20). The object of the game is to eliminate the bug (just like programming). A bug is eliminated by "swatting" it, that is, by clicking the mouse when the pointer is positioned over the bug. These are tough bugs, and it takes several swats to kill one. When the first bug is eliminated, another faster bug takes its place. If a bug is missed (i.e., the mouse button is clicked, but the pointer is not over a shape), the player loses the game. A player wins when he or she eliminates both the slow bugs and the fast bugs without any misses.

Before beginning to design Bug Hunt, we need a more precise statement of what the program should do. A more precise problem statement follows.

The game Bug Hunt consists of a window containing an image of a bug. A bug moves in random directions within the window. There are two types of

Figure 1.20

The Bug Hunt game

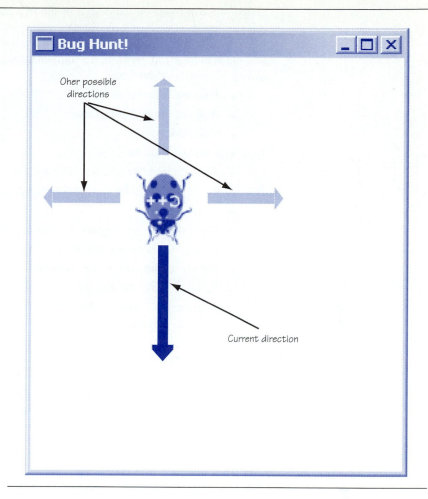

bugs—a slow bug and a fast bug. Obviously, a slow bug moves more slowly than a fast bug moves. In addition, the two types of bugs move differently. When a slow bug hits the border of the window, it reverses directions as if it hit a wall. When a fast bug hits a window border, it goes right on through and comes out the opposite window border.

To swat the bug, the user positions the mouse pointer over a bug and clicks a mouse button. If the mouse button is clicked when the pointer is not positioned over a bug (i.e., the player misses), a pop-up window tells the player that he or she missed and the game starts at the beginning. It takes several swats to kill a bug. The game ends when the fast bug is eliminated.

The first step in the object-oriented design process is to determine the objects we will be working with. From the problem statement, we can extract the objects by identifying the nouns that are objects according to our definition of object on page 34. The objects named in the problem statement are window, mouse, and bug. To illustrate the features available in an object-oriented language, we will focus on the design of the two bug objects. The design of the window and mouse objects are similar and are left as an exercise.

For each bug, we need to determine the properties associated with the bug and the actions it can perform. To implement Bug Hunt, a bug needs the following properties or attributes:

- Position in the window.
- A display image or picture.
- Current speed.
- Current direction.
- Strength (i.e., the number of swats it takes to eliminate the bug).

A bug needs to be able to handle the following messages or commands:

- Draw.
- Move the bug (i.e., update its current position).
- Change the direction in which the bug is moving.
- Hit (i.e, tell the bug it was swatted).
- Kill (i.e., make the bug die).
- Is-pointed-at, which asks the bug to determine whether the mouse cursor is pointing inside it.

These properties and messages form our abstraction of Bug Hunt's bugs.

Object-oriented languages provide a way of forming an abstraction by encapsulating properties and messages into a single concept. Such a concept is sometimes called a *class*. When a set of properties and messages are encapsulated in a class, we often say they are members of the class. The member properties of a class are sometimes called *data members* because they hold information. The messages a class of objects can handle are sometimes called *methods* or *member functions*.

The difference between a class and an object is subtle but important. Whereas a class is an abstract concept, an object is a concrete entity. For example, the concept of a car is a class, but a blue Ford Taurus with leather interior and a V-6 engine is an object. In practical terms, a class can be thought of as a stencil or mold for an object. From the class, objects with specific properties can be created, or instantiated.

The notion of instantiating a concrete object from a class abstraction is illustrated in Figure 1.21. Here, three different bugs, each with its own position, image, direction, and strength, are instantiated from the Bug class. The dotted enclosure for the class distinguishes it from a concrete object. In essence, a class defines an object's properties and messages. Instantiation creates an object with specific values for each of the properties.

At this point, we could create one class for each type of bug (slow and fast) and instantiate different kinds of bugs as required. However, an important feature of object-oriented languages is that it lets the programmer exploit the similarity of objects. If we think about it, a fast bug and a slow bug have many common characteristics. Whether a bug is slow or fast, it has a position, a velocity, an image, a direction, and a strength. In fact, the distinguishing fea-

Figure 1.21

*Instantiation of three
bug objects from class
Bug*

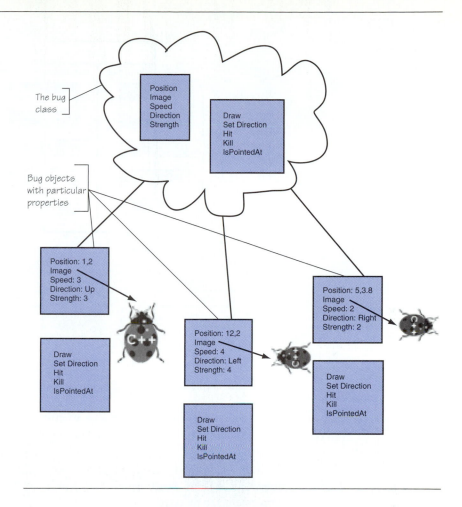

ture of a slow and a fast bug is how they move. A slow bug just reverses directions when it hits the edge of the window, whereas a fast bug tunnels through and reappears at the opposite side of the window. Thus we can think of creating a basic Bug that captures the attributes and behaviors that all bugs have in common and using it to create two special types of bugs, SlowBug and FastBug, that behave differently when they hit the edge of the window. Thus both Slow-Bug and FastBug are special types of Bug. These relationships, sometimes known as the *is-a* relationship, define a hierarchy. This hierarchy is shown in Figure 1.22.

At the top of the diagram is the Bug class. This class, our most general class, is sometimes referred to as the *base class* or *super class*. Below the base class are the *subclasses* or *derived classes*. Derived classes inherit the properties and messages of their ancestors. Thus both SlowBug and FastBug have the properties position, image, velocity, direction, and strength. Similarly, a FastBug and SlowBug understand the following messages or commands: draw, set

Figure 1.22

Abstraction and inheritance of bugs with different behaviors

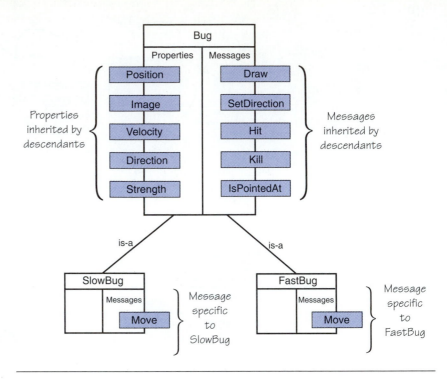

the direction, hit, kill, and determine whether the mouse is pointing at it. The notion of inheritance is a defining characteristic of object-oriented languages.

The ability of a class to inherit properties and member functions from an ancestor class supports the principle of reuse. Both bug types share the member functions of Draw, SetDirection, Hit, Kill, and IsPointedAt. These need to be implemented only once.

Our class hierarchy for bugs illustrates another feature of object-oriented languages—polymorphism. *Polymorphism* is the capability of something to assume different forms. In an object-oriented language, polymorphism is the property that a message can mean different things depending on the object receiving it. The message Move means one thing if it is sent to a SlowBug and something different if it is sent to a FastBug object. A SlowBug reverses directions when it hits the border of the window, whereas a FastBug tunnels through to the other side. This use of polymorphism is illustrated in Figure 1.22 by including Move as a message for both the FastBug class and the SlowBug class.

Polymorphism is a natural concept to apply to objects. Similar objects often accept the same message but do different things. For example, consider the graphical user interface of a computer. Here the objects consist of icons that represent files. We use the mouse to send messages to these objects. A typical message is a double-click, which is sent to the object by moving the mouse cursor over the object and double-clicking a mouse button. For an executable file, the double-click message means execute the program, whereas for a text file, the double-click message means start up the text editor and open the file for editing.

The development of the Bug hierarchy illustrates many of the features available in an object-oriented language. However, to fully demonstrate the power of object-oriented design and programming, we need to discuss how we can create a complete system from a group of objects. We can do this by sketching the high-level design of Bug Hunt.

Recall from the earlier description of Bug Hunt that the other objects explicitly mentioned were mouse and window. We will certainly need realizations of these objects. However, another very important object is mentioned in the description: the game itself! It's easy to overlook because the problem statement is a description of this object. If you think about it a moment, it makes sense to think of the game as an object. From an abstract point of view, the game object is the thing that coordinates the activities of the other objects, and it makes sure that the rules of the game are obeyed. We will call the object that is the game, the Game Controller.

We are now ready to complete the high-level design of Bug Hunt. As we mentioned, we certainly need mouse and window objects. For now, we can ignore the window object. Although it is necessary for the implementation of the game, creation and control of a window does not play a major role in the operation of the game. The mouse, on the other hand, is a key component of the game. Indeed, most of the game's action centers around the activities of the mouse. Our abstract view of the mouse object, Mouse, is that it can send messages to the Game Controller. The Mouse sends a message to the Game Controller whenever a button is clicked. The message contains the screen location of the mouse pointer, or sprite.

With the abstraction of the Mouse and Bug in hand, the design and operation of Bug Hunt is quite simple. The overall operation is illustrated in Figure 1.23. When a mouse button is clicked, the Mouse sends a MouseClick message to the Game Controller. The Game Controller extracts the mouse location from the message and sends an IsPointedAt message containing the location of the Mouse to the Bug on the screen. The Bug determines whether the location in the message is within it. If the Mouse is pointing at the Bug, it responds yes to the IsPointedAt message; otherwise, it responds no. If the Game Controller receives a yes response, then the Game Controller sends a Hit message to the Bug. If the Bug's strength has been sapped, the bug responds to the Hit message saying it has no strength. If this response is received, the Game Controller kills the Bug. If it was the SlowBug, the Game Controller creates a FastBug and the game continues. The interaction between the Game Controller and the Bug is illustrated in Figure 1.23.

If the Bug responds no, the Mouse is not pointing at it; then the Game Controller creates a new window and displays a message telling the player that he or she missed the bug. If all the Bugs are removed without a miss, the Game Controller displays a nice message in the window congratulating the player on

Figure 1.23

Interaction of the game controller, mouse, and bug

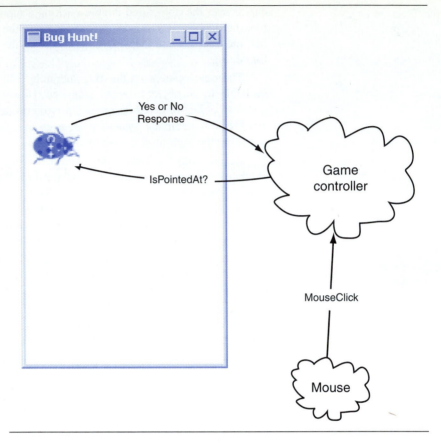

her or his skill with a mouse. Of course, there are many details that still need to be worked out to complete the implementation of Bug Hunt. However, the high-level design is set, and in Chapter 15, we will complete the design and implementation of Bug Hunt. So don't go away!

Self-check Questions

12.   What is a hierarchical ordering based on natural relationships?

13.   What is the name of the program that translates a high-level language program to machine code?

14.   What is the name of the program that combines object files and library files so they can be produced as a unit?

15.   What is the process of extracting the relevant properties of an object while ignoring the nonessential details?

16.   What is the process of separating the aspects of an object into external and internal aspects?

17.   What is the process of dividing an object into smaller pieces or modules so that some goal is easier to obtain?

18.   What is the object-oriented property where a message can mean different things depending on the object receiving it?

1.5 POINTS TO REMEMBER

✔ The speed of a computer is usually expressed in cycles per second. Typical machines operate at 100 to 200 megahertz or 100 million to 200 million cycles per second.

✔ Computers use the binary number system. A binary digit is called a bit.

✔ The basic unit of storage in a computer is a byte, or 8 bits.

✔ Negative numbers are usually stored in two's complement representation. In this representation, an n-bit number can represent values in the range -2^{n-1} through $2^{n-1} - 1$.

✔ The central processing unit, or CPU, is the brain of a computer. It is where arithmetic and logical functions are performed.

✔ The size of a computer's random access memory, or RAM, is measured in megabytes (MB). Current desktop machines have memories that range from 64 to 512MB.

✔ The capacity of the hard disks found on current desktop machines ranges from 10 to 75 gigabytes (GB).

✔ A programming language is a language that gives commands or instructions to a computer.

✔ A compiler translates a programming language to machine language. A machine language consists of primitive operations that a computer can perform directly.

✔ Application software is software that solves a particular problem or provides a particular service.

✔ Systems software is software that supports the development and execution of other programs.

✔ An operating system is system software that controls and manages the computing resources such as the memory, the input and output devices, and the CPU.

✔ Information is stored on a disk in a hierarchy of files, so it can be found and retrieved quickly.

✔ An algorithm is a detailed, step-by-step description of how to perform some task.

✔ The goal of a software engineer is to produce software that is reliable, understandable, cost effective, adaptable, and reusable.

✔ Abstraction is the process of isolating the essential, inherent aspects of an object while ignoring nonessential or irrelevant details.

History of Computing

Algorithms

Any system of counting or calculation, whether mentally or by means of a device, involves following a set of steps or directions. Computer scientists use the word *algorithm* to describe such a set of directions. The derivation of this word is of some interest. At the beginning of the ninth century, Caliph Al-Mamum established a great academic center in Baghdad. The center was known as the House of Wisdom. One of the scholars wrote a very influential textbook called *Kitab al jabr w'al-muqabala (Rules of Restoration and Reduction)*. The word *algebra* comes from the title of this book. The textbook introduced the use of Hindu numerals and included a systematic discussion of fundamental operations on integers. The book was influential because it fostered the use of Hindu numerals throughout the entire Arab empire and beyond. The word *algorithm* comes from the name of the scholar, Abu Ja'far Mohammed ibn Mûsâ al-Khowârizmî (literally, Father of Ja'far, Mohammed, son of Moses, native of Khowârizm).

A well-known example of an algorithm is Euclid's algorithm, which is a process for calculating the greatest common divisor (GCD) of two integers m and n. The algorithm is

Step 1.   Let r be the remainder of m divided by n.

Step 2.   If r is 0, the algorithm terminates and n is the GCD. Otherwise, set $m \leftarrow n$ and $n \leftarrow r$, and go back to step 1.

To illustrate the use of the algorithm, let's calculate the GCD of 12 and 8. We perform each step in sequence.

Step 1.   *Step 1*: $r \leftarrow 4$ (remainder of 12 divided by 8 is 4).

Step 2.   *Step 2*: r is not 0, so $m \leftarrow 8$ and $n \leftarrow 4$, and we go back to step 1.

Step 3.   *Step 1*: $r \leftarrow 0$ (remainder of 8 divided by 4 is 0).

Step 4.   *Step 2*: $r = 0$, so the algorithm terminates. The GCD of 12 and 8 is 4.

Notice that the algorithm is expressed as a set of steps. Each step describes some action to take. In this algorithm, we have used English to describe the actions to perform at each step. In many algorithms, the steps are described using a combination of a natural language and mathematical notation. The notation we use to describe the steps is largely irrelevant; the important thing is to describe the actions to be performed clearly and unambiguously. In later chapters of this text, as we construct a program to perform a particular task, we will often begin with algorithms that describe how to do the task. We will use a notation similar to that shown above.

✔ Encapsulation, or information hiding, is the process of separating the external aspects of an object, which can be viewed or accessed by other objects, from the internal implementation details, which should be hidden from other objects.

✔ Modularity is the process of dividing an object into smaller pieces so each smaller object or module can be dealt with individually.

✔ An inheritance hierarchy is a way of organizing a set of abstractions from most general to least general.

✔ Object-oriented design and programming is a paradigm of programming in which a software system is modeled as a set of objects that interact with each other.

✔ In C++ an abstraction is formed by creating a class. A class encapsulates the properties and behaviors of an object.

✔ The data members of a class are the properties or attributes of a class.

✔ The member functions of a class are the behaviors of a class.

✔ A base class is one from which other, more specialized classes can be derived.

✔ A derived class inherits properties from a base class.

✔ Polymorphism is the capability of something to assume different forms. In an object-oriented language, polymorphism is provided by allowing a message or member function to mean different things depending on the type of object that receives the message.

✔ Instantiation is the process of creating a concrete object from the class abstraction.

1.6 TO DELVE FURTHER

The following books are excellent sources for learning more about the history of computing.

- Stan Augarten, *Bit by Bit: An Illustrated History of Computers*, New York: Ticknor & Fields, 1984.

- Jon Palfreman and Doron Swade, *The Dream Machine: Exploring the Computer Age*, London: BBC Books, 1991.

- Harry G. Stine, *The Untold Story of the Computer Revolution*, New York: Arbor House, 1985.

- Michael R. Williams, *A History of Computing Technology*, Los Alamitos, CA: IEEE Computer Society Press, 1997.

1.7 EXERCISES

1.1 Suppose a microprocessor's clock rate is 120 MHz. If an addition operation can be done in one clock tick, how long, in nanoseconds, does it take to perform an addition?

1.2 Explain the difference between RAM and ROM.

1.3 Suppose a computer has a memory capacity of 16 megabytes. How many bits do we need to represent an address?

1.4 A computer has 640K bytes of memory. Exactly how many bytes of memory does it have?

1.5 How many bytes of information does a typical CD-ROM hold?

1.6 Find out all you can about one of the machines in a computer laboratory at your school. At a minimum, you should obtain the following information:

   a) The name of the company that manufactured the microprocessor in the machine.

   b) The clock speed of the processor.

   c) The amount of RAM in the machine.

   d) The size of the hard disk.

   e) The resolution of the graphics display.

   f) The name and version of the operating system.

1.7 Find an advertisement for one of the mail-order companies that sells computers. Find out what the acronyms and terms in the advertisement mean. Some of the terms and acronyms you might see are cache, Plug-and-Play, SCSI, EIDE, burst mode, EDO, EPP, and 56K.

1.8 The capacity of hard disk drives doubles every three years with cost remaining constant. Current 3.5-inch hard drives have a capacity of approximately 30 gigabytes and cost about $450. In six years, how much can we expect to pay for a one terabyte disk drive?

1.9 For the operating system you are using, name the commands that manipulate files. In particular, name the command that performs the following actions:

   a) Delete a file.

   b) Rename a file.

   c) Copy a file.

   d) Move a file.

   e) Create a directory.

   f) Delete a directory.

1.10 Give the decimal value of the following numbers:

   a) 01001_2

   b) 0374_8

   c) 0110100_2

      d) 4033_5

      e) $A32E_{16}$

      f) 2345_8

      g) 1211_4

      h) 0111111_2

      i) $02F3D_{16}$

      j) 010100100011_2

      k) 1776_8

      l) $ABBA_{16}$

      m) $ACDC_{16}$

1.11   Convert the following numbers to the specified base:

      a) 777_8 to hexadecimal

      b) $AD11_{16}$ to binary

      c) 01001011_2 to octal

      d) 1111_{16} to octal

      e) 01001111_2 to hexadecimal

      f) 01001111_2 to octal

      g) 3771_8 to binary

      h) 4356_{16} to octal

1.12   Give the decimal value of the following 8-bit, two's complement numbers:

      a) 10101100_2

      b) 10000001_2

      c) 11000000_2

      d) 10100101_2

      e) 11111111_2

      f) 10000000_2

1.13   Compute the following sums and products. Your answers should be in binary.

      a) $01000110 + 0001010$

      b) $00111011 + 0101100$

      c) $00000111 + 0000001$

      d) $00100111 + 0001111$

      e) $00010101 \, ´ \, 0001000$

      f) $00001000 \, ´ \, 0000011$

      g) $00001001 \, ´ \, 0000101$

      h) $00001011 \, ´ \, 0000100$

1.14   Interview a computer scientist at your institution. Write a two-page summary of the interview. Here are some questions you might ask the interviewee:

a) Why did you choose to become a computer scientist?

b) What are your areas of research expertise?

c) What are the most important research problems in your research area?

d) What are the most important research problems in the field of computer science?

e) Do you work with industry in your research? Which companies are your industrial partners? What are the advantages/disadvantages of working on research with industrial partners?

1.15 Consider an automated teller machine (ATM) at a bank. What are the relevant properties of an ATM for the following people?

a) ATM user.

b) ATM repair person.

c) Bank teller.

d) Bank president.

1.16 Give an example of encapsulation at work in a telephone-answering machine.

1.17 Most organizations have a hierarchical structure. Pick an organization that you belong to and produce a diagram that illustrates its hierarchy.

1.18 Are the following objects? Justify your answer.

a) Beauty

b) Time

c) Jealousy

d) Tree

e) Forest

1.19 Most electronic devices are designed using the principle of modularity, which makes the devices easier to manufacture and repair. Name the major components or modules of the following devices:

a) Television

b) VCR

c) Microwave oven

d) Boom box

e) Radio

f) Telephone

g) Washing machine

h) Bicycle

1.20 In an object-oriented inheritance hierarchy, the objects at each level are more specialized than the objects at the higher levels. Give three real-world examples of a hierarchy with this property.

1.21 Sketch the design of the Window class for the Bug Hunt game. Be sure to give the attributes (i.e., data members) and the actions (i.e., the member functions) that the class will have.

1.22 Sketch the design of the Mouse class for the Bug Hunt game. Be sure to give the attributes (i.e., data members) and the actions (i.e., the member functions) that the class will have.

1.23 Sketch the design of the Game Controller class for the Bug Hunt game. Be sure to give the attributes (i.e., data members) and the actions (i.e., the member functions) that the class will have.

1.24 Using the designs from questions 1.21 through 1.23, draw a diagram that shows how a Game Controller object, a Bug, a Mouse, and a Window might interact.

1.25 Sketch the object-oriented design of the card game blackjack. What are the key objects? What are the attributes and behaviors of these objects? How do the objects interact?

1.26 Sketch the object-oriented design of a system to control a pop machine. What are the key objects? What are the attributes and behaviors of these objects? How do the objects interact?

1.27 The inheritance example in Figure 1.22 ignored some details. Consider the following issues:

   a) Position is a property of all bugs. How might the position of a bug be specified?

   b) Outline the actions that a bug takes when it receives a Kill message.

1.28 Extend the class hierarchy of Figure 1.22 to include a WarpBug class. A WarpBug occasionally disappears and reappears in a new position. Do you need to make any changes to the properties of Bug?

CHAPTER 2

C++: The fundamentals

Introduction

In this chapter, we examine and write several small C++ programs and introduce the fundamental objects supported by C++. The intent is to give you an overall feel for the general structure of a C++ program and to help you become familiar with fundamental objects provided by C++. Indeed, a characteristic that often distinguishes one programming language from another is the primitive objects provided by the language. C++ has a rich set of fundamental objects, which allow integers, reals, and characters to be created and operated on.

Key Concepts

- function `main()`
- include
- comments
- definitions
- simple interactive input and output
- integer, floating-point, and character types
- integer, floating-point, and character literals
- C++ names
- declarations
- expressions
- usual unary conversions
- usual binary conversions
- operator precedence
- operator associativity
- iostream insertion and extraction

2.1   PROGRAM ORGANIZATION

Most programming languages have the concept of an executable unit. An *executable unit* is a named set of program statements. A program consists of a collection of these executable units. In languages such as FORTRAN and BASIC, the units are called subroutines or subprograms. In other languages, they are called procedures. In C++ the executable unit is called a function. These C++ executable units may be in one file or in several. A file containing C++ code is called a *translation unit*.

The ability to group program statements and functions into a named units has many advantages. First, it enables the programmer to structure the code as small, understandable units that perform specific, well-defined tasks. This structure can reduce the complexity of the program significantly. Reduced complexity means the program is easier to understand, easier to modify, and more likely to run correctly. Organizing a program into translation units and functions is analogous to structuring a book into a series of chapters (translation units) where each chapter consists of several sections (executable units). A well-thought-out organization helps the reader (programmer) understand the book (program).

The judicious use of functions can reduce the size of a program. In most programs, a particular task must be performed at several points during the execution. For example, an interactive program frequently asks users whether to proceed and perform some action. The user typically responds with a yes or no. If such queries occur often in a program, the size of the program can be reduced by placing the statements that prompt users and accept their responses in a separate function. Whenever user input is required, the programmer simply calls the function. In this chapter, we examine several simple C++ programs that consist of a single function.

2.2   A FIRST PROGRAM

Following a long-standing tradition, the first program we examine consists of a single function that outputs the following message:

Hello world!

Program 2.1 contains the source code for this program. Let's inspect this program in detail. The first three lines of the program are comments. *Comments* are program text that begin with two slashes. Comments are not translated by the compiler into executable code; they are inserted to describe and explain the operation of the program. The above program is so simple, we need not explain its operation. However, it is always useful to include comments that name the authors of the program. Later, if other programmers have questions about the program, they know who to ask. In Section 2.4 we will say much more about including comments in your programs.

Program 2.1

Hello world program

```cpp
// Program 2.1: Display greetings
// Authors: James P. Cohoon and Jack W. Davidson
// Date: 1/25/1998
#include <iostream>
#include <string>
using namespace std;
int main() {

    cout << "Hello world!" << endl;
return 0;

}
```

Lines 4 through 6 of the program

```cpp
#include <iostream>
#include <string>
using namespace std;
```

are three lines that will begin almost all our programs. These lines will appear at the beginning of any program that uses the iostream library to perform input or output. Lines 4 and 5 are preprocessor directives. The *preprocessor* is a program that runs before the compiler. Its job is to handle directives that control what source code the compiler sees as input. The `include` directive instructs the preprocessor to copy the contents of the specified file into the program. Essentially, the preprocessor replaces the directive with the contents of the specified file. The two files included, `iostream` and `string`, contain the output facilities that the program will use. The left and right angle brackets surrounding the filenames indicate that these are system files that can be found in a special system directory.

Line 6 of the program

```cpp
using namespace std;
```

says the program will be using objects that are named in a special region called `std`. This special region contains the names of many predefined objects that we will find useful as we write programs.

Line 7 of the program names the function and specifies the type of result the function will return. In a standard C++ program, the function named `main` is the first function called when the program is compiled and executed. The parentheses after the function name are used to delimit any arguments to the function. In this program, function `main()` requires no arguments, and hence nothing appears between the parentheses. The word `int` that appears before `main` indicates the type of result `main()` should return. The word `int` is C++'s name for an integer. By definition, `main()` always returns an integer result.

Following the parentheses is `'{'`, a left brace character. Much like parentheses, braces are used to group things. In this case, the left brace and the right brace at the end of the function group the program statements that make up the function. This function consists of two statements:

```cpp
cout << "Hello world!" << endl;
return 0;
```

The first statement is actually an expression like a + b + c. The operand cout is an object. Its definition along with the descriptions of the operations on it are found in the file iostream within the namespace std. The objects described in iostream are part of the iostream library, and they are used for doing input and output. cout is an output stream, and it typically corresponds to the display. The second operand is a string literal. String literals are enclosed in double quotes. In C++ terminology, we say that the << operator inserts the string into the named stream. The result is that the string Hello World! is sent to the display. The third operand, endl, is also part of the iostream library. It is called a manipulator. A *manipulator* is a value that can be inserted into a stream to cause some special action to take place. The manipulator endl inserts a new-line character in the output stream (so that the next output will begin on a new line), and it forces all output that has been sent to the display to be printed immediately on the screen.

The second and final statement of the program is

```
return 0;
```

This statement ends execution of the function main, and control is returned to the code that called main. This code does some cleanup (e.g., files are closed), and then control is returned to the operating system. The zero in the return statement is the value returned by main. The convention is that a zero result from main indicates that the program ran successfully and no errors occurred. A nonzero result indicates that some type of error occurred, and the calling program or operating system can take appropriate action.

2.3 A SECOND PROGRAM

Program 2.1 introduced several C++ components. However, it did not accept input, and it performed no calculations. Program 2.2 reads the value of a purchase and computes the sales tax on it. The following lines illustrate the execution of the program.

```
Purchase price ? 55.50
Sales tax on $55.50 is $2.22
```

The underlined text was typed by the user in response to the request to input the amount of the purchase. We will use this convention for indicating user input throughout the textbook.

The first executable statement

```
cout << "Purchase price ? ";
```

prompts the user to enter the purchase price. Such prompts are common in programs that interact with users. Notice that we did not use the endl manipulator, because we wanted the cursor to remain on the same line as the prompt.

To read the value of the purchase, we need a place to store the value. Line 9 of the program

```
float Price;
```

Program 2.2

Compute sales tax on a
purchase

```
// Program 2.2: Compute sales tax on purchase
// Authors: James P. Cohoon and Jack W. Davidson
// Date: 4/25/1998
#include <iostream>
#include <string>
using namespace std;
int main() {
    // Input price
    cout << "Purchase price ? ";
    float Price;
    cin >> Price;

    // Compute and output sales tax
    cout << "Sales tax on $" << Price << " is ";
    cout << "$" << Price * 0.04 << endl;
    return 0;
}
```

is a definition that instructs the C++ compiler to create an object named `Price` that can hold a floating-point value (i.e., a real). A floating-point object is used because we wish to enter the price as a decimal number.

The statement

```
cin >> Price;
```

waits for a number to be typed on the keyboard. When a value is typed, the value is converted to the internal format for floating-point numbers and stored in the object `Price`. The first operand, `cin`, is an object. Like `cout`, its definition along with the operations on it are found in the file `iostream`. `cin` is an input stream object, and it typically corresponds to the keyboard. The operator `>>` is called the *extraction operator,* and we say that it extracts a value from the named stream. The value extracted is stored in the right operand. The net effect is that the number typed on the keyboard is read and stored in `Price`.

The last two statements

```
cout << "Sales tax on $" << Price << " is ";
cout << "$" << Price * 0.04 << endl;
```

write the results to the display. The first statement writes a string, and the value stored in `Price`. The second statement outputs the result of the computation `Price * 0.04`, which is the sales tax. So we see that the insertion operator can output the value of an object as well as the value of a computation. These two statements could have been written as a single statement, but they were split to fit nicely on a line.

2.4   COMMENTS

A concept that is often difficult for beginning programmers to appreciate is that although a program is meant to be executed on a computer, it will be read by other human beings. Therefore, we want the program to be legal C++ (i.e., understandable by the computer), and we also want other programmers to understand the program. Hundreds of programmers often work on large commercial software systems. Some might be adding new features while others are fixing bugs. To accomplish their tasks, the programmers must be able to understand how the program works. Thus it is important to write our programs so that other people can understand them.

It is our experience that even when we write programs for our personal use, modification is often necessary. Although we surely understood how the program worked when we wrote it, after a few months or more have passed, we may have forgotten some important details about how the program works. *Comments* are a mechanism that enable us to include prose or commentary in the program that is not processed by the compiler. This commentary should explain how the program works.

In C++ there are two types or styles of comments. In the first type, the character '/' is immediately followed by another '/'. The compiler ignores the // and everything that follows it on the line. The following

```
// Comment
```

is a legal C++ comment, whereas the following statement is not a legal comment.

```
/ / Not a comment due to the space between the /'s
```

We used comments at the beginning of Programs 2.1 and 2.2 to identify the program, tell who wrote the program, and record when it was written. Including this information at the beginning of the program should be standard practice. Later, if other programmers have questions about the program, they know who to ask. Another common practice is for each programmer who changes a program to add a comment after the comment naming the original authors, giving the modifier's name and a description of the changes. Program 2.3 gives an example.

Program 2.3

Modified hello world program

```
// Program 2.3: Display greetings updated
// Authors: James P. Cohoon and Jack W. Davidson
// Date: 4/25/1998

// Modified by:
//    Jane Student: added a goodbye message
//    Date: 8/1/1998
#include <iostream>
#include <string>
using namespace std;
int main() {
    cout << "Hello world!" << endl;
    cout << "Goodbye world!" << endl;
    return 0;
}
```

The second form of C++ comment begins with the characters /* and ends with a */. Such comments can span one or more lines. The compiler ignores everything between the beginning /* and the closing */. For example:

```
/* This is a multiline comment. It
   can span several lines.           */
```

Program 2.4 illustrates the use of this style of comment.

Program 2.4

Program with /*...*/
style comments

```
/*****************************************************
 * Program 2.4: Greetings variant                    *
 * Authors: James P. Cohoon and Jack W. Davidson     *
 * Date: 4/25/1998                                    *
 *****************************************************/
#include <iostream>
#include <string>
using namespace std;
int main() {
    cout << "Hello world!" << endl;
    cout << endl; /* output blank line */
    cout << "Bye world!" << endl;
    return 0;
}
```

Generally, C++ programmers use the // style of comment exclusively. The second form is used when blocks of code need to be temporarily removed, perhaps for debugging purposes. The block of code to be removed is surrounded by a /* */ pair. One must use this convention carefully because this style of comment does not nest. Thus if the block of code in question includes a /* */ style comment, the results will not be as expected. Again, let's consider Program 2.4.

If we attempt to temporarily remove the last two statements by commenting them out, we get Program 2.5.

Program 2.5

Program with /*...*/
block-style comments

```
/*****************************************************
 * Program 2.5: Greetings variant                    *
 * Authors: James P. Cohoon and Jack W. Davidson     *
 * Date: 4/25/1998                                    *
 *****************************************************/
#include <iostream>
#include <string>
using namespace std;
int main() {
    cout << "Hello world!" << endl;
/*
    cout << endl; /* output blank line */
    cout << "Bye world!" << endl;
*/
    return 0;
}
```

The third insertion statement is not removed because the */ at the end of the previous line terminates the comment. In addition, the line following the third insertion statement (i.e., the */) is treated as source code, but it is not a valid C++ expression. When the program is compiled, the compiler will report a syntax error.

Self-check Questions

1.   What manipulator inserts a new line character in the output stream?

2.   Write a C++ statement that extracts an integer from the stream `cout` and places it in the object `Count`.

3.   Under what circumstances should function `main()` return a nonzero value?

4.   Write a C++ program that computes a tip on a meal purchase. Since you are generous, use 17 percent as the tipping rate.

2.5 ASSIGNING A VALUE

The third program we examine computes the *y*-coordinate of a point on a line. The inputs to the program are the characteristics of the line (i.e., the slope and *y*-intercept) and the *x*-coordinate of the point of interest. The problem is illustrated in Figure 2.1.

Figure 2.1

Equation for a line

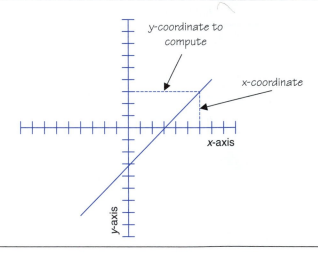

Program 2.6 contains the code. Although this program is obviously larger than the previous two, it uses only one new C++ construct: the assignment expression. The first few lines of the program prompt the user for and read the slope of the line, the *x*-intercept, and the *x*-coordinate of interest. The statement

```
y = m * x + b;
```

computes the value of the *y*-coordinate. This statement does not say that `y` is equal to `m * x + b`, but rather it says to store the result of the computation m * x + b in the object y. The ability to compute and store values is fundamental to all computing.

Program 2.6

Compute y-coordinate of a point on a line

```cpp
// Program 2.6: Compute the y-coordinate of a
// point on a line given the line and an x-coordinate
// Authors: James P. Cohoon and Jack W. Davidson
// Date: 4/25/1998
#include <iostream>
#include <string>
using namespace std;
int main() {
    // Input line s parameters
    cout << "Slope of line (integer)? ";
    int m; // Line slope
    cin >> m;
    cout << "Intercept of y-axis (integer)? ";
    int b;  // y-intercept
    cin >> b;

    // Input x-coordinate of interest
    cout << "x-coordinate of interest (integer)? ";
    int x;  // x-coordinate of interest
    cin >> x;

    // Compute and display y-coordinate
    int y;
    y = m * x + b;
    cout << "y = " << y << " when m = " << m << ";";
    cout << " b = " << b << "; x = " << x << endl;

    return 0;
}
```

Programmer Alert

2.6 FUNDAMENTAL C++ OBJECTS

C++ is notable because it has a large number of fundamental or built-in object types. The motivation was to give the programmer access to all the object types supported by typical hardware. The fundamental object types fall into one of three groups: the integer objects, the floating-point objects, and the character objects. Each of these groups contains several variants. In the following sections, we discuss each group and the most commonly used variants. Other specialized variants of the fundamental types are introduced throughout the text as they are needed.

2.6.1   Integer object types

Most programming languages have an object type for storing and manipulating integer values. The basic integer object type in C++ is called **int**. The definition of C++ does not specify the size of an **int**. The size of an **int** depends on both the underlying hardware and the compiler. Computer scientists say that the size of an **int** is *implementation dependent* or that the implementer of the compiler is free to choose the size of an **int**. Usually an **int** is chosen to be the most efficient integer data type on the underlying hardware. For most PC-based systems this size is 16 bits. A two's complement 16-bit **int** can represent integers from −32,768 to 32,767. For UNIX workstations, an **int** is usually 32 bits, although newer machines provide support for 64-bit integers. For these machines, the compiler designer could choose to use 64 bits to represent an **int**.

C++ provides several other integer object types. There is also **short** and **long**. Again, the specification of C++ does not dictate the size in bits of the **short** and **long** object type; however, it does specify that **long** be no shorter than **int** and that **int** be no shorter than **short**. That is,

$$NumberOfBits_{short} \leq NumberOfBits_{int} \leq NumberOfBits_{long}$$

The intent, however, is that **short** be smaller than **int** and **long** be greater than **int**. On PC-based systems, a **short** is usually 8 bits, and a **long** is 32 bits. On UNIX-based systems, a **short** is typically 16 bits, whereas a **long** is usually either 32 or 64 bits.

The question arises as to why C++ supports three different integer object types (actually, it provides support for others as well, but we defer discussion of those until later). Today many everyday objects are controlled by a computer. Examples include microwave ovens, automobiles, VCRs, and stereos. Systems in which a computer plays a central role in the operation of the system are called *embedded systems*. In most embedded systems, the memory used to hold the program that controls the system is a valuable resource that should not be wasted.

For example, many microwave ovens include a simple CPU that accepts input from a touch pad on the front and controls the operation of the oven. One of the costs associated with producing the oven is the number of memory chips required to hold the program that controls the operation of the oven. By providing support for integer objects of various sizes, C++ permits the programmer to optimize the usage of memory in the program. By picking the appropriate size object type, the programmer can reduce the memory requirements of the program. If this design results in fewer memory chips, the cost of the oven is lower.

As we mentioned earlier, an *object* is a set of attributes or values and behaviors or operations on the object. For the integer objects types **short**, **int**, and **long**, C++ provides the usual arithmetic operations such as addition, subtraction, multiplication, and division. C++ also has operators for comparing two integer objects. The six comparison operations are equal, not equal, less than, less than or equal, greater than, and greater than or equal.

2.6.2   Character object types

Closely related to the integer object type is the character object type **char**. Characters are encoded using some scheme where an integer represents a particular character. For example, the integer 98 might represent the letter *a*. The encoding scheme used is known as the *character set*. The two character sets in use today are ASCII and EBCDIC. Most computers use the ASCII character set; however, the EBCDIC character set is used on IBM mainframe computers. The ASCII character set encodes the characters using 7 bits, and the EBCDIC character set uses 8 bits. For this reason, **char** is usually 8 bits in length regardless of the character set in use. But again, we must point out that the definition of C++ leaves this decision to the implementer of the compiler.

Because the underlying representation of **char** is an integer, the operators defined on the integer types are defined on the character types as well. Regardless of the character set being used, we can always assume that the following relationships hold.

```
'a' < 'b' < 'c' < ... < 'z'
'A' < 'B' < 'C' < ... < 'Z'
```

and

```
'0' < '1' < '2' < ... < '9'
```

These relationships are useful, since they allow values that are made up of sequences of characters to be sorted into alphabetic order.

Additionally, with the ASCII character set we can assume that

```
'a' + 1
```

yields an integer that is the encoding for the character `'b'` and that

```
'A' + 1
```

produces an integer that is the encoding for the character `'B'`. That is, for any uppercase or lowercase letter *c* except for 'z' and 'Z', the expression

```
'c' + 1
```

yields the next letter in the alphabet. Similarly, the expression

```
'2' + 1
```

yields an integer that is the encoding for the character `'3'`. That is, for any digit *d* except for '9', the expression

```
'd' + 1
```

yields the next sequential digit. These relationships are useful, as they permit a character to be classified efficiently as to whether it represents a lowercase character, an uppercase character, or a digit.

For the EBCDIC character set, the preceding relationships do not hold for all characters. For example, with the EBCDIC character set the expression

```
'i' + 1
```

yields an integer that is the encoding of the character `':'`, not the letter `'j'`. For this reason, when dealing with the object type **char**, from this point forward we will assume that the encodings are defined by the ASCII character set.

The integer and character object types, along with the enumeration types that are discussed in Chapter 4, form the set of types known as the integral types. They are called the *integral* types because they are represented by a binary encoding of the integers.

2.6.3   Floating-point object types

The floating-point object types are used to represent real numbers, that is, numbers that have both an integer part and a fractional part. For example,

```
3.1412
```

has an integer part of 3 and a fractional part of `.1412`. C++ provides three floating-point object types: **float**, **double**, and **long double**. Analogous to the situation with **int**, **short**, and **long**, the specification of C++ does not dictate the sizes of **float**, **double**, and **long double**. It depends on the underlying hardware. However, we can assume that values represented by the **float** type are a subset of the values represented by the **double** type and that values represented by the **double** type are a subset of the values represented by the **long double** type.

For a processor that supports only a single floating-point format, the **float**, **double**, and **long double** types would be equivalent. On a processor that supports two distinct formats, it is likely that the type **float** would be mapped to the smaller of the two formats and that **double** and **long double** would be mapped to the larger format.

As a concrete example, consider personal computers based on Intel's x86 family of architectures. This family supports two floating-point representations. One is called *single real*. It is stored in 32 bits, and it can represent numbers in the range

$$1.18 \times 10^{-38} \le X \le 3.40 \times 10^{38}$$

with a precision of about seven decimal digit.

The second is called *double real,* and it can represent numbers in the range

$$2.23 \times 10^{-308} \le X \le 1.80 \times 10^{308}$$

with a precision of about 15 decimal digits. Double real requires 64 bits of storage. On this architecture, the type **float** would be mapped to single real. The types **double** and **long double** would be mapped to double real.

C++ provides the usual arithmetic operations on the floating-point data types as well as comparison operations.

One can guess that the rationale for different floating-point object types is somewhat analogous to that justifying the need for integer object types of different sizes. The larger floating-point formats are capable of representing numbers with a greater range and precision. It is up to the programmer to pick the format that best suits the application.

2.7 | CONSTANTS

In the previous section, we discussed C++'s fundamental object types. We now examine how to write *constants* of each of these types. Again, in comparison with many other programming languages, C++ has a variety of ways that constants of each type can be written. We begin by examining string constants.

2.7.1   String and character constants

In Program 2.1, the string constant

```
"Hello World!"
```

was used. A *string constant* is a sequence of zero or more characters enclosed in double quotes.

This simple mechanism works well for characters that have a symbolic representation, but we also need to be able to specify special characters that do not have an obvious printable representation such as the bell, carriage return, or form feed. To include a special character in a string constant, C++ defines an *escape mechanism.* The idea is that a special character, called the escape character, is used to change the meaning of the character following it. In C++, the escape character is the backslash '\', so, for example, to write a string constant that has the special newline character at the end, we would write

```
"Hello World!\n"
```

The backslash indicates that the character n is not to be interpreted as a constant n, but rather as a newline character.

Suppose we wish to write a string constant that includes the double quote. Again, we can use the escape mechanism and write

```
"\"Hello World!\""
```

The statement

```
cout << "\"Hello World!\"" << endl;
```

writes the string (including the double quotes)

```
"Hello World!"
```

to the display. Table 2.1 contains a list of the C++ character escape codes.

	Character Name	ASCII Name	C++ Escape Sequence
Table 2.1 *Character escape codes*	newline	NL	\n
	horizontal tab	HT	\t
	vertical tab	VT	\v
	backspace	BS	\b
	form feed	FF	\f
	alert or bell	BEL	\a
	carriage return	CR	\r
	backslash	\	\\
	single quote	'	\'
	double quote	"	\"
	question mark	?	\?

C++ provides one additional escape mechanism for specifying characters in a string constant in which the numeric value of the character (from the ASCII character set definition) is given. Interestingly, the base of the number used must be either octal or hexadecimal. Decimal notation is not allowed. Thus a character can be included using one of the forms

ooo

or

\x*hh*

where *ooo* and *hh* are, respectively, octal or hexadecimal numbers. For example, the string constant

```
"Hello World!\012"
```

is exactly the same string as

```
"Hello World!\n"
```

because 12_8 is the ASCII encoding of the newline character. Generally, it is better to use the C++ character escape sequence for special characters because if the program is moved to a machine with a different character set, the C++ compiler will figure out the correct encoding for any special characters.

When a string constant is stored in memory, the individual characters are stored in consecutive memory locations. After the last character of the string, a null character ('\0') is added. This convention of terminating strings with the null character allows for easy checking for the end of the string. It also means that the length of the string need not be stored as part of the representation of the string. The memory allocation of the string

```
"Hello World!"
```

is shown in Figure 2.2.

Figure 2.2

Memory allocation
for a string literal

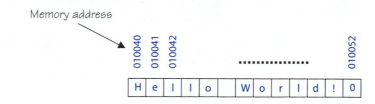

Each character takes up 1 byte of storage. The null character at the end of the string literal is not included when counting the number of characters in a string. Thus, the string literal above has 12 characters. This count is sometimes referred to as the *size of the string*.

The string constant with zero characters

```
""
```

is often called the *null string,* or *empty string*. It contains zero characters, or has size 0. Remember, however, that it too has the null character at the end, so it takes up 1 byte of memory.

Sometimes we will need the representation of a single character. In C++ a character constant is created by enclosing the character desired with the ' character. For example,

```
'a' '1' '+' ';'
```

are valid C++ character constants.

We can use the character escape mechanism described for string constants to create character constants for any special characters that do not have an obvious printable representation. So, for example, to write a character literal that is the special newline character we write

```
'\n'
```

Again, the backslash indicates that the character n is not to be interpreted as a constant n, but rather as a newline. Suppose we wish to write a character constant that has the value of the single quote? Again, we can use the escape mechanism and write

```
'\''
```

The backslash again indicates the middle single quote is the character being defined.

We can also use the numeric escapes to write a character constant. A character constant can be written using one of the forms

    `'\ooo'`

or

    `'\xhh'`

where `ooo` and `hh` are octal or hexadecimal numbers. The following are legal C++ character constants using the octal form:

    `'\033' '\06' '\0177'`

They denote the ASCII characters ESC (escape), ACK (acknowledge), and DEL (delete), respectively. It is typical C++ style to include the leading zero to further indicate the number is base 8. The following are the same constants:

    `'\33' '\6' '\177'`

The literals

    `'\x1b' '\x6' '\x7f'`

use the hexadecimal format, and they denote the same characters.

For both octal and hexadecimal character constants, the compiler should report an error if the number specified is too large to fit in a character object.

2.7.2   Integer constants

The simplest way to write an integer constant in C++ is to just write the number. For example,

    `23 45 101 55`

are four valid C++ integer literals. When we write an integer constant, the compiler assigns it a C++ object type. Generally, it will usually be the type **int**, but the type assigned depends on the size of the constant and whether it has a suffix. For example, to write an integer constant that will be treated as type **long**, the C++ programmer can append either an 1 or an L at the end of the number. Thus the constants

    `23L 451 101L 55L`

all have type **long**. We do not recommend using a lowercase 1, as it is easily confused with the digit 1. There is no way to specify an integer constant that is type **short**.

If the integer constant does not have a suffix, then the compiler chooses the type based on the size of the value. If the value can be stored as an **int**, then its type is **int**. However, if the value is too large to be stored as an **int**, but it can be stored as a **long**, then the compiler will treat the constant as type **long**. If the value is too large to be stored as a **long**, the compiler should report an error.

It is sometimes convenient to specify integer constants using a different base. C++ supports writing integer constants using both the base 8 and base 16.

C++ Language

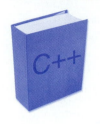

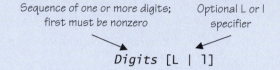

Specifying C++ syntax

There are a variety of ways to form an integer constant. Looking at some examples is a good way to get a general idea of what constitutes a valid C++ constant, but it would be nice if we had a notation for describing how to construct valid constants as well as other C++ constructs we will discuss. In this textbook, C++ syntax is described using annotated syntax diagrams. For example, the syntax diagram that describes decimal constants is

Sequence of one or more digits;   Optional L or l
first must be nonzero   specifier

Digits [L | l]

To specify one of several alternatives, the vertical bar ('|') is used. Square brackets around an item indicate that it is optional. Thus a type specifier can either be an L or an l, and it may be omitted. In a syntax diagram, italic symbols are known as *nonterminals*. That is, they represent a set of possibilities. In the diagram above, the symbol Digits represent the digits 0, 1, 2, ..., 9. The annotation notes that the first digit may not be a zero.

An integer constant that begins with a leading zero is assumed to be a base 8 number. The C++ constants

    023 077L 045 010

are all base 8 numbers and represent the decimal values 19, 63, 37, and 8. All but the second are type **int**. The second is type **long**. If the constant is base 8, then the characters 8 or 9 cannot appear in the constant. Thus the constants

    038 093 0779

are not valid C++ constants.

To use base 16, the prefix 0x or 0X is used. In a hexadecimal constant, the characters a through f or A through F represent the digits 10 through 15. The literals

    0x2a 0x45 0XffL 0xA1e

represent the decimal values 42, 69, 255, and 2590. The third value has type **long**; the others have type **int**.

The general syntax for octal and hexadecimal integer constants is

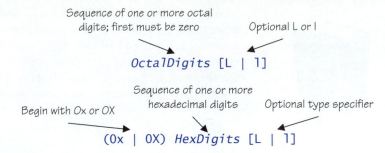

Program 2.7 outputs the decimal values for octal, decimal, and hexadecimal constants.

Program 2.7

Output different base constants

```
// Program 2.7: Output different base constants
#include <iostream>
#include <string>
using namespace std;
int main() {
    cout << "Display integer constants\n" << endl;

    cout << "Octal constant 023 is " << 023 << " decimal"
      << endl;    // outputs decimal value 19
    cout << "Decimal constant 23 is " << 23 << " decimal"
      << endl;    // outputs decimal value 23
    cout << "Hexadecimal constant 0x23 is " << 0x23
      << " decimal" << endl; // outputs decimal value 35

    return 0;
}
```

When executed, the program produces the following output:

```
Display integer constants

Octal constant 023 is 19 decimal
Decimal constant 23 is 23 decimal
Hexadecimal constant 0x23 is 35 decimal
```

Using different bases to represent numbers is the basis for the following really bad computer science riddle. Question: Why did the programmer get Halloween and Christmas confused? Answer: Because Oct 31 = Dec 25.

The observant reader might note that we have made no mention of negative numbers. The reason is that integer constants are always nonnegative. To form a negative value, a minus sign can be applied to a constant, but the formal interpretation is that a unary minus operator is applied to the constant. The minus sign is not part of the constant. A plus sign can also be applied to an integer constant. It does not change the value of the constant. The plus sign is included in C++ for symmetry with the unary minus operator.

2.7.3 Floating-point constants

C++ also provides a variety of ways to write floating-point constants. The syntax for one form of floating-point constant is

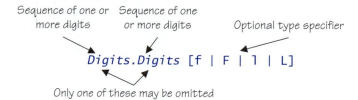

For example,

2.34 3.1416 29.00 .23 0.32

are all valid C++ floating-point constants. For floating-point constants, the type is always **double** unless otherwise specified. In a manner similar to that used for integer constants, the type can be specified using the letters f, F, l, and L as a suffix. The letters f or F specify that the constant is to be type **float**; the letters l or L specify that the constant is to be of type **long double**. The types of the floating-point constants

23.4f 0.21L 45.3F 7456.1

are **float**, **long double**, **float**, and **long double**.

C++ also provides the ability to express floating-point constants using scientific notation. Recall that in standard scientific notation, a number is expressed as a power of 10. The number

$$1.23 \times 10^3$$

is in scientific notation. This number is read as "one point two three times ten to the third power." The above number is equal to

1230.0

The general form for a number in scientific notation is

$$mantissa \times 10^{exponent}$$

The syntax for C++ scientific notation is

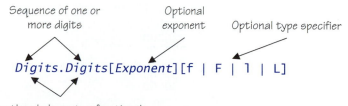

where Exponent is

One or more
Starting e or E   Optional sign   digits

(e | E) [+ | -] Digits

The mantissa can be an integer or a decimal number. The exponent is a signed integer. Examples of valid C++ floating-point constants using the scientific notation are

    1.23E10   0.23E-4   45.e+23   23.68E12

These constants represent, respectively, the values

$$1.23 \times 10^{10} \quad 0.23 \times 10^{-4} \quad 45.0 \times 10^{23} \quad 23.68 \times 10^{12}$$

in standard scientific notation. The type of a floating-point constant can be specified using the previously mentioned suffixes. In the preceding example, since there is no type suffix, all of the above numbers are type **double**. The C++ constants

    1.23E10F   0.23E-4f   45.e+23L   23.68E12L

have the same values as the preceding numbers expressed in scientific notation, but the first two are type **float** and the second two are type **long double**.

Program 2.8 illustrates the use of the various forms of floating-point constants.

Program 2.8

Output different forms of floating-point constants that represent the same value

```
// Program 2.8: Illustrate different forms of
// floating-point constants that have the same value
#include <iostream>
#include <string>
using namespace std;
int main() {
    cout << 230.E+3 << endl;
    cout << 230E3 << endl;
    cout << 230000.0 << endl;
    cout << 2.3e5 << endl;
    cout << 0.23E6 << endl;
    cout << .23e+6 << endl;
    return 0;
}
```

When the program is executed, it outputs the following values:

    230000
    230000
    230000
    230000
    230000
    230000

As the output shows, all the constants represent the same value.

Analogous to the situation with integer literal constants described in Section 2.7.2, floating-point constants are not signed. A constant can be negated by applying a minus sign to it.

Self-check Questions

5.   Suppose a short is 16 bits on a particular machine. How big must an `int` be?

6.   How many bits does the ASCII character set use to encode a character?

7.   What type of C++ object is used to represent real numbers?

8.   What is the C++ escape sequence for including a newline in a string?

9.   What is the C++ escape sequence for including a double quote (' ') in a string?

10.   What is the size (i.e., number of bytes of storage occupied) of the following string?
      `Ben Rush`

11.   Name the two numeric components of a floating-point number.

12.   What is the type of the C++ floating-point constant `2.3E10`?

13.   What is the type of the C++ floating-point constant `1.45E5L`?

14.   Give the standard scientific notation for the C++ floating-point constant `1.13E-10`.

2.8   NAMES

A fundamental requirement of computing is the ability to store and retrieve information. In the early days of computing, before assemblers and high-level programming languages, programmers wrote programs in machine language and they were required to keep track of where in the computer's memory values were stored. These values were accessed by specifying the address of the memory location that contains the value. To see first-hand how tedious and error-prone this process can be, let's write a simple machine-language program that computes a 6 percent sales tax on five items.

The prices of the five items are stored in memory. Figure 2.3 shows the layout of memory. The item prices are stored in memory locations 2000 through 2016. We also need memory locations to store the sum of the prices of the items and the computed tax. We must ensure that the locations we choose do not overlap with the memory locations where the cost of the items is stored. We arbitrarily pick memory location 2028 for the sum and memory location 2024 to hold the sales tax.

Figure 2.3

Memory layout for machine-language programming example

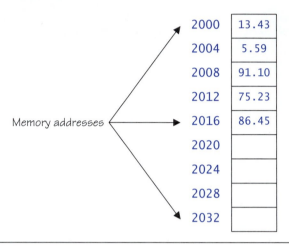

A memory location is accessed by writing M[n] where n is the address to access. The operation M[n] → expr stores the value of expr in the memory location M[n]. A machine-language program to compute the sales tax is

```
M[2028]  → 0
M[2028]  → M[2028] + M[2000]
M[2028]  → M[2028] + M[2004]
M[2028]  → M[2028] + M[2008]
M[2028]  → M[2028] + M[2012]
M[2028]  → M[2028] + M[2016]
M[2024]  → M[2028] * .06
```

The first thing to notice about this program is that if you looked at it without knowing beforehand what it is supposed to do, it would be difficult to tell what it is computing. If we rewrite the instructions using symbolic names instead of machine addresses, we get the program

```
TotalCost  → 0
TotalCost  → TotalCost + Price1
TotalCost  → TotalCost + Price2
TotalCost  → TotalCost + Price3
TotalCost  → TotalCost + Price4
TotalCost  → TotalCost + Price5
SalesTax   → TotalCost * .06
```

which is much easier to understand and less prone to errors.

Because of the overwhelming advantages of using symbolic names, all modern programming languages support the use of names to denote program values or objects. All high-level programming languages allow a programmer to use symbolic names to represent values as well as other program entities.

An important component of a programming language is the rule for forming valid names. In C++ a valid name is a sequence of letters (upper- and lowercase), digits, and underscores with the additional restriction that the name cannot begin with a digit. Examples of valid C++ names are

```
x _digit x1 Score date AverageScore temp Nbr_Trials
```

Examples of strings that are not valid C++ names are

```
2BORNOT2B ToHot? $a1 A#
```

Names are case sensitive. That is, for two names to be the same, they must have exactly the same spelling, including the case of the characters. For example, the names

```
NbrOfTrials      NbrofTrials
```

are different because of is capitalized in the first, but not in the second.

A question of interest is, How long can a name be? The definition of C++ sets no limit on the length of name. However, some C++ implementations are deficient in this area, and they may use only the first *n* characters of a name to determine uniqueness. For example, the Turbo C++ compiler uses the first 32 characters of the name. Other compilers may use more or less. Thus it is important to make sure that two long names for different objects are unique in the first part of the name rather than at the end. Otherwise, two names that appear different to the programmer may be treated as the same name by the compiler.

Like many other programming languages, C++ has two classes of names: keywords and identifiers. These names are discussed in the following sections.

2.8.1 Keywords

Some words are reserved as part of the language, and they cannot be used by the programmer to name things. These special names are usually called *reserved words*; in C++ terminology they are called *keywords*. Table 2.2 lists the C++ keywords.

Keywords have special meaning to the compiler, and they cannot be changed by the programmer. We have already discussed a few of these keywords. The keywords **short**, **int**, **long**, **float**, **double**, and **char** are C++ fundamental types. As we delve deeper into C++, we will discuss the meaning of the other keywords.

Recall that names are case sensitive, and by definition keywords consist of lowercase letters only. Thus the strings

```
Continue DO Char
```

are not keywords. However, as we discuss in the next section, they are valid C++ identifiers.

2.8.2 Identifiers

An *identifier* is a name defined by and given meaning to by the programmer. For example, in Program 2.1 on page 51 main, cout, and endl are symbolic

Table 2.2

C++ keywords

asm	else	operator	throw
auto	enum	private	true
bool	explicit	protected	try
break	extern	public	typedef
case	false	register	typeid
catch	float	reinterpret_cast	typename
char	for	return	union
class	friend	short	unsigned
const	goto	signed	using
const_cast	if	sizeof	virtual
continue	inline	static	void
default	int	static_cast	volatile
delete	long	struct	wchar_t
do	mutable	switch	while
double	namespace	template	
dynamic_cast	new	this	

names. main is the name of the function; cout is the name of an object that is used to do output to the display; and endl is the name of a manipulator.

The rule for forming a valid identifier is that it must be a valid C++ name and cannot clash with the keywords. Examples of valid C++ identifiers are

TaxRate   n   price   flow   first_value   tmp

Choosing identifiers that connote the purpose of the object being named is good programming practice. For example, suppose we are writing a program to compute and store the number of students in a class. We could choose the identifier

s

to name the object that will hold the number of students in the class, but this identifier is not very descriptive. At the other end of the spectrum, we could use

Number_of_Students_in_Class

but this identifier would be tedious to write all the time. Usually, there is a reasonable middle ground. The identifier

NbrStudents

is much shorter and almost as clear. In this text, we will adopt several conventions for picking and constructing identifiers to name objects. First, we will strive to use single word identifiers. However, when we use identifiers constructed of two or more words so that the purpose of the object is clear, we will follow the convention of capitalizing the first letter of each word. So, for instance, we might use the identifiers

WordCount   Time   BitsPerSecond   LapTime

Second, we will often use abbreviations for obvious words. For example, abbreviations such as Nbr for *Number*, Obj for *Object*, and Cnt for *Count* decrease the length of the identifier without loss of clarity. Identifiers illustrating this style of abbreviation are

WindowObj   EmployeeNbr   WordCnt

As we develop programs and the need for additional naming conventions becomes apparent, we will introduce them.

C++ Language

Use of underscores

Although underscores are permitted at the beginning of C++ names, their use should be avoided. Identifiers beginning with a double underscore are reserved for use by the C++ compiler. Similarly, names that begin with a single underscore should be avoided as they are reserved by some C implementations for naming operating system routines. Some C++ implementations use C libraries.

2.9 DEFINITIONS

In C++, before we can use an object, we must define the object. A *definition* introduces the name of the object into the program, and it specifies the type of the object.

A common form of a C++ definition is

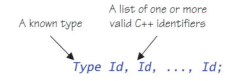

A known type   A list of one or more
                    valid C++ identifiers

Type Id, Id, ..., Id;

where *Type* is a fundamental type or a type that has been previously defined by the programmer and *Id* is a C++ identifier. The definition

int Sum;

defines an object called Sum that has type **int** with no initial value. That is, the object is named, memory is allocated, but the object is given no initial value. Additional examples of this form of definition are

int x;
int WordCnt, Radius, Height;
float FlightTime, Mileage, Speed;

None of these objects is given an initial value. In general, it is not a good idea to define an object without initializing it. For example, if we attempt to use

`Mileage`'s value before we have explicitly given it one, the value we get is unknown or undefined.

Programming Tip

> ### *What is an object?*
>
> Some texts make a distinction between objects and the fundamental data types. In their view, an object is an instance of a programmer-defined data type where the data and the functions that operate on that data are combined into a single unit. Also in their view, a declaration of a fundamental data type is not an object, but a variable. Such a distinction is artificial. In our view, an object is a region of memory that contains values. How these values are interpreted depends on the type of the object and how it is accessed. Whether the type was created by the programmer or provided by the programming language is irrelevant.

Program 2.9 illustrates the danger of using uninitialized objects. The program defines four uninitialized objects and then outputs their values. When the program is run, the output is unpredictable.

When executed, the program outputs:

```
f's value is 1.81825e+11
i's value is 8653
c's value is e
d's value is 1.12975e-231
```

Thus it is always a good idea to initialize an object when it is defined.

Another form of definition allows objects to be initialized when they are defined. The C++ syntax for this type of definition is

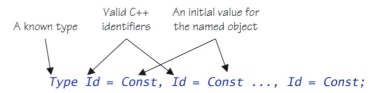

```
Type Id = Const, Id = Const ..., Id = Const;
```

The definition

```
int Sum = 0;
```

is equivalent to the first definition, but it initializes `Sum` to zero. Other examples of this form of definition are

```
float TaxRate = 0.06;
char letter = 'a';
```

The first definition creates a **float** object called `TaxRate` with an initial value of `0.06`; the second creates an object named `letter` that has type **char** with an initial value of `'a'`.

Program 2.9

*Output the values of
uninitialized objects*

```
// Program 2.9: Output the values of uninitialized objects
#include <iostream>
#include <string>
using namespace std;
int main() {
    float f;
    int i;
    char c;
    double d;
    cout << "f's value is " << f << endl;
    cout << "i's value is " << i << endl;
    cout << "c's value is " << c << endl;
    cout << "d's value is " << d << endl;

    return 0;
}
```

We will often use comments in conjunction with definitions to explain what the object represents. Some examples are

```
int Temp = 32;      // current Temperature (Fahrenheit)
char c;             // current input character
float PayRate;      // hourly rate of pay (Dollars)
```

Notice that when the object is a measure, it is helpful to state the units of measure in the comment.

Several objects can be defined and initialized in a single statement. For example, the C++ declaration

```
int Count = 0, Bits = 16, Small = -1;
```

declares three objects, all of type **int**. Count is initialized to 0, Bits is initialized to 16, and Small is initialized to -1.

Besides allowing us to use symbolic names for program objects, the use of definitions passes the burden of deciding where to place objects in memory to the compiler. In our machine-language sales tax program, we had to ensure that the memory locations for the various objects did not conflict or overlap. This process of assigning memory locations to objects is called *memory allocation*. To allocate memory manually, we had to know the amount of memory required to store each item. In our example, we assumed that a price was represented as a floating-point value and required 4 bytes of storage.

For a program with just a few objects, a programmer could probably keep track of where to store the objects. However, this task would be difficult for large programs with many objects, and perhaps more importantly, it would detract from the important job of writing a correct program.

Thus, a definition directs the compiler to do several things. Using the type information to determine the number of memory locations to hold the object, the compiler allocates memory locations to store the object. These memory locations are then reserved and cannot be used to hold subsequently defined objects. The compiler records that information along with the name so that when the name is used subsequently, the location of the object in memory can be found. And finally, it gives the object an initial value.

Programmer Alert

> *Always give objects an initial value*
>
> A common error is to forget to give an object an initial value. To avoid this, it is a good idea to give an object an initial value when it is defined. The only exception is when the object will be initialized immediately after the definition by extracting a value from an input stream and storing it in the object. For example, the code
>
> ```
>     float Price;
>     cin >> Price;
> ```
>
> is acceptable. However, it certainly would not hurt to write
>
> ```
>     float Price = 0.0;
>     cin >> Price;
> ```
>
> However, some would argue that the above fragment could confuse the reader because the object Price is given a value that is immediately overwritten.
>
> Our code follows the convention of always giving an object an initial value unless the object is immediately given a value through an extraction operation.

The two forms of definitions introduced above can be used together. The following C++ definition

```
    int i, j = 4, k, l = 10;
```

creates four **int** objects: i, j, k, and l. The objects i and k have no initial value, whereas j and l are initialized to 4 and 10, respectively.

In this text, our rule of thumb is to use a definition that initializes the object. Furthermore, we typically define only one object per line. This convention enables us to include a comment with each definition that explains the purpose of the object.

Self-check Questions

15.   What are the allowable characters for forming a valid C++ name?

16.   Is Window$Cost a valid C++ name?

17.   In C++ a name that has a special meaning to the C++ compiler is called a
      _____.

18.   Write a C++ definition that defines and initializes the **int** object Head-Count to 25.

19.   Write a C++ definition that defines and initializes the **float** object MovingAverage to 25.0.

2.10   EXPRESSIONS

In Chapter 1, we introduced the notion of an object. Recall that an object is a set of attributes or values and the operations that can be performed on them. An *expression* is C++'s mechanism for applying operations to objects. Conceptually, an expression is the means by which we calculate new objects from old ones. The objects or values being operated on are called the *operands*. The process of applying the operation to the operands is referred to as *evaluating the expression*. The evaluation of an expression yields a result that has a type as well as a value. The notion that the evaluation of an expression yields a result that has value and a C++ type is very important. To make this notion very clear, in the following sections that discuss expressions, we will present the result of evaluating an expression as a 2-tuple of the form

<value, type>

where *value* is the value of the expression and *type* is the C++ type associated with the value. Do not be put off by the term *2-tuple*. It is just a formal way of saying that a result consists of two components. As a reminder that we have adopted this convention for clarity, results expressed as 2-tuples will be italicized. In later sections, we drop the notation and give only the value with the assumption that the type is implicitly part of the result.

2.10.1   Simple expressions

The simplest form of a C++ expression is a constant with no operation applied. For example, the evaluation of the expression

```
23;
```

yields the result *<23, int>*. The semicolon after the expression is the C++ delimiter that separates or terminates an expression.

Similarly, the expression

```
18.53;
```

evaluates to *<18.53, double>*. The expression

```
'a';
```

evaluates to *<97, int>*.

An expression can also be an object with no operation applied. The result of evaluating this type of expression is the value of the object. For example, consider the following declaration and expression:

```
int XCoord = 23;        // x-coordinate of point
XCoord;
```

The result of evaluating the expression is *<23, int>*. In some sense, an operation is being applied to the operand XCoord. The operation being applied is one that fetches the value stored in XCoord. Consider the following longer example:

```
double BattingAvg = .253;// current batting average
int AtBats = 301;         // at bats this season
short StolenBases = 34;  // stolen bases this season
float EarnedRunAvg = 1.7;     // Earned run average
                              // (pitchers)

char c = 'x';

// Begin expressions
AtBats;
BattingAvg;
EarnedRunAvg;
c;
StolenBases;
```

The results of the expressions are *<301, int>*, *<0.253, double>*, *<1.7, float>*, *<120, int>*, and *<34, short>*, respectively.

2.10.2 Binary arithmetic operations

C++ has several binary operators for performing arithmetic on the integer and floating-point types. The term *binary* indicates that the operator is applied to two operands. Because the C++ rules for performing binary operations are rather complicated, we first consider the binary operators applied to integer values. We then consider expressions involving binary operators applied to floating-point values. The section concludes with a discussion of how C++ handles expressions involving values of both integer and floating-point types.

The binary integer arithmetic operators are listed in Table 2.3. All the examples are done using the type **int**. As the table shows, the binary integer arithmetic operators, for the most part, do just what you think they should do. The simple expression

```
2 + 3;
```

produces the value *<5, int>*. Similarly, the expression

```
4 - 7;
```

produces the value *<3, int>*. The division and modulus operators, however, deserve special attention. Notice that the expression

```
6 / 4;
```

produces the value 1, not 1.5. When applied to two positive integer values, the C++ division operator produces an integer result. If the divisor does not evenly divide the dividend, the fractional part of the quotient is discarded and the whole part of the quotient is the value component of the result. The process of discarding the fractional part is called *truncation*. In the second division example, the expression

```
11 / 4;
```

evaluates to the result *<2, int>*. That is, the result of the division 2.75 is truncated to produce the value 2. Note that truncation is not the same as *rounding*. In the previous example, rounding would have produced the value 3.

Table 2.3

Binary integer
arithmetic operators

Operation	Operator	Example	Result
Addition	+	2 + 3; 5 + 10;	*<5, int>* *<15, int>*
Subtraction	–	13 – 4; 4 – 7;	*<9, int>* *<–3, int>*
Multiplication	*	3 * 4; 5 * 11;	*<12, int>* *<55, int>*
Division	/	8 / 2; 6 / 4; 11 / 4; 4 / 5; 6 / 0;	*<4, int>* *<1, int>* *<2, int>* *<0, int>* *<undef, int>*
Remainder	%	10 % 3; 23 % 4; 5 % 0;	*<1, int>* *<3, int>* *<undef, int>*

What happens if one of the operands is negative and the result is inexact? In this case, the definition of C++ allows one of two choices. The two choices are the integers that are closest to the mathematical quotient. The implementer of the compiler is free to choose the result that is most convenient for the target machine. For example, the choices for the value component of the expression

        -11 / 2;

are –5 and –6. Thus depending on the compiler and the machine, either of the results, *<–5, int>* or *<–6, int>*, may be produced.

Finally, there is a case that deserves special attention. If the divisor is zero, the result of the division operation is undefined. Indeed, for most machines, dividing by zero will cause the program to halt with an error. In many of the examples in this book, we take special care to ensure that we do not inadvertently perform a division by zero.

Closely related to division is the remainder operator %, which produces as a result the remainder of the division. It is also sometimes referred to as the *modulus* operator. The result of the expression

        19 % 5

is *<4, int>* because 19 divided by 5 yields a quotient of 3 and a remainder of 4.

Because the remainder operator is typically implemented using the target machine's division instruction, it shares many characteristics of the division operator. First, if the right operand is zero, the result of the operation is undefined. Second, if either operand is negative and the result is not zero (i.e., there is a remainder), the value component of the result depends on how the target machine performs division. It is always the case that the expression

```
(a / b) * b + a % b
```

is equal to a if b is not 0. So, for example, if

```
7 / -2
```

produces the result <–4, int>, the expression

```
7 % -2
```

must produce <–1, int>. On the other hand, if the expression

```
7 / -2
```

produces the result <–3, int>, the remainder operator must produce the result <1, int>.

All the binary integer arithmetic operators have the potential to produce a value that is larger than the host machine can handle. This situation is called *overflow*. If an integer arithmetic operation produces an overflow, the value produced by the operation is undefined and the behavior of the program is unpredictable.

If you recall from Section 2.6.1, C++ has three integer types—**short**, **int**, and **long**—as well as the **char** type. Up to this point, we have assumed that the operands are all of type **int**. How is arithmetic performed on the other integer types? For example, is the addition of two values of type **long** different from the addition of two values of type **int**? What if one value is of type **int** and the other of type **long**? With four types, there are 10 different possibilities for addition.

To reduce the number of cases that must be handled, C++ defines a set of conversions that is applied to operands before any operations are performed. These conversions are called the *usual unary conversions*. The usual unary conversions specify that values of type **char** and **short** should be converted to type **int** before any operations are performed. At this point, the operands of an integer binary operation can be either of type **int** or of type **long**. In addition, a set of conversions are applied to operands before binary operations are applied. These conversions are called the *usual binary conversions*. If the operands are the same type, no conversion is done and the type of the result is the type of the operands. If the types of the operands are not the same, then the one that is type **int** is converted to type **long**, a **long** operation is performed, and the type of the result is **long**.

The above may seem a bit complicated, but it really is not that difficult. Just remember, the result is always **int** unless one of the operands is type **long**; then the result is type **long**. This rule is summarized in Table 2.4.

All the arithmetic operators, except for the remainder operator (%), can be applied to floating-point operands (i.e., **float**, **double**, and **long double**). The binary floating-point arithmetic operators are listed in Table 2.5. Again, for illustrative purposes, all operands are type **double**.

Table 2.4

Result types for integer binary operations

		Type of Right Operand			
		char	short	int	long
Type of Left Operand	char	int	int	int	long
	short	int	int	int	long
	int	int	int	int	long
	long	long	long	long	long

Table 2.5

Binary floating-point arithmetic operators

Operation	Operator	Example	Result
Addition	+	2.0 + .33; 5.1 + 10.0;	<2.33, double> <15.1, double>
Subtraction	-	13.6 - 4.2; 4.0 - 7.0;	<9.4, double> <-3.0, double>
Multiplication	*	3.0 * 4.4; 7.5 * 11.0;	<13.2, double> <82.5, double>
Division	/	8.6 / 2.0; 5.0 / 4.0; -11.0 / 4.0; 6.0 / 0.0;	<4.3, double> <1.25, double> <-2.75, double> <undef, double>

The remainder operator makes no sense when applied to floating-point operands. The C++ compiler will flag as illegal an expression where a floating-point value is an operand to the remainder operation.

The other binary floating-point arithmetic operators act as you would expect. Just as with the binary integer arithmetic operators, overflow is a possibility, and a floating-point division by zero will cause the program to halt.

Similar to the situation with the binary integer arithmetic operations, the usual binary conversions are applied when operands are of different floating-point types. The rule is similar in spirit to the rule for the integer types. That is, the less precise operand is converted so that it is at least as precise as the other operand. To do otherwise would mean that we would unnecessarily lose precision in the result. For example, if one operand is type **float** and the other is type **double**, the operand that is type **float** is converted to type **double**. The operation performed is a double-precision addition, and the type of the result is **double**. The possibilities for the results of binary floating-point operators with operands of different precisions are summarized in Table 2.6.

	Type of Right Operand		
	`float`	`double`	`long double`
`float`	`float`	`double`	`long double`
`double`	`double`	`double`	`long double`
`long double`	`long double`	`long double`	`long double`

(Type of Left Operand on the vertical axis)

To help understand the usual binary conversions when the operands are different floating-point types, let's study a code fragment that requires conversions.

```
float Temp = 23.3;
double Volume = 3.2;
long double AvogadroConstant = 6.023E23;
cout << Volume * AvogadroConstant;
cout << Temp / Volume;
```

In the arithmetic expression in the first insertion to `cout`, `Volume` is promoted from **double** to **long double** because `AvogadroConstant` is **long double**. In the following statement, `Temp` is promoted from **float** to **double** because `Volume` is **double**. Again, the key idea is that the operands are promoted so that the operation can be done using arithmetic that is as precise as the most precise operand.

2.10.3   Unary arithmetic operations

C++ has several unary operators. The term *unary* means that the operator is applied to a single operand. As we mentioned in Section 2.7.2 and Section 2.7.3, C++ has a *unary minus operator* for negating a value. The expression

```
-23;
```

is interpreted as

```
0-23
```

and obviously the result is *<−23, int>*. The unary minus operator can be applied to named objects that hold numeric values. For example, in the code fragment

```
int i = 10;
float x = 12.3;
long Time = 33;
// begin expressions
-i;
-x;
-Time;
```

the last three lines of code are expressions where the unary minus operator has been applied to the objects `i`, `x`, and `Time`. In each case, the value of the object is subtracted from zero to yield the result. The results are *<−10, int>*, *<−12.3, float>*, and *<−33, long>*.

C++ also has a *unary plus operator*, which is included for symmetry with the unary minus operator. The expression

    +244

is interpreted as

    0+244

and the result is *<244, int>*.

2.10.4 Area of a circle

To illustrate the concepts covered thus far, let's write a program to solve a simple problem. The problem statement is

Compute the area and circumference of a circle given the radius. The input/output behavior of the program should be

```
Circle radius (real number)? 5.1
Area of circle with radius 5.1 is 81.7104
Circumference is 32.0433
```

Before we can write the program, we must consider a number of issues. Recall that the area of a circle is $Area = \pi r^2$. C++ does not have a exponentiation operator, but this operation is easily handled by multiplying the radius by itself. Thus if the name of the object that holds the radius is `Radius`, the area of the circle can be computed by the expression

```
3.1415 * Radius * Radius
```

Because we wish to allow the user to input a floating-point value as the radius, `Radius` should be a C++ floating-point type. Since the problem statement did not specify the possible size of the radius, or the accuracy of the result, we will arbitrarily choose type **float** for `Radius`. Program 2.10 contains the code that solves the problem.

Program 2.10

Compute area and circumference of a circle

```
// Program 2.10: Compute area and circumference
// of circle given radius
#include <iostream>
#include <string>
using namespace std;
int main() {
    cout << "Circle radius (real number)? ";
    float Radius;       // Radius of circle
    cin >> Radius;

    cout << "Area of circle with radius " << Radius
        << " is " << (3.1415 * Radius * Radius) << endl;
    cout << "Circumference is " << 3.1415 * 2 * Radius
        << endl;

    return 0;
}
```

2.10.5 Mixed-mode expressions

Up to this point we have discussed the conversions that are done when an expression involves values that are either integer values or floating-point values. Mixed-mode expressions involve values with both integer and floating-point types. For example, in the expression

```
23 - 13.2;
```

the left operand is type **int**, and the right operand is type **double**. We need rules that tell us how to evaluate the expression so that the result makes sense. The only thing that makes sense is to convert the left operand to type **double** and perform a double-precision subtraction, which produces the result *<9.8, double>*. In general, in a binary expression where either operand is a floating-point value, the operation will be performed using floating-point arithmetic, and the result will be one of C++'s floating-point types.

Because the usual unary conversions always convert an integer operand to either **int** or **long**, we need only to add two additional rows and columns to our table of usual binary conversions to cover mixed-mode arithmetic. Table 2.7 summarizes the possibilities.

Consider the following code fragment:

```
int MyDebt = 150;
double NationalDebt = 3.5E9;
float InterestRate = 0.06;
long USPopulation = 200000000;

MyDebt * InterestRate;
NationalDebt / USPopulation;
```

The first expression, which computes the interest due on MyDebt, yields the result *<9, float>*. The second expression, which computes the per capita national debt for each person in the United States, yields the result *<17.5, double>*.

Table 2.7

Result types for mixed-mode operations

		Type of Right Operand				
		int	long	float	double	long double
Type of Left Operand	int	int	long	float	double	long double
	long	long	long	float	double	long double
	float	float	float	float	double	long double
	double	double	double	double	double	long double
	long double	long double	long double	long double	long double	long double

2.10.6 Precedence

Like many programming languages, C++ allows the programmer to write expressions of arbitrary complexity using the binary and unary operators. As an example, consider the code fragment

```
int i = 4;
int j = 5;
i + 2 * j;
```

Depending on the order of operations, there are several possible results. Applying the operators in order from left to right, the result is *<30, int>*. Applying operators in order from right to left, the result is *<14, int>*. Clearly, we need a set of rules that tell us the order in which to apply the operators. These rules are called the *associativity* and *precedence* rules of the language.

Let us begin by discussing precedence. Each operator is assigned a precedence level. Table 2.8 contains the precedence level of the integer arithmetic operators we have discussed thus far. Informally, operators with higher precedence are applied before operators with lower precedence. Essentially, arithmetic expressions are evaluated just as we learned in high-school algebra. The two unary operators have highest precedence, and multiplication, division, and remainder have higher precedence than addition and subtraction. In the expression

```
i + 2 * j;
```

multiplication has higher precedence than addition, so the multiplication is done first, and the result of that operation is added to the value of i to yield the value 14.

Table 2.8

Operator precedence and associativity

Operator	Operation	Precedence	Associativity
+ -	Unary plus and minus	15	Right
* / %	Multiplication, division, and remainder	13	Left
+ -	Addition and subtraction	12	Left

As other examples, consider the following expressions:

```
2 / 3 + 5;
-8 * 4;
8 + 7 % 2;
```

In the first expression, division has higher precedence than addition, so division is performed first. The result is 0, which is then added to 5 to yield a final value of 5. In the second example, the unary minus operator is applied to 8, and the resulting value -8 is multiplied by 4 to yield the final value of -32. In the third expression, the remainder operation is performed and yields the value 1. The final value of the expression is 9.

We will often want to override C++'s precedence rules. For example, consider writing an expression to compute the sales tax on five items. The expression

```
Price1 + Price2 + Price3 + Price4 + Price5 * 0.06
```

is obviously incorrect. The multiplication operator will be applied to `Price5`, and the product is added to the other four prices. C++ permits expressions to be parenthesized. Expressions enclosed in parentheses are evaluated first. Using parentheses, we can rewrite the expression as

```
(Price1 + Price2 + Price3 + Price4 + Price5) * 0.06
```

In this expression, the five prices are summed first, and then 6 percent of the total is computed.

Parenthesized expressions can be nested. In other words, a parenthesized expression can contain other parenthesized expressions. In these cases, the innermost parenthesized expressions are evaluated first. Consider the following expression:

```
(2 + (3 + 2) * 5) / (4 - 2);
```

The parenthesized subexpression (3+2) is nested within another parenthesized expression and is evaluated first. Now the expressions contained in the outer sets of parentheses can be evaluated. The final value is 13.

2.10.7 Associativity

Let's now consider the expression

```
3 * 5 / 2;
```

In this expression, the operators have the same precedence level. Depending on whether the multiplication is performed first or last, the value of the expression is either 7 or 6. In the case where an operand is surrounded by operators of the same precedence level, we need a rule that tells us which operator to apply to the operand. This characteristic is called the *associativity* of the operator. As shown in Table 2.8, multiplication and division are *left associative*. Therefore, in the preceding example, the operand 5 "associates" with the operator on its left, and the correct value of the expression is 7. (Remember, integer division truncates!)

As a final check on the concepts covered thus far, consider the following code fragment:

```
int t1 = 17;
int t2 = 3;
int t3 = 7;
t1 % t2 * 5 / t3;
t3 * (-5 / 2) + t2;
t3 + t1 * 4 + t1;
```

The values of these expressions are

```
1
-11
92
```

Style Tip

> ### *Use of parentheses*
> Although it is important to know the rules of precedence, we recommend the use of parentheses to make the order of evaluation explicit even in cases where they are not needed. This technique helps the reader of the code, and it means that if the code gets changed later, other programmers are less likely to introduce an error.
>
>   Consider the unparenthesized expression
>
> ```
> a * b + c / d - 3.0;
> ```
>
> and the equivalent parenthesized expression
>
> ```
> (a * b) + (c / d) - 3.0;
> ```
>
> Both expressions perform exactly the same computation, but the meaning of the second one is much clearer.
>
>   The code in this book always uses parentheses to make the order of evaluation explicit in complicated expressions.

Self-check Questions

20.   Using the notation *<value, type>* give the value of the C++ expression `23.0 + 8`.

21.   Using the notation *<value, type>* give the value of the C++ expression `10 / 12`.

22.   Using the notation *<value, type>* give the value of the C++ expression `23 % 6`.

23.   Using the notation *<value, type>* give the value of the C++ expression `15 / 14`.

24.   Using the notation *<value, type>* give the value of the C++ expression `10L / 2`.

25.   Using the notation *<value, type>* give the value of the C++ expression `25.5L / 5`.

26.   Using the notation *<value, type>* give the value of the C++ expression `5 / 2`.

27.   Write a C++ program that converts U.S. dollars to Canadian dollars. Assume a conversion rate of 1.54 Canadian dollars for each U.S. dollar.

28.   Using the notation *<value, type>* give the value of the C++ expression `2 + 5L`.

29.   Using the notation *<value, type>* give the value of the C++ expression `2.3f + 5.2`.

30.   Using the notation *<value, type>* give the value of the C++ expression `5.1f + 3L`.

31.   Using the notation *<value, type>* give the value of the C++ expression `3.4L + 3L`.

32.   Using the notation *<value, type>* give the value of the C++ expression `2 + 5L`.

33.   Give the value of the C++ expression `3 / 2 + 5`.

34.   Give the value of the C++ expression `5 / 1 + 2`.

35.   Give the value of the C++ expression `3 * 2 + 4 * 5`.

36.   Give the value of the C++ expression `4 - 2 + 5 / 3 + 2`.

37.   Give the value of the C++ expression `10 - 2 + 7 % 2 - 1`.

2.11 OUTPUT STATEMENTS

At this point, we have discussed how to declare and initialize simple integral and floating-point objects and perform computations on these objects. These activities are not very useful unless we can display the results of the computation. We need a mechanism to output information computed by the program to the user.

Interestingly, unlike some other languages such as FORTRAN, Pascal, and BASIC, C++ does not have special language constructs for doing output. Rather, output capability is provided by libraries that are implemented using ordinary C++.

Recall that in Program 2.1, we said that the C++ statement

```
cout << "Hello World!" << endl;
```

displays the message

```
Hello World!
```

on the user's screen. A complete description of how this statement achieves the desired effect requires understanding some of the more advanced features of C++, so we will not discuss all the details at this point. However, the statement does illustrate one of the nice features of C++: We can use objects developed by others without completely understanding exactly how they work. We do, however, need to know how to access these objects.

We will come back to our first program shortly, but for now let's discuss a simpler example. Consider the following statement:

```
cout << "C++";
```

The object we are accessing is cout (pronounced "C out"). It is an output stream object. The term *stream* refers to a flow of data to or from a device. Because cout is an output stream object, the data is written to the device rather than being read from it. Normally, the device that cout is associated with is the display. cout is part of the iostream library. Thus to make data appear on the display, we must insert data into the stream. This is done via the insertion operator <<. In the example above, the characters 'C', '+', and '+' are inserted into the output stream, as illustrated in Figure 2.4.

Figure 2.4

Output with cout

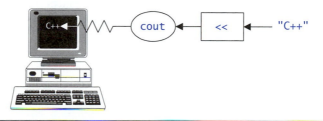

In Program 2.1, we used the special object endl. When endl is inserted into the output stream, it causes two things to happen. First, a newline character ('\n') is inserted into the stream. Second all the characters that have been inserted into the stream are written to the display device immediately. We say that the output is *flushed* to the output device. endl is a special class of object called a manipulator. A *manipulator* is an object that can be inserted into a stream to have some effect.

We could rewrite our previous example as

```
cout << "C++";
cout << endl;
```

and the second statement would ensure that a carriage return is inserted after the string "C++" and that the output is written to the display immediately.

The preceding insertion statements can be simplified into a single one. Like the arithmetic operators, the insertion operator can be composed or cascaded to output multiple values in a single statement. The two lines above can be written as the following single statement:

```
cout << "C++" << endl;
```

There is no limit on the number of insertion operations that can be cascaded in a single statement. The contrived statement

```
cout << "C++" << " is a " << "breeze" << endl;
```

illustrates this concept. It outputs the message

```
C++ is a breeze
```

to the display.

C++ Language

> ### *Tying of cout to cin*
>
> Earlier versions of C++ required the programmer to explicitly flush the characters inserted into cout before extracting input from cin. The current version of C++ eliminates this need by tying cout to cin. The stream cout is automatically flushed whenever an extraction operation from cin requires new input characters to satisfy the extraction operation. Consequently, it is no longer necessary to flush cout explicitly when writing a prompt to the display device.

Cascading really becomes useful when we wish to output different types of values in the same statement. The insertion operator enables us to output any of C++'s fundamental types. For example, the statement

```
cout << "18 % 4 = " << 18 % 4 << endl;
```

outputs the following:

```
18 % 4 = 2
```

The statement outputs a string literal and the result of an arithmetic expression that produced a value of type **int**. The preceding statement also revisits the concept of precedence. Notice that depending on the relative precedence levels of the << and % operators, the operand 18 could bind with either the << operator or the % operator. Fortunately, % has higher precedence than << has, so the statement does what we wanted it to do. However, as we have pointed out before, it's a good idea to add parentheses around the expression 18 % 4 so that the meaning of the statement is crystal clear.

We can also use the << operator to output the values of objects. When the code fragment

```
int Hours = 11;
cout << Hours << " hours is " << (Hours * 60)
 << " minutes " << endl;
```

is executed

```
11 hours is 660 minutes
```

is output. In this code, the << operator handles inserting an **int** object operand, several string literal operands, and the result of an arithmetic expression into the stream cout.

The insertion operator can also output floating-point values. The expression

```
cout << (5.0 / 2.0) << " " << (1.0 / 3.0) << endl;
```

writes

```
2.5 0.33333
```

to the display.

When a floating-point value is inserted into the output stream, the insertion operator attempts to output the value in a minimum amount of space. Thus the code fragment

```
float x = 6.0;
cout << (x / 2.0) << endl;
```

writes

```
3
```

to the display. Later we will discuss some techniques for controlling the display of floating-point values.

As we do more programming, we will introduce other aspects of doing output using the iostream library. For now, it is sufficient to remember the following points:

- You must include the system header files `iostream` and `string` at the beginning of your program.

- You must indicate that you are using the objects within the namespace `std`.

- The `<<` operator can output any of C++'s fundamental types.

- The `<<` operator can be cascaded to output several values in a single statement.

2.12   COMPUTING AVERAGE VELOCITY

As a final case study, let's write a program that computes the average velocity of a car traveling on a road periodically marked with mileposts. The inputs to the program are the starting milepost and an ending milepost and time. Times are entered in hours, minutes, and seconds. The program should compute and output the average velocity in miles per hour. The problem statement is

Compute the average velocity in miles per hour of a car. The input/output behavior of the program should be

```
All inputs are integers!
Start milepost? 321
Elapsed time (hours minutes seconds)? 2 15 36
End milepost? 458
Car traveled 137 miles in 2 hrs 15 min 36 sec
Average velocity was 60.6195 mph
```

The steps to solving this problem follow.

     Step 1.   Issue the prompts and read the input.

     Step 2.   Compute the elapsed time in hours.

     Step 3.   Compute the distance traveled.

     Step 4.   Compute the average velocity.

Each step seems relatively straightforward but converting each step to C++ code involves making some subtle, but important, decisions.

To implement step 1, we must select the types of the objects to store the input. The input/output behavior of the program shows that all values will be entered as integers. Thus it seems natural to use the type `int` to store the value of the starting point and ending point and the starting and ending time. However, if we use this method, we introduce a subtle problem that occurs in step 4. Recall that the formula for computing the average velocity of an object is

$$Velocity = \frac{Distance}{ElapsedTime}$$

Remember that in C++ division truncates. In most cases, truncation will not be a problem, but in the rare case where the elapsed time is greater than the distance traveled, the division will produce a zero result. This scenario points out one of the most difficult parts of programming. It's usually easy to write code that handles the common cases, but anticipating and handling the rare case is hard. Failure to anticipate a rare situation that could occur is the source of bugs in many programs. This type of error is particularly prevalent in interactive programs where the input is coming from a human.

Programming Tip

Interactive input and output

When writing an interactive program, it is important to tell the user what he or she is expected to do. For example, in Program 2.10, the user is told to input the radius and that a real number is expected. This prompt may seem unnecessary: we know to enter a real number because we wrote the program and the source code is right in front of us. However, remember that someone else may run the program without seeing the source, so it is important for the program to inform the user of what is expected. Program 2.11 also tells the user what is expected.

In addition to telling the user what form the input should take, another general principle of good interactive I/O is to echo the input typed by the user. This practice gives the user some assurance that the input was received and interpreted correctly. In Program 2.10, the radius along with the computed area is printed. Thus the user can see whether the program received the correct input. Similarly, in Program 2.11, when the output is produced, both the distance and the elapsed time are echoed along with the computed velocity.

There are a couple of solutions to this problem. We could make all the objects floating-point and thus ensure that floating-point arithmetic would be used for all computations. This approach is certainly the easiest, but it seems like overkill. A better solution is to accept the input as integers as was intended, but when a floating-point result is needed, make sure a floating-point result is computed. For example, we must convert the time that is entered as hours, minutes, and seconds into a single value that represents the elapsed time. The conversion can be done with the definition

```
float ElapsedTime = EndHour + (EndMinute / 60.0)
   + (EndSecond / 3600.00);
```

Because we used floating-point constants as the divisors, both divisions will be floating-point and the additions will also produce floating-point results.

Notice that the preceding definition is slightly different from the form we presented in section 2.9 on page 73. There we said that the initial value could be a literal. Actually, C++ allows the initial value to be an arbitrary expression. Thus the general form is

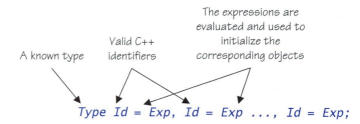

where Exp is an arbitrary expression.

We can now compute the velocity with the following definition

```
float Velocity = Distance / ElapsedTime;
```

where Distance was computed earlier by the definition

```
int Distance = EndMilePost - StartMilePost;
```

The complete program is contained in Program 2.11.

Self-check Questions

38.   Write a C++ statement that inserts the value of the expression 25 / 4 in the stream cout.

39.   What two files must be included in a C++ program to use the iostream library?

40.   Write a C++ program that prompts for and accepts a time and computes the number of seconds elapsed since midnight. The time should be entered in the format HH:MM:SS.

Program 2.11

Compute average
velocity of a car

```cpp
// Program 2.11: Compute average velocity of car
#include <iostream>
#include <string>
using namespace std;
int main() {
    cout << "All inputs are integers!\n";
    cout << "Start milepost? ";
    int StartMilePost;
    cin >> StartMilePost;

    cout << "End time (hours minutes seconds)? ";
    int EndHour, EndMinute, EndSecond;
    cin >> EndHour >> EndMinute >> EndSecond;

    cout << "End milepost? ";
    int EndMilePost;
    cin >> EndMilePost;

    float ElapsedTime = EndHour + (EndMinute / 60.0)
     + (EndSecond / 3600.0);
    int Distance = EndMilePost - StartMilePost;
    float Velocity = Distance / ElapsedTime;

    cout << "\nCar traveled " << Distance << " miles in ";
    cout << EndHour << " hrs " << EndMinute << " min "
     << EndSecond << " sec\n";
    cout << "Average velocity was " << Velocity << " mph"
     << endl;
    return 0;
}
```

Style Tip

Placement of declarations

In older style programs, the convention was to place all declarations at the beginning of the function. C++ permits declarations to appear almost anywhere in a function. As with any stylistic issue, there are pros and cons to each method.

Placing a declaration at the point of the first use of an object has the advantage that you don't have to look back at the beginning of the function to determine the type of the object. In addition, if you change the code, so that the object is no longer needed, you are much more likely to delete the now unnecessary declaration. We have encountered older style code that, after several years of maintenance, contains many useless declarations.

On the other hand, having all the declarations in a central location has some advantages. You know right where to look for the declaration. With the advent of integrated development environments and browsing tools, this advantage seems less significant. In our code, we always place the declaration at or near the point of first use.

2.13 POINTS TO REMEMBER

✔ The statement `#include <iostream>` is a preprocessor directive that includes the necessary definitions so that a program can do input and output using the iostream library.

✔ The statement

```
using namespace std;
```

makes the objects defined in the namespace `std` available for use. The iostream objects (i.e., `cin` and `cout`) are defined in the namespace `std`.

✔ The C++ operator `<<` is called the insert operator. It is used to insert text into an output stream.

✔ The output stream `cout` normally corresponds to the display.

✔ The C++ operator `>>` is called the extraction operator. It is used to extract characters from an input stream.

✔ The input stream `cin` normally corresponds to the keyboard.

✔ The manipulator `endl` inserts a newline in the output stream. In addition, it forces all the output that has been sent to the stream to be written to the corresponding device.

✔ Standard C++ programs begin executing in function `main()`. Function `main()` returns an integer value that indicates whether the program executed successfully or not. The value 0 indicates successful execution, whereas the value 1 indicates that a problem or error occurred during the execution of the program.

✔ A value is returned from a function using the **return** statement. The statement

```
return 0;
```

returns the value 0.

✔ A C++ style comment begins with `//` and continues to the end of the line.

✔ Including descriptive and useful comments in a program is an important part of good programming. Remember, other programmers will read your program.

✔ The assignment operator = assigns or gives a new value to an object.

✔ The C++ object types **short**, **int**, and **long** hold integer values. On the PC, a **short** is stored in 8 bits, an **int** in 16 bits, and a **long** in 32 bits.

✔ The C++ object type **char** holds a character. For most machines, characters are encoded using the ASCII character set. Appendix A contains the ASCII character set.

✔ The C++ object types, **float**, **double**, and **long double** hold real values. On the PC, a **long** is stored in 32 bits, and a **double** is stored in 64 bits. On most PCs, a **long double** is the same size as a **double**, but on other machines it can be larger. For example, on some machines **long double** is 128 bits.

History of Computing

Napier's bones and the slide rule

One of the early influential contributions to computing was by John Napier, Baron of Merchison (1550–1617). Up until the 1600s, most computing was done by hand. Multiplication and division, in particular, were tedious to perform, requiring many individual calculations. Napier invented the principle of logarithms, which reduce multiplication and division to the simpler operations of addition and subtraction. This principle, that numerical powers can be added and subtracted (e.g., $x^4 \times x^3 = x^7$ and $x^7 \div x^4 = x^3$), had far-reaching effects.

To aid in computing logarithms, Napier also developed a device that came to be known as "Napier's bones." The device was essentially a multiplication table cut up into movable columns. The term *bones* was coined because the columns were from bone or ivory. Although primitive by our standards, Napier's bones were considered an indispensable computing device in the early 1600s.

The development of logarithms and Napier's bones spawned several "next generation" computing devices. One device, developed in the 1600s and still in use as late as the 1970s, is the slide rule. A *slide rule* is essentially a physical analog of logarithms. A slide rule consists of three pieces of wood or metal with one piece sliding between two fixed pieces (see Figure 2.5). Scales etched on the pieces correspond to the logarithms. Numbers can be multiplied and divided by adding and subtracting distances. A cursor is used to help read the result. Later versions of slide rules had many different scales and could perform very complicated calculations. One problem with the slide rule is that the accuracy is limited to four or five decimal places.

Figure 2.5

A slide rule

✔ A C++ string constant is a sequence of characters enclosed in double quotes. Special characters such as the newline, tab, and bell can be included in a string constant using special escape characters. These are listed in Table 2.1 on page 62.

✔ A C++ integer constant can be written in one of three bases: octal, decimal, or hexadecimal. An octal integer constant begins with a zero digit. Thus, the constant 040 is octal and represents the decimal value 32. Decimal constants begin with a digit other than zero, and hexadecimal constants begin with the prefix 0x or 0X. The constant 0x40 represents the decimal value 64.

✔ C++ provides several ways to write a floating-point constant. The simplest way is to use standard decimal notation: 3.1416, 2.53, 0.3512. Floating-point constants can also be written using scientific notation. The C++ floating-point constant, 2.3E5, represents the value 2.3×10^5 or 230,000.

✔ A C++ name consists of a sequence of letters (uppercase and lowercase), digits, and underscores. A valid name cannot begin with a digit character.

✔ C++ names are case sensitive. For example, the names Temp and temp refer to two different objects.

✔ It is very important to pick meaningful and descriptive names for the objects in a program. Descriptive names help other programmers understand what your program is doing.

✔ An object must be defined before it can be used. Smart programmers give an object an initial value when it is defined.

✔ Integer division always produces a truncated result. The expression 5 / 2 produces the result 2, not 2.5.

✔ The usual unary conversions specify that operands of type **char** or **short** are converted to type **int** before proceeding with the operation.

✔ For an arithmetic operation involving two integral operands, the usual binary conversions specify that when the operands have different types, the one that is type **int** is converted to **long** and a **long** operation is performed to produce a **long** result.

✔ For an arithmetic operation involving two floating-point operands, the usual binary conversions specify that when the operands have different types, the operand with lesser precision is converted to the type of the operand with greater precision. The arithmetic operation is performed using the operation that produces a result with the same type as the operand with the greater precision. Thus for an addition operation involving a **float** operand and a **double** operand, the **float** operand is converted to **double** and a double-precision addition is performed.

✔ A mixed-mode arithmetic expression involves integral and floating-point operands. The integral operand is converted to the type of the floating-point operand, and the appropriate floating-point operation is performed.

✔ The precedence rules of C++ define the order in which operators are applied to operands. For the arithmetic operators, the precedence from highest to lowest is unary plus and minus; multiplication, division, and remainder; and addition and subtraction.

2.14 EXERCISES

2.1   What is the range of a 32-bit integer?

2.2   How many null bytes are at the end of the following string literal?

```
"What's going on here?\0"
```

2.3   Describe how integer division of two **int**s can produce a result that overflows.

2.4   Remove the statement

```
return 0;
```

from Program 2.1. Compile the modified program. Does the compiler report an error or warning? If so, what is the message?

2.5   Remove the statement

```
#include <iostream>
```

from Program 2.1. Compile the modified program. Does the compiler report an error or warning? If so, what is the message?

2.6   Remove the statement

```
using namespace std;
```

from Program 2.1. Compile the modified program. Does the compiler report an error or warning? If so, what is the message?

2.7   What is printed by the following code fragment?

```
int i = 2;
int j = 3;
i = j + j;
j = i * 1.5;
cout << "i = " << i << "  j = " << j << endl;
```

2.8   Remove the **include** statement from Program 2.1 and compile the modified program. For which line of the modified program does the compiler first report an error?

2.9   Write a program that accepts the weight of an object in pounds and outputs the weight of the object in kilograms.

2.10   Write a program that computes the volume of an object. The program should ask the user to input the object's mass and density. The mass will be given in grams; the density will be in grams per cubic centimeter. The relationship of mass, density, and volume of an object is given by

$$Density = \frac{Mass}{Volume}$$

Your program should output the volume in cubic centimeters.

2.11 Write a program to compute the mass of a block of aluminum. The program should input the dimensions of the block (i.e., length, width, and height) in centimeters. The density of aluminum is 2.7 g/cm^3.

2.12 Modify Program 2.2 so that `Price` is of type `int`. Run the program. Explain why the output of the program is different.

2.13 In C++ the result of applying a backslash to a character that is not a character escape code is undefined. Many compilers do not catch this error. Try it with a compiler available to you and report the result.

2.14 Modify Program 2.11 so that it uses type `float` for all objects. Does the input/output behavior of the program remain the same?

2.15 Which of the following are invalid C++ identifiers?

a) `GPA` b) `Grade.pnt` c) `GradePtAvg` d) `Int` e) `1stNum` f) `Num1` g) `X-ray` h) `R2D2`

i) `T2` j) `3CPO` k) `Avg_cost` l) `$Cost` m) `Era` n) `int` o) `PDQBach` p) `ReturnV`

q) `A` r) `_dog` s) `Not!` t) `_123` u) `Cat s` v) `main` w) `Cost$`

2.16 What is the result of the following expressions? Express your answer as *<value, type>*.

a) `25 / 7` b) `21 / 3` c) `26 / 2L` d) `14 % 3` e) `31 % 3` f) `22.1 + 1.0` g) `30L % 5`

h) `7 - 21` i) `28 + 3 * 5` j) `(27 / 3) + 15` k) `2` l) `-23 + 7 * 2`

2.17 Write a program that accepts a Fahrenheit temperature and outputs the equivalent centigrade temperature. The equation for converting a Fahrenheit temperature to Celsius is

$$Celsius = \frac{5}{9}(Fahrenheit - 32)$$

2.18 Write a program that accepts a centigrade temperature and outputs the equivalent Fahrenheit temperature. The equation for converting a Celsius temperature to Fahrenheit is

$$Fahrenheit = \frac{9}{5}Celsius + 32$$

2.19   Assume the following declarations:

```
float f1 = 23.3;
float f2 = 1.0;
double d1 = 3.1;
int i1 = 5;
int i2 = 10;
int i3 = 7;
short s1 = 11;
short s2 = 5;
char c1 = '0';
```

What is the result of the following expressions? Express your answer as *<value, type>*.

a) `f1 + d1`

b) `i1 + d1`

c) `i1 + i2 * i3`

d) `i2 % i3`

e) `i3 / i2 + i1 * i3`

f) `f1 - f2`

g) `f1 - i3`

h) `f1 / i2 + d1`

i) `i2 + i3 + 3.0`

j) `i2 * f2 + 4`

k) `s1 / i3`

l) `c1 + f2`

m) `s1 + s2`

n) `i3 + c1`

o) `c1 - s2`

2.20   Write C++ expressions that are equivalent to the following mathematical formula:

a) $b^2 + 4ac$

b) $a + \dfrac{b}{c} + d$

c) $\dfrac{1}{1 + x^2}$

d) $\dfrac{4}{3}\pi r^2$

e) $-(a^2 - b^3)$

f) $a\left(\dfrac{b}{c}\right)$

g) $(a + b)(c + d)(e + f)$

2.21   Write a program that prompts for and reads a distance in kilometers and outputs the distance as miles.

2.22   Write a program that prompts for and reads five integers and computes the average.

2.23   Write a C++ statement that implements the following equation.

$$q = \left(\frac{T_1 \times T_2}{D - k}\right) + T_2$$

Your assignment statement should use the following objects.

```
float q;              // result
float k = 1.35;       // constant of irritation
float D = 9.2;        // duration
float T1 = 98.4;      // start time
float T2 = 101.12;    // end time
```

2.24   Write a program that prompts for and reads a distance in miles and outputs the distance as kilometers.

2.25   Write a program that prompts for and reads the distance an object travels in miles and the time it takes to travel that distance. The program should compute and display the speed of the object.

2.26   Write a program that accepts an integer between 10 and 12 digits long and writes the integer with commas between every third digit starting from the right.

2.27   Write a program that prompts for and reads a floating-point number and evaluates the polynomial

$$3x^4 - 10x^3 + 13$$

The program should display both the number read and the result of evaluating the polynomial.

2.28   Write a program that prompts for and reads a floating-point number and evaluates the polynomial

$$23x^5 - 6x^4 + 11$$

The program should display both the number read and the result of evaluating the polynomial.

2.29   Write a program that prompts for and reads your age in years and outputs your age in days. You may assume that there are 365 days in a year.

2.30   Write a program that computes the number of minutes it takes for light to reach the Earth from the Sun. You will need to know the speed of light and the distance between the Earth and Sun.

2.31   Write a program that prompts for a person's age and heart rate. The program computes and displays the number of heart beats since the person was born. You may assume that there are 365 days in a year.

2.32   Suppose every person in China drank two bottles of beer a week. To brew a case of beer (24 bottles) requires a half bushel of barley. There are approximately 1 billion people in China. Write a program to determine the number of bushels of wheat that must be grown to satisfy the demand for beer.

2.33   Interest on credit card accounts can be quite high. Most credit card companies compute interest on an average daily balance. Here is an algorithm for computing the average daily balance and the monthly interest charge on a credit card.

Step 1.   Multiply the net balance shown on the statement by the number of days in the billing cycle.

Step 2.   Multiply the net payment received by the number of days the payment was received before the statement date.

Step 3.   Subtract the result of the calculation in step 2 from the result of the calculation in step 1.

Step 4.   Divide the result of step 3 by the number of days in the billing cycle. This value is the average daily balance.

Step 5.   Compute the interest charge for the billing period by multiplying the average daily balance by the monthly interest rate.

Here is an example to illustrate the algorithm. Suppose your credit card statement showed a previous balance of $850. Eleven days before the end of the billing cycle, you made a payment of $400. The billing cycle for this month is 31 days, and the monthly interest rate is 1.32%. The calculation of the interest charge is as follows:

Step 1. $850 \times 31 = \$26{,}350$

Step 2. $400 \times 11 = \$4{,}400$

Step 3. $\$26{,}350 - \$4{,}400 = \$21{,}950$

Step 4. $\$21{,}950 \div 31 = \$708.06$

Step 5. $\$708.06 \times .0132 = \$9.34$

Write a program that computes the monthly interest charge on a credit card account. Your program should prompt for and accept the previous balance, the payment amount, the number of days in the billing cycle, the day of the billing cycle the payment was made, and the monthly interest rate.

2.34   We all like to exercise because it's good for us. Experts tell us that to get the maximum aerobic effect from exercise we should try to keep our pulse rate in a training zone. The training zone is computed as follows. Subtract your age from 220; 72% of that value is the low end of the range and 87% of that value is the high end of the range. Write a program that accepts an age and computes the training range.

CHAPTER 3

Modifying objects

Introduction

In this chapter, we introduce operators that can modify objects and the use of programmer-defined object types. The operators are the assignment operators and the extraction operator. Of particular importance is =, the assignment operator. The assignment operation is common to most programming languages, and understanding the concept of assignment and its implementation in a language is a key concept that all programmers must master. The extraction operator >> modifies an object by extracting a value from a stream and storing that value in an object. The chapter concludes by introducing two programmer-defined object types: `SimpleWindow` and `RectangleShape`. We show how to define and manipulate instances of these programmer-defined object types by writing programs that produce graphical displays.

Key Concepts

- assignment operation

- assignment conversions

- assignment precedence and associativity

- extraction operations

- **const** declarations

- compound assignment operations

- input with `cin`

- increment and decrement operation

- strings

- EzWindows

3.1 ASSIGNMENT

The C++ assignment operator is the =. This operator stores a value into an object. The code fragment

```
int x = 0;
x = 10;
```

stores the value 10 into the memory location assigned to x. The expression is read as "x gets 10" or "x is assigned 10."

To see better what the assignment operator does, let's examine the following code fragment:

```
float GrossSalary = 0.0;
float WithHolding = 0.0;
float TakeHomePay = 0.0;
GrossSalary = 50000.0;
WithHolding = GrossSalary * .05;
TakeHomePay = GrossSalary - WithHolding;
```

This fragment contains three objects, each of type **float**. Each object has memory allocated for it. As we discussed in Chapter 2, the C++ compiler assigns the objects to memory locations. Some people find it convenient to think of these memory locations as "mailboxes." The assignment operator places information in the mailbox. The object name acts like the address.

In Figure 3.1, the left diagram represents the state of memory before execution of the three assignment statements in the preceding code fragment. Notice that all three objects have zeros in their mailboxes. These initial values were given when these objects were defined. The right diagram of Figure 3.1 represents the state of memory after the assignment expressions execute. Notice that the value of TakeHomePay was computed using the value of WithHolding that was computed and assigned in the previous statement.

A common programming job is to swap or exchange the values of two objects. For example, let's suppose that the following objects are defined and initialized and we want to swap their values.

```
int Score1 = 90;
int Score2 = 75;
```

We want to copy the value of Score1 into Score2 and the value of Score2 into Score1. It is tempting to write the assignment statements as follows:

```
Score2 = Score1;    // Copy Score1 into Score2
Score1 = Score2;    // Copy Score2 into Score1
```

Unfortunately, this code would result in both Score1 and Score2 having the original value of Score1, which is 90. The problem was that the first assignment statement overwrote the value of Score2.

To do the job correctly, we need a temporary object where we can store the value of one of the objects before we change its value. Assuming a temporary **int** object named Temp has been defined, a correct sequence for swapping the values of Score1 and Score2 is

Figure 3.1

Illustration of assignment statement changing the value of objects

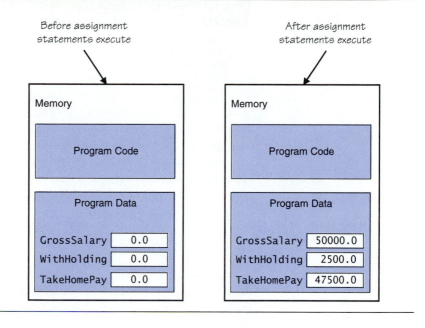

The step-by-step process is illustrated in the following diagram:

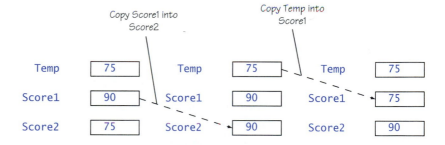

```
int Temp = Score2;    // Copy original value of Score2
Score2 = Score1;      // Copy Score1 into Score2
Score1 = Temp;        // Copy original value of Score2
                      // into Score1
```

3.1.1 Assignment conversions

In the previous section, we used the simplest form of assignment statement.

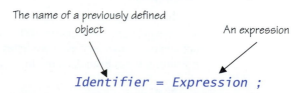

The rules of C++ state that the types of the left and right operands should be the same. In the following code fragment

```cpp
int x;
float y;
double z;
x = 1;
y = 2.3F;
z = 0.81;
```

the left and right operands of each assignment expression match. If the left and right operands do not have the same type, it is necessary to convert the operands appropriately. In the case of the assignment operator, the generated code converts the right operand so that its type matches that of the left operand. This type of conversion is called the *assignment conversion*.

For example, in the fragment

```cpp
int x = 0;
x = 2.3;
```

the type of the left operand is **int**, and the type of the constant right operand is **double**. Before performing the assignment, the assignment conversion conventions convert the right operand *<2.3, double>* to *<2, int>*. Recall that a conversion from a floating-point type to an integral type causes a truncation to occur.

For the most part, the assignment conversions behave exactly as you would expect. The only situation where unexpected results occur is when the type of the left operand is less precise than the type of the right operand and the value of the right operand is larger than what can be stored in the memory that corresponds to the left operand. The following code fragment shows this problem.

```cpp
short s1 = 0;
long i2 = 65536;
s1 = i2;
cout << "i2 is " << i2 << endl;
cout << "s1 is " << s1 << endl;
```

When this fragment is executed on a machine where a **short** is 16 bits and a **long** is 32 bits (like most PCs), the following output is produced.

```
i2 is 65536
s1 is 0
```

In this case, assignment conversion maps i2's value from a **long** to a **short** by discarding the most significant 16 bits and storing the least significant 16 bits, which are all zero.

In the previous discussions of the assignment operator, we used the term *assignment expression* to emphasize that the assignment operator, besides storing a value in memory, also produces a result just like the arithmetic operators. Assuming x has been declared to be an **int**, the statement

```cpp
x = 1;
```

stores a one in the object x, but it also produces the result *<1, int>*. The type of the result of the assignment operator is the type of the left operand, and the value of the result is the value stored into the left operand.

3.1.2   Assignment precedence and associativity

Because assignment is an operator, we can write expressions such as

```
x = y = z + 2;
```

The question is, Exactly what does this expression mean? The answer lies in knowing the precedence and associativity of the assignment operator. First, let's consider precedence. Because z is surrounded by two different operators, the relative precedences of the operators determine whether z binds with + or =. The natural interpretation is that z and 2 are added together. Thus the precedence of = must be lower than that of +. Indeed, assignment has a very low precedence. Therefore, the interpretation of the previous expression is

```
x = y = (z + 2);
```

Appendix A.2 contains a complete precedence table for all C++ operators.

Continuing with this example, we notice that y is surrounded by the = operator. In this situation, the associativity of = determines whether y binds with the = on the right or the = on the left. Unlike the arithmetic operators, assignment is right associative. Consequently, the interpretation of the previous expression is

```
x = (y = (z + 2));
```

which says that the result of the assignment of the sum of z + 2 to y is assigned to x. Again this interpretation is natural because if assignment was left associative, the interpretation would be

```
(x = y) = (z + 2);
```

which makes no sense.

Style Tip

C++ assignment idiom

It is often the case that several objects need to be initialized to the same value. For example, it is common to have to initialize several objects to zero. To initialize the three **int** objects i, j, and k to zero, one could write

```
i = 0;
j = 0;
k = 0;
```

In C++ it is standard practice to write the previous code as

```
i = j = k = 0;
```

This is shorter (generally always a good thing), and just as clear. In terms of efficiency, it is likely there will be no difference—a good optimizing compiler should produce the same machine code for each C++ fragment.

3.2 CONST DEFINITIONS

In addition to the definitions that we have seen thus far, C++ has another form of definition that is very handy. It is called a **const** definition. For a fundamental type object, a **const** definition has the following form:

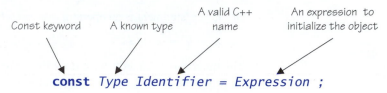

Const keyword   A known type   A valid C++ name   An expression to initialize the object

```
const Type Identifier = Expression ;
```

For example, the declarations

```
const double AvogadroNmber = 6.02E23;
const float SpeedOfLight = 186000;
```

are valid **const** definitions.

A **const** definition is similar to a normal definition in that the object named *Identifier* is defined and given the value of the expression *Expression*. However, the keyword **const** tells the compiler that this object can no longer be modified once it has been assigned its initial value. This convention seems strange, but it is very useful. In most programs, we use literals to represent an unchanging value. For example, many scientific and engineering programs use physical constants (e.g., Avogadro's number, the speed of light, and π). Rather than use the literal value, it is better to define a **const** object that holds the value and use the object name throughout the program rather than the literal value.

For example, Program 3.1 is a rewrite of Program 2.10 using a **const** definition. The object Pi holds the constant 3.1415, and the **const** definition signals the compiler that this value is a constant and should not be changed.

Program 3.1

Compute area and circumference of a circle

```
// Program 3.1: Compute area and circumference of circle
// given radius. Program modified to use const declaration.
#include <iostream>
#include <string>
using namespace std;
int main() {
    cout << "Circle radius (real number)? ";
    float Radius;
    cin >> Radius;

    const float Pi = 3.1415;
    cout << "Area of circle with radius " << Radius
     << " is " << (Pi * Radius * Radius) << endl;
    cout << "Circumference is " << Pi * 2 * Radius << endl;
    return 0;
}
```

One of the advantages of using **const** definitions to declare program constants is that if we decide to change the constant, we need to make a change at only one place in the program. For example, in Program 3.1, if we decide to use more precision for π, we would need to change only the **const** declaration and recompile. On the other hand, Program 2.10 requires two changes. For a large program, where a constant may be used in many places, changing all occurrences is tedious and error prone. In addition, if we choose a name that connotes the value of the constant, the program will be easier to understand.

Programming Tip

> *Using const*
>
> A good programming practice is to use a **const** object for any value that will not change during the execution of the program. The **const** definition tells the reader of the program that the value of this object will not change. Furthermore, if someone modifies the program and accidentally inserts a statement that would change the value of the object, the compiler will report the error. Additionally, if the compiler knows that an object will not change during the execution of a program, it can often generate more efficient code than it could if the object can be modified.

3.3 INPUT STATEMENTS

In Chapter 2, we discussed how to do output using the `cout` object and the insertion operator `<<`. The iostream library also provides an object for doing input. This object, `cin` (pronounced "C in"), is an input stream object. It is normally associated with the keyboard. That is, as we type characters on the keyboard the sequence of characters typed forms the input stream. For input, we must extract data from the stream via the extraction operator `>>`. The code fragment

```
int Value;
cin >> Value;
```

reads a single integer from the `cin` input stream and places the value in the **int** object `Value`. At this point, it would be counterproductive to try to cover all the details of input. However, we do need to understand the basic behavior of the extraction operator when applied to the fundamental types.

When extracting integers or floating-point numbers, by default the extraction operator skips whitespace characters while looking for a character that can begin a number. The whitespace characters are the blank, the vertical and horizontal tabs, the form feed, and the newline. The characters that can begin an integer are the digits and the sign characters (+ and –). For a floating-point type, the possible initial values also include the period (i.e., the decimal point). When extracting a **char** value, the extraction operator also by default skips white space and stores the next character into the **char** object.

What happens if we are trying to extract an integer, but the next non-whitespace character encountered is not one that can begin an integer? In this case, the input stream object `cin` is put into an error state. When a stream object is in an error state, no additional characters can be extracted from the stream. Subsequent extractions do not change the value of the object being modified. In later chapters, we discuss how to test for errors in processing input and how to recover from them.

To illustrate `cin`'s behavior, let's consider the operation of the following code fragment when the user has typed the input shown in Figure 3.2.

```
int Ivalue;
cin >> Ivalue;
float Fvalue;
cin >> Fvalue;
char Cvalue;
cin >> c;
```

Figure 3.2

Input from stream cin

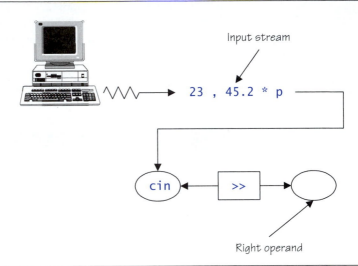

For the first extraction operator, the leading blanks are skipped. On encountering the character 2, the characters that constitute the integer are read and converted to the internal machine representation of an **int** and this value is stored in the object. No further input is consumed, and subsequent extraction operations will begin processing the input stream at this point (i.e., the next character of the input stream is the blank following the three). Thus the object `Ivalue` now has the value 23 stored in it.

The next operation is to extract a floating-point value from the input stream. In our example, the next nonwhitespace character is a comma. At this point, `cin` is placed into an error state, and the remaining extraction operations have no effect. Both `Fvalue` and `Cvalue` remain uninitialized.

Recall that integer literals can take several forms. For example, 0x40 is a hexadecimal literal that has the decimal value 64. Similarly, 0100 is an octal literal with that same value. The extraction operator knows how to interpret these numbers correctly when they are encountered in a stream. When the input

```
0x52 034
```

is processed by the code fragment

```
int Ivalue1;
```

```
int Ivalue2;
cin >> Ivalue1 >> Ivalue2;
```

the objects `Ivalue1` and `Ivalue2` are given the decimal values 82 and 28, respectively. Notice that the extraction operator can be cascaded just like the insertion operator.

The iostream library provides a variety of mechanisms for extracting data. For example, at times we will want to process every character in an input file and not skip any. Similarly, we may wish the extraction operator to interpret the numbers being extracted as being in a different base. Chapter 5 provides a thorough introduction to the various stream libraries.

Self-check Questions

1. Using the notation *<value, type>* give the value and type assigned to the object on the left side of the assignment operator.

    ```
    int k;
    k = 2.4;
    ```

2. Using the notation *<value, type>* give the value and type assigned to the object on the left side of the assignment operator.

    ```
    int j;
    j = 5.9;
    ```

3. Using the notation *<value, type>* give the value and type assigned to the object on the left side of the assignment operator.

    ```
    int t;
    t = 2.3L;
    ```

4. Using the notation *<value, type>* give the value and type assigned to the object on the left side of the assignment operator.

    ```
    float x;
    x = 3;
    ```

5. Give the primary reason for using a **const** definition as opposed to an equivalent non-**const** definition.

6. What values are extracted into the objects `Value1` and `Value2` when the input

    ```
    2.4,4
    ```

    is processed by the following code fragment?

    ```
    int Value1;
    int Value2;
    cin >> Value1 >> Value2;
    ```

7.   What values are extracted into the objects `Value1` and `Value2` when the input

      7.8,0

is processed by the following code fragment?

```
float Value1;
int Value2;
cin >> Value1 >> Value2;
```

8.   What values are extracted into the objects `Value1` and `Value2` when the input

      2e3,6

is processed by the following code fragment?

```
int Value1;
int Value2;
cin >> Value1 >> Value2;
```

3.4 COMPUTING THE NUMBER OF MOLECULES IN A HYDROCARBON

A common problem in elementary chemistry is to compute the number of atoms or molecules contained in a particular amount of a substance. The substances we are interested in are the hydrocarbons. These are substances that contain only two elements: carbon and hydrogen. Examples of familiar hydrocarbons are the fuels methane, propane, and butane.

The computation of the number of molecules in a hydrocarbon is best illustrated with an example. Recall that a mole of any substance contains 6.02×10^{23} molecules. This number is known as Avogadro's constant. It is the case that 1 mole of a substance is always equal to the formula weight in grams. The formula weight is the sum of the atomic weights of the constituent elements. The computation of formula weight of methane, CH_4, is

1 carbon atom	=	1×12.0 amu	=	12.0
4 hydrogen atoms	=	4×1.0 amu	=	4.0
1 mole of CH_4			=	16.0 g

Therefore, 16 grams of methane contain 6.02×10^{23} molecules. The following equation expresses the relationship between the mass of a substance and the number of molecules.

$$Molecules = Mass \times \frac{1\,mole}{Formula\,Weight} \times \frac{6.02 \times 10^{23}\,molecules}{1\,mole}$$

We can now write the problem statement:

> Compute the number of molecules in an amount of hydrocarbon. The amount of hydrocarbon will be given in grams. Carbon's atomic weight is 12 amu, and hydrogen's is 1 amu. An example of the input/output behavior of the program follows.

```
Enter mass of hydrocarbon (in grams)
followed by the number of carbon atoms
followed by the number of hydrogen atoms
(e.g. 10.5 2 6): 16 1 4
16 grams of a hydrocarbon
with 1 carbon atom(s) and 4 hydrogen atom(s)
contains 6.02e+23 molecules
```

This algorithm computes the number of molecules in any hydrocarbon substance:

Step 1.   Prompt for and read the mass of hydrocarbon, the number of carbon atoms, and the number of hydrogen atoms.

Step 2.   Compute the formula weight of one mole.

Step 3.   Compute the number of molecules in given mass of hydrocarbon (using the preceding formula).

Step 4.   Output the input and the computed result.

Program 3.2 implements this algorithm. The definitions and insertion and extraction statements

```
cout << "Enter hydrocarbon mass (in grams)\n"
  "followed by the number of carbon atoms\n"
  "followed by the number of hydrogen atoms\n"
  "(e.g. 10.5 2 6):";

float Mass;
int CarbonAtoms;
int HydrogenAtoms;
cin >> Mass >> CarbonAtoms >> HydrogenAtoms;
```

implement step 1 of the algorithm. Because the mass need not be an integral value, we have defined it to be type **float**. Notice that we cascaded the extraction operation. This technique is more efficient than three separate statements, and it is shorter.

The next three lines compute the formula weight of 1 mole of hydrogen. They are

```
const int CarbonAMU = 12;
const int HydrogenAMU = 1;
long FormulaWght = (CarbonAtoms * CarbonAMU)
  + (HydrogenAtoms * HydrogenAMU);
```

The atomic weights of carbon and hydrogen are defined to be **const int**. The **const** tells the compiler and other readers of the program that these values are constant values that will not change during the execution of the program. We

Program 3.2

Compute number of molecules in a hydrocarbon

```
// Program 3.2: Compute number of molecules in a
// hydrocarbon
#include <iostream>
#include <string>
using namespace std;
int main() {
   cout << "Enter mass of hydrocarbon (in grams)\n"
     "followed by the number of carbon atoms\n"
     "followed by the number of hydrogen atoms\n"
     "(e.g. 10.5 2 6): ";

   float Mass;
   int CarbonAtoms;
   int HydrogenAtoms;
   cin >> Mass >> CarbonAtoms >> HydrogenAtoms;

   const int CarbonAMU = 12;
   const int HydrogenAMU = 1;
   long FormulaWght = (CarbonAtoms * CarbonAMU)
     + (HydrogenAtoms * HydrogenAMU);

   const double AvogadroNmbr = 6.02e23;
   double Molecules = (Mass / FormulaWght) *
     AvogadroNmbr;
   cout << Mass << " grams of a hydrocarbon\nwith "
     << CarbonAtoms << " carbon atom(s) and "
     << HydrogenAtoms << " hydrogen atom(s)\ncontains "
     << Molecules << " molecules" << endl;

   return 0;
}
```

chose type **long** for the formula weight because for very complex hydrocarbons, the computation might have overflowed an object of type **int**.

In the computation of the formula weight, the subexpression

```
(HydrogenAtoms * HydrogenAMU)
```

appears. Because HydrogenAMU's value is 1, we could argue that this expression is useless and the entire statement can be written as

```
long FormulaWght = (CarbonAtoms * CarbonAMU)
  + HydrogenAtoms;
```

However, recall that an important part of programming is to write your program so others can easily understand it and possibly modify it. Thus we argue that the first way of writing the expression is clearer. Furthermore, compilers routinely do code optimizations like the one above, so there is no need for us to worry about such minor details.

The remaining statements in Program 3.2 compute and display the number of molecules. Because we are dealing with the number of molecules in a substance, the values involved can become quite large. Because we wish to be as precise as possible, we have used type **double** for the objects that hold

Style Tip

Multiline expressions

As Program 3.2 illustrates, we often need to write long expressions that will not conveniently fit on the screen or a printed page. This is particularly true of output statements where we wish to label and output a number of values. For example, the expression

```
cout << "X-coordinate: " << Xcoord <<
"Y-coordinate: " << Ycoord << "Z-coordinate: " <<
Zcoord << endl;
```

is quite long and will most likely not fit in the window. A good convention to follow for breaking a long expression into a multiline expression is that the continuation line should always begin with an operator and that it should be indented one space. Both of these serve to signal the reader that the line is a continuation of the previous line.

For example, we write the previous expression as

```
cout << "X-coordinate: " << XCoord
  << "Y-coordinate: " << YCoord
  << "Z-coordinate: " << ZCoord << endl;
```

As another example, we can write a long arithmetic expression as

```
((XCoord1 - YCoord1) / 2) * Distance1 + ((XCoord2
  - YCoord2) / 2) * Distance2;
```

Taking some care as to where you break an expression can also improve the readability of the code. The above arithmetic expression can be written more clearly as

```
((XCoord1 - YCoord1) / 2) * Distance1
  + ((XCoord2 - YCoord2) / 2) * Distance2;
```

For insertion statements where the value being inserted is a long string, we can split the line wherever we choose and just continue the string on the next line. The compiler will automatically handle concatenating the strings together into one large string and inserting it into the stream in a single operation. The last insertion statement of Program 3.2 illustrates this technique.

Avogadro's number and the number of molecules. Of course, the **const** modifier is used to define Avogadro's number.

3.5 COMPOUND ASSIGNMENT

C++ has several special operators for performing commonly occurring operations. One can think of these operators as idioms or the shorthand of the language. For example, a common operation is to apply an operator to an object and then store the result back into the object. As an example, consider adding 5 to an object called i. In many programming languages, this operation might be written as

```
                        i = i + 5;
```

C++, on the other hand, has a compound assignment operator that accomplishes the same thing. In C++, the above expression is more properly written as

```
                        i += 5;
```

C++ has compound assignment operators for all of the binary arithmetic operators. Program 3.3 demonstrates the use of this type of operator.

Program 3.3

Illustrate use of the compound assignment operators

```
// Program 3.3: Illustrate compound assignments
#include <iostream>
#include <string>
using namespace std;
int main() {
    int i = 5;
    int k = 2;
    i /= k;
    cout << "i is " << i << endl;

    int j = 20;
    j *= k;
    cout << "j is " << j << endl;

    int m = 15;
    m %= 4;
    cout << "m is " << m << endl;
    return 0;
}
```

The output from this program is

```
    i is 2
    j is 40
    m is 3
```

What happens when the operands of a compound assignment operator are not the same type? For example, consider the following code fragment:

```
    int i = 10;
    float y = 3.2;
    i += y;
```

What conversions/operations are performed, and what is the type and value of the result? To answer these questions, it is convenient to think of the preceding assignment operation as

```
    i = i + y;
```

We can then use the conversion rules for applying binary operators and doing assignment. First, the usual unary and binary conversions of the operands are performed and then the operation is done. In our example, i is converted to **float**, and a floating-point addition is done, yielding a result of *<13.2, float>*.

Next, assignment conversion is done. Thus the value 13 is stored in i. Just as with simple assignment, the result of the expression is *<13, int>*.

Programming Tip

> ### *Don't sacrifice clarity for speed*
> Even the most experienced programmers are tempted to "optimize" their programs so they run faster. While efficiency is important, clarity and correctness are always more important. Who wants to use a program that runs fast but produces incorrect results? Thus we should never sacrifice clarity and correctness for efficiency. Furthermore, it is very hard for a programmer to "tweak" a program so that it runs measurably faster. One rule of thumb in programming is that 90 percent of a program's running time is spent in 10 percent of the code. Consequently, without some idea of where a program spends most of its time, most changes to a program to speed it up will have little or no effect on the overall running time. If efficiency becomes an issue, a more effective approach is to wait until the program is complete and then use a special tool called a *profiler* to identify the program's hot spots. *Hot spots* are where the programs spends most of its time running. These areas of the program can be tuned to reduce the running time of the program.

3.6   INCREMENT AND DECREMENT

C++ also has special operators for incrementing or decrementing an object. The operator ++ is the increment operator, and the operator -- is the decrement operator. Now the reason for the name C++ is clear. It is really "C incremented!"

When applied to the arithmetic objects, these operators add or subtract 1 from the value of the object. For example, the following code fragment:

```
int i = 4;
++i;
cout << "i is " << i << endl;
```

results in the output

```
i is 5
```

For all intents and purposes, the expression

```
++i
```

is equivalent to

```
i += 1;
```

but it is shorter still. Interestingly, there are two forms of the increment and decrement operators—prefix and postfix. The term *prefix* means the operator appears before the operand. The expression ++i is an example. There is also a postfix form. The previous code fragment could have been

```
int i = 4;
i++;
cout << "i is " << i << endl;
```

which would produce exactly the same output. So what is the difference between the postfix and prefix versions of the increment operator? The difference becomes apparent when the operation is used as part of a larger expression. Consider this code fragment:

```
int i = 4;
int j = 5;
int k = j * ++i;
cout << "k is " << k << ", i is " << i << endl;
```

Is the multiplication operation performed before or after i is incremented? In the case of the ++ prefix operator, i is incremented first and then the multiplication is performed. The output is therefore

```
k is 25, i is 5
```

If the fragment is modified to be

```
int i = 4;
int j = 5;
int k = j * i++;
cout << "k is " << k ", i is " << i << endl;
```

the output would be

```
k is 20, i is 5
```

Thus the *postfix* increment returns the value of the object before it is incremented, whereas the *prefix* increment returns the value of the object after it has been incremented. The decrement operator is similar to the increment operator except that it subtracts 1.

The increment and decrement operators can also be applied the floating-point objects **float**, **double**, and **long double**, and they do exactly what you think they would do. Respectively, they add or subtract one from the object. Consider this code fragment

```
float f = 5.2F;
double d = 8.6;
++f;
--d;
cout << "f is " << f << ", d is " << d << endl;
```

the output would be

```
f is 6.2, d is 7.6
```

An important point to note is that the increment and decrement operators can be applied only to objects. For example, it is tempting to interpret the expression

```
(x - 2)++;
```

to mean

```
x - 2 + 1;
```

However, the previous expression is illegal and will not compile. The increment operator is being applied to an expression. See Appendix A.2 for the precedence and associativity of the increment and decrement operators.

Style Tip

Increment and decrement

As was noted in the text, the increment and decrement operators are C++ shorthand for adding or subtracting 1 from an arithmetic object. A good C++ programmer would never write

```
i = i + 1;
```

Whether to use prefix or postfix incrementing in this situation is a question of style. Our experience is that most good C++ programmers seem to favor the prefix version. Believing that imitation is the sincerest form of flattery, we also use the prefix version. Whichever you choose, the really important thing is to be consistent!

Self-check Questions

9.   Using the notation *<value, type>* give the value and type assigned to the object on the left side of the compound assignment operator.

```
int i = 3;
float f = 6.1;
i += f;
```

10.   Using the notation *<value, type>* give the value and type assigned to the object on the left side of the compound assignment operator.

```
int i = 4;
float f = 6.8;
f += i;
```

11.   Using the notation *<value, type>* give the value and type assigned to the object on the left side of the compound assignment operator.

```
short i = 4;
int k = 6;
i -= k;
```

12.   Using the notation *<value, type>* give the value and type assigned to the objects k and j.

```
int i = 5;
int j = 0;
int k;
```

```
k = ++i;
j = i;
```

13.   Using the notation *<value, type>* give the value and type assigned to the
      objects k and j.

```
int i = 6;
int j;
int k;
k = i++;
j = i;
```

14.   Using the notation *<value, type>* give the value and type assigned to the
      objects y and z.

```
float x = 3.2;
float y;
float z;
y = x++;
z = x;
```

3.7   ESTIMATING YEARLY SAVINGS OF CHANGE

If you are like most people, you collect a fair amount of change in your pocket.
A painless savings plan is to dump all the loose change into a jar at the end of
the week. However, we'd like some idea of the amount of money we'll have
saved in a year so we can start thinking about what we want to buy. The final
case study of this chapter is the construction of a program to estimate the
yearly savings based on four weeks of data. The problem statement is as
follows:

> Compute the estimated yearly savings based on the amount of change
> saved at the end of each of four weeks. The amount of change saved at the
> end of each week is recorded as four numbers: the number of pennies, the
> number of nickels, the number of dimes, and the number of quarters. Here
> is an example of the input/output behavior of the program:

```
For each week enter 4 numbers:
 pennies nickels dimes quarters (e.g.: 3 2 4 1)

Week 1 data: 8 2 5 3
Week 2 data: 4 3 3 5
Week 3 data: 8 5 6 3
Week 4 data: 5 2 7 6
Over four weeks you have collected
 25 Pennies
 12 Nickels
 21 Dimes
 17 Quarters
```

which is 7 dollar(s) and 20 cent(s).
This is a weekly average of 1 dollar(s) and 80 cent(s).
Estimated yearly savings: 93 dollar(s) and 60 cent(s).

The algorithm for solving this problem is straightforward:

Step 1.   Prompt for and read each week's data and keep a running total of the number of pennies, nickels, dimes, and quarters saved.

Step 2.   Print the number of pennies, nickels, dimes, and quarters saved.

Step 3.   Compute and print the total amount saved and the weekly average.

Step 4.   Compute and print the estimated year-end savings.

Listing 3.1 contains the code that implements the first two steps of the algorithm. The program begins by displaying directions telling the user how to input the data. The next four sections of code read each week's data and update the total number of pennies, nickels, dimes, and quarters. Notice the use of the += operator to update the totals. The fifth section prints the totals.

Listing 3.1

Part 1 of change.cpp

```cpp
// Compute estimated yearly savings by saving pocket change
#include <iostream>
#include <string>
using namespace std;
int main() {
    cout << "For each week enter 4 numbers:\n"
        " pennies nickels dimes quarters (e.g.: 3 2 4 1)\n"
        << endl;

    // Prompt for and read the amount of change for 4 weeks
    cout << "Week 1 change: ";
    int Pennies, Nickels, Dimes, Quarters;
    cin >> Pennies >> Nickels >> Dimes >> Quarters;
    int TotalPennies = Pennies;
    int TotalNickels = Nickels;
    int TotalDimes = Dimes;
    int TotalQuarters = Quarters;

    cout << "Week 2 change: ";
    cin >> Pennies >> Nickels >> Dimes >> Quarters;
    TotalPennies += Pennies;
    TotalNickels += Nickels;
    TotalDimes += Dimes;
    TotalQuarters += Quarters;

    cout << "Week 3 change: ";
    cin >> Pennies >> Nickels >> Dimes >> Quarters;
    TotalPennies += Pennies;
    TotalNickels += Nickels;
    TotalDimes += Dimes;
    TotalQuarters += Quarters;

    cout << "Week 4 change: ";
    cin >> Pennies >> Nickels >> Dimes >> Quarters;
    TotalPennies += Pennies;
    TotalNickels += Nickels;
    TotalDimes += Dimes;
    TotalQuarters += Quarters;

    cout << "Over four weeks you collected\n " <<
        TotalPennies << " Pennies\n " << TotalNickels
        << " Nickels\n " << TotalDimes << " Dimes\n "
        << TotalQuarters << " Quarters" << endl;
```

The second part of the program computes the total amount saved and the weekly average (see Listing 3.2). Displaying the dollar amounts in the proper format is the only complicated part of the program. This step is done by computing the number of dollars and the number of cents separately, using the division and remainder operators. The statement

```cpp
int TotalDollars = Total / 100;
```

computes the number of dollars; the statement

```cpp
int TotalCents = Total % 100;
```

computes the cents. This sequence of operations is done whenever we need to print out a dollar and cents amount. An amount is output by inserting a dollar sign, followed by the dollar amount, followed by a period, followed by the cents. This technique is also used to output the average savings and the estimated year-end savings computed in step 4.

Listing 3.2

Part 2 of change.cpp

```cpp
// Compute and print total savings and the
// weekly average
int Total = TotalPennies + TotalNickels * 5
  + TotalDimes * 10 + TotalQuarters * 25;
int Average = Total / 4;
int TotalDollars = Total / 100;
int TotalCents = Total % 100;
int AverageDollars = Average / 100;
int AverageCents = Average % 100;
cout << "which is " << TotalDollars << " dollar(s) and "
  << TotalCents << " cent(s)." << endl;
cout << "This is a weekly average of "
  << AverageDollars << " dollar(s) and " << AverageCents
  << " cent(s)." << endl;
// Compute and print estimated yearly savings
int YearSavings = Average * 52;
int YearDollars = YearSavings / 100;
int YearCents = YearSavings % 100;
cout << "Estimated yearly savings: "
  << YearDollars << " dollar(s) and "
  << YearCents << " cent(s)." << endl;
return 0;
}
```

3.8   THE STRING CLASS

Up to now, we have worked with the fundamental objects in C++: **char**, **int**, **long**, **float**, **double**. In addition to these fundamental objects, the C++ language definition specifies a standard library. This library contains many additional useful objects. Part of becoming a good C++ programmer is to learn what facilities are available in the standard library and to use them when appropriate. As we proceed through our exploration of C++, we will introduce some of the more useful classes found in the standard C++ library.

One useful abstraction found in the standard C++ library is the **string** class. A string is a sequence of characters treated as a single object. We have made use of string constants—a sequence of zero or more characters enclosed in double quotes. However, C++ does not provide a fundamental object for naming and storing strings. Fortunately, the standard C++ library provides a class for that purpose. The class `string` is used to instantiate objects that can hold sequences of characters. To use the `string` class, the program must contain the include directive

```
#include <string>
```

Library objects are created just like fundamental type objects are created—they are defined. For example, the code fragment

```
string Greeting = "Hello";
```

defines a `string` object named `Greeting` and initializes it to the sequence of characters found between the quotes. One thing to notice about this definition is that it uses the same syntax we use to define and initialize a fundamental or built-in object. Interestingly, although a string can be initialized with a string constant, it cannot be initialized with a character constant. The following definition is illegal.

```
string ExclamationMark = '!';
```

As we mentioned in Chapter 1, a class has a set of attributes and messages that it understands. Among others, the class `string` has the following attributes:

- The characters that comprise the string.
- The number of characters in the string.

Consequently, we can visualize the definition

```
string Message = "Help!";
```

as creating the object depicted below:

Unlike string constants, the characters stored in a `string` object do not have a terminating í\0í character.

There are many behaviors or messages that a `string` object understands and several operations that can be performed on `string` objects. Strings can be written and read using the insertion and extraction operators. The following statement writes the contents of `Prompt` to the stream `cout`

```
string Prompt = "Enter your password";
cout << Prompt;
```

which would cause the following characters to be written to the display

```
Enter your password
```

The following code fragment extracts strings from stream `cin`.

```
string Account;
string Password
cin >> Account;
cin >> Password;
```

The extraction operator skips initial whitespace and reads a whitespace-terminated word to its `string` operand. So for the previous code fragment, if we typed

```
Hot      Stuff!
```

the word `Hot` would be extracted and stored in `Account` and the word `Stuff!` would be stored in `Password`.

Like fundamental objects, one `string` object can be assigned to another. For example, the code fragment

```
string Message1 = "Hello!";
string Message2;
Message2 = Message1;
```

copies the contents of `Message1` to `Message2` as shown in Figure 3.3. Thus two distinct strings with the same value exist.

Figure 3.3

Assignment of string objects

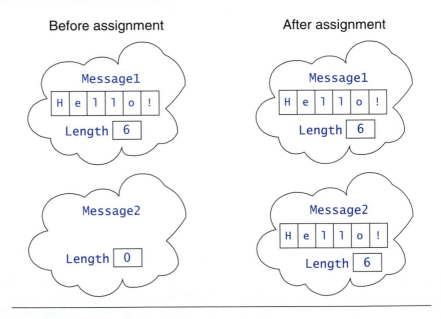

In addition to the assignment operation, the class `string` provides the ability to *concatenate* two strings to produce a new string. Concatenation constructs a new string out of two strings by placing one after another. The + is the string concatenation operator. Consider the following code fragment:

```
string FirstName = "Zach";
string LastName = "Davidson";
string FullName = FirstName + í í + LastName;
```

The `string FullName` is initialized to

```
Zach Davidson
```

Notice the concatenation operator allows a **char** to be concatenated to a `string`.

Another operation provided by the class `string` is append. The append operation, +=, adds characters to the end of a string. Like concatenation, the append operation can add another string or a character to the end of a string. The code fragment

```
string Message = "Help";
Message += í!í
cout << Message << endl;
```

writes

```
Help!
```

Similarly, the code fragment

```
string Message = "Help";
string Who = " Me!";
Message += Who
cout << Message << endl;
```

writes

```
Help Me!
```

In addition to understanding the operators, a `string` object also understands many behaviors or messages. We will mention only a few of the most useful at this time. One useful message understood by a `string` object is `size`. This message requests the string object to return the number of characters in the string. The C++ syntax for sending an object a message is

Object name   *Message type*   *Optional list of arguments (the message contents)*

```
Identifier.Message([Arg₁, Arg₂, ... Argₙ]) ;
```

The C++ fragment

```
string Date = "March 7, 1994";
int i = Date.size();
```

initializes `i` to 13. Notice that the size message does not require any arguments.

Another capability provided by the class `string` is `substr`, which returns a substring of a string. The substring to select is specified by giving a

starting position and a length as arguments to `substr`. In C++ the first character of a string is located at position 0. The code fragment

```
string Date = "March 7, 1994";
string Year = Date.substr(9, 4);
cout << "Year is" << Year << endl;
```

specifies that the substring of `Date` starting at position 9 and four characters
long be assigned to `Year`. Thus the text

```
Year is 1994
```

is written to the display. It is an error to give `substr` a position that is not
within the string. If the sum of the position specified and the length of substring requested are greater than the size of the string, `substr` returns the substring starting at the position specified through the end of the string. Thus the
code fragment

```
string Date = "March 7, 1994";
string Year = Date.substr(9, 10);
cout << "Year is" << Year << endl;
```

also displays

```
Year is 1994
```

The class `string` also provides the ability to find a substring within a
string. This message is called `find`. The find message accepts two arguments—a substring to find and the position within the subject string to start the
search. The `find` message returns the position within the string where the substring is found. If the substring is not found, `find` returns a number that is
larger than any legal position within a string.

Consider the following code fragment:

```
string SpockSays = "Live long and prosper!";
int i = SpockSays.find("and", 0);
cout << "i is " << i << endl;
```

This second statement searches the `string SpockSays` for the substring `and`
starting at position 0 of `SpockSays`. The text

```
i is 10
```

is written to the display.

Finally, the `string` library provides `getline()`, which reads an entire
line of input into a string. Unlike the other `string` capabilities we have just
discussed, `getline()` is not a message that is sent to a string object—it is an
auxiliary capability provided by the `string` library. The following code illustrates the use of `getline()` to read a line of input from stream `cin`:

```
cout << "Please enter some text:";
string InputLine;
getline(cin, InputLine, i\ni);
cout << "Your input is \"" << InputLine << "\"" << endl;
```

The first argument to `getline()` is the stream to read from, the second argument is the string that receives the input line, and the third argument is the

character that terminates the extraction. The following illustrates what happens when the previous code is executed:

```
Please enter some text: a man a plan a canal panama
Your input is "a man a plan a canal panama"
```

To illustrate the usefulness of the string library, let's write a program that converts dates from American format (e.g., December 29, 1953) to international format (e.g., 29 December 1953). The problem statement is simple:

Read a date in American format and output that date in international format.

The algorithm for solving this problem is equally simple.

Step 1.   Prompt for and read the date in American format.

Step 2.   Locate the month and store it in an object called Month.

Step 3.   Locate the day and store it in an object called Day.

Step 4.   Locate the year and store it in an object called Year.

Step 5.   Display the date as Day Month Year.

The following code prompts for and reads the date.

```
// Prompt for and read the date
cout << "Enter the date in American format "
  << "(e.g., December 29, 1953) : ";
string Date;
getline(cin, Date, i\ni);
```

To extract the month, we use find() to locate the blank that separates the month from the day and then we use substr to pick out this substring. The following code accomplishes this task.

```
int i = Date.find(" ");
string Month = Date.substr(0, i);
```

To locate and extract the day, we first locate the comma that follows the day. Using this position and the position of the blank just located, we can compute the number of characters in the day portion of the date and extract it. The following code accomplishes step 3 of the algorithm.

```
int k = Date.find(",");
string Day = Date.substr(i + 1, k - i - 1);
```

Step 4 of the algorithm locates the year by getting the substring that begins two positions beyond the comma and extends through the end of the string.

```
string Year = Date.substr(k + 2, Date.size());
```

The last step is to create the date in the new format and display it. We use the concatenation operator to assemble the components of the date into the proper order.

```
string NewDate = Day + " " + Month + " " + Year;
cout << "Original date: " << Date << endl;
cout << "Converted date: " << NewDate << endl;
```

Program 3.4 contains the complete program.

We have only touched on some of the many capabilities and behaviors of the **string** class. Appendix C contains a complete description of the **string** class.

Program 3.4

Convert a date from American format to international format

```
// Program 3.4: Convert a date from American format to
// international format
#include <iostream>
#include <string>
using namespace std;
int main() {
    // Prompt for and read the date
    cout << "Enter the date in American format "
      << "(e.g., December 29, 1953) : ";
    string Date;
    getline(cin, Date, í\ní);

    // Get the month by finding the first blank character
    int i = Date.find(" ");
    string Month = Date.substr(0, i);

    // Get the day by finding the comma character
    int k = Date.find(",");
    string Day = Date.substr(i + 1, k - i - 1);

    // Get the year by getting the substring from the blank
    // following the comma through the end of the string
    string Year = Date.substr(k + 2, Date.size());
    string NewDate = Day + " " + Month + " " + Year;

    cout << "Original date: " << Date << endl;
    cout << "Converted date: " << NewDate << endl;
    return 0;
}
```

Self-check Questions

15. What include directive must a program contain to use the **string** class?

16. What is the name of the **string** library function for reading a string from a stream?

17. Give the output of the following code fragment.

    ```
    string Message = "Wallyball!";
    Message = "!!";
    cout << Message << endl;
    ```

18. Give the output of the following code fragment.

    ```
    string Time = "1:42";
    string AM = "AM";
    cout << Time + AM << endl;
    ```

19. Give the output of the following code fragment.

```
string Time = "11:15";
Time += "PM";
cout << Time << endl;
```

20. Give the output of the following code fragment.

```
string s = "";
cout << s.size() << endl;
```

21. Give the output of the following code fragment.

```
string s = "Go Wahoos!";
cout << s.size() << endl;
```

22. Give the output of the following code fragment.

```
string s = "Beam Me Up Scotty";
cout << s.substr(5, 2) << endl;
```

23. Give the output of the following code fragment.

```
string s = "The Picard Maneuver";
cout << s.substr(4, s.size() - 1) << endl;
```

24. Give the output of the following code fragment.

```
string s = "Resistance is futile!";
cout << s.find( is , 4) << endl;
```

25. Give the output of the following code fragment.

```
string s = "You will be assimilated";
int i = s.find("a", 0);
cout << s.substr(i, s.size()) << endl;
```

26. Consider the following code fragment.

```
string Message;
getline(cin, Message, í,í);
cout << "Message is "<< Message << endl;
```

Give the output if the input is

```
Spock, you laughed, you laughed!
```

27. Write a program that reads a date in the format *mm/dd/yy* from the stream `cin` and writes the date to stream `cout` as follows:

```
Month: mm
Day: dd
Year: yy
```

28.   Write a program that reads an assignment statement (e.g., a = b + c;)
       from the stream cin and outputs the left and right sides of the assign-
       ment statement to stream cout.

3.9   EZWINDOWS

Although the standard C++ library provides many useful objects, the real power
of C++ comes from the ability to use object types that are specially developed
for the task at hand. For example, in Chapter 1 we discussed creating a new
type or class called Bug in order to implement the Bug Hunt game.

We are not quite ready to discuss how to create classes; however we can
write programs that use programmer-defined classes of objects that have
already been designed and implemented. To begin, we will use a library called
EzWindows that contains objects designed to enable us to write programs that
use the graphical display capabilities available on most computers. The first
programmer-defined classes we will use are SimpleWindow and Rectangle-
Shape.

3.9.1   Class SimpleWindow

SimpleWindow is a class that lets us create window objects that we can use to
display graphical objects. Objects of type Label and Rectangle can be displayed in a SimpleWindow window. SimpleWindow has the following
attributes:

- The text to display in the title bar at the top of the window.
- The width and height of the window.

The behaviors or messages that a SimpleWindow object understands are Open
and Close. The Open message causes the window to appear on the screen, and
it enables the window so that objects can be displayed in it. The Close message
causes the window to shut down and remove its image from the screen. So, for
example, the C++ statement to send SimpleWindow object W an Open message
is

```
W.Open();
```

In this instance, the Open message does not require any arguments.

For example, the code fragment

```
SimpleWindow W;
W.Open();
```

creates and displays the window shown in Figure 3.4.

Since we made such a big deal about initializing objects, you might wonder
why W was not initialized. Actually, W was initialized. For most programmer-
defined classes, when a class is designed, the designer can specify default initial
values for the attributes of an object when it is defined without initializing it
explicitly. We can, however, define an object and give its attributes different initial values by using a slightly different syntax than we used for initializing

Figure 3.4

*A SimpleWindow with
default attributes*

fundamental objects when we defined them. The reason is that we need a way to
specify several initial values, one for each attribute. The syntax for defining an
object and explicitly giving initial values for its attributes is

For the `SimpleWindow` class, for example, the definition

```
SimpleWindow N("Narrow Window", 8, 2);
N.Open();
```

creates the following window:

The window title is Narrow Window, and the window is 8 centimeters wide and 2 centimeters high. Thus when defining a `SimpleWindow` object, the first argument is the title of the window and the second and third arguments are the width and the height of the window, respectively.

This new syntax for initializing objects can also be used to initialize fundamental objects. For example, the definition

```
int x(2);
```

is equivalent to the definition

```
int x = 2;
```

The first definition can be used to initialize a complex object with several attributes, but the second definition can be used to initialize a simple object only.

Style Tip

C++ definition styles

Because the new definition style works with both programmer-defined objects and fundamental objects, we could use this style of definition for all our objects. This convention would have the advantage of uniformity, which is definitely a plus. However, the new style of definition can be confusing for a fundamental object, especially when the object is being initialized with the value of an expression. Consider the following definition from Program 3.2 rewritten to use the new style of definition:

```
double Molecules((Mass / FormulaWght) *
   AvogadroNmbr);
```

We think that this definition is much harder to read and understand than the original.

Our convention will be to continue to use the = style of definition for fundamental objects and to use the new style of definition only for complex objects that have more than one attribute that needs to be initialized.

Definitions of complex objects can be long, so we need a convention for splitting this type of definition into multiple lines. Our convention will be to split the definition between arguments. The following definition illustrates this style:

```
SimpleWindow Display("A Window for Display",
   DisplayLength, DisplayWidth);
```

3.9.2   Class RectangleShape

Now that we have a window, we need something that we can draw in a window.
A simple but useful type of object is a rectangle. The class `Rectangle` has the
following properties or attributes:

- A `SimpleWindow` object in which the rectangle is displayed.
- A position in the window.
- A color.
- A width and height.

A `Rectangle` object understands the following messages:

- `Draw`—display the rectangle in the window.
- `GetColor`—return the color of the rectangle.
- `GetWidth`—return the width of the rectangle.
- `GetHeight`—return the height of the rectangle.

The following code

```
SimpleWindow W("A Blue Rectangle", 8, 4);
W.Open();
RectangleShape R(W, 4.0, 2.0, Blue, 3, 2);
R.Draw();
```

creates and displays the following window and the object inside it.

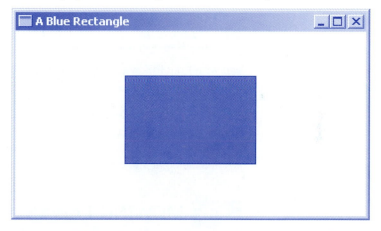

The definition of R instantiated a blue `RectangleShape` named R whose center is 4 centimeters from the left edge of the window and 2 centimeters from
the top edge of the window. R is 3 centimeters wide and 2 centimeters high.
Thus R is centered within `SimpleWindow` W.

We can use the messages to obtain information about an object. For the
object R above, the statement

```
int Width = R.GetWidth();
```

sends a message to `RectangleShape` R requesting that it return its width. The
value is stored in the `int` object `Width`. As another example, let's write code

that displays the default width and height of a `RectangleShape`. The code fragment

```
SimpleWindow W("Default Rectangle", 8, 5);
W.Open();
RectangleShape D(W, 4.0, 2.0);
D.Draw();
cout << "Dis width is " << D.GetWidth() << endl;
cout << "Dis height is " << D.GetHeight() << endl;
```

creates the following display window

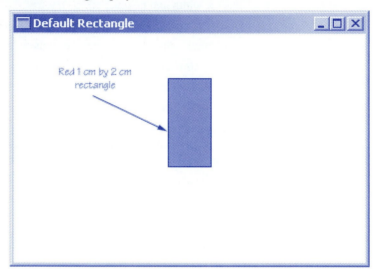

and writes the following output to the text output window:

```
Dis width is 1
Dis height is 2
```

We see that when the color and size of a `RectangleShape` are not specified in the definition, the default color of a `RectangleShape` is red, and the default width and height are, respectively, 1 centimeter and 2 centimeters.

3.10 MOWING LAWNS

Your kid brother plans to start a lawn-mowing service this summer, and he wants to earn $6 an hour. He wants you to write a program that computes how much he should charge to mow a lawn. The problem statement is

The input to the program is (1) the length and width of a rectangular lawn and (2) the length and width of a house situated on the lawn. All inputs will be in meters. The average speed of mowing is 1 square meter a second. This average takes into account water breaks and periodically refueling the lawn mower. The amount to charge should be printed in dollars and cents.

Programmer Alert

The input and output should look like the following:

```
Please use meters for all input
Please enter the length of the lawn: 150
Please enter the width of the lawn: 100
Please enter the length of the house: 25
Please enter the width of the house: 20
Yard size: 150 by 100 meters
House size: 25 by 20 meters
Approximate time to cut: 4 hour(s) and 1 minute(s)
Cost to cut: 24 dollar(s) and 16 cent(s)
```

In addition, the program should create a window that graphically displays a plot of the house and the lawn. The scale of the display should be 100 meters equals 1 centimeter. The lawn should be green, and the house should be yellow.

The steps necessary to solve the problem are straightforward.

Step 1.   Prompt for and read the inputs.

Step 2.   Print the input so the user can verify that it was correctly entered.

Step 3.   Compute the mowable area. The mowable area is the total size of the lawn minus the area the house takes up.

Step 4.   Compute and print the time required to mow the lawn.

Step 5.   Compute and print the amount to charge for mowing the lawn.

Step 6.   Create a display showing the lawn and the house.

Before implementing the first step of the program, we should define any constants we will use. We will group these at the beginning of the program so that they are easy to find and modify if necessary.

We need the following constants:

```cpp
// Mowing rate in meters per second
const float MowRate = 1.0;

// Pay rate desired
const float PayRate = 6.0;

// Seconds in a minute
const int SecondsPerMinute = 60;
// Seconds in an hour
const int SecondsPerHour = SecondsPerMinute * 60;

// Length and width of display window
const int DisplayWidth = 20;
const int DisplayHeight = 20;

// Scale factor for display: 100 meters equals
// 1 centimeter
const float ScaleFactor = 0.01;
```

To prompt for and read the input is straightforward. The code is

```cpp
cout << "Please use meters for all input\n" << endl;

int LawnLength; // Length of the lawn in meters
cout << "Please enter the length of the lawn: ";
cin >> LawnLength;

int LawnWidth; // Width of the lawn in meters
cout << "Please enter the width of the lawn: ";
cin >> LawnWidth;
```

In both code fragments, notice the use of descriptive names for the objects.

The code to echo the input is equally straightforward:

```cpp
cout << endl;
cout << "Yard size: " << LawnLength << " by "
  << LawnWidth << " meters" << endl;
cout << "House size: " << HouseLength << " by "
  << HouseWidth << " meters" << endl;
```

The next step is to compute the mowable area. The following statement accomplishes this task.

```cpp
int MowableArea = (LawnLength * LawnWidth)
  - (HouseLength * HouseWidth);
```

Using `MowableArea` and `MowRate`, we can compute the time needed to mow the lawn. We initially compute the time to mow in seconds and then use that value to calculate the number of hours and minutes. The code to calculate and display the time is

```cpp
int MowTimeInSeconds = MowableArea / MowRate;
int Hours = MowTimeInSeconds / SecondsPerHour;
int Minutes = (MowTimeInSeconds % SecondsPerHour)
  / SecondsPerMinute;
cout << "Approximate time to cut: " << Hours
  << " hour(s) " << Minutes << " minute(s)" << endl;
```

Step 5 is to compute and display the amount to charge for the job. To compute the cost we simply convert the pay rate, which is in dollars per hour, to dollars per second and multiply this amount by the time in seconds to mow the lawn. The cost calculation is

```
float DollarCost = MowTimeInSeconds
  * (PayRate / SecondsPerHour);
```

and the output calculation is

```
int Dollars = DollarCost;
int Cents = (DollarCost - Dollars) * 100;
cout << "Cost to cut: " << Dollars << " dollar(s)"
  << " and " << Cents << " cent(s)" << endl;
```

Notice that the number of dollars was obtained by assigning `DollarCost`, which is a **float**, to `Dollars`, which is an **int**. Recall that assignment from a floating-point type to an integral type results in a truncated value being stored. Using `DollarCost` and `Dollars`, the number of cents in the amount is computed.

The final step of the program is to produce the graphical display. Like our previous examples, the first step is to instantiate and open a window. The code

```
SimpleWindow Display("Lawn and House Plot",
  DisplayWidth, DisplayHeight);
Display.Open();
```

instantiates a window named `Display` with the title Lawn and House Plot. The window is `DisplayWidth` centimeters wide and `DisplayHeight` centimeters high.

To create the display we want, we will first draw the lawn and then we will draw the house. If we did it the other way, the larger rectangle would overwrite the smaller rectangle, and it would not be visible. The code to display a scaled image of the lawn is

```
RectangleShape Lawn(Display, DisplayWidth / 2.0,
  DisplayHeight / 2.0, Green, LawnLength
  * ScaleFactor, LawnWidth * ScaleFactor);
Lawn.Draw();
```

The position attributes of `Lawn` are set to the values

```
DisplayWidth / 2.0
```

and

```
DisplayHeight / 2.0
```

so it is positioned in the center of the window.

The final step is to draw the rectangle representing the house in the proper position. This code is similar to the previous code

```
RectangleShape House(Display, DisplayWidth / 2.0,
  DisplayHeight / 2.0, Yellow, HouseWidth * ScaleFactor,
  HouseHeight * ScaleFactor);
House.Draw();
```

The final action of the program is to close the display window. The statements

```
cout << "Type a character followed by a\n"
  << "return to remove the display and exit" << endl;
```

```
char AnyChar;
cin >> AnyChar;
Display.Close();
```

display a message in the console window and wait for the user to type a character followed by a return. Waiting for a character to be typed pauses the program
so that the display window does not disappear. When the user types a character
and a return, the program continues and sends the close message to the
window.

Program 3.5 contains the complete code for the program and Figure 3.5
shows the display window that the program creates. There are several important things to notice about this program. First, the include statement

```
#include "rect.h"
```

incorporates the file `rect.h` into the program. This file contains the definitions
necessary to access and use the programmer-defined types `SimpleWindow` and
`RectangleShape`. Including an `.h` file is the standard way to gain access to
new types and classes of objects.

Program 3.5

*Compute time and cost
to mow a lawn*

```cpp
// Program 3.5: Compute the time and cost required to mow
// a lawn
#include <iostream>
#include <string>
#include "rect.h"
using namespace std;

int ApiMain() {
    // Mowing rate in square meters per second
    const float MowRate = 1.0;
    // Pay rate desired
    const float PayRate = 6.0;

    // Seconds in a minute
    const int SecondsPerMinute = 60;
    // Seconds in an hour
    const int SecondsPerHour = SecondsPerMinute * 60;

    // Length and width of display window
    const int DisplayWidth = 20;
    const int DisplayHeight = 20;

    // Scale factor for display. 100 meters equals
    // 1 centimeter
    const float ScaleFactor = 0.01;

    cout << "Please use meters for all input\n" << endl;

    int LawnLength; // Length of the lawn in meters
    cout << "Please enter the length of the lawn: ";
    cin >> LawnLength;

    int LawnWidth; // Width of the lawn in meters
    cout << "Please enter the width of the lawn: ";
    cin >> LawnWidth;

    int HouseLength; // Length of the house in meters
    cout << "Please enter the length of the house: ";
    cin >> HouseLength;

    int HouseWidth; // Width of the house in meters
    cout << "Please enter the width of the house: ";
    cin >> HouseWidth;
```

```cpp
// Echo the input so they can be verified
cout << endl;
cout << "Yard size: " << LawnLength << " by "
   << LawnWidth << " meters" << endl;
cout << "House size: " << HouseLength << " by "
   << HouseWidth << " meters" << endl;

// Compute the mowable area
int MowableArea = (LawnLength * LawnWidth)
   - (HouseLength * HouseWidth);

// Compute the time to cut and display it
int MowTimeInSeconds = MowableArea / MowRate;
int Hours = MowTimeInSeconds / SecondsPerHour;
int Minutes = (MowTimeInSeconds % SecondsPerHour)
   / SecondsPerMinute;

cout << "Approximate time to cut: " << Hours
   << " hour(s) " << Minutes << " minute(s)" << endl;
// Compute the cost and display it
float DollarCost = MowTimeInSeconds * PayRate
   / SecondsPerHour;
int Dollars = DollarCost;
int Cents = (DollarCost - Dollars) * 100;
cout << "Cost to cut: " << Dollars << " dollar(s)"
   << " and " << Cents << " cent(s)" << endl;

// Open the window and display the lawn
SimpleWindow Display("Lawn and House Plot",
   DisplayWidth, DisplayHeight);
Display.Open();

RectangleShape Lawn(Display, DisplayWidth / 2.0,
   DisplayHeight / 2.0, Green, LawnLength * ScaleFactor,
   LawnWidth * ScaleFactor);
   Lawn.Draw();
// Display the house
RectangleShape House(Display, DisplayWidth / 2.0,
   DisplayHeight / 2.0, Yellow, HouseLength * ScaleFactor,
   HouseWidth * ScaleFactor);
House.Draw();

cout << "Type a character followed by a\n"
   << "return to remove the display and exit" << endl;
char AnyChar;
cin >> AnyChar;
Display.Close();

return 0;
}
```

The second thing to notice is that this program does not contain a function main(), but rather the code is contained in a function called ApiMain(). Because we are creating our own windows and managing the display of objects within these windows, we must bypass the normal window creation mechanism provided by the C++ compiler. The reason we need this special function is described more completely in Chapter 10, where we discuss the mechanics of graphical programming. So for now, just remember that when we write a program that creates a separate window for the display of graphical objects, the starting point for the execution of the program is in a function called ApiMain(), not main().

Figure 3.5

*A graphical depiction
of the house and lawn*

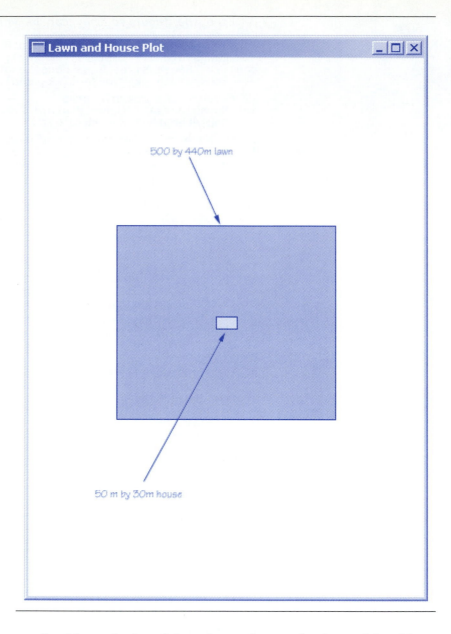

Careful examination of the code reveals a couple of potential problems. What would happen if the size of the lawn was so large that when it was scaled, it was larger than the display window? Similarly, what if the house size is larger than the size of the lawn? You could try running the program and see what happens, but clearly these are situations that we should avoid. In an interactive program, it is important to validate the input and make sure it is reasonable. We do not yet have a mechanism for doing this type of checking, but the next chapter introduces several C++ constructs that will allow us to check user input to make sure it is acceptable.

Self-check Questions

29.   Write a C++ definition that creates a `SimpleWindow` object `Try`. The title bar should say "Good Job!" and the window should be 6 centimeters wide and 3 centimeters high.

30.   Write a program that creates a `SimpleWindow` with the title "Nice Job!" and draws a blue square in the middle of the window. The window should be 5 centimeters wide and 6 centimeters high, and the rectangles should be 3 centimeters wide and 2 centimeters high.

31.   What is the message for obtaining the width of a `RectangleShape`?

32.   What is the message for obtaining the height of a `RectangleShape`?

33.   Describe the rectangle created and drawn by the following code fragment. How big is the rectangle and what color is it?

```
SimpleWindow T( Check Your Knowledge , 10, 10);
T.Open();
Rectangle P(T);
T.Draw();
```

3.11 POINTS TO REMEMBER

✔ Always initialize an object when it is declared.

✔ When a floating-point value is stored in an integer object, the floating-point value is converted to an integer value by truncating its value. For example, after the code

```
int x = 0;
x = 23.6;
```

is executed, the value of x is 23.

✔ The assignment operator is right associative and has lower precedence than the arithmetic operators.

✔ The C++ keyword **const** is used to define objects that should not be modified. This technique is useful for defining objects that hold values that represent physical constants, values that are conversion factors, and other values that should not be changed during the execution of the program.

✔ The iostream object `cin` is an input stream. It is normally associated with input from the keyboard.

History of Computing

Mechanical devices

The 17th century saw the development of the first primitive mechanical calculators. The person now credited with constructing the first mechanical calculator is Wilhelm Schickard (1592–1635). The principal innovation of Schickard's device, which he called the "calculating clock" (see Figure 3.6), was the use of gears to propagate a carry from one digit place to the next highest digit place. This mechanism was used in one form or another in many of the later mechanical calculating devices. Unfortunately, the details of Schickard's invention were lost until the 1960s when references to his work were discovered in letters to the great mathematician and astronomer, Johannes Kepler. Because of this accident of history, much more attention has been paid to another inventor of a mechanical calculator—Blaise Pascal.

Blaise Pascal (1623–1662) was certainly a child prodigy. At an early age, he discovered several mathematical theorems and wrote several highly regarded essays. In his 30s, not long before he died, he invented the syringe and the hydraulic press. Pascal is best known for his design and construction of a mechanical calculator known as the Pascaline (see Figure 3.7). The *Pascaline* was a small box that had a series of toothed wheels. Each wheel corresponded to a digit, and the digit was displayed above the wheel in a small window. Addition was performed by dialing the numbers to be added on the wheels and reading the result in the windows above the wheels. The machine could also be used to do subtraction, but it was a bit more complicated. This may seem like a simple device, but in Pascal's day, it was a great accomplishment. To produce the machine, Pascal had to overcome several difficult problems. One of the most serious, and one that has plagued inventors throughout history, was that his ideas outstripped the technology of the time. Pascal designed several machines only to find that the craftsmen of the day could not build the components required.

Pascal addressed one of the problems with Schickard's calculating clock. The problem of using simple gears to propagate a carry to the next digit is that if the carry must be propagated in several places, the force required to turn all the gears is quite large and the gears could break. Pascal devised a device that used a gravity-assisted mechanism to help propagate carries. Essentially, when a carry was needed, a weight would fall to activate a spring mechanism that would advance the next wheel. This mechanism eliminated any strain on the gears.

✔ Input is extracted from an input stream using the extraction operator >>. The extraction operator can extract integer, floating-point, and character values from an input stream.

✔ When writing a program that accepts input from a human user, the program must issue prompts that clearly indicate what input is requested and the form of the input.

Figure 3.6

*Wilhelm Schickard
(1592–1635) and his
calculating clock*

Gottfried Wilhelm Leibnitz (1646–1716) was a man of many talents. He worked in the areas of logic, mathematics, philosophy, law, and theology. He is best known for his independent invention of differential calculus, which he invented 20 years after Sir Isaac Newton but in a more usable form.

Leibnitz also invented a calculator, called the "stepped reckoner" (see Figure 3.8), with a special drum that acted as mechanical multiplier. The wheel had nine teeth that ran horizontally across the drum. The first tooth went one-tenth the distance of the drum, the second two-tenths, and so on. By adjusting a sliding gear the appropriate distance, a multiplier was shifted one decimal place to the left. Leibnitz, like Pascal, could not find craftsmen able to do the exacting work required to construct his calculator. The only surviving device was found to not work properly, in large part because of construction flaws. Indeed, some scholars feel that it is unlikely that the stepped reckoner ever worked properly. Nonetheless, the use of the "Leibnitz wheel" in later working calculators was common.

Figure 3.7

Blaise Pascal (1623–1662) and his Pascaline

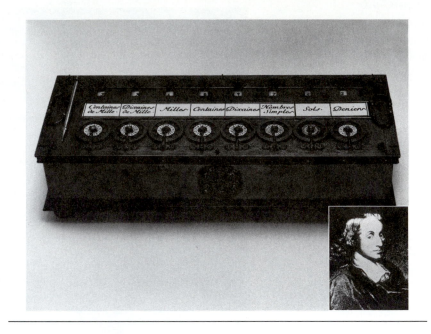

Figure 3.8

Gottfried Wilhelm Leibnitz (1646–1716) and his Stepped Reckoner

✔ The most important characteristic of a program is correctness and comprehensibility. When faced with the choice between clarity and a possible gain in performance, the correct choice is almost always clarity.

✔ The C++ standard library includes many useful classes. Part of mastering C++ is learning what facilities exist and when to use them.

✔ The `string` class is designed for storing and manipulating sequences of characters.

✔ The directive

```
#include <string>
```

must be included to access the facilities provided by the `string` library.

✔ A `string` can be initialized with another `string` or a `string` constant. A `string` cannot be initialized with a character.

✔ The sequence of characters that constitute a `string` object does not include a terminating `í\0í` character.

✔ Concatenation is the process of creating a new string by "gluing" together two strings. The + operator is the concatenation operator. For example, the following code concatenates the strings `FirstName` and `LastName` to create the string `FullName`.

```
FullName = FirstName + í í + LastName;
```

✔ When applied to two strings, the `+=` operator performs an append operation. The following statement appends the string `Year` to the string `Date`.

```
Date += Year;
```

✔ The C++ compound assignment operators +=, -=, *=, /=, and %= perform an arithmetic operation on an object and store the resulting value back into the object. For example, the statement

```
x += 5;
```

is equivalent to

```
x = x + 5;
```

✔ C++ has special operators, ++ and --, for incrementing and decrementing integral and floating-point objects. There are *pre* and *post* versions of these operators. With the *post*increment and *post*decrement operators, the value of the expression is the value of the object before it is modified. For example, when the code fragment

```
int x = 10;
int i = x++;
```

is executed, the value of i is set to 10 and the value of x becomes 11. With the *pre*increment and *pre*decrement, the value of the expression is the incremented value of the object. For example, when the code fragment

```
int x = 9;
int i = --x;
```

is executed, the value of i is set to 8 and the value of x becomes 8.

✔ The C++ syntax for sending a message to an object is

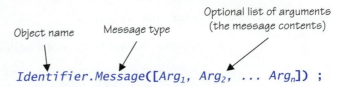

$$Identifier.Message([Arg_1, Arg_2, \ldots Arg_n]) ;$$

✔ The **string** class provides, among others, the ability to obtain the size in characters of a string (**size()**), find a substring within a string (**find()**), extract a substring from a string (**substr()**), insert a string in an output stream (**<<** operator), and extract a string from an input stream (**>>** operator).

✔ An entire line can be read into a string using **getline()**. The following code reads an input line from **cin** into the string **StudentRecord**.

```
getline(cin, StudentRecord, í\ní);
```

✔ Objects with more than one attribute or value are defined and initialized using a special syntax. The syntax is

$$Type \; Identifier(Exp_1, \; Exp_2, \; \ldots, \; Exp_n);$$

3.12 EXERCISES

3.1   What is the name of the C++ >> operator?

3.2   Explain why the following code fragment is illegal.
```
int x = 5;
int y;
int z;
(z = y) = x;
```

3.3   Explain why the following code fragment is illegal.
```
const float PayRate = 6.50;
OldSalary = PayRate * 40;
PayRate = 7.25;
NewSalary = PayRate * 40;
```

3.4   What is the collective name of the C++ operators *=, +=, -=, /=, and %=?

3.5   What file must be included before the stream **cin** can be used?

3.6   For the following expressions, give the final values of the objects **Cost** and **Price**. The objects of interest are

```
int Cost = 5;
int Price = 10;
```

a) ++Cost;

b) Cost++;

c) Cost = Price++;

d) Cost = ++Price;

e) Cost = Price++
       + ++ Price

f) Cost += Price;

g) Cost *= 5;

h) Cost += Price * 5;

i) ++Cost++;

j) Cost = ++Price++;

k) Price /= Cost++

3.7 Give a single assignment statement that is equivalent to

```
j += 1;
i = j;
```

3.8 Give a single assignment statement that is equivalent to

```
i = j;
j += 1;
```

3.9 Add a statement to Program 3.1 directly before the computation of the circumference that attempts to change the value of π to 3.1415926. Compile the modified program. Does the compiler report an error? If so, what is the error message?

3.10 Modify Program 3.1 to accept the diameter of the circle instead of the radius.

3.11 Modify Program 3.2 so that it computes the number of molecules in a sugar. Sugars are composed of hydrogen, oxygen, and carbon. You will need to look up the atomic weight of oxygen. Use your program to compute the number of molecules in 10 grams of glucose ($C_6H_{12}O_6$).

3.12 For each of the assignment statements below, give the value that is stored into the object on the left side of the assignment operator. For this exercise, assume that a **char** is 8 bits, a **short** is 16 bits, and an **int** is 32 bits. The objects of interest are declared as

```
char c;
short s;
int i;
```

Give your answer as a decimal value.

a) i = 101.3;

b) i = 59.8;

c) s = 0x3a1;

d) i = 25;

e) i = 3e2;

f) c = íaí;

g) i = 31 + 0.7;

h) s = 12.2 + 13;

i) c = 55L;

j) c = 0xff1;

k) s = 0773451;

l) i = 0.23;

m) i = 0x143F;

n) c = í0í;

o) i = í9í;

p) s = 31000;

3.13   Give the values of the defined objects after the execution of the following objects. If the value of an object is unknown, report its value as undefined.

a) `int i = 15;`
   `int k = 10;`
   `int j = 0;`
   `j = k;`
   `k = j;`
   `j = i;`

b) `int i = 5;`
   `int j = 6;`
   `int k = 7;`
   `j = i;`
   `i = 3;`
   `k = j;`

c) `int i = 21;`
   `int j = 0;`
   `int k = 11;`
   `j = k;`
   `k = i;`
   `j = k;`

d) `double x = 5.2;`
   `double y = 0.0;`
   `double z = 0.0;`
   `y = x;`
   `z = y;`
   `x = z;`

e) `double x = 32.1;`
   `double y = 45.0;`
   `double z = 0.0;`
   `x = z;`
   `y = z;`
   `x = y;`
   `y = x;`

f) `char a = íaí;`
   `char b = íbí;`
   `char c = ící;`
   `a = b;`
   `b = c;`
   `c = a;`

3.14   For each assignment expression below, give the result (using the *<value, type>* notation). If the assignment is invalid, give the result *<undef, undef>*. The objects of interest are declared as

```
char c = íAí;
int i = 23;
float x = 3.1;
double z = 5.0;
```

The value portion of your answer should be expressed as a decimal value.

a) `i = c;`
b) `i = x;`
c) `c = i;`
d) `x = i;`
e) `z = x;`
f) `x = i = c;`
g) `x = i = z;`
h) `i = x = z;`
i) `z = x = i;`
j) `z = i = c;`
k) `i = c = z;`

3.15   For each of the following **const** definitions, indicate whether or not they are valid C++ definitions.

a) **const** x = 23;
b) **const float** z = 5;
c) **const int** i = 5;
d) **const double int** = 5;
e) **const double** x = 33;
f) **const char** Blank(040);
g) **const float** f = +3;
h) **const double** x = 3.0;
i) **const float** z(2e3);

3.16   Consider the following code fragment:

```
int NumberOfDays = 30;
float PayRate = 5.0;
float AverageHours = 5;
cin >> PayRate >> NumberOfDays >> AverageHours;
cout << "Salary is " << PayRate * NumberOfDays
    * AverageHours << endl;
```

Give the output when the input stream contains the following characters.

a)   4.50 023 4
b)   6.00 23 010
c)   7.00,5,12
d)   7.00*5*12

3.17   Find a machine with a C++ compiler where a **double** is more precise than a float (this is true for most implementations of C++ on PCs). On this machine, write a C++ program that demonstrates that a **double** is more precise than a **float**.

3.18   Increase the precision of the value of π in Program 3.1. Do you see a difference in the output? Explain your observation.

3.19   Modify the program shown in Listing 3.1 so that a daily average is computed, rather than weekly average. Does this change make a difference in the estimated year-end savings? If so, explain why.

3.20   Modify the program shown in Listing 3.1 so that it handles half-dollar coins.

3.21   Modify Program 3.5 so that it handles lawns that have two buildings. Assume the second building is an attached garage.

3.22   Write a program that creates a checkerboard pattern of red and blue squares in a window that is 8 centimeters wide and 8 centimeters high. The squares should be 2 centimeters on a side.

3.23   Write a program that draws a tower consisting of five rectangles. The rectangles should be displayed in a window that is 8 centimeters wide and 10 centimeters high. The base rectangle should be 6 centimeters long and 1 centimeter high. Each succeeding rectangle is 75 percent of the length of the one underneath. The height of all the rectangles is the same. The rectangles should be blue.

3.24   Write a program that draws an empty square. An empty square can be constructed by drawing two vertical rectangles that are tall and very narrow and two horizontal rectangles that are short and wide. The rectangles are positioned so their ends meet to form a square. The rectangles should be yellow.

3.25   Write a program that prompts for and accepts a telephone number in the form *ddd–ddd–ddd*, where *d* is a digit, and prints it out in the following format: (*ddd*) *ddd–dddd*.

3.26   Write a program that prompts for and reads a distance in inches. The program prints the distance as miles, feet, and inches.

3.27   Write a program to compute a water and sewer bill. The input is the number of gallons consumed. A water and sewer bill is computed as follows:

- Water costs 0.021 cents per 100 gallons.

- Sewer service is 0.001 cents per 100 gallons consumed.

- A service charge of 2 percent is applied to the total of the water and sewer service charges.

3.28   Write a program that prompts for and reads a floating-point value. The program prints the whole part on one line and the decimal part on a second line. For example, if the program was given the input 23.45, it would output

```
23
0.45
```

3.29   A safe way to invest is to buy Treasury bills. Typically, Treasury bills are sold in denominations that are multiples of $1,000. For example, you might pay $960 for a $1,000 Treasury bill maturing in 91 days. At the end of 91 days, you receive $1,000. To compare this investment to other investments, it is useful to compute the annual interest rate. The steps to compute the annual interest rate are as follows:

- Compute the interest factor per period. For our example, this value is $1000 \div 960 = 1.0416$. The interest rate is .0416.

- Compute the annual interest rate by multiplying the interest rate by the number of periods in a year. In our example, there are four periods in a year, so the annual interest rates is $4 \times .0416 = 16.64\%$.

Write a program that prompts for and reads the denomination of a Treasury bill, the cost of the Treasury bill, and the number of days until the bill matures. The program uses this information to compute the annual interest rate.

3.30   Modify Program 3.4 so that it outputs the international date format using only the first three characters of the month and the last two characters of the year. For example, the date March 18, 1983, would be output as

```
18 Mar 83
```

3.31   Write a program that reads a name in the format

```
Tom Paris
```

and outputs it as

```
Paris, Tom
```

3.32   Write a program that creates a `SimpleWindow` that is 20 centimeters wide and 20 centimeters high. The window created is then tiled with yellow and blue squares.

3.33   We all know that air pressure decreases as altitude increases. The exact air pressure at a particular altitude depends on a number of factors such as the density of the air and the temperature. A rule of thumb for computing altitude based on air pressure is that air pressure drops about 1 millibar for each 8 meters of altitude gain.

Write a program that prompts for the air pressure at sea level (in millibars) and the air pressure at a particular location and computes the altitude in meters at that location.

3.34   Write a program that prompts for and reads an elapsed time in the following format

```
hh:mm:ss
```

and then computes the elapsed time in seconds and outputs it. Try your program on the following times:

a) `2:5:10`

b) `5:30:4`

c) `10:4:30`

3.35   Write a program that creates a `SimpleWindow` that is 10 centimeters wide and 8 centimeters high. Draw a blue `RectangleShape` that is 5 centimeters wide and 4 centimeters high. The `RectangleShape`'s center should be 3 centimeters from the left edge of the window and 5 centimeters from the top edge of the window. Run your program and explain the behavior you observe.

CHAPTER 4

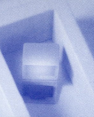

Control constructs

Introduction

Up to this point, our programs—whether defined in a function `main()` or an `ApiMain()`—have had the property that each time they are run, the exact same sequence of statements is executed. Execution begins with the first statement in the function and proceeds in a straight-line manner to the last statement in the function with every statement along the way being executed once. This form of programming is adequate for solving simple problems. However, for general problem solving we need the ability to control which statements are executed and how often. In this chapter, we consider two *conditional constructs*—the **if** and **switch**—that control whether a statement list is executed and three *iterative constructs*—the **while**, **for**, and **do**—that control how many times a statement list is executed. Except for the **switch** construct, which performs a matching process to determine which statements are executed, these control constructs use logical expressions to determine their course of action. To support these constructs, C++ has the logical type **bool**. Our control construct examination begins with logical expressions and the type **bool**.

Key Concepts

- logical values and operators
- truth tables
- **bool** type
- relational operators
- short-circuit evaluation
- **if-else** statement
- **switch** statement

- **break** statement
- **enum** statement
- **for** construct
- **while** construct
- **do** construct
- infinite loops
- invariants

4.1   BOOLEAN ALGEBRA

A *logical expression* is an expression whose value is either the logical value *true* or the logical value *false*. For example, two logical expressions are

- Zero degrees Celsius is the same as 32 degrees Fahrenheit (true).

- A triangle has four sides (false).

The area of mathematics associated with the manipulation of logical values is called Boolean algebra. It is named after the 19th-century British mathematician George Boole who formalized its study.

Logical values and expressions are important mathematically because they are the fundamental building blocks of formal proofs. In the realm of computers, besides being used to control statement execution, logical expressions are important because they can be used to model hardware behavior.

We use three primary logical operators to combine logic values into logical expressions. These logical operators are *and*, *or*, and *not*. The three primary operators are used in the following examples:

- Angela is amazed *and* Michael is happy.

- Kyle is going skiing *or* Michelle is going skiing.

- Veronica is *not* walking the dog.

In normal conversation, there may be mild confusion over the meaning of a logical operator. For example, if Kyle is going skiing or Michelle is going skiing, can it be the case that they are both going skiing? However, there is no mathematical ambiguity—each operator has a well-defined specification for the value of the operation given the values of the operands.

4.1.1 Truth tables

A *truth table* is the principal way of specifying the conditions that make a logical operation true and the conditions that make it false. A truth table lists all possible combinations of operand values and the result of the operation for each combination.

The truth table for the logical operator *and* is given in Table 4.1. In this and successive truth tables, we use *P* and *Q* as placeholders to represent the left and right operands of the binary logical operator being discussed. We also use *P* in the discussion of the unary logical operator *not*.

Binary logical operators have four possible logic value combinations and therefore four entries in their truth tables. Unary logic operators have only two table entries.

The logical *and* truth table shows that the operation is true only if both of its operands are true; otherwise, the operation is false. For example, the second entry of the truth table indicates that when *P* is true and *Q* is false, an *and* operation has the value false. In the fourth entry where both *P* and *Q* are true, an *and* operation has the value true.

Table 4.1

Truth table for logical and

P	Q	P and Q
false	false	false
false	true	false
true	false	false
true	true	true

Table 4.2 gives the truth table for the logical *or* operator. This truth table indicates that the *or* operation is true if at least one of its operands is true; otherwise, the operation is false.

Table 4.2

Truth table for logical or

P	Q	P or Q
false	false	false
false	true	true
true	false	true
true	true	true

Table 4.3 gives the logical *not* operator. The *not* operation is true if its operand is false, and the operation is false if its operand is true.

Table 4.3

Truth table for logical not

P	not P
false	true
true	false

4.1.2 Logical expressions

We can form *compound* expressions by combining logical operations. For example, the following expression is true when both *P* and *Q* are false; otherwise, the expression is false.

$$not\ (P\ or\ Q)$$

When *P* and *Q* are both false, subexpression (*P or Q*) is false and the negation of subexpression (*P or Q*) is true, making the overall expression *not* (*P or Q*) true. Any other combination of values for *P* and *Q* makes subexpression (*P or Q*) true, and the negation of that subexpression false, making the overall expression *not* (*P or Q*) false. The truth table in Table 4.4 verifies this analysis. Note that the table has entries for both the subexpression (*P or Q*) and the overall expression *not* (*P or Q*).

Table 4.4

Truth table for not (P or Q)

P	Q	P or Q	not (P or Q)
false	false	false	true
false	true	true	false
true	false	true	false
true	true	true	false

As another example, the following expression is true only when *P* is false and *Q* is true.

$$(not\ P)\ and\ Q$$

Table 4.5 verifies this analysis.

Table 4.5

Truth table for
(not P) and Q

P	*Q*	*not P*	*(not P) and Q*
false	false	true	false
false	true	true	true
true	false	false	false
true	true	false	false

The exercises at the end of the chapter consider other operators and logical equivalences including DeMorgan's law.

4.2   A BOOLEAN TYPE

The representation of logical values in C++ has evolved over time. Early versions of C++ used the same convention as the C programming language[†], where a logical false is represented by the value 0 and all other numeric values are representations of logical true. Using these rules, the following expressions are true:

```
1
979 * 3
```

And the following expressions are false.

```
0
17 % 17
```

C++ now includes a logical type. It is named **bool**, and associated with this type are two symbolic constants **true** and **false**. Consider the following definitions:

```
bool MoreDataToProcess = true;
bool ErrorHasBeenDetected = false;
```

The definitions show that by using the **bool** type and its symbolic constants we can contribute to program readability and in turn programmer understanding. Because of this effect, we will use **bool** objects when representing logical concepts.

4.2.1 Boolean operators

There are three logical C++ operators: &&, ||, and !. Operator && is used to perform a logical *and* operation, operator || is used to perform a logical *or*

---

†.   C++ was derived from C, hence the ++ in C++.

operation, and operator ! is used to perform a logical *not* operation. Suppose the following object definitions are in effect.

```
bool P = true;
bool Q = false;
bool R = true;
bool S = false;
```

The following expressions are then true.

```
P          // P has value true
P && R     // logical and is true when both operands
           // are true
P || Q     // logical or is true when at least one of
           // the operands is true
!S         // logical not is true when the operand is
           // false
```

And the following expressions are false.

```
Q          // Q has value false
P && S     // logical and is false when at least one
           // of the operands is false
Q || S     // logical or is false when both of the
           // operands are false
!R         // logical not is false when the operand
           // is true
```

The insertion and extraction operators are defined for **bool** objects. By default, **bool** objects are displayed in binary notation. Thus if P is a **bool** object, the insertion statement

```
cout << P << endl;
```

displays either 1 or 0, depending on whether P is, respectively, **true** or **false**. If the next value in standard input is a 0, then the statement

```
cin >> P;
```

causes P to be assigned the value **false**. If instead the next value in standard input is not a 0, then the statement

```
cin >> P;
```

causes P to be assigned the value **true**.

The logical operators are also defined for the integral type objects such as **int** and **char**. When using the logical operators with integral type objects, the previously mentioned convention, where only zero represents a logical false, is used. We demonstrate this capability through some examples. Suppose the following definitions are in effect.

```
int i = 1;
int j = 0;
int k = -1;
int m = 0;
```

The following expressions are then true.

```
i          // i is nonzero
i && k     // both operands are nonzero
```

```
!j            // not is true when operand is zero
```

And the following expressions evaluate to false.

```
j             // j is zero
j || m        // both operands are zero
!k            // not is false when the operand is nonzero
```

4.2.2 Relational operators

In addition to the logical operators that manipulate logical values, there are also the relational operators that produce logical values. There are two kinds of relational operators: equality and ordering.

The *equality operators* are defined for the fundamental and pointer types (pointer types are discussed in Chapter 11). The two equality operators are == and !=. They can be used for determining whether two objects represent the same or different values.

An == operation is true if its two operands have the same value; otherwise, the operation is false. A != operation performs in the opposite manner. If its two operands represent different values, the operation is true; otherwise, the operation is false.

The *ordering operators* are also defined for the fundamental and pointer types. They are used to determine the relative size of two values. There are four ordering operators: <, >, <=, and >=.

The < operator corresponds to the mathematical concept of less than. A < operation is true if its left operand occurs before the right operand in an ordering of the two values; otherwise, the operation is false. The operator > corresponds to the mathematical concept of greater than. A > operation is true if its left operand occurs after the right operand in an ordering of the two values; otherwise, the operation is false. The operator <= corresponds to the mathematical concept of less than or equal to. A <= operation is true if its left operand can occur before the right operand in an ordering of the two values; otherwise, the operation is false. The operator >= corresponds to the mathematical concept of greater than or equal to. A >= operation is true if its left operand can occur after the right operand in an ordering of the two values; otherwise, the operation is false.

For the **bool** type, the value of the constant **false** is less than the value of the constant **true**. We are not guaranteed any particular integral values for **true** and **false**.

We now consider some examples. Suppose the following object definitions are in effect.

```
int i = 1;
int j = 2;
int k = 2;
char c = '2';
char d = '3';
char e = '2';
```

The following expressions are then true.

```
c == e             // == is true when the values of the two
```

```
                          // operands are the same
      i != k              // != is true when the two operands have
                          // different values
      i < j               // < is true when the value of the left
                          // operand is smaller than the value
                          // of the right operand
      d > e               // > is true when the value of the left
                          // operand is larger than the value
                          // of the right operand
      i <= k              // <= is true when the value of the left
                          // operand is not larger than the value
                          // of the right operand
      j >= k              // >= is true when the value of the left
                          // operand is not smaller than the value
                          // of the right operand
```

And the following expressions are false.

```
      i == j              // == is false when the values of the
                          // two operands are different
      c != e              // != is false when the values of the
                          // two operands are the same
      j < k               // < is false when the value of the left
                          // operand is not smaller than the value
                          // of the right operand
      c > e               // > is false when the value of the left
                          // operand is not larger than the value
                          // of the right operand
      d <= c              // <= is false when the value of the left
                          // operand is larger than the value of
                          // the right operand
      i >= k              // >= is false when the value of the
                          // left operand is smaller than the
                          // value of the right operand
```

Programmer Alert

Confusing assignment and equality

A common programming error is misuse of the = operator. A programmer may intend to write the following expression:

```
    i == 0
```

But instead writes this expression:

```
    i = 0
```

The first expression is an equality expression and is true whenever i is 0. The second expression is an assignment expression and is never true, because the value of that expression is the value assigned to i, which is 0.

4.2.3 Operator precedence revisited

More complicated expressions can be built by using multiple operators in the same expression. To evaluate such expressions requires knowing the precedence of the relational and logical operators with respect to the other operators.

The not operator ! has the same high precedence as other unary operators. Among the binary operators, the relational and logical operators have lower precedence than the arithmetic operators and greater precedence than the assignment operators. Relational operators have greater precedence than the logical operators. Among the relational operators, the ordering operators have greater precedence than the equality operators. Among the logical operators, **&&** has greater precedence than **||**. Because of operator precedence, the following expressions are equivalent:

```
i + 1 < j * 4 && ! P || Q
(((i + 1) < (j * 4)) && (!P)) || Q
```

And the next expressions are also equivalent.

```
P != i < j || Q && S
(P != (i < j)) || (Q && S)
```

To ensure readability and understanding, we stress the use of parentheses.

The relative precedence of the arithmetic, relational, and logical operators is summarized in Table 4.6. A complete specification of the operator precedence is described in Appendix A.

Table 4.6

Precedence of selected operators arranged from highest to lowest

Operation
Unary operators
Multiplicative arithmetic
Additive arithmetic
Relational ordering
Relational equality
Logical and
Logical or
Assignment

4.2.4 Short-circuit evaluation

In the evaluation of a logical expression, we sometimes know the value of the expression before all the operands have been considered. For example, if one operand of an **&&** operation is known to be false, then we know that the result of **&&** operation is false, since the **&&** operation is true only when both operands are true. Similarly, if one operand of an **||** operation is known to be true, then we know that the result of the **||** operation is true, since the **||** operation is true when at least one of its operands is true.

When evaluating a logical operation, C++ requires that the left operand be evaluated before the right operand. It also requires that if the value of an operation can be determined from the left operand, that the right operand should not evaluated. This kind of evaluation is known as *short-circuit evaluation*.

Short-circuit evaluation is typically used in a logical expression to ensure that the objects being considered have a particular property before they are manipulated. For example, consider

```
(i != 0) && ((j / i) > 5)
```

Since the left operand of the **&&** is evaluated first, we know that if the right operand of the **&&** is evaluated, i cannot be 0 and therefore dividing by i

Programmer Alert

> *Rounding errors*
>
> Beware of using the equality operators with the floating-point types. The finite precision of the floating-point types permits round-off errors to be introduced with repeated operations. For example, suppose the following definition is in effect:
>
> ```
> float Sum = .1 + .1 + .1 + .1 + .1 + .1 + .1 + .1
>     + .1 + .1;
> ```
>
> The following expression, which should be mathematically true, is unlikely to be true within a program:
>
> ```
> Sum == 1.0
> ```
>
> Rather than directly testing for equality or inequality, we check whether the two values are sufficiently close to each other. The checking is done by specifying a maximal error tolerance and verifying that the absolute value of the difference is smaller than that tolerance. For example, suppose our maximum error tolerance is specified as the following constant:
>
> ```
> const float Delta = 0.0001;
> ```
>
> The following expression would detect whether the two values are sufficiently close. The expression makes use of the math library function `fabs()` that returns the absolute value of its floating-point parameter. (The math library is discussed in the Chapter 5 examination of libraries.)
>
> ```
> fabs(Sum - 1.0) <= Delta
> ```

makes sense. Without short-circuit evaluation, the right operand of the **&&** could be evaluated with i being 0, causing an illegal division to occur.

Self-check Questions

1. Suppose the following definitions are in effect.
    ```
    bool Q1 = true;
    bool Q1 = true;
    bool Q3 = false;
    ```

    What is the value of the following expression?
    ```
    (Q1 && Q2) || Q3
    ```

2. Suppose the following definitions are in effect.
    ```
    bool Q1 = true;
    bool Q2 = true;
    bool Q3 = false;
    ```

    What is the value of the following expression?
    ```
    (!(Q1 && Q2)) || Q3
    ```

3.   Suppose the following definition is in effect.

```
bool Q3 = false;
```

What is the value of the following expression?

```
(!(!(!Q3)))
```

4.   Suppose the following definitions are in effect.

```
bool Q1 = true;
bool Q2 = true;
bool Q3 = false;
```

What is the value of the following expression?

```
(Q3 || Q1) && Q2
```

5.   Suppose the following definitions are in effect.

```
bool Q1 = true;
bool Q2 = true;
bool Q3 = false;
```

What is the value of the following expression?

```
(!(Q3 && Q1)) || Q2
```

6.   Suppose the following definitions are in effect.

```
bool Q1 = true;
bool Q2 = true;
bool Q3 = false;
```

What is the value of the following expression?

```
(!(!Q3 && Q1)) || Q2
```

7.   Suppose the following definitions are in effect.

```
bool Q1 = false;
bool Q2 = true;
bool Q3 = true;
```

What is the value of the following expression?

```
(!(!Q3 && Q1)) || Q2
```

8.   Suppose the following definitions are in effect.

```
bool Q1 = false;
bool Q2 = true;
bool Q3 = false;
```

What is the value of the following expression?

```
(!(!Q3 && Q1)) || Q2
```

9.	Suppose the following definitions are in effect.

```
int i = 5;
int j = 10;
int k = 30;
```

What is the value of the following expression?

```
(i < j) && (k > 10)
```

10.	Suppose the following definitions are in effect.

```
int i = 5;
int j = 10;
int k = 30;
```

What is the value of the following expression?

```
(i > j) && (k > j)
```

11.	Suppose the following definitions are in effect.

```
int i = 5;
int j = 10;
int k = 30;
```

What is the value of the following expression?

```
(j <= 10) && (k == 30)
```

12.	Suppose the following definitions are in effect.

```
int i = -3;
int j = 10;
int k = 30;
```

What is the value of the following expression?

```
(i != j) && ((i < 5) || (j < 10) || (k >= 30))
```

13.	Suppose the following definitions are in effect.

```
int i = -3;
int j = 10;
int k = 30;
```

What is the value of the following expression?

```
((i < 5) || (j > 9))
```

14.	Suppose the following definitions are in effect.

```
int i = -3;
int j = 10;
int k = 30;
```

What is the value of the following expression?

$$(i \; != \; j) \; \&\& \; ((i \; < \; 5) \; \&\& \; (j \; < \; 10) \; || \; (k \; >= \; 30))$$

15. Suppose the following definitions are in effect.

```
int i = 3;
int j = 13;
int k = 30;
```

What is the value of the following expression?

$$(i \; != \; j) \; \&\& \; (((i \; < \; 5) \; || \; (j \; < \; 10)) \; \&\& \; (k \; >= \; 30))$$

16. Suppose the following definitions are in effect.

```
int i = 3;
int j = 13;
int k = 30;
bool B1 = false;
```

What is the value of the following expression?

$$(i \; != \; j) \; \&\& \; (((i \; > \; 5) \; || \; (j \; < \; 10)) \; \&\& \; B1)$$

17. Suppose the following definitions are in effect.

```
int i = 3;
int j = 13;
int k = 30;
bool B1 = true;
```

What is the value of the following expression?

$$(i \; = \; j) \; \&\& \; (((i \; > \; 5) \; || \; (j \; < \; 10)) \; \&\& \; B1)$$

4.3 CONDITIONAL EXECUTION USING THE IF STATEMENT

The first control construct that we consider is the **if** statement. The **if** statement has two possible forms. The simpler of the two has the following syntax:

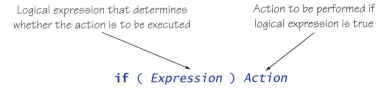

Logical expression that determines
whether the action is to be executed

Action to be performed if
logical expression is true

if (*Expression*) *Action*

When an **if** statement is reached within a program, the parenthetic expression *Expression* following the keyword **if** is evaluated. If *Expression* is true, *Action* is executed; otherwise, *Action* is not executed (in its simplest form, *Action* is a single statement). Either way, program execution continues with the next statement in the program. This description of the execution process of an **if** statement is its *semantic* definition. The semantics are demonstrated pictorially in Figure 4.1. The representation in that figure is called a *flow-chart*—the chart indicates the flow of program execution.

Figure 4.1

Flowchart representation of a basic if statement

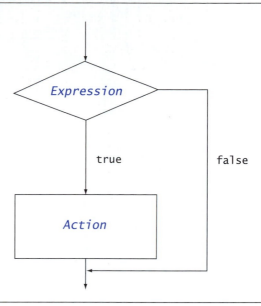

Our first example using an **if** statement is Program 4.1 which echoes the absolute value of its input. The input is stored in the object `Value`. If the expression (`Value < 0`) is true, then `Value` is negative and reassigning it with the complementary value changes `Value` to the equivalent positive number. If instead the expression (`Value < 0`) is false, then `Value` must be nonnegative and no action needs to be performed. In Program 4.1 and in the rest of the examples of this section, we are zealous in our commenting. We use the comments to reinforce new concepts. In practice, most of these comments should be eliminated. A flowchart of Program 4.1 is given in Figure 4.2.

Program 4.1

Demonstration of an if statement

```cpp
// Program 4.1: Display absolute value of input
#include <iostream>
#include <string>
using namespace std;

int main() {
    cout << "Please enter a number: ";
    int Value;
    cin >> Value;
    if (Value < 0)   // is Value less than zero?
        Value = -Value;// it is, so change its sign
    cout << Value << " is positive" << endl;
    return 0;
}
```

We use an **if** statement in the following code segment to report whether an input is an even number. As in Program 4.1, the input is stored in the object

Figure 4.2

*Flowchart
representation of
Program 4.1*

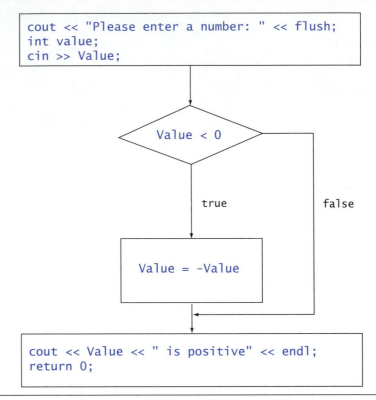

```
cout << "Please enter a number: " << flush;
int value;
cin >> Value;
```

Value < 0

true   false

```
Value = -Value
```

```
cout << Value << " is positive" << endl;
return 0;
```

named `Value`. The term `(Value % 2)` is the remainder of `Value` divided by 2. If that value is not 0, then the input cannot be even.

```
cout << "Please enter a number: ";
int Value;
cin >> Value;
cout << Value << " is ";
if ((Value % 2) != 0)   // is Value odd?
    cout << "not ";      // Value is odd
cout << "even" << endl;
```

It is more often the case that several statements need to be executed based on the value of an expression. To indicate that a group of statements is to be executed, the statements in the group are surrounded by left and right curly braces. The individual statements in the group are separated by semicolons. The semicolons are necessary so that the individual statements can be distinguished. An example of this kind of **if** statement is demonstrated in the following code segment where two input values `Value1` and `Value2` are extracted and echoed back in sorted order.

```
cout << "Please enter two numbers: ";
int Value1;
int Value2;
cin >> Value1 >> Value2;
```

```
if (Value1 > Value2) { // is Value1 larger?
    // as Value1 is larger, we need to do a swap
    int RememberValue1 = Value1;
    Value1 = Value2;
    Value2 = RememberValue1;
}
cout << "The input numbers in sorted order: "
    << Value1 << " " << Value2 << endl;
```

In the preceding segment, after the two numbers are extracted, they are compared. If `Value2` is smaller than `Value1`, the two values are swapped. The object `RememberValue1` assists with the interchange. Once the **if** statement has been completed, the objects `Value1` and `Value2` are displayed.

4.3.1 The if-else statement

A second form of the **if** statement deals with programming situations where different actions are to be taken based on the value of a logical expression. This form of the **if** statement has the following syntax:

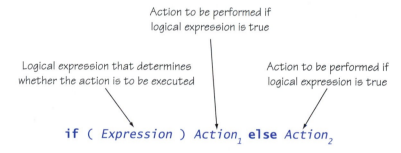

where $Action_1$ and $Action_2$ are individually either a single statement with a terminating semicolon (;) or a group of statements surrounded by curly braces. When this type of **if** statement is executed, *Expression* is evaluated. If *Expression* is true, $Action_1$ is executed; otherwise, $Action_2$ is executed. The flowchart in Figure 4.3 demonstrates the semantics of the **if-else** statement.

Suppose S and T are properly initialized objects of type `Rectangle-Shape`. The following code segment correctly reports whether these two objects have the same color.

```
if (S.GetColor() == T.GetColor()) // equal colors?
    cout << "Rectangles have the same color";
else // colors are not equal
    cout << "Rectangles have different colors";
cout << endl;
```

If the color of the rectangles is the same, then the equality operator returns true and the statement

```
cout << "Rectangles have the same color";
```

Figure 4.3

*Flowchart
representation of an
if-else statement*

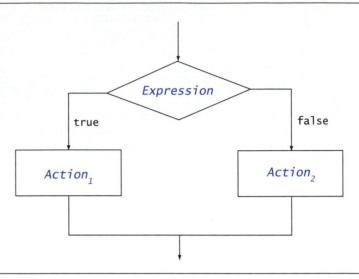

is executed, which displays the message denoting similarity. If the rectangles have different colors, then the equality operator returns false and the statement

```
cout << "Rectangles have different colors";
```

is executed, which displays the message denoting difference. Either way execution continues with the statement

```
cout << endl;
```

In the following code segment, two input values are extracted, and the larger of the values is displayed.

```
cout << "Please enter two numbers: ";
int Value1;
int Value2;
cin >> Value1 >> Value2;
int Larger;
if (Value1 < Value2)     // is Value2 larger?
    Larger = Value2;     // yes, Value2 is larger
else // (Value1 >= Value2)
    Larger = Value1;     // no, Value1 is larger
cout << "The larger of " << Value1 << " and "
    << Value2 << " is " << Larger << endl;
```

After extracting input values `Value1` and `Value2`, the code segment evaluates the expression (`Value1 < Value2`) in an **if-else** statement.

```
if (Value1 < Value2)     // is Value2 larger?
    Larger = Value2;     // yes, Value2 is larger
else // (Value1 >= Value2)
    Larger = Value1;     // no, Value1 is larger
```

If the expression is true, `Value2` is the larger of the two inputs and it is used to set object `Larger`. Observe the semicolon following this assignment; it indicates that the action associated with a true test expression is completed.

Programmer Alert

Consistent indentation and curly brace location

By examining the programs in this chapter, you see that we have indented the *Action* statements associated with the **if** statements. The indentation is a clue to the reader that the execution of an *Action* statement depends on the less-indented **if** statement expression. A consistent indentation scheme is necessary for program readability. Most programmers typically use three or four characters per level of indentation. We will use a similar indentation scheme for actions associated with other control statements.

The placement of the curly braces that group the statement list is a matter of personal taste. The basis for our curly-brace placement is the following: We include the opening left brace on the initial line of the **if** statement to conserve line space. We place the closing brace on its own line at the same indentation level as the associated **if** as a visual clue that subsequent statements in the program are not associated with this **if** statement.

To get a sense of how hard it is to understand a program, consider the following code segment, which is a nonindented version of our program that sorted two values:

```cpp
#include <iostream>
#include <string>
using namespace std;
int main() {
cout << "Please enter two numbers: ";
int Value1;
int Value2;
cin >> Value1 >> Value2;
if (Value1 > Value2) {
int RememberValue1 = Value1;
Value1 = Value2;
Value2 = RememberValue1; }
cout << "The input numbers in sorted order: " <<
Value1 << " " << Value2 << endl;
return 0;
}
```

If the expression (Value1 < Value2) is instead false, Value1 is at least as large as Value2. Therefore, in the **else** part, Value1 is used to set object Larger.

Thus our analysis shows that when this **if else** statement is completed, Larger is appropriately set and can be used as needed.

Our next example, Program 4.2, extracts three values and determines the smallest of those values. This program uses **if-else** statements embedded within other **if-else** statements to accomplish its task.

After extracting the three input values Value1, Value2, and Value3, Program 4.2 compares Value1 with Value2. If Value1 is no larger than Value2, then the program proceeds to evaluate whether Value1 is no larger than Value3. If Value1 is no larger than Value3, then Value1 is the smallest

Program 4.2

*Demonstration of an
embedded if statement*

```cpp
// Program 4.2: Determines smallest of three numbers
#include <iostream>
#include <string>
using namespace std;
int main() {
   cout << "Please enter three numbers: ";
   int Value1;
   int Value2;
   int Value3;
   cin >> Value1 >> Value2 >> Value3;
   int Smallest;
   if (Value1 <= Value2) {
      // Value1 is at most Value2
      if (Value1 <= Value3)
         // Value1 is also at most Value3
         Smallest = Value1;
      else // Value3 < Value1
         // Value3 is less than Value1, which is at most
         // Value2
         Smallest = Value3;
   }
   else { // Value2 < Value1
      // Value2 is less than Value1
      if (Value2 <= Value3)
         // Value2 is also at most Value3
         Smallest = Value2;
      else // Value3 < Value2
         // Value3 is less than Value2, which is at most
         // Value1
         Smallest = Value3;
   }
   cout << "The smallest of "
    << Value1 << ", " << Value2 << ", and " << Value3
    << " is " << Smallest << endl;

   return 0;
}
```

of the three values. If `Value1` is larger than `Value3`, `Value3` must be the smallest of the three inputs because `Value3` is smaller than `Value1`, which in turn is no bigger than `Value2`.

If, in the initial comparison of `Value1` and `Value2`, `Value1` is larger than `Value2`, then the smaller of `Value2` and `Value3` is the smallest of the three input values. Program 4.2 makes this determination within the **else** statement associated with the initial **if** statement.

As noted previously, a consistent indentation scheme makes the logic more understandable to a reader, but it does not affect the translation of the program. Language syntax and semantics rules precisely determine how a program is to be translated. They ensure that there is no ambiguity in determining which **else** is associated with which **if**. The rules in this regard are quite simple. Preceding the **else**, there must be either a single statement or a group of statements within curly braces. In front of this statement or statement list, there must be an **if** followed by a parenthetic expression. The **else** is associated with that **if**. For example, consider

```cpp
if (P)
   if (Q)
```

```
            cout << "A" << endl; // P is true, Q is true
        else // not Q
            cout << "B" << endl; // P is true, Q is false
                                 // true
```

In this segment, the **else** and its statement are associated with the **if** statement that evaluates Q. For the string "B" to be displayed, expression P must be true and expression Q must be false.

In the next code segment, curly braces surround the inner **if** statement:

```
if (P) {
    if (Q)
        cout << "A" << endl; // P is true, Q is true
}
else
    cout << "B" << endl;     // P is false, Q is
                             // unknown
```

Because of these braces, the **else** is matched to the first **if** statement. Therefore, string "B" is displayed whenever P is false, regardless of the value of Q.

4.3.2 Sorting three numbers

Sometimes we want to test which one of several expressions is true and then execute the appropriate action. For example, Program 4.3 extracts three input numbers and displays those numbers in sorted order, that is, nondecreasing order. We use the term *nondecreasing* rather than "ascending" because the input values may contain duplicates.

For three numbers, there are only six possible number orderings:

- $Value1 \le Value2 \le Value3$
- $Value1 \le Value3 \le Value2$
- $Value2 \le Value1 \le Value3$
- $Value2 \le Value3 \le Value1$
- $Value3 \le Value1 \le Value2$
- $Value3 \le Value2 \le Value1$

The program first tests whether the inputs `Value1`, `Value2`, and `Value3` are already sorted. If the input values are sorted, then they are copied to `Output1`, `Output2`, and `Output3`. These three "output" objects record the correct sorted ordering. Observe that the test expression is

```
(Value1 <= Value2) && (Value2 <= Value3)
```

and not

```
(Value1 <= Value2 <= Value3)
```

This alternative expression has the right mathematical look but is wrong in terms of programming. Because of operator precedence, the alternative expression is equivalent to

```
(Value1 <= Value2) <= Value3
```

Program 4.3

*Demonstration of an
if-else-if construct*

```cpp
// Program 4.3: Sorts three numbers
#include <iostream>
#include <string>
using namespace std;
int main() {
    // extract inputs and define outputs
    cout << "Please enter three numbers:";
    int Value1;
    int Value2;
    int Value3;
    cin >> Value1 >> Value2 >> Value3;
    int Output1;
    int Output2;
    int Output3;
    // determine which of the six orderings is applicable
    if ((Value1 <= Value2) && (Value2 <= Value3)) {
        // Value1 <= Value2 <= Value3
        Output1 = Value1;
        Output2 = Value2;
        Output3 = Value3;
    }
    else if ((Value1 <= Value3) && (Value3 <= Value2)) {
        // Value1 <= Value3 <= Value2
        Output1 = Value1;
        Output2 = Value3;
        Output3 = Value2;
    }
    else if ((Value2 <= Value1) && (Value1 <= Value3)) {
        // Value2 <= Value1 <= Value3
        Output1 = Value2;
        Output2 = Value1;
        Output3 = Value3;
    }
    else if ((Value2 <= Value3) && (Value3 <= Value1)) {
        // Value2 <= Value3 <= Value1
        Output1 = Value2;
        Output2 = Value3;
        Output3 = Value1;
    }
    else if ((Value3 <= Value1) && (Value1 <= Value2)) {
        // Value3 <= Value1 <= Value2
        Output1 = Value3;
        Output2 = Value1;
        Output3 = Value2;
    }
    else { // (Value3 <= Value2) && (Value2 <= Value1)
        // Value3 <= Value2 <= Value1
        Output1 = Value3;
        Output2 = Value2;
        Output3 = Value1;
    }
    // display results
    cout << Value1 << " " << Value2 << " " << Value3
     << " in sorted order is " << Output1 << " "
     << Output2 << " " << Output3 << endl;
    return 0;
}
```

which compares a logical value (the result of comparing `Value1` to `Value2`) to `Value3`. Thus the alternative expression does not accomplish what is needed and should not be used.

If the three input values are not in sorted order, then a test is made to determine whether `Value1` is the smallest, `Value3` is the middle value, and `Value2` is the largest value. If this test evaluates true, then `Value1` is copied to `Output1`, `Value2` is copied to `Output3`, and `Value3` is copied to `Output2`. If instead this test evaluates false, another ordering is considered. The testing process continues until five different orderings have been considered and rejected. At that point, there is only one untried ordering, and it must represent the sorted ordering.

The multiple occurrences of **else if** in Program 4.3 are not applications of a new statement. Instead they are a repositioning of the **else** occurrences and the action statements associated with those occurrences. The indentation scheme and structuring of Program 4.3 reflects that the program is testing a series of expressions and executing the actions associated with the first expression that evaluates to true.

If in Program 4.3, we had instead consistently increased the indentation level as the **if** statements are embedded within the **else** statements, there would have been a considerable shifting of the code towards the right. That shifting would make it hard to present the statements in a coherent manner.

Self-check Questions

18.   Consider the following code segment:

```
int i = 5;
int j = 7;
int k = 6;
if ((i < j) && (k < 5))
    cout << "Yes" << endl;
else
    cout << "No" << endl;
```

What does the code fragment output?

19.   Consider the following code segment:

```
int i = 10;
int j = 7;
int k = 4;
if ((i < j) && (k < 5))
    cout << "Yes" << endl;
else
    cout << "No" << endl;
```

What does the code fragment output?

Writing effective conditional expressions

Execution of control structures depends on conditional expressions to determine which statements to execute. Writing easy to understand and clear conditional expressions is key to producing code that is bug-free and easy to maintain.

One should simplify conditional expressions as much as possible so they are clear. One rule of thumb is to avoid negated expressions. For example, the **if** statement

```
if (!(command == 'u' || command == 'U'))
    return;
```

can be simplified using DeMorgan's Laws. The code

```
if (command !='u' && command != 'U')
    return;
```

is simpler to understand.

Similarly, the **if** statement

```
if (!InputOK) {
    // do error processing
    ...
}
else {
    // input is OK
    ...
}
```

is clearer if the negation is removed and the code in the arms of the if-then-else is swapped.

```
if (InputOK) {
    // input is OK
    ...
}
else {
    // do error processing
    ...
}
```

20.   Consider the following code segment:

```
int i = 10;
int j = 7;
int k = 4;
if ((i >= j) || (5 < j))
    cout << "Yes" << endl;
else
    cout << "No" << endl;
```

What does the code fragment output?

21.   Write a C++ code fragment that extracts an integer from the stream `cin` into integer object `Score` if the integer j is less than 25 but greater than 10.

22.   Write a C++ code fragment that sets integer k to 10 if the integer j is less than 5; otherwise k should be unchanged.

23.   Write a C++ code fragment that sets integer k to 3 if the integer m is less than 5 and j is less than 0; otherwise k should be unchanged.

24.   Write a C++ code fragment that sets integer k to 3 if the integer m is less than 5 and j is less than 0; otherwise k should be unchanged.

25.   Write a C++ code fragment that sets integer k to 34 if the integer m is odd and divisible by 3; otherwise set i to 44.

26.   Consider the following code segment:

```cpp
int i = 10;
int j = 7;
int k = 4;
if ((i < 11) && (j != 7))
    cout << "Yes" << endl;
else if (k < 10 || j == 7)
    cout << "No" << endl;
else
    cout << "Maybe" << endl;
```

What does the code fragment output?

27.   Consider the following code fragment:

```cpp
bool A;
bool B;
bool C;
bool D;
if (A && B)
    if (!C && !D)
        cout << "1" << endl;
    else if (!D)
        cout << "2" << endl;
    else
        cout << "3" << endl;
else if (C == D)
    cout << "4" << endl;
else if (C)
    cout << "5" << endl;
else
    cout << "6" << endl;
```

Give values for A, B, C, and D that cause the code fragment to display 3 to the standard output stream.

28.   Write a C++ program that computes a luxury tax. If the item costs between \$30,000 and \$50,000 (inclusive), the tax rate is 4 percent. If the item costs more than \$50,000 but less than \$70,000 the tax rate is 4.5 percent. Items that cost \$70,000 and higher have a 5 percent tax applied.

4.4 CONDITIONAL EXECUTION USING THE SWITCH STATEMENT

A software engineer is sometimes confronted with a programming task where the action to be executed depends on the value of a specific integral expression. The **if-else-if** construct can be used to solve such tasks by separately comparing the desired expression to a particular value and, if the expression and value are equal, then executing the appropriate action. For example, suppose we need to report whether the current character **command** is a valid command character ('u', 'd', 'l', 'r' for up, down, left, and right respectively) for indicating which way to move an object on the screen. Using **if** statements, the code would look like the following:

```cpp
if (command == 'u')
    cout << "Move Up command received" << endl;
else if (command == 'd')
    cout << "Move Down command received" << endl;
else if (command == 'l')
    cout << "Move Left command received" << endl;
else if (command == 'r')
    cout << "Move right command received" << endl;
else
    cout << "Invalid command received" << endl;
```

Because such programming tasks occur frequently, the C++ language includes a **switch** statement. Our command character reporting task can be done in a more succinct and readable manner using that statement.

```cpp
switch (command) {
    case 'u':
        cout << "Move Up command received" << endl;
        break;
    case 'd':
        cout << "Move Down command received" << endl;
        break;
    case 'l':
        cout << "Move Left command received" << endl;
        break;
    case 'r':
        cout << "Move Left command received" << endl;
        break;
    default:
        cout << "Invalid command received" << endl;
}
```

As our example suggests, the **switch** statement has the following syntax:

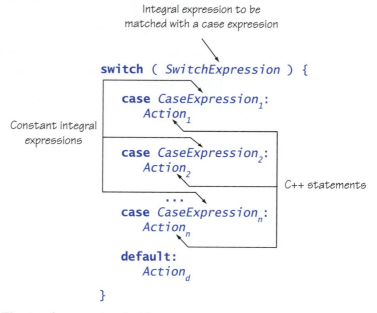

Integral expression to be
matched with a case expression

switch (*SwitchExpression*) {

　　　case *CaseExpression*$_1$:
　　　　Action$_1$

Constant integral
expressions

　　　case *CaseExpression*$_2$:
　　　　Action$_2$

C++ statements

　　　...

　　　case *CaseExpression*$_n$:
　　　　Action$_n$

　　default:
　　　Action$_d$

}

The *Action* associated with a **case** expression is either a single statement or a group of statements. Even if the *Action* is a group of statements, no surrounding curly braces are required.

When a **switch** statement is executed, its *SwitchExpression* is evaluated; if the value of that expression equals the value of a *CaseExpression* in that **switch** statement, then flow of control is transferred to the *Action*$_i$ associated with the matching *CaseExpression*$_i$.

If no *CaseExpression* equals the value of the *SwitchExpression* and if a **default** case is supplied, then the **default** *Action*$_d$ code is executed. In the command character example, the **default** case issues an error message if an invalid command is received. If no *CaseExpression* equals the value of the *SwitchExpression* and no **default** case is supplied, then control continues with the statement following the **switch** statement—none of the *Actions* are executed. In practice, most **switch** statements include a **default** *Action* that checks for unexpected conditions.

What happens after the selected *Action* is executed depends on the statements that make up *Action*. Normally, the last statement in an *Action* is a **break** statement. The **break** statement indicates that the **switch** statement has completed its task and that the flow of control should continue with the statement after the **switch** statement. If a **break** statement is not supplied, then control continues with the next statement. In the following code fragment, if the value of i is 3, then the string "Hello, world" is displayed 3 times. If the value of i is 2, then the string "Hello, world" is displayed 2 times.

```
switch (i) {
    case 3:
        cout << "Hello, world" << endl;
```

```
            case 2:
                cout << "Hello, world" << endl;
            default:
                cout << "Hello, world" << endl;
        }
```

Multiple string insertions occur for these cases because the flow of control is allowed to continue through the various actions; that is, there are no **break** statements. If the value of i is neither 2 nor 3, then the **default** action is executed and the string is displayed just once. A flowchart illustrating the flow of control of this segment is given in Figure 4.4.

Figure 4.4

Flowchart of switch statement without break statements

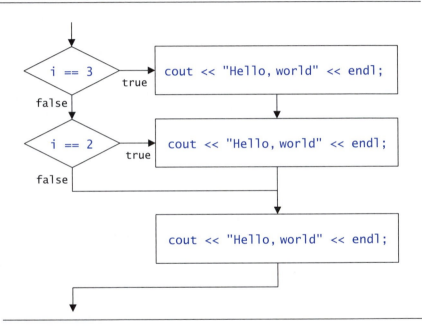

Normally, one should avoid using the "fall-through" behavior of the switch statement to achieve a desired effect. The *Action* of a case should almost always end with a **break** statement. However, there is one situation where using the fall-through behavior makes sense.

What if we would like the same *Action* to be performed for different values of the *SwitchExpression*? For example, suppose we wanted to allow a movement command character to be entered in either lower or uppercase. In this situation, we can use the fall-through behavior to write clear code. For example, to handle upper and lowercase 'u', the **case** statements would be:

```
        case 'u':
        case 'U':
            cout << "Move up command received" << endl;
            break;
```

The *Action* for the **case** 'u' is empty, and control flows into the **case** 'U' and its *Action* is executed. The following code fragment uses this fall-through technique to allow movement commands to be entered in either lower or upper-case. It is common to place the cases for identical code on a single line.

```
switch (command) {
    case 'u': case 'U':
        cout << "Move Up command received" << endl;
        break;
    case 'd': case 'D':
        cout << "Move Down command received" << endl;
        break;
    case 'l': case 'L':
        cout << "Move Left command received" << endl;
        break;
    case 'r': case 'R':
        cout << "Move Left command received" << endl;
        break;
    default:
        cout << "Invalid command received" << endl;
}
```

One final note about the **switch** statement. Because of the requirement that both the *SwitchExpression* and the individual *CaseExpressions* be integral, the **switch** statement cannot be used to determine actions based on the value of a floating-point object. Such processing requires **if-else-if** statements.

Programming Tip

Using the switch statement effectively

Appropriate use of the **switch** statement makes programs easier to understand and can result in more efficient programs. Here are some guidelines for effective use of the **switch** statement.

Keep the *Action* code short. This helps make the structure of the **switch** statement clear. A piece of *Action* code that runs several pages obscures the structure of the code.

Always provide a **default** case. Failing to provide a **default** case leads to undetected errors.

Avoid fall-through cases. They make the code hard to understand and difficult to maintain. The only time a fall-through case is appropriate is when the cases have identical *Action* statements.

Order the cases in some meaningful way. Depending on the situation, it may make sense to order the cases alphabetically or according to frequency of occurrence (i.e., put the case that occurs most often at the beginning).

4.5 **COMPUTING A REQUESTED EXPRESSION**

We now develop a simple calculator program that computes and displays the result of a single requested operation. Our problem has the following description:

The input to the problem is a pair of operand numbers separated by an arithmetic operator. If the requested operation is defined for the values of its operands, then the operation is computed and displayed to the standard output stream. If either the requested operation is not defined or its operands are inappropriate, then an error message is displayed to the standard output stream.

For example, if the input is

```
15 * 20
```

then the program displays

```
15 * 20 equals 300.
```

If the operator is not legal, as in the following example

```
24 ~ 25
```

then the program displays

```
~ is unrecognized operation.
```

As a final example, if the denominator for a division operation is 0, as in the following input

```
23 / 0
```

then the program displays the following

```
23 / 0 cannot be computed: denominator is 0.
```

An algorithm for the problem would have three simple steps:

Step 1.   Prompt and extract expression to be calculated. The expression operands are integers; the expression operator is a character.

Step 2.   Validate and compute expression.

Step 2.1   Determine type of operator.

Step 2.2   Determine whether operands are appropriate.

Step 2.3   Compute expression that corresponds to input operands and operator.

Step 3.   Display result.

Although an argument can be made that the validation and the computation of the expression should be made in separate steps, it is more easily done in a combined step. The translations of step 1 and step 3 into C++ are straightforward and can be found in Program 4.4.

The translation of step 2 in Program 4.4 is easily accomplished using a **switch** statement. The **switch** statement stores the result of the operation in object `Result`. The operands to be manipulated are objects `LeftOperand` and `RightOperand`. The operator is maintained in object `Operator`.

The **switch** statement treats each of the four arithmetic operators as a separate **case**. For addition, subtraction, and multiplication, no validation of the operands is necessary, so the result can be immediately determined. If the input expression is a division operation, `RightOperand` must be checked to determine whether it is nonzero. If `RightOperand` is nonzero, the division is computed. If instead `RightOperand` is zero, an error is displayed and the pro-

Program 4.4

Calculate a simple input arithmetic expression

```cpp
// Program 4.4: Compute a simple arithmetic expression
#include <iostream>
#include <string>
using namespace std;
int main() {
    // prompt and extract desired operation
    cout << "Please enter a simple expression "
        << "(number operator number): ";
    int LeftOperand;
    int RightOperand;
    char Operator;
    cin >> LeftOperand >> Operator >> RightOperand;

    // validate and compute desired operation
    int Result;
    switch (Operator) {
        case '+':
            Result = LeftOperand + RightOperand;
            break;
        case '-':
            Result = LeftOperand - RightOperand;
            break;
        case '*':
            Result = LeftOperand * RightOperand;
            break;
        case '/':
            if (RightOperand != 0)
                Result = LeftOperand / RightOperand;
            else {
                cout << LeftOperand << " / "
                    << RightOperand << "cannot be computed:"
                    << " denominator is 0." << endl;
                return 1;
            }
            break;
        default:
            cout << Operator
                << " is unrecognized operation." << endl;
            return 1;
    }
    // display result
    cout << LeftOperand << " " << Operator << " "
        << RightOperand << " equals " << Result << endl;
    return 0;
}
```

gram returns with a nonzero value. As noted previously, a program return value of zero indicates success, whereas a nonzero value indicates that the desired activity could not be properly performed. The flowchart for the switch statement is given in Figure 4.5.

4.6   VALIDATING A DATE

We next develop a program that prompts a user for a date and then determines whether that date is valid. The program is expanded in the exercises to compute

Figure 4.5

*Flowchart for switch
statement using break
statements*

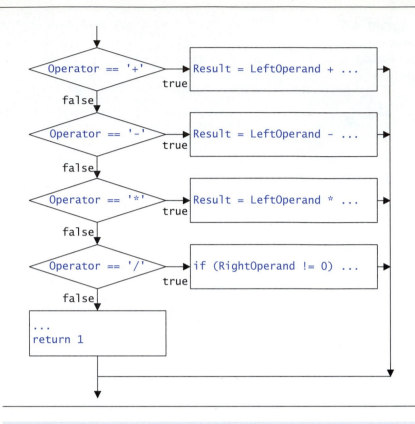

C++ Language

The ? : operator

The operator ? : can sometimes be used in place of a conditional statement.
The operator has the following form:

$$TestExpression \text{ ? } Expression_1 \text{ : } Expression_2$$

When executed, *TestExpression* is evaluated first. If *TestExpression*
is true, then the value of the operation is $Expression_1$; otherwise, the
value of the operation is $Expression_2$. A colon separates the two
expressions.

The operator is used in the following code segment to assign the
lesser of two input values to Min:

```
int Input1;
int Input2;
cin >> Input1 >> Input2;
int Min = Input1 <= Input2 ? Input1 : Input2;
```

the day of the year (e.g., February 12 is the 43rd day of the year). Our problem
description is simple.

Extract a month, day, and year and determine whether the date is valid. If the program is given a valid date, an appropriate message is displayed. If instead the program is given an invalid date, an explanatory message is given. Note: To recognize whether the date is valid, we must be able to determine whether the year is a leap year.

An example of the expected input/output behavior for a valid date follows.

```
Please enter a date (mm dd yyyy): 4 30 2001
4/30/2000 is a valid date.
```

An example of the expected input/output behavior for a date with an invalid month is

```
Please enter a date (mm dd yyyy): 13 1 2001
Invalid month: 13
```

Finally, an example of the expected input/output behavior for a date with an invalid day in a month is

```
Please enter a date (mm dd yyyy): 2 29 1899
Invalid day of month: 29
```

Before developing an algorithm for the problem, we first give the rules for determining whether a year is a leap year:

To be a leap year, the year must be evenly divisible by 4. However, not all years evenly divisible by 4 are leap years. Years whose last two digits are zero are *century years*; for example, 1800, 1900, and 2000 are century years. Noncentury years that are evenly divisible by four are always leap years. However, century years are leap years only if they are evenly divisible by 400. The years 1600 and 2000 are leap years; 1700, 1800, and 1900 are not leap years. These rules are captured in the Venn diagram given in Figure 4.6.

Figure 4.6
Venn diagram capturing leap year specification

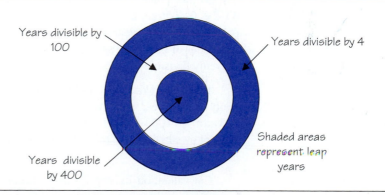

Using the problem description and the rules for determining whether a year is a leap year suggests the following algorithm:

Step 1. Prompt and read the month, day, and year.
Step 2. Determine whether year is a leap year.
Step 2.1 If the year is not evenly divisible by 4, the year is not a leap year.

Step 2.2	If the year is evenly divisible by 400, the year is a leap year.
Step 2.3	If the year is a century year and not evenly divisible by 400, the year is not a leap year.
Step 2.4	If none of the previous situations apply, the year is a leap year.
Step 3.	Validate date.
Step 3.1	If the month is invalid, display an error message and quit.
Step 3.2	If the day is invalid for the month, display an error message and quit.
Step 3.3	If the month and day are valid, announce date is valid.

Translating step 1 is straightforward, and a code segment to accomplish it appears in Program 4.5 on page 187. Translating step 2 can be accomplished by examining the input year to determine which of the four cases applies. The important piece of information to be derived in this step is knowing the number of days in February for the given year. This information is maintained in object DaysInFebruary. An **if-else-if** construct can be used to set that object.

```
int DaysInFebruary;
if ((Year % 4) != 0)
    DaysInFebruary = 28;
else if ((Year % 400) == 0)
    DaysInFebruary = 29;
else if ((Year % 100) == 0)
    DaysInFebruary = 28;
else
    DaysInFebruary = 29;
```

In the preceding code segment, if the test expression ((Year % 4) != 0) is true, then the input year is not a leap year and February has 28 days for the input year. If instead ((Year % 4) != 0) is false, then in the remainder of the **if-else-if** construct, it must be the case that the input year is evenly divisible by 4.

If the test ((Year % 400) == 0) is true, then the input year is automatically a leap year and therefore February has 29 days. If instead, the test ((Year % 400) == 0) is false, then the input year can be a leap year only if it is not evenly divisible by 100. The last **else-if** test determines whether this is true.

The validation in step 3 can be accomplished by first determining how many days are in the input month and then making sure the input day lies in the interval defined by the first and last days of the month.

The number of days in the input month can be calculated by determining to which group the input month belongs: months with 31 days, months with 30 days, or February. Although an **if-else-if** construct would work, a **switch** statement provides a more readable code segment.

```
int DaysInMonth;
switch (Month) {
    case January: case March: case May: case July:
    case August: case October: case December:
        DaysInMonth = 31;
        break;
    case April: case June: case September:
    case November:
        DaysInMonth = 30;
        break;
    case February:
        DaysInMonth = DaysInFebruary;
        break;
    default:
        cout << "Invalid month: " << Month << endl;
        return 1;
}
```

The cases for the preceding **switch** statement use named constants for the various months that must be previously defined. The definition of these constants can be done in two ways. One method is to define each constant separately.

```
const int January = 1;
const int February = 2;
const int March = 3;
const int April = 4;
const int May = 5;
const int June = 6;
const int July = 7;
const int August = 8;
const int September = 9;
const int October = 10;
const int November = 11;
const int December = 12;
```

However, C++ provides the **enum** statement to define a collection of related symbolic constants. The collection of constants forms a type. In an **enum** definition, the constants are listed in ascending order of value. We can use the following **enum** statement to define a type MonthsOfYear whose values are 1 through 12.

```
enum MonthsOfYear {January = 1, February = 2,
    March = 3, April = 4, May = 5, June = 6, July = 7,
    August = 8, September = 9, October = 10,
    November = 11, December = 12};
```

This statement is our first definition of a nonfundamental type. Such types are called *programmer-defined* types. The use of the **enum** method is usually preferred over the first method because the **enum** enables the programmer to define objects of that derived type. Such a definition gives more information to a reader of code about the possible values for the object, even if the name of the object itself does not. For example:

```
MonthsOfYear M;
MonthsOfYear BirthdayMonth = April;
MonthsOfYear SpringBreak = March;
```

enum constants, while integral, are not **int** objects, which means that we cannot use **int** arithmetic operators on **enum**-type objects. Also note that in referring to an **enum** constant, we do *not* use quotes. For example, to refer to our constant for the fourth month of the year, we use April and not "April". April is an identifier, whereas "April" is a string.

If the input month is a valid month, the **switch** statement correctly assigns the object DaysInMonth. An invalid month is processed by the **default** case of the **switch** statement. An invalid value causes an appropriate error message to be displayed and causes the program to terminate by returning a nonzero (unsuccessful) value.

After object DaysInMonth is determined, an **if** statement can be used to test whether Day is valid. If Day is less than 1 or if it exceeds DaysInMonth, an error message is displayed and the program terminates with a return value of 1.

```
if ((Day < 1) || (Day > DaysInMonth)) {
    cout << "Invalid day of month: " << Day << endl;
    return 1;
}
```

C++ Language

Specifying "valueless" constants

Although **enum** type MonthsOfYear needs particular values for its constants, the programmer does not always have to supply actual values for **enum** constants. C++ will automatically generate values for the constants, as is the case in this definition of musical genres.

```
enum Music {Classical, Country, Jazz, Popular, Soul,
    Rap, Rock};
```

Our type color used to describe the color of our various RectangleShape objects is also defined automatically.

```
enum color {White, Red, Green, Blue, Yellow, Cyan,
    Magenta};
```

If the programmer does not supply a value, then the first constant in the list will have value 0, the second constant will have value 1, and so on. This feature is useful when concepts with no specific values need to be represented.

If the expression ((Day < 1) || (Day > DaysInMonth)) is false, then the input date is a valid date. It is not necessary to group the remaining actions in the program within an **else** statement because the program terminates with the execution of the **return** statement if the expression is true. Therefore, if program execution reaches the insertion statement that follows this **if** statement, we know that Day has a proper value.

Our analysis and development of the date validation program is now complete. The entire implementation is given in Program 4.5.

Program 4.5

*Determine whether an
input date is valid*

```cpp
// Program 4.5: Determine whether user date is valid
#include <iostream>
#include <string>
using namespace std;
int main() {
    enum MonthsOfYear {January = 1, February = 2,
     March = 3, April = 4, May = 5, June = 6,
     July = 7, August = 8, September = 9,
     October = 10, November = 11, December = 12};
    // prompt and extract date
    cout << "Please supply a date (mm dd yyyy): ";
    int Month;
    int Day;
    int Year;
    cin >> Month >> Day >> Year;

    // compute days in February
    int DaysInFebruary;
    if ((Year % 4) != 0)
        DaysInFebruary = 28;
    else if ((Year % 400) == 0)
        DaysInFebruary = 29;
    else if ((Year % 100) == 0)
        DaysInFebruary = 28;
    else
        DaysInFebruary = 29;

    // if month is valid, determine how many days it has
    int DaysInMonth;
    switch (Month) {
        case January: case March: case May: case July:
        case August: case October: case December:
            DaysInMonth = 31;
            break;
        case April: case June: case September:
        case November:
            DaysInMonth = 30;
            break;
        case February:
            DaysInMonth = DaysInFebruary;
            break;
        default:
            cout << "Invalid month: " << Month << endl;
            return 1;
    }

    // determine whether input day is valid
    if ((Day < 1) || (Day > DaysInMonth)) {
        cout << "Invalid day of month: " << Day << endl;
        return 1;
    }

    // display result
    cout << Month << "/" << Day << "/" << Year
     << " is a valid date" << endl;

    return 0;
}
```

Self-check Questions

29.   Convert the following code into a switch statement.

```
int i;
int n;
int k;
if (i == 3) {
    n = 1;
    k = 5;
}
else if (i == 4)
    n = 5;
else if (i == 6)
    n = 6;
else
    n = 0;
```

30.   Convert the following code into a switch statement.

```
int i;
int n;
bool TryAgain;
if (i == 3 || i == 5) {
    ++n;
    TryAgain = false;
}
else if (i == 4 || i == 10)
    n = 5;
else if (i == 6)
    n = 6;
else {
    n = 0;
    TryAgain = true;
}
```

31.   Consider the following **switch** statement:

```
switch (i++) {
    case 1: case 2: case 3:
        cout << "Yes" << endl;
        break;
    case 5: case 6:
        cout << "No" << endl;
        break;
    case 10: case 11:
        cout << "Maybe" << endl;
        break;
    default:
        cout << "Sometimes" << endl;
}
```

If i is 4, what is the output of the above code?

32.   Consider the following **switch** statement:

```
switch (++i) {
    case 1: case 2: case 3:
        cout << "Yes" << endl;
    case 5: case 6:
        cout << "No" << endl;
    case 10: case 11:
        cout << "Maybe" << endl;
        break;
    default:
        cout << "Sometimes" << endl;
}
```

If i is 6, what is the output of the above code?

33.   Implement a program that extracts a single character from the stream cin. The character indicates a color. The possible characters are 'y' (yellow), 'r' (red), 'b' (blue), 'g' (green), and 'm' (magenta). If the input is 'y', the program should draw a 2 by 3 centimeter yellow rectangle; if the input is 'r' the program should draw a 3 by 3 centimeter red square; if the input is 'b' the program should draw a 1 by 2 centimeter blue rectangle; if the input is 'g' the program should draw a 3 by 4 green rectangle; and if the input is 'm' the program should draw a 4 by 4 magenta rectangle. All the shapes should be drawn in the middle of the window. The SimpleWindow should be 8 centimeters wide and 6 centimeters high. If the input is not a legal character, then no shape should be drawn and an error message should be written to the stream cerr.

4.7   ITERATION USING THE WHILE STATEMENT

Suppose we want to calculate the average of a list of five numbers that are to be extracted from the standard input stream. We might write something similar to the following code segment:

```
float Value1;
float Value2;
float Value3;
float Value4;
float Value5;
cin >> Value1 >> Value2 >> Value3 >> Value4
 >> Value5;
float Average = (Value1 + Value2 + Value3 + Value4
 + Value5)/5;
```

Now suppose that we needed to calculate the average of a list with 1,000 values. Simply modifying the previous code segment is too unwieldy. A better way is to write a code segment with an iterative component that repeatedly gets the next input value and then adds that value to a sum of values processed so far.

       Step 1.   Set the running total to 0.
       Step 2.   Set the number of values processed so far to 0.
       Step 3.   If the number of values processed so far is equal to the list size proceed to step 6.
       Step 4.   Process the next value.
       Step 4.1   Extract the next value.
       Step 4.2   Add the new value to the running total of values.
       Step 4.3   Increment the number of values processed so far by 1.
       Step 5.   Repeat step 3.
       Step 6.   Divide the running total by the list size to compute the average.

A simple way of having an action repeatedly executed in a program is through the **while** statement. The construct has the following form:

where *Expression* is a logical expression and *Action* is either a statement or a list of statements nested within curly braces. The *Action* is often called the *body* of the **while** statement.

When a **while** statement is executed, its *Expression* is first evaluated. If the *Expression* is true, the *Action* is executed. The evaluation process is then repeated; if the *Expression* is again true, the *Action* is repeated. This process is called *looping*, and it continues until the *Expression* is false. At that point, execution continues with the next statement in the program. This process is demonstrated pictorially in the flowchart of Figure 4.7.

Program 4.6 uses a **while** statement to succinctly solve our problem of averaging five input values. The program first defines a constant `ListSize` to represent the number of values to be processed. Object `ValuesProcessed` is then defined. Its role is to reflect the number of values that have been processed. Because no values have yet been processed, `ValuesProcessed` is initialized to 0.

An *invariant* is a programmer-stated rule regarding program behavior. In discussing Program 4.6, we will show that throughout its execution the value of `ValuesProcessed` always reflects the number of values that have been processed. As a result, the behavior of `ValuesProcessed` is an invariant of the program. Ensuring that programmer claims regarding object behavior are invariants is an important part of programming with loops. The correct operation of loops can break down when an object's role is ambiguous.

A running total of the input values processed so far is maintained in `ValueSum`, which is initialized to 0. The fact that object `ValueSum` reflects the sum of the values processed is another invariant of our program.

Figure 4.7

Flowchart
representation of a
while construct

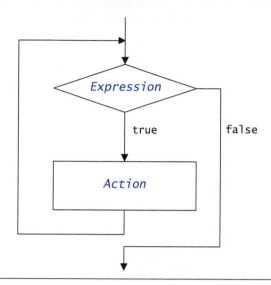

Program 4.6

Demonstration
program for the while
statement

```cpp
// Program 4.6: Compute average of five numbers
#include <iostream>
#include <string>
using namespace std;

int main() {
    const int ListSize = 5;

    int ValuesProcessed = 0;   // no values processed yet
    float ValueSum = 0;        // no running total

    cout << "Please enter " << ListSize
        << " numbers" << endl;

    while (ValuesProcessed < ListSize) {
        // there are more values to process
        float Value;
        cin >> Value;            // extract the next value
        ValueSum += Value;       // add value to running total
        ++ValuesProcessed;       // increment number of values
                                 // that have been processed
    }

    float Average = ValueSum / ValuesProcessed;
    cout << "Average: " << Average << endl;

    return 0;
}
```

At this point in Program 4.6, we are ready to process the inputs, so a prompt is issued to the user.

As long as the number of values processed so far is less than the size of the list, there are more values to consider. This condition corresponds to the **while** loop's test expression (ValuesProcessed < ListSize). If the expression is true, there are still additional values to process; if the expression is false, there are no more values to extract. Because processing a value requires several statements, the **while** loop's body is surrounded by curly braces.

```
while (ValuesProcessed < ListSize) {
    float Value;
    cin >> Value;
    ValueSum += Value;
    ++ValuesProcessed;
}
```

The first statement within the body defines an object local to the loop, named Value, to hold the extraction. The extraction then occurs, and the input value is added to the running total ValueSum. The processing of the current value is now finished. Therefore, the number of values that have been processed, ValuesProcessed, is incremented. Thus our invariants regarding ValueSum and ValuesProcessed remain true.

The expression (ValuesProcessed < ListSize) is then reevaluated. If the expression evaluates to true, the **while** loop body is again executed. This process continues until ListSize values have been processed. At that point, expression (ValuesProcessed < ListSize) evaluates to false.

Execution then continues at the statement following the **while** statement, where the object Average is defined and initialized using the running total divided by the list size, which is the number of values processed.

```
float Average = ValueSum / ValuesProcessed;
```

We know that the average is correctly computed because ValueSum and ValuesProcessed have been correctly maintained.

By using this repetitive action approach, we gain flexibility. If the list size subsequently changes, updating the code segment is straightforward—just use the new list size value in the definition of constant ListSize.

Let's trace through Program 4.6 to better understand how it works. Suppose the input stream contains the values

```
3 9 4 7 17
```

After the first three definitions in our program, the objects defined so far have the following representation:

ListSize	5
ValuesProcessed	0
ValueSum	0.0

When the **while** test expression is evaluated, 0 is less than 5, so the body of the loop is executed. The extraction assigns a 3 to object Value because the 3 is the first value in our input stream. The two assignments then respectively

increment ValueSum by 3 and ValuesProcessed by 1. After the first iteration, the objects have the following representation:

ListSize	5
ValuesProcessed	1
ValueSum	3.0
Value	3.0

The **while** test expression is then reevaluated. Because 1 is less than 5, the
body of the loop is again executed. The extraction now assigns a 9 to Value (9
is the second value in the input stream). The assignment statements then
respectively increment ValueSum by 9 and ValuesProcessed by 1. After the
second iteration, the objects have the following representation:

ListSize	5
ValuesProcessed	2
ValueSum	12.0
Value	9.0

The **while** test expression is then evaluated for a third time. Because 2 is
less than 5, the body of the loop is again executed. The extraction assigns a 4 to
object Value (4 is the third value in the input stream). The two assignments
then respectively increment ValueSum by 4 and ValuesProcessed by 1.
After this iteration, the objects have the following representation:

ListSize	5
ValuesProcessed	3
ValueSum	16.0
Value	4.0

The **while** test expression is then evaluated for a fourth time. Because 3 is
less than 5, the body of the loop is again executed. The extraction assigns a 7 to
object Value (7 is the fourth value in the input stream). The two assignments
then respectively increment ValueSum by 7 and ValuesProcessed by 1.
After this iteration, the objects have the following representation:

ListSize	5
ValuesProcessed	4
ValueSum	23.0
Value	7.0

The **while** test expression is then evaluated for a fifth time. Because 4 is less than 5, the body of the loop is again executed. The extraction assigns a 17 to object Value (17 is the fifth value in the input stream). The two assignments then respectively increment ValueSum by 17 and ValuesProcessed by 1. After this iteration, the objects have the following representation:

ListSize	5
ValuesProcessed	5
ValueSum	40.0
Value	17.0

The **while** test expression is then evaluated for a sixth time. Because 5 is not less than 5, the **while** statement is terminated and execution continues with the definition of Average, which is set to 8.0.

The average calculation problem can be solved in an alternative manner that provides even greater list-processing flexibility. This alternative method is given in Program 4.7. This new program differs from Program 4.6 in one

Program 4.7

Computing the average of an arbitrary list of values

```cpp
// Program 4.7: Computes average of a list of values
#include <iostream>
#include <string>
using namespace std;

int main() {
    cout << "Please enter list of numbers" << endl;

    int ValuesProcessed = 0;
    float ValueSum = 0;
    float Value;

    while (cin >> Value) {
        ValueSum += Value;
        ++ValuesProcessed;
    }
    if (ValuesProcessed > 0) {
        float Average = ValueSum / ValuesProcessed;
        cout << "Average: " << Average << endl;
    }
    else
        cout << "No list to average" << endl;

    return 0;
}
```

significant way. In Program 4.6, it is necessary to know the size of the list at the beginning of the computation, whereas in Program 4.7 the list size so far is calculated during program execution through the object ValuesProcessed. Note that the invariants regarding ValuesProcessed and ValueSum do not change.

The test expression in Program 4.7 that determines whether to execute the **while** loop body is (cin >> Value). The value of an extraction operation is normally a reference to the input source stream. However, if the source stream has been exhausted (i.e., there are no more values to extract), then the value of the extraction operation is zero. Thus the expression (`cin >> Value`) is non-zero if and only if a value has been extracted. Consequently, the extraction expression can be used as the basis for determining whether another value needs to be processed. To indicate that there are no more input values, the user types an operating-system-specific escape sequence. For UNIX systems, the sequence is normally `Ctrl+d`; for DOS and Windows-based systems, the sequence is `Ctrl+z`.

The processing of the current extracted value, `Value`, again requires that the value be added to the running total `ValueSum`. Similarly, the program must also increment `ValuesProcessed`, as its value represents the size of the list so far.

If a nonempty list was processed, the average can be calculated. To determine whether any values were extracted, a test is made using an **if** statement. If some input values were extracted, then `ValuesProcessed` is greater than zero. If instead no values were provided, then no extractions were made and `ValuesProcessed` keeps its initial value of zero.

The **break** statement is sometimes used for the early termination of loops. The following code segment extracts and displays input values from the standard input stream `cin` until a specified value is found.

```
int KeyValue;
cin >> KeyValue;
int Input;
while (cin >> Input) {
    if (Input != KeyValue)
        cout << Input << endl;
    else
        break;
}
```

Use of the **break** statement in loops is sometimes discouraged because it can make the program's behavior harder to understand. In particular, it makes invariant claims more difficult to verify. Often, such loops can be easily rewritten to eliminate the **break** statements.

```
int KeyValue;
cin >> KeyValue;
int Input;
while ((cin >> Input) && (Input != KeyValue)) {
    cout << Input << endl;
}
```

4.8 SIMPLE STRING AND CHARACTER PROCESSING

There are two common ways to view a stream of text. In one view, text is seen as consisting of an unknown number of strings. In the other view, text is seen as consisting of an unknown number of lines with each line composed of an unknown number of characters. For either view, because the amount of

Programmer Alert

material to process is unknown, **while** constructs are typically used to process the text. In this section, we give examples of both types of processing.

Listing 4.1 gives a model code segment composed of three sections for processing a stream of strings from the standard input stream **cin**. The first section does whatever preparatory work is necessary. The second section performs the actual extraction and processing of individual strings. The third section performs any final postprocessing activities.

Listing 4.1

Model for text processing

```
// prepare for string processing
...
// extract and process strings
while (cin >> s) {
    // prepare to process string s
    ...
    // process current string s
    ...
    // prepare to process next string
    ...
}
// finish string processing
...
```

The middle section is implemented with a **while** loop that iterates one time for each extracted string. The loop body consists of three subsections. The first subsection does any preparatory work for processing the current string. Next the actual processing of the current string is performed. Then any postprocessing to prepare for the next iteration is performed.

Demonstrations using the model segment are given in Program 4.8 and Program 4.9. Program 4.8 examines standard input and determines the number of words in the input and the number of words that are articles (i.e., *the*, *an*, or *a*), under the assumption that each extracted string is a word. For example, if the following text is given as input to Program 4.8

```
There once was a course on discourse.
Where the instructor was quite hoarse.
He mumbled. And he fumbled.
And once took a tumble.
```

> When he realized his remarks were too coarse!

then the program outputs

> Text contains 31 words of which 3 are articles

Program 4.8 begins with three definitions.

```
int NumberOfWords = 0;
int NumberOfArticles = 0;
string s;
```

Program 4.8

Computing word statistics

```
// Program 4.8: Computes number of words and articles
#include <iostream>
#include <string>
using namespace std;
int main() {
    // initialize counters for text analysis
    int NumberOfWords = 0;
    int NumberOfArticles = 0;
    // begin string processing
    string s;
    cout << "Enter text for analysis" << endl << endl;
    while (cin >> s) {
        // found another word
        ++NumberOfWords;
        // test if the word an article
        if ((s == "the") || (s == "The") || ( s == "an")
          || (s == "An") || (s == "a") || (s == "A")) {
            // the word an article
            ++NumberOfArticles;
        }
    }
    // display test statistics
    cout << endl;
    cout << "Text contains " << NumberOfWords
      << " words of which " << NumberOfArticles
      << " are articles" << endl;
    return 0;
}
```

Objects NumberOfWords and NumberOfArticles are used as running totals, respectively, for the number of words that have been extracted so far and for the number of articles in those words. String s represents the current string. These definitions along with the prompt statement make up the string preprocessing section.

As indicated in Listing 4.1, the **while** loop body performs the processing of the current string. For Program 4.8 this string processing consists of two statements. The first statement increments the NumberOfWords counter because the newly extracted string s represents the next word.

```
++NumberOfWords;
```

String s is then tested to see whether it is an article. Because an article may or may not appear with its initial letter capitalized, the test expression for determining whether s is an article has six terms—one capital and one lowercase term for each possible article. As s is an article if anyone of the terms is true, the terms are combined using the or operator.

```
((s == "the") || (s == "The") || (s == "an")
   || (s == "An") || (s == "a") || (s == "A"))
```

If s is found to be an article, then the counter NumberOfArticles is incremented.

```
++NumberOfArticles;
```

Program 4.9

Reporting duplicate inputs

```
// Program 4.9: Detects and reports duplicate strings
// in input
#include <iostream>
#include <string>
using namespace std;
int main() {
    // prepare for string processing of duplicates
    string prev = "";
    string s;
    int count = 0;
    cout << "Enter text for duplication detection"
     << endl << endl;
    // extract and process strings
    while (cin >> s) {
        // process current string s
        if (s == prev) { // s is a duplicate
            ++count;
        }
        else { // s is not a duplicate
            if (count > 1) {
                // previous duplicate run needs to be
                // reported
                cout << "\"" << prev << "\" occurs " << count
                 << " times in a row" << endl;
            }
            // s is a run of size 1 so far
            prev = s;
            count = 1;
        }
    }
    // finish up string processing of duplicates
    if (count > 1) {
        // text ended with a string of duplicates
        cout << "\"" << prev << "\" occurs " << count
         << " times in a row" << endl;
    }
    return 0;
}
```

When the loop is finished, all the strings have been extracted and we are ready to display the text statistics. The display is accomplished by inserting to cout the counters NumberOfWords and NumberOfArticles with appropriate labels.

```
cout << "Text contains " << NumberOfWords
 << " of which " << NumberOfArticles
 << " are articles" << endl;
```

Our other string demonstration program is Program 4.9, which examines its input strings for consecutive duplicates. For example, if standard input contains the following

```
We are even loonier than you you think
But we are not as funny as as we think
Ha ha ha ha
```

then the program displays the following duplicate information:

```
"you" occurs 2 times in a row
"as" occurs 2 times in a row
"ha" occurs 3 times in a row
```

Observe that the test processing performed by Program 4.9 is case sensitive. For example, the *Ha* that starts the third line is distinct from the *ha* that immediately follows it. In the exercises, we consider an alternative version of Program 4.9 that finds duplicates regardless of case.

Program 4.9 prepares for the processing of the strings by defining string objects prev and s:

```
string prev = "";
string s;
```

String s represents the string currently being processed; string prev represents the string that was processed immediately before s. Because there is no previous string when the program begins, prev is initialized to the empty string. An object count is also defined. Object count represents the number of consecutive occurrences seen so far of the string represented by prev. Its initial value is 0.

```
int count = 0;
```

The simplicity of the problem is reflected in its **while** loop body. No pre- or postprocessing of the current string s is required. The action taken for the current string s depends only whether s duplicates the value of the previously extracted string prev.

If strings s and prev represent the same value, count is incremented.

```
if (s == prev) { // s is a duplicate
    ++count;
}
```

The program does not report the duplications at this point, because additional duplicates may occur.

If instead strings s and prev represent different values, we must determine whether a series of duplicates has ended. We can do so by examining count, which maintains the number of consecutive occurrences of the string value maintained in prev. If count is greater than 1, there were duplicates. The insertion statement

```
cout << "\"" << prev << "\" occurs " << count
    << " times in a row" << endl;
```

correctly reports the duplication information for this case. If instead, `count` is not greater than 1, then no particular action is required. Regardless of the value of `count`, current string `s` is copied into `prev` for future duplication detection.

```
prev = s;
```

In addition, the value of `count` is set to 1:

```
count = 1;
```

Thus `count` continues to reflect the number of consecutive occurrences of the value of the string maintained by `prev`.

When the loop is finished, duplication reporting might be necessary for the last string that was extracted. The test that was performed for the processing of duplicates within the loop also works here:

```
if (count > 1) {
    // text ended with a string of duplicates
    cout << "\"" << prev << "\" occurs " << count
        << " times in a row" << endl;
}
```

Listing 4.2 gives a model code segment for processing a stream of characters. One advantage of this method over the method of Listing 4.1 is that this method can determine the layout of individual lines of text. This detection is not possible with Listing 4.1 because it views the input solely as a sequence of strings. The disadvantage of the Listing 4.2 method is that it makes the programmer build the string structures out of the individual characters.

The Listing 4.2 code segment begins with a section that does whatever preparatory work is necessary for processing the text. A **bool** object `MoreLinesToProcess` is defined and initialized to keep track of whether additional processing is necessary. A **while** loop processes the individual lines. Iteration of the **while** loop is controlled by `MoreLinesToProcess`. The **while** body begins with a preparatory section for processing the characters on the current line. A **bool** object `MoreCharactersOnCurrentLine` is defined and initialized in this section. The purpose of the object is to indicate whether to process additional characters on the current line.

The values of the two **bool** objects `MoreLinesToProcess` and `MoreCharactersOnCurrentLine` are invariants with respect to the text processing: as long as they are true, there are more lines to process and more characters to process on the current line.

As soon as the preprocessing of a line is finished, the actual processing begins. A **while** loop is used to process the individual characters. This inner **while** loop iterates for each character that needs to be processed. Embedding loops within loops is a powerful programming mechanism; it enables programs to accomplish a significant amount of work because the inner loop is run for each iteration of the outer loop.

The body of the inner **while** begins with a preparatory section for an individual character. Part of this preparation is defining a **char** object `CurrentCharacter` for representing the character that will be extracted.

```
// prepare for processing text
bool MoreLinesToProcess = true;
...
while (MoreLinesToProcess) {
    // process next line
    bool MoreCharactersOnCurrentLine = true;
    ...
    while (MoreCharactersOnCurrentLine) {
        // prepare to process next character
        ...
        char CurrentCharacter;
        if (cin.get(CurrentCharacter)) {
            // process CurrentCharacter on current line
            ...
            if (CurrentCharacter == '\n') {
                // current line has no more characters
                MoreCharactersOnCurrentLine = false;
            }
            ...
        }
        else { // no more characters
            MoreCharactersOnCurrentLine = false;
            MoreLinesToProcess = false;
        }
    }
    // finish processing of current line
    ...
}
// finish overall processing
...
```

The extraction into `CurrentCharacter` occurs in the test expression of an **if** statement. The extraction is not done via the extraction operator <<, but rather through a member function of `cin`. Like `RectangleShape` objects, object `cin` has member functions. This member function `get()` of `cin` attempts to extract the next character from the standard input stream and store it in `CurrentCharacter`. If the attempt is successful, the expression `(cin.get(CurrentCharacter))` evaluates to true; if the extraction is not possible, the expression evaluates to false. The reason we use `get()` rather than << is that `get()` does not ignore whitespace—function `get()` extracts all characters. We discuss other member functions of `cin` in the next chapter.

If function `get()` does extract a character, then that character is processed. The particular nature of the processing depends on the specific character and the specific task intended for the code segment. The processing of the inner loop generally ends when the `CurrentCharacter` is found to be the newline character.

Once the characters on the current line have been individually processed and the inner **while** loop is terminated, the next section of code does any post-processing of the line that might be necessary. The outer **while** loop expression is then tested to see whether an additional iteration of the inner **while** loop is necessary.

If function `get()` is unable to extract a character, then the code segment sets the two **bool** objects to indicate that the inner and outer **while** loops are to be terminated. Once the outer **while** loop is terminated, a final postprocessing section may occur.

This model segment is used in Program 4.10, which echoes each line of the input stream to the output stream. The echoing is done in a manner that displays uppercase input letters in the lowercase equivalent.

Program 4.10

Echoing input in its lowercase equivalent

```
// Program 4.10: Echo input to standard output
// converting uppercase to lowercase along the way
#include <iostream>
#include <string>
using namespace std;

int main() {
    // prepare for processing text
    bool MoreLinesToProcess = true;
    while (MoreLinesToProcess) {
        // process next line
        bool MoreCharactersOnCurrentLine = true;
        cout << "Please type a line of text: ";
        while (MoreCharactersOnCurrentLine) {
            // process next character on current line
            char CurrentCharacter;
            if (cin.get(CurrentCharacter)) {
                // process current character on current line
                if (CurrentCharacter == '\n') {
                    // found newline character that ends line
                    MoreCharactersOnCurrentLine = false;
                }
                else if ((CurrentCharacter >= 'A')
                  && (CurrentCharacter <= 'Z')) {
                    // CurrentCharacter is uppercase
                    CurrentCharacter = CurrentCharacter - 'A'
                      + 'a';
                    cout << CurrentCharacter;
                }
                else { // nonuppercase character
                    cout << CurrentCharacter;
                }
            }
            else { // no more characters
                MoreCharactersOnCurrentLine = false;
                MoreLinesToProcess = false;
            }
        }
        // finish processing of current line
        cout << endl;
    }
    // finish overall processing
    return 0;
}
```

The processing of the CurrentCharacter depends on whether CurrentCharacter is a newline character; an uppercase alphabetic character; or neither a newline nor an uppercase alphabetic character. This determination is made using an **if-else-if** statement.

```
if (CurrentCharacter == '\n') {
    // found newline character that ends line
    MoreCharactersOnCurrentLine = false;
```

```
    }
    else if ((CurrentCharacter >= 'A')
      && (CurrentCharacter <= 'Z')) {
        // CurrentCharacter is uppercase
        CurrentCharacter = CurrentCharacter - 'A' + 'a';
        cout << CurrentCharacter;
    }
    else { // nonuppercase character
        cout << CurrentCharacter;
    }
```

If the `CurrentCharacter` lies in the ASCII interval `'A'` through `'Z'`, it is uppercase alphabetic. An uppercase alphabetic character can be converted to its lowercase equivalent by subtracting the representation of `'A'` from the representation of that uppercase alphabetic character and then adding to this difference the representation of `'a'`. (The difference represents an offset of how far the `CurrentCharacter` is from the beginning of the alphabet.)

```
    CurrentCharacter = CurrentCharacter - 'A' + 'a';
```

The only postprocessing needed is the issuing of the newline character. (By using `endl` rather than `'\n'`, the insertion is immediately displayed.)

Self-check Questions

34. Consider the following code segment:

```
int i = 1;
while (i < n) {
    if ((i % 2) == 0) {
        ++i;
    }
}
cout << i << endl;
```

What is output if n is 9?

35. Consider the following code segment:

```
int i = 1;
while (i < n) {
    if ((i % 2) == 0) {
        ++i;
    }
}
cout << i << endl;
```

What is output if n is 10?

36. Consider the following code segment:

```
int i = 1;
int j = 3;
while (i < 15 && j < 20) {
    ++i;
    j += 2;
```

```
    }
    cout << i + j << endl;
```

What is the output?

37.   Write a **while** loop that generates the values of the equation

$$x^2 + x + 49$$

for the *x* values 2 through 40.

38.   Write a program that reads text from the stream **cin** and counts the
       number of digit characters (i.e., '0', '1', '2', '3', '4', '5', '6', '7', '8',
       '9') in the input.

4.9 ITERATION USING THE FOR CONSTRUCT

Although the **while** construct has sufficient flexibility to handle all iteration
needs, C++ provides two other iteration constructs—the **for** and **do**. These
constructs make some common programming tasks simpler to code. We first
consider the **for** construct, as it is used more often; we then briefly consider
the **do** construct.

The **for** construct has the form

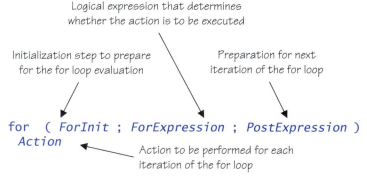

where *ForInit* is either an object definition(s) or an expression; *ForExpression* is a logical expression; *PostExpression* is an expression, and *Action*
is either a single statement or it is a group of statements nested within curly
braces. Any of *ForInit*, *ForExpression*, and *PostExpression* may be
omitted. The flowchart in Figure 4.8 gives the semantics for the **for** construct.

When a **for** statement is reached within a program, *ForInit* is first executed and then *ForExpression* is evaluated. (Note that if *ForExpression* is
not supplied, the value true is used instead.) If *ForExpression* is true, first
Action is executed and then *PostExpression* is executed. *ForExpression*
is then reevaluated, and if it is again true, the execution of *Action* and

Programming Tip

> ***Writing effective conditional expressions***
>
> Conditional expressions that test whether an object is in a certain range of numeric values are often complicated. One way to make them simpler is to order the individual tests so they are in number line order. For example, consider the **while** statement
>
> ```
> while (NumberOfElements > i) {
>     // Process the ith element
>     ...
> }
> ```
>
> The idea is that i should be less than NumberOfElements. Since i is always smaller than NumberOfElements, it should appear first in the test.
>
> ```
> while (i < NumberOfElements) {
>     // Process the ith element
>     ...
> }
> ```
>
> This guideline really helps when testing to make sure a value falls in a range bounded by two values. Suppose we need to write a test to see whether *MinElement < i < MaxElement*. Which of the following fragments is clearer?
>
> ```
> while (i < MaxElement && i > MinElement) {
>     ...
> }
> ```
>
> or
>
> ```
> while (MinElement < i && i < MaxElement) {
>     ...
> }
> ```
>
> Certainly, the second one more closely resembles the mathematical expression of the relationship. It is also clearer because the order of the elements in the expression give a clue as to the ordering of the values being tested.

PostExpression is repeated. This testing of *ForExpression* and execution of *Action* and *PostExpression* continues until *ForExpression* evaluates to false. Evaluation then continues with the next statement in the program.

If *ForExpression* is initially false, then neither *Action* nor *PostExpression* is ever executed—the program immediately continues with the next statement in the program. Most programmers use *ForInit* to do the necessary initialization for the **for** statement and *PostExpression* to do the necessary work to prepare for the next iteration of the **for** statement body.

Figure 4.8

*Flowchart
representation of a
for construct*

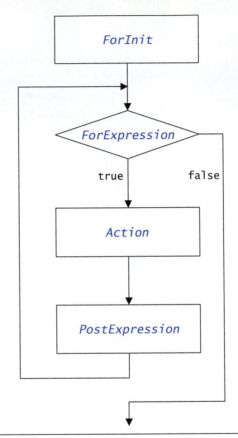

Our next example computes the product of the integers 1 through n. Mathematically this value is called $n!$ (pronounced "en-factorial") and its definition is

$$n! = \begin{cases} 1 & \text{if } n = 0 \\ n \times (n-1) \times \dots \times 1 & \text{if } n \geq 1 \end{cases}$$

The following code segment first prompts and extracts an integer value n. It then uses a **for** statement to compute the desired factorial. For simplicity in this and successive examples, we do not validate that the input has the correct form—this testing is left as an exercise.

```
cout << "Please enter a positive integer: ";
int n;
cin >> n;
int nfactorial = 1;
for (int i = 2; i <= n; ++i) {
    nfactorial *= i;
}
cout << n << "! = " << nfactorial << endl;
```

Suppose the extraction from the input stream supplies the value 4 for n. The code segment next defines nfactorial and initializes it to 1. These objects have the following representation:

n	4
nfactorial	1

The **for** statement begins with a *ForInit* that defines and initializes an object i with the value 2 (the first factor with which we must be concerned). In traditional programming terminology, i would be known as the *index variable*—its value changes with each iteration. The value of i reflects the current factor used in our factorial computation. Because the factors are generated in ascending order, nfactorial always reflects the product of n's factors 1 through i–1. This behavior is our invariant. By appropriately updating nfactorial with the current factor i and then updating i to the next largest factor, our computation will be successful. At this point, our objects have the following representation:

n	4
nfactorial	1
i	2

The **for** statement next compares i with n. Because 2 is less than 4, the **for** loop body is executed. The body scales nfactorial by i. The result is that object nfactorial has value 2. The expression ++i is then evaluated, causing index i to be incremented by 1 so that it has the value 3:

n	4
nfactorial	2
i	3

The loop then reevaluates the expression i <= n. Because 3 is less than 4, the **for** loop body is again executed. In the body, object nfactorial is again scaled by index i. The result is that object nfactorial has value 6. The expression ++i is then evaluated, causing index i to be incremented by 1 so that it has the value 4:

n	4
nfactorial	6
i	4

The loop then reevaluates the expression i <= n. Because 4 equals 4, the **for** loop body is again executed. The scaling of nfactorial by index i gives it the value 24. The expression ++i is then evaluated, causing index i to be incremented by 1 so that it has the value 5:

n	4
nfactorial	24
i	5

The loop then reevaluates the expression i <= n. Because 5 is not less than or equal to 4, the **for** statement is over. Execution continues with the statement

```
cout << n << "! = " << nfactorial << endl;
```

which causes the following output:

```
4! = 24
```

Observe that if object n had been either 0 or 1, the *ForExpression* i <= n would be initially false. As a result, the value of nfactorial would remain 1, which is the correct value for 0! and 1!.

Programming Tip

Representing a for statement using a while statement

Any **for** statement

```
for (ForInit; ForExpression; PostExpression)
    Action;
```

can be converted into a **while** statement. For example, the following code segment is equivalent to the preceding **for** statement:

```
{
    ForInit;
    while (ForExpression) {
        Action;
        PostExpression;
    }
}
```

The outer braces are necessary to limit the scope of any definition in *ForInit*.

In Program 4.11, we use a **for** statement as the iterative construct to solve our earlier problem of computing the average of a list of input values. The objects used in this program have the same role as they had in Program 4.7, and the same invariants apply regarding their values.

The initialization of ValuesProcessed is the initialization expression of the **for** construct. The definition of ValuesProcessed preceded the **for** statement because the C++ standard states that objects defined in the *ForInit* of a **for** loop can be used only in that **for** statement. If we had defined

Program 4.11

Computing the average of a list of numbers using a for statement

```cpp
// Program 4.11: Compute the average of an arbitrary
// list of numbers
#include <iostream>
#include <string>
using namespace std;
int main() {
    cout << "Please enter list of numbers" << endl;
    float ValueSum = 0;
    float Value;
    int ValuesProcessed;
    for (ValuesProcessed = 0; cin >> Value;
     ++ValuesProcessed) {
        ValueSum += Value;
    }
    if (ValuesProcessed > 0) {
        float Average = ValueSum / ValuesProcessed;
        cout << "Average: " << Average << endl;
    }
    else
        cout << "No list to average" << endl;
    return 0;
}
```

ValuesProcessed in the **for** statement, we would be unable to use it after the loop in the calculation of the average.

The incrementing of ValuesProcessed is the *PostExpression* for the next possible iteration. Alternatively we could have made the incrementing part of the **for** loop *Action*. However, it is more appropriate as the *PostExpression* because the processing of the current value is properly viewed as updating the running total.

Our next example using a **for** statement involves an important mathematical series known as the Fibonacci sequence. We consider this sequence in more detail in Chapter 6. The sequence starts with the following numbers: 1, 1, 2, 3, 5, 8, 13, 21. After the initial two 1s, each number in the sequence is the sum of the two previous numbers. For example, $1 + 1 = 2$, $1 + 2 = 3$, $2 + 3 = 5$, $3 + 5 = 8$, and so on. The following code segment extracts a value n. A **for** loop is then used to display the first n numbers in the sequence. It is assumed that n is at least 2.

```cpp
cout << "Please enter an integer greater than 2: ";
int n;
cin >> n;
cout << "The first " << n << " Fibonacci numbers:"
 << endl << 1 << endl << 1 << endl;
int PreviousNumber = 1;
int CurrentNumber = 1;
for (int i = 3; i <= n; ++i) {
    int Sum = PreviousNumber + CurrentNumber;
    cout << Sum << endl;
    PreviousNumber = CurrentNumber;
    CurrentNumber = Sum;
}
```

After the extraction of n, the code segment displays the first two numbers in the sequence. Next, objects `PreviousNumber` and `CurrentNumber` are defined. They represent the two previously processed numbers in the sequence. The **for** loop then iterates n–2 times. Object i is the loop index variable, and it takes on the values 3 through n. Each loop iteration begins by defining and displaying an object Sum whose value is the sum of the two previously processed numbers. The iteration then updates the values of `PreviousNumber` and `CurrentNumber` to reflect that another number has been processed.

In our next code segment, we use a **for** loop to display three square `RectangleShape` objects in a diagonal fashion. The output of the code segment is given in Figure 4.9.

```
SimpleWindow W("One diagonal", 5.5, 2.25);
W.Open();
int i = 0;
for (int j = 1; j <= 3; ++j) {
    RectangleShape S(W, i + j*0.75 + 0.25,
    j*0.75 - 0.25, Blue, 0.4, 0.4);
    S.Draw();
}
```

Figure 4.9

Displaying squares along a diagonal

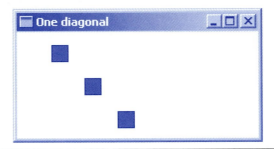

The diagonal-producing segment begins by defining a `SimpleWindow` object W that has a suitable label and size for the task at hand. An object i is then defined and initialized to zero (our next example uses i in a generalization of this code segment to display three diagonals of rectangles). The **for** loop uses j as the index variable. Index j takes on, in turn, the values 1, 2, and 3. The index variable takes on these values because it is initialized to 1, and it is incremented by 1 after each iteration.

`Window W`, object i and index j are used in the definition of a `RectangleShape` S. Object S is redefined each time through the loop. Each definition assigns to `Window W` a blue square `RectangleShape` whose sides are 0.4 centimeters long. In the first iteration, the center of the `RectangleShape` being defined is at coordinate (i + j*0.75 + 0.25, j*0.75 – 0.25) = (1, 0.5). In the second iteration, the center of the `RectangleShape` being defined is (1.75, 1.25). In the third and final iteration, the center of the `RectangleShape` being defined is (2.5, 2). Thus, each time through the loop, S is redefined and redrawn to occupy a different position in the window W. However, the previous versions of S also remain part of the display. This behavior is a characteristic of most windowing systems—an object is removed from a display only by actively invoking some kind of erasing command.

Our next code segment embeds the loop of the previous code segment within another **for** loop.

```
SimpleWindow W("Three diagonals", 5.5, 2.25);
W.Open();
for (int i = 0; i <= 2; ++i) {
    for (int j = 1; j <= 3; ++j) {
        RectangleShape S(W, i + j*0.75 + 0.25,
        j*0.75 - 0.25, Blue, 0.4, 0.4);
        S.Draw();
    }
}
```

The outer **for** loop uses an index i, which takes on, in turn, the values 0, 1, and 2. Because this loop iterates three times, the inner **for** loop is executed three times, and because each execution of the inner loop causes three squares to be drawn, a total of nine squares are drawn altogether. The output of a run of this segment is given in Figure 4.10.

Figure 4.10

Displaying nine squares along three diagonals

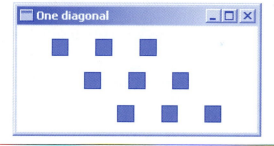

When the outer **for** loop is initiated, i has value 0, so the first three rectangles have centers (1, 0.5), (1.75, 1.25), and (2.5, 2) (as in our previous example). In the second iteration of the outer **for** loop, i has value 1. This causes the inner **for** loop to generate rectangles with centers (2, 0.5), (2.75, 1.25), and (3.5, 2). The final iteration of the outer **for** loop generates three more rectangles. They have centers (3, 0.5), (3.75, 1.25), and (4.5, 2).

Programmer Alert

Infinite loops

All our **while** and **for** examples include some action that causes the iteration statement to eventually complete. Without such an occurrence, the programs would have what is known as an *infinite loop*—they would continue to execute until some operating system command eventually terminated them. To avoid this problem in your programs, make sure that you understand what is going on in your iteration statements. In particular, make sure that your iteration statements are designed to terminate.

We next consider two application problems whose solutions are appropriately solved using **for** statements.

4.10 SIMPLE DATA VISUALIZATION

Suppose we are given the following data set that represents 15 observations of some phenomenon. What statements can we make?

```
4.90 2.41 0.82 0.77 2.60 5.10 7.52 9.45 9.65
7.81 5.04 2.51 0.95 0.80 2.62
```

One statement we can make by performing statistical analysis is that the phenomenon being observed appears to come from the interval 0 … 10 with an average value of 4.97. We could perform further statistical analysis and report, for example, the standard deviation 2.95 of the observations.

Another approach for attempting to understand the nature of the phenomenon is to try to detect whether our sequence of observations represents a pattern. For example, are the numbers arranged in descending or Fibonacci-type order? If no patterns are recognized, data visualization is sometimes attempted. For example, a natural way to plot the data set values in a two-dimensional manner would be to have the y-axis correspond to data set values and the x-axis correspond to positions in the data set sequence (e.g., the first two data set values correspond to points (1, 4.9) and (2, 2.41)). Such a plot for the data set is given in Figure 4.11. The plot indicates that the numbers do have structure—the numbers appear to be generated in a sine-line manner.

Program 4.12 is a simple data visualization tool that translates a numeric data set into a set of plotted points for analysis. It produced the plot of Figure 4.11. Program 4.12 accomplishes its task by iteratively drawing squares using the EzWindows `RectangleShape` class, where the ith square is centered at the position whose x-coordinate is i and whose y-coordinate is the ith value in the data set.

The program begins by defining a constant `Unit`. Each plot point will be displayed as a square with sides of length `Unit`.

```
const float Unit = 0.25;
```

The size `n` of the data set is then extracted.

```
cout << "Size of data set: ";
int n;
cin >> n;
```

The program then defines and opens a `SimpleWindow` object `W` to contain the data set plot:

```
SimpleWindow W("Data set display", n+2, 10);
W.Open();
```

The size of the window is fixed to be `n+2` × 10 centimeters. (The exercises develop a more robust version of the program.)

Figure 4.11

Plot of data set with numbers paired to form points

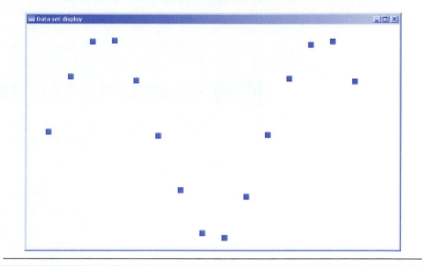

Program 4.12

Plotting data set values

```
// Program 4.12: Simple visualization tool
#include <iostream>
#include <string>
#include "rect.h"
using namespace std;

int ApiMain() {
    const float Unit = 0.25;
    cout << "Enter size of data set: ";
    int n;
    cin >> n;
    SimpleWindow W("Data set display", n+2, 10);
    W.Open();
    for (float x = 1; x <= n; ++x) {
        cout << "Enter data value (n): ";
        float y;
        cin >> y;
        RectangleShape Point(W, x, y, Blue, Unit, Unit);
        Point.Draw();
    }
    return 0;
}
```

A **for** loop displays the data set. The loop iterates n times. Index x is used to count the number of iterations so far. In each iteration, the body of the loop first extracts the next data set value y.

```
cout << "Enter data value (n): ";
float y;
cin >> y;
```

A RectangleShape object Point is then defined and drawn in window W. Point represents a blue square centered at position (x, y) with sides of length Unit:

```
RectangleShape Point(W, x, y, Blue, Unit, Unit);
Point.Draw();
```

Once `Point` is drawn, the postexpression for the **for** loop is evaluated, which increments `i`. The increment indicates that another data set value has been processed. We are then ready to reevaluate the loop test expression to determine whether there is another data set value to be extracted and processed.

4.11 SOLVING THE LAZY HOBO RIDDLE

The following riddle dates back to the late 19th century. (Its revival is credited to Will Shortz, crossword puzzle editor of *The New York Times*.)

> There were once four hoboes traveling across the country. During their journey they ran short on funds, so they stopped at a farm to look for some work. The farmer said there were 200 hours of work that could be done over the next several weeks. The farmer went on to say that how they divided up the work was up to them. The hoboes agreed to start the next day. The following morning, one of the hoboes—who was markedly smarter and lazier than the other three—said there was no reason for them all to do the same amount of work. This hobo went on to suggest the following scheme: The hoboes would all draw straws. A straw would be marked with a number. The number would indicate both the number of days the drawer must work and the number of hours to be worked on each of those days. For example, if the straw was marked with a 3, the hobo who drew it would work 3 hours a day for 3 days. It goes without saying that the lazy hobo convinced the others to agree to this scheme and that through sleight of hand, the lazy hobo drew the best straw. The riddle is to determine the possible ways to divide up the work according to the preceding scheme.

A solution to the riddle consists of four numbers a, b, c, and d such that $a^2 + b^2 + c^2 + d^2 = 200$. So what we need to do is to systematically generate combinations of four numbers and check whether the current combination has the property that the squares of its numbers sum to 200.

Since the squares of numbers that are 15 or greater exceed 200, the only values that we need to consider for a, b, c, and d occur in the interval 1 to 14. As there is no advantage in evaluating the same combination more than once, we should generate the combinations in a manner that eliminates duplicate combinations. An easy way to ensure no duplications is to generate the combinations in ascending order. As a result, each generated combination will have the property that $a \leq b \leq c \leq d$.

To solve the riddle, we consider the various possibilities for a from the interval 1 to 14. For a given value of a, we consider all possibilities of b, c, and d subject to the constraints discussed above. In particular, the possibilities for b are a through 14. In a similar manner, given that a and b are fixed, we consider all possibilities for c and d. The possible values for c are b through 14. Once a, b, and c have been fixed, the possibilities for d are c through 14. This strategy is implemented in Program 4.13. The program consists essentially of four nested **for** statements where a, b, c, and d are index variables.

The output of a program run follows.

```
Lazy hobo possible solutions
2 4 6 12
6 6 8 8
```

Program 4.13

Solving the lazy hobo riddle

```cpp
// Program 4.13: Display solutions for lazy hobo riddle
#include <iostream>
#include <string>
using namespace std;
int main() {
    cout << "Lazy hobo possible solutions" << endl;
    for (int a = 1; a <= 14; a++) {
        for (int b = a; b <= 14; b++) {
            for (int c = b; c <= 14; c++) {
                for (int d = c; d <= 14; d++) {
                    if (a*a + b*b + c*c + d*d == 200) {
                        cout << a << " " << b << " " << c
                             << " " << d << endl;
                    }
                }
            }
        }
    }
    return 0;
}
```

It is interesting to determine how many possible solutions were considered during a run of the program. This task can be done by modifying the program to keep track of how many times the **if** expression is evaluated. It turns out that the **if** statement is executed 2,380 times. This number is large, but it is still small compared to $14 \times 14 \times 14 \times 14 = 38,416$, which is the number of sequences we would have considered if we had not generated unique combinations in ascending order. We can improve the efficiency of the program by causing the innermost **for** loop to terminate when a*a + b*b + c*c + d*d is greater than 200. Doing so will not cause any legal solutions to be missed (given that the a, b, and c are fixed, any unconsidered value for d will result in a sum of squares also bigger than 200). This modification turns out to lower the number of considered solutions to 1,214.

4.12 ITERATION USING THE DO CONSTRUCT

In some situations an action needs to be done at least once and possibly multiple times. To explicitly show this, a programmer can use the **do** construct. The **do** construct has the following form where *Expression* is a logical expression and *Action* is again either a single statement or a group of statements enclosed with curly braces.

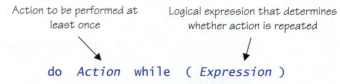

Action to be performed at least once   Logical expression that determines whether action is repeated

do   *Action*   while   (*Expression*)

The construct begins by executing *Action*. The *Expression* is then evaluated. If *Expression* is true, then the *Action* is repeated. This process continues until *Expression* is false. The semantics are demonstrated pictorially by the flowchart in Figure 4.12.

Figure 4.12
Flowchart for do-while statement

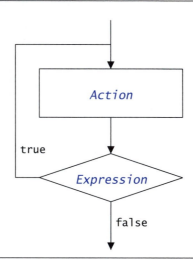

The **do** is sometimes used in the processing of a user reply to a prompt. For example, the following code segment repeatedly issues a prompt and then extracts a single character reply until the reply indicates yes or no. If a reply is not given, the code segment assumes no.

```
char reply;
do {
    cout << "Decision (y, n): ";
    if (cin >> reply)
        reply = tolower(reply);
    else
        reply = 'n';
} while ((reply != 'y') && (reply != 'n'));
```

To simplify the processing of this task, a reply is converted to its lowercase equivalent through the use of the **ctype** library function **tolower()** rather than mimicking the manual conversion of Program 4.10. The use of library functions is the focus of our next chapter.

Self-check Questions

39. Write an easy to understand conditional expression that is true when
     $ArraySize > j > 0$.

40. Consider the following code segment:

```
int n = 0;
for (i = 0; i < 10; ++i)
    for (j = 0; j < i; ++j)
        ++n;
cout << n << endl;
```

What is output?

41. Consider the following code segment:

```
int n = 10;
for (i = 0; i < n; i += 2) {
    ++n;
}
cout << i << endl;
```

What is output?

42. Consider the following code segment:

```
int n = 10;
for (i = 1; ; ++i) {
    if ((i % 5) == 0)
        break;
    else
        ++i;
}
cout << i << endl;
```

What is output?

43. Consider the following code segment:

```
int n = 10;
for (i = 0; i < n; ) {
    ++n;
    i += 3;
}
cout << i << endl;
```

What is output?

44. Consider the following code segment:

```
int n = 10;
for (i = 1; i <= n; ++i) {
    if ((i % 5) == 0)
        break;
}
```

```
cout << i << endl;
```

What is output?

45.   Consider the following code segment:

```
int n = 10;
for (i = 1; i <= n; i += 2) {
    if ((i % 3) == 0)
        break;
}
cout << i << endl;
```

What is output?

46.   Consider the following code segment:

```
int n = 0;
for (i = 0; i < 10; ++i)
    for (j = 0; j < i; ++j) {
        if (i == 5)
            break;
        ++n;
    }
cout << n << endl;
```

What is output?

4.13   POINTS TO REMEMBER

✔ The type **bool** is used in C++ for representing logical values.

✔ A logical expression evaluates to true if the value of the expression is either a nonzero integer value or the **bool** value **true**.

✔ A logical expression evaluates to false if the value of the expression is integer 0 or the **bool** value **false**.

✔ Logical expressions can contain the logical operators **&&**, **||**, and **!**. These operators correspond, respectively, to *and*, *or*, and *not*.

✔ A truth table is the traditional representation for a logical operation. A table will contain an entry for each possible logical operand combination.

✔ The relational operators also produce logical values. The relational operators fall into two categories: equality and ordering.

✔ The equality operators **==** and **!=** and the ordering operators **<**, **<=**, **>**, and **>=** are defined for all fundamental and pointer types, and the string class.

✔ Because of its limitations in accuracy, floating point values are typically not tested for equality. Instead tests are made to determine whether floating point values are approximately equal.

✔ A logical expression that is being evaluated is subject to the short-circuit rule. This rule states that once the overall value of an expression is known, evaluation ceases; that is, if P is true, then the term Q is not evaluated in

History of Computing

The Difference Engine

A major milestone in the march toward the age of the computer occurred in the early 19th century. One of the great problems of that day was the accurate calculation and transcription of the various tables used by scientists and mathematicians. Accuracy was a very important problem because surveyors, bankers, navigators, and engineers relied on these tables. The problem was that the computation and printing of the tables was done largely by hand, and the process was extremely tedious. A young mathematician named Charles Babbage (1792–1871) had an idea for a solution. His idea was to use a machine to compute the tables. The proposed machine, called the "Difference Engine," would be powered by steam and perform all computations mechanically; the results would be recorded on metal plates. The metal plates would be used to print the tables, thereby eliminating the possibility of transcription and printing errors.

To understand the name *Difference Engine* and how it was to be used to automate the computation of mathematical tables, it is necessary to briefly discuss how tables were computed back in the 1800s. Most mathematical and physical functions can be approximated by evaluating a polynomial of the form $dx^n + \ldots + cx^2 + bx + a$. For a series of values, polynomials of this form can be evaluated by calculating a table of differences. To illustrate the concept, consider the second-degree polynomial $n^2 + 2n + 22$ and the following table.

n	$n^2 + 2n + 22$	Difference$_1$	Difference$_2$
0	22	—	—
1	25	3	—
2	30	5	2
3	37	7	2
4	46	9	2
5	57	11	2
6	70	13	2
7	85	15	2

The last row in the table can be easily computed without evaluating the formula. The value of Difference$_2$ is always 2. The value of Difference$_1$ for a row n is the sum of Difference$_1$ and Difference$_2$ for the previous row. Thus the entries for row 7 are 85, 15, and 2. In general, a polynomial of degree n can be evaluated by computing n differences. The Difference Engine was designed to handle polynomials of degree 6.

Babbage realized that construction of the Difference Engine would require considerable resources. He also realized that the construction of the engine required manufacturing methods far superior to those available.

He addressed the first problem by petitioning the government for funds to support the construction of the equipment. With the support of the Royal Society of London, a preeminent scientific society, Babbage was able to secure £1,500 (about $7,500 in 1823) from the British government. This support is one of the first examples of a government grant to carry out research. Babbage attacked the second problem by making a complete study of the manufacturing methods of the day. He found that better methods for building machine parts were necessary, and he focused his efforts on that aspect of the project. Although this effort greatly advanced the state of the art in the milling of machine parts, it did little to advance the construction of the engine. The project suffered a setback when Babbage lost two children and his wife in the space of a year. The project moved on slowly, and only a portion of the Difference Engine was ever completed (see Figure 4.13).

It worked and could solve second-degree equations to six-digit accuracy. Unfortunately, Babbage never completed a full Difference Engine. He had conceived of a grander machine, the Analytical Engine, and he chose to devote his time to it.

The Analytical Engine was designed to be general purpose; that is, it could compute any mathematical function, not just one involving differences. Babbage attempted to convince the government to support the development of the Analytical Engine, but his request was refused. Babbage continued to work on the design of the Analytical Engine until his death. Despite the failure to build either the Difference Engine or the Analytical Engine, Babbage's influence should not be underestimated. The ideas embodied in his two engines had a profound influence on computing. For example, the Analytical Engine essentially had all the components that are a part of today's modern computers. It was programmed via punched cards. It had a memory, called the store, and a portion that performed computations that is similar in concept to the processing unit of today's computers.

P || Q because the overall expression is true, and if P is false, then the term Q is not evaluated in P && Q because the overall expression is false.

✔ The **if** statement has two forms. In both forms, a logical expression is evaluated, and if that expression is true, an action is executed. In one of the forms, an action is also specified when the evaluated expression is false.

✔ The expression used to determine the course of action for a conditional or iterative construct is known as a test expression.

✔ The **switch** statement takes actions based on the value of an integral expression. The programmer specifies the case values of interest for that expression, and for each case value the desired action is specified. The switch statement allows for an optional **default** case that handles non-specified values.

✔ Types defined by a programmer are known as programmer-defined or derived types.

Figure 4.13

*A portion of the
Difference Engine
along with an inset of
Charles Babbage*

- ✔ The **enum** statement is a method for organizing a collection of integral constants into a type.
- ✔ A loop is a group of statements whose actions are repeated using an iterative construct.
- ✔ The **while** statement permits actions to be repeated while a given logical expression evaluates to true. If the logical expression is initially false, then the action of the construct is never executed; otherwise, the action is repeatedly executed until the test expression evaluates to false.
- ✔ Because a **while** test expression can be initially false, it is possible for the body of a while loop not to be executed.
- ✔ The **do** statement is similar in nature to the **while** statement; however, its action is always executed at least once. It has this property because its test expression is not evaluated until after its body is executed.
- ✔ The **for** statement is a specialization of the **while** construct that has a test expression and both a one-time loop initialization action and an action that is to be performed once for each execution of the loop body. All parts of a **for**

statement are optional. In particular, if the test expression is omitted, then the value true is used instead.

✔ An object defined in the *ForInit* section of a **for** loop can be used only in that loop.

✔ A **break** statement causes the innermost **switch**, **while**, **for**, or **do** control structure that contains the statement to be exited.

✔ As in other parts of programming, loops should be carefully constructed. Actions taken before and during the loop should ensure that the test expression for the loop always makes sense. These actions should also ensure that the loop eventually terminates.

✔ An invariant is a rule that should be always true. In developing a loop, the designer should be aware of the invariants that the loop can affect.

✔ A **typedef** statement creates a new name for an existing type. Both the new and old names can be used in subsequent definitions.

4.14 EXERCISES

4.1   Suppose the following definitions are in effect.

```
bool P = true;
bool Q = false;
bool R = false;
string s = "a";
string t = "b";
int i = 10;
int j = 0;
```

Evaluate the following expressions:

a) !P == Q

b) s != t

c) R == (P && Q)

d) Q && (P || R)

e) Q || (P && !R)

f) P && !Q && !R || (P == !Q)

g) s < t

h) s + t << t

i) i * j

j) i && j

4.2   Suppose the following object definitions are in effect.

```
bool P = false;
bool Q = true;
bool R = true;
int i = 1;
int j = 0;
```

Evaluate the following expressions:

a) `P && Q || !P && !Q`
b) `P || Q && !P || !Q`
c) `0 == 1 || 0 < 1`
d) `0 == 1 == true`
e) `P && (Q || R)`
f) `!!P`
g) `!j`
h) `false < true`
i) `j = i`

4.3 Using the operator precedence rules, parenthesize the following expressions:

a) `1 + 2 == 3 * 4`
b) `1 + 2 == 3 * 4 && 5 / 6 == 7`
c) `P == Q <= R`
d) `P < Q == R`
e) `P == Q || R`
f) `P == Q && R`
g) `! 5 < 3 < 4`
h) `P || Q && R || S`
i) `- 5 < 9 == P && 3 == 17`

For Exercises 4.4 through 4.9 assume that `i` and `j` are **int** objects.

4.4 Define an expression that is true when `i` equals `j`.

4.5 Define an expression that is true when `i` lies in the interval 6 ... 9.

4.6 Define an expression that is true only when `i` is even and `j` is odd, or when `i` is odd and `j` is even.

4.7 Define an expression that is true only if the following conditions are all met: `i` is greater than 11, `j` is at most 28, and `m` and `n` have different values.

4.8 Define an expression that is true only if none of the following conditions are met: `i` plus `j` equals 30, `i` is less than 4, and `i` times `j` is greater than 54.

4.9 Define an expression that is true if any of the following conditions are met: `i` is twice the value of `j`, `j` is smaller than `k` but larger than `n`, or `m` is negative.

4.10 Consider the following code segment:

```
if (i <= j)
    cout << "1" << endl;
else
    cout << "2" << endl;
cout << "3" << endl;
```

a) If `i` is 1 and `j` is 2, what is the output?
b) If `i` is 2 and `j` is 1, what is the output?

c) If i is 2 and j is 2, what is the output?

4.11   Consider the following code segment:

```
if (i == j)
    cout << "1" << endl;
else if ((i % j) < 3)
    cout << "2" << endl;
else if (i < (j-1))
    cout << "3" << endl;
else
    cout << "4" << endl;
cout << "5" << endl;
```

a) If i is 9 and j is 4, what is the output?

b) If i is 4 and j is 9, what is the output?

c) If i is 5 and j is 6, what is the output?

d) If i is 5 and j is 9, what is the output?

4.12   Write code segments that implement the following actions:

a) If i divided by j is 4, then i is set to 100.

b) If i times j is 8, then i is set to 50; otherwise, j is set to 60.

c) If i is less than j, then j is doubled; if instead i is even, then i is doubled; otherwise, both i and j are incremented by 1.

d) If both i and j are 0, then i is set to 1 and j is set to 2; if instead only i is 0, then i is set to 5 and j is set to 10; if instead only j is 0, then i is set to 10 and j is set to 5; otherwise, both i and j are set to 4.

4.13   Consider the following **if** statement:

```
if ((i == 3) || (j == 4)) {
    cout << "yes" << endl;
}
else {
    cout << "no" << endl;
}
```

Are there values that cause the display of both "yes" and "no"? Why?

4.14   Assume the following object definitions are in effect:

```
bool P = false;
bool Q = true;
bool R = true;
```

Consider the following expressions. Determine whether they have short-circuit evaluations and, if so, where.

a) Q && P && R

b) Q && P || R

c) !Q || (i != j)

d) (P || Q && R) && (3 <= 4)

e) R || (P || !Q || !R && (4 > 3))

4.15 Consider the following code segment using **bool** objects A, B, C, and D.

```
if (A && B)
    if (!C || !D)
        cout << "1" << endl;
    else if (D)
        cout << "2" << endl;
    else
        cout << "3" << endl;
else if (C != D)
    cout << "4" << endl;
else if (C)
    cout << "5" << endl;
else
    cout << "6" << endl;
```

a) Give values for A, B, C, and D that cause the code segment to display 1 to the standard output stream.

b) Give values for A, B, C, and D that cause the code segment to display 2 to the standard output stream.

c) Give values for A, B, C, and D that cause the code segment to display 3 to the standard output stream.

d) Give values for A, B, C, and D that cause the code segment to display 4 to the standard output stream.

e) Give values for A, B, C, and D that cause the code segment to display 5 to the standard output stream.

f) Give values for A, B, C, and D that cause the code segment to display 6 to the standard output stream.

4.16 Write the truth table that the following code segment computes.

```
if (P)
    Operation = true;
else if (Q)
    Operation = false;
else
    Operation = true;
```

4.17 Write the truth table that the following code segment computes.

```
if (P)
    if (Q)
        Operation = true;
    else
        Operation = false;
else
    Operation = false;
```

4.18 Write the truth table for the logical binary operation of isomorphism (*iso*). The operation evaluates to true if the operands evaluate to the same value; otherwise, *iso* evaluates to false. Is there a C++ operator that computes *iso*? Explain.

4.19 Write the truth table for the logical binary operation of exclusive-or (*xor*). The operation evaluates to true if exactly one of its operands evaluates to true; otherwise, *xor* evaluates to false. Write a code segment that tests whether P *xor* Q is true, where P and Q are **bool** objects.

4.20 Write the truth table for the logical binary operation for the complement of and (*nand*). The operation evaluates to false if both of its operands evaluate to true; otherwise, *nand* evaluates to true. Write a code segment that tests whether P *nand* Q is true, where P and Q are **bool** objects.

4.21 Provide the truth table for the following logical expressions:

a) (*not P*) *and Q*

b) *P and* ((*not P*) *or Q*)

4.22 DeMorgan's law states that for logical variables *P* and *Q*:

▪ *not* (*P and Q*) is equivalent to (*not P*) or (*not Q*).

▪ *not* (*P or Q*) is equivalent to (*not P*) and (*not Q*).

Prove these two equivalences through the use of truth tables. Hint: For the first equivalence, your truth table should have headings *P*; *Q*; *P and Q*; *not* (*P and Q*); *not P*; *not Q*; (*not P*) *or* (*not Q*).

4.23 Develop a Boolean expression using an integer object `year` that is true if and only if the value of `year` corresponds to a leap year.

4.24 Develop flowchart representations of the following programs:

a) Program 4.2

b) Program 4.6

c) Program 4.7

d) Program 4.13

4.25 Demonstrate that any **switch** statement can be reimplemented using an **if-else-if** statement.

4.26 Demonstrate that some **if-else-if** statements cannot be reimplemented as a **switch** statement.

4.27 Implement a program that extracts a single integer value as input. The program should display whether the input value is positive, negative, or zero.

4.28 Implement a program that extracts two integer values as input. The program should display whether the inputs are both positive, both negative, or one positive and one negative.

4.29 Implement a program that extracts two floating-point values as input. The program should determine whether the difference in the two values is at most `Epsilon`, where `Epsilon` is a program-defined constant equal to 0.00001.

4.30 Rewrite Program 4.2 so that it uses an **if-else-if** statement to determine the smallest value.

4.31 Suppose we want to sort four numbers. How many different orderings can there be?

4.32 Design and implement a program that sorts four input values.

4.33 Consider the following **switch** statement:

```
switch (i*j) {
    case 1: case 2: case 3: case 6:
        cout << "1" << endl;
    case 5:
        cout << "2" << endl;
        break;
    case 10:
        cout << "3" << endl;
        break;
    default:
        cout << "4" << endl;
}
```

a) If i is 11 and j is 2, what is the output?

b) If i is 1 and j is 5, what is the output?

c) If i is 3 and j is 2, what is the output?

d) If i is 5 and j is 2, what is the output?

4.34 Implement a program that extracts a single integer value. The input value should be in the range 1 through 10. The program should display whether the input value is a prime number. The program should categorize the input value using a **switch** statement.

4.35 Modify Program 4.4 so that it also computes remainder expressions of the form *LeftOperand % RightOperand* where % is the modulus operator.

4.36 Modify Program 4.4 so that it also computes simple relational expressions of the form *LeftOperand Operator RightOperand* where *Operator* is either less than (<) or greater than (>).

4.37 Convert the following code segment into a **switch** statement.

```
if ((i == 1) || (i == 4)) {
    n = 1;
}
else if (i == 3) {
    n = 4;
}
else {
    n = 3;
}
```

4.38 What is wrong with the following code segment? How can it be corrected?

```
cout << "Enter key value (n): "
int key;
cin >> key;
int value;
cout << "Enter a list of numbers (n1 n2 ...): "
for (int i = 0; cin >> value; ++i) {
    if (key == value) {
        ++counter;
    }
}
```

```
cout << counter << " of the " << i
    << " values equal " << key << endl;
```

4.39   What is wrong with the following code segment? How can it be corrected?

```
int equal1 = 0;
int equal2 = 0;
int equal3 = 0;
cout << "Enter a list of numbers: (n1 n2 ...):";
int value;
while (cin >> value) {
    switch (value) {
        case 1: ++equal1;
        case 2: ++equal2;
        case 3: ++equal3;
    }
}
cout << equal1 << " inputs equals 1" << endl;
cout << equal2 << " inputs equals 2" << endl;
cout << equal3 << " inputs equals 3" << endl;
```

4.40   Define an **enum** type Days for days in the week.

4.41   Define an **enum** type for card suits.

4.42   Show how a **do** statement can be converted into a **while** statement.

4.43   Suppose c is an object of **enum** type color. Write a **switch** statement to insert the name of its value to the standard output stream cout. For example, if c has the value red, then the string "red" is inserted.

4.44   Add input validation to Program 4.6.

4.45   Rearrange the following code segment so that it is properly indented.

```
if ((n > 0) && (m > 0)) { for (int i = 0; i < n;
++i) { for (int j = 0; j < m; ++j) { if (i ! =
j) { cout << "0" << endl; } else { cout << "1";
} } } } else { cout << "2" << endl; }
```

4.46   Provide a code segment that prompts a user for an extracted value in the interval 0 ... 99. The segment then displays the value in words. For example, if the input value is 21, then twenty-one is displayed.

4.47   What is the output of the following code segment?

```
int counter1 = 0;
int counter2 = 0;
int counter3 = 0;
int counter4 = 0;
int counter5 = 0;
for (int i = 0; i < 10; ++i) {
    ++counter1;
    for (int j = 0; j < 10; ++j) {
        +counter2;
        if (i == j) {
            ++counter3;
        }
        else {
            ++counter4;
        }
```

```
            }
        ++counter5;
    }
    cout << counter1 << " " << counter2 << " "
         counter3 << " " << counter4 << " " << counter5;
```

4.48 Correct the following code segment so that it displays the number of inputs that are bigger than the first input.

```
int FirstValue;
int CurrentValue;
int Sum = 1;
cin >> FirstValue;
while (cin >> FirstValue) {
    if (FirstValue == CurrentValue) {
        ++Sum;
    }
}
cout << Sum << endl;
```

4.49 Correct the following code segment so that it displays the sum of odd integers from 1 to n.

```
int i = 0;
for (int Sum = 1; Sum < n; ++i) {
    if (i % 2) {
        Sum += n;
    }
    cout << Sum << endl;
}
```

4.50 Provide a code segment that iteratively prompts and extracts from standard input a rectangle description and then displays the corresponding RectangleShape to window W. In reaction to a prompt, the user should provide the width and height of the rectangle, the x- and y-values that correspond to the center of the rectangle, and the color of the rectangle. The rectangle dimension and center characteristics are given as floating point values; the color of the rectangle is given as a string. A sample prompt and user response are given below:

```
Enter rectangle characteristics (w h x y color)
: 4 5 2 2 red
```

4.51 Provide a code segment that uses a **for** statement to display the sum of the integers in the interval 11 … 29.

4.52 Provide a code segment that iteratively extracts n pairs of integers. For each extracted pair of integers a and b, the program displays the product $a \times a+1 \times \ldots b$.

4.53 Design and implement a program that displays the absolute value of its inputs.

4.54 Correct the following code segment so that it displays the product of the integers in the inclusive interval 5 through 15.

```
int Factor = 5;
int Product = 1;
```

```
do {
    ++Factor;
    Product *= Factor;
} until (Factor == 15);
cout << Product << endl;
```

4.55 Consider the following code segment:

```
int i = 1;
while (i <= n) {
    if ((i % n) == 0) {
        ++i;
    }
}
cout << i << endl;
```

a) What is the output if n is 0?

b) What is the output if n is 1?

c) What is the output if n is 3?

4.56 Consider the following code segment:

```
for (i = 0; i < n; ++i) {
    --n;
}
cout << i << endl;
```

a) What is the output if n is 0?

b) What is the output if n is 1?

c) What is the output if n is 3?

d) What is the output if n is 4?

4.57 Design and implement a program that counts the number of its inputs that are positive, negative, and zero.

4.58 Design and implement a program that extracts values from the standard input stream and then displays the smallest and largest of those values to the standard output stream. The program should display appropriate messages for special cases where there are no inputs and only one input.

4.59 Design and implement a program that prompts the user for a nonnegative value n. The program then displays the value of n in reverse binary notation. For example, if n is 19, then 11001 is displayed.

4.60 Design and implement a program that prompts the user for a nonnegative value n. The program then displays the value of n in standard binary notation. For example, if n is 21, then 10101 is displayed.

4.61 Modify Program 4.4 so that it extracts a series of expressions and displays the output of each expression.

4.62 Design and implement a program that accepts a date as input. The program should display the date's position in the year. For example, if the date is 12 29 2002, then the displayed number is 363.

4.63 Design and implement a program that accepts as input starting and ending dates in the form expected by Program 4.5. The program then computes the number of days between the dates.

4.64 A sequence of numbers is monotonic nondecreasing if the values are in sorted order, that is, they are arranged in a nondecreasing order. For example, 1, 1, 3, 4, 9 is a monotonic sequence, but 1, 3, 2, 4, 9 is not a monotonic sequence because 3 is greater than 2. Design and implement a program that determines whether its input sequence is in monotonic nondecreasing order.

4.65 Design and implement a program that prompts its user for a nonnegative value n. The program then displays as its output:

```
1 2 3 ... n-1 n
1 2 3 ... n-1
...
1 2 3
1 2
1
```

(Note the …s are to be filled in with the appropriate numbers.)

4.66 A character is whitespace if it is a blank (' '), a tab ('\t'), a newline character ('\n'), or a formfeed ('\f'). Design and implement a program that counts the amount of whitespace in its input.

4.67 Design and implement a program that determines the number of strings and average string length in its input.

4.68 Redesign and reimplement Program 4.9 using the character processing method of Listing 4.2 to detect duplicates regardless of letter case.

4.69 Redesign and reimplement Program 4.12 to prompt and extract the approximate range in which the data set values occur. The size of the SimpleWindow in which the points are plotted should be proportional to the size of the range. The plots should be displayed in a normalized manner. For example, if the low end of the range is named a, then a pair of values n1 and n2 should be plotted, centered around (n1-a, n2-a).

CHAPTER 5

Function basics

Introduction

Functions improve clarity and enable software reuse. A function is like an assistant that goes off to perform a particular task and then returns with its solution. In the next two chapters, the design and use of functions is considered in detail. We begin this exploration by examining fundamental concepts such as invocation and parameter passing. We do so by developing programs that use functions from standard software libraries including the iostream library. The iostream library is important because it permits an extensible method of displaying and extracting objects. The use of libraries is facilitated through preprocessor commands. The preprocessor commands support file inclusion, macro definitions, and conditional compilation.

Key Concepts

- functions
- value parameters
- invocation and flow of control
- header files
- function prototyping
- activation records
- define directives
- file inclusion
- conditional compilation
- iostream functionality
- pseudorandom numbers

- iomanip manipulators
- formatted output
- fstream class `ifstream`
- fstream class `ofstream`
- file manipulation
- stdlib library
- `exit()` function
- assert library
- translation unit
- casting

5.1 FUNCTION BASICS

The programs presented in previous chapters are interesting, but they are not typical software. Aside from their use of the iostream library and our EzWindows graphical library, the actions in those programs were completely specified within their individual function's `main()` and `ApiMain()`. This approach was possible because the tasks were simple and easy to code. However, significant software applications require hundreds of thousands, if not millions, of lines of code. It would be practically impossible to correctly produce a single piece of code for such large applications—a huge monolithic program of such magnitude would be far too complex to understand and validate. Even if the application could be built in this fashion, it would be a waste of resources—there are already many software modules that perform common computing tasks in readily available software libraries. For these reasons, all major application developments and even most simple programs use programming schemes that organize their information and its manipulation in a modular fashion. A principal part of all such schemes is the use of *functions*. Not surprisingly, functions are a crucial component of object-oriented programming.

Functions help programs to solve particular tasks. In C++ a program waits until an assisting function completes its task before continuing to the next statement. To solve its task, the assisting function can use other functions. In fact, as strange as it may seem, a function can even use another instance of itself. (This process is known as *recursion*, and it is considered in the next chapter.)

Program 5.1 is a small program that uses a function `sqrt()` to assist its function `main()` compute the roots of a quadratic expression whose coefficients are user-supplied input values. A quadratic expression is normally written with coefficients a, b, c in the form:

$$ax^2 + bx + c = 0.$$

The roots of the expression are given by the formula:

$$\frac{-b \pm \sqrt{b^2 - 4ac}}{2a}.$$

For pedagogical purposes, Program 5.1 limits its computation to a quadratic expression with two real roots (the general quadratic problem is left to the exercises).

The act of using a function is referred to as an *invocation* or *call* of the function. In Program 5.1, function `sqrt()` is invoked in the definition of **double** object `radical`.

```
double radical = sqrt(b*b - 4*a*c);
```

During invocation, a function can be passed information to perform its task. The information is referred to as the function's *parameters* or *arguments*.

Program 5.1

Computing roots of a
quadratic equation
$ax^2 + bx + c$

```
// Program 5.1: Determines roots of a quadratic equation
#include <iostream>
#include <string>
#include <cmath>
using namespace std;
int main() {
   cout << "Coefficients for quadratic equation: ";
   double a;
   double b;
   double c;
   cin >> a >> b >> c;
   if ((a != 0) && ((b*b - 4*a*c) > 0)) {
      double radical = sqrt(b*b - 4*a*c);
      double root1 = (-b + radical) / (2*a);
      double root2 = (-b - radical) / (2*a);
      cout << "The roots of " << a << "x**2 + " << b
           << "x + " << c << " are " << root1 << " and "
           << root2 << endl;
   }
   else {
      cout <<   a << "x**2 + " << b << "x + " << c
           << " does not have two real roots" << endl;
   }
   return 0;
}
```

For example, function `sqrt()` expects a **double** floating-point value to be passed as its parameter. It then computes the square root of that parameter.

When a function is invoked, the *flow of control* is temporarily *transferred* to that function, which means that the next statement to be executed is the first one in the function that was invoked. To prepare for the execution of the function definition, a correspondence is established between the actual values used in the invocation with the parameters in the definition. After the invoked function completes its task, the flow of control returns to the statement that invoked the function.

5.1.1 Interface specification

During program translation, three things must have been specified about a function before it can be used: the type of value (if any) that the function will return, the function's name, and a description of its parameters. These three items form the function's *interface*. Note that the actual function definition is not required (although the definition must be eventually supplied so that the compilation process can be completed).

We have seen examples of a function interface in the various definitions of `main()` in our sample programs. The interface is the portion of the definition of `main()` that appears before the left curly brace. Thus the interface for function `main()` in our programs has been

```
int main()
```

For Program 5.1 the interface for function `sqrt()` is specified in the math library *header file* `cmath`, where a header file is a collection of function interfaces, constant and variable object definitions, and class descriptions. The header file is incorporated into the program through an include directive.

```
#include <cmath>
```

The initial c in cmath indicates that the math library has been adopted from the C language.

C++ Language

> ***To c or not to c***
>
> Older C++ compilers may not support the standard naming conventions for the standard libraries. Be aware that your compiler may require that the math library and other C-based libraries be invoked without the prefix c in the header file name. Also, some compilers require a file extension suffix h to be used for some standard header files. For example, some compilers require that the math library be included in the following manner:
>
> ```
> #include <math.h>
> ```
>
> Note that how you include a library can affect how you reference the objects, types, and functions that it specifies. Header files whose names do not have an h suffix typically place their elements in a namespace. To use the elements of such header files, we normally also use a **using namespace** statement. Header files whose names do have an h suffix typically place their elements in a general namespace that does not require a **using namespace** statement. A discussion of namespaces appears in Appendix D.

The interface statement for function sqrt() in the math header file resembles

```
double sqrt(double number);
```

The first part of an interface specification indicates what type of value (if any) the function produces as its result. We call that type the *function type* or *return type*. A function type can be any of the standard types or even a programmer-defined type. For sqrt(), the function type is **double**.

If the function does produce a value, we call the produced value in a particular invocation the *return value*. If a function's type is not **void**, then the function must *always* return a single value of the specified type. The return value that is produced by a function can vary with each invocation of the function. For example, if sqrt() is given the value 6.25 as its parameter, its return value is 2.5. If sqrt() is instead given the value 1.44 as its parameter, its return value is 1.2.

If a function's type is **void**, then the function *never* returns a value. It may seem strange to have a function that does not produce a return value, but **void** functions can be quite useful. For example, they are often used to display messages to the user.

The next part of the interface specification is the name of the function. The name must be an identifier. Programmers normally follow the same naming convention with function names as they follow with object names, which means using good names with a consistent capitalization scheme. Our naming convention, unless special conditions dictate otherwise, capitalizes the first letter in each word that makes up the name. Such a scheme makes it easier for readers of the code to recognize which functions are programmer-defined and which are part of the standard libraries (most standard library functions have lowercase names, e.g., `sqrt()`).

The last part of the interface specification describes the form of the parameters to be given to the function. The parameters are enclosed between a pair of parentheses. In our program examples so far, neither `main()` nor `ApiMain()` have required any information other than what was available through the standard input stream. Therefore, their parameter lists are empty. This is not the case for `sqrt()`. It requires a single piece of information to perform its computation—the value whose square root is to be determined. The description of that piece of information is called a *parameter declaration*. Functions that require multiple pieces of information have corresponding multiple parameter declarations; the individual declarations are separated by commas.

The interface specification for a function has the following form:

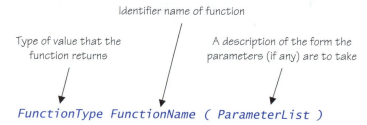

and *ParameterList* has the form:

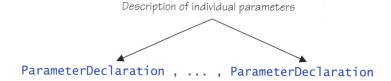

C++ provides programmers with an extensive set of options for specifying a parameter. For now, we limit ourselves to the *value* parameter declaration form. Other possibilities are considered in the next chapter. In its basic form, a value parameter declaration resembles a object declaration, since it consists of an identifier preceded by its type:

Function `sqrt()` uses the basic form for its parameter declaration, so the declaration of its parameter resembles the following:

```
double number
```

5.1.2 Function prototyping

A *function prototype* statement indicates that a function of a particular form may be used to perform a program subtask. A function prototype statement resembles an interface specification followed by a semicolon. As mentioned earlier, at least the interface must be specified before a function can be used within a program. Function prototype statements are typically placed near the beginning of the program file after the `#include` statements.

Some simple prototype declarations follow.

```
int PromptAndExtract();
float CircleArea(float radius);
bool IsVowel(char CurrentCharacter);
```

The `PromptAndExtract()` prototype indicates that the function does not expect a parameter but does return a value of type **int**. The prototype of `CircleArea()` indicates that the function computes and returns a value of type **float**. In addition, `CircleArea()` requires a single **float** value be given to it or, in programmer terminology, *passed* to it. The prototype for function `IsVowel()` indicates that it returns a **bool** value. The function expects to be passed a single **char** value.

If a complete function definition is being given, the interface specification is followed by the list of statements directing the function's actions. The statement list is surrounded by left and right curly braces. This is the case for function `main()` in Program 5.1.

We say that a function prototype resembles an interface specification because the names of the parameters are not necessary in a prototype. However, it is our practice to include good names so as to contribute to program understandability.

5.1.3 Invocation and flow of control

The interesting statement in Program 5.1 is the definition of `radical`, which in its initialization invokes function `sqrt()`.

```
double radical = sqrt(b*b - 4*a*c);
```

The invocation supplies the value whose square root is desired, which in this case is the value of the expression `b*b - 4*a*c`. We call the expression `b*b - 4*a*c` the *actual parameter*. The object used in the definition of `sqrt()` to represent the actual parameter is called the *formal parameter*. At this point in the execution of the program, the flow of control is temporarily transferred from `main()` to `sqrt()`. Figure 5.1, depicts the flow of control for Program 5.1.

Transfer of control to function `sqrt()` requires establishing a correspondence between the actual parameter given in the invocation and the object used

Figure 5.1

Depiction of the flow of control in Program 5.1 as it proceeds from main () to sqrt () back to main ()

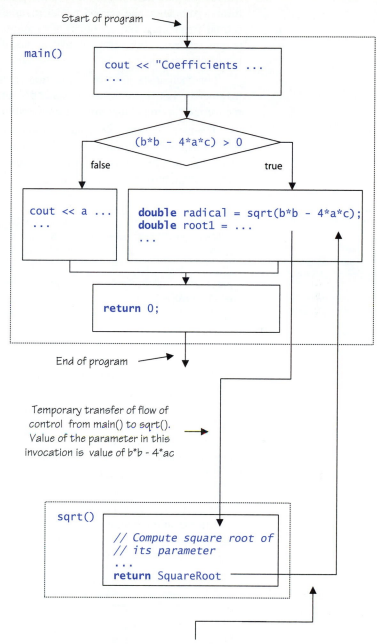

by **sqrt()** to represent that parameter. In general, the relative positions of the parameters determines the correspondence between the actual parameters and the formal parameters. The first actual parameter is associated with the first formal parameter, the second actual parameter is associated with the second formal parameter, and so on. If a function's interface uses the basic value parameter declaration form, all invocations of the function must have that number of parameters

For each invocation of a function, memory is set aside for its formal parameters. For functions such as sqrt() that have a value formal parameter, the formal parameter memory is initialized to the value of the actual parameter.

The memory that is set aside for the formal parameters of a function is part of the function's *activation record*. A fresh activation record is created for each invocation of a function. Even function main(), which is invoked by the operating system, has an activation record.

C++ Language

The right type

The type of the actual parameter used in a function invocation should agree with the type of the corresponding formal parameter as specified in the function interface. If there is a mismatch between the type of the actual parameter and the type of the formal parameter, the usual conversions are tried automatically. If the usual conversions cannot convert the actual parameter to the type of the corresponding formal parameter, a compilation error occurs.

The activation record for a function is large enough to store the values associated with each object that is defined within the function. Depending on the compiler, other information may be maintained in the activation record (e.g., a pointer to the current statement in the function being executed; a pointer to the statement in the function that invoked the function being executed; and if there is a return value, memory to temporarily hold that value).

The activation record for function main() in Program 5.1 includes the objects a, b, c, radical, root1, and root2. Suppose that the values supplied by the user for a, b, and c are, respectively, 6, 5, and 1 and that we are about to execute the initialization statement of radical in main(). In the following snapshot of main()'s activation record a question mark indicates that the value of the object has not yet been set by the program.

main()	
a	6
b	5
c	1
radical	?
root1	?
root2	?

When function `sqrt()` is invoked to initialize `radical`, an activation record is also created for `sqrt()`. In its activation record, its value formal parameter is initialized to the value of the actual parameter, the expression `b*b - 4*a*c`, which in this case has the value 1.

Once the expression `b*b - 4*a*c` has been used to initialize the value formal parameter, the actual parameter and formal parameter are then independent of each other. Whenever the formal parameter is used in `sqrt()`, the value used for the formal parameter is the one stored in the current activation record for `sqrt()`. Even if the invocation of `sqrt()` makes a change to the formal parameter, the change occurs within the memory of that invocation's activation record and the expression `b*b - 4*a*c` would be unaffected. This type of formal parameter–actual parameter relationship is referred to as *pass by value*. Essentially, the formal parameter is an object that can be used only within function `sqrt()`. The formal parameter is created with the invocation of `sqrt()`, and the formal parameter is destroyed when function `sqrt()` completes and releases its activation record memory.

The following code segment demonstrates some other legal invocations of `sqrt()`.

```
double ScaledRoot = 25 * sqrt(1000);
sqrt(15.0);
```

The first of the two invocations initializes `ScaledRoot`. The invocation demonstrates that a function invocation can be used in combination with operators. The function invocation is permissible because it produces a return value and that return value can be used like any other value. In particular, the return value can be used in composing an expression. The second of the two invocations seems peculiar because nothing is done with the return value of the invocation. However, the statement is legal—an expression is a valid statement in C++, and a valid function invocation is a valid expression.

Next consider the statement

```
cout << sqrt(14) - sqrt(12);
```

This insertion statement twice invokes function `sqrt()`. Therefore, the flow of control is twice passed to function `sqrt()`, and two `sqrt()` activation records are created during the execution of the insertion statement. The two activation records are distinct and occur one after the other (i.e., they do not exist simultaneously). In each of the invocations, memory storage for the activation record—possibly different storage locations per invocation—is set aside to hold the value for the `sqrt()` formal parameter. In one invocation, that storage is initialized to the value 14, and in the other invocation that storage is initialized to the value 12.

The return value of the invocation with actual parameter 14 is used as the left operand for the subtraction, and the return value of the invocation with actual parameter 12 is used as the right operand of the subtraction.

Conceptually, the following code segment *could* represent the insertion of `sqrt(14) ó sqrt(12)`:

```
double LeftOperand = sqrt(14);
double RightOperand = sqrt(12);
cout << LeftOperand - RightOperand;
```

Although these statements first evaluate the left operand and then the right operand of the subtraction, the original insertion statement did not require this evaluation ordering. C++ precedence rules specify the exact order of operator evaluation, but except for short-circuit evaluation of logical expressions, the precedence rules do not specify which operand of an operator is evaluated first—the order of evaluation is left to the compiler. Thus the invocation of `sqrt(12)` can occur before the invocation `sqrt(14)`. Therefore, the following code segment could also represent the insertion of `sqrt(14) – sqrt(12)`.

```
double RightOperand = sqrt(12);
double LeftOperand = sqrt(14);
cout << LeftOperand - RightOperand;
```

Programmer Alert

Function side effects

For the evaluation of the expression `sqrt(14) - sqrt(12)`, either operand can be evaluated first. However, as we shall see in later chapters, it is possible to write functions where the value of an expression depends upon the order of evaluation. This evaluation dependency can happen when a function modifies objects whose definitions are external to the function. Such modifications are known as *side effects*, as they are produced in addition to the function's return value. For ease of comprehension, a function invocation that produces side effects should not be part of a larger expression.

The ability to perform multiple invocations in a single statement is not limited to using return values as operands. A return value can also be used as the actual parameter in another function invocation. An example of such an invocation follows.

```
double QuarticRoot = sqrt(sqrt(5));
```

In this example, there are again two invocations and consequently two distinct activation records are created for `sqrt()`. However, this time the order of the invocations is specified. The expression `sqrt(5)` is computed first, and then its return value is used by the second invocation. This invocation sequence means that a `sqrt()` activation record is first created with memory storage for the formal parameter that is initialized to the value 5. The function then performs its computation using that activation record and produces a return value. The activation record is then discarded, and a new one is created that initializes the formal parameter to the return value of the previous `sqrt()` invocation. Using this value, the function again performs its computation and produces the return value that is used to initialize `QuarticRoot`. Thus the following actions occur (conceptually).

```
double Temporary = sqrt(5);
double QuarticRoot = sqrt(Temporary);
```

Not all function invocations are valid. For example, the following two invocations are invalid. The first has too few parameters and the second has too many.

```
double x = sqrt();     // illegal
double y = sqrt(5,3); // illegal
```

Before we begin a detailed discussion of some of the more useful C++ libraries, we consider the *preprocessor*, which incorporates the prototypes and definitions of a library header file into the program file.

5.2   THE PREPROCESSOR

The preprocessor examines the input program file for *file inclusion directives* and *conditional compilation directives*. Because the preprocessor carries out these directives on the input program file to produce the actual file to be compiled, the processing of these directives is the first step in program translation. The file produced by the preprocessor is called a *translation unit*.

5.2.1 File inclusion directives

A file inclusion directive specifies the name of a file that is to be part of the translation unit. The file named in the directive replaces the directive itself. If the file to be included cannot be found in the standard directories, the translation process is typically aborted and an error message is produced.

There are two file inclusion directive forms. One of the forms is given below.

```
#include <filename>
```

The octothorp symbol # indicates a preprocessor directive is to follow. The # must be the first nonwhitespace character on the line. The angle brackets < and > both delimit the filename and indicate that the file is to be found in one of the standard directories of the system. The location of these standard directories is implementation dependent; that is, different systems can place the standard directories in different locations. For PC-based systems, the standard directories are typically within subdirectories of the directory that contains the compiler. These libraries are normally created when the compiler is installed on the PC.

The size of the translation unit is typically much bigger than the input program file. For example, using one popular PC-based compiler, the following five-line program file has an 884-line translation unit. This size increase indicates that the iostream library provides many capabilities other than just standard stream insertion and extraction.

```
#include <iostream>
#include <string>
using namespace std;
int main() {
    cout << "Hello, World." << endl;
    return 0;
}
```

The second file inclusion directive has the following form:

```
#include "filename"
```

The quotes surrounding the filename indicate that an alternative set of directories should be searched to find the file in question. The process of considering alternative directories is implementation dependent. In practice, almost all compilers behave in the following manner:

- If the filename is given in terms of an absolute file system pathname, then the file is taken from that absolute location. For example, the following directive states that the included file is `sample.h` and it can be found in the directory `\example\source` on the C: drive of the PC system.

  ```
  #include "C:\example\source\sample.h"
  ```

- If an absolute pathname is not specified, then the filename is taken to be a relative name with respect to the user's current directory on the computer system. For example, the following directive would look in the current directory for the file `hold.txt`. If the file was not found in that directory, the standard directories would then be searched.

  ```
  #include "hold.txt"
  ```

It is legal for included files to contain preprocessor directives. If the files do contain directives, those directives are also processed. The processing of the directives in an included file is done before the processing of any remaining directives in the current file. For example, suppose the following line represents the contents of the input file to the preprocessor.

```
#include "a.txt"
```

File `a.txt` contains the following lines:

```
#include "b.txt"
#include "b.txt"
```

and file `b.txt` contains, for purposes of exposition, the following line:

```
hello world
```

The output of the preprocessor would be a file with the following lines:

```
hello world
hello world
```

Note that the preprocessor does not consider whether the lines it is creating are legal C++ statements. The preprocessor just executes its directives.

5.2.2 Conditional compilation

In our programs so far, each statement in the program file has always been compiled. This feature can be overridden with the `#ifndef` (if not defined) and `#ifdef` (if defined) conditional compilation directives.

The preprocessor directive `#ifndef` serves as the opening delimiter for a section of the file. An occurrence of the preprocessor statement `#endif` serves as the closing delimiter for the section. The delimited section is compiled only if the macro name following the `#ifndef` has not been previously defined. A macro name is defined using the `#define` statement. For example, the preprocessor statement

```
#define I386
```

defines the name I386.

The ability to determine which statements should be compiled is useful because it enables us to prevent the illegal redefinition of an object due to multiple inclusions. For example, many programs start off with

```
#include <iostream>
#include <iomanip>
```

even though the iomanip library includes the iostream library. Without the use of `#ifndef` statements by the iostream library, such programs would be illegal because there would be repeated definitions of standard streams `cin` and `cout`.

In the following example, objects a and b can be defined at most once, no matter how many times this code segment is included into a program file.

```
#ifndef NO_MORE_A_AND_B
int a;
int b;
#define NO_MORE_A_AND_B
#endif
```

This behavior is the case, as one of the lines within these conditional compilation directives defines the macro NO_MORE_A_AND_B. Once this macro is defined, subsequent inclusions of the code segment will not redefine a and b.

It is also possible to embed a conditional compilation directive within another conditional compilation directive. (The embedding process is known as *nesting*.) For example, in the following code segment, objects a and c are defined if the macro NO_INTS is undefined. Object b is defined only if macros NO_INTS and NO_B are both undefined. When conditional compilation directives are nested, a `#endif` statement is matched to the most recently occurring `#if` statement.

```
#ifndef NO_INTS
int a;
#ifndef NO_B
int b;
#endif
int c;
#endif
```

The #ifdef directive works in analogous manner. However, it requires that the macro name be defined for the associated statements to be part of the compilation process.

We next provide additional detail on how libraries are incorporated to produce a complete program. In particular, we discuss how to reference the elements of a header file and the mechanics of linking library definitions to the program object file. Then we explore several useful libraries.

Self-check Questions

1.   Give the function prototype for a function called Scale that accepts two parameters. The first parameter is an **int**, and the second is a **double**. Function Scale returns an **int**.

2.   Give the function prototype for a function called Blend that takes no parameters. Function scale returns a **double**.

3.   Give the function prototype for a function called Dither that accepts three parameters. The first two parameters are type **double**, and the third parameter is a **float**. Function Dither returns no value.

4.   Give the file inclusion directive for including the programmer-created include file stats.h in a program.

5.   Give the file inclusion directive for including the C++ include file iostream in a program.

6.   Create an include file called objects.h that contains the definition of two objects. One object is an **int** named Count initialized to 0. The second object is a **double** called Average initialized to 1.0. Implement the include file so that the objects Count and Average are defined just once no matter how many times objects.h is included by another module.

5.3   USING SOFTWARE LIBRARIES

Including a header file at the start of a program file enables programmers to use the header file declarations throughout the program file. A declaration that can be used throughout a program file is called a *global* declaration. The collection of all global declarations is called the *global namespace*. Besides providing a global namespace, C++ gives programmers the ability to place declarations in program-defined namespaces. We discuss how to create such namespaces in Appendix D.

As noted previously in this chapter, header files that make their declarations globally available typically have the file extension h. And header files that place their declarations within a nonglobal namespace typically do not use any filename extension. Thus `iostream` is a header file whose declarations are placed into a nonglobal namespace. In particular, they are placed in the namespace `std`. Similarly, `rect.h` is one of the header files for the EzWindows library, and its declarations are not assigned to a particular namespace. Therefore, its declarations are part of the global namespace.

An object, type, or function declared in a global namespace can be referenced without any special syntax. For example, when we want to use the globally defined type `RectangleShape`, we just use it:

```
RectangleShape R(W, 5, 4, blue);
```

However, referencing an object, type, or function from a nonglobal namespace requires some additional syntax. One way to handle this is to prepend each reference with the namespace name and the scope resolution operator `::`, as in the following statement using `cout`.

```
std::cout << "Hello, World" << endl;
```

A second alternative is to employ a **using** statement to make all the declarations in the desired namespace accessible:

```
using namespace std;
//
cout << "Hello, World" << endl;
```

Most programmers prefer this alternative because the individual references to namespace elements are less clumsy. However, the first alternative specifies more precisely the source of the object, type, or function in question.

There are generally no function definitions in a library header file. Instead, the definitions are placed in another file or files that are combined with the program during the linking stage of the translation process. By linking only the library object modules to the program, the compilation process is greatly speeded up—no translation of the library is needed because it has been done previously. The translation process was discussed in Chapter 1 and is reviewed in Figure 5.2.

If a library is standard, then the linking is usually performed automatically by the compiler. If a library is nonstandard, then compiling commands specify where the definitions can be found. The linking of libraries can be automated through the use of *make* or *project* tools associated with the compiler. In Appendix F, we discuss how to create and manipulate project files for several popular compilers.

In the next several sections we consider in detail the iostream library and several other libraries: iostream, iomanip, fstream, and assert. The functions, classes, and objects defined by these libraries are used in examples here and elsewhere in the text.

Note that C++ compilers also provide other standard libraries and sometimes even nonstandard libraries. For example, there are standard libraries for creating various kinds of lists (discussed in detail in Chapter 9), handling exceptions, and accessing time and date information. Because these other libraries are often very useful, we suggest that, in addition to the appendixes

Figure 5.2

Translation process

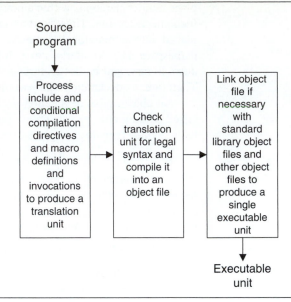

here, you consult both a C++ language reference manual and the reference manual for your compiler.

5.4 THE IOSTREAM LIBRARY

As in many programming languages, input/output (I/O) operations are not officially part of the C++ language. The I/O operations are instead defined in libraries that are associated with the language. Although separating the I/O operations from the language definition may seem quirky, it enables software developers to choose the right library for the task at hand.

C++ I/O libraries provide an interface between the program and the hardware devices that make up the computer system. The interface spans two levels of abstraction. At the lower level is a file. In this context, a *file* is a logical concept that represents a particular hardware device like a monitor, modem, or keyboard or represents a particular portion of a hardware device like a disk file on a floppy or on a CD-ROM. At the higher level of abstraction is a stream. The *stream* is a hardware-independent view of the actual device. The data coming from or going to the hardware device is just a sequence of bytes.

The stream and file views are both important. The stream view allows a program to issue generic I/O requests on flows of data while being unconcerned about how the requests are to be carried out. The file view captures the important physical characteristics of the actual device. The I/O requests of the stream view are translated automatically by the compiler into file-level specific actions that accomplish the desired requests.

An important characteristic of the iostream library is its extensibility. This characteristic is not true of the major alternative I/O library, the *stdio library*. The stdio library is the library C programmers use to do I/O. There are stdio functions for performing I/O requests for standard type values and for character strings, but there are no methods for extending or redefining these functions to operate on programmer-defined data types. And because pointers (discussed in Chapter 11) are frequently required in the processing of stdio-based input, many programmers make mistakes when using the stdio library. For these reasons, we recommend the use of the iostream library and confine our discussion to it.

Although the iostream library provides a hierarchy of basic I/O functionality, our concern here is the top level of the hierarchy that supports stream manipulation.

5.4.1 Standard streams

Header file `iostream` defines a collection of stream classes that are capable of input, output, or both input and output. Part of this collection are four standard stream objects that are automatically created when program execution begins. We have been using two of these stream objects, `cin` and `cout`, in most of our programs. The actual type of stream `cin` is `istream`, and the actual type of stream `cout` is `ostream`. The two other standard streams are `cerr` and `clog`. Like `cout`, these two standard streams are both of type `ostream`.

5.4.2 Standard error stream objects

Streams `cerr` and `clog` display output to the default error log. This log is normally the console monitor. Because `cerr` and `clog` are stream objects, they have values, member functions, and member operators. In particular, the insertion operator << is one of their members.

If a program detects an abnormal situation, it is good practice to display a message indicating the nature of the problem to the user. Such a message typically goes to the monitor so that it is immediately viewable. Because the output associated with stream `cout` is sometimes redirected to a file using operating system commands, `cout` is inappropriate for error or system status messages—you do not want the viewing of such messages to wait until the user gets around to looking at the output file. The preferred stream for error messages is `cerr`. Like `cout`, its insertion requests are directed by default to the monitor. However, unlike `cout`, `cerr` is normally never redirected to a file.

The streams `cout` and `cerr` are also different with respect to buffering. Buffering is generally inappropriate for error messages because they tend to be time critical. So each insertion request to stream `cerr` is sent immediately for display. Several example error messages are given below:

```
cerr << "System being rebooted in 2 minutes\n";
cerr << "Zero balance: withdrawal ignored\n";
cerr << "Modem is not online, no call possible\n";
```

If for reasons of efficiency, it is necessary to have buffered error and system status messages, the buffered error stream `clog` should be used. Like cerr, clog is normally always directed to the monitor. Some sample messages are given below.

```
clog << UserName << " has logged onto system\n";
clog << "Backup was successfully performed\n";
clog << "Mail has arrived\n";
```

5.4.3 The iostream manipulators

The iostream library also defines some input and output stream manipulators. Several of these manipulators are listed in Table 5.1. Different I/O manipulators can occur as the right operand of either an insertion operator << or of an extraction operator >>.

Table 5.1

Selected iostream manipulators

Manipulator	Purpose
dec	Display numeric values in decimal notation
endl	Output a newline character and flush the stream
ends	Output a null character and flush the stream
flush	Flush the stream buffer
hex	Display numeric values in hexadecimal notation
oct	Display numeric values in octal notation

We have already used the iostream manipulator endl. Manipulator endl, when inserted to an output stream, appends a newline character to the stream and causes the stream to be flushed. Manipulator ends operates in a similar manner except that it inserts a null character (the literal '\0') to the target stream. This manipulator is sometimes useful in string processing.

Manipulators dec, hex, and oct are used to specify the base in which numbers are displayed to the associated output stream. Manipulator dec is used to specify decimal (the default base); manipulator hex is used to specify hexadecimal (base 16), and manipulator oct is used to specify octal (base 8). The three manipulators are all *persistent* (i.e., all numbers are expressed in the requested base for the affected stream until another base change is specified).

Manipulator flush, when applied to an output stream, does what its name implies—it causes the output buffer to be immediately flushed. Thus a flush operation is similar to endl except that flush does not insert the newline character before flushing.

The following small example demonstrates some of these manipulators:

```
int i = 10;
int j = 20;
int k = 30;
cout << i << " " << j << " " << k << endl;
cout << i << " " << j << " " << k << "\n" << flush;
cout << oct << i << " " << j << " " << k << endl;;
cout << hex << i << " " << j << " " << k << endl;
```

The first two insertion statements are effectively the same—they both cause i, j, and k to be displayed in the default decimal base. The statements differ only in how the newline character is displayed and how flushing is requested. In the first insertion statement, the end1 manipulator issues a newline character and flushes the output buffer, whereas the second statement explicitly inserts a newline character and explicitly invokes the manipulator flush.

The use of the oct manipulator in the third insertion statement of main() causes the subsequent insertion of i, j, and k to be displayed in octal format. The use of the hex manipulator in the last insertion statement causes that insertions of i, j, and k to be displayed in hexadecimal. The output of the code segment follows.

```
10  20  30
10  20  30
12  24  36
a  14  1e
```

5.5 THE IOMANIP LIBRARY

The iomanip library defines a collection of I/O stream manipulators to modify the behavior of insertions and extractions. Its manipulators are not strictly necessary, because other functions associated with the stream objects can accomplish these tasks. However, invoking those other functions is generally more cumbersome than applying the iomanip manipulators.

The iomanip manipulators are defined in the standard header file iomanip. It is common practice for C++ programs to include the iomanip header file along with the iostream header file.

```
#include <iostream>
#include <iomanip>
```

A selected list of the manipulators provided by iomanip is given in Table 5.2. Except for manipulator setw(), all the manipulators are persistent. *Be aware that some compilers have not yet implemented all of these manipulators.*

Manipulator setw() sets the desired width of an insertion. As noted above, to the annoyance of many programmers the setw() manipulator is not persistent. The width specified to the manipulator affects *only* the next insertion. After that next insertion, default behavior is again used.

If the requested width to setw() is too small for the display of the next value, then the width of the next insertion is minimally increased to display the value correctly. Determining the minimal width necessary to display a value depends on the type of the value. In particular, for character strings if the width specified to setw() is less than the string length, then the string length is used. For integers, the entire number is always displayed along with a sign if one is necessary. For floating-point values, the necessary width varies according to whether scientific or decimal notation is being used. For either form, the minimal width is only large enough to include both the whole number and decimal portion, and if scientific notation is being used, the exponent. If the specified width to setw() is larger than needed, then the value is displayed by default in a right-adjusted manner with the extra width portion filled with the fill character. By default, the fill character is a space.

	Output Manipulators	Purpose
Table 5.2	`setw(int w)`	Set field width to w
Selected iomanip	`setfill(int c)`	Set the fill character to c
manipulators	`left`	Fill characters are padded after the display
	`right`	Fill characters are padded before the display
	`setbase(int b)`	Set the numeric base to b
	`fixed`	Display floating-point values in decimal notation
	`scientific`	Display floating-point values in scientific notation
	`showpoint`	Floating-point values are always displayed with a decimal point
	`noshowpoint`	Decimal points are displayed for floating-point values only if the decimal portion is nonzero
	`setprecision(int d)`	Set number of places of accuracy to d
	`skipws`	Whitespace characters are ignored during extractions
	`noskipws`	Whitespace characters are extractable.
	`showpos`	Positive numbers are displayed with a leading +
	`noshowpos`	Positive numbers do not have a leading +
	`showbase`	Octal displays are preceded with 0, and hexadecimal displays are preceded with 0x
	`noshowbase`	Numbers are not displayed with a base indicator
	`boolalpha`	Display logical values symbolically as true and false
	`noboolalpha`	Display logical values as 0 and 1
	`resetiosflags(long f)`	Set flags indicated in f to 0
	`setiosflags(long f)`	Set flags indicated in f to 1

Consider the following insertions of the character string `"Hello world"`.

```
cout << setw(1)  << "Hello world" << endl
     << setw(15) << "Hello world" << endl
     << "Hello world" << endl;
```

The insertions produce as their output

```
Hello world
    Hello world
Hello world
```

The middle output line differs from the first line because of the differing setw() invocations that precede the display of the string. The first invocation with setw(1) does not allow sufficient display width for the string, so the display width is temporarily increased to the length of the string. The second invocation with setw(15) provides more than sufficient display width for the string; therefore, the string is displayed in a right-adjusted manner (i.e., four copies of the space fill character are displayed prior to the display of the string). The final display of the string again starts an output line. This behavior happens because the setw() manipulator is not persistent—the default width behavior, which uses minimal width, is again in effect.

Manipulator setfill() sets the fill character to be displayed when the width of an insertion request is larger than necessary. The following statement demonstrates the use of this manipulator:

```
cout << setfill('#') << setw(15) << "Hello" << endl;
```

In this insertion statement, the string "Hello" is right adjusted through the display of the octothorp character '#'.

```
##########Hello
```

Manipulators left and right control whether an insertion is displayed in a left- or right-adjusted manner. Consider the following examples, which insert three names to standard output. Each of the names are displayed with a field width of 6.

```
cout << ":" << left << setw(6) << "JJ" << ":"
 << endl;
cout << ":" << right << setw(6) << "Jenna" << ":"
 << endl;
cout << ":" << left << setw(6) << "Hannah"<< ":"
 << endl;
```

It produces the following as its output:

```
:JJ    :
: Jenna:
:Hannah:
```

The first line of output occurred in this manner because the string "JJ" has length 2, requiring its display to be padded with four blanks. Because of the manipulator left, the padding occurs after the name. The string "Jenna" has length 5; therefore, its display is padded with one blank. Because of the use of the manipulator right, the padding occurs before the name. The string "Hannah" has length 6, which is equal to the field width, so no adjustment is performed. Note that the main use of the left and right manipulators is to obtain tablelike displays.

Manipulator setbase() is for output streams and requires a single parameter. The parameter specifies the base to be used in the display of numeric data (decimal, octal, or hexadecimal). The manipulator is not generally used because iostream manipulators dec, oct, and hex are also available. One typically uses setbase() only when the desired base for inserting a value is the result of an earlier computation or input request. An example with some unintended consequences follows.

```
int number;
int base;
cout << "Provide a number and a base: ";
cin  >> number >> base;
cout << number << " in decimal is "
  << setbase(base) << number << " in base " << base
  << endl;
```

If the input values for number and base are 9 and 8, then the output would be

```
9 in decimal is 11 in base 10
```

This result is not what we intended; the 10 in the preceding output is the representation of 8 in octal. This output happens because the effect of a set-base() invocation is persistent, so the cout insertions for number and base that occurred after the setbase() invocation are displayed in octal. To achieve the intended output, the insertion statement in the preceding code segment should be modified in the following manner:

```
cout << number << " in decimal is "
  << setbase(base) << number << " in base " << dec
  << base << endl;
```

This modification produces the desired output.

```
9 in decimal is 11 in base 8
```

If the input values for number and base are 19 and 16, then the output would be the following:

```
19 in decimal is 13 in base 16
```

Manipulators fixed and scientific specify, respectively, whether floating-point values should be displayed in decimal or scientific notation. By default, floating-point values are displayed in *automatic* mode. When automatic mode is in effect, large values, small values, and values close to zero are displayed in scientific notation while other values are displayed in decimal notation. For example, the following code segment under automatic mode

```
cout << 1000000000000.0 << endl;
cout << 0.0000000000001 << endl;
cout << 921.28 << endl;
cout << -1000000000000.0 << endl;
```

produces as its output

```
1e+012
1e-013
921.28
-1e+012
```

However, if fixed mode is in effect as in the following code segment

```
cout << fixed <<   1000000000000.0 << endl;
cout << 0.0000000000001 << endl;
cout << 921.28 << endl;
cout << -1000000000000.0 << endl;
```

the output is

```
1000000000000.000000
0.000000
921.280000
-1000000000000.000000
```

Observe that fixed mode causes six-place decimal accuracy to also be in effect.

If instead scientific mode is in effect as in the following code segment

```
cout << scientific << 1000000000000.0 << endl;
cout << 0.0000000000001 << endl;
cout << 921.28 << endl;
cout << -1000000000000.0 << endl;
```

the output is

```
1.000000e+012
1.000000e-013
9.212800e+002
-1.000000e+012
```

Observe that scientific mode also causes six-place decimal accuracy to be in effect.

Manipulator `setprecision()` sets the number of digits of precision when displaying a floating-point value. For automatic mode, the precision value is the preferred number of digits to be displayed. For fixed and scientific modes, the precision value is the number of places after the decimal. Note that, when in automatic mode, output stream insertions do not display trailing zeroes. The following example exhibits this behavior.

```
cout << setprecision(6)
  << 12.01234 << endl
  << 12.0123 << endl
  << 12.012 << endl
  << 12.01 << endl
  << 12.0 << endl;
```

The output of the fragment is given below.

```
12.0123
12.0123
12.012
12.01
12
```

The first two lines of the output are identical because six-place accuracy is the maximal display given the `setprecision(6)` invocation. The output serves as a warning that the display of floating-point values should always be considered approximate. In fact, given that there is finite precision to represent values, a reader must always be cautious no matter how many places after the decimal are displayed. The next three output lines reflect that, by default, only nonzero trailing digits are displayed. The last output line also shows that if all the decimal places are zero, by default even the decimal point is dropped. However, we can require the decimal point be displayed using the manipulator `showpoint`. This behavior can be subsequently turned off with the manipulator `noshowpoint`.

Now consider the following example:

```
cout << setprecision(0) << 12.01234 << endl;
```

The output of the insertion statement is

```
12.01234
```

This output occurred because a parameter of 0 in a `setprecision()` invocation indicates that the automatic precision is desired.

Now consider the following insertion statement that displays representations of the floating-point value `10.12345`.

```
cout << setprecision(5)
  << setw(5) << 10.12345 << endl
  << setprecision(4)
  << setw(9) << 10.12345 << endl
  << setw(5) << 10.12345 << endl;
```

For the first insertion of `10.12345`, the requested decimal-place accuracy is 5 and the total display width is also 5. These widths are due to the `setprecision(5)` and `setw(5)` invocations. The request for a five-decimal accuracy takes precedence, so the total display width is increased 6 to allow for the display of five digits and a decimal point.

```
10.123
```

The next insertion, which invokes `setprecision(4)`, causes four-place accuracy in the future.

```
10.12
```

This insertion of `10.12345` differs from the first one because the requested total display is now nine due to the `setw(9)` invocation. Because this width is more than necessary (given that four-place accuracy is in effect), the value is right adjusted by first displaying four fill characters. Because `setw()` is not persistent and `setprecision()` is persistent, the next insertion of `10.12345` starts off the output line and again uses four-place accuracy.

```
10.12
```

For large floating-point values, such as `123456789.123456789`, scientific notation is used by default. Consider the following insertion statement:

```
cout << setw(6) << 123456789.123456789 << endl
  << setprecision(3)
  << setw(15) << 123456789.123456789 << endl;
```

This statement produces these lines of output:

```
1.23457e+08
       1.23e08;
```

The lines differ because of the `setw()` and `setprecision()` invocations in the insertion statement. Observe that the first insertion rounded the value to be displayed (rounding is standard practice).

Persistent manipulators `boolalpha` and `nobool alpha` specify how **bool** objects are to be displayed (the default for **bool** objects is to display them in binary notation). For example, the code segment

```
cout << true << endl;
cout << false << endl;
```

produces as its output

```
1
0
```

If string notation is preferred over binary notation, use the manipulator `boolalpha`. For example, the code segment

```
cout << boolalpha << true << endl;
cout << false << endl;
```

produces as its output

```
true
false
```

The binary notation for **bool** objects can be restored using the manipulator `noboolalpha`.

The persistent manipulators `showbase` and `noshowbase` specify whether octal and hexadecimal numbers are displayed with identifying prefixes (the default is no identifying prefix). If manipulator `showbase` is used, then octal numbers are displayed with a leading 0 and hexadecimal numbers are displayed with a leading 0x. The use of identifying prefixes for subsequent insertions can be turned off with the manipulator `noshowbase`.

The persistent manipulators `showpos` and `noshowpos` do for positive numbers what `showbase` and `noshowbase` do for nondecimal displays. When invoked, manipulator `showpos` causes subsequent insertions of positive numbers to use the prefix +. This behavior can be turned off using the manipulator `noshowpos`.

These number-identifying manipulators are demonstrated in the following code segment:

```
cout << oct << showbase << 8 << " " << hex << 8
    << endl;
cout << dec << showpos << 8 << " " << noshowpos << 8
    << endl;
```

The segment produces as its output

```
010 0x8
+8 8
```

Manipulators `skipws` and `noskipws` are input stream manipulators. They control whether whitespace is ignored or extracted. As previously observed, the default C++ mode is to ignore whitespace. These manipulators are demonstrated in the following code segment:

```
char s1, t1, s2, t2, s3, t3;
cout << "Enter text: ";
cin >> s1 >> t1;
```

```
cout << "[" << s1 << "]" << endl;
cout << "[" << t1 << "]" << endl;
cin >> noskipws >> s2 >> t2;
cout << "[" << s2 << "]" << endl;
cout << "[" << t2 << "]" << endl;
cin >> skipws >> s3 >> t3;
cout << "[" << s3 << "]" << endl;
cout << "[" << t3 << "]" << endl;
```

If the code segment was run with a b c d e entered as input, the segment would have the following input/output behavior:

```
Enter text: a b c d e
[a]
[b]
[ ]
[c]
[d]
[e]
```

This behavior occurs because whitespace is initially ignored. Thus the whitespace between the a and b is ignored giving objects s1 and t2, the values 'a' and 'b'. The use of the manipulator noskipws causes the space before the c to be extracted. Thus objects s2 and t2 are assigned the values ' ' and 'c'. The subsequent use of manipulator skipws causes whitespace to again be ignored. Therefore, objects s3 and t3 are assigned the values 'd' and 'e'.

5.6 THE FSTREAM LIBRARY

In the Chapter 4, we developed a program that extracts values from the standard input stream cin and then displays the average of those values to the standard output stream cout. The program is reproduced below.

```
#include <iostream>
#include <string>
using namespace std;
int main() {
    cout << "Please provide list of numbers" << endl;
    int ValuesProcessed = 0;
    float ValueSum = 0;
    float Value;
    while (cin >> Value) {
        ValueSum += Value;
        ++ValuesProcessed;
    }
    if (ValuesProcessed > 0) {
        float Average = ValueSum / ValuesProcessed;
        cout << "Average: " << Average << endl;
    }
    else
        cout << "No list to average" << endl;
    return 0;
}
```

For a list with 10 or so values, running the program would be reasonable. But if we had a substantially larger list to process, we would like a program that gets its values from a file. By having the values in a file, their accuracy can

be checked and, if necessary, errant values can be corrected. Simil~
gram generates a significant amount of output, we would prob~
capture that output to a file so that we can review the information. Throu~
use of the standard library `fstream`, we can perform such file extractions and
insertions. The interface for the library is specified in the standard header file
`fstream`.

The fstream library defines stream class types `ifstream`, `ofstream`, and
`fstream`. Class `ifstream` is derived from the class `istream`. Class
`ifstream` creates input streams for extracting values from files. The class
`ofstream` is derived from the class `ostream`. Class `ofstream` creates output
streams for inserting values to files. The class `fstream` is for defining file-
oriented streams capable of both input and output. Class `fstream` is derived
from the class `iostream`.

Suppose we need an input stream `fin` for extracting values from the file
`mydata.nbr`. The desired stream can be created by defining an `ifstream`
object `fin` that uses the string `"mydata.nbr"` in its initialization.

```
ifstream fin("mydata.nbr");
```

As seen in the definition, the name of the file that we want to process is passed
as a string in defining the `ifstream` object. The definition sets up a correspondence between the stream `fin` and the file `mydata.nbr`.

Because class `ifstream` is derived from `istream`, the `istream` extraction operator `>>` is defined for `ifstream` objects. However, when the extraction operator is applied with an `ifstream` object, the data comes from the
associated file rather than from the standard input stream `cin`.

We can use both the iostream input manipulators and member functions,
as well as the iomanip input manipulators, on `ifstream` objects. Likewise, we
can use iostream output manipulators and member functions, as well as iomanip output manipulators, on `ofstream` objects.

For example, given the previous initialization of `fin`, the following statement extracts the next value from file `mydata.nbr`.

```
fin >> Value;
```

If we define an `ofstream` object, we can use it to capture insertions to a
file. In the following example, we associate `ofstream` object `fout` with the
file `average.nbr` and then insert the average of the inputs to that file. By
default, the file associated with the `ofstream` object is made empty during the
initialization of the object. This default behavior is known as *truncation mode*.

```
ofstream fout("average.nbr");
fout << Average << endl;
```

If we do not want the file that is to be the target of our insertions to lose its
current contents, then we need to specify an extra parameter in the stream definition. In particular, the extra parameter needs to indicate that *append mode* is
in effect. In append mode, insertions are added immediately after the existing
file contents. The way to express this parameter is with the expression

(ios_base::out | ios_base::app). The expression specifies two options—the file is to be opened for writing and insertions are to be appended to the end of the file. In the following definition, the output stream myout is associated with the file dataset.txt in such a manner.

```
ostream myout("dataset.txt",
  (ios_base::out | ios_base::app));
```

Given this definition, insertions to myout are added after the current contents of dataset.txt.

Using the fin and fout stream definitions, we can modify our average calculation program to extract values from file mydata.nbr and create a file average.nbr that holds the average of the inputs. The result is Program 5.2.

Program 5.2

Calculates average of a file of numbers

```cpp
// Program 5.2: Calculates average of file mydata.nbr
#include <fstream>
#include <string>
using namespace std;
int main() {
    ifstream fin("mydata.nbr");
    int ValuesProcessed = 0;
    float ValueSum = 0;
    float Value;
    while (fin >> Value) {
        ValueSum += Value;
        ++ValuesProcessed;
    }
    if (ValuesProcessed > 0) {
        ofstream fout("average.nbr");
        float Average = ValueSum / ValuesProcessed;
        fout << "Average: " << Average << endl;
    }
    else {
        cerr << "No list to average" << endl;
    }
    return 0;
}
```

The **while** loop of Program 5.2 iterates until there are no more values to extract from the stream fin. The loop test expression fin >> Value behaves similarly to the expression cin >> Value—the expression evaluates to true if and only if the extraction is successful. If an extraction is unsuccessful (i.e., there are no more values to extract), then the expression evaluates to false. We say that a stream with this property has reached *end of file*, or *eof* for short.

Sometimes a requested input or output file is wrongly supplied or unavailable for some reason. There is a method of checking whether this is the case. If the stream of interest can be used, a nonzero value (i.e., a logical true value) will be associated with it; otherwise, its value will be zero (i.e., a logical false value). The following code segment uses an **if** statement to test whether the input file is available before attempting an extraction.

```cpp
ifstream fin("mydata.nbr");
int Number;
if (fin) {
    fin >> Number;
```

```
        cout << Number << endl;
    }
    else {
        cout << "mydata.nbr is unavailable, 1 used "
          << endl;
        Number = 1;
    }
```

A way to achieve greater flexibility in file processing is to prompt the user for a filename and then process the file that the user specifies. The extraction of the filename could be done easily through the use of type `string`. However, the fstream library is not `string` aware, which means that the following code does not compile.

```
string s;
cout << "Enter name of file to process: ";
cin >> s;
ifstream fin(s);      // s is not a valid parameter
```

But string objects do have a member function `c_str()` that returns a representation of the string, which can be used wherever a conventional character string is expected. In particular, the representation returned by `c_str()` is valid for initializing an `ifstream` or `ofstream` object. Thus the correct way to initialize input stream `fin` is the following:

```
string FileName;
cout << "Enter name of file to process: ";
cin >> FileName;
ifstream fin(FileName.c_str());
```

Once we initialize `fin`, it is prudent to test that we have a valid stream for extracting values. As noted above, such a test can be made by examining the value of the `ifstream` object of interest. The following code segment performs such a test.

```
if (! fin) {
    cerr << "Cannot open " << FileName
      << " for averaging." << endl;
    exit(1);
}
// ready to process file stream represented by fin
```

If the initialization is not successful, an error message is generated and the program is exited. Function `exit()` is defined in the C-based `stdlib` library, which is a collection of miscellaneous utility functions. The header file for this library is `cstdilb`. When invoked, function `exit()` immediately terminates the program. The parameter to `exit()` is used as the program return value. Therefore, if the comment at the end of the code segment is reached, it must be the case that the expression (`! fin`) evaluates to false and that input stream `fin` represents a file that is available for processing. By adapting Program 5.2 and using this code segment, we can create a general-purpose average-calculating program. The resulting program is given as Program 5.3.

Objects of type `ifstream` and `ofstream` have several member functions. Two member functions of interest are `close()` and `open()`. Member function `close()`, when applied to a stream, indicates that the processing of the associated file is complete. For example, the following statements indicate that there are to be no more insertions or extractions to the files currently associated with fin and fout.

```
fin.close();
fout.close();
```

Invocations of close() are typically made only if new file associations will be assigned to the streams later.

Program 5.3

A general-purpose average calculator

```
// Program 5.3: Prompts user for a file and then calculates
// the average of the values in that file
#include <fstream>
#include <iostream>
#include <cstdlib>
#include <string>
using namespace std;

int main() {
    cout << "File of values to be averaged: ";
    string FileName;
    cin >> FileName;
    ifstream fin(FileName.c_str());
    if (! fin) {
        cerr << "Cannot open " << FileName
            << " for averaging." << endl;
        exit(1);
    }
    int ValuesProcessed = 0;
    float ValueSum = 0;
    float Value;
    while (fin >> Value) {
        ValueSum += Value;
        ++ValuesProcessed;
    }
    if (ValuesProcessed > 0) {
        float Average = ValueSum / ValuesProcessed;
        cout << "Average of values from " << FileName
            << " is " << Average << endl;
    }
    else {
        cerr << "No values to average in "
            << FileName << endl;
        exit(1);
    }
    return 0;
}
```

There are conceptually two versions of the member function open(). Both versions require a character string parameter representing the name of the file to be associated with the stream. One version also allows a second parameter that specifies the mode in which the file is to be opened (e.g., append).

The following code segment uses an ifstream object sin to process two different files. The first file, in1.txt, is associated with sin during its definition. The second file, in2.txt, becomes associated with sin as the result of an open() invocation. The processing of the two files is quite simple. The first file is copied to out1.txt by making insertions to sout. Stream sout is associated with out1.txt by a definition that uses the default truncation mode.

Programmer Alert

> ***Backslash backlash***
>
> Consider the following object definition:
>
> ```
> ifstream InStream("num\nbr.txt");
> ```
>
> If you are familiar with Windows, you would expect that the file being associated with object `InStream` is `nbr.txt`, which can be found in the directory `num`. However, this assumption is wrong. As literal backslash character sequences are interpreted by the preprocessor, the `\n` in the filename is interpreted as the newline character. So the file in question is supposed to contain a newline as its fourth character. Because the newline is an illegal character in an MS-DOS filename, `InStream` is improperly initialized. To achieve the correct initialization, we must use the `\\` literal sequence as in the following statement:
>
> ```
> ifstream InStream("num\\nbr.txt");
> ```

The second file is copied to `out2.txt` by associating `sout` to `out2.txt` with an `open()` invocation that specifies append mode.

```cpp
ifstream sin("in1.txt");      // extract from in1.txt
ofstream sout("out1.txt");    // insert to out1.txt
string s;
while (sin >> s) {
    sout << s << endl;
}
sin.close();                  // done with in1.txt
sout.close();                 // done with out1.txt
sin.open("in2.txt");          // now extract from in2.txt
sout.open("out2.txt",         // now append to out2.txt
  (ios_base::out | ios_base::app));
while (sin >> s) {
    sout << s << endl;
}
sin.close();                  // done with in2.txt
sout.close();                 // done with out2.txt
```

Observe that before `sin` is associated with `in2.txt`, the association with `in1.txt` is finished using an invocation of `close()`. Similarly, before the association of `out2.txt` with `sout`, the association with `out1.txt` is finished using an invocation of `close()`. The disassociations are necessary for the proper processing of `in1.txt` and `out2.txt`.

5.7 RANDOM NUMBERS

Random number sequences have an important role in many computer applications. For example, they are used in games to ensure that players do not experience the same situations each time they play the game. Random number sequences are also used in the design of complex systems such as a new highway. Before a highway is constructed, it is typically modeled and simulated on a computer. By using random number sequences that reflect the expected frequency and behavior of automobiles on the proposed highway, designers can estimate the impact of adding a lane or an interchange.

A particularly useful random number sequence is the *uniform random number sequence*. A uniform random number sequence has a specified set of numbers from which the sequence takes or *draws* its random numbers. In each position of the random number sequence, any number from the set is equally likely to occur.

Suppose you wanted to create a uniformly distributed random number sequence drawn from the set {1, 2, 3, 4, 5, 6}. One way to do so is to get a normal six-sided die that has each of its sides labeled with a different element from that set. When the die is thrown, one of its sides will be facing up after the throw. For any given throw, each side is equally likely to be facing up. The sequence of values appearing on the face-up side will be a uniform random number sequence from the set {1, 2, 3, 4, 5, 6}.

Because a random number sequence is supposed to be random, there cannot be any computer algorithm that iteratively computes truly random numbers. The instructions that constitute an algorithm are deterministic rules—knowing them tells you the next number. However, some functions do produce sequences of numbers that appear to be random. These sequences are properly called *pseudorandom number sequences*, although most people are imprecise and drop the prefix *pseudo*.

The C++ stdlib library provides two functions that are useful in generating pseudorandom number sequences. They are `rand()` and `srand()`, and they are declared in `stdlib.h`. Function `rand()` takes no parameters. Each time it is invoked, it returns a uniform pseudorandom number from the *inclusive* interval 0 to RAND_MAX, where RAND_MAX is an implementation-dependent preprocessor macro constant defined in `stdlib.h`. In most implementations of `rand()`, the generation of the current pseudorandom number is a function of the previously generated pseudorandom number. The generation of the first pseudorandom number by a program is based on a similar function of an initial value, called the *seed*, that is supplied to the pseudorandom number generator.

Program 5.4 displays five pseudorandom numbers through repeated invocations of function `rand()`.

Program 5.4

Displays five random numbers without using srand()

```
// Program 5.4: Display of pseudorandom numbers
#include <iostream>
#include <string>
#include <stdlib.h>
using namespace std;
int main() {
   for (int i = 1; i <= 5; ++i)
      cout << rand() << endl;
   return 0;
}
```

The program was run on a system where RAND_MAX equals 32,767. The output of the first run is as follows:

346
130

```
10982
1090
11656
```

The program was run a second time and produced the following output:

```
346
130
10982
1090
11656
```

That the two runs produce the same output is not a defect in the design of `rand()`. In fact, the repetition is part of the design of the function. By default, `rand()` always produces the same pseudorandom number sequence. That way, while a program is being tested or examined, it is possible to reproduce the same statement execution sequence.

To produce a different sequence of pseudorandom numbers, the function `srand()` is used. Function `srand()` expects an **unsigned int** as its parameter (the type modifier **unsigned** indicates that the value being represented does not use a sign bit in its representation, i.e., all values are nonnegative). The parameter is used to set the seed for generating the first pseudorandom number. Once the seed is set, `rand()` should produce a different sequence of pseudorandom numbers.

Program 5.5 is a modification of Program 5.4; in the new program, the user provides the seed value that is to be passed to `srand()`.

Program 5.5

Display five random numbers using prompted value for srand()

```
// Program 5.5: Display five pseudorandom numbers
#include <iostream>
#include <string>
#include <stdlib.h>
using namespace std;
int main() {
   cout << "Random number seed (number): ";
   unsigned int seed;
   cin >> seed;
   srand(seed);
   for (int i = 1; i <= 5; ++i)
      cout << rand() << endl;
   return 0;
}
```

The following is an example of the input/output behavior of Program 5.5.

```
Random number seed (number): 12
4155
30526
32049
23353
29576
```

Another run of Program 5.5 produced the following input/output behavior:

```
Random number seed (number): 13
4501
30310
10132
```

13461
7374

Program 5.6 is a modification of Program 5.5; the new program automatically generates the seed. Program 5.6 uses the current time as the basis for the seed value. By using the current time as the seed, the seed should be different for each run of the program, which, in turn, should produce a different sequence of numbers for each run. The current time is determined using the function `time()`, which is defined in the time standard library. Function `time()` returns a value of type `time_t`, which is an integral type that is also defined in the time library. If the value passed to function `time()` is zero, function `time()` supplies the current time through its return value.

Program 5.6

Automatic display of different pseudo-random number sequences

```cpp
// Program 5.6: Display pseudorandom numbers
#include <iostream>
#include <string>
#include <stdlib.h>
#include <time.h>
using namespace std;
int main() {
    srand((unsigned int) time(0));
    for (int i = 1; i <= 5; ++i)
        cout << rand() << endl;
    return 0;
}
```

The following is an example of the input/output behavior of Program 5.6.

1372
20765
3967
26247
6928

The following is a display of another run of Program 5.6.

7084
8706
20276
6944
8322

The following statement in Program 5.6 is an example of a C++ cast expression.

```cpp
srand((unsigned int) time(0));
```

A *cast expression* directs the compiler to convert the value of its operand to an explicit type. In this statement, the expression directs the compiler to convert the result of the call to `time()`, which is type `time_t`, to an **unsigned int**.

Casting expressions have several common uses. You have just seen one. In this example, the cast expression is actually not required as casting of argument functions would have handled the conversion. However, it is good programming practice to use the cast expression so that it is clear to other programmers that a conversion is taking place and that this conversion is intended.

Another common use of cast expressions is to prevent the use of integer addition that produces a truncated result. Suppose that we wanted to compute a batting average. A *batting average* is defined as the number of hits divided by the official number of times at bat. The following code fragment will not produce the correct results.

```
int AtBats = 3;
int NbrOfHits = 1;
float BattingAverage = NbrOfHits / AtBats;
```

The problem is that integer division truncates and `BattingAverage` is set to 0.0. One solution would be to define one of the objects, `AtBats` or `NmbrOf-Hits`, to be a floating-point type. However this solution is artificial because you cannot have a fractional number of at bats or number of hits. The best solution is to use a cast expression. By casting either operand of the division to type `float`, we can force the compiler to perform floating-point division.

```
float BattingAverage = ((float) NmbrOfHits) / AtBats;
```

The above statement correctly computes the average .333. There are a few other situations where cast expressions can help clarify the code. We will point these out as we encounter them.

We conclude this section by developing two functions that are very useful in applications that use random numbers to pick something at random from a selection of choices. One is a function that sets the random number seed so that a new random number sequence is generated each time the application is run. The other function generates a random number in a specified interval. We shall use these functions in several programming examples. Later, we will generalize and encapsulate the capability of generating random numbers in a user-defined class. Listing 5.1 contains the prototypes for these utility functions.

Listing 5.1

Header file uniform.h

```
// Interface to random number utility functions
#ifndef UNIFORM_H
#define UNIFORM_H
void InitializeSeed();
int Uniform(int Low, int High);
#endif
```

Function `InitializeSeed()` sets the random number seed. It uses the same statement as Program 5.6 to set the pseudorandom number generator seed. The purpose of function `Uniform()` is to produce a pseudorandom number from a specified interval. The interval is specified to the function via its two parameters `Low` and `High`. The name `Uniform` indicates that the numbers generated will be uniformly chosen from the specified interval. That is, each number in the interval is equally likely to be generated. Listing 5.2 contains the implementations of the two functions.

```
// Implementation of InitializeSeed and Uniform
#include <iostream>
#include <string>
#include <stdlib.h>
#include <time.h>
#include "uniform.h"
using namespace std;
// InitializeSeed(): set the random number generator seed
void InitializeSeed() {
   srand((unsigned int) time(0));
}
// Uniform(): generate a uniformly distributed random
// number between Low and High
int Uniform(int Low, int High) {
   if (Low > High) {
      cerr << "Illegal range passed to Uniform" << endl;
      exit(1);
   }
   else {
      int IntervalSize = High - Low + 1;
      int RandomOffset = rand() % IntervalSize;
      return Low + RandomOffset;
   }
}
```

The definition of `InitializeSeed()` is straightforward. It uses the same statement as function `main()` did in Program 5.6 to set the pseudorandom number generator seed. Function `Uniform()` is a bit more complicated. It first ensures that a valid interval has been specified, i.e., that `Low` is no bigger than `High`. If `Low` is bigger than `High`, an error message is issued and the function exits signaling an error.

If the interval is proper, the number of integers in the specified interval is then computed and assigned to `IntervalSize`.

```
int IntervalSize = High - Low + 1;
```

Next, a pseudorandom number produced by `rand()` is taken modulus `IntervalSize` and assigned to `RandomOffset`.

```
int RandomOffset = rand() % IntervalSize;
```

The expression `rand() % IntervalSize` produces pseudorandom numbers in the interval 0 to `IntervalSize - 1` in an equally likely manner. Because the value of `RandomOffset` is a pseudorandom number from the interval 0 to `IntervalSize - 1`, the value of the expression `Low + RandomOffset` is a pseudorandom number from the interval `Low` to `Low + IntervalSize - 1`. Because `IntervalSize` equals `High - Low + 1`, the expression `Low + IntervalSize - 1` equals `High`. Therefore, the value returned by `Uniform()` is a pseudorandom number from the interval `Low` to `High`.

5.8   THE ASSERT LIBRARY

The assert library provides a preprocessor macro `assert` that is useful during program development. The `assert` macro expects an integral expression as its single parameter. When an `assert` macro is invoked, its parameter expression is tested to see whether it has the value zero. If the expression is nonzero, the program continues in the normal fashion. If the expression is zero, the program produces a message to the standard error stream displaying the expression that caused the program to terminate, the name of the source file, and the line in that file where the failed `assert` expression occurred. After displaying the information, the program terminates.

The assert library is similar to math library in that it is a C-based library. Therefore, when including this library in a program, use `cassert`.

Program 5.7 uses an `assert` statement to make sure that the denominator it is processing is nonzero. Suppose the program is contained in the file `my.cpp`. If a zero is extracted for its object `Denominator`, then the `assert` macro will test to zero and the program will terminate after displaying an error message similar to the following:

`Assertion failed: Denominator, file my.cpp, line 12`

Assertion failure information, although useful to a programmer, is usually meaningless to a user. Thus the use of `assert` macros should not replace input validation or user-friendly error messages. Programmers normally use `assert` macros during debugging to help verify that their program logic is correct.

Program 5.7

Asserting a denominator is zero

```
// Program 5.7: Computes quotient and remainder of two
// inputs
#include <cassert>
#include <iostream>
#include <string>
using namespace std;
int main() {
    int Numerator;
    cout << "Enter numerator: ";
    cin >> Numerator;
    int Denominator;
    cout << "Enter denominator: ";
    cin >> Denominator;
    assert(Denominator); // really should be if test
    int Ratio = Numerator / Denominator;
    int Remainder = Numerator % Denominator;
    cout << Numerator << "/" << Denominator << " = "
      << Ratio << " with remainder " << Remainder << endl;
    return 0;
}
```

Self-check Questions

7. Explain what the statement

    `using namespace std;`

    accomplishes.

Controlling the evaluation of assert invocations

For the expression in an `assert` invocation to be evaluated, the macro NDE-BUG must be undefined. Thus the default behavior of an `assert` invocation is to evaluate assertions. Through the use of the following preprocessor statement, the evaluation of subsequent assertions can be turned off.

```
#define NDEBUG
```

In some implementations, evaluation of assertions can be turned on again through the use of the following preprocessor statement:

```
#undef NDEBUG
```

This process works because the actions performed by an assert invocation are nested within a conditional evaluation directive that checks whether NDEBUG is defined.

It is normal practice to include the definition of NDEBUG at the start of a program that is distributed to users.

8.   Assume that a `namespace` directive for `iostream` has not been used in a program module, but the programmer needs to write the string "Fatal Error" to the stream `cout`. Give the C++ statement to do this.

9.   What are the names of the two streams used for displaying and recording error messages?

10.   Give a C++ statement that inserts into stream `cout` the octal representation of the **int** object HeadCount.

11.   The manipulators `oct`, `dec`, and `hex` are said to be persistent. What does this mean?

12.   What does the following code fragment output?
```
int i = 16;
int j = 25;
int k = 56;
cout << hex << i << endl;
cout << oct << j << "" << dec << k << endl;
```

13.   What does the following code fragment output?
```
cout << "123456789" << endl;
cout << setw(10) << "Hello" << endl;
cout << "Good bye" << endl;
```

14.   What does the following code fragment output?
```
int k = 3;
cout << setfield('$') << setw(5) << k << endl;
```

15.   What does the following code fragment output?

```
cout << "123456789" << endl;
cout << "$" << left << setw(5) << "z" << "$"
  << endl;
cout << "$" << left << setw(4) << "z" << "$"
  << endl;
```

16.   What does the following code fragment output?

```
cout << "123456789" << endl;
cout << "$" << right << setw(5) << "z" << "$"
  << endl;
cout << "$" << right << setw(4) << "z" << "$"
  << endl;
```

17.   What does the following code fragment output?

```
bool Yes = true;
cout << noboolalpha << Yes << endl;
```

18.   What does the following code fragment output?

```
int i = 16;
int j = 25;
int k = 56;
cout << setbase(16) << i << endl;
cout << setbase(8) << j << " " << setbase(10) << k
  << endl;
```

19.   What does the following code fragment output?

```
int i = 16;
cout << showpos << i << endl;
```

20.   What does the following code fragment output?

```
int i = 16;
cout << oct << showbase << i << endl;
```

21.   What is the name of the stdlib function that returns a pseudorandom integer?

22.   What is the name of the stdlib function that sets the seed value for the random number generator.

23.   Write a program that simulates flipping a coin 1,000 times and reports the percentage of time heads occurred.

24.   Write a program that reads integers from a file named `data.txt`. The program should output a count of the odd numbers in the file. The output should look like the following.

```
There are 25 odd number(s) in the file data.txt
```

25.   Write a statement using the assert macro that will cause an assertion error if the **int** object Count is 0.

26.   Write a statement using the assert macro that will issue an assertion error if the **int** function Index returns a negative number.

5.9   POINTS TO REMEMBER

History of Computing

Punch card computing

The U.S. census department must perform a census every 10 years. In 1880 the actual head count required only a few months, but tabulating and analyzing the data took nine years to complete. Recognizing a problem in need of a solution, Herman Hollerith developed a system that used punched cards and special machines that could tabulate the data recorded on the cards. The system was quite simple. Data about a person, such as age, sex, and marital status, were recorded on a card by punching holes in the proper positions. The data on the card were counted by a machine operated by a human. The card was placed in a reader station. The operator applied a press containing pins that corresponded to each possible position where a hole could be punched. In locations where a hole was punched, a pin would make contact with a connection on the other side of the card and a counter would be incremented.

Through various trials and tests, Hollerith's system proved to be a vast improvement over previous tabulation methods. Hollerith formed a company, called the Tabulating Machine Company, and rented machines to the census department to perform the 1890 census. The tally of the total number of people in the United States was available six weeks after the head count began, and the final statistics were available in seven years. A two-year reduction may not seem like much of an improvement, but the 1890 census included a far more thorough and detailed analysis of the raw data.

Hollerith's system was featured on the cover of the August 1890 issue of *Scientific American*, and it was adopted by countries all over Europe. Eventually, companies began using the system to do accounting and inventory. Hollerith's company experienced phenomenal growth and eventually merged with several others; it ultimately became one of the giants in the computing industry, International Business Machines (IBM).

✔ Software reuse is important if programs are to be developed quickly and efficiently. One of the major sources of software is the standard libraries.

✔ C++ provides a significant number of libraries for a variety of application areas. Some of the more important stream libraries are the iostream, iomanip, and fstream libraries. These libraries provide mechanisms for inserting and extracting information in a controlled manner.

✔ A header file is a collection of function interfaces, constant and variable object definitions, and class descriptions. The header file is incorporated into the program through an include directive.

✔ Information to a function is passed via parameters. The function's computation is normally brought back as the return value. The type of value brought back by a function is the return type. A function that does not return a value has the type **void**.

✔ The parameters in the invocation are called the actual parameters. The actual parameters are represented in the invoked function by its formal parameters.

✔ When a function is invoked, flow of control is transferred from the invoking function to the invoked function. When the invoked function completes, control is transferred back to the invoking function. If the invoked function returns a value, then that value is essentially substituted for the invocation.

✔ Every function invocation creates an activation record. The values of the formal parameters and other objects defined in the function are kept in the activation record.

✔ Before a function is invoked, it must be prototyped or defined. A prototype is a description of the function's interface. A function definition contains both a description of the function's interface and its statement body. A description of the interface specifies the return type, function name, and the form of the parameter list.

✔ One way of passing actual parameters is the pass-by-value parameter-passing style. When an actual parameter is passed in this style, the formal parameter is called a value parameter because it is initialized to the value of the actual parameter. Subsequent changes to the formal parameter do not affect the actual parameter.

✔ All the standard libraries have header files that prototype the functions defined in those libraries. Depending on the library, the header file may also contain object, class, and function definitions.

✔ When including a standard library in a program, it is also standard practice to have the statement

```
using namespace std;
```

If this statement is not included then each reference to the library must be prepended with std::.

✔ The preprocessor is responsible for processing three kinds of commands in a program file. The file inclusion directives specify files that are to be part of the translation unit that is to be compiled. Macro definitions and invocations provide textual substitution. Conditional compilation directives allow a programmer to restrict the lines of code that are compiled.

✔ A hierarchy of classes exists for representing input and output streams. The root of this hierarchy is the class ios_base.

✔ Two important stream classes are istream and ostream. Class istream is a root of the subhierarchy for input streams; class ostream is a root of the subhierarchy for output streams.

✔ Classes ifstream and ofstream are for defining streams that manipulate files. These streams process extractions and insertions, respectively.

✔ Classes iostream and fstream define streams capable of both extractions and insertions.

✔ The iostream library defines two streams for error messages. Stream cerr is for unbuffered error messages; stream clog is for buffered error messages.

✔ The iostream library also defines manipulators for specifying how to perform stream insertions and extractions.

✔ A manipulator that controls successive I/O operations is persistent.

✔ The iostream manipulators dec, oct, and hex control the base in which numbers are displayed.

✔ The iostream manipulator flush causes the contents of the output buffer to be displayed immediately.

✔ The iomanip library also provides stream manipulators. Two of its important manipulators are setw() and setprecision(), which allow the width and precision of an insertion to be specified.

✔ The iostream manipulators fixed and scientific control whether a numeric value is displayed in decimal or scientific notation.

✔ The iostream manipulators skipws and noskipws control whether whitespace is extractable using the insertion operator.

✔ The assert library defines an assert macro that enables an integral expression to be evaluated. If the expression is false, the program is terminated. If the expression is true, program execution continues in a normal manner. The assert library is a C-based library. To include the library, we use either header file cassert or header file assert.h.

✔ The stdlib library is a collection of miscellaneous utility functions. To include the library, we use either header file cstdlib or header file stdlib.h.

✔ The stdlib library function exit(), when invoked, immediately terminates the program. The parameter to exit() is used as the program return value.

✔ The stdlib library provides a function rand() that returns a pseudorandom number from the interval 0 through RAND_MAX, where RAND_MAX is a stdlib constant.

✔ The stdlib library provides a function srand() to alter the sequence of pseudorandom numbers that can be obtained through the use of rand(). The function invocation srand((**unsigned int**) time(0)) should initiate a different pseudorandom number sequence for each invocation.

✔ Cast expressions explicitly convert one type to another.

✔ A cast expression is useful when the programmer wants to force the compiler to perform a particular type of operation, such as floating-point division rather than integer division.

✔ A cast expression is useful for converting values that library functions return to the appropriate type. This feature signals other programmers that the conversion was intended and avoids unnecessary warnings from the compiler.

5.10 TO DELVE FURTHER

The description of the functions and components of the various libraries in this chapter is adapted from the following sources:

- B. Stroustrup, *The C++ Programming Language: Third Edition*, Reading, MA: Addison-Wesley, 1998.

- X3 Secretariat, *Draft Standard — The C++ Language*, X3J16/97-14882, Washington, DC: Information Technology Council (NSITC), 1997.

- P. J. Plauger, *The Standard C Library*, Englewood Cliffs, NJ: Prentice-Hall, 1992.

5.11 EXERCISES

5.1 Suppose you must create a library to facilitate computer-assisted telephone calls. What functions should be in the library to support client applications?

5.2 Suppose you must create a library to facilitate computer-assisted checkbook management. What functions should be in the library to support client applications?

5.3 Specify two application areas other than telephony and checkbook management where computing assistance is appropriate. What functions should be in these libraries to support client applications?

5.4 Search the directories on your system to find where the header files are stored.

5.5 Discuss flow of control.

5.6 Speculate on possible parameter-passing styles other than pass by value. Discuss how they could be effective.

5.7 Most operating systems designate one character as the end-of-file character. This character is different from the iostream **int** constant EOF. When this character is reached in standard input, the user is indicating that there are no more input values to follow. On most PC-based systems, the end of file character is Ctrl+z. On many other systems, it is Ctrl+d. Determine the end-of-file character on your system. Indicate how you determined it.

5.8   Suppose a `cout` output request was unsuccessful; that is, it returned zero. What could cause such an event? How could you inform the user of the program?

5.9   Prototype a function `QuarticRoot()` that takes a double-precision floating-point value `x` as its parameter and returns a value of that same type.

5.10   Prototype a function `Area()` that takes two integer values `width` and `height` and returns an integer result.

5.11   Prototype a function `IsMathSymbol()` that takes a character value `c` and returns a Boolean value.

5.12   Prototype a function `GetNumber()` that does not take any parameters and returns an integer.

5.13   Prototype a function that returns the volume of a specified sphere.

5.14   Prototype a function that returns the speed of an object starting at rest that accelerates at a specified rate for a specified number of seconds.

5.15   Prototype a function that converts a Celsius temperature to a Fahrenheit temperature.

5.16   Prototype a function that displays five spaces to the standard output stream `cout`.

5.17   Prototype a function that displays a specified number of spaces to the standard output stream `cout`.

5.18   What is a persistent manipulator? Speculate why `setw()` was not designed to be a persistent manipulator.

5.19   Determine whether your implementation of the iostream library displays a **float** number by default in decimal or scientific notation. Does the default behavior have anything to do with how big or how small the number is? Does the default behavior have anything to do with where the most significant digit is found?

5.20   Modify Program 5.1 so that it correctly processes quadratic equations whose roots are imaginary or whose coefficient a is zero.

5.21   Is Program 5.1 a candidate for having its input coming from a file stream? Why?

5.22   Modify Program 5.3 so that the input comes from a user-specified file.

5.23   Should a program prompt a user for an input value using stream `cout` or `cerr`? Give reasons for the possible use of either stream.

5.24   What is the output of the following program? Why?

```cpp
int main () {
    cout << "12345678901234567890" << endl;
    cout << setw(5) << 100 << endl;
    cout << 100 << endl;
    cout << setprecision(4) << 71.498000000001
      << endl;
    cout << setfill('0');
    cout << setw(10) << 88 << endl;
    cout << setw(20) << "Hello World" << endl;
```

```
        return 0;
    }
```

5.25 Write C++ expressions for the following formulas. Use functions from the math library described in Appendix B.

a) $(\sin x)^2 \times (\cos x)^2$

b) $e^{\frac{1}{2}\sqrt{\tan \cos x}}$

c) $\dfrac{\left\lfloor \log\left(\dfrac{x^2}{1-x}\right) \right\rfloor}{\left\lceil x^{5+x} \right\rceil}$

5.26 Write a program that displays the following strings to standard output. The strings should be displayed one per line with each line centered within a field length that is extracted from standard input.

```
Greetings earth inhabitants
Take me to your leaders
Is that all there is
It is not our fault
```

5.27 Implement a program that extracts a character from standard input and then inserts a nicely displayed and labeled table to standard output. The information in the table is the values produced by the various functions in the ctype library (see Appendix B) when invoked with the extracted character as the parameter.

5.28 Rewrite your solution to Exercise 5.27 so that its output is inserted to the file ctype.tbl.

5.29 Implement a program without any loops that extracts five input values. The program displays these values in histogram form using asterisks. For example, if the input is

```
5 9 4 12 7
```

then the output should be

```
 5: *****
 9: *********
 4: ****
12: ************
 7: *******
```

Hint: Use the iostream to modify the fill character.

5.30 Rewrite your solution to Exercise 5.29 so that setw() is the only stream manipulator used. You may use loops but no strings.

5.31 Design and implement a program that prompts a user for a filename and string. The program then counts the numbers of occurrences of that string in the specified file.

5.32 Design and implement a program that prompts a user for the sides a, b, and c of a triangle, and if these sides do represent a triangle, the program displays the area of that triangle. The sides represent a valid triangle if the sum of the lengths for any two sides is greater than the length of the remaining side. The area of a triangle can be computed from its sides using the formula

$$\sqrt{s \cdot (s - a) \cdot (s - b) \cdot (s - c)}$$

where s is half of the sum of the sides (i.e., it is half the perimeter).

5.33   Design and implement a program that prompts a user for a starting amount and a number of years. The program determines the percentage rate that allows the amount to double in the required number of years.

5.34   Design and implement a program that prompts a user for a starting amount and a percentage rate. The program determines how many years are necessary for the amount to double given the percentage rate.

5.35   Is the starting amount a necessary input for Exercises 5.33 and 5.34? Explain.

5.36   Write a program that copies the characters in standard input stream `cin` to standard output stream `cout` except for the alphanumeric characters, which are to be ignored.

5.37   Write a program that copies the characters in standard input stream `cin` to standard output stream `cout` except for the digit characters. For a digit character, the program instead displays the digit's name; that is, zero for 0, one for 1, and so on.

5.38   Write a program that copies the characters in standard input stream `cin` to standard output stream `cout` while replacing all whitespace characters with the corresponding escape code. For example, if the input contains a tab, then the character `\t` is inserted.

5.39   Write a program that draws blue `RectangleShapes` at random locations in a `SimpleWindow`. The `RectangleShapes` should have random sizes.

5.40   Write a program that draws `RectangleShapes` at random locations in a `SimpleWindow`. The `RectangleShapes` should have random sizes and colors.

5.41   Write a program that translates normal text into Pig Latin. Pig Latin translates words in the following way: words that start with consonants have the consonants stripped and added as a suffix along with the string "ay"; words that start with a vowel are appended with the string "ay". Sample input/output behavior of the program follows.

```
Enter sentence:
    You speak great Pig Latin
Translation:
    Ou-yay eak-spay eat-gray Ig-pay Atin-lay
```

In implementing the program, you should use string object member functions `front()` and `erase()`. For a string s, `s.front()` returns the value of the first character in the string, and `s.erase(0)` removes the first character from `s`.

The next two exercises are based on formulas given by the U.S. National Weather Service. [†]

5.42 The wind chill factor is the perceived temperature when taking temperature and wind into account. The standard formula for wind chill factor is $0.0817(3.71\sqrt{Wind} + 5.81 - 0.25\sqrt{Wind})(Temp - 91.4) + 91.4$, where *Wind* is the current wind speed in miles per hour and *Temp* is the current Fahrenheit temperature. Write a program that prompts its user for a Fahrenheit temperature and a wind speed. The program reports back to the user the wind chill value for the supplied temperature-wind combination.

5.43 Heat index is the perceived temperature taking temperature T and relative humidity R into account. The formula for Fahrenheit heat index is

$$16.293 + 0.185212 \cdot T + 5.37941 \cdot R - 0.100254 \cdot T \cdot R$$
$$+ 9.41695\text{e}{-}3 \cdot T^2 + 7.28898\text{e}{-}3 \cdot R^2 - 3.45372\text{e}{-}4 \cdot T^2 \cdot R$$
$$- 8.14971\text{e}{-}4 \cdot T \cdot R^2 + 1.02102\text{e}{-}5 \cdot T^2 \cdot R^2 - 3.8646\text{e}{-}5 \cdot T^3$$
$$+ 2.91583\text{e}{-}5 \cdot R^3 + 1.42721\text{e}{-}6 \cdot T^3 \cdot R + 1.97483\text{e}{-}7 \cdot T \cdot R^3$$
$$- 2.18429\text{e}{-}6 \cdot T^3 \cdot R^2 + 8.43296\text{e}{-}10 \cdot T^2 \cdot R^3 - 4.81975\text{e}{-}11 \cdot T^3 \cdot R^3$$

Write a program that prompts its user for a Fahrenheit temperature and a relative humidity. The program should compute powers of T and R using `pow()`. The program reports back to the user the heat index value for the supplied temperature-relative humidity combination. The program should display an alert if the heat index is greater than 90, a warning if the heat index is greater than 100, and a severe warning if the heat index is greater than 110.

5.44 The formula for computing interest compounded on an annual basis is as follows:

$$StartingAmount \cdot (1 + InterestRate / 100)^{Years}$$

Write a program that prompts its users for the amount of deposit, the interest rate, and the term of deposit. After extracting these values, the program then computes and displays how the principal will change.

[†] Note that the formulas are approximations that are intended for normal temperature ranges.

CHAPTER 6

Programmer-defined functions

Introduction

Chapter 5 explored the use of library functions to accomplish tasks. However, any significant software project also requires that new functions be designed and implemented. In this chapter, we consider the basics of programmer-defined functions with value parameters. Our examination includes a discussion of invocation, parameters, and the local and global scopes.

Key Concepts

- programmer-defined functions
- invocation and flow of control
- parameters
- prototypes
- activation records
- return statement
- local object
- scope
- global objects
- name reuse
- implementation file
- header file

- standard class `ostringstream`
- standard class `istringstream`
- class `Label`
- Standard Template Library (STL)
- reference parameters
- constant parameters
- default parameters
- function overloading
- function overload resolution
- side effects
- recursion

6.1 BASICS

Using existing software libraries to accomplish programming tasks is the pre-ferred problem-solving strategy. This preference reflects the expectation that library use will be cost-effective with respect to both time and money. How-ever, for most software tasks using only library functions is not possible—it is also necessary to create programmer-defined functions.

Besides being concerned with correctness and efficiency when you design your own functions, you must also be concerned with software reuse. Reuse helps to minimize the expenses of maintenance and future projects.

With the exception of one program that demonstrates the use of global objects, the functions that we design in this chapter have two properties:

- External information to be used by a function comes from its value parameter list or by extractions from an input stream.

- Information to be communicated from a function is sent through its return value or by insertions to a output stream.

Such control over the information flow makes it easier for a function to be implemented and understood. This information flow is depicted in Figure 6.1.

Figure 6.1

Model for flow of information to and from a function using value parameters

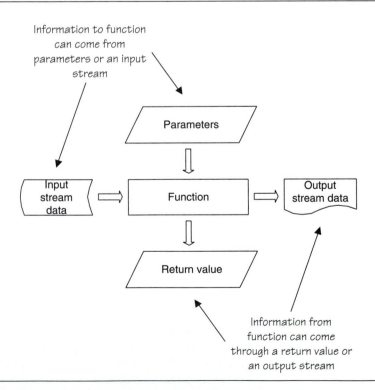

6.1.1 Function definition syntax

A *function definition* includes both a description of the interface and the statement list that comprises its actions. Since C++ allows multiple functions to have the same name, giving the function name alone is insufficient for a complete and unambiguous definition. Instead, C++ uses the entire interface, including the names and types of the formal parameters, to indicate which function is being defined.

Program 6.1 contains the definition of a function `CircleArea()`. This function computes the area of a circle, and it is invoked by function `main()` in that same program. Function `CircleArea()` has a single **float** parameter r and has a **float** return type.

Program 6.1

*Calling a user-defined
function from main()*

```
// Program 6.1: Compute area of a user-specified circle
#include <iostream>
#include <string>
using namespace std;

// CircleArea(): compute area of circle of radius r
float CircleArea(float r) {
    const float Pi = 3.1415;
    return Pi * r * r;
}

// main(): manage computation and display of the area of
// a user-specified circle
int main() {
    // prompt and read the radius
    float DesiredRadius;
    cout << "Circle radius (number): ";
    cin >> DesiredRadius;

    // compute the area
    float Area = CircleArea(DesiredRadius);
    cout << "Area of circle with radius "
         << DesiredRadius << " is " << Area << endl;

    // all done
    return 0;
}
```

As in previous examples using a function `main()`, the actions to be performed by a function are given in the function body. The *function body* is a statement list that is nested within left and right curly braces. The body of function `CircleArea()` from the definition in Program 6.1 is

```
    const float Pi = 3.1415;
    return Pi * r * r;
```

There are no restrictions on what kind of statements can be used in a function body. Any statement that would be permissible in function `main()` is permissible in any other function. The first statement defines an approximation `Pi` to the mathematical constant π. The next statement is the **return** statement for the function. It makes use of constant `Pi` and the circle area formula πr^2 to compute a **float** expression that corresponds to the area of a circle with a radius specified by parameter r.

A function uses a **return** statement to indicate that its task is completed. If the function return type is non-**void**, the statement also supplies the function's return value to the invoker of the function. A **return** statement has the form

For non-void functions, this value is returned to the invoking function; for void functions, it is empty

return *ReturnExpression* ;

where *ReturnExpression* evaluates to a value whose type should be the same as the return type that is specified in the interface for the function. (If the type of *ReturnExpression* is not the same as the return type, conversions are automatically attempted to transform the value of *ReturnExpression* to the return type.) For function CircleArea(), the return value is the value of the **float** expression Pi * r * r. Once a *ReturnExpression* is computed, execution continues at the invocation using the value of *ReturnExpression*.

Although it is not necessary, functions of type **void** can use **return** statements. In a **void** function, a **return** statement is an explicit indication that the function is finished and that flow of control should return to the function that did the call. The **return** statement for a **void** function is not permitted to have an expression.

6.1.2 Invocation and flow of control

As with library function invocations, the correspondence between the actual parameters in an invocation and the formal parameters of a programmer-defined function is determined by the relative positions of the parameters. The first actual parameter is associated with the first formal parameter, the second actual parameter is associated with the second formal parameter, and so on.

For function main() in Program 6.1, its activation record includes the objects DesiredRadius and Area. Suppose that the value extracted for DesiredRadius is 10 and that in terms of the execution of main() we are about to execute the definition of Area. A depiction of a snapshot of the activation record of main() follows. (A question mark indicates that the object's value has not yet been set by the program.)

main()	
DesiredRadius	10.000
Area	?

When function CircleArea() is invoked to initialize Area, an activation record is also created for it. In that activation record, formal parameter r is initialized to the value of the actual parameter, which in this case is the value of

DesiredRadius. The activation record for this invocation has the following depiction:

CircleArea()	
r	10.0000
Pi	3.1415

Because the formal parameter r is a value parameter, once DesiredRadius has been used to initialize r, DesiredRadius and r are independent of each other. Whenever r is used in CircleArea(), the value used for r is the one stored in the current activation record for the function. If CircleArea() were to make a change to r, the change would occur within the memory of CircleArea()'s current activation record and object DesiredRadius would be unaffected. Essentially, formal parameter r is an object that is *local* to function CircleArea(). The parameter is created with an invocation of CircleArea(), and it is destroyed when function CircleArea() completes and releases its activation record memory.

For our invocation of CircleArea(), the return value is 314.15, and this value is used to initialize Area. At that point, main()'s activation record has the following depiction:

main()	
DesiredRadius	10.000
Area	314.150

As noted in Chapter 5, an invocation cannot appear until the function being invoked has been prototyped or defined. In Program 6.1, the definition of function CircleArea() occurs before the definition of function main(). This ordering allows main() to invoke CircleArea(). Although CircleArea() is defined before main(), program execution begins in main().

6.2   A TASTY PROBLEM

Suppose we are interested in computing the size of a donut. For our purposes, a donut is a cylinder with a cylindrical core removed. This shape is demonstrated in Figure 6.2.

The size of a cylinder with radius r and height h is given by the formula $\pi r^2 h$. Based on our experience of computing the size of a circle, computing

Programming Tip

Constant value parameters

With one exception, the functions that we define in this chapter effectively use their formal parameters as constants that are initialized using the actual parameters. Because the formal parameters are used in this manner, we could have declared them to be **const** value parameters. For example, the following code segment defines function CircleArea() using a **const** parameter declaration.

```
float CircleArea(const float r) {
    const float Pi = 3.1415;
    return Pi * r * r;
}
```

In previous situations, when an object was not to be changed, we applied the **const** modifier to provide extra information to the compiler and to the client programmer. However, in this context we are giving information to the client regarding the implementation of the function that is not needed—the client cares only that the function does its job and that the actual parameter not be modified. Making the formal parameter a value parameter is generally sufficient to handle client concerns.

Figure 6.2

A donut can be approximated as a cylinder with a cylindrical core removed

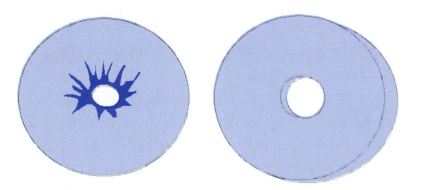

---

the size of a cylinder is straightforward. We use the function CylinderVolume():

```
// CylinderVolume(): compute the size of a cylinder
// with radius r and height h
float CylinderVolume(float r, float h) {
    const float Pi = 3.1415;
    return Pi * r * r * h;
}
```

The size of a donut can be calculated by taking the difference in the sizes of two cylinders. Function DonutSize() does this job for us. This function expects the radii of two corresponding cylinders as its parameters, along with the thickness of the donut, and returns the difference in the cylinder volumes defined by those parameters.

```
// DonutSize(): compute the size of a donut with
// outer edge radius Outer from the donut center,
// inner edge radius Inner from the donut center,
// and thickness Width
float DonutSize(float Outer, float Inner, float
  Width) {
    float OuterSize = CylinderVolume(Outer, Width);
    float HoleSize = CylinderVolume(Inner, Width);
    return OuterSize - HoleSize;
}
```

Note that just as the invocation of `CircleArea()` in Program 6.1 requires that memory be set aside for an activation record to store the value associated with its parameter r, so do invocations of `DonutSize()` and `CylinderVolume()` require that memory be set aside for activation records to store the values of the parameters and objects that they use.

When the `DonutSize()` parameter initialization is completed parameters `Outer` and `Inner` are independent of the objects or expressions used to initialize them. As discussed previously, this independence is a characteristic of value parameter passing. Inside `DonutSize()`, we are free to use `Outer`, `Inner`, and `Width` as **float** objects. In particular, we can use them in function invocations. Thus in the definition of `OuterSize`, there is no problem using `Outer` and `Width` to initialize parameters r and h in the first invocation of `CylinderVolume()`. Likewise, in the definition of `HoleSize`, there is no problem using `Inner` and `Width` to initialize the parameters of `Cylinder-Volume()` in its second invocation.

The two invocations of `CylinderVolume()` by `DonutSize()` do require that `CylinderVolume()` be previously defined or prototyped in the program file. In Program 6.2, our complete solution to the donut problem, `Cylinder-Volume()` is prototyped before `DonutSize()` is defined.

In Program 6.2, we follow convention and define function `main()` before defining other functions. We also follow the convention of placing prototypes of the other functions defined in the program file prior to the definition of the `main()`. Because C++ allows a function to be used as soon as it has been prototyped, placing these prototypes at the beginning of the program file enables us to define `DonutSize()` and `CylinderVolume()` in any order.

The prototyping of `CylinderVolume()` calls the parameters `Radius` and `Width`, even though the definition of `CylinderVolume()` uses r and h. This difference is perfectly fine—a prototype declaration describes only the form of a function's interface. As remarked in Chapter 5, supplying identifier names is optional in a prototype—specifying the types of the formal parameters is sufficient. However, supplying a meaningful name helps programmers understand the code. Because most software development effort is spent modifying existing code, making code easy to understand should pay off.

We now trace through a sample run of the program. Suppose the dimensions extracted for `OuterEdge`, `InnerEdge`, and `Thickness` are 2.5, 0.5, and

Program 6.2

Computing the area of
a donut through user-
defined functions

```cpp
// Program 6.2: Compute size of a user-specified donut
#include <iostream>
#include <string>
using namespace std;

// prototyping
float DonutSize(float Outer, float Inner, float Width);
float CylinderVolume(float Radius, float Width);

// main(): manage computation and display of user-
// specified donut size
int main() {
    // prompt for donut dimensions
    cout << "Outer edge donut radius: ";
    float OuterEdge;
    cin >> OuterEdge;
    cout << "Hole radius: ";
    float InnerEdge;
    cin >> InnerEdge;
    cout << "Donut thickness: ";
    float Thickness;
    cin >> Thickness;

    // compute and display the size of our donut
    cout << endl << "Size of donut with" << endl
     << "    radius " << OuterEdge << endl
     << "    hole radius " << InnerEdge << endl
     << "    thickness " << Thickness << endl
     << "is "
     << DonutSize(OuterEdge, InnerEdge, Thickness)
     << endl;

    return 0;
}

// DonutSize(): compute the size of a donut with outer
// edge radius Outer from the donut center, inner edge
// radius Inner from the donut center, and thickness
// Width
float DonutSize(float Outer, float Inner, float Width) {
    float OuterSize = CylinderVolume(Outer, Width);
    float HoleSize = CylinderVolume(Inner, Width);
    return OuterSize - HoleSize;
}

// CylinderVolume(): compute the size of a cylinder with
// radius r and height h
float CylinderVolume(float r, float h) {
    const float Pi = 3.1415;
    return Pi * r * r * h;
}
```

0.75, respectively. After the three extractions, the activation record for function
`main()` has the following depiction:

main()	
OuterEdge	2.5000
InnerEdge	0.5000
Thickness	0.7500

The invocation of DonutSize() in the insertion statement causes a temporary transfer of control to a copy of function DonutSize(). The parameters Outer, Inner, and Width are initialized using the values 2.5 from Outer-Edge, 0.5 from InnerEdge, and 0.75 from Thickness. The activation record associated with this invocation of DonutSize() after parameter initialization has the following depiction:

DonutSize()	
Outer	2.5000
Inner	0.5000
Width	0.7500
OuterSize	?
HoleSize	?

The initialization of Outer causes a temporary transfer of control from DonutSize() to a copy of CylinderVolume(). The parameters r and h of CylinderVolume() are initialized using the values 2.5 and 0.75 of Outer and Width.

CylinderVolume()	
r	2.500
h	0.750

After defining Pi, CylinderVolume() computes and returns the value of expression Pi * r * r * h, which is approximately 14.7258. The return causes control to be transferred back to DonutSize() and the memory for CylinderVolume()'s activation record to be released. The activation record for DonutSize() now has the following depiction:

DonutSize()	
Outer	2.5000
Inner	0.5000
Width	0.7500
OuterSize	14.7258
HoleSize	?

The initialization of Inner in DonutSize() causes another temporary transfer of control from DonutSize() to a copy of CylinderVolume(). The parameters r and h of CylinderVolume() are now initialized using the values 0.5 and 0.75 of Inner and Width.

CylinderVolume()	
r	0.500
h	0.750

After defining Pi, CylinderVolume() computes and returns the value of expression Pi * r * r * h, which for this invocation is approximately 0.5890. The return causes control to be transferred back to DonutSize() and the memory for CylinderVolume()'s activation record to be released. The activation record for DonutSize() now has the following depiction:

DonutSize()	
Outer	2.500
Inner	0.500
Width	0.750
OuterSize	14.7258
HoleSize	0.5890

The return statement of DonutSize() is then executed. The return expression has value 14.1368. The return causes the activation record memory of DonutSize() to be released and control transferred back to main(), which uses the value 14.1368 in its insertion statement.

The input/output behavior of this tracing through Program 6.2 follows.

```
Outer edge donut radius: 2.5
Hole radius: 0.5
Donut thickness: 0.75
Size of donut with
     radius 2.5
     hole radius 0.5
     thickness 0.75
is 14.1368
```

6.3   SOME USEFUL FUNCTIONS

Two useful functions for many programs are Max() and Min(). For current purposes, both functions return an **int** value and require two **int** parameters. Function Max() returns the larger value of its two parameters, and Min() returns the smaller value of its two parameters.

Function `Max()` can be implemented in the following manner:

```
// Max(): determine larger of its two parameters
int Max(int a, int b) {
    if (a < b)
        return b;
    else
        return a;
}
```

The function begins by comparing the values of its two parameters. If the expression a < b, which tests whether parameter a is less than parameter b, is true, then b is the larger of the values and the value of b is returned. If the test a < b is instead false, then a is no smaller than b, so the value of a is returned. The preceding function demonstrates that a function can have more than one **return** statement.

The implementation of function `Min()` is similar to the implementation of function `Max()`. The only change is using the > operator rather than the < operator to compare the values of the two parameters.

```
// Min(): determine smaller of its two parameters
int Min(int a, int b) {
    if (a > b)
        return b;
    else
        return a;
}
```

Suppose we are required to prompt and extract two input values and then indicate the larger of the two values and the smaller of the two values. The following code segment using `Max()` and `Min()` accomplishes this task.

```
cout << "Please enter a number (integer): ";
int Value1;
cin >> Value1;
cout << "Please enter a number (integer): ";
int Value2;
cin >> Value2;
cout << "Max: " << Max(Value1, Value2) << endl;
cout << "Min: " << Min(Value1, Value2) << endl;
```

As noted previously, the actual parameters in the invocation of a function do not need to have the same name as the formal parameters. The correspondence between actual and formal parameters is always established using their positions in the parameter list. In the invocation of `Max()` in the preceding code segment, the first formal parameter a is associated with the first actual parameter `Value1`, and the second formal parameter b is associated with the second actual parameter `Value2`. Once the correspondence is set, function `Max()` performs its computation and returns the appropriate value. A similar correspondence is established between the actual parameters in the invocation of `Min()` in the preceding code segment and the formal parameters contained in `Min()`'s definition.

Note that the algorithm library component of the Standard Template Library (STL) provides generic versions of functions `Max()` and `Min()`. These generic versions, named `max()` and `min()`, make use of templates (template functions are discussed in Chapter 14). To have these generic versions available for your program, place the following statement at the beginning of your program file along with the include directives.

```
#include <algorithm>
```

Another useful function is **int** function `PromptAndGet()`, which first issues a prompt for a number to output stream `cout`. The function then extracts the response from the input stream `cin`. The response is used as the return value for `PromptAndGet()`. The function does not require any parameters because the invoking function provides no information to `PromptAndGet()` for its computation.

```
// PromptAndGet(): prompt and extract next integer
int PromptAndGet() {
    cout << "Please enter a number (integer): ";
    int Response;
    cin >> Response;
    return Response;
}
```

Our code segment for determining the larger and smaller of two input values can be rewritten to use `PromptAndGet()` for acquiring the input.

```
int Value1 = PromptAndGet();
int Value2 = PromptAndGet();
cout << "Max: " << Max(Value1, Value2) << endl;
cout << "Min: " << Min(Value1, Value2) << endl;
```

In Chapter 5, we developed a code segment for determining whether a character is a vowel. For purposes of software reuse, it makes sense to encapsulate that code segment into a function so that it is not necessary to reproduce the statements every time such a computation is necessary. An appropriate name for this function is `IsVowel`. The function requires a single **char** value as its parameter and returns a **bool** value indicating whether that value is a vowel.

```
// IsVowel(): determine whether parameter is a vowel
bool IsVowel(char ch) {
    switch (ch) {
        case 'a': case 'A':
        case 'A': case 'E':
        case 'i': case 'I':
        case 'o': case 'O':
        case 'u': case 'U':
            return true;
        default:
            return false;
    }
}
```

In our next example, we define a function to compute the factorial of a number. As discussed in Chapter 4, this expression is denoted mathematically as $n!$ where

$$n! = \begin{cases} 1 & \text{if } n = 0 \\ n \times (n-1) \times \ldots \times 1 & \text{if } n \geq 1 \end{cases}$$

Our function is named `Factorial()`. It expects a single **int** parameter n, and it returns an **int**.

```
// Factorial(): determine n! for parameter n
int Factorial(int n) {
    int nfactorial = 1;
    while (n > 1) {
        nfactorial *= n;
        --n;
    }
    return nfactorial;
}
```

Function `Factorial()` uses its parameter n to represent the current factor for updating the running product `nfactorial`. Once n has the value 1, all factors have been considered. Because n is a value parameter, the change made to it by the function does not affect the actual parameter. This independence is illustrated in the following code segment:

```
int i = 5;
int Result = Factorial(i);
cout << i << "! equals " << Result << endl;
```

which displays

```
5! equals 120
```

Our implementation of function `Factorial()` does not perform any checking to make sure that the value of n is sensible. Adding such a check is left as an exercise.

Our next example develops a function that computes the area under a curve for a quadratic polynomial. Being able to compute the area under a curve is necessary for a variety of applications in both the natural and social sciences.

6.4 INTEGRATING A QUADRATIC POLYNOMIAL

A polynomial $f(x)$ of degree n is a function whose value is the sum of $n + 1$ terms where the terms are of the form $a_i x^i$, $0 \leq i \leq n$, with the restriction that a_n is not 0. The two standard ways to write a polynomial of degree n are

$$a_n x^n + a_{n-1} x^{n-1} + \ldots + a_2 x^2 + a_1 x + a_0$$

or using summation notation

$$\sum_{i=0}^{n} a_i x^i \, .$$

Figure 6.3 depicts a graph of a degree 2 polynomial $x^2 + 2x + 5$. The graph highlights the area of the two-dimensional plane that lies between the curve and the x-axis interval (1, 4). By using calculus, we can determine that the area in question is 51.

Figure 6.3

Plot of $x^2 + 2x + 5$ with x-axis interval (1, 4) highlighted

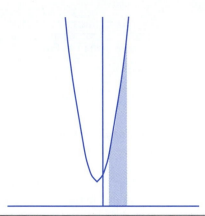

An integral sign ∫ is the calculus symbol that indicates that the area under the curve is to be computed. The mathematical notation for expressing the problem of computing the area under the curve along the x-axis interval (s, t) for a polynomial of degree n has the following form:

$$\int_s^t a_n x^n + a_{n-1} x^{n-1} + \dots + a_2 x^2 + a_1 x + a_0 \, dx$$

The solution to our integral is given by the formula

$$\sum_{i=0}^{n} \frac{a_i t^{i+1}}{i+1} - \sum_{i=0}^{n} \frac{a_i s^{i+1}}{i+1}$$

which is equal to the following

$$\sum_{i=0}^{n} \frac{a_i}{i+1} (t^{i+1} - s^{i+1}).$$

For a quadratic polynomial, this formula can be rewritten as

$$a_2(t^3 - s^3)/3 + a_1(t^2 - s^2)/2 + a_0(t - s).$$

Function `QuadraticArea()` of Program 6.3 is a **double** function with five **double** parameters: a2, a1, a0, s, and t.

```cpp
double QuadraticArea(double a2, double a1,
    double a0, double s, double t);
```

Program 6.3

Computing the area under a quadratic curve

```cpp
// Program 6.3: Computes area under the curve for a user-
// specified quadratic polynomial and x-interval
#include <iostream>
#include <string>
using namespace std;
// prototype
double QuadraticArea(double a2, double a1, double a0,
  double s, double t);
// main(): manage the computation of area under the
// curve for a quadratic polynomial
int main() {
    // prompt and extract quadratic polynomial
    cout << "Enter quadratic coefficients (a2 a1 a0): ";
    double a2;
    double a1;
    double a0;
    cin >> a2 >> a1 >> a0;
    // prompt and extract x-axis interval
    cout << "Enter interval of interest (n1 n2): ";
    double s;
    double t;
    cin >> s >> t;
    // compute and display area
    double Area = QuadraticArea(a2, a1, a0, s, t);
    cout << "The area of quadratic polynomial "
      << a2 << "x*x + " << a1 << "x + " << a0
      << " for the x-interval (" << s << ", " << t << ")"
      << " is " << QuadraticArea(a2, a1, a0, s, t) << endl;
}
// QuadraticArea(): compute area for a2*x*x + a1*x + a0
// for x-axis interval (s,t)
double QuadraticArea(double a2, double a1, double a0,
  double s, double t) {
    double term2 = a2*(t*t*t - s*s*s)/3.0;
    double term1 = a1*(t*t - s*s)/2.0;
    double term0 = a0*(t - s);
    return term2 + term1 + term0;
}
```

Parameters a2, a1, and a0 correspond to the coefficients of a quadratic polynomial; parameters s and t represent an *x*-axis interval. The function returns the area under the curve for the given polynomial and *x*-axis interval by computing the three terms from the preceding formula and returning their sum.

```cpp
double term2 = a2*(t*t*t - s*s*s)/3.0;
double term1 = a1*(t*t - s*s)/2.0;
double term0 = a0*(t - s);
return term2 + term1 + term0;
```

The program itself prompts the user for the quadratic formula and a desired interval to pass to function `QuadraticArea()`.

```
cout << "Enter quadratic coefficients (a2 a1 a0): ";
double a2;
double a1;
double a0;
cin >> a2 >> a1 >> a0;
cout << "Enter interval of interest (n1 n2): ";
double s;
double t;
cin >> s >> t;
```

By invoking function `QuadraticArea()` on these inputs, the program correctly computes the size of the desired area.

```
double Area = QuadraticArea(a2, a1, a0, s, t);
```

In the exercises, we consider functions for computing the areas under the curve for polynomials of other degrees.

6.5   THE LOCAL SCOPE

Consider Program 6.4. Why doesn't this program compile? It does not compile because the references to a and b in function `main()` are illegal. Objects a and b do not exist in the *scope* of function `main()`. According to the C++ language specification, a function's parameters and the objects declared within the function can be used only within the function itself. Such objects are said to be *local* to the function. Depending on where the definition occurs and what other definitions occur in the function, scope rules can also limit a local object or parameter to particular sections of code within the function.

6.5.1   Local scope rules

A *block* is a list of statements nested within curly braces. By this definition, a function body is a block. It is legal in C++ to put a statement block anywhere a statement would be legal, and there is no restriction on what type of statements the block can include. This flexibility allows us to have a block within a block within a block and so on. A block contained within another block is called a *nested* block.

The statement list that comprises a block is naturally delimited, or *terminated* in C++ terminology, from the statement that follows it by the right curly brace. Thus no semicolon is needed after the right curly brace, as shown in the following example:

```
{
    int a = 1; // semicolon is necessary
}             // semicolon is not necessary
```

C++'s scope rules state that a local object can be used only in the block and in the nested blocks of the block in which it has been defined. In particular, a local object can be used only in a statement or nested block that occurs after its

Program 6.4

Program with a scope problem

```
// Program 6.4: Has a scope problem
#include <iostream>
#include <string>
using namespace std;

void Mystery(int a, int b); // prototype

int main() {
    int i = 10;             // local object definition
    int j = 20;             // local object definition
    Mystery(i, j);          // invocation of mystery with
                            // local objects i and j
    cout << a << endl;      // insert?
    cout << b << endl;      // insert?
    return 0;
}

void Mystery(int a, int b) {
    cout << a << endl;
    cout << b << endl;
    a = 1;
    b = 2;
    cout << a << endl;
    cout << b << endl;
    return;
}
```

definition. Note that a formal parameter is considered to be defined at the beginning of its associated function body. This convention means that a formal parameter can normally be used throughout the function body.

6.5.2 Name reuse with objects

One more scope rule limits the statements in which an object can be used. This limitation has to do with the reuse of an object's name. Although it often seems disconcerting to beginning programmers to reuse names, imagine how difficult it would be to write programs if name reuse was not permitted. Programmers would then need to know the name of every object used in every function in the software project, regardless of the function's author. Not only would this task tend to be unmanageable; it would encourage poor names for the sake of uniqueness.

C++ allows identifier names to be reused as long as the declarations naming the duplicating identifier occur in different blocks. This policy means that the following definition of main() is legal.

```
int main() {
    int a = 10;
    int b = 20;
    Mystery(a, b);
    cout << a << endl;
    cout << b << endl;
    return 0;
}
```

Function main()'s local objects a and b are different from the formal parameters a and b in the earlier definition of function Mystery(). The local objects a and b of main() exist only within main()'s statement block, and the formal parameters a and b of Mystery() exist only within Mystery()'s statement block.

This name reuse is reflected in the activation records for the two functions. They both contain entries for an a and b, but the a and b in one are independent of the a and b in the other.

main()	
a	10
b	20

Mystery()	
a	1
b	2

The output of the program is

```
10
20
1
2
10
20
```

Name reuse in two different blocks is permitted, even if one of the blocks is nested within the other block. As soon as the nested block that reused the name is complete, the declaration of the encompassing block is back in effect. The following example demonstrates this rule.

```cpp
{
    int i;
    // statement here using i references int object i
    {
        // statement here using i references int
        // object i
        char i;
        // statement here using i references char
        // object i
        {
            // statement here using i references char
            // object i
            float i;
            // statement here using i references float
            // object i
        }
        // statement here using i references char
        // char object i
    }
    // statement here using i references int object
    // i
}
// none of the preceding i s can be used here
```

The name reuse in the preceding code segment did not depend on the use of different types for the various object i's. For example, the following code segment defines two objects with the same name and type.

```
{ // outer block
    int i;
    // statement here using i references outer
    // block i
    { // inner block
        int i;
        // statement here using i references inner
        // block i
    }
    // statement here using i references outer
    // block i
}
```

Although a name can be reused in a nested block, a name cannot be redefined in the same block in which it is initially defined. This restriction means the following program fragment is illegal.

```
int i;
float i; // illegal: cannot reuse i within same block
```

Redefining a name within the same block is illegal, even when a nested block occurs between the two definitions.

```
int i;
{
    char i; // legal: reuse occurs in different blocks
}
float i;    // illegal: cannot reuse i within same block
```

6.6 THE GLOBAL SCOPE

Although an object can be defined within a statement block, a function definition is not allowed to occur within another function's statement block. This restriction does not contradict our use of function prototypes. A prototype is a declaration that describes a function's interface—it is not a definition. C++ requires that functions be defined at the *global* scope. The global scope occurs in the parts of your program that are not contained within any statement block. Object definitions and declarations, type definitions and declarations, as well as function prototypes are allowed to occur in the global scope.

6.6.1 Scope rules and name reuse with global objects

An object defined in the global scope is called a *global object*. The scope rules for global objects are similar to, but not the same as, the rules for local objects. As with local objects, a global object may be referenced by simply using its name in any desired block that occurs after its definition as long as no reuse for the object's name is in effect in the given block. Similarly, just as it is illegal to redefine a local object in the same block as it is initially defined, it is also illegal to reuse a global object's name for another object while the global scope is in effect.

C++ provides the unary scope operator :: as a way to use global objects when name reuse has occurred in a local block. A :: placed in front of an object indicates that the definition being used is the global one. Consequently, it is illegal to use the scope operator on a local object.

To help understand these scope rules, let's consider the following example:

```
int i;
int main() {
    // statement here using i references global
    // int object i
    // statement here using ::i references global
    // int object i. the :: is unnecessary
    return 0;
}
void f() {
    // statement here using i references global
    // int object i
    // statement here using ::i references global
    // int object i. the :: is unnecessary
    char i;
    // statement here using i references local
    // char object i
    // statement here using ::i references global
    // global int object i
    {
        // statement here using i references local
        // char object i
        // statement here using ::i references global
        // int object i
        int i;
        // statement here using i references local
        // int object i
        // statement here using ::i references global
        // int object i
    }
    // statement here using i references local
    // char object i
    // statement here using ::i references global
    // int object i
    return;
}
void g() {
    // statement here using i references global
    // int object i
    // statement here using ::i references global
    // int object i. the :: is unnecessary
    return;
}
```

In our example, both functions main() and g() can use the global **int** object i throughout their entire function bodies. The scope resolution operator :: can be used there, but it is not necessary. Without using the scope resolution operator, function f() can make use of the global **int** object i in its outermost block until the definition of the local **char** object occurs. From that point on in that block and in its nested blocks, access to global **int** object i is possible only through the use of the scope operator. In the innermost nested block of function f(), a local **int** object i is in use. This object and the global object i are distinct. Changes to the local object will not affect the global object. The scope operator can also be applied to functions and programmer-defined types. This application is normally useful only in class definitions. We examine this use of the scope operator in later chapters.

6.6.2 Initialization of global objects

Unlike local objects, global objects are always initialized. If no explicit initialization is given for a fundamental type global object, then the value 0 is used. For example, the following program displays the value 0.

```
#include <iostream>
#include <string>
using namespace std;
int a;
int main() {
    cout << a << endl;
    return 0;
}
```

Self-check Questions

1.   What type of function uses the C++ statement

```
return;
```

to return?

2.   Explain why it is unnecessary to declare a value parameter to be a **const**.

3.   Write a **bool** function nor() that takes two **bool** arguments x and y and returns the value of x nor y.

4.   Write a **float** function that takes two integers and returns their average.

5.   Write a function Compare() that returns an integer. Function Compare() accepts two integer arguments, a and b. It returns −1 if a is less than b, 0 if a is equal to b, and 1 if a is greater than b.

6.   What is the output of the following program?

```
#include <iostream>
using namespace std;
int main() {
    int i = 10;
    int j = 12;
    cout << i << "   " << j << endl;
    {
        i++;
```

```
        int i = 3;
        cout << i << "   " << j << endl;
        {
            int j = 11;
            i++;
            cout << i << "   " << j << endl;
        }
        j++;
        cout << i << "   " << j << endl;
        return 0;
        }
    }
```

7.   What is the output of the following program?

```
#include <iostream>
using namespace std;
int a = 0;
void Demo(){
    int b = 4;
    cout << "a = " << a << endl;
    cout << "b = " << b << endl;
}
int main() {
    int a = 2;
    int b = 3;
    cout << "b = " << b << endl;
    cout << "a = " << a << endl;
    Demo();
    cout << "b = " << b << endl;
    return 0;
}
```

8.   What is the output of the following program?

```
#include <iostream>
using namespace std;
int a = 0;
void Demo() {
    int b = 4;
    cout << "a = " << a << endl;
    cout << "b = " << b << endl;
}
int main() {
    int a = 2;
    int b = 3;
    cout << "b = " << b << endl;
    cout << "a = " << ::a << endl;
    Demo();
    cout << "b = " << b << endl;
```

```
            return 0;
    }
```

9.   Many problems can most easily be solved on a computer via an iterative process. The user makes an initial estimate of the solution, and a program iteratively refines the answer to the desired accuracy. This iterative solution of complicated problems is a common and powerful approach to solving all sorts of difficult problems.

For this self-check exercise, you are to develop an iterative solution to an engineering problem, that of determining the depth of a flow through a channel. A formula that describes the flow of water through a channel is

$$Q = \frac{1.49}{N} A R^{2/3} S^{1/2}$$

where Q is the flow of water (cubic feet per second), N is the roughness coefficient (unitless), A is the area (square feet), S is the slope (feet/foot), and R is the hydraulic radius (feet). This is known as Manning's equation. The hydraulic radius is the cross-sectional area divided by the wetted perimeter. For square channels, the hydraulic radius is

$$R = (depth \times width) \div (2.0 \times depth + width)$$

The channel in question has vertical walls and is 15 feet wide. It is 10 feet deep, and has a slope of 0.0015 feet/foot, and a roughness coefficient of 0.014. The question to be answered is: How deep will the water be when 1,000 cubic feet per second is flowing through the channel?

To solve this problem, you should design and implement a program that allows the user to guess a depth and then calculate the corresponding flow. If the flow is too little, the user should guess a depth a little higher; if the flow is too high, the user should guess a depth a little lower. The guessing is repeated until the computed flow is within 0.1 percent of the flow desired.

Programmer Alert

Beware of global objects

There is strong potential for a programmer to lose track of just what a global object is supposed to represent. Consider the following scenario: A function f() neither changes nor even uses a global object in its function body. However, the function f() does invoke a function that invokes a function that invokes a function that does change a global object. Keeping track of this situation would be most difficult. To avoid such difficulties, the use of global objects is severely limited by most programming methodologies. Note that our implementation of the stock-charting problem in Section 6.15 requires a SimpleWindow object with global scope because we have not yet introduced reference parameters.

6.7 REFERENCE PARAMETERS

One of the advantages of the call-by-value parameter transmission method is that it simplifies the understanding of a program. If the parameters are passed using the call-by-value method, we know that the called function cannot change the values of the actual parameters. For example, when reading a program encountering a call to a function with all call-by-value parameters, we know, without looking at the body of the function, that when the function returns, the actual parameters will have the same value as they did before the call.

Consider the following code fragment:

```
// Prototype section
// Compute flow (gallons per second) through a channel
// Depth - depth of water
// Width - width of channel
float Flow(float Depth, float Width);
// more prototypes
...
int main() {
    ...
    f = Flow(CurrentDepth, ChannelWidth);
    ...
}
```

Without examining the body of function Flow, we can tell based on just the prototype for Flow that the objects CurrentDepth and ChannelWidth will not be changed by Flow. A function that does not modify the parameters passed to it and changes only values in the calling function via the function return value is said to have no *side effects*.

Because programs that use functions with no side effects are, in general, easier to understand than those with side effects, we should use call by value whenever possible. However, allowing a function to change the values of the actual parameters that are passed to it is sometimes useful—for example, when the natural design of a function calls for it to return more than one value. For these and other situations, C++ provides *reference parameters*. In contrast to a value parameter where a copy of the actual parameter is passed, a reference parameter passes a reference or pointer to the actual parameter. Thus when a formal reference parameter is changed in a function, the actual parameter is changed also.

Recall that the C++ syntax for specifying the interface of a function with value parameters is

Type of value that the   A description of the form the
function returns   parameters (if any) are to take
                    Identifier name of function

```
FunctionType FunctionName (ParameterList) ;
```

where the *ParameterList* is a list of declarations of the following form:

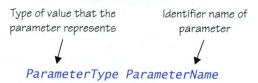

To indicate that a parameter is a reference parameter, the syntax of a parameter declaration is extended slightly as follows:

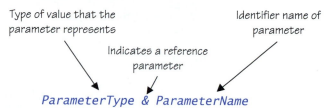

The ampersand indicates that a reference to *ParameterName*, rather than a copy of *ParameterName*'s value, is to be passed to the called function.

To illustrate how reference parameters work, let's revisit the Mystery program from the previous chapter. In the original program, the interface to Mystery() was

```
void Mystery(int a, int b);
```

That is, Mystery() requires two **int** parameters that are passed by value. In addition, Mystery() does not return a value. It is a **void** function. We shall change the interface of Mystery() to use a reference parameter. The new interface is

```
void Mystery(int a, int &b);
```

The first parameter, a, is still a value parameter, but b is now a reference parameter. Program 6.5 is a complete program that uses Mystery(). Examination of the operation of this program helps illustrate the difference between call by value and call by reference. The output of Program 6.5 follows.

```
Output at beginning of main
i is 10
j is 20
Output at beginning of Mystery
a is 10
b is 20
Output after Mystery assignments
a is 5
b is 6
Output after Mystery returns
i is 10
j is 6
```

Thus when Mystery() changed b, main()'s j was changed!

```
// Program 6.5: Demonstrate call by reference
#include <iostream>
#include <string>
using namespace std;
void Mystery(int a, int &b) {
    cout << "Output at beginning of Mystery" << endl;
    cout << "a is " << a << endl;
    cout << "b is " << b << endl;
    a = 5;
    b = 6;
    cout << "Output after Mystery assignments" << endl;
    cout << "a is " << a << endl;
    cout << "b is " << b << endl;
    return;
}
int main() {
    int i = 10;            // local object definition
    int j = 20;            // local object definition
    cout << "Output at beginning of main" << endl;
    cout << "i is " << i << endl;
    cout << "j is " << j << endl;
    Mystery(i, j);         // invocation of Mystery with
                           // local objects i and j
    cout << "Output after Mystery returns" << endl;
    cout << "i is " << i << endl;
    cout << "j is " << j << endl;
    return 0;
}
```

To understand exactly what is happening, we need to look at the activation records of main() and Mystery(). The left side of Figure 6.4 depicts the two activation records before the assignment statements in Mystery() are executed. Notice that in Mystery()'s activation record, the value of parameter object b is an arrow that points to object j in main()'s activation record. The arrow signifies that when Mystery() accesses b, it really accesses j in main(). We can say it this way: When we *refer* to b in Mystery(), we are really *referencing* j in main(). Hence b is a reference parameter, and objects that are passed via a reference parameter are *passed by reference*.

Figure 6.4

Activation records of main() and Mystery()

main()	
i	10
j	20

Mystery()	
a	10
b	&j

Before assignments
in Mystery()

main()	
i	10
j	6

Mystery()	
a	5
b	&j

After assignments
in Mystery()

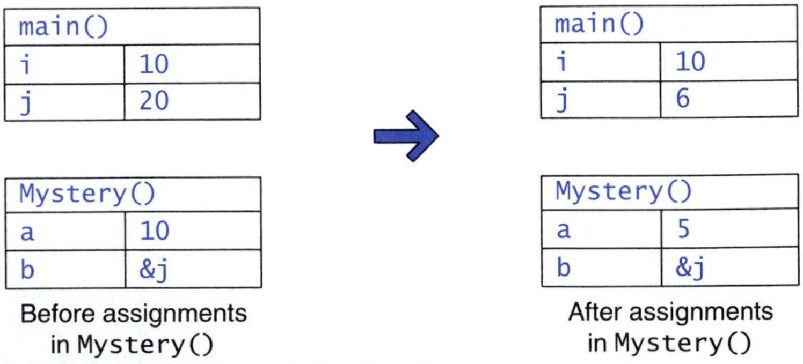

The right side of Figure 6.4 shows the activation records of main() and Mystery() after the assignment statements in Mystery() are executed. Notice that j in main() has changed, whereas i has not. This result occurs because a is a value parameter, so i was passed by value. Instead of a reference to i, a copy of i's value was passed.

To illustrate the usefulness of reference parameters, let's revisit a program we wrote in Chapter 4. This program read three values and output the values in sorted order. To obtain the proper ordering, the program checked for each of the possible six orderings of three values and executed the appropriate assignment statements to produce the correct order of the values. We can achieve the same effect with much less code by using a function that employs reference parameters. Our approach will be to write a function that sorts three integer values. The function accepts three integer reference parameters and arranges the values such that when the function returns, the first parameter contains the smallest of the three values, the second parameter contains the next smallest, and the third parameter is the largest.

The strategy we use is to compare pairs of values and swap them if they are out of order. First, we compare the values contained in the first and second parameters, and if they are not in the correct order, we swap the values they contain. We repeat this operation on the first and third parameters. After these two steps, we know that the first parameter contains the smallest value. The last step is to compare the second and third parameters and swap their values if they are not in the correct order. In the case where the values are the same, we do not swap values. Thus to sort the three values we do three comparisons and, based on the results of the comparisons, potentially perform three swap operations.

The following code implements these operations.

```cpp
void Sort3(int &a, int &b, int &c) {
    if (a > b) {
        int t = a;      // swap a and b
        a = b;
        b = t;
    }
    if (a > c) {
        int t = a;      // swap a and c
        a = c;
        c = t;
    }
    if (b > c) {
        int t = b;      // swap b and c
        b = c;
        c = t;
    }
    return;
}
```

For the function to work correctly, all three parameters must be reference parameters. Otherwise, any changes the function makes to the values of the parameters would not change the values of the actual parameters.

Using this function, we can now rewrite Program 4.3. Program 6.6 contains the revised program, which is shorter and easier to understand than the original.

Program 6.6

Sorting three numbers

```cpp
// Program 6.6: Input three numbers and output
// them in sorted order
#include <iostream>
#include <string>
using namespace std;
// sort three numbers into nondescending order
void Sort3(int &a, int &b, int &c) {
    if (a > b) {
        int tmp = a;    // b is smaller, swap a and b
        a = b;
        b = tmp;
    }
    if (a > c) {
        int tmp = a;    // c is smaller, swap a and c
        a = c;
        c = tmp;
    }
    if (b > c) {
        int tmp = b;    // c is smaller, swap b and c
        b = c;
        c = tmp;
    }
    return;
}
int main() {
    // Input the three numbers
    cout << "Please provide three integers: ";
    int Input1;
    int Input2;
    int Input3;
    cin >> Input1 >> Input2 >> Input3;
    int Output1 = Input1;
    int Output2 = Input2;
    int Output3 = Input3;

    // Sort the three numbers
    Sort3(Output1, Output2, Output3);

    // Output the sorted numbers
    cout << Input1 << " " << Input2 << " " << Input3
        << " in sorted order is "
        << Output1 << " " << Output2 << " " << Output3 << endl;

    return 0;
}
```

To make sure we understand the operation of the program, let's look at the activation records of `main()` and `Sort3()` at several key points. We will assume that the inputs to the program are the integers 20, 5, and 9. On entry to `Sort3()`, the activation records appear as shown in the left diagram of Figure 6.5. Notice that the parameters of `Sort3()`, a, b, and c, refer to `Output1`, `Output2`, and `Output3` of function `main()`. `Sort3()` now compares the values of a and b, and because a is greater than b, it swaps them. Of course, it really swaps the values of `Output1` and `Output2`. The activation records after this step are shown in the middle part of Figure 6.5. Notice that the values of Output1 and Output2 have been exchanged.

Figure 6.5

Activation records during execution of Program 6.6

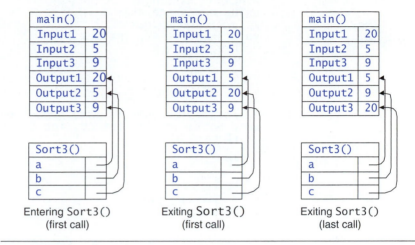

main()	
Input1	20
Input2	5
Input3	9
Output1	20
Output2	5
Output3	9

Sort3()
a
b
c

Entering Sort3()
(first call)

main()	
Input1	20
Input2	5
Input3	9
Output1	5
Output2	20
Output3	9

Sort3()
a
b
c

Exiting Sort3()
(first call)

main()	
Input1	20
Input2	5
Input3	9
Output1	5
Output2	9
Output3	20

Sort3()
a
b
c

Exiting Sort3()
(last call)

Next, the values of a and c are compared. Because they are already in sorted order, nothing happens. Next, the values of b and c are compared. Because they are out of order, they are swapped. The activation records just before Sort3() returns to function main() are shown in the right-most diagram of Figure 6.5. The values in the output variables are now in sorted order. The output of the program follows.

20 5 9 in sorted order is 5 9 20

Our program is fairly simple, but we can make it simpler still. Notice that Sort3() performs the same operation, a swap, on three different pairs of values. If we can write a function to do this, we can replace the three instances of the swap code with calls to a swap function. This function will shorten and simplify the code. Using reference parameters to write a function that swaps two values is easy. The code for swapping two integer values follows.

```
void Swap(int &x, int &y) {
    int tmp = x;
    x = y;
    y = tmp;
    return;
}
```

Program 6.7 contains the final code for our sorting program. This program is interesting because it contains a call to a routine that uses reference parameters (i.e., main() calls Sort3()) and that routine calls another routine that uses reference parameters (i.e., Sort3() calls Swap()). What do the activation records look like?

Using the input from the previous example (20, 5, and 9), we can step through the program as we did before. Sort3() compares parameters a and b and determines that they are out of order. In this program, rather than swapping

Program 6.7

*Sort three numbers
using a swap function*

```
// Program 6.7: Input three numbers and output them
// in sorted order
#include <iostream>
#include <string>
using namespace std;
// swap two values
void Swap(int &x, int &y) {
    int tmp = x;
    x = y;
    y = tmp;
    return;
}

// sort three numbers into nondecreasing order
void Sort3(int &a, int &b, int &c) {
    if (a > b)
        Swap(a, b);
    if (a > c)
        Swap(a, c);
    if (b > c)
        Swap(b, c);
    return;
}

// read three numbers and output them in sorted order
int main() {
    cout << "Please enter three integers: ";
    int Input1;
    int Input2;
    int Input3;
    cin >> Input1 >> Input2 >> Input3;
    int Output1 = Input1;
    int Output2 = Input2;
    int Output3 = Input3;

    // Sort the three numbers
    Sort3(Output1, Output2, Output3);

    // Output the sorted numbers
    cout << Input1 << " " << Input2 << " " << Input3
      << " in sorted order is "
      << Output1 << " " << Output2 << " " << Output3 << endl;

    return 0;
}
```

them directly, Sort3() calls Swap(), passing it a and b. Because Swap()'s formal parameters, x and y, are both reference parameters, rather than pass the values of a and b, references to a and b are passed. However, because a and b are themselves reference parameters, the values that they reference are passed instead!

The left-most diagram of Figure 6.6 depicts the activation records just before the first statement of Swap() is executed. The parameters x and y refer to main()'s local variables Output1 and Output2. The action Swap() takes will switch their values. The middle diagram of the figure depicts the activation records after Swap() has completed its operation, but before it returns to Sort3().

Figure 6.6

*Activation records for
sorting program with
swap*

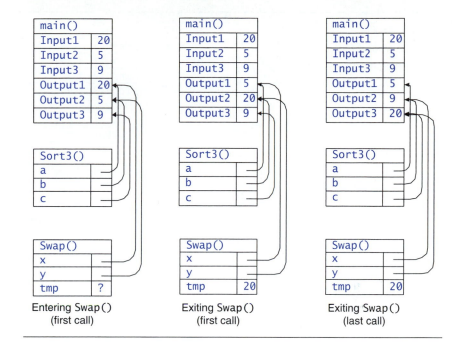

Function Swap() is called again to swap the values of b and c. The right-most diagram in Figure 6.6 shows the activation records after Swap() completes the exchange. Notice that in this diagram, x and y refer to Output2 and Output3, respectively.

Although the pictures of the activation records accurately depict what is happening with value and reference parameters, it is awkward to draw arrows all the time. A simple way to think about a reference parameter is that the formal parameter name is an *alias* for the actual parameter. In Sort3(), a is an alias for Output1 in main(). When we get or change a's value, we get or change the value of Output1. If we adopt this more convenient view, we can simplify our pictures by putting the actual name in the box that corresponds to the formal parameter's value instead of drawing a line that connects a formal reference parameter to the actual parameter. However, we need a way to show that the parameter is not a value, but really a reference to a named object. By putting an ampersand (&) in front of the name, we can indicate that an actual parameter is a reference to an object. Figure 6.7 reflects this simpler notation. It shows that when we access a in function Sort3(), we are really referencing Output1 in function main(). Similarly, in Swap() the formal parameter x references Output2 in Sort3().

Figure 6.7

*Activation records for
sorting program with
swap*

main()	
Input1	20
Input2	5
Input3	9
Output1	5
Output2	9
Output3	20

Sort3()	
a	&Output1
b	&Output2
c	&Output3

Swap()	
x	&Output2
y	&Output3
tmp	20

Exiting Swap()
(last call)

6.8   PASSING OBJECTS BY REFERENCE

One situation where it is absolutely mandatory to use a reference parameter is when we pass a stream object to a function. The reason, of course, is that when we extract data from a stream or insert data into a stream, we are changing the stream. This change must be reflected in the stream object. As we know, if we passed the stream object by value, any changes that we made to the stream object would be made to a copy of the stream object, not to the actual object. Thus whenever we need to pass a stream to a function, we must pass the stream by reference. In fact, most compilers make sure that when a stream object is passed to a function, the stream is passed by reference. If it is not, a compilation error occurs and no object file is produced.

The following function writes an integer value to a stream that is passed as the first parameter to the function.

```
void OutputValue(ostream &out, int Value) {
    out << "Value is " << Value << endl;
    return;
}
```

The next line of code uses the `OutputValue()` to write the value k to the stream `cout`.

```
OutputValue(cout, k);
```

Similarly, the code

```
OutputValue(cerr, k);
```

invokes OutputValue() that writes the value of k to the stream cerr.

Functions that output values to a stream are useful when we need to output several values along with labeling information from several places in a program. We might use such a function to write data to the display as well as to a log file for later examination. Another use would be to help debug the program. We can also use the function to output values of interest at strategic points in the program. Let's examine this latter use.

Suppose, for example, that we wish to "watch" our Sort3() function from Program 6.7 as it sorts the values. We want to show the values of a, b, and c after each step of the function. Rather than add three insertion statements after each **if** statement, we can call a function that outputs the three values. We want this function to be as general as possible, so one of its parameters is the stream to write the output to. The code for the function, called ShowValues(), is

```
void ShowValues(ostream &out, int a, int b, int c) {
    out << "a: " << a << endl;
    out << "b: " << b << endl;
    out << "c: " << c << endl;
    return;
}
```

and the revised code for Sort3() that uses ShowValues() to write the values to stream clog is

```
// sort three numbers into ascending order
void Sort3(int &a, int &b, int &c) {
    if (a > b)
        Swap(a, b);
    ShowValues(clog, a, b, c);
    if (a > c)
        Swap(a, c);
    ShowValues(clog, a, b, c);
    if (b > c)
        Swap(b, c);
    ShowValues(clog, a, b, c);
    return;
}
```

We can also put the ability to pass an input stream as a parameter to a function to good use. For example, suppose we are writing a program to process data from a file. Program development and testing will go faster if the program takes input from the keyboard. We can quickly test the program by typing in data, rather than creating a test file each time we want to test the program on different data. However, eventually the program will be reading data from a file. We do not want to write the program so that it accepts input from the keyboard and then, when the program is complete, have to make extensive changes to the program so that it operates on a different stream. We can handle this situation by writing any functions that extract input to accept as a parameter the stream to read data from. This way, if we decide to take the data from a different source, the function need not be changed.

The function `ReadValues()` reads three values from the stream that is passed as its first parameter.

```cpp
bool ReadValues(istream &in, int &v1, int &v2,
  int &v3) {
    if (in == cin)
        cout << "Please enter three numbers";
    if (in >> v1 >> v2 >> v3)
        return true;
    else
        return false;
}
```

The function is, for the most part, straightforward, However, the two **if** statements in the function deserve further discussion. When `ReadValues()` is used for interactive input (for example, during testing), we want it to prompt us for data. However, when it is used in the system that will read data from a file, we do not want it to output a prompt. The first **if** statement handles this requirement. If the stream being read from is `cin` (i.e., the keyboard), then a prompt is output.

Because `ReadValues()` is intended to be used as part of a larger system, it must tell the calling function whether it was able to read three values successfully. As was discussed in Chapter 5, an extraction expression returns true if the extraction operation succeeded; otherwise, it returns false. The second **if** statement checks to make sure that three values were read. If three values were read successfully, `ReadValues()` returns true; otherwise, it returns false.

Using `ReadValues()`, we can modify the main function of Program 6.7 so that it reads values from a file called `test.dat`. Program 6.8 contains the revised function. Notice the function checks to make sure that the file was successfully opened and that `ReadValues()` reports successfully reading three values. If either of these actions fails, the program writes an error message to `cerr` and returns a 1 to the operating system, indicating that some type of failure occurred. This type of "defensive programming" is key when we are writing code that other programmers will use.

6.9 VALIDATING TELEPHONE ACCESS CODES

Many organizations require users of their telephone system to first provide a valid access code. This security measure helps prevent unauthorized long-distance calls. A computer that connects the internal phone system with the outside world validates the access code.

An example of a simple access and validation method is to have a user type a five-digit number. The first three digits are added together. The remainder of this sum when divided by the fourth digit should be equal to the fifth

Program 6.8

Sorting numbers read
from a file

```cpp
// Program 6.8: Sorting numbers read from a file
#include <iostream>
#include <fstream>
#include <string>
using namespace std;
int main() {
    // Open the input file
    ifstream fin("test.dat");
    if (!fin) {
        cerr << "Could not open test.dat" << endl;
        return 1;
    }
    int Input1;
    int Input2;
    int Input3;
    if (!ReadValues(fin, Input1, Input2, Input3)) {
        cerr << "Could not read three values" << endl;
        return 1;
    }
    int Output1 = Input1;
    int Output2 = Input2;
    int Output3 = Input3;
    // Sort the three numbers
    Sort3(Output1, Output2, Output3);
    // Output the sorted numbers
    cout << Input1 << " " << Input2 << " " << Input3
      << " in sorted order is "
      << Output1 << " " << Output2 << " " << Output3 << endl;
    return 0;
}
```

digit. If this is the case, the user is allowed to make the phone call; otherwise, access is denied. As long as the algorithm that determines whether a number sequence is a valid access code is secret, the probability that a randomly typed number is valid is reasonably low.

Program 6.9 demonstrates the basics of access validation. After the include directives for the `iostream` and `ctype` libraries, the program prototypes **bool** functions `Get()` and `Valid()`.

The purpose of function `Get()` is to set its five reference parameters with the next five inputs supplied by the user. The purpose of the function `Valid()` is to examine the digit inputs and determine whether they represent a valid access code.

Function `main()` begins by defining five **int** objects to store the input values. The function then invokes `Get()` and, if it is successful, then invokes function `Valid()`. Finally, function `main()` uses its return value to signal whether the access code is valid. As noted previously, if a program returns zero, the program is indicating a successful computation. If the computation was not successful, the program should return a nonzero value. Different nonzero values can be used to indicate how the program failed. Function `main()` follows this convention. It returns zero only if both `Get()` and `Valid()` return true. Otherwise it returns a one—this indicates that either an incomplete or invalid access code was supplied.

Program 6.9

*Validate a telephone
access code*

```
// Program 6.9: Validate a telephone access code
#include <iostream>
#include <string>
#include <ctype.h>
using namespace std;

// Prototypes for utility functions that main will use
bool Get(istream &in, int &d1, int &d2, int &d3,
 int &d4, int &d5);
bool Valid(int d1, int d2, int d3, int d4, int d5);

int main() {
    int d1;
    int d2;
    int d3;
    int d4;
    int d5;

    if (Get(cin, d1, d2, d3, d4, d5)
     && Valid(d1, d2, d3, d4, d5))
        return 0;
    else
        return 1;
}
bool Get(istream &sin, int &d1, int &d2, int &d3,
 int &d4, int &d5) {
    char c1;
    char c2;
    char c3;
    char c4;
    char c5;

    if (sin >> c1 >> c2 >> c3 >> c4 >> c5) {
        if (isdigit(c1) && isdigit(c2) && isdigit(c3)
                && isdigit(c4) && isdigit(c5)) {
            d1 = c1 - '0';
            d2 = c2 - '0';
            d3 = c3 - '0';
            d4 = c4 - '0';
            d5 = c5 - '0';
            return true;
        }
        else
            return false;
    }
    else
        return false;
}
bool Valid(int d1, int d2, int d3, int d4, int d5) {
    if (d4 == 0)
        return false;
    else
        return ((d1 + d2 + d3) % d4) == d5;
}
```

In our version of function `Get()`, the inputs are extracted from the stream
`sin`, which is passed as the first parameter. The inputs are extracted as **char**
objects in case the user supplies illegal values. The function uses the fact that
an extraction operation returns a nonzero value only if the extraction was

successful. Therefore, if the user did not supply five inputs, execution would flow to the **else** statement of the construct and the function would indicate that it was unsuccessful by returning **false**. If the user did supply five inputs, function Get() verifies that they are digits by calling the library function isdigit(), whose definition is obtained from the include file ctype.h. This function returns true if its parameter is a decimal digit; otherwise, it returns false. If all the input characters are digits, then the reference parameters are appropriately set with the numeric equivalent of the digits. In this case the function was successful, and it returns **true**. If the inputs are not all digits, the function instead executes the **else** statement, where it signals that it was unsuccessful by returning **false**.

The conversion of the character representation of a digit to a numeric representation by Get() assumes that characters are encoded in ASCII format. As discussed in Chapter 2, the ASCII characters' digits are arranged in a contiguous ascending order (i.e., '1' equals '0' + 1, '2' equals '1' + 1, and so on). By subtracting the character 0 from the character digit, Get() computes the numeric version of the digit. For example, '3' - '0' yields the integer value 3.

Program 6.9 next defines the function Valid() that examines its parameters and returns **true** if they correspond to a valid access code and returns **false** if they do not. The first step of the validation process is to examine the fourth digit—it must be nonzero, since its role is to be a divisor in the access algorithm. If the fourth digit is zero, Valid() returns **false**. If the fourth digit is not zero, then the first three digits are summed. If this sum modulus the fourth digit is equal to the fifth digit, Valid() returns **true**, indicating a valid access code; otherwise, it returns **false**, indicating an invalid access code.

Self-check Questions

10.   Consider the following valid program

```
#include <iostream>
using namespace std;
int main() {
    int x = 1;
    f(x);
    cout << "x is " << x << endl;
    return 0;
}
```

When this program runs, the output is

x is 2

Give the function prototype for function f().

11.   What is the output of the following program?

```
#include <iostream>
using namespace std;
void f(int a, int &b) {
    int t;
    t = b;
    a = b;
    b = a;
}
int main() {
    int x = 10, y = 20;
    f(x, y);
    cout << "x is " << x << endl;
    cout << "y is " << y << endl;
    return 0;
}
```

12.   What is the output of the following program?

```
void X(int a, int &b, int &c) {
    a = c;
    b = a;
    c = b;
}
int main() {
    int i, j;
    i = 3;
    j = 5;
    X(j, i, j);
    cout << i << " " << j << endl;
    return 0;
}
```

13.   What is the output of the following program?

```
#include <iostream>
int funny(int &a, int b) {
    int c = a + b;
    a = b;
    b = c;
    return c;
}
int main() {
    int x = 3;
    int y = 4;
    int z = 5;
    cout << funny (x, y) << endl;
    cout << "x is: " << x << " and y is: " << y
        << endl;
    z = funny (x, z);
    cout << "z is: " << z << " and x is: " << x
        << endl;
```

```
        return 0;
    }
```

14.   Draw the activation records for functions `main()` and `funny()` just before `funny()` returns to `main()`.

15.   Explain why a stream object must be passed by reference.

16.   Explain why a `SimpleWindow` object must be passed by reference.

17.   Write a C++ function called `ZeroSmaller` that accepts two **int** arguments by reference and sets to zero the number with the smaller absolute value.

6.10 CONSTANT PARAMETERS

For the programs that we have written thus far, we have used the **const** modifier to define program objects that represent constant values. These objects could be accessed, but not modified. There are two justifications for using **const** objects. First, they make our programs easier to modify. For example, if we need to change the value of a literal constant that appears in many different places throughout a large program, we have to find each instance of the literal constant and change it. Clearly, for a large program this task would be tedious and time-consuming, and we would probably miss some of the literals. Any oversight could introduce a bug into the program.

The other justification for using a **const** modifier is that it gives anyone reading the program additional, useful information about the object. When we encounter a definition of an object that has the **const** modifier, we know that the program cannot change that object. That is, the object is "read only." This information is useful if we are trying to understand or modify the program.

The **const** modifier can also be used with parameter declarations. The meaning is exactly the same as when it is applied to a local declaration—the function cannot change the object. Consider the following function that accepts three integer value parameters where the first is a **const** value parameter.

```
void Example(const int a, int b, int c) {
    b = a + 3;      // legal assignment
    a = c + 5;      // illegal assignment
    return;
}
```

The first assignment statement is legal because it reads, but does not modify, a. The second statement is illegal because it attempts to modify a. The C++ compiler will report the violation and not produce an executable.

Here is another example illustrating the use of **const** parameters.

```
void AnotherExample(const RectangleShape &R1,
    RectangleShape &R2) {
    R2.SetColor(Blue);    // Legal
```

The second statement in the preceding function is illegal because R1 is a **const** parameter and the SetColor message will change the color of R1. Function AnotherExample() cannot change its color, even though it is passed by reference.

Programming Tip

> ***Using const reference parameters for efficiency***
>
> When an object is passed by value, a copy of the object is made and the copy is passed to the called function. For large objects, copying can add considerable overhead to the program and may in some instances adversely affect the performance of the program. For such objects, we can obtain efficiency, yet retain safety, by passing the object as a constant reference parameter. Thus a reference to the object is passed, which is usually more efficient than passing a copy, but the **const** modifier ensures that the called function does not modify the actual object. For example, in Program 6.10 the argument FullName is passed as a **const** reference parameter. This approach is efficient (the string is not copied), and we know that Parse-Name() cannot modify FullName. Sometimes you can have your cake and eat it too!

A **const** parameter indicates that the function cannot change the value of the parameter. It does not say anything about whether the argument passed to the function is a constant or not. Consider the valid program shown in Program 6.10.

Program 6.10

Reformat a name

```
// Program 6.10: Reformat a name from LastName, FirstName
// to FirstName <space> LastName
#include <iostream>
#include <string>
using namespace std;
void ParseName(string &FirstName, string &LastName, const
  string &FullName) {
    int i = FullName.find(",");
    LastName = FullName.substr(0, i);
    FirstName = FullName.substr(i + 2, FullName.size());
    return;
}
int main() {
    string Name = "Stroustrup, Bjarne";
    string FirstName;
    string LastName;
    ParseName(FirstName, LastName, Name);
    Name = FirstName + " " + LastName;
    cout << Name << endl;
    return 0;
}
```

In function `ParseName()` the third formal parameter, `FullName`, is a **const** parameter, but the call to `ParseName()` in `main()` passes `Name`, which is not a **const** object. This sequence is perfectly fine. The **const** modifier applied to `FullName` in the formal parameter list of `ParseName()` only specifies that `ParseName()` cannot change the string `FullName`. In fact, notice that `Name` is changed immediately after the call to `ParseName()` in function `main()`.

Using the **const** modifier for parameters that a function will not change is a good software-engineering practice. It provides additional information to readers of the code, and it allows the compiler to automatically verify that the object is not intentionally or unintentionally changed.

Programmer Alert

Compiler limitations on enforcing the const modifier

Most C++ compilers will issue an error message if they detect a **const** object on the left side of an assignment. However, if a **const** object is passed by reference to another function, the compiler might issue a warning message only or no message at all.

Consider the following example:

```
void foo(int &p1, int p2) {
    p1 = p2 + p1 + 10;
    return;
}
void example(const int CValue) {
    foo(Cvalue, 3);
    return;
}
```

In function `foo()`, reference parameter `p1` is changed. Of course, there is no problem with this. However, when function `example()` calls `foo()` and passes the **const** object `CValue` by reference, the value of `CValue` could be changed. Most compilers will not issue an error message for this situation. However, some compilers will issue a warning message to tell you that you passed a **const** object to a function that expects a reference parameter.

In general, when passing a **const** object to another function, we should take care that the function the object is passed to does not modify the object. We cannot rely on all compilers to catch this potential hazard.

6.11 DEFAULT PARAMETERS

Normally when we call a function, we must pass exactly the number of parameters to the function that the function expects. For example, suppose the prototype for a function called `ThreeArgs` is

```
int ThreeArgs(int a, int b, int c);
```

and it is invoked with the following code:

```
int x = ThreeArgs(1, 2);
```

The compiler will issue an error message because we did not pass a value for c.

Generally, we want the compiler to let us know if we have not supplied all the values necessary to invoke a function. However, it would be nice to not have to pass a value for each parameter a function expects, yet still have that parameter receive a value. This technique is useful when we want to write a function that has a default behavior, but occasionally we want to change or override that behavior. In this case we can use *default parameters*.

The following function uses a default parameter to control whether the output should be double-spaced.

```cpp
void OutputValues(ostream &out, int Value1,
  int Value2, bool DoubleSpace = false) {
    out << "Value 1 is " << Value1 << endl;
    if (DoubleSpace)
        out << endl;
    out << "Value 2 is " << Value2 << endl;
    if (DoubleSpace)
        out << endl;
    return;
}
```

The code

```cpp
OutputValue(cout, 20, 30);
```

calls OutputValues() and passes values for the first three parameters. Because a fourth parameter value was not supplied, when the function executes, the fourth parameter DoubleSpace is given the value specified in the function header. Thus when the above code executes, the output inserted into stream cout is

```
Value 1 is 20
Value 2 is 30
```

If we want the output to be double-spaced, we can invoke OutputValues and pass **true** as the fourth parameter. Because we supplied a fourth parameter, the default value for the fourth parameter is ignored and the value passed is used. Thus the function call

```cpp
OutputValues(cout, 20, 30, true);
```

inserts the output

```
Value 1 is 20

Value 2 is 30
```

When defining a function with default parameters, the default parameters must appear after any mandatory parameters. For example, the following function declaration is illegal.

```cpp
void f(int x = 5, double z, int y); // illegal
```

This rule makes sense because the compiler does not know whether a nontrailing parameter is missing.

We can use default parameters to simplify writing generalized input and output functions. In Program 6.9, we wrote an input function Get() that accepted an input stream as its first parameter. It read the access code from that stream. We can rewrite `Get()` so that unless specified otherwise, it reads from the stream `cin`, but it can also read from another stream if desired. The prototype for the new `Get()` is

```
bool Get(int &d1, int &d2, int &d3, int &d4,
   int &d5, istream &in = cin);
```

and when `Get()` is invoked as

```
if (Get(d1, d2, d3, d4, d5)
   && Valid(d1, d2, d3, d4, d5))
      return true;
else
      return false;
```

it will read from stream `cin`. When we want to use `Get()` to read from a file, we can do so by supplying the sixth parameter. Thus the code

```
ifstream fin("telcodes.dat");
if (Get(d1, d2, d3, d4, d5, fin)
   && Valid(d1, d2, d3, d4, d5))
      return true;
else
      return false;
```

causes `Get()` to read from the stream `fin`, which is the file `telcodes.dat`.

Programmer Alert

> ### *Default parameters cannot be redefined*
>
> C++ does not allow the redefinition of a default parameter—not even to the same value—within a translation unit. The following code is illegal.
>
> ```
> void f(int x, int y = 3);    // prototype for f
> ...
>
> ...
> void f(int x, int y = 3) {    // illegal
> // body of f
> ...
> }
> ```
>
> In effect, either the prototype or the definition of the function, but not both, must specify the default values of the parameters. It will be our convention to specify the default value in the prototype of the function because we view the prototype as the interface to the function. However, you may encounter code that follows the opposite convention, or worse, sometimes specifies the default in the prototype and sometimes in the function definition.

6.12 CASTING OF FUNCTION PARAMETERS

One way to think about a function call is that it is just like an operator except that the function can take many operands and it may or may not produce a value. For example, the statement

```
int Sum = Plus(a, b, c);
```

can be thought of as applying the Plus operator to the operands a, b, and c. Indeed, in many respects C++ takes this view of functions, and many of the concepts that we discussed as applying to operators also apply to function calls.

For example, consider the following prototype and corresponding function invocation.

```
// ComputeInterest: compute simple compound interest
double ComputeInterest(double Principle,
 double InterestRate, int Days);
...

...
double Interest = ComputeInterest(4500, .075, 365);
```

Notice that in the call to function ComputeInterest() the type of the first parameter is **int**, whereas the prototype of the function specifies that ComputeInterest() expects a **double**. Similar to the way the C++ compiler converted operands of arithmetic operators to the appropriate type, it will convert parameter expressions to the appropriate type. In the above example, the compiler will convert the 4500 to a **double** and pass that as the first value.

Similarly, in the function invocation

```
double Interest = ComputeInterest(500.0, 0.8,
 155.8);
```

the third parameter 155.8 will be converted to an **int**. Thus the parameter Days will receive the value 155.

6.13 FUNCTION OVERLOADING

Previously we discussed how C++, like many programming languages, has operators that are *overloaded*. That is, what an operator means or does depends on the type of its operands. For example, the plus operator is overloaded. If its operands are integers, then it performs an integer addition. If its operands are floating point, then it performs a floating-point addition.

C++ also supports *function overloading*. That is, we can create several functions of the same name that behave differently. Function overloading is useful when we need to write functions that perform similar tasks but need to operate on different data types. The following function Swap() from Section 6.7 illustrates the use of function overloading.

```
void Swap(int &x, int &y) {
    int tmp = x;
    x = y
    y = tmp
    return;
}
```

The function accepts two reference integer parameters and swaps their values. Suppose that we also needed a function that swapped two **double** values. Without function overloading, we would be forced to choose a different name for this function. We might call it `SwapDouble()`. Inventing new names could become awkward, especially if we had many different versions of the swap function.

With function overloading, we do not need to think up different names for functions that perform similar tasks on different data types. We can create two functions that have the same name but different parameter lists.

Suppose that we had defined the following two `Swap()` functions.

```
// integer version of Swap
void Swap(int &x, int &y) {
    int tmp = x;
    x = y
    y = tmp
    return;
}
// double version of Swap
void Swap(double &x, double &y) {
    double tmp = x;
    x = y
    y = tmp
    return;
}
```

When the compiler encounters a call to function `Swap()`, how does it decide which one to invoke? The answer is that the compiler uses a technique similar to the one it uses to decide which type of operation to perform when it encounters an overloaded operator. With an overloaded operator, the types of the operands determine which operation to perform. With overloaded functions, the specifications of the actual parameters determine which function to invoke. The *signature* of a function is its parameter list. The compiler examines the parameter list of the function call, and it invokes the function whose signature best matches the actual parameter list.

For example, the code fragment

```
double w = 1.2;
double z = 3.4;
Swap(w, z);
```

would cause the double version of `Swap()` to be invoked because both actual parameters are type **double**. On the other hand, the statements

```
int i = 2;
int j = 4;
Swap(i, j);
```

invoke the integer version of `Swap()` because the parameters are integers. Determining which function to invoke when more than one function has the same name is called *function overload resolution*.

Function overload resolution is simple when there is a function definition in which the types of the formal parameters exactly match the types of the actual parameters. The matching function is invoked. When no exact match exists and the compiler must convert the actual parameters so that a function can be invoked, function overload resolution can become quite complicated. For example, the invocation of Swap() in the following statements

```
double z = 2.4;
int k = 4;
Swap(z, k);
```

is illegal because there is no "best match" between the actual parameter list and the formal parameter lists of the two function definitions. There is no best match because there are two equally reasonable ways the compiler could cast the actual parameters to match the formal parameter lists. The compiler could convert the first actual parameter to an integer and call the integer version of Swap(), or it could cast the second actual parameter to a **double** and call the **double** version of Swap().

As an indication of the complexity of overload resolution, the discussion of parameter matching requires 14 pages of discussion and examples in *The Annotated C++ Reference Manual* by Ellis and Stroustrup. Because of the complexity of function overload resolution when parameter conversions are required, we will not rely on its use. Rather, we will always ensure that a function definition exists with a parameter list where the types of the formal parameters exactly match the types of the actual parameters of any call. The interested or brave reader is referred to the annotated reference for the full details.

Programmer Alert

The Standard Template Library (STL)

The STL contains implementations of many useful functions that can be specialized based on the type. These are called *templates*. For example, the STL contains a template for creating specialized min and max functions discussed in Chapter 6. Similarly, it contains a template for creating swap functions for different types. Templates and how to use them are discussed in Chapter 14. As we have mentioned before, a good C++ programmer is aware of the features provided by the STL and uses them when appropriate.

Self-check Questions

18.   What is the signature of a function?

19.   What is function overload resolution?

20.   What is the output of the following program.

```
#include <iostream>
using namespace std;
void g(int i, int &j, int k = 9) {
    i = j;
    j = i - k;
    k = j * i
}
```

```
int main() {
    int i = 5;
    int j = 3;
    g(j, i, j);
    cout << i << endl;
    return 0;
}
```

21. What is the output of the following program?

```
#include <iostream>
using namespace std;
void g(int i, int &j, int k = 9) {
    i = j;
    j = i - k;
    k = j * i
}
int main() {
    int a = 5;
    int b = 8;
    g(a, b);
    cout << b << endl;
    return 0;
}
```

22. What is the output of the following program?

```
#include <iostream>
using namespace std;
void f(int a, float b, char c) {
    cout << "a is " << a << endl;
    cout << "b is " << b << endl;
    }
void f(float b, int a, char c) {
    cout << "b is " << b << endl;
    cout << "a is " << a << endl;
    }
int main() {
    int i = 3;
    float x = 5.0;
    f(x, i, 'd');
    f(i, x, 'd');

    return 0;
}
```

23. What is wrong with the following program?

```
#include <iostream>
using namespace std;
void g(int i, int &j, int k = 9)
int main() {
```

```
        int a = 5;
        int b = 8;
        g(a, b);
        cout << b << endl;
        return 0;
}

void g(int i, int &j, int k = 9) {
        i = j;
        j = i - k;
        k = j * i
}
```

6.14 RECURSIVE FUNCTIONS

Many programming languages, C++ included, support the use of recursion to solve problems. *Recursion* is the ability of a function to call itself. To illustrate what we mean by recursion and its use, let's reconsider the implementation of the factorial function. Our earlier definition of factorial

$$n! = \begin{cases} 1 & \text{if } n = 0 \\ n \times (n-1) \times \ldots \times 1 & \text{if } n \geq 1 \end{cases}$$

is not mathematically precise because we use an ellipsis (…). The ellipsis tells a reader to use her or his intuition to recognize the pattern. A formal definition of factorial removes any ambiguity.

$$n! = \begin{cases} 1 & \text{if } n = 0 \\ n \times (n-1)! & \text{if } n > 0 \end{cases}$$

In the preceding formal definition, we see that factorial is defined in terms of itself. That is, if $n > 0$, then $n!$ is $n \times (n-1)!$.

Using recursion, we can write a short and simple C++ function that computes factorial. The function is

```
int Factorial(int n) {
if (n == 0)
     return 1;
else
     return n * Factorial(n-1);
}
```

This function exactly mirrors the mathematical definition of factorial. If the value of n is 0, the value 1 is returned. If the value of n is not equal to 0, the product of n and Factorial(n-1) is returned.

To understand how recursion works, it is useful to visualize what is happening when a function calls itself. One way to do so is to picture the activation records that are created for each recursive call. Let's assume that we have the following main program:

```cpp
#include <iostream>
#include <string>
using namespace std;
int main() {
    cout << "Please enter a positive integer: ";
    int n;
    cin >> n;
    cout << n << "! = " << Factorial(n) << endl;
    return 0;
}
```

The activation records after `main()` calls `Factorial()` are

Activation records

In `Factorial()`, n is 3, so the **else** part

```cpp
return n * Factorial(n-1);
```

of the **if** statement is executed. The **else** part calls `Factorial()` again, this time with an actual parameter with value 2. In this invocation of function `Factorial()`, n is 2, so the **else** part

```cpp
return n * Factorial(n-1);
```

of the **if** statement is executed again with an actual parameter with value 1. As shown in Figure 6.8, the process continues until n equals 0. At this point, the **if** test expression evaluates to true, and

```cpp
return 1;
```

is executed. This statement causes the recursion to start to *unwind* (i.e., no more recursive calls).

As the recursion unwinds, values are returned to the calling invocation of the function. In effect, the return value is substituted for the call. The process of the recursion unwinding is illustrated in Figure 6.9. Using the returned value, the factorial of the n (for this invocation) is computed and returned to the next level. This process continues until the call to `Factorial()` from function `main()` returns to `main()` with the value of 3!.

When the first call to `Factorial()` returns to `main()`, the insertion statement produces the following output:

```
3! = 6
```

Figure 6.8

Activation records for recursive calls to Factorial()

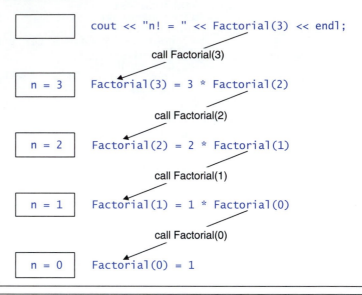

Figure 6.9

Unwinding the recursive calls to Factorial()

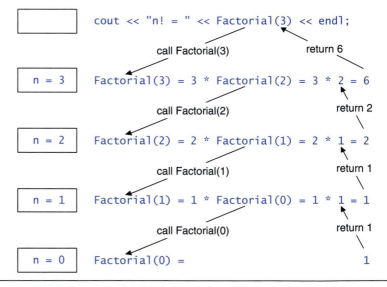

One of the nice things about recursion is that it is a succinct way of expressing certain mathematical formulas, and the corresponding C++ implementation is equally short. A recursive function generally has two parts:

- A recursive call with simpler parameters.

- A termination part that stops the recursion.

In the factorial code, the recursive call and the termination part were the two action parts of the **if-else** statement.

$$
\left.
\begin{aligned}
&\texttt{if (n == 0)}\\
&\qquad\texttt{return 1;}
\end{aligned}
\right\} \text{ Termination part}
$$

$$
\text{Recursive part }
\left\{
\begin{aligned}
&\texttt{else}\\
&\qquad\texttt{return n * Factorial(n - 1);}
\end{aligned}
\right.
$$

Let's consider the development of a recursive function to compute x^n. The C++ prototype of our power function is

```
int Power(int x, int n);
```

We know that x^0 is 1 for all x. This fact will be the termination part of our recursive function. We also know that $x^n = x \times x^{n-1}$ when n > 0, which will be the recursive part. Observe that because n is getting smaller, the recursion is sure to terminate. Writing the recursive version of the power function is simple.

```
int Power(int x, int n) {
    if (n == 0)
        return 1;
    else
        return x * Power(x, n-1);
}
```

As a final example of simple recursion, let's write a function that computes the nth Fibonacci number. We first considered this number sequence in Chapter 4. The Fibonacci sequence is denoted $F_1, F_2, F_3, \ldots, F_n$ where $F_1 = F_2 = 1$ and every further term is the sum of the preceding two. The first eight numbers in the sequence are 1, 1, 2, 3, 5, 8, 13, 21. The Fibonacci sequence was developed in 1202 by the Italian mathematician Leonardo Pisano, who was investigating how fast rabbits could breed in ideal circumstances. He assumed that a pair of rabbits (male and female) breed and always produce another pair of rabbits (male and female, too). Furthermore, a rabbit becomes sexually mature after one month, and the gestation period is also one month. Thus a pair produces one new pair every month from the second month on. Assuming a rabbit never dies, how many rabbits would there be after one year?

We can work out a solution by hand. At the end of the first month, there is still only one pair. At the end of the second month, another pair is born so there are now two pairs. At the end of the third month, the original pair produces another pair, but the second pair is just getting started, so there are only three pairs. At the end of the fourth month, the original pair has produced another pair and so has the second pair, so now there are five pairs. At the end of the fifth month, there will be eight pairs. In the sixth month, there will be thirteen pairs. The sequence being generated is

1, 1, 2, 3, 5, 8, 13, 21, 34, …

That is, the number of pairs for a month is the sum of the number of pairs in the two previous months. At the end of 12 months, there will be 144 pairs of rabbits.

The mathematical definition of the nth Fibonacci number is

$$F_n = \begin{cases} F_n = 1 & \text{if } n = 1 \\ F_n = 1 & \text{if } n = 2 \\ F_n = F_{n-1} + F_{n-2} & \text{if } n > 2 \end{cases}$$

The definition is a bit more complicated than our previous recursive functions, but we can use the same strategy. The pattern for our previous recursive functions has been

```
if (termination code satisfied)
    return value;
else
    make simpler recursive call;
```

and this pattern will work for the Fibonacci numbers, too. The code for the function is

```
int Fibonacci(int n) {
    if (n <= 2)
        return 1;
    else
        return Fibonacci(n-1) + Fibonacci(n-2);
}
```

The main difference between the current code and the code for the previous recursive functions is that the current code makes two "simpler" recursive calls. We know that these recursive calls eventually unwind because each recursive call is passing an n that is getting smaller. Figure 6.10 illustrates the recursive calls made by this code when computing F_5.

The Fibonacci numbers are interesting because they model many things in nature. For example, they model the reproductive behavior of bees, the number of branches in a tree, and the number of petals on a flower (e.g., buttercups have 5 petals; some asters have 21 petals; and there are daisies with 34, 55, and 89 petals). In the exercises, we explore some other interesting aspects of the Fibonacci numbers.

Self-check Questions

24.   What is the output of the following program?

```
#include <iostream>
using namespace std;
int f(int n) {
    if (n <= 1)
        return n;
    else
        return f(n-1) + f(n-2);
}
```

```
int main() {
    cout << f(4) << endl;
    return 0;
}
```

Figure 6.10

Computation of F_5

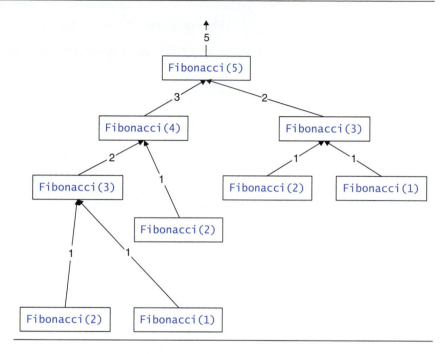

25. Write a recursive function `Reverse()` that accepts two string arguments, s and r. Function `Reverse()` uses recursion to reverse the characters in string s and place the reversed string in string r.

26. Write a recursive function `PrintNumber()` that accepts an integer argument. Function `PrintNumber()` uses recursion to print out the value of its argument a character at a time.

6.15 DISPLAYING A PRICE-INTERVAL STOCK CHART

Serious investors spend a lot of time trying to figure how the stock market is going to behave. Many of the software tools they use present information in a graphical manner to make any patterns in the market's behavior more apparent. The problem we now consider is how to graphically display a series of weekly high–low price intervals for a given stock. The problem description is

The input to the price-interval problem comes from a file that contains a collection of weekly prices for the stock of interest. The name of the file is supplied by the user in response to a prompt (the filename and prices within the file should be tested for validity). Conceptually, the prices in the file come in pairs. A pair represents the low and high price of the stock for a week. All of the pairs are to be extracted, and a line interval is plotted on a labeled graph for each pair. For example, given the following sample input/output behavior for extracting the stock filename

```
Please enter file to be processed: stock.dat
```

where file `stock.dat` contains the following values

```
2 4
1 5
4 6
4 8
5 9
3 8
```

Figure 6.11 shows the expected display. The graph includes labels for the axes, the file being processed, origins for both axes, the number of weeks of stock data, and the maximum occurring stock price.

Figure 6.11

Price-interval chart for file stock.dat

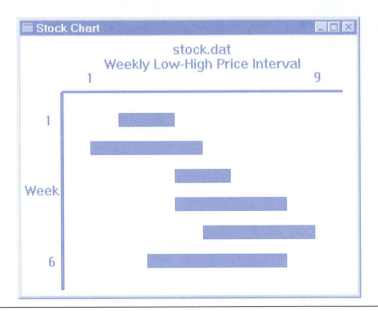

Properly representing the weekly data is crucial to solving this problem. In a pure object-oriented design, we would probably create an object whose representation captures both the weekly low and high, along with member functions that can test validity and chart the associated interval. Starting in Chapter 7, we introduce the class mechanism that allows us to define such objects. One of the exercises in that chapter is to rethink this problem. However, for now we need two independent objects to represent the weekly low and high. Given these two weekly values and the window for the display, displaying a price interval, using an object of type `RectangleShape`, is straightforward.

The display of the *x*-axis requires that we have a record of the maximum stock price seen over all weeks, and the display of the *y*-axis requires that we have a record of the number of weeks of stock data. Computing these two values is simple. For the maximum price, we iteratively compare the current weekly high with the maximum price seen so far and, if necessary, update the maximum price seen so far. To do the comparison, we use the function `Max()` discussed in Section 6.3. For the number of weeks, we maintain a counter that is incremented once per weekly extraction.

An algorithm for the problem quickly follows from our analysis.

Step 1.   Prompt and extract filename.

Step 2.   Define an input stream associated with extracted filename.

Step 3.   Set-up weekly counter and overall stock high.

Step 4.   While we can read another valid weekly low and high do

Step 4.1   Increment week counter.

Step 4.2   Compare weekly high with overall stock high so far and update the overall stock high so far if necessary.

Step 4.3   Chart weekly interval.

Step 4.4   Repeat step 4.

Step 5.   Display *x*-axis.

Step 6.   Display *y*-axis.

The steps of the algorithm provide a framework for our program. The steps are captured in the following code segment.

```
// steps 1 and 2: extract filename and setup stream
string StockFile = GetFileName();
ifstream fin(StockFile.c_str());
if (! fin) {
    cerr << "Cannot open: " << StockFile << endl;
    exit(1);
}
// step 3: setup
float StockHigh = 0;
int WeekNbr = 0;
// step 4: iteratively process stock-price intervals
int WeeklyHigh;
int WeeklyLow;
while (ReadStockInterval(fin, StockFile, WeeklyLow,
  WeeklyHigh, WeekNbr) {

    // step 4.1: have another week of data
    ++WeekNbr;

    // step 4.2: update the overall high if necessary
    StockHigh = Max(StockHigh, WeeklyHigh);

    // step 4.3: chart it
    ChartWeek(WeekNbr, WeeklyLow, WeeklyHigh);
}
// steps 5 and 6: display axes
DrawXAxis(StockFile, StockHigh);
DrawYAxis(WeekNbr);
```

In the code segment, the portions of the algorithm that require further refinement are assigned to functions in what is essentially a *top-down design*. In this design method, you determine the basic tasks that must be performed to solve the problem. You also determine how these tasks must interface and interact. If necessary, the basic tasks are decomposed until all actions are well understood and (relatively) easy to implement. For our problem, we decompose six of the tasks into functions.

- `GetFilename()`: get the name of the file that contains the stock intervals to be charted.
- `ReadStockInterval()`: read the weekly stock prices and verify that they are sensible.
- `Max()`: assist in the updating of the highest stock price seen so far.
- `ChartWeek()`: display the current weekly interval.
- `DrawXAxis()`: draw the x-axis and its associated labels.
- `DrawYaxis()`: draw the y-axis and its associated labels.

When developing functions to solve a problem, the functions are typically placed in files that group them by purpose. Essentially the function files are private libraries. At the same time, a software engineer will also create header files for these function files. If a private library is needed, the associated header file is then typically included at the start of the program file that requires the functions. It is the header file that is included rather than the implementation file. The implementation file is separately compiled just once and then linked as needed during the translation of applications that use the private library. The result is a faster application compilation.

Our stock-charting program consists of two implementation files, `stock.cpp` and `utility.cpp`, and one header file, `utility.h`.

Implementation file `stock.cpp` principally contains `ApiMain()`. In fact, except for some additions regarding windowing features, the previous code segment is the function body of `ApiMain()`. As discussed in Chapter 3 when using our graphical classes, `ApiMain()` is where your program logically starts. The complete contents of `stock.cpp` are shown in Listing 6.1.

Besides defining `ApiMain()`, implementation file `stock.cpp` includes the necessary standard library header files and our local library header files `ezwin.h` and `utility.h`. Library header file `ezwin.h` prototypes our basic graphical functionality. Header file `utility.h` prototypes the six functions from `utility.cpp` used by `ApiMain()`.

Listing 6.2 gives the contents of `utility.h`. The function prototypes are nested within preprocessor directives. The directives ensure that the prototypes are declared once per translation unit. The header file for a programmer-defined library is normally included at the beginning of an implementation file right after the inclusions of the header files for the standard libraries.

The contents of `utility.cpp` are given in Listings 6.3 to 6.5. Listing 6.3 shows the initial portion of `utility.cpp`. Observe that the file includes header file `utility.h`. This inclusion ensures that the function definitions actually have the proper interface—if they did not, an error message would be generated by the compiler regarding an improper overloading of the function in question. After the file inclusions, several constants are defined. The constants describe axis and interval bar characteristics and how far the graph should be offset from the origin of the window.

Listing 6.1

Program with a scope problem

```cpp
#include <iostream>
#include <fstream>
#include <string>
#include <stdlib.h>
#include "ezwin.h"
#include "utility.h"
using namespace std;

// ApiMain(): manage display of a stock chart
int ApiMain() {
   // extract filename and setup stream
   string StockFile = GetFileName();
   ifstream fin(StockFile.c_str());
   if (! fin) {
      cerr << "Cannot open: " << StockFile << endl;
      exit(1);
   }

   // setup
   SimpleWindow W("Stock Chart", 12, 9);
   W.Open();
   float StockHigh = 0.0f;
   int WeekNbr = 0;

   // iteratively process stock-price intervals
   int WeeklyHigh;
   int WeeklyLow;
   while (ReadStockInterval(fin, StockFile, WeeklyLow,
    WeeklyHigh, WeekNbr)) {
      // have another week of data
      ++WeekNbr;

      // chart it
      ChartWeek(W, WeekNbr, WeeklyLow, WeeklyHigh);

      // update the overall high if necessary
      StockHigh = Max(StockHigh, WeeklyHigh);
   }

   // display axes
   DrawXAxis(W, StockFile, StockHigh);
   DrawYAxis(W, WeekNbr);

   cout << "Type a character followed by a\n"
    << "return to remove the graph and exit" << endl;
   char AnyChar;
   cin >> AnyChar;
   W.Close();

   // all done
   return 0;
}
```

Functions GetFileName(), Valid(), and Max() follow next in Listing 6.3. These functions are presented without comment, as they are either simple or have been previously discussed.

Listing 6.3 also contains the **void** function ChartWeek() from utility.cpp. Function ChartWeek() has four parameters. The first parameter, W, is the SimpleWindow that holds the graph. This parameter must be a reference parameter because the function will modify the window by plotting the current week's interval. Indeed, all the plotting functions, ChartWeek(), DrawX-Axis(), DrawYAxis(), have a reference parameter for the SimpleWindow

Listing 6.2

*Utility.h prototypes the
functions of utility.cpp*

```
#ifndef UTILITY_H
#define UTILITY_H
#include <iostream>
#include <string>
using namespace std;
// prototypes
string GetFileName();
bool Valid(float low, float high);
void ChartWeek(SimpleWindow &W, int week, float low,
   float high);
void DrawXAxis(SimpleWindow &W, const string &StockFile,
   float StockHigh);
void DrawYAxis(SimpleWindow &W, float WeekNbr);
int Max(int a, int b);
bool ReadStockInterval(istream &file, const string &FName,
   int &Low, int &High, int WeekNbr);
#endif
```

where the graph will be rendered. The three **float** value parameters, Week, Low, and High, representing the week number and endpoints of the interval. The function displays a bar representing a weekly stock-price interval in the chart graph.

The *x*-coordinate of the center of the stock-price interval bar is the sum of the chart's *x*-axis constant offset ChartXOffset and the average of the values Low and High. The *y*-coordinate of the center of the bar is the value Week shifted by the chart's *y*-axis constant offset ChartYOffset. The length of the bar is given by the difference High – Low. The height of the bar is given by the constant BarThickness. The color of the bar is given by the constant Bar-Color. Once a RectangleShape object Bar has been defined with these characteristics, its Draw() member function displays the stock-price interval.

Listing 6.3 also contains function ReadStockInterval(). As explained in Section 6.8 for flexibility, the input function of the program is placed in a separate function. The first argument to function ReadStockInterval() is the stream to read the data. Similar to function ReadValues() presented in Section 6.8, if the stream to extract the data is cin, the function prompts the user for input. Thus function ReadStockInterval() can be used to read data interactively or from a file. As always, the input is tested to ensure it is valid data.

Listing 6.4. of utility.cpp defines the **void** function DrawXAxis(), which displays the *x*-axis and its various labels. To accomplish the display, the function makes uses of two classes that we have not used before: Label and ostringstream.

Class Label is another of our graphical classes. Label objects are used to display messages in a SimpleWindow. In initializing a Label object, we need only specify the SimpleWindow object to which the label will be displayed, its position in that window, and the desired message.

Class ostringstream is part of the iostream hierarchy. An object of class ostringstream is known as an *in-memory* or *in-core* stream because insertions to it are stored in a stringlike memory buffer rather than being sent to the monitor or to a file. Once the insertions to an ostringstream object have

Listing 6.3

*Contents of initial
portion of utility.cpp*

```cpp
#include <iomanip>
#include <sstream>
#include <string>
#include "rect.h"
#include "label.h"
#include "utility.h"

using namespace std;

// utility constants
const float AxisThickness = 0.1f;
const color AxisColor = Blue;
const float BarThickness = 0.5f;
const color BarColor = Blue;
const float ChartXOffset = 1.5f;
const float ChartYOffset = 2.0f;

// GetFileName(): prompt and extract filename
string  GetFileName() {
    cout << "Please enter file to be processed: ";
    string s;
    cin >> s;
    return s;
}

// Valid(): are weekly stock prices sensible
bool Valid(float low, float high) {
    return (0 <= low) && (low <= high);
}

// Max: determine larger of its two parameters
int Max(int a, int b) {
    if (a < b)
        return b;
    else
        return a;
}

// ChartWeek(): display current week's interval
void ChartWeek(SimpleWindow &W, int Week, float Low,
 float High) {
    float x = ChartXOffset + (Low + High)/2.0;
    float y = ChartYOffset + Week;
    float Length = High - Low;
    RectangleShape Bar(W, x, y, BarColor, Length,
     BarThickness);
    Bar.Draw();
    return;
}

// ReadStockInterval(): read weekly low and high for stock
bool ReadStockInterval(istream &fin,
 const string &FileName, int &Low, int &High, int Week) {
    if (fin == cin)
        cout << "Enter the low and high stock price";
    fin >> Low >> High;
    // if no more data return false
    if (! fin)
        return false;
    // check for valid data
    if (! Valid(Low, High)) {
        cerr << FileName << ": Bad data for week "
         << Week + 1 << endl;
```

```
        exit(1);
    }
    return true;
}
```

been completed, the constructed string can be accessed via the `ostring-stream` member function `str()`. The `ostringstream` class is declared in the standard header file `sstream`. This header file also declares an in-memory input stream class `istringstream` and an in-memory class `stringstream` capable of both insertions and deletions.

Listing 6.4

DrawXAxis() from utility.cpp

```
// DrawXAxis(): display x-axis with labels
void DrawXAxis(SimpleWindow &W, const string &StockFile,
 float MaxX) {
    // draw axis
    float AxisLength = MaxX + 1;
    float CenterX = ChartXOffset + MaxX/2.0 + 0.5;
    float CenterY = ChartYOffset;
    RectangleShape Axis(W, CenterX, CenterY, AxisColor,
     AxisLength, AxisThickness);
    Axis.Draw();

    // display filename
    float FilenameX = CenterX;
    float FilenameY = ChartYOffset/4.0;
    Label Filename(W, FilenameX, FilenameY, StockFile);
    Filename.Draw();

    // display axis legend
    float LegendX = CenterX;
    float LegendY = ChartYOffset/2.0;
    Label Legend(W, LegendX, LegendY,
     "Weekly Low-High Price Interval");
    Legend.Draw();

    // display low label over axis
    float LowX = ChartXOffset + 1;
    float LowY = ChartYOffset/2.0 + 0.5;
    Label Low(W, LowX, LowY, "1");
    Low.Draw();

    // display high label over axis
    float HighX = ChartXOffset + MaxX;
    float HighY = ChartYOffset/2.0 + 0.5;
    ostringstream HighValue;
    HighValue << setw(3) << MaxX;
    Label High(W, HighX, HighY, HighValue.str());
    High.Draw();

    // all done
    return;
}
```

Function `DrawXAxis()` begins by defining the length of the axis. For aesthetic purposes, the axis is one unit greater than parameter `MaxX`, which represents the maximum *x*-coordinate used in displaying the price-interval bars. The *x*- and *y*-coordinates `CenterX` and `CenterY` of the center of the *x*-axis are then defined. Like the display of price-interval bars, the center coordinates of the axis are shifted over from the origin of the window. Having defined these values, the axis is represented as a `RectangleShape` object and then drawn.

The name of the file being processed through the `string` parameter `FileName` and a character string legend for the axis are displayed next, using `Label` objects. The positions of these two `Label` objects are relative to the center of the *x*-axis.

Function `DrawXAxis()` next constructs and displays the labels for low and high values on the *x*-axis. Because the low value is known to be 1, which can be represented as the string "1", it is easy to define a `Label` object `Low` for labeling the left end of the axis. However, labeling the right end of the axis is not as straightforward, because there is no automatic conversion of a numeric value to a string. We can construct a string representation by inserting the value of `MaxX` to `ostringstream` object `HighValue`. The `setw(3)` manipulator ensures that the field width is (at least) 3. Together, the two insertions produce a suitable string representation of the value `MaxX`, which can then be accessed by invoking `HighValue.str()`.

Listing 6.5 of `utility.cpp` defines the **void** function `DrawYAxis()`. Its operation is analogous to `DrawXAxis()`, and therefore the function is not discussed.

Listing 6.5

DrawYAxis() from utility.cpp

```
// DrawYAxis(): display y-axis with labels
void DrawYAxis(SimpleWindow &W, float MaxY) {
    // draw axis
    float CenterX = ChartXOffset;
    float CenterY = ChartYOffset + MaxY/2.0 + 0.5;
    float AxisLength = MaxY + 1;
    RectangleShape Axis(W, CenterX, CenterY, AxisColor,
     AxisThickness, AxisLength);
    Axis.Draw();

    // display legend
    float LegendX = ChartXOffset/2.0;
    float LegendY = CenterY;
    Label Legend(W, LegendX, LegendY, "Week");
    Legend.Draw();

    // display low label over axis
    float LowX = ChartXOffset/2.0 + 0.25;
    float LowY = ChartYOffset + 1;
    Label Low(W, LowX, LowY, "1");
    Low.Draw();

    // display high label over axis
    float HighX = ChartXOffset/2.0 + 0.25;
    float HighY = ChartYOffset + MaxY;
    ostringstream HighValue;
    HighValue << setw(3) << MaxY;
    Label High(W, HighX, HighY, HighValue.str());
    High.Draw();

    // all done
    return;
}
```

This analysis completes the discussion of our stock-charting program.

History of Computing

A universal calculator

The period from 1900 to 1930 saw the refinement of mechanical calculators—they became faster and more sophisticated. Similarly, the punched card equipment developed by Hollerith was steadily improved and put to new uses. As of 1930, Babbage's dream of a general-purpose computer had not been advanced; however, from 1930 onward, advances occurred at a breakneck pace. Indeed, new developments happened so fast that historians have had a hard time determining who should be given credit for various inventions and ideas.

Two noteworthy ideas are credited to Konrad Zuse. Zuse was a German engineer, who like many before him, hated doing tedious engineering calculations. To make such calculations easier, Zuse decided to develop a universal calculator. Previous machines had used the decimal number system. Zuse recognized that a calculation machine could be made much simpler if it used the binary number system. Indeed, all of today's modern high-speed computers use the binary number system. Zuse's second contribution was that instead of using mechanical wheels, the calculator used mechanical switches to manipulate the data. Again, all of today's modern machines use switches, although they are in the form of very small transistors.

Zuse's first machine was called the Z1. The Z1, besides being an innovative machine, is also notable because it may have been the first "homebrew" computer. Zuse constructed the Z1 in the living room of his parents' apartment in Berlin. Using the knowledge and experience gained from building the Z1, he built a larger machine called the Z2. The distinguishing feature of the Z2 was that it was an electromechanical calculator. In this machine, electrical relays replaced the mechanical switches. This replacement greatly increased the speed of the calculator. During World War II, Zuse continued to refine his designs, producing the Z3 and Z4. After the war, the Z4 (see Figure 6.12) was installed at the Federal Polytechnical Institute (ETH) in Switzerland and was used until 1955. Zuse, himself, went on to found a small computer company.

6.16   POINTS TO REMEMBER

✔ A function is a mechanism that permits modular programming and software reuse.

✔ The simplest functions take parameters in a manner similar to mathematical functions and then compute and return a value to be used in an expression.

✔ A statement block is a list of statements within curly braces.

✔ A nested block is a statement block occurring within another statement block.

✔ To define a function, a programmer must completely specify its interface and actions. The actions occur within the function body. The function body is a statement block.

Figure 6.12

Konrad Zuse and the Z4

✔ A **return** statement supplies a value from the invoked function to the invoking function.

✔ A local object is an object defined within a statement block.

✔ A global object is an object defined outside of any function interface or function body.

✔ To complete their tasks, functions can use local and global objects and even other functions.

✔ To invoke a function, a programmer supplies actual parameters of the correct types. If the actual parameters do not match the types of the formal parameters, the compiler will attempt to perform conversions to put the actual parameters in the correct form.

✔ An activation record is memory that the function uses to store its parameters and local objects.

✔ For each function invocation, a new activation record is created.

✔ Typical programming efforts span multiple files. The files are individually compiled and linked together to produce an executable version of the program.

✔ A header file is often used to prototype functions that are defined in implementation files. Through the use of header files, functions defined in one implementation file can be invoked within another implementation file.

✔ Names can be reused as long as the declarations associated with the names occur in different blocks.

✔ The unary scope resolution operator :: can be used to reference a global object whose name has been reused in the local scope.

✔ Global fundamental objects are initialized to zero by default.

✔ A reference to a global object in an implementation file requires that the global object be either defined or declared using an **extern** statement within the translation unit of that implementation file.

✔ A global object can be defined only once in the global scope of the program.

✔ In top-down design, you determine the basic tasks that must be performed and how these tasks must interface and interact. If necessary, the basic tasks are decomposed until all actions are well understood and can be easily implemented.

✔ The `sstream` library provides in-memory streams that can act like string buffers.

✔ Through a series of insertions, an `ostringstream` object can create a string representation of the values of other objects.

✔ Recursion is when a function calls itself. A recursive function must have two parts. It has a termination part that ends the recursion and a recursive call with simpler parameters.

✔ C++ supports two types of parameters—value parameters and reference parameters.

✔ When a parameter is passed by value, a copy of the object is passed to the called function. Any modifications made to the parameter by the called function change the copy, not the original object.

✔ When a reference parameter is used, instead of passing a copy of the object, a reference to the original object is passed. Any modifications made to the parameter by the called function change the original object.

✔ One common reason for using a reference parameter is that the called function needs to modify the object being passed, for example, when the called function needs to return several values to the calling function. The parameters that are used to pass values back to the calling function should be reference parameters.

✔ When an `iostream` object is passed to a function, either an extraction or an insertion operation implicitly modifies the stream. Thus stream objects should be passed as reference parameters.

✔ A reason to use a reference parameter is for efficiency. When an object is passed by value, a copy of the object is passed. If the object is large, making a copy of it can be expensive in terms of execution time and memory space. Thus objects that are large or objects whose size is not known are often passed by reference. We can ensure that the objects are not modified by using the **const** modifier.

✔ A **const** modifier applied to a parameter declaration indicates that the function may not change the object. If the function attempts to modify the object, the compiler will report a compilation error.

✔ C++'s default parameter mechanism provides the ability to define a function so that a parameter gets a default value if a call to the function does not provide a value for that parameter. Thus for most calls to the function, only the necessary parameters are listed in the call; default values are provided for the other parameters. When necessary, the function can be called with values provided for all the parameters.

✔ To make a function maximally useful, especially a library function, try to make the function as general as possible. The function should accept more parameters than are needed in the common, most heavily used cases.

✔ Default parameters can be specified for trailing parameters only.

✔ A function's parameter list is the signature of the function.

✔ Function overloading is when two or more functions have the same name.

✔ The compiler resolves overloaded function calls by calling the function whose signature best matches that of the call.

6.17 TO DELVE FURTHER

The Annotated C++ Reference Manual by Margaret Ellis and Bjarne Stroustrup contains a complete discussion of function overload resolution.

6.18 EXERCISES

6.1 What is the purpose of name reuse?

6.2 Describe what happens during a function call.

6.3 How does a function prototype differ from a function definition?

6.4 What is an activation record?

6.5 What are the differences between an actual parameter and a formal parameter?

6.6 What is a local object?

6.7 What is a global object?

6.8 Can the name of a formal parameter be the same name as an actual parameter?

6.9 Does a **void** function necessarily contain a **return** statement? Explain.

6.10 Does a non-**void** function necessarily contain a **return** statement? Explain.

6.11 Write a **int** function Cube() that returns the cube of its single **int** formal parameter n.

6.12 Write a **float** function Triangle() that computes the area of a triangle using its two **float** formal parameters h and w, where h is the height and w is the length of the base of the triangle.

6.13 Write a **float** function Rectangle() that computes and returns the area of a rectangle using its two **float** formal parameters h and w, where h is the height and w is the width of the rectangle.

6.14 Write a **void** function DoubleSpace() that inserts two newline characters ('\n') to the standard output stream cout.

6.15   Write a **void** function EndLine() with a single **int** formal parameter n that indicates the number of newline characters to be displayed by the function.

6.16   Write a **float** function GetRadius() that prompts the user for a radius, extracts the user's response, and then returns the response as its value.

6.17   Rewrite Program 6.1 so that it uses the function GetRadius() from Exercise 6.16.

6.18   As discussed in Chapter 2, the formula for a line is normally given as $y = mx + b$. Write a function Line() that expects three **float** parameters, a slope m, a y-intercept b, and an x-coordinate x. The function computes the y-coordinate associated with the line specified by m and b at x-coordinate x.

6.19   Write a **bool** function Intersect() with four **float** parameters m1, b1, m2, and b2. The parameters come conceptually in two pairs. The first pair contains the coefficients describing one line; the second pair contains coefficients describing a second line. The function returns **true** if the two lines intersect; otherwise, the function returns **false**.

6.20   Write a **bool** function Parallel() with four **float** parameters m1, b1, m2, and b2. The parameters come conceptually in two pairs. The first pair contains the coefficients describing one line; the second pair contains coefficients describing a second line. The function returns **true** if the two lines are parallel; otherwise, the function returns **false**. Why does the function take four parameters?

6.21   Write functions for the following tasks. Discuss your choice of which values are parameters, which values are local constants, and what their types should be.

a)   Speed(): Compute the speed of an object after t seconds of acceleration given that the object was initially traveling at v_0 meters per second and then accelerated at a meters per second per second, where $speed = v_0 + at$.

b)   Distance(): Compute the distance traveled in t seconds by an object that started at rest and then accelerated at a meters per second per second, where $distance = at^2/2$.

c)   BarVolume(): Compute the volume of a rectangular bar with width w, length l, and height h, where $bar\ volume = wlh$.

d)   SphereVolume(): Compute the volume of a sphere with radius r, where $sphere\ volume = 4\pi r^3/3$.

6.22 What is the output of the following program? Explain.

```cpp
#include <iostream>
#include <string>
using namespace std;
int i = 0;
int I = 1;
int main() {
    int i = 2;
    int I = 3;
    ::i = i + 10;
    I = ::I + I + 20;
    ::I = ::i + 30;
    i = I + 40;
    cout << i << endl;
    cout << ::i << endl;
    cout << I << endl;
    cout << ::I << endl;
    return 0;
}
```

6.23 What is the output of the following program? Explain.

```cpp
#include <iostream>
#include <string>
using namespace std;
int counter = 0;
void f() {
    ++counter;
}
void g() {
    f();
    f();
}
void h() {
    f();
    g();
    f();
}
int main() {
    f();
    cout << counter << endl;
    g();
    cout << counter << endl;
    h();
    cout << counter << endl;
    return 0;
}
```

6.24 What is the output of the following program? Explain.

```cpp
#include <iostream>
#include <string>
using namespace std;
void f() {
    int i = 1;
    int j = 2;
    cout << "f: i = " << i << endl;
    cout << "f: j = " << j << endl;
    return;
```

```
}
int main() {
    int i = 10;
    int j = 20;
    f();
    cout << "main: i = " << i << endl;
    cout << "main: j = " << j << endl;
    return 0;
}
```

6.25   What is the output of the following program? Explain.

```
#include <iostream>
#include <string>
using namespace std;
void f(int i, int j) {
    cout << "f: i = " << i << endl;
    cout << "f: j = " << j << endl;
    return;
}
int main() {
    int i = 10;
    int j = 20;
    f(i, j);
    cout << "main: i = " << i << endl;
    cout << "main: j = " << j << endl;
    return 0;
}
```

6.26   What is the output of the following program? Explain.

```
#include <iostream>
#include <string>
using namespace std;
void f(int i, int j) {
    i = i + j;
    j = j + i;
    cout << "f: i = " << i << endl;
    cout << "f: j = " << j << endl;
    return;
}
int main() {
    int i = 10;
    int j = 20;
    f(50, j);
    f(i, 50);
    cout << "main: i = " << i << endl;
    cout << "main: j = " << j << endl;
    return 0;
}
```

6.27   What is the output of the following program? Explain.

```
#include <iostream>
#include <string>
using namespace std;
void f(int i, int j) {
    int temp;
    temp = i;
    i = j;
```

```
        j = temp;
        cout << "f: i = " << i << endl;
        cout << "f: j = " << j << endl;
        return;
}
int main() {
        int a = 10;
        int b = 20;
        f(a, b);
        f(b, a);
        cout << "main: a = " << a << endl;
        cout << "main: b = " << b << endl;
        return 0;
}
```

6.28   Write a function SwissCheese() with eight parameters w, 1, h, m, b, n, r, and d that computes the volume of a rectangular hunk of Swiss cheese, where the hunk has width *w*, length *l*, height *h*, *m* internal spherical air bubbles of radius *b*, and *n* surface cylindrical holes of radius *r* and height *d*. The function should use function CylinderVolume() defined in this chapter and functions BarVolume() and SphereVolume() developed in Exercise 6.21. Then develop a complete program that prompts a user for the characteristics of a Swiss cheese hunk and then appropriately displays the volume of the hunk.

6.29   In the U.S. coin system, the penny is the basic coin, and it is equal to 1 cent, a nickel is equivalent to 5 cents, a dime is equivalent to 10 cents, a quarter is equivalent to 25 cents, and a half-dollar is equivalent to 50 cents. Write the following **int** functions. Each function has a single **int** formal parameter Amount.

   a) HalfDollars(): Compute the maximum number of half-dollars that could be used in making change for Amount.

   b) Quarters(): Compute the maximum number of quarters that could be used in making change for Amount.

   c) Dimes(): Compute the maximum number of dimes that could be used in making change for Amount.

   d) Nickels(): Compute the maximum number of nickels that could be used in making change for Amount.

6.30   Write a **void** function MakeChange() that expects a single **int** parameter Amount that displays to the standard output stream cout how to make change for Amount using a minimal number of U.S. coins. The function should use the functions developed in the previous exercise. Also develop a complete program that prompts a user for an amount, and if the amount is sensible, the program then invokes MakeChange(), using that amount as its actual parameter.

6.31   Modify function `PromptAndGet()` to take a single parameter `s` of type `string` from the library `string`. Parameter `s` is to be the prompt message.

6.32   Modify the stock program to extract a third data value per week. The additional value is the weekly closing price. Modify `ChartWeek()` to use this value as a parameter and to display a marker for the value in the appropriate spot on the price-interval bar.

6.33   The declaration of window `W` in Listing 6.1 is a potential problem in that its size is set before analyzing the data. Because the data comes from a file, it is possible to process the information more than once. Write functions `NumberOfWeeks()` and `HighStockPrice()` that respectively determine the number of weeks of stock data and the highest stock price in the file. Replace the definition of `W` in `stock.cpp` to use these functions in the initialization of `W` as the following code segment shows:

```
extern const float ChartXOffset;
extern const float ChartYOffset;
string StockFile = GetFileName();
SimpleWindow W("Stock Chart",
  HighStockPrice(StockFile) + ChartXOffset+1,
  NumberOfWeeks(StockFile) + ChartYOffset+1);
```

6.34   Rewrite function `Factorial()` so that it returns a double value.

6.35   Develop a program that uses the function `Factorial()` of Exercise 6.34 to compute an approximation of e (Euler's number). Base your approximation on the following formula for e:

$$1 + \frac{1}{1!} + \frac{1}{2!} + \frac{1}{3!} + \dots .$$

6.36   Write a **float** function `ftoc()` that returns the Celsius temperature corresponding to the Fahrenheit temperature represented by its value **float** parameter `t`. The conversion formula for Fahrenheit to Celsius is $C = 5(F - 32)/9$.

6.37   Write a **float** function `ctof()` that returns the Fahrenheit temperature corresponding to the Celsius temperature represented by its value **float** parameter `t`. The conversion formula for Fahrenheit to Celsius is $F = (9C/5) + 32$.

6.38   Write a **float** function `mtok()` that returns the distance in kilometers corresponding to the distance in miles represented by its float value `d`. Note that a mile = 1.609344 kilometers.

6.39   Write a **float** function `ktom()` that returns the distance in miles corresponding to the distance in kilometers represented by its float value `d`.

6.40   Write a **bool** function `IsPrime()` that has a single parameter `i` of type integer. The function returns **true** if `i` is a prime number; otherwise, the function is **false**.

6.41   Write a **bool** function `IsEndOfSentence()` that has a single value **char** parameter `c`. The function returns **true** if `c` is either a period, a question mark, or an exclamation point; otherwise, the function returns **false**.

6.42 Write an **int** function Sum() that expects a single integer number as its parameter. The function should return the sum of the integers from 1 to that number.

6.43 Modify the recursive version of function Factorial() given in Section 6.14 so that it terminates if the value of its parameter is negative. Note that 0! is defined mathematically to be 1, so your modification should not affect this computation.

6.44 Design a program that takes as its input two integer numbers that represent a range of integers. The program should display the sum of the integers in that range. Which functions from the chapters and exercises should be used? Explain.

6.45 Write a **void** function PrintChar() that expects two parameters: a character object c and an integer amount n. The function should make n copies of the character c to the standard output stream cout.

6.46 Write a **float** function EvaluateQuadraticPolynomial() that expects four **float** parameters a, b, c, and x. The function should return the value

$$ax^2 + bx + c$$

6.47 Write a **double** function CubicArea() that computes the area under the curve for the cubic polynomial $a_3x^3 + a_2x^2 + a_1x + a_0$ along the x-interval (s, t).

6.48 Write a **double** function QuarticArea() that computes the area under the curve for the quartic polynomial $a_4x^4 + a_3x^3 + a_2x^2 + a_1x + a_0$ along the x-interval (s, t).

6.49 An angle is normally measured in either degrees or in radians where 360 degrees equal 2π radians. Write **float** functions DegreesToRadians() and RadiansToDegrees() that each expect a single **float** parameter. Function DegreesToRadians() treats its parameter as a value in degrees and returns the equivalent number of radians. Function RadiansToDegrees() treats its parameter as a value in radians and returns the equivalent number of degrees.

6.50 Write a function StripVowels() that extracts and processes the current input line. The function returns, as a string, the consonant portion of the input.

6.51 Write a function DistanceToLightYears() that takes a distance in kilometers and returns the amount in light years to travel that distance. The speed of light is approximately $2.997925 * 10^8$ meters per second. What types should the parameter and return value be? Why?

6.52 Write a string function PigLatin() with a single parameter w of type string. The function returns the translation of the word represented by w into Pig Latin. The translation should be according to the rules of Exercise 5.41.

6.53 Write a **double** function WindChill() with two **double** parameters t
and w representing temperature and wind speed. The function returns the
perceived temperature according to the formula of Exercise 5.42.

6.54 Write a **double** function HeatIndex() with two **double** parameters t
and h representing temperature and relative humidity. The function
returns the perceived temperature according to the formula of Exercise
5.43.

6.55 Consider the following function scramble():

```
void scramble(int i, int &j, int k) {
    i = 10;
    j = 20;
    k = 30;
    return;
}
```

a) What is the output of the following program fragment?

```
#include <iostream>
#include <string>
using namespace std;
int main() {
        int i = 1;
        int j = 2;
        int k = 3;
        scramble(i, j, k);
        cout << "i = " << i << " j = " << j
             << " k = " << k << endl;
    return 0;
}
```

b) What is the output of the following program fragment?

```
#include <iostream>
#include <string>
using namespace std;
int main() {
    int i = 1;
    int j = 2;
    int k = 3;
    scramble(j, j, j);
    cout << "i = " << i << " j = " << j
         << " k = " << k << endl;
    return 0;
}
```

6.56 Consider the following function scramble():

```
void scramble(int i, int &j, int &k) {
    i = 10;
    j = 20;
    k = 30;
    return;
}
```

a) What is the output of the following program fragment?

```cpp
#include <iostream>
#include <string>
using namespace std;
int main() {
    int i = 1;
    int j = 2;
    int k = 3;
    scramble(k, j, i);
    cout << "i = " << i << " j = " << j
         << "k = " << k << endl;
    return 0;
}
```

b) What is the output of the following program fragment?

```cpp
#include <iostream>
#include <string>
using namespace std;
int main() {
    int i = 1;
    int j = 2;
    int k = 3;
    scramble(j, j, j);
    cout << "i = " << i << " j = " << j
         << "k = " << k << endl
    return 0;
}
```

6.57 Consider the following function `scramble()`:

```cpp
void scramble(int &i, int &j, int &k) {
    i = 10;
    j = 20;
    k = 30;
    return;
}
```

a) What is the output of the following program fragment?

```cpp
#include <iostream>
#include <string>
using namespace std;
int main() {
    int i = 1;
    int j = 2;
    int k = 3;
    scramble(k, j, i);
    cout << "i = " << i << " j = " << j
         << "k = " << k << endl;
    return 0;
}
```

b) What is the output of the following program fragment?

```cpp
#include <iostream>
#include <string>
using namespace std;
```

```
int main() {
    int i = 1;
    int j = 2;
    int k = 3;
    scramble(j, j, j);
    cout << "i = " << i << " j = " << j
         << "k = " << k << endl
    return 0;
}
```

6.58 Consider the following C++ program:

```
#include <iostream>
#include <string>
using namespace std;
int funny(int &a, int b) {
    int c = a + b;
    a = b;
    b = c;
    return c;
}
int main() {
    int x = 3;
    int y = 4;
    int z = 5;
    cout << funny (x, y) << endl;
    cout << "x is: " << x << " and y is: " << y
         << endl;
    z = funny (x, z);
    cout << "z is: " << z << " and x is: " << x
         << endl;
    return 0;
}
```

What does the program display when it is executed?

6.59 Consider the following valid program:

```
#include <iostream>
#include <string>
using namespace std;
int main() {
    int x = 1;
    f(x);
    cout << "x is " << x << endl;
    return 0;
}
```

When this program runs, the output is

```
x is 2
```

Write the function prototype for **void** function f().

6.60 Consider the following valid function tricky():

```
void tricky(const int x, int &y, int z) {
    x = 3;
    y = 3;
    z = 3;
}
```

When the function is compiled which assignment statements generate a compilation error? Write Yes beside the assignment statement if a compilation error occurs; write No if a compilation error does not occur.

a) x = 3; _____

b) y = 3; _____

c) z = 3; _____

6.61   What is the output of the following C++ program?

```cpp
#include <iostream>
#include <string>
using namespace std;
void f(int &a) {
    cout << "int " << a << "\n";
    return;
}
void f(char &a) {
    cout << "char " << a << "\n";
    return;
}
int main() {
    int  i = 1;
    char c = 'c';
    f(i);
    f(c);
    return 0;
}
```

6.62   Find the errors in the following program fragments:

a)
```cpp
int Update(const int &x, int y, int z) {
    y = z % 3;
    x = y + z;
    return x;
}
```

b)
```cpp
int sum(int x, int y = 3, int z) {
    return x + y + z;
}
```

c)
```cpp
void Flow(double x, int y) {
    return x + y;
}
```

d)
```cpp
double Mul(const double a, const double b) {
    return a * b;
}
```

e)
```cpp
double Mul(double x, double y) {
    return x * y;
}
```

f)
```
#include <iostream>
#include <string>
using namespace std;
bool GetInput(istream in, int &Value) {
    if (in >> Value)
        return true;
    else
        return false;
}
```

g)
```
#include <iostream>
#include <string>
using namespace std;
bool GetInput(const istream &in, int &Value) {
    if (in >> Value)
        return true;
    else
        return false;
}
```

6.63   Write a program that reads a telephone number from a file called num-ber.dat. The program should determine whether the input is a valid telephone number. A valid telephone number has the following syntax:

$$D\ D\ D\ '-'\ D\ D\ D\ '-'\ D\ D\ D\ D$$

where the first *D* cannot be a zero.

If the telephone number is valid, the program should print the telephone number followed by a colon (:) followed by a space and the word *Valid*. If the telephone number is invalid, the program should print the telephone number followed by a colon (:) followed by a space and the words *Not Valid*.

6.64   Write a program that prompts for and accepts two characters as input. The program determines whether the two characters are a valid state abbreviation. If the characters are a valid state abbreviation, the program prints the characters (in uppercase) followed by a colon (:) followed by a space and the word *Valid*. If the characters are not a valid state abbreviation, the program prints the characters (in uppercase) followed by a colon (:) followed by a space and the words *Not Valid*. For example, for the input

```
Va
```

the program should display

```
VA: Valid
```

For the input,

```
tz
```

the program should display

```
TZ: Not Valid
```

6.65   Consider the following functions:

```cpp
#include <iostream>
#include <string>
using namespace std;
void f(int a, double b) {
    cout << "f(int, double) says a is "
        << a << endl;
    cout << "f(int, double) says b is "
        << b << endl;
    return;
}
void f(int a, int b) {
    cout << "f(int, int) says a is "
        << a << endl;
    cout << "f(int, int) says b is "
        << b << endl;
    return;
}
void f(double a, double b) {
    cout << "f(double, double) says a is "
        << a << endl;
    cout << "f(double, double) says b is "
        << b << endl;
    cout << endl;
    return;
}
```

a) What is output when the following program is executed using these
    functions?

```cpp
int main() {
    int i = 1;
    int j = 2;
    double x = 3.5;
    double y = 10.2;
    f(i, j);
    f(i, y);
    f(y, x);
    return 0;
}
```

b) What is output when the following program is executed using these
    functions?

```cpp
int main() {
    f(1, 2.3);
    f(2, 4);
    f(2.6, 10.5);
    return 0;
}
```

c) When the following program is compiled using these functions, a
    compilation error occurs. What is wrong with the program?

```cpp
int main() {
    f(1, 2.3);
    f(2.3, 4);
```

```
f(2.6, 10.5);
return 0;
}
```

6.66 The function `Valid()` in Program 6.9 contains the following if statement:

```
if (d4 == 0)
    return false;
else
    return ((d1 + d2 + d3) % d4) == d5;
```

Rewrite the if statement so that it is a single return statement. Which version of the program do you think is clearer? Why?

6.67 What is the output of the following program?

```
#include <iostream>
#include <string>
#include <assert.h>
using namespace std;
void DisplayString(ostream &sout, char c = '*',
  int count = 1) {
    assert(count >= 0);
    for (int i = 0; i < count; ++i)
        sout << c;
    sout << endl;
}
int main() {
    DisplayString(cout);
    DisplayString(cout, '-', 10);
    DisplayString(cout, '+');
    return 0;
}
```

6.68 Modify Program 6.9 to read a file of access codes. The access codes are contained in a file called `access.dat`, one access code per line. For each access code, the program determines whether the code is valid or not. The program creates a file called `tested.dat` that contains each access code followed by either the word *Valid* or the word *Invalid*.

6.69 Write a program that computes final averages for a set of grades. The program reads the grades from a file called `scores.dat`. The file `scores.dat` begins with a header line followed by a set of scores for each student. The format of the header line is

$$n \qquad weight_1 \ weight_2 \ ... \qquad weight_n$$

where n is the number of scores for each student and $weight_i$ is the weight of the ith score. The header line is followed by grades for each student. The format of a grade line is

$$name \qquad score_1 \quad score_2 \quad ... \qquad score_n$$

where *name* is the last name of the student and $score_i$ is the ith score. All scores must be between 0 and 100.

The program reads the file `score.dat` and writes a file called `aver-age.dat` that has the following format:

$$name \ \ score_1 \ \ score_2 \ \ ... \ \ score_n \ \ => \ \ nn.nn \ \ \text{Average}$$

where *name* and *score$_i$* are as before and *nn.nn* is the weighted average of the student's scores. The weighted average is computed as

$$\frac{\displaystyle\sum_{i=1}^{n} score_i \times weight_i}{n}$$

Your program should validate its input. That is, it should make sure each score is between 0 and 100 and that each student has *n* scores. If a student's scores are invalid, the program should write an error message to `cerr` and that student's scores should not be written to the output file `average.dat`. Design hint: Your program should contain a routine that handles input and a routine that handles validating the input.

6.70   Extend Exercise 6.69 so that the program also determines a final letter grade. The letter grade ranges are

Average	Letter Grade
0–59	F
60–69	D
70–79	C
80–89	B
90–100	A

The lines written to `average.dat` should have the following format:

$$name \ \ score_1 \ \ ... \ \ score_n \ \ => \ \ nn.nn \ \ \text{Average} \ \ (Letter)$$

where *Letter* is the letter grade.

6.71   Extend Exercise 6.69 so that the program computes and displays an overall average for the class.

6.72   An interesting baseball statistic is the slugging average. This statistic measures the ability of a batter to hit for power. The definition of *slugging average* is the total number of bases reached divided by the official number of times at bat. For example, in 12 official at-bats (walks and sacrifices do not count as official at-bats), a player has 2 singles (2 bases), 2 doubles (4 bases), a home run (4 bases), and a strike out (0 bases), the player's slugging average is 10 ÷ 12 = .833. Incidentally, Babe Ruth holds the record for lifetime slugging average of .690.

Write a program to compute the slugging average of a set of players. The data for the players is contained in a file. The file has the following format:

name   AtBats   Singles   Doubles   Triples   HomeRuns   StrikeOuts

Name is the last name of the player. All other items are integer values. Your program should prompt the user for the name of the file that contains the data to be processed. Your program should create a new file called `slugging.dat` that contains the computed slugging average. The format of each line of this file should be

name `Total Bases:` *bb* `At-Bats:` *aa* `Slugging Avg:` `.`*nnn*

all on one line. *Name* is the last name of the player, *bb* is the total bases for the player, *aa* is the number of at-bats, and `.`*nnn* is the slugging average.

6.73   Write a function named `TimeToSeconds()` that takes a single argument that represents a time. The time is a string with the following format

`hh:mm:ss`

where `hh` is hours, `mm` is minutes, and `ss` is seconds. Function `TimeToSeconds()` returns the equivalent time in seconds. If `TimeToSeconds()` receives an invalid time (e.g., 02:23:67), it should use `assert()` to report an error.

Test your function by writing a program that reads a string that represents a time and calls `TimeToSeconds()` to convert it. Your test program should display the input time and the equivalent time in seconds. Test your function with the following times:

a) `00:00:00`   h) `00:59:49`
b) `00:00:59`   i) `03:20:20`
c) `00:00:60`   j) `05:55:30`
d) `00:01:30`   k) `30:00:00`
e) `00:44:30`   l) `11:11:11`
f) `00:60:59`
g) `10:50:05`

6.74   Write a function called `ElapseTime()` that takes two parameters— `EndTime` and `StartTime`. Both `EndTime` and `StartTime` are strings that represent times in the following format:

`hh:mm:ss`

Function `ElapseTime()` computes the elapsed time in seconds between `StartTime` and `EndTime`. Implement your function so that `StartTime` is an optional parameter. If `StartTime` is not supplied, it defaults to the time 00:00:00. Your implementation of `ElapsedTime()` should make use of function `TimeToSeconds()` described in Exercise 6.73. Your implementation should assert an error if `StartTime` or `EndTime` do not represent valid times or if `StartTime` is greater than `EndTime`.

Write a driver program to test your implementation. Test your implementation for the following starting and ending times:

Start Time	End Time
00:00:00	00:01:00
00:20:00	00:25:50
01:30:40	00:35:50
01:10:51	01:11:61
20:10:10	21:09:08

6.75 Write a function called FormatTime() that takes a single parameter that is a time in seconds. Your function should return a string that represents the time in the following format:

hh:mm:ss

Write a driver program to test your implementation for FormatTime(). Verify that your implementation of FormatTime() works for the following times:

Time
0
59
60
3600
10000
50000

6.76 Write a recursive function to compute the greatest common divisor (gcd) of two integers. The gcd of two integers is the largest integer that divides them both. A working definition of gcd is

$$gcd(m, n) = \begin{cases} n & \text{if } n \text{ divides } m \\ gcd(n, \text{remainder of } m \text{ divided by } n) & \text{otherwise} \end{cases}$$

6.77 Develop a program that prompts a user for a number n and then computes and displays for integer values i in the interval 1 through n the nearest integer to the expression

$$\frac{1}{\sqrt{5}} \cdot \left(\left(\frac{1 + \sqrt{5}}{2} \right)^i - \left(\frac{1 - \sqrt{5}}{2} \right)^i \right)$$

Compare the output of the program with the output of function Fibonacci() for the same values. Discuss their similarity.

6.78 If we take the ratio of successive numbers in the Fibonacci sequence, we see that the ratio is approaching a particular value. For example, 5/3 is 1.66666…; 8/5 is 1.6; and 13/8 is 1.625. The value to which these ratios are converging is called the *golden ratio* or *golden mean*. Develop a program to compute an approximation of the golden mean. To get an accurate estimation of its value, compute the golden mean of successive pairs of Fibonacci numbers until the difference between the computed golden means is less than 0.0005.

6.79   Below is a picture that illustrates the relationship between successive Fibonacci numbers.

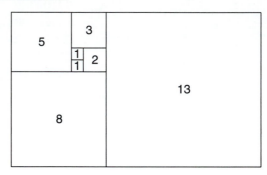

This picture was drawn by starting with two squares of size 1 drawn on top of each other. To the right, a square whose size is the sum of the previous two squares is drawn (i.e., a square of size 2). Each succeeding square's size is the sum of the size of the last two squares drawn. Let's call a diagram drawn in this fashion the Fibonacci squares picture. Develop an EzWindows program using `RectangleShape` that draws a Fibonacci squares picture. Your program should prompt for and accept the number of squares to draw.

Interestingly, if you draw quarter circles in each square, you get a spiral like the one shown below. This spiral is very similar to the spirals that occur in nature in seashells and snail shells.

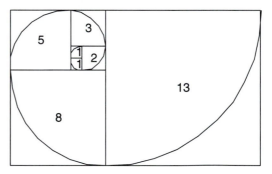

CHAPTER 7

The class construct and object-oriented design

Introduction

Objects are the basic unit of programming in object-oriented languages like C++. Objects are models of information and are implemented as software packages that can encapsulate both attributes and behavior. The construct for defining new types of encapsulated objects in C++ is the **class**. A **class** is the "blueprint" from which an object can be created. In this chapter, we explain how to create these blueprints, or specifications of objects. We do so by showing the class declaration of a programmer-defined type that we used in previous chapters—RectangleShape.

Key Concepts

- **class** construct
- information hiding
- encapsulation
- data members
- member functions
- constructors
- inspectors
- mutators
- facilitators
- **const** functions
- access specification: **public** and **private**
- object-oriented analysis and design

7.1 INTRODUCING A PROGRAMMER-DEFINED DATA TYPE

The preceding chapters provided the basics of programming and software-engineering practices. Knowing that material makes it possible for you to solve simple problems. However, to solve more complex problems, you must master additional language features, algorithmic skills, and engineering techniques. In this chapter, we introduce the C++ **class** construct for defining new types of objects. This construct is the basis of object-oriented programming using C++.

A fundamental-type object is an object that is provided by the programming language. For example, in C++ the type **int** and the operations on it are part of the language definition of C++. That is, all C++ compilers must provide **int** objects. In addition to its fundamental types, C++ provides several mechanisms to define other types. These other types are called *programmer-* or *user-defined types*.

In the previous chapters we used the C++ **enum** construct to create new types. The type `color`, which we used in conjunction with the object `RectangleShape`, was created using the **enum** construct. In addition to the **enum** construct, C++ provides several other methods for creating new types. For example, C++ allows the programmer to define a type that is a list of objects. These objects are called *arrays*. A second example is the pointer mechanism that allows a programmer to define a type whose values are the memory addresses of other objects. Both of these mechanisms are considered in subsequent chapters.

The **class** construct that is introduced in this chapter is the most important mechanism for defining new types. With this construct, software engineers can define class-type objects that contain or *encapsulate* both an *attribute* component and a *behavior* component.

To illustrate the basics of creating a new object type using the **class** construct, we discuss the declaration of a programmer-defined type that we used in previous chapters—`RectangleShape`. Whenever one is designing something, it helps to know how the thing will be used. Our goal in designing `RectangleShape` is that we want a graphical object that is easy to create and simple to use. It can then be used, as we have seen in the previous chapters, whenever a rectangle shape can represent a real object.

The first thing to do when creating a class type is to determine the attributes of the object. For objects in our graphical display system, the necessary attributes of a rectangle are its size, its location within the viewport or display window, the window it will be displayed in, and its color. In C++ the attributes of a class-type object are referred to as the *data members* of the class. Later in this chapter when we consider how classes are defined, you will see that the data members are simply subobjects of the class-type object.

The second step when creating a class-type object is to determine the messages the object can receive and the operations that can be performed on the object. This is its behavior component. The behavior component of a class-type object is a collection of *member functions* that can send messages to an object requesting it to perform some action. Continuing with the development of a class for a rectangle shape in a windowed graphical display system, a rectangle needs to handle two classes of messages. One set of messages returns the value of an attribute of a rectangle, and one set of messages changes the value of an attribute.

Messages that return the value of an attribute are called *inspectors*. For maximum flexibility, our definition of RectangleShape will include inspectors for all data members. Thus RectangleShape's inspectors are Get-Color(), GetSize(), GetWidth(), GetHeight(), GetPosition(), and GetWindow(). Notice that the inspectors provide some duplication of functionality. In addition to GetSize(), which returns both the width and height of the rectangle, we have GetWidth() and GetHeight(). These inspectors are provided as conveniences in case the client needs to fetch either the width or the height, but not both.

Messages that change or set an attribute are called *mutators*. Again, to make the RectangleShape as flexible as possible, we will have mutators for the attributes that control the appearance and location of a RectangleShape. Thus RectangleShape's mutators are SetColor(), SetPosition(), and SetSize(). Each member function sets the attribute indicated by its name.

One additional message is neither an inspector nor a mutator. The draw message tells the rectangle to display itself in the window. Draw() is an example of a facilitator. A *facilitator* causes an object to perform some action or service.

Notice that RectangleShape has an inspector GetWindow(), but there is no corresponding mutator SetWindow(). Once a RectangleShape is created, it is bound to a display window, and once a shape is bound to a display window, it cannot be changed. Thus we prevent a user from changing the window by not providing the necessary mutator. As we will see shortly, there are several good reasons for having this restriction.

Figure 7.1 illustrates our abstraction of a rectangle for our simple graphical display system. The dotted cloud shape indicates that this entity is a class definition of a rectangle, not an actual instance of a rectangle. Our convention is to label the class name with the letter C, the data members with the abbreviation DM, and the member functions with the abbreviation MF.

You might wonder why we say that class RectangleShape is an abstraction of a rectangle. After all, there are some concrete details about the rectangle such as size, color, and position within the window. Abstraction eliminates the irrelevant and focuses on the essential properties of an object. In our case, the essential properties are those that are required for making a RectangleShape useful for developing graphical programs. These properties are the size, color, and position of a rectangle within a window. The irrelevant details are how a RectangleShape is drawn in a window. Our abstraction of a rectangle says nothing about that. By eliminating unessential details, we make Rectangle-Shape easy to use. Furthermore, how we use RectangleShape is independent of the windowing system we use. Thus our programs can run on a variety of operating systems without modification.

Figure 7.1

Data members and member functions for class RectangleShape

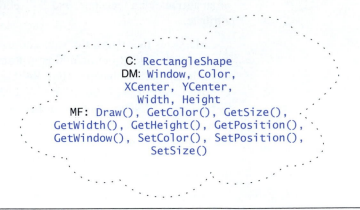

C: RectangleShape
DM: Window, Color,
XCenter, YCenter,
Width, Height
MF: Draw(), GetColor(), GetSize(),
GetWidth(), GetHeight(), GetPosition(),
GetWindow(), SetColor(), SetPosition(),
SetSize()

7.2   THE RECTANGLESHAPE CLASS

Now that we have determined an abstraction for a rectangle, we are ready to see how to declare a C++ **class** corresponding to an object abstraction. The syntax for declaring a class-type object is

```
                          Class keyword          A valid C++ name


                       class ClassName {
 Public          ──►      public:
 keyword                       // Prototypes for constructors
                               // and public member functions
                               // and declarations for public
                               // data attributes go here.
                                     . . .
                                     . . .
 Private         ──►      private:
 keyword                       // Prototypes for private data
                               // members and declarations for
                               // private data attributes go here.
                                     . . .
                                     . . .
                       };
```

The declaration begins with the keyword **class** followed by the name of the class. Inside the class declaration are the prototypes for the functions that implement the inspectors, mutators, and facilitators. The class declaration also contains declarations for any member data that are part of the class.

For example, the **class** declaration for RectangleShape is

```
class RectangleShape {
    public:
        RectangleShape(SimpleWindow &Window,
         float XCoord, float YCoord, const color &Color,
         float Width, float Height);
        void Draw();
        color GetColor() const;
        void GetSize(float &Width, float &Height) const;
        float GetWidth() const;
        float GetHeight() const;
        void GetPosition(float &XCoord,
         float &YCoord) const;
        SimpleWindow& GetWindow() const;
        void SetColor(const color &Color);
        void SetPosition(float XCoord, float YCoord);
        void SetSize(float Width, float Height);
    private:
        SimpleWindow &Window;
        float XCenter;
        float YCenter;
        color Color;
        float Width;
        float Height;
};
```

and the following program uses the class to create a 2-centimeter-by-3-centimeter blue rectangle named R in a window.

```
#include "rect.h"
SimpleWindow W("MAIN WINDOW", 8.0, 8.0);
int ApiMain() {
    W.Open();
    RectangleShape R(W, 4.0, 4.0, Blue, 2.0, 3.0);
    R.Draw();
    return 0;
}
```

Figure 7.2 shows the resulting window.

A C++ **class** declaration begins with the keyword **class** followed by the name of the **class**. As you would expect, the name of the **class** must be a valid C++ identifier. The data members and member functions of the **class** are enclosed in curly braces. Inside the curly braces, the data member and member function declarations are divided into two sections labeled **public** and **private**. For now, we will ignore the meaning of these labels.

Let's begin by examining the data attribute declarations that appear after the reserved word **private**. One declaration corresponds to each attribute of the object. For example, the declaration

```
SimpleWindow &Window;
```

declares a subobject called Window that will hold a reference to the SimpleWindow that will display the RectangleShape object. You are probably

Figure 7.2

*RectangleShape R in
SimpleWindow W*

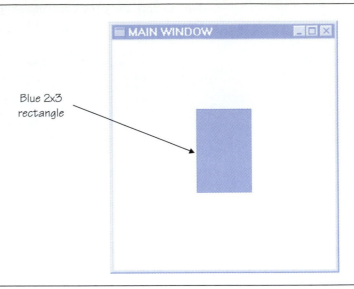

wondering why the declaration uses the reference operator &. If the declaration had been

```
SimpleWindow Window;
```

then a `RectangleShape` would contain a `SimpleWindow` object (not a reference to one). Just like the call-by-value parameter passing mechanism, this declaration means that when a new `RectangleShape` object is instantiated, a copy of a `SimpleWindow` object is made. This action is confusing because what should happen when you make a copy of a `SimpleWindow` object is unclear. Normally, when you copy an object, you get another identical object. Do we really want another window to appear each time we create a `RectangleShape`? Clearly, no. Therefore, rather than copy the `SimpleWindow` object, we just keep a reference to it. Just like the reference parameter passing mechanism, you can think of the reference attribute `Window` as an alias for the actual window that contains the object.

The declarations

```
float XCenter;
float YCenter;
```

are the declarations for the subobjects that will hold the coordinates of the center of the rectangle, and the declaration

```
color Color;
```

declares the data member that will hold the color of the rectangle. The attributes for the size of the rectangle are held in the following data members:

```
float Width;
float Height;
```

Now that we understand the attributes of a `RectangleShape`, let's examine the various public functions. The first prototype in `RectangleShape`'s class declaration

```
RectangleShape(SimpleWindow &Window,
    float XCoord, float YCoord, const color &Color,
    float Width, float Height);
```

is a *constructor* for `RectangleShape`. A constructor function is automatically invoked when an object is defined. The constructor can initialize some or all of the object's data members to appropriate values. Constructor functions are easily recognized because they have the same name as the class.

The definition

```
RectangleShape R(W, 4.0, 4.0, Blue, 2.0, 3.0);
```

creates a `RectangleShape` called R; invokes the constructor; and passes it the values W, `4.0`, `4.0`, `Blue`, `2.0`, and `3.0` to initialize the data members of R. As you can guess, `Window` is initialized to the value W. `XCenter` and `YCenter` are given the values `4.0` and `4.0`, `Color` is set to `Blue`, and `Width` and `Height` are set to `2.0` and `3.0`, respectively. The process of creating an object and initializing its data members is called *instantiation*.

Similarly, the definitions

```
RectangleShape R1(W, 1.0, 4.0, Cyan, 3.0, 3.0);
RectangleShape R2(W, 6.0, 4.0, Red, 1.0, 2.0);
```

instantiate two objects of type `RectangleShape` named R1 and R2. The process of instantiating a particular instance of an object from its abstraction is illustrated in Figure 7.3. The solid cloud shape indicates that the entity is an actual instance of the abstraction. Our convention is to label the name of the object with the letter O. The data members and member functions will be labeled with the same notation used with the illustration of a class.

The next part of `RectangleShape`'s definition lists the prototypes for the messages that a `RectangleShape` object can receive. The definitions of these functions and the constructors are contained in another module. Although it is possible to include the definition of a member function or constructor in the class declaration, the principle of information hiding encourages us to put the implementation details in a separate module. The inclusion of the implementation of the constructor or member functions within the class would complicate the class declaration and make the interface to the class harder to see.

In C++ messages are sent to objects by invoking member functions. Recall that the syntax for sending a message to an object by invoking a member function is

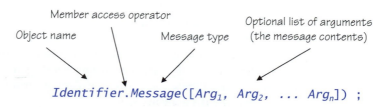

Object name   Member access operator   Message type   Optional list of arguments
(the message contents)

```
Identifier.Message([Arg₁, Arg₂, ... Argₙ]) ;
```

Figure 7.3

Instantiation of two
RectangleShape
objects R1 and R2

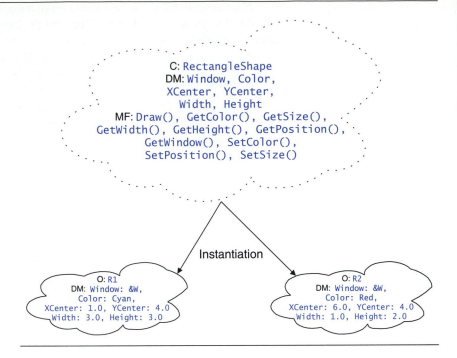

The dot between the identifier and the message type is called the member access operator. The *member access operator* selects a member function or data member of an object.

Our class `RectangleShape` contains eight member functions. The first member function, `Draw()`, sends a message telling the object that it should make itself visible in the window. When a `RectangleShape` is instantiated, it does not appear in the window. Rather the programmer must explicitly tell a `RectangleShape` object to draw itself in the window by sending the object a draw message. For example, for `RectangleShape` object R, the code

`R.Draw();`

sends a message telling R to draw itself in the `SimpleWindow` that contains it.

You might wonder why we need a draw function at all. Why not just have the object appear in the window when it is instantiated? This is a reasonable question. As we shall see, having an explicit draw function makes `Rectangleshape` more flexible. We will often want to create a shape before we know exactly what characteristics the shape should have. Similarly, we will often reuse an existing shape by giving it a new color, changing its position, and drawing it in its new location. By separating the actions of instantiation from the action of drawing, we can create a shape with default values, determine and set its attributes, and then when we are ready, cause the shape to appear by sending it a draw message.

Following the draw member function declaration are declarations for the member functions `GetColor()`, `GetSize()`, `GetWidth()`, `GetHeight()`, `GetPosition()`, and `GetWindow()`. These are the declarations of the inspectors that return the attributes of a `RectangleShape`. Notice that the inspectors `GetSize()` and `GetPosition()` use reference parameters to return both values of their attributes. For example, `GetSize()` returns both the width and height of a `RectangleShape`. The declaration for `GetWindow()` specifies that it returns a reference to the `SimpleWindow` that contains the `RectangleShape`. Again, we use this method because we don't want to make a copy of the window that contains the shape.

You should also notice that each inspector has the reserved word **const** as part of its declaration. For example, the declaration of inspector `GetColor()` indicates that the member function is a constant function.

```
color GetColor() const;
```

That is, this function does not modify or change the object. Knowing that a function is specified to not change an object helps us read the code, and it allows the compiler to make sure that we do not mistakenly change the value of the object. If a constant function tries to change the value of the object or call a nonconstant function, the compiler will report the error.

Following the declaration of the inspectors are the declarations of the mutators. The mutator member functions are `SetColor()`, `SetPosition()`, and `SetSize()`. Each attribute that can be changed has a mutator. For example, the code

```
R2.SetColor(Blue);
```

sends R2 a set color message with the argument `Blue`. When R2 receives this message, it will set its color attribute to `Blue`. The code

```
R2.SetPosition(2.5, 6.0);
R2.SetSize(1.0, 4.0);
```

sends messages to set R2's other attributes. The first message tells R2 that its center should be 2.5 centimeters from the left edge of the window and 6.0 centimeters from the top edge of the window. The final message tells R2 that its width should be 1.0 centimeters and its height 4.0. After setting the various attributes, we can display R2 in the window by sending it a draw message. The invocation

```
R2.Draw();
```

sends a message telling R2 to draw itself in its window at its x, y coordinates, with its color, and size. The process of instantiation, initialization of data members, and the drawing of R2 is illustrated in Figure 7.4.

7.2.1   Public and private access

One of the principles of software engineering that we discussed in Chapter 1 was information hiding or encapsulation. Recall that this process separates the aspects of an object into external and internal aspects. The external aspects of

Figure 7.4

Instantiation, initialization, and drawing of a RectangleShape R2

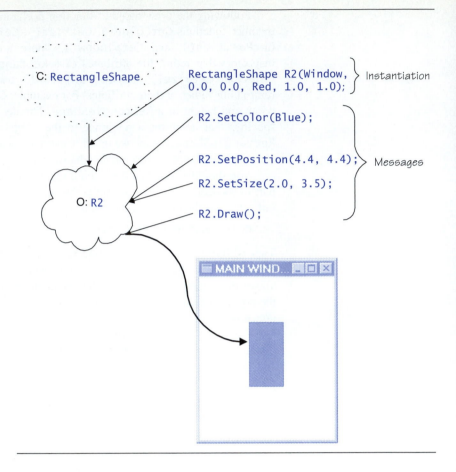

an object are those that need to be visible or known to other objects in the system. The internal aspects of an object are those that should not affect other parts of the system and therefore need not and should not be known to or available to other objects in the system. The labels **public** and **private** within a class declaration are one of the features that C++ provides to support information hiding or encapsulation.

Style Tip

Public before private

In a C++ class declaration, the public and private sections may appear in any order. Some programmers prefer to put the private section first, because it contains the data attributes. We believe that the public section should be first because the public member functions and the constructors are the user's interface to the class. Indeed, the data attributes in the private section are somewhat secondary to the use of the class, and with a properly defined class, we really should never need to see how the data attributes are declared.

Data members and member functions declared following a **private** label are accessible only to other member functions of the class. Class members following a **public** label are accessible to functions that are not members of the class. This notion of controlling access to the members of a C++ **class** is illustrated in Figure 7.5.

Figure 7.5

Controlling access to class members with public and private sections

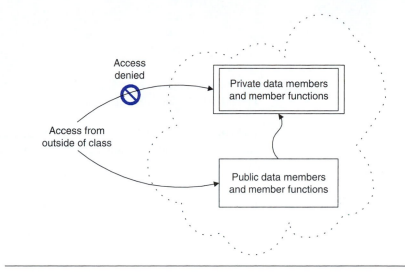

Although public and private sections can be used to control access to data members and member functions, a more important use of access specifiers is to implement information hiding. The information hiding principle states that all interaction with an object should be constrained to use a well-defined interface that allows underlying object implementation details to be safely ignored. Thus the member functions and data members in the **public** section form the external interface to the object, whereas the items in the **private** section are the internal aspects of the object that do not need to be accessible to use the object.

In the RectangleShape class, the member functions Draw(), Get-Color(), GetSize(), GetPosition(), GetWidth(), GetHeight(), GetWindow(), SetColor(), SetPosition(), and SetSize() are the public interface to RectangleShape. Using RectangleShape's public interface, we were able to write a code fragment that created a rectangle within a window by defining a RectangleShape object called R and by calling the appropriate member functions to set R's attributes. The exact details of how a RectangleShape is represented and implemented are irrelevant.

For example, RectangleShape's public interface says the size and position of a RectangleShape are specified using centimeter values that are stored in floating-point objects. However, the underlying window system uses a system based on pixels, not centimeters. RectangleShape's public interface lets us use a more familiar measurement system to position and size shapes. Furthermore, we do not know anything about the underlying coordinate system

C++ Language

Default access

When objects are declared without a preceding **public** or **private** label, the default access is **private** for those objects. For example, in the class declaration

```cpp
class Obj {
    int x;
    int y:
    public:
        Obj();
};
```

the integer objects x and y have private access since no access label preceded their declarations.

in which windows are represented. The beauty of encapsulation is that irrelevant and complicating details can be hidden, which simplifies the use of the object.

Self-check Questions

1.   What is the term for member functions that return the value of an attribute?

2.   What is the term for member functions that change an attribute?

3.   What is the term for member functions that perform some action or service?

4.   What is the term for a member function that creates the object?

5.   What is the term for the process of creating an object and initializing its data members?

6.   Write the statement that sets the RectangleShape BigBox to green.

7.   Write the statement that sets the size of the RectangleShape Button to 4 centimeters wide and 3 centimeters high.

8.   Write the statement that sets the position of the RectangleShape Door 2 centimeters from the top of the window and 4 centimeters from the left side of the window.

9.   Consider the following class declaration.
```cpp
class Person {
    public:
        Person();
```

```
                string GetName();
            private:
                bool Citizen();
                string LastName;
                string FirstName;
                string PhoneNumber;
        };
```

Explain what is wrong with the following code fragment.

```
        int main() {
            Person P;
            ...
            string PNumber = P.PhoneNumber;
            return 0;
        }
```

10.   Consider the following class declaration.

```
        class Person {
                Person();
                string GetName();
            private:
                bool Citizen();
                string LastName;
                string FirstName;
                string PhoneNumber;
        };
```

Is the access to the inspector `GetName()` **public** or **private**?

7.3 USING THE RECTANGLESHAPE CLASS

Now that we understand the basics of declaring a class, instantiating objects of that class, and interacting with the object via the member functions, we can explore the use of class `RectangleShape` in more detail. Recall that the coordinate system used to position rectangles in a window assumes that the origin is the upper-left corner of the window. Figure 7.6 shows the `SimpleWindow` coordinate system.

The units on the axes are centimeters. Thus the definition

`RectangleShape T(ExampleWindow, 2, 3, Red, 2, 2);`

creates a `RectangleShape` named T with its center 2 centimeters from the left side of the window and 3 centimeters from the top of the window.

The unit of measure of all the arguments to `RectangleShape`'s member functions that have to do with position or size is centimeters. Having a consistent or uniform interface to a class of object is a key object-oriented design principle. For example, the following program creates and draws blue rectangle B 1 centimeter on a side and positioned 3 centimeters from the left and top of window W. Then the program creates rectangle M. M's width and height is 2 centimeters, its color is set to magenta, and it is set to be displayed in window W.

Figure 7.6

The SimpleWindow coordinate system

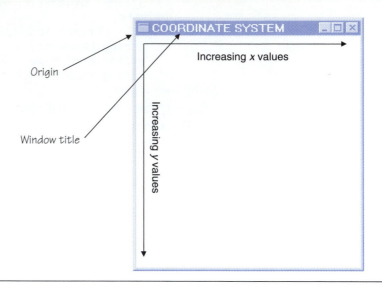

M's position is set to coordinates (2.5, 2.5) so that its bottom-right corner touches B's upper-left corner.

```
#include "rect.h"
SimpleWindow W("Double Square", 8, 8);
int ApiMain() {
    W.Open();
    RectangleShape B(W, 4, 4, Blue, 1, 1);
    B.Draw();

    // Create and draw another rectangle so that its
    // bottom-right corner touches the upper-left
    // corner of B
    RectangleShape M(W, 2.5, 2.5, Magenta, 2, 2);
    M.Draw();

    return 0;
}
```

Figure 7.7 shows the resulting window.

Another important characteristic of a window system is the color scheme that can be used. The color scheme is sometimes referred to as the *palette*. Let's write a program called Colors that displays all the colors that a RectangleShape object can be.

Recall that the colors a RectangleShape object can be are specified by the enumeration

```
enum color { Black, White, Red, Green, Blue, Yellow,
    Cyan, Magenta };
```

Thus we need to display six squares—one for each color except Black and White. Because white is the background color, we wouldn't be able to see it. We will display the six colors using 1-centimeter squares laid out side-by-side so that the screen resembles a color spectrum. Of course, we want to center the

Figure 7.7

Display created by double square

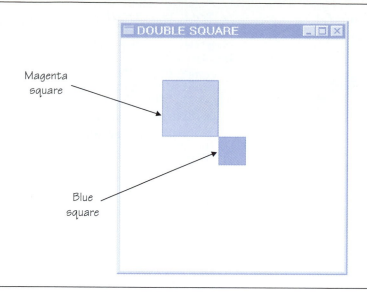

color spectrum within the window so it looks nice. Program 7.1 contains the code for this program.

With one minor exception, the code is quite straightforward. First, a few constants specify the size of the rectangle and the position of the first color patch. Following those definitions, the RectangleShape object ColorPatch is instantiated.

The **for** statement loops over the colors. The **for** loop contains another use of a cast expression. The increment expression of the **for** loop is

```
c = (color) (c + 1)
```

This statement sets c to the next color. You might ask why we did not write ++c to advance to the next color. C++ does not allow enumeration objects to be incremented. The reason is that given a member of an enumeration, the next member may not be represented by the next integer. However, because the underlying implementation of an enumeration type is integer, we can perform arithmetic enumeration objects. The result is an integer. Because we know that the members of color are consecutive integers, we can safely cast the result of the expression c + 1 to color to obtain the next color. This approach allows us to write the **for** loop in a natural way.

The body of the **for** statement sets the object Colorpatch to the appropriate color, draws the patch, and then repositions the patch so the next patch

Program 7.1

Create and display a color palette

```
// Program 7.1: Display color palette
#include "rect.h"
SimpleWindow ColorWindow("Color Palette", 8.0, 8.0);
int ApiMain() {
    const float SideSize = 1.0;
    float XPosition = 1.5;
    const float YPosition = 4;

    ColorWindow.Open();

    // Create a RectangleShape to use
    RectangleShape ColorPatch(ColorWindow,
     XPosition, YPosition, White, SideSize, SideSize);

    // Loop over colors drawing ColorSquare with
    // that color next to the previous square
    for (color c = Red; c <= Magenta;
     c = (color)(c + 1)) {
        ColorPatch.SetColor(c);
        ColorPatch.SetPosition(XPosition, YPosition);
        ColorPatch.Draw();
        XPosition += SideSize;
    }
    return 0;
}
```

will appear adjacent to the previous one. Figure 7.8 shows the window created by the program.

Figure 7.8

Display created by the color palette program

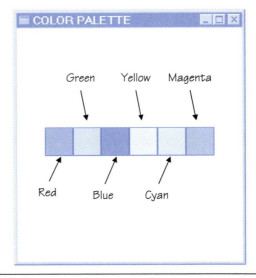

7.4 CONSTRUCTORS

In the previous examples, each time we defined a `RectangleShape`, we had to provide initial values for all the data members because the `Rectangle-Shape` constructor required them. We need a way to create a class-type object without having to specify all the data member values, especially if we are immediately going to change them or set them as we did in the color palette program. However, creating an object without specifying values for the attributes would be dangerous. For example, if we created a `Rectangle-Shape`, didn't give it a position, and then sent it a message to draw itself, any number of strange things might happen—including our program crashing the system.

Fortunately, C++ provides a way to do exactly what we want. Remember the default parameters we discussed in Chapter 6? We can also use this mechanism in a constructor.

We can change the prototype of `RectangleShape`'s constructor to be

```
RectangleShape(SimpleWindow &Window, float XCoord = 0,
    float YCoord = 0, const color &c = Red,
    float Width = 1, float Height = 2);
```

Using default parameter values in a constructor works just like using default parameter values in a function prototype. For example, the definition

```
RectangleShape C(ControlWindow);
```

creates a `RectangleShape` named C and sets its `SimpleWindow` attribute to `ControlWindow`. The other attributes are given the default values as specified in the constructor's prototype. Thus the position attributes `XCenter` and `YCenter` are given the value 0.0, the data member `Color` is set to `Red`, and the data members `Width` and `Height` are set to the values 1.0 and 2.0, respectively.

Similarly, the definition

```
RectangleShape D(ControlWindow, 3, 5);
```

instantiates a `RectangleShape` named D that is in the window `ControlWindow` with its center 3 centimeters from the left edge of the window and 5 centimeters from the top edge of the window. Because the definition did not specify the values of the color and size attributes, they are given the default values of `Red`, 1.0, and 2.0.

Notice the argument `Window` does not have a default value. Thus the definition

```
RectangleShape E;
```

is illegal, and the C++ compiler will flag it as an error because reference data members must be initialized when the object is constructed. In addition, once a reference data member is initialized, it cannot be changed.

Programmer Alert

EzWindows source code

If you are interested in examining the interface to `RectangleShape` class and its implementation, the interface (`rect.h`) and the implementation (`rect.cpp`) can be found on the CD accompanying this book. The interface files for all the EzWindow shapes including `rect.h` can be found in the directory

```
{BaseDirectory}\ezwin\include
```

Similarly, implementation files for the corresponding shapes can be found in the directory

```
{BaseDirectory}\ezwin\src
```

In both cases, `{BaseDirectory}` is the location on your hard drive where the EzWindows software was installed. The latest version of the EzWindow software can be downloaded from the following Web site:

```
http://www.cs.virginia.edu/c++programdesign
```

Self-check Questions

11. Give an appropriate C++ class declaration for a "date" object. The class `Date` should contain the following information:

-   The year
-   The month
-   The day of the month

Your class declaration should be designed using information hiding principles; that is, you should have the appropriate inspectors and mutators.

The single constructor for `Date` should support constructing a `Date` object where:

-   No specific date is given. In this case, all the data fields should be initialized to 1.
-   Only the year is given. In this case, all the other data fields should be initialized to 1.
-   Only the year and month is given. In this case, the day gets a default value of 1.

12. For example, the following are legal declarations of `Date` objects

```
Date Date1;
Date Date2(1999);    // Year set to 1999
                     // Month set to Jan
```

```
                                    // Day set to 1

        Date Date3(1999, 1);    // Year set to 1999
                                // Month set to Jan
                                // Day set to 1

        Date Date4(2000, 2, 13);   // Year set to 2000
                                   // Month set to Feb
                                   // Day is 13
```

Your class declaration does not need to include any other member functions beyond the mandatory constructor (only one constructor!), inspectors, and mutators.

13. Give the appropriate C++ class declaration for a "book" object. The class **Book** should contain the following data:

- Title of book.

- Authors (assume a maximum of **MaxAuthors** where **MaxAuthors** is a constant).

- A unique identifying number (assume an integer).

Your class declaration should be designed using information hiding principles; that is, you should have the appropriate inspectors and mutators. *Hint!* Pay particular attention to the inspector and mutator for the authors data. There should be only one inspector and one mutator for this data member.

The single constructor for **Book** should support constructing a **Book** object where:

- The title is specified, a single author is given, and an identifying number is given.

- The title is specified, a single author is given, but no identifying number is given. In this case, the identifying number should default to the value 0.

- A title is specified, but no author and no identifying number are specified. In this case, the author is the string "No author", and the identifying number is set to zero.

- No title, author, or identifying number is specified. In this case, the title should default to the value "No title", and the other fields are as in the previous case.

For example, the following are legal declarations

```
Book Book1("My Friend Linda", "Monica Lewinsky", 2);
Book Book2("Eat a Peach", "Greg Allman");
Book Book3("My Life As a Dog");
Book Book4;
```

Your class declaration does not need to include any other member functions beyond the mandatory constructor, inspectors and mutators.

14.   Give the complete header (.h) file and constructor implementation for an object called Latitude that is used to represent a latitude. Your class should be designed and implemented using good object-oriented design techniques. One property is that the class should support information hiding.

A latitude is specified by four values: degrees, minutes, and seconds, and whether the latitude is north or south. Thus class Latitude should have exactly three integer data members: one for degrees, one for minutes and one for seconds; and one data member that specifies whether the latitude is north or south. The north/south indicator should be stored using an enumeration type which you should declare in your header file. In addition to the standard inspectors and mutators, your class should have a constructor. The constructor should provide default values for all four data members. For example, the declaration

```
Latitude Equator;
```

would create a Latitude object with each of its integer data members set to zero and its north/south indicator set to North. Make your code as efficient as possible.

15.   Design and implement a program that displays the colors supported by EzWindows. Your program should construct a SimpleWindow that is 8 centimeters high and 5 centimeters wide. In the window, draw stripes 1 centimeter high and 5 centimeters wide of each color down the window.

7.5   BUILDING A KALEIDOSCOPE

As a final demonstration of the use of class RectangleShape, we now design and implement a program that simulates a kaleidoscope display in a window. In this first implementation of a program to simulate a kaleidoscope, we will use objects, but the design of the program is not object-oriented. Chapter 13 contains an improved program that simulates a kaleidoscope. This version was designed using the object-oriented approach.

The kaleidoscope, invented in 1816 by Sir David Brewster, is a device, somewhat similar in size and shape to a small telescope, that creates symmetrical multicolored patterns that can be viewed through an eyepiece. Many of us are familiar with the child's version of a kaleidoscope that is constructed from cardboard tubes. One tube contains bits of colored glass and mirrors; the other tube contains the eyepiece for viewing the image. The image created is the result of combining reflections of the bits of colored glass. The pattern can be changed by rotating the tube with the colored glass and mirrors. As the bits of colored glass shift, they create new patterns.

A kaleidoscope image can be simulated by displaying images symmetrically positioned in a display window. In this first version of our kaleidoscope program, the images displayed will be squares of various sizes and colors. Rather than refer to the images as squares, which are their concrete representation, we will call them trinkets, which is more in keeping with the way a real kaleidoscope works

Thus we need to write a routine, `Kaleidoscope()`, that displays trinkets of various sizes and colors symmetrically within the window to create a kaleidoscope effect. To simulate the changing patterns, `Kaleidoscope()` will be called repeatedly to add new trinkets to the display window.

Our strategy for creating the symmetrical patterns will be to partition the window into four quadrants (see Figure 7.9). To simulate the mirrorlike reflection, identical trinkets are displayed in diagonally opposite quadrants. All four trinkets are positioned symmetrically about the center of the window. The net effect is that the trinkets in opposite quadrants look like reflections. Four additional trinkets are positioned similarly with the color scheme reversed. Thus two trinkets are drawn in each quadrant for a total of eight trinkets.

Figure 7.9

Window layout to simulate a kaleidoscope

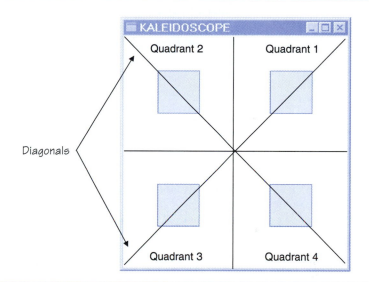

Three of the subtasks we need to do are to randomly pick a color, a trinket size, and an offset from the center of the window to position the trinkets. For all these tasks, we can use the function `Uniform()` that we developed in Section 5.7.

Generating a random color is easy using `Uniform()` and a cast expression. The following three-line function generates a random color.

```
color RandomColor() {
    return (color) Uniform(1, MaxColors - 1);
}
```

Notice that in the return statement the random number returned by `Uniform()` is cast to be the type **color**. This technique works because **color** is an enumeration type and its underlying implementation is a sequence of integers starting at 0. Thus the value 1 is mapped to red, 2 is mapped to green, 3 is mapped to blue, and so on. The cast expression explicitly states that we want to convert the integer returned by Uniform() to a color.

To generate a random trinket size, we can do something similar. We would like to generate a size that is between 1 and some maximum that we pick. We need to control the maximum size because we do not want the trinket to be larger than the window. To get some variability in the display, we want to use a range of trinket sizes and allow trinkets with fractional sizes. As a starting point, we decide that we will generate trinket sizes in the range 1 to some maximum size in 0.1 centimeter increments. The function

```
float RandomTrinketSize(int MaxSize) {
    return Uniform(10, MaxSize * 10) / 10.0;
}
```

generates a number in the range 1 to MaxSize in 0.1 increments. Using simple algebraic substitution, you can convince yourself that the function returns a number from the sequence of numbers 1, 1.1, 1.2, ..., MaxSize.

We also need to generate a random offset to position the trinkets along the diagonals. Generating the offset is somewhat more difficult because we need to make sure that the offset is large enough so that when the trinket is drawn it does not overlap the center of the window. Consequently, the offset depends on the size of the trinket. Additionally, if the offset is too large, part of the square will be displayed outside the window.

To take into account the size of the trinket, we need to make sure that the offset is at least as large as half the length of the trinket's side. Thus if we make sure the offset is at least this length, we can be assured that the trinkets will not overlap at the center when drawn. The following function generates a random offset that meets our requirements.

```
float RandomOffset(int Range, float TrinketSize) {
    float offset = (Uniform(0, Range * 10)) / 10.0;
    if (offset < (TrinketSize / 2))
        offset = TrinketSize / 2;
    return offset;
}
```

We can now write Kaleidoscope(), the function that will draw the required eight trinkets. The following code creates the first four trinkets.

```
const float Center = WindowSize / 2.0;
float TrinketSize = RandomTrinketSize(MaxSize);
float Offset = RandomOffset(TrinketSize, MaxSize);
color FirstColor = RandomColor();
color SecondColor = RandomColor();

// Create four trinkets, one in each quadrant
RectangleShape TrinketQuad1(KaleidoWindow,
  Center + Offset, Center + Offset, FirstColor,
  TrinketSize, TrinketSize);
RectangleShape TrinketQuad2(KaleidoWindow,
  Center - Offset, Center + Offset, SecondColor,
  TrinketSize, TrinketSize);
RectangleShape TrinketQuad3(KaleidoWindow,
  Center - Offset, Center - Offset, FirstColor,
  TrinketSize, TrinketSize);
RectangleShape TrinketQuad4(KaleidoWindow,
```

```
            Center + Offset, Center - Offset, SecondColor,
            TrinketSize, TrinketSize);
```

The first part of the code computes various values needed to create the trinkets. The first line computes the center coordinate of the square window. Following that, the program computes the size of the trinkets and their offsets from the center of the window by calling the appropriate functions. The last bit of setup code gets two colors for the trinkets. Using this information, trinkets in each quadrant are instantiated. Once the trinkets are instantiated, the following code draws the trinkets.

```
            TrinketQuad1.Draw();
            TrinketQuad2.Draw();
            TrinketQuad3.Draw();
            TrinketQuad4.Draw();
```

The next job is to reposition the trinkets and draw them in their new positions. We call `RandomOffset()` to get a new offset. Using this offset, the trinkets are repositioned using `RectangleShape`'s `SetPosition()` mutator. The code for drawing the other four squares is identical to the preceding code. Program 7.2 contains the complete Kaleidoscope program.

The function `ApiMain()` contains calls to library functions that we have not seen before. To simulate the kaleidoscope turning slowly, we need to call function `Kaleidoscope()` periodically. The `SimpleWindow` class contains a timer object that is designed specifically for this purpose. The `SimpleWindow SetTimerCallback()` member function sets up the timer and tells the EzWindows system to call the `Kaleidoscope()` function when the timer goes off. The `SimpleWindow` member function `StartTimer()` starts the timer and tells it to go off every 1,000 milliseconds or once a second.

Despite its simplicity, function `Kaleidoscope()` creates a display that looks very much like an image created by a real kaleidoscope. Figure 7.10 shows the image created after the program has been running for about 30 seconds.

Program 7.2

Simulate a kaleidoscope

```
// Program 7.2: Simulate a simple kaleidoscope
#include "uniform.h"
#include "rect.h"

// Size of the window
const float WindowSize = 10.0;

// Maximum size of a trinket
const float MaxSize = 4.0;

// Create a square window
SimpleWindow KaleidoWindow("Kaleidoscope",
 WindowSize, WindowSize);

color RandomColor() {
   return (color) Uniform(0, MaxColors - 1);
}

// RandomOffset - generate a random amount to offset
// a trinket from the center of the window. Generate
// a random offset in the interval 0..Range-1 in
// .1-centimeter increments. The size of the offset
// must take into account the size of the trinket so
```

```
                       // the shapes do not overlap at the center.
                       float RandomOffset(int Range, float TrinketSize) {
                          float Offset = Uniform(0, Range * 10) / 10.0;
                          if (Offset < TrinketSize / 2)
                             Offset = TrinketSize / 2;
                          return Offset;
                       }
                       // RandomSize - generate a random size in
                       // the interval 1 to MaxSize in .1-centimeter
                       // increments (i.e., 1, 1.1, 1.2, ..., MaxSize)
                       float RandomTrinketSize(int MaxSize) {
                          return Uniform(10, MaxSize * 10) / 10.0;
                       }

                       int Kaleidoscope() {

                          const float Center = WindowSize / 2.0;

                          const float TrinketSize = RandomTrinketSize(MaxSize);
                          float Offset = RandomOffset(MaxSize, TrinketSize);
                          const color FirstColor = RandomColor();
                          const color SecondColor = RandomColor();

                          // Create four trinkets, one in each quadrant
                          RectangleShape TrinketQuad1(KaleidoWindow,
                           Center + Offset, Center + Offset, FirstColor,
                           TrinketSize, TrinketSize);
                          RectangleShape TrinketQuad2(KaleidoWindow,
                           Center - Offset, Center + Offset, SecondColor,
                           TrinketSize, TrinketSize);
                          RectangleShape TrinketQuad3(KaleidoWindow,
                           Center - Offset, Center - Offset, FirstColor,
                           TrinketSize, TrinketSize);
                          RectangleShape TrinketQuad4(KaleidoWindow,
                           Center + Offset, Center - Offset, SecondColor,
                           TrinketSize, TrinketSize);

                          // Draw the trinkets
                          TrinketQuad1.Draw();
                          TrinketQuad2.Draw();
                          TrinketQuad3.Draw();
                          TrinketQuad4.Draw();

                          // Reset their color
                          TrinketQuad1.SetColor(SecondColor);
                          TrinketQuad2.SetColor(FirstColor);
                          TrinketQuad3.SetColor(SecondColor);
                          TrinketQuad4.SetColor(FirstColor);

                          // Relocate the trinkets to a new position for
                          // a kaleidoscope effect
                          Offset = RandomOffset(MaxSize, TrinketSize);
                          TrinketQuad1.SetPosition(Center + Offset,
                           Center + Offset);
                          TrinketQuad2.SetPosition(Center - Offset,
                           Center + Offset);
                          TrinketQuad3.SetPosition(Center - Offset,
                           Center - Offset);
                          TrinketQuad4.SetPosition(Center + Offset,
                           Center - Offset);

                          // Draw the trinkets at the new positions
                          TrinketQuad1.Draw();
                          TrinketQuad2.Draw();
                          TrinketQuad3.Draw();
                          TrinketQuad4.Draw();
```

```
      return 0;
   }
int ApiMain() {
   InitializeSeed();
   KaleidoWindow.Open();
   KaleidoWindow.SetTimerCallback(Kaleidoscope);
   KaleidoWindow.StartTimer(1000);
      return 0;
   }
```

Figure 7.10

Kaleidoscope display after several calls to Kaleidoscope

7.6 OBJECT-ORIENTED ANALYSIS AND DESIGN

The class construct is the key C++ construct for realizing an object-oriented design. Object-oriented design, like most worthwhile disciplines, is difficult to master. However, it ultimately pays for itself by reducing the cost of maintaining and extending the life of the software. Figure 7.11 illustrates the difference between object-oriented and traditional software development methods. With traditional software development methods, implementation and testing consume the largest portion of development time. With the object-oriented approach, design consumes the largest portion of overall development time. In object-oriented design less time is spent on implementation and maintenance because a good design is easier to implement and has fewer errors; however a larger percentage of time is spent on the design itself because designing for reuse, maintenance, and extensibility is quite difficult. Although both methods require about the same amount of overall development time, software designed using the object-oriented method costs less to maintain, is easier to extend, and parts of it can be reused in other applications. Thus the cycle time for these efforts is greatly reduced.

Figure 7.11

Comparison of the software life cycle of traditional and object-oriented software projects

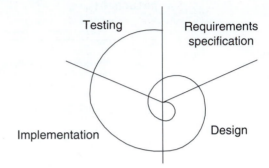

Traditional software life cycle

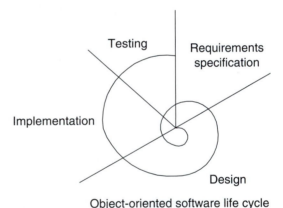

Object-oriented software life cycle

To illustrate the basics of object-oriented analysis (OOA) and object-oriented design (OOD) and the realization of an object-oriented design using classes, let's walk through the OOA and OOD for a realistic application.

Most modern factories use automation wherever possible to reduce costs and to speed up the manufacturing process. Despite the advances in factory automation, many jobs are difficult to automate and require human input. For example, humans are still much better than machines at recognizing subtle differences in colors and recognizing complex patterns. Our task is to design and implement a program for training people to perform a particular task in a factory.

In this factory, groups of three parts move down a conveyor belt to an inspection station. At the inspection station, a video image of the parts is sent to a display that is being watched by a human inspector. Figure 7.12 illustrates the operation of the inspection process. The inspector examines the video image of the three parts and determines whether they should be accepted or rejected. To be accepted, two of the parts must be the same color. If two parts are the same color, the inspector punches the accept button and the parts proceed down the line and are assembled with other components. If no two parts are the same color, the inspector punches the reject button and the three parts are routed to a recycling station.

Figure 7.12

Factory automation system

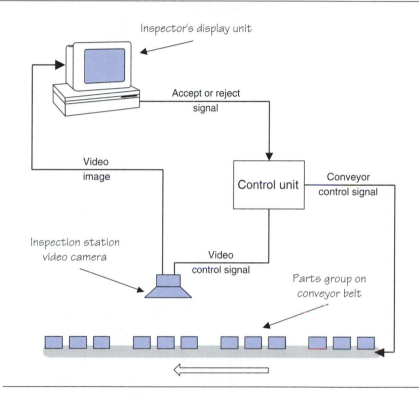

Our job is to write a program that can be used to train and evaluate the performance of potential part inspectors. In addition, the program can be used to help determine at what rate inspectors can reliably inspect parts. This information is used to set the rate at which parts move through the system. Before starting the detailed design and implementation of the trainer, we need a more precise description of exactly how the trainer should operate.

The parts-inspection trainer will simulate the operation of the inspection component of the assembly line. To simulate parts moving down the conveyor belt, we will create three rectangles with randomly chosen colors. The display system will consist of a display window where the three rectangles produced by the conveyor will be displayed. The input by the inspector will be accepted through the control window. The inspector can accept a group of parts by typing the letter *a* (for accept) or can reject a group of parts by typing the letter *r* (for reject). A group of parts is acceptable if two of the parts are the same color. If no two parts are the same color, the parts should be rejected.

The trainer should maintain statistics about the inspector's performance. It should also record the number of parts groups the inspector handles and the number of correct and incorrect decisions the inspector makes. After the training session is complete, the trainer should print the following statistics: the length of the training session, the number of part groups inspected during the session, the number of correct and incorrect decisions, and the percentage of correct decisions.

The first step of an object-oriented design is to discover or determine the objects that constitute the system. Generally, this task is not too difficult, especially for concrete objects, such as a camera, an ATM machine, a sensor, or a telephone. Objects that represent some intangible entity in the system are more difficult to identify. Examples of such objects are a video image, a banking transaction, a sensor signal, or a telephone call.

From Figure 7.12, we can identify some of the classes we would need to realize in an object-oriented design. We do not necessarily need all the objects in Figure 7.12 because we are writing a training system—not a simulation of the entire factory automation system. Clearly, we need a video camera, a display device, an input device, and parts. For the training system, there's no need to simulate the conveyor belt. Because we are implementing a simulation, it will be useful to have a simulation controller that coordinates the operation of the simulation. Additionally, Figure 7.12 contains references to items like a video image, an accept or reject signal, and a video control signal. It's not so obvious as to whether we want objects to represent these entities. We will keep these objects in mind, but will not commit to creating classes for them just yet.

Once we have determined the objects we need, it is useful to draw a diagram showing how the objects interact. This step is important because how the objects interact affects their behaviors or responsibilities. Figure 7.13 shows the interaction of the objects. Not surprisingly, it corresponds closely to Figure 7.12. One of the strengths of object-oriented analysis and design is that the design closely models the actual system. From Figure 7.13, we see that the video camera interacts with the control unit by sending it the video image, which the control unit forwards to the video display. Remember, we are building a training system for the factory automation system, so the control unit needs the video image to determine whether the trainee gave the correct response. In addition, the control unit interacts with the video camera, the conveyor belt, and the operator console.

After determining how the objects will interact, we can think about the behaviors or responsibilities of an object. Let's determine the responsibilities and attributes of the video camera. The camera takes a picture of the parts as they pass under the camera, so one of its responsibilities is to capture an image of the parts when signaled by the control unit.

A common attribute of a physical device is its mode or *state*. For example, a photocopier has several states that it displays on a LCD panel: off, warming up, on, out of paper, and malfunction. A video camera also has state, and the

Figure 7.13

Interaction of objects in the factory automation trainer

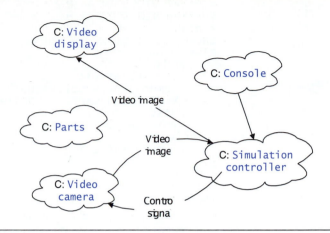

C: Video display

C: Console

Video image

C: Parts

Video image

C: Simulation controller

C: Video camera

Control signal

various states depend on the type of camera. Typical states include on, off, or error. In determining the state of an object it is important to use abstraction, which means to eliminate the irrelevant and focus on the essential. For the factory automation trainer, the essential state is whether the camera is on or off. If it's on, then it can take a picture; if it's off, it cannot. Thus our abstraction of a video camera will have a state attribute that can have two values: on and off. We will want to manipulate the state of the camera so it accepts messages that turn it on and off. We will also want to determine the state of the camera. These actions will be additional behaviors of the camera.

Our abstraction of the video camera has a single attribute—its status—and the following behaviors:

- Capture an image.
- Turn on the camera.
- Turn off the camera.
- Get the status of the camera.

Using our picture notation, the class `VideoCamera` is

C: VideoCamera
DM: Status
MF: CaptureImage(), TurnOn(),
TurnOff(), GetStatus()

We can realize this abstraction through the C++ class declaration in Listing 7.1.

Notice that our design process has three steps:

1. Determine the object or classes in the system.

2. Determine how the objects interact.

3. Determine the responsibilities (behaviors) and attributes of the objects.

Listing 7.1

Declaration of class
VideoCamera from
vcam.h

```
#ifndef VIDEOCAMERA_H
#define VIDEOCAMERA_H
#include "image.h"
enum CameraStatus { CameraOn, CameraOff };
class VideoCamera {
   public:
      VideoCamera();
      CameraStatus GetStatus() const;
      VideoImage CaptureImage();
      void TurnOn();
      void TurnOff();
   private:
      CameraStatus Status;
};
#endif
```

These are the typical steps in any object-oriented design methodology. Like most design processes, the steps are repeated as the design is refined. For example, when determining the behaviors of an object, you might discover that you overlooked an interaction between that object and another. Similarly, when determining the attributes of an object, you are likely to discover that you need additional objects to represent the attributes.

In the declaration of the class `VideoCamera`, the member function `CaptureImage()` returns a `VideoImage` object. This object is an abstraction of a video image. It is the object sent from the camera to the simulation controller. Let's apply the OOA/OOD process to realize this object. The video image is an interesting object because it is not at all clear how to represent it. From Figure 7.13, we see that the video image is sent to the simulation controller. The simulation controller forwards it to the display unit. Because the display unit will display the image of the parts group, clearly the video image needs enough information so the video display can synthesize an appropriate image (e.g., a `RectangleShape` of the appropriate size and color). Consequently, it is tempting to represent this object using our graphical object `RectangleShape`. However, we would be making a common design mistake.

Using `RectangleShape` to realize the object `VideoImage` would prematurely tie the abstraction of the video image object to how we plan to display it. To illustrate our erroneous logic, suppose we decided to move the simulation to a machine that did not have a windowing system like EzWindows. On this machine, we need to output a character string that indicates the parts group under the camera (e.g., output the string `Red Blue Red` for a parts group with a red part, a blue part, and another red part). To make this change when the video image is represented by a `RectangleShape` would be time-consuming and would require changing more code than we would like. In general, it is a good idea to decouple the display of information from the operation of the rest of the system because we often want to change how information is displayed.

To solve this problem, we again apply abstraction—eliminate the irrelevant and focus on the essential. For the factory automation trainer, the essential aspects of the video image are the parts viewed. Thus a video image can consist of three parts. Listing 7.2 contains the class declaration for `VideoImage`.

Listing 7.2

Declaration of class
VideoImage from
image.h

```
// class VideoImage
#ifndef VIDEOIMAGE_H
#define VIDEOIMAGE_H
#include "part.h"
class VideoImage {
    public:
        VideoImage(const color &c1, const color &c2,
          const color &c3);
        Part GetPart1() const;
        Part GetPart2() const;
        Part GetPart3() const;
    private:
        Part Part1;
        Part Part2;
        Part Part3;
};
#endif
```

Since VideoImage contains a Part, let's design it next. Part has no uses outside of VideoImage. For our simulation, the essential properties or state of a part is its color. As usual, we will want an inspector for the color attribute. We will not need a corresponding mutator, because once a part is created we will never need to change its color. Listing 7.3 contains the class declaration for Part.

Listing 7.3

Declaration of class
Part from part.h

```
#ifndef PART_H
#define PART_H
#include "ezwin.h"
class Part {
    public:
        Part(const color &c = Red);
        color GetColor() const;
    private:
        color Color;
};
#endif
```

The final two objects in the training simulator are the video display and the console. These objects are the user interface objects. The operator views the parts of the video display, and he or she records a response using the console. Let's begin with the video display unit. The responsibility of the video display is to project the image so the operator can view it and make a decision as to whether to accept or reject the parts group. Like the video camera, the video display maintains state information about whether it is on or off. To display the images of the parts, we will use the SimpleWindow class from the EzWindows library. The SimpleWindow used for the display will be another attribute of the display unit. This approach is appropriate because we want to encapsulate all aspects of how we display the parts in the video display unit class. The declaration of class VideoDisplayUnit is shown in Listing 7.4.

The constructor requires a string parameter, which is the string displayed in the title bar of the SimpleWindow that is created. The member function DisplayImage() is the message that causes the VideoDisplayUnit to display the images of the parts. The content of the message is the video image.

```
#ifndef DISPLAYUNIT_H
#define DISPLAYUNIT_H
#include <string>
#include "ezwin.h"
#include "image.h"
enum DisplayStatus { DisplayOn, DisplayOff };
class VideoDisplayUnit {
    public:
        VideoDisplayUnit(const string &Title);
        void DisplayImage(const VideoImage &Image);
        void TurnOn();
        void TurnOff();
    private:
        SimpleWindow W;
        DisplayStatus Status;
};
#endif
```

The final object in our design is the console. The console's responsibilities are to display any instructions to the trainee, to accept all input from the operator trainee, and to display the results of the training session. The only attribute of the console is its state: on or off. Listing 7.5 contains the declaration of class `Console`.

Member function `TurnOn()` sets the state of the console to on, and it prints the introductory message that directs the operator to resize the windows. `GetResponse()` reads the response and returns it to the simulation controller so it can be verified. Member function `PrintSessionResults()` displays the results of the training session on the console when the simulation is finished.

Using these class definitions, we can design the operation of the training simulator. A high-level description of the steps of the simulation follows.

Step 1.   Get part images.

Step 2.   Display parts images in the display window.

Step 3.   Read and record the response of the trainee.

Step 4.   Score the response.

Step 5.   Check to see whether the training session should end. If time is not up, go back to step 1. If time is up, the final statistics of the training session are computed and printed.

These steps will form the main loop of the simulation.

Listing 7.6 contains code that implements the training simulator. The first part of the code creates the central objects of the simulation—`TrainingMonitor`, `InspectionCamera`, and `TrainingConsole`. Immediately after construction these devices are turned on. The second part of the code initializes various counters need and records the starting time of the simulation. The main part of the code is the main loop of the simulation which closely corresponds to the steps listed previously.

Four points about the simulation program are worth noting. First, we have chosen to keep most of the logic of the program in the routine `ApiMain()`. We could have created a simulation control object and placed the code there, but this approach seemed like overkill, and so we opted against it. Second, the

Listing 7.5

*Declaration of class
Console from console.h*

```cpp
#ifndef CONSOLE_H
#define CONSOLE_H
enum ConsoleStatus { ConsoleOn, ConsoleOff };
class Console {
    public:
        Console();
        void TurnOn();
        void TurnOff();
        char GetResponse();
        void PrintSessionResults(long Time, int Attempts,
          int Correct, int Wrong);
    private:
        ConsoleStatus Status;
};
#endif
```

Listing 7.6

*Implementation of the
factory automation
training simulator in
trainer.cpp*

```cpp
// ApiMain(): a factory automation training simulator
#include <iostream>
#include "uniform.h"
#include "dunit.h"
#include "ezwin.h"
#include "vcam.h"
#include "console.h"
using namespace std;

// Length of the session (60 seconds)
const long TestTime = 60 * 1000L;

// Determine if the appropriate response was given
bool CheckResponse(char Response,
 const VideoImage &v) {
    Part Part1 = v.GetPart1();
    Part Part2 = v.GetPart2();
    Part Part3 = v.GetPart3();
    if (Part1.GetColor() == Part2.GetColor()
      || Part1.GetColor() == Part3.GetColor()
      || Part2.GetColor() == Part3.GetColor())
        return Response == 'a';
    else
        return Response == 'r';
}

int ApiMain() {
    VideoDisplayUnit TrainingMonitor("PARTS DISPLAY");
    VideoCamera InspectionCamera;
    Console TrainingConsole;
    TrainingMonitor.TurnOn();
    TrainingConsole.TurnOn();
    InspectionCamera.TurnOn();

    InitializeSeed();
    // Define objects for scoring the trainee
    int Attempts = 0;       // Number of tests done
    int CorrectResponses = 0;
    int IncorrectResponses = 0;

    // Record starting time
    const long StartTime = GetMilliseconds();
    long ElapsedTime;

    do {
```

```
        VideoImage Image =
         InspectionCamera.CaptureImage();
        TrainingMonitor.DisplayImage(Image);

        char Response;
        Response = TrainingConsole.GetResponse();

        ++Attempts;
        if (CheckResponse(Response, Image))
            ++CorrectResponses;
        else
            ++IncorrectResponses;
        ElapsedTime = GetMilliseconds();
    } while ((ElapsedTime - StartTime) < TestTime);

    TrainingConsole.PrintSessionResults(TestTime,
     Attempts, CorrectResponses, IncorrectResponses);
    TrainingMonitor.TurnOff();
    TrainingConsole.TurnOff();
    InspectionCamera.TurnOff();
    return 0;
}
```

heart of the program, the do-while loop in function `ApiMain()`, reads very naturally. The program closely corresponds to a physical realization of the trainer. Third, this implementation will be easy to maintain and extend. For example, an exercise in a later chapter is to modify the program so that the operator can use the mouse to indicate whether a parts group should be accepted or rejected. Because of the object-oriented design, this change will be simple and easy to make. Fourth, the objects we developed can be reused in implementations of other simulations. Suppose we were asked to implement a simulator of a central highway traffic monitoring station. Much of the code we developed for the factory training simulator could be reused. In the highway traffic monitoring system, an operator sits in a control room and monitors video screens showing traffic moving down a highway. Video cameras are placed at key points on the highways. If there is some interruption in traffic, the operator notifies the highway patrol. To implement this system, we could reuse many of the objects we developed for the factory automation trainer. We could reuse the class `VideoImage`, but instead of parts, the video image would consist of cars. The classes `VideoDisplayUnit` and `VideoCamera` could be reused with little or no modification. Because of reuse, we could likely design, implement, and test the simulation of the highway monitoring system in half the time it would take to do it from scratch. The third and fourth points, extensibility and reuse, are two of the key benefits of object-oriented design and implementation.

7.7 POINTS TO REMEMBER

✔ New data types that represent real-world objects are created using C++'s class construct.

✔ A class-type object has two components—a set of attributes and a set of behaviors. The attributes are called the data members, and the behaviors are called the member functions.

✔ When creating a new class type, two important initial steps are determining the attributes and the behaviors of the objects.

✔ Member functions that return the value of an attribute of an object are called inspectors.

✔ Member functions that set or change the value of an attribute of an object are called mutators.

✔ Member functions that direct an object to perform some function or action are called facilitators.

✔ A constructor is a special member function that is invoked when an object is created. It is typically used to initialize the attributes of an object.

✔ A class declaration is divided into two sections: public and private. The public section contains declarations for the attributes and behaviors of the object that are meant to be accessible to users of the object. Constructors must always be declared in the public section. The private section contains the member functions and data members that are hidden or inaccessible to users of the object. These member functions and data attributes are accessible only by the object's member function.

✔ The process of creating an object is called instantiation.

✔ Data members and member functions are accessed using a dot (.), the member access operator.

✔ A constant member function is one that cannot change its objects' attributes.

✔ Default arguments make a constructor more flexible and useful.

✔ Reference data members must be initialized when an object is instantiated. Once initialized, a reference data member cannot be changed.

✔ Abstraction eliminates the irrelevant properties of an object and focuses on the essential.

✔ Object-oriented design consists of three basic steps: (1) determine the objects in the system, (2) determine how the objects collaborate or interact, and (3) determine the behaviors and attributes of the objects.

History of Computing

Stored programs

The next major advance in computing involved how computers were programmed. The ENIAC computer was programmed with plug boards that consisted of an array of sockets into which wires could be plugged. By connecting the appropriate sockets, the machine circuitry could be changed and a different computation could be performed. The problem was that this task was very time-consuming. For complex problems, it could take several days to reprogram the machine.

This problem was solved with the development of the Electronic Discrete Variable Computer (EDVAC). Although there is some controversy over the development of the ideas embodied in EDVAC, most historians agree that John von Neumann played a pivotal role in the design of the stored-program computer.

John von Neumann was a well-known, highly respected and brilliant mathematician. In addition to his contributions to computing, which we are about to discuss, von Neumann made significant contributions in areas such as game theory, physics, pure mathematics, and meteorology. Von Neumann, a consultant to BRL, became interested in computers after visiting the University of Pennsylvania to review the work on ENIAC. After meeting with Eckert and Mauchly, von Neumann produced a paper, "First Draft of a Report on EDVAC," that outlined the components and basic operation that would be part of all modern computers. One of the most important ideas was to store the program that controlled the computer in memory along with the data. This concept meant that the program could be manipulated like data, an ability that is fundamental to all computers.

At this point, it is worthwhile to step back and discuss some of the controversy over the development of the ideas embodied in ENIAC and EDVAC. Many researchers at the University of Pennsylvania believed that von Neumann slighted them by omitting their names from his paper and not mentioning their contributions to the project. Indeed, because of this and other conflicts involving intellectual property, Eckert and Mauchly left the university in 1946 and founded a company to design, build, and sell electronic computers. To protect their invention, they filed for a patent to cover the operation of their electronic computer.

In 1942, three years before the completion of ENIAC, John Atanasoff, a professor at Iowa State University, and Clifford Berry, a graduate student, constructed the Atanasoff-Berry Computer, or ABC for short. The ABC also used vacuum tubes, and it performed binary arithmetic. In fact, Mauchly visited Atanasoff in Iowa and reviewed a proposal written by Atanasoff to build an electronic calculator. Many of the ideas in the proposal found their way into the ENIAC. Unfortunately for Atanasoff, his attorney never filed for a patent to cover the innovations in the ABC, and the credit rightfully due him never materialized.

It was not until 1964, when the Mauchly–Eckert patent for the ideas in ENIAC was finally granted, that the full story of the development of the electronic computer was revealed. At that time, the patent was held by Sperry Rand. In 1968, Sperry decided to begin enforcing the patent and collecting royalties. One company, Honeywell, rather than pay royalties, decided to fight in court. Honeywell's strategy was to have the ENIAC patents declared invalid. A patent can be declared invalid if it can be shown that the idea in the patent was developed previously. As you can probably guess, Atanasoff was a star witness during the lawsuit. After a five-year court battle, the judge hearing the case invalidated the ENIAC patents, and the judgment stated, "Eckert and Mauchly did not themselves first invent the automatic electronic digital computer, but instead derived that subject matter from one Dr. John Vincent Atanasoff." After more than 25 years, Atanasoff's contributions to the development of the electronic digital computer were finally made public.

With the development of the concept of a stored-program computer, systems for storing information became a critical issue. In this area, researchers in Britain had the lead because of their work with radar, and the first operational stored-program machine was constructed there. A prototype machine employing the stored-program concept, called the Manchester Mark I, was completed in 1948 at the University of Manchester in Manchester, England. It had a memory of 32 words, each containing 32 bits. One year later, in Cambridge, England, another stored-program computer, the Electronic Delay Storage Automatic Computer (EDSAC) was unveiled. The EDVAC, whose original design spawned all this development, was not completed until 1952.

✔ Good design is hard. Do not be afraid to spend time designing a system. In the long run, it will save time.

7.8   TO DELVE FURTHER

Several excellent books that discuss object-oriented analysis and design follow.

- G. Booch, *Object-Oriented Analysis and Design with Applications*, Redwood City, CA: Benjamin-Cummings, 1994.

- R. Martin, *Designing Object-Oriented C++ Applications Using the Booch Method*, Englewood Cliffs, NJ: Prentice-Hall, 1995.

- J. Rumbaugh, M. Blaha, W. Premerlani, F. Eddy, and W. Lorensen, *Object-Oriented Modeling and Design*, Englewood Cliffs, NJ: Prentice-Hall, 1991.

- R. Wirfs-Brock, B. Wilkerson, and L. Wiener, *Designing Object-Oriented Software*, Englewood Cliffs, NJ: Prentice-Hall, 1990.

7.9 EXERCISES

7.1   A _____ is a function that is called to create an instance of a class.

7.2   A _____ is a member function that gets the value of a data member of an object.

7.3   A _____ is a member function that changes or sets the value of a data member of an object.

7.4   A _____ is a member function that performs some action or service.

7.5   Structured design is the traditional design method. Find out about structured design and compare it to object-oriented design.

7.6   Give a C++ **class** declaration to represent the following geometric objects.

    a)   Circle

    b)   Rectangle

    c)   Ellipse

    d)   Triangle

    e)   Quadrilateral

7.7   Consider the following class declaration:

```
class Top {
    public:
        Top ();
        int Look();
    private:
        int Value;
        void Change(int v);
};
```

and the following code fragment:

```
int main() {
    Top t;
    t.value = 3;        // legal or illegal?
    int k = t.Look();   // legal or illegal?
    t.Change(3);        // legal or illegal?
    return 0;
}
```

For the commented statements, indicate whether they are legal or illegal statements.

7.8   Give a C++ **class** declaration to represent the following objects:

    a)   Digital clock.

    b)   Home thermostat.

    c)   Digital timer.

    d)   Cassette player.

7.9   Make an object-oriented design like the one for the factory automation trainer for the following applications:

a) Calculator.

b) Calendar.

c) Bank ATM.

d) Library checkout system.

e) Computer version of a Las Vegas slot machine.

f) Spelling checker.

In your design, be sure to show how the objects collaborate or interact.

7.10   Other messages can be useful with `RectangleShape`, for example, an erase message that directs a rectangle to remove its image from the display. Can you think of other useful messages? Extend class `RectangleShape` to include member functions for each message.

7.11   Write a program that reads a file where each line specifies a position within a `SimpleWindow`. The floating-point numbers that make up the position are separated by a blank. For each position read, draw a red rectangle 1 centimeter wide and 2 centimeters high at that position. The `SimpleWindow` you create should be 10 centimeters by 10 centimeters. Your program should make sure that the coordinates read represent valid coordinates (i.e., they fall within the window).

7.12   For questions *a*) through *d*), use the following declaration for a square object:

```
class Square {
    public:
        Square(SimpleWindow &W);
        void Draw();
        void SetColor(const color &Color);
        void SetPosition(float XCoord,
          float YCoord);
        void SetSize(float Length);
    private:
        color Color;
        float XCenter;
        float YCenter;
        float SideLength;
        SimpleWindow &Window;
};
```

a) Write a code fragment that defines and draws a square object with 1.5-centimeter sides called `GreenSquare` that is displayed in the window `Sample`. Position `GreenSquare`'s center 3.5 centimeters from the left edge of the window and 2.5 centimeters from the top edge of the window. `GreenSquare` should be green.

b) Write a code fragment that defines and draws a square object with 2-centimeter sides called `MagentaSquare`. `MagentaSquare` is displayed in the window `Sample`. Position the upper-left corner of

MagentaSquare's at the upper-left corner of the window. Color MagentaSquare magenta.

c) Write a code fragment that defines and draws two square objects both with 2.5-centimeter sides. Display both squares in the window DoubleSquare. One square should be called TopSquare, and the other square should be called BottomSquare. Position TopSquare 3 centimeters from the left edge of the window and 1.5 centimeters from the top edge of the window. Position BottomSquare below TopSquare so that BottomSquare's top side touches Top-Square's bottom side. Color TopSquare red and BottomSquare blue.

d) Write a code fragment that defines and draws three square objects. One square is 3 centimeters on a side, another square is 2 centimeters on a side, and the last square is 1 centimeter on a side. Display all three squares in the window OverlappedSquares. Position all three squares at the screen coordinates contained in the variables XCenterWindow and YCenterWindow. The 3-centimeter square is called BigSquare and is yellow. The 2-centimeter square is called MiddleSquare and is green. The 1-centimeter square is called SmallSquare and is red.

7.13 Redo Exercise 7.12 assuming the following declaration for Square is available.

```
class Square {
    public:
        Square(SimpleWindow &W, float XCoord = 0,
            float YCoord = 0, const color &c = Red,
            float Length = 1);
        void Draw();
        void SetColor(const color &Color);
        void SetPosition(float XCoord,
            float YCoord);
        void SetSize(float Length);
    private:
        color Color;
        float XCenter;
        float YCenter;
        float SideLength;
        SimpleWindow &Window;
};
```

7.14 You have been asked to write a program to help visualize the spatial relationships of structures within a two-dimensional space. To represent structures, you will use the EzWindow shape RectangleShape. Your program should read a file that contains the dimensions of the structure, its location, and the color to use to display the structure. The format of an input line is

width height xcoordinate ycoordinate color

where width and height are the size of the rectangle to display (in centimeters), xcoordinate and ycoordinate are the location within the window to draw the structure, and `color` is the color of the rectangle to draw. All input data except for the color are floating-point data. The input data color is a string indicating the color of the structure. The possible values are Red, Green, Blue, Yellow, Cyan, and Magenta. For example, when the program reads the following data file, it produces the display shown in Figure 7.14.

```
0.5 0.3 3.0 3.0 Red
0.3 0.2 5.0 5.0 Green
1.0 1.0 8.0 5.0 Blue
0.5 0.5 1.0 1.0 Magenta
0.5 1.0 2.0 6.0 Yellow
```

Figure 7.14

Structure relationship display for Exercise 7.14

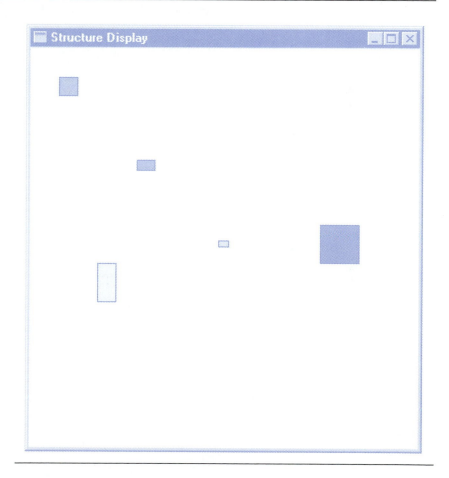

7.15   Design a Kaleidoscope class.

7.16   Design a class for the following objects. Give a C++ class declaration that corresponds to your design.

a) A screen position for use in the EzWindows graphical system.

b) A line object for use in the EzWindows graphical system.

c) A mouse object for use in the EzWindows graphical system.

7.17 Redesign the `VideoImage` class of the factory automation trainer so a parts group consists of five objects. What other classes must you modify?

7.18 Redesign the `Part` class of the factory automation trainer so that a part has a width and a height. What other classes must you modify?

7.19 Revise the Kaleidoscope program so that the color of each trinket is picked randomly.

7.20 Revise the Kaleidoscope program so that it also draws trinkets along axes that divide the screen into the four quadrants (see Figure 7.15). The program should randomly decide whether to place the trinkets on the diagonals or on the vertical axes.

Figure 7.15

Trinkets positioned on vertical and horizontal axes

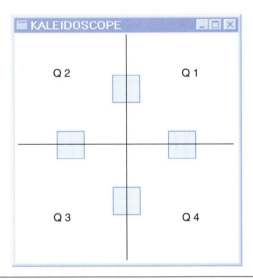

CHAPTER 8

Implementing abstract data types

Introduction

A data abstraction is a representation of information and the operations to be performed on the information. An abstract data type, or ADT, is a well-defined and complete data abstraction that uses the information-hiding principle. ADTs make it possible to create and manipulate objects in a natural manner. In this chapter, we introduce ADTs in the C++ framework of classes, functions, and operators. We do so by developing ADTs for rational numbers, uniform pseudorandom numbers, and a simple guessing game. Our development of ADTs includes discussion of their interfaces and implementations.

Key Concepts

- data abstraction
- abstract data type (ADT)
- rule of minimality
- class minimality principle
- default constructors
- copy constructors
- member assignment
- inspectors
- mutators
- facilitators
- **const** member functions
- destructors
- auxiliary functions and operators
- operator overloading
- overloading insertion and extraction operators
- reference return
- pseudorandom number sequence

8.1   INTRODUCING ABSTRACT DATA TYPES

All the problems that we previously considered were carefully chosen so that if an object was used in the solution, it was best represented using a fundamental type or a class type that was defined in an available library. More sophisticated problem solving requires that we develop our own representations for the information to be manipulated. In object-oriented programming terminology, the representation and the operations to be performed on the representation form a *data abstraction*. In this chapter, we develop abstractions for rational numbers, for random numbers, and for a simple guessing game. The abstractions are developed using classes, functions, and operators.

In developing an abstraction, the information-hiding principle is normally followed. Enforcing information hiding through encapsulation helps to maintain the integrity of the data (e.g., prevent a rational number with a denominator of zero). In addition, by using public methods, client programs are generally immune to changes in the implementation of the abstraction.

A well-defined abstraction allows its objects to be created and used in an intuitive manner. Therefore, the programming syntax for the definition and manipulation of objects of an abstraction should have a form analogous to fundamental-type and standard-class objects doing comparable activities. For example, suppose we have an abstraction `Rational` for rational numbers and we want to display the result of summing 1/2 and 1/3. A code segment such as the following should be possible.

```
Rational a(1,2);          // a = 1/2
Rational b(2,3);          // b = 2/3
cout << a << " + " << b << " = " << (a + b) << endl;
```

The insertion has the same form as the corresponding display of the sum of two **int** or **float** objects would have. This analogous form would not be the case in traditional, non-object-oriented languages like C. In traditional languages, a programmer can neither have objects with methods nor extend existing operators to work with new types of objects. The programmer is forced to define functions and additional temporary objects. The resulting code is generally unnatural and awkward.

We will call a well-defined class using the information-hiding principle coupled with the appropriate library functions an *abstract data type*, or ADT.

8.2   RATIONAL ADT BASICS

Our exploration of ADTs begins with development of an ADT `Rational` for representing rational numbers. A rational number is the ratio of two integers and is typically represented in the manner *a/b*. We call *a* the numerator and *b* the denominator. The denominator must be nonzero. The basic arithmetic operations have the following definitions:

Programming Tip

- Addition: $\dfrac{a}{b} + \dfrac{c}{d} = \dfrac{ad + bc}{bd}$

- Subtraction: $\dfrac{a}{b} - \dfrac{c}{d} = \dfrac{ad - bc}{bd}$

- Multiplication: $\dfrac{a}{b} \times \dfrac{c}{d} = \dfrac{ac}{bd}$

- Division: $\dfrac{a/b}{c/d} = \dfrac{ad}{bc}$

Our goal in developing `Rational` is to create a type whose objects are as natural to use as objects defined using the fundamental types.

To represent a rational number, we need to represent a numerator and denominator. This necessity implies that a class representing rational numbers should define objects with two data members—one member to represent the particular numerator and the other member to represent the particular denominator of the object. Both data members will be `int` objects.

Previous experience with rational numbers tells us that the member functions of our `Rational` ADT should provide methods to initialize and manipulate a rational number object in the following ways:

- Construct the rational number with default or particular attributes.

- Add, subtract, multiply, and divide the rational number to another rational number.

- Copy the value of the rational number to another rational number.

- Compare the rational number to another rational number.

- Display the value of the rational number.

- Extract the value of the rational number.

To support these client-programmer activities and information hiding, the following methods should also be present for a rational number object:

- Inspect the values of the numerator and denominator.

- Set the values of the numerator and denominator.

To supplement the Rational class, we also need to define some auxiliary operators in the class library. The *auxiliary operators* are not members of the class but are overloaded versions of the arithmetic, relational, and stream operators. They use the public members of the class to accomplish their tasks. These operators are vital because they enable Rational objects to be manipulated in a consistent, natural manner. Together the class and the auxiliary operators compose the rational library. A discussion of why these operators are auxiliary, rather than members of the Rational class, is deferred until the next section.

The definitions of objects a and b in the earlier code segment are depicted in Figure 8.1. The figure shows that the memory associated with a rational

Figure 8.1

Depiction of two Rational objects being instantiated from a class definition

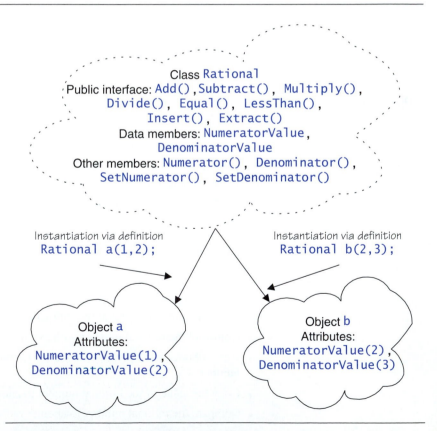

number object has portions that are reserved for the numerator and the denominator being represented. Other portions of memory are reserved for the code associated with the various member functions.

Programming Tip

> **Rule of minimality**
>
> Deciding which behaviors to include in an ADT library generally relies on the *rule of minimality*. This rule states that unless a behavior is needed, it should not be part of the ADT. There are several reasons for the rule. Software engineers have found that client application developers prefer a minimal size library. That way client programs that include the library can remain as small as possible and thus run on a wide range of machine configurations. In addition, when changes need to be made to the library, there is less source code to be considered. The preference for minimality is sometimes traded off with program efficiency.
>
> A corollary to the rule of minimality is the class minimality principle that states: If a function or operator can be defined such that it is not a member of the class, then do not make it a member. This practice makes a nonmember function or operator generally independent of changes to the class's implementation.

8.2.1 A client program using the rational library

Before presenting a C++ implementation of the rational number ADT, we first consider Program 8.1. This client program is a simple illustration of the look

Program 8.1

Demonstration of some Rational ADT capabilities

```
// Program 8.1: Demonstrate Rational ADT
#include <iostream>
#include <string>
#include "rational.h"
using namespace std;
int main() {
   Rational r;
   Rational s;
   cout << "Enter rational number (a/b): ";
   cin >> r;
   cout << "Enter rational number (a/b): ";
   cin >> s;

   Rational t(r);
   Rational Sum = r + s;
   Rational Product = r * s;

   cout << r << " + " << s << " = " << Sum << endl;
   cout << r << " * " << s << " = " << Product << endl;

   return 0;
}
```

and feel that we want in the various components of the Rational ADT. If the rational library truly represents an abstract data type, Program 8.1 should be easy to understand.

Suppose the two inputs to our client program are the rational numbers 1/2 and 1/3. The input/output behavior of the program is then

```
Enter rational number (a/b): 1/2
Enter rational number (a/b): 1/3
1/2 + 1/3 = 5/6
1/2 * 1/3 = 1/6
```

Program 8.1 begins by including the header files for both the standard iostream library and the nonstandard rational library. Header file `rational.h` is similar to header file `iostream` in that the file is really an interface specification for an ADT (the implementations of `Rational` and the auxiliary operators are in file `rational.cpp`). By convention, the header file suffix `h` indicates that the include statement adds the library interface to the global namespace.

Function `main()` of Program 8.1 first defines `Rational` objects r and s.

```
Rational r;
Rational s;
```

No initialization is specified for these objects, so their initial values are determined by the default constructor for the class `Rational`.

The default constructor takes no parameters and assigns default values to the various data members of the object. It is standard practice that constructors initialize all data members to some appropriate value. We have chosen the default rational representation to be 0/1.

A class can often have several different constructors. The constructors will differ in their parameter list specifications. If no constructor has a parameter list that matches the actual initialization parameters given in the object definition, then an error message is generated.

One constructor that is always present is the copy constructor. The *copy constructor* has a single constant reference parameter that is of the same type as the new object. The new object becomes a copy of the actual parameter. The copy constructor is always present because if the class designer does not specify a copy constructor, one is automatically supplied by the compiler. In Program 8.1 the copy constructor makes t a duplicate of r.

```
Rational t(r);          // t is a copy of r
```

Another member of a class that is always present, regardless of whether the designer includes it, is the assignment operator, which modifies an existing object.

The copy constructor and assignment operator provided by the compiler do what is known as a memberwise copying of the data members of the source object to the target object. In a *memberwise copy*, the various data members are copied member by member with each member being directly copied in a bit-by-bit manner from the source data member to the corresponding target data member. This bit-by-bit assignment is the same kind of assignment performed on an object defined using one of the fundamental types. Because memberwise copying of data members is appropriate for the ADTs that we consider in this chapter, we use the compiler-supplied copy constructor and member assignment operator in our basic implementations. However, in Section 8.5 we do explore how to define such members if there is a need for explicit definitions.

In spite of the difference in form from the definition of object t, the copy constructor is also used by Program 8.1 in the definitions of objects Sum and Product.

```
Rational Sum = r + s;
Rational Product = r * s;
```

In a definition where an initialization expression follows the assignment operator (=), the invoked constructor is the one whose definition allows a single parameter of the same type as the expression. The invoked constructor uses the initialization expression as its actual parameter. Thus the definitions of Sum and Product both invoke the copy constructor because the type of values produced by Rational addition and multiplication is Rational.

In the following code segment, Rational object v is copied to Rational objects w and x. Object v is copied to w using the assignment operator and to x through copy construction.

```
Rational v(6,21);  // v is 6/21
Rational w;         // w is 0/1
w = v;              // w is 6/21 by assignment
Rational x = v;     // x is 6/21 by copy construction
```

Observe that w initially represents 0/1 through its construction with the default constructor. Object w is then modified by assignment to represent 6/21. The assignment operator, rather than the copy constructor, is being used on w because w is being modified, not defined. The statement involving x is a definition; therefore, construction, rather than assignment, is being performed. In particular, copy construction is occurring.

A class may also define other constructors depending on what kind of information is reasonable for initializing a new object of the desired class. For a Rational ADT, another constructor should exist. This constructor would expect either one or two integer values as parameters. The first parameter is the initial value of the new object's numerator. The second parameter is an optional parameter that supplies the initial value of the new object's denominator with a default value of one. Examples of this constructor's application are given in the following code segment:

```
Rational x(3,4);   // x = 3/4
Rational y(5);     // y = 5/1
```

The modifier **const** can be used in conjunction with creating **class** objects. If the modifier is applied, then after the construction of the object, it is illegal to modify the values of its data members. In the following statement, a **const** Rational object representing 1/2 is defined.

```
const Rational OneHalf(1,2);
```

Program 8.1 performs two extractions from `cin` to assign values to objects r and s.

```
cout << "Enter rational number (a/b): ";
cin >> r;
cout << "Enter rational number (a/b): ";
cin >> s;
```

The `Rational` number extraction operator `>>` is not a member operator of the `Rational` class, but is an auxiliary operator. `Rational` extraction is not a member method, because we expect a particular form for an extraction. We expect that the left operand of the extraction operator is the source stream and the right operand is the target object. If operator `>>` is instead overloaded to be a member operator of the `Rational` class, then the two operands need to be reversed to comply with the proper form for member operators (it is the left operand that invokes the method). This reversal would result in extractions with form

```
r >> cin;
```

which would be confusing to a reader of the code and should be avoided. Thus the extraction operator and, for similar reasons, the insertion operator are defined as auxiliary operators in the rational library. By making them auxiliary operators, we are free to define their left and right operands as we choose.

As noted previously, Program 8.1 contains definitions of `Rational` objects Sum and Product. The expressions used in their definitions demonstrate that + and * have also been overloaded. Like the stream operators, the arithmetic operators are auxiliary operators rather than member operators. The reason to make the arithmetic operators auxiliary operators, rather than member operators, is for promotional consistency.

In Chapter 3, we discussed how promotions are automatically attempted during expression evaluation if operands of mixed fundamental types are present. The same is true if the mixed-type operands involve class-type objects. For example, in the following code segment the right operand of the addition and the left operand of the subtraction are promoted to `Rational` objects.

```
Rational u(3,4);
cout << (u + 2) << endl;
cout << (2 - u) << endl;
```

Promotions are attempted when there is no definition for the relevant combination of operator and operands. A promotion is achieved by invoking a constructor on an operand. In the preceding example, the `Rational` constructor with the default second parameter can construct a `Rational` from the `int` 2. Thus the preceding example is equivalent to the following code segment:

```
Rational u(3,4);
Rational Two(2,1);
cout << (u + Two) << endl;
cout << (Two - u) << endl;
```

The complete promotion rules are quite involved. For a formal definition of these rules, examine a C++ reference manual. However, an important thing to note regarding them is that when dealing with a member operator, only the right operand can be promoted; but when dealing with an auxiliary operator, either operand can be promoted. Thus the statement

```
cout << (u + 2) << endl;
```

would work regardless of whether the plus operator is a member or auxiliary operator. In contrast, the statement

```
cout << (2 + u) << endl;
```

only works if the plus operator is an auxiliary operator. Therefore, for consistency and client ease, we make the arithmetic operators auxiliary operators.

This discussion completes our overview of the behavior that we expect with `Rational` class objects. We are now ready to proceed with the actual development of the rational library. The only rational arithmetic operations we consider are addition and multiplication. The other rational arithmetic operations, as well as the rational relational operations, are left to the exercises.

The rational library encompasses two files: a header file, `rational.h`, and an implementation file, `rational.cpp`. We begin with an examination of the header file.

8.3 RATIONAL INTERFACE DESCRIPTION

A copy of the header file `rational.h` is given in Listing 8.1. This header file is strictly an interface description, but this property is not necessarily the case with all class header files. For example, header files like `iostream` define global objects (e.g., `cin` and `cout`).

The two major declaration sections in `rational.h` are surrounded by preprocessor statements. The first section is the definition of the `Rational` class. Following that description is a prototyping of the auxiliary operators. Neither the definitions of the member functions nor the definitions of auxiliary operators are given in the header file. The definitions of these functions and operators are given in implementation file `rational.cpp`.

Preceding the two declaration sections in Listing 8.1 are several preprocessor statements of familiar form. The first two preprocessor statements coupled with the final line in the header file ensure that the file is included only once into a translation unit. The other preprocessor statement in the header file includes the iostream library. The iostream library is included because of the auxiliary overloading of the insertion and extraction operators.

8.3.1 Access restrictions

As demonstrated by our definition of `RectangleShape` for the kaleidoscope program in Chapter 7, a class declaration or definition begins with the reserved word **class**. It is then followed by the name of the class. If only the class name is being introduced, then the declaration is immediately followed by a semicolon. If it is a definition (i.e., the data members and member functions

Listing 8.1

Header file rational.h

```
// rational.h: declaration of Rational ADT
#ifndef RATIONAL_H
#define RATIONAL_H

#include <iostream>
#include <string>

using namespace std;

// Rational ADT: class description
class Rational {
   public: // member functions
      // default constructor
      Rational();
      // a second constructor
      Rational(int numer, int denom = 1);
      // some arithmetic and stream facilitators
      Rational Add(const Rational &r) const;
      Rational Multiply(const Rational &r) const;
      void Insert(ostream &sout) const;
      void Extract(istream &sin);
   protected:
      // inspectors
      int GetNumerator() const;
      int GetDenominator() const;
      // mutators
      void SetNumerator(int numer);
      void SetDenominator(int denom);
   private:
      // data members
      int NumeratorValue;
      int DenominatorValue;
};
// Rational ADT: auxiliary operator description
Rational operator+(const Rational &r, const Rational &s);
Rational operator*(const Rational &r, const Rational &s);

ostream& operator<<(ostream &sout, const Rational &s);
istream& operator>>(istream &sin, Rational &r);
#endif
```

and operators are also being declared), then the name is followed by a sequence of declarations and definitions. The sequence is delimited by a pair of left and right curly braces. Through the use of *access-specifier* labels, the sequence is divided into sections with different access permissions.

The Rational class definition in Listing 8.1 has three sections. They begin, respectively, with the access-specifier labels **public**, **protected**, and **private**. The members declared within a **public** section can be directly used by client programs. For that reason, Program 8.1 can make use of the various Rational constructors. Members declared within a **protected** section of a class definition can normally be used only by other member functions and operators of the class and by member functions and operators from a derived class (e.g., istream is derived from ios, so an istream object has access to its ios members). Members declared within a **private** section can normally be used only by other member functions and operators of that class.

8.3.2 Constructor member functions

The prototypes of the two `Rational` constructors in Listing 8.1 are different from typical function prototypes.

```
Rational();
Rational(int numer, int denom = 1);
```

As observed for the class `RectangleShape` in Chapter 7, a constructor prototype does not specify a return value. Because a constructor function for a class is required to have the same name as the class, no other special syntax is necessary to identify the function as a constructor.

The first constructor being declared is the default constructor because it uses no parameters.

The second constructor expects either one or two `int` objects as parameters. As the two parameter names suggest, they are used, respectively, to set the new `Rational` object's numerator and denominator data members. The default value for the denominator is one.

As neither a copy constructor nor a member assignment operator is declared in its class definition, the `Rational` class uses the definitions provided by the compiler.

8.3.3 Facilitator member functions

To reference a data member or member function of an object, a client code uses the access operator (.). The left operand of the access operator is an object; the right operand is the particular member of that object being referenced. We previously used the access operator with `string` and `RectangleShape` objects. For example, the following code segment displays the length of an extracted string.

```
cout << "Enter a string: ";
string s;
cin >> s;
cout << "Length of " << s << " is " << s.size();
```

Our next example uses the access operator to invoke several `Rational` member functions.

```
Rational r;
Rational s;
r.Extract(cin);
s.Extract(cin);
Rational t = r.Add(s);
t.Insert(cout);
```

Although the access operator provides the mechanism to access a member, it must also be the case that the operator is used in a valid context. In the preceding code segment, the `Rational` members that are accessed are all declared in the public section of the class declaration; therefore, they can be accessed in both client and member code.

Because the information-hiding principle is generally followed, data members are almost never public members. Consequently, data members cannot normally be referenced with the access operator in nonmember functions and operators. The nonpublic access rights act as a barrier that helps ensure the integrity of the data.

Without access restrictions, the improper use of an object can introduce inconsistencies or illegal values. Therefore, a well-constructed public interface supplies member functions and operators to safely manipulate the data members. Their presence supports information hiding. These member functions fall into three categories: inspectors, mutators, and facilitators. Inspector functions provide methods to access representations of the data members of an object. Mutator functions provide methods to modify the representations of the data members of an object. Facilitator functions provide methods for achieving the operations intended with the object.

After the constructor declarations, Listing 8.1 prototypes a collection of four arithmetic and stream facilitator functions. (We leave the relational facilitators and the other arithmetic facilitators to the exercises.)

```
// arithmetic and stream facilitators
Rational Add(const Rational &r) const;
Rational Multiply(const Rational &r) const;
void Insert(ostream &sout) const;
void Extract(istream &sin);
```

The two arithmetic facilitators Add() and Multiply() each have a single formal parameter r. The facilitators use the invoking object's value and the actual parameter's value to determine the result of the member function.

Stream facilitator Insert() expects a reference to an ostream as its parameter. The facilitator inserts a representation of its rational number to that stream. Stream facilitator Extract() expects a reference to an istream as its parameter. The facilitator extracts a representation of a rational number from that stream to be used for its object. In this regard, Extract() is also a mutator. The two stream facilitators have reference parameters because the act of inserting or extracting modifies the stream.

Because the Rational facilitators are public members, they can be used by client programs. However, they are not used in practice. Instead the auxiliary operators with their natural interfaces are used. The roles of the Rational facilitators are to be the underlying mechanisms that allow the auxiliary arithmetic and stream operators to do their jobs.

In the following code segment, we use the four Rational facilitators to accomplish the task of Program 8.1.

```
Rational r;
Rational s;
cout << "Enter rational number (a/b): ";
r.Extract(cin);
cout << "Enter rational number (a/b): ";
s.Extract(cin);
Rational t(r);
Rational Sum = r.Add(s);
Rational Product = r.Multiply(s);
r.Insert(cout);
cout<< " + ";
s.Insert(cout);
```

```
cout << " = ";
Sum.Insert(cout);
cout << endl;
r.Insert(cout);
cout<< " * ";
s.Insert(cout);
cout << " = ";
Product.Insert(cout);
cout << endl;
```

The code segment shows the importance of the auxiliary operators in making the code natural looking. Clearly, the statements in Program 8.1 are preferable to the use of the facilitators.

You should have observed that the declarations of facilitators Add(), Multiply(), and Insert() in the Rational class definition make use of the *qualifier* **const** at the end of their declarations.

```
Rational Add(const Rational &r) const;
Rational Multiply(const Rational &r) const;
void Insert(ostream &sout) const;
```

The **const** in this context indicates that the member's invocation does not change any of the invoking object's data members. Member functions and operators with the qualifier **const** can be used by **const** and non-**const** objects. Member functions without this qualification cannot be used by **const** objects. In the following example, the **const** object OneHalf can invoke the Insert() facilitator, but cannot invoke the Extract() facilitator.

```
const Rational OneHalf(1,2);
OneHalf.Insert(cout); // legal
OneHalf.Extract(cin); // illegal
```

8.3.4 Inspector member functions

The next declarations in the definition of the Rational class in Listing 8.1 are two prototypes of **protected** inspector member functions.

```
int GetNumerator() const;
int GetDenominator() const;
```

These inspectors give access to representations of the numerator and denominator. Their use of the qualifier **const** allows them to be invoked on **const** objects. Because they are in a **protected** section, a client program cannot use these two inspectors. However, they can be used by other Rational member functions. For example, the following code segment is legal in Rational member functions, but not in a client program.

```
// legal in member code, illegal in client code
Rational z;
cout << z.GetNumerator() << z.GetDenominator();
```

8.3.5 Mutator member functions

The `Rational` class definition in Listing 8.1 next declares two **protected** mutators.

```
void SetNumerator(int numer);
void SetDenominator(int denom);
```

The declarations indicate that both member functions are of type **void** and expect a single **int** object as a parameter. The mutators are used, respectively, to set the numerator and denominator of the rational number being represented. Like the two inspectors, because they are declared in a **protected** section, the two mutators cannot be used in a client program. However, the mutators can be used by other `Rational` member functions.

Because mutators modify data members, they cannot use the qualifier **const**. Therefore, mutator methods cannot be used by **const** objects once the objects have been constructed.

8.3.6 Data members

Data members are normally declared in a **private** section. This convention requires that any access or modification to data members by client programs or by other classes derived from this class use the public member inspector and mutator functions. As noted previously, information hiding helps ensure the integrity of the data members and also normally makes it possible to update or correct the library without requiring changes to code developed by clients. When the library is updated, clients need only relink their code.

Non-**const** data members cannot be initialized in their class declaration. Constructors are instead used to perform the initialization of the data members. Good software-engineering practice makes sure that every data member of an object is initialized by its constructor to some appropriate value. If all constructors and mutators guarantee that only appropriate values are set for the data members, the other member functions and operators do not need to validate that the data members contain appropriate values.

The definition of the `Rational` class in Listing 8.1 indicates that all `Rational` objects have two **int** data members associated with them.

```
int NumeratorValue;
int DenominatorValue;
```

The intended use of these two data members is self-explanatory from their names—data member `NumeratorValue` holds a representation of the numerator of the rational number being represented, and data member `DenominatorValue` holds a representation of the denominator of the rational number being represented.

The two data members are declared within a **private** section, so it is illegal to directly reference them in a nonmember function or operator. Thus an error message would occur if the following statement is placed in function `main()` of Program 8.1 to display the value of r's numerator.

```
cout << "Numerator of rational number: "
```

```
          << r.NumeratorValue << endl; // illegal access
```

The error message would indicate that a nonpublic member is being illegally referenced.

This completes our introduction of the `Rational` class definition in Listing 8.1. We next consider the prototypes of the `Rational` auxiliary operators.

8.3.7 Overloaded operators

The prototypes of the `Rational` auxiliary arithmetic operators are also in Listing 8.1. These prototypes are our first examples of operator overloading declarations.

```
Rational operator+(const Rational &r,
  const Rational &s);
Rational operator*(const Rational &r,
  const Rational &s);
```

Operator prototypes serve the same purpose as function prototypes—they describe an interface that enables other functions and operators to invoke the prototyped operator. The reserved word **operator** indicates that operator overloading is being performed.

Whether an operator prototype declaration or definition is being given, the interface to the operator is described first. The interface description begins with the return type of the operator. Unless it is a member operator being defined outside of the class definition, the operator return type is followed by the reserved word **operator**. (If a member operator is being defined outside of its class definition, then the class name and the scope operator (::) precede the reserved word **operator**.) The reserved word **operator** is followed by the actual operator to be overloaded. The interface is completed with the declaration of the operands. The declaration of the operands is given as a parameter list.

Because the result of rational arithmetic is a rational value, the `Rational` arithmetic operator declarations have `Rational` as their return types. Both `Rational` arithmetic operator declarations specify two operands (parameters). The left operand is declared first and then the right operand. Since the operands should not be modified as a result of an operation, the operands are declared as **const** parameters. The operands are defined as **const** reference parameters for efficiency reasons. (If they were value parameters, then copies of the objects would be created and passed into the arithmetic operators.)

The ability to overload the insertion operator for `Rational` objects is an example of why software engineers prefer the iostream library with its *extensibility* to the stdio library. The functionality designed into the iostream library makes its possible to overload the insertion and extraction operators so that there is a consistent interface for all input and output requests. This expressiveness is not possible with the stdio library, which constrains all input and output requests to involve only the fundamental types and character strings.

The prototypes of the insertion and extraction operators also specify two operands.

```
ostream& operator<<(ostream &sout, const Rational &r);
istream& operator>>(istream &sin, Rational &r);
```

The left operands of the insertion and extraction operators are declared as reference parameters. The left operands are reference parameters because inserting or extracting a `Rational` object modifies the stream and this change is permanent with respect to the client program. Type `ostream` is a base class for all output streams. Type `istream` is a base class for all input streams. By using these base classes, the operators can be invoked with standard streams, file streams, and in-memory string streams.

The insertion and extraction operators perform *reference returns*. The modifier & in conjunction with a return type indicates this type of return. In a standard return, the return value of a function or operator is a temporary object that is created to hold the value being returned. The existence of the temporary object is bound to the invocation expression. In a reference return, no temporary object is created. The return value is instead supplied in an object with the property that its scope includes the scope of the function or operator that contained the invocation. For a member operator or function, the invoking object has this property. A reference parameter also has this property.

With a reference return, a `Rational` object insertion or extraction can be part of a larger insertion or extraction operation. For example, in the following code segment, first `Rational` r is displayed and then a newline character is displayed.

```
Rational r(1,2);
cout << r << endl;
```

The insertion statement works correctly because the result of the operation `cout << r` is actually `cout` and not some temporary stream. Therefore, the subsequent insertion request using manipulator `endl` also goes to `cout`. If instead, a value return had been performed, the `endl` insertion would go to a temporary copy, rather than to `cout`, which would not be the desired result.

Without the ability to do a reference return, the insertion operator would need to be of type **void**, forcing two separate insertion expressions to achieve the desired result.

```
cout << r;
cout << endl;
```

Note that a reference return is more efficient than a standard return—no temporary object needs to be created. This efficiency is particularly obvious when using classes more complex than `Rational`.

If a reference return uses a local object to supply a reference return value, the compiler should generate an error message. If it did not, then any use of that object in the invoking function would have undefined behavior. The behavior is undefined because any use of the return value would be to activation record memory that has already been released.

C++ Language

> *Struct*
>
> The **class** construct is a generalization of the **struct** construct of C, which permits public data members but not member functions or operators. In addition, there cannot be any **protected** or **private** sections. This restriction prevents information hiding and makes C less suitable than C++ for significant software-engineering applications.
>
> C++ also has a **struct** construct. However, it is more like the **class** construct than its counterpart in C. The C++ **struct** permits data members, member functions, and operators, as well as access specifiers. The **struct** construct differs from the **class** construct only in that the default access specification is **public**.
>
> The **struct** construct is rarely used in C++ programs because the class construct with its default access specification of **private** better supports the information-hiding principle.

Self-check Questions

1. Give the meaning of the acronym ADT.

2. What kind of copy does the compiler-supplied copy constructor perform?

3. Explain why it is best to use auxiliary operators for overloaded versions of the binary arithmetic operators.

4. Design an ADT for a point in a cartesian space. Make your ADT as flexible as possible

5. Can two classes have member functions with identical names?

6. Explain why insertion and extraction operators perform reference returns.

7. Consider the following class declaration.

```cpp
class Obj {
    public:
        Obj();
        int F1(int x);
        void F2(int x);
        void F3(int x) const;
    protected:
        void F4(int x);
```

```
        private:
            void F5(int x);
            int Count;
    };
```

Is the following a legal program? If it is not legal, explain what is wrong.

```
#include <iostream>
#include <string>
using namespace std;
int main() {
    Obj Object1;
    Obj Object2;
    Object1.Count = 0;
    Object2.Count = 0;
    return 0;
}
```

8. Consider the class declaration of Self-check Question 7 and the following program.

```
#include <iostream>
#include <string>
using namespace std;
int main() {
    Obj Object1;
    Object1.F1(3);
    return 0;
}
```

Is the preceding program a valid C++ program? If not, explain why.

9. Consider the class declaration of Self-check Question 7 and the following program.

```
#include <iostream>
#include <string>
using namespace std;
int main() {
    Obj Object1;
    Object1.F4(3);
    return 0;
}
```

Is the preceding program a valid C++ program? If not, explain why.

10. Consider the class declaration of Self-check Question 7 and the following program.

```
#include <iostream>
#include <string>
using namespace std;
```

```
int main() {
    Obj Object1(3);
    Object1.F3(3);
    return 0;
}
```

Is the preceding program a valid C++ program? If not, explain why.

11.   Design an ADT for a modulo counter. A modulo counter is a counter that can count up. When counting up, if the counter reaches its maximum value, the counter wraps back around to zero. Give the class declaration for your ADT.

12.   Design an ADT for a wrap-around counter. A wrap-around counter is a counter that can count up or down. When counting up, if the counter is at its maximum value, the counter wraps back around to zero. When counting down, if the counter is at zero, it wraps around to the maximum value. Give the class declaration for your ADT.

13.   Design an ADT for scientific notation numbers (i.e., numbers in the form 2.34×10^{-5}). Only give the class declaration and the prototypes of any auxiliary functions that you feel are appropriate for the ADT.

8.4 IMPLEMENTING THE RATIONAL CLASS

Thus far the description of the rational library has neither included the definitions of the member functions nor the definitions of the auxiliary operators. Listings 8.2 through 8.7 contain a possible implementation of the functions and operators described in `rational.h`.

As you examine the listings you will see that in the definitions of the Rational member functions, the name of the function being defined is always preceded by the class name and the scope operator. For example, the definition of the Rational mutator SetNumerator() has the following syntax:

```
void Rational::SetNumerator(int numer) {
    NumeratorValue = numer;
}
```

The scope identification is necessary because a source file can contain definitions of member functions and operators from different classes that use the same member name and interface. Without some scope resolution, it is not possible to match the definitions with the appropriate class.

Within a member definition, there is no similar difficulty in recognizing which member function or operator is being referenced by default. The lack of difficulty is because the default nonlocal scope in a member function is the class scope. Therefore, inside member definitions it is not necessary to use the scope resolution operator in conjunction with the class name to reference members of that class.

Programming Tip

8.4.1 Constructor definitions

Both constructors in Listing 8.2 use the mutators `SetNumerator()` and `Set-Denominator()` to do their actual work.

Listing 8.2

Implementation of Rational constructors from rational.cpp

```cpp
#include <iostream>
#include <string>
#include "rational.h"
using namespace std;
// default constructor
Rational::Rational() {
    SetNumerator(0);
    SetDenominator(1);
}
// (numer, denom) constructor
Rational::Rational(int numer, int denom) {
    SetNumerator(numer);
    SetDenominator(denom);
}
```

The default constructor is defined first, and it invokes the mutators with parameters 0 and 1, respectively, to initialize the new object so that it represents the rational number 0/1.

```cpp
SetNumerator(0);
SetDenominator(1);
```

The use of mutators `SetNumerator()` and `SetDenominator()` isolates the underlying data member implementation. The information-hiding principle encourages localizing data member manipulations to as few functions and operators as possible. This localization generally makes it simpler to incorporate changes in the data representation.

The second constructor defined in Listing 8.2 uses the values of its parameters `numer` and `denom` in its invocations of mutators `SetNumerator()` and

SetDenominator(), respectively, to initialize the new object so that it represents the rational number numer/denom.

```
SetNumerator(numer);
SetDenominator(denom);
```

For this constructor, the second parameter is an optional parameter. The C++ language rules specify that the declaration of the default value should occur only once. Therefore, the declaration of the default value can occur either in the class definition or in the definition of the member function. It is our practice to specify the default value in the class definition—for it is this section of the ADT library that is normally examined by client programmers.

8.4.2 Inspector definitions

As noted previously, the Rational class supports information hiding, so it provides inspector and mutator member functions to control references to the data members.

Listing 8.3

Implementation of Rational inspectors and mutators from rational.cpp

```
// get the numerator
int Rational::GetNumerator() const {
    return NumeratorValue;
}
// get the denominator
int Rational::GetDenominator() const {
    return DenominatorValue;
}
// set the numerator
void Rational::SetNumerator(int numer) {
    NumeratorValue = numer;
}
// set the denominator
void Rational::SetDenominator(int denom) {
    if (denom != 0) {
        DenominatorValue = denom;
    }
    else {
        cerr << "Illegal denominator: " << denom
            << "using 1" << endl;
        DenominatorValue = 1;
    }
}
```

The definitions of the inspectors GetNumerator() and GetDenominator() in Listing 8.3 are straightforward. The numerator of the rational number being represented is maintained in the data member NumeratorValue. Therefore, to accomplish its task inspector GetNumerator() simply returns the current value of this data member.

```
    return NumeratorValue;
```

Similarly, as the denominator is maintained in the data member `Denomina-torValue`, inspector `GetDenominator()` simply returns the current value of that data member.

```
return DenominatorValue;
```

There is no need to use the scope operator or even the access operator within the inspector function body to qualify which `NumeratorValue` and `DenominatorValue` are being referenced—by default, references are to the data members of the object whose inspector is invoked.

8.4.3 Mutator definitions

The definitions of the mutators `SetNumerator()` and `SetDenominator()` in Listing 8.3 are also straightforward. These functions each have a single **int** parameter that is used as the new value of the object's data members `NumeratorValue` and `DenominatorValue`. For example, mutator `SetNumerator()` uses its parameter `numer` to set `NumeratorValue`.

```
NumeratorValue = numer;
```

As any integer value is reasonable for the numerator of a rational number, `SetNumerator()` performs no validation. However, it is generally the responsibility of the mutator to validate manipulation requests. In particular, as a denominator of 0 does not make sense, `SetDenominator()` must check the proposed denominator value before using it.

```
if (denom != 0) {
    DenominatorValue = denom;
}
else {
    cerr << "Illegal denominator: " << denom
        << "using 1" << endl;
    DenominatorValue = 1;
}
```

If the requested value is nonzero, the requested value is used to reset data member `DenominatorValue`. If instead the requested value is 0, the function displays an error message and uses 1 for the value of the denominator. The error processing performed by `SetDenominator()` is a form of *exception handling*. C++ provides a mechanism known as **try-throw-catch** for general-purpose exception handling. This mechanism is discussed in Appendix D.

8.4.4 Arithmetic facilitator definitions

The two arithmetic facilitators in Listing 8.4 are direct implementations of rational arithmetic. The parameter supplied to each of the facilitators is conceptually the right operand of the arithmetic operation being computed where the left operand is the object doing the invoking.

Listing 8.4

Implementation of the arithmetic facilitators from rational.cpp

```
// adding Rationals
Rational Rational::Add(const Rational &r) const {
    int a = GetNumerator();
    int b = GetDenominator();
    int c = r.GetNumerator();
    int d = r.GetDenominator();
    return Rational(a*d + b*c, b*d);
}

// multiplying Rationals
Rational Rational::Multiply(const Rational &r) const {
    int a = GetNumerator();
    int b = GetDenominator();
    int c = r.GetNumerator();
    int d = r.GetDenominator();
    return Rational(a*c, b*d);
}
```

For example, the following segment sums `Rational` objects x and y by invoking x's member function `Add()` with y as the parameter. The result of the operation is used in the construction of `Rational` object z.

```
Rational x(1,2);
Rational y(1,3);
Rational z = x.Add(y); // 1/2 + 1/3 is 5/6
cout << z << endl;
```

The definition of member function `Add()` begins by defining two **int** objects a and b.

```
int a = GetNumerator();
int b = GetDenominator();
```

These objects hold copies of the invoking object's numerator and denominator. For the preceding example, a would be initialized to 1 and b to 2.

Next the function defines two **int** objects c and d. These objects hold copies of the parameter's numerator and denominator. For the preceding example, c would be initialized to 1 and d to 3.

```
int c = r.GetNumerator();
int d = r.GetDenominator();
```

These four objects are used to define a `Rational` object representing the rational sum of a/b + c/d. The constructed object is used as the return value for the facilitator.

```
return Rational(a*d + b*c, b*d);
```

Observe that the construction of the `Rational` object holding the sum is unnamed—the return expression directly invokes the constructor with parameters a*d + b*c and b*d. This invocation is permissible because no subsequent statement needs to reference this value using a name.

The definition of facilitator `Multiply()` is analogous to `Add()` and warrants no additional discussion.

8.4.5 Insertion and extraction definitions

The definition of facilitator `Insert()` and `Extract()` are given in Listing 8.5.

Listing 8.5

Implementation of stream facilitators from rational.cpp

```
// inserting a Rational
void Rational::Insert(ostream &sout) const {
    sout << GetNumerator() << '/' << GetDenominator();
    return;
}

// extracting a Rational
void Rational::Extract(istream &sin) {
    int numer;
    int denom;
    char slash;
    sin >> numer >> slash >> denom;
    SetNumerator(numer);
    SetDenominator(denom);
    return;
}
```

Facilitator `Insert()` has an `ostream` reference parameter `sout` that is the target output stream for the insertion that it performs. The process to insert a `Rational` object is quite simple—display its numerator, display a slash character, and display its denominator.

```
sout << GetNumerator() << '/' << GetDenominator();
```

Observe that the information-hiding principle is in effect in the displaying of the rational number—the numerator and denominator of the invoking object are accessed by using inspectors `GetNumerator()` and `GetDenominator()`.

The definition of the facilitator `Extract()` in Listing 8.5 specifies a single `istream` reference parameter `sin`. Parameter `sin` is the source stream of the rational number representation that is to be extracted into the invoking object.

The definition begins by extracting an **int** value `numer` that should correspond to the numerator of the rational number being extracted.

```
sin >> numer >> slash >> denom;
```

A character is then extracted; in this case, it should be the slash that separates the numerator from the denominator. Proper exception handling would verify that the extracted character is indeed a slash. This modification is left to the exercises. Finally, the desired value for the denominator is extracted into an **int** object `denom`.

Facilitator `Extract()` next uses the two extracted values in its invocations of mutators `SetNumerator()` and `SetDenominator()` to reset the invoking object's data members.

```
SetNumerator(numer);
SetDenominator(denom);
```

No validation is needed by `Extract()` for checking the new value of the denominator. The checking is unnecessary as mutator `SetDenominator()` performs that validation.

8.4.6 Auxiliary arithmetic operator definitions

The two overloaded arithmetic operators in Listing 8.6 each use the appropriate facilitator to perform the desired action.

Listing 8.6

Implementation of the arithmetic operators from rational.cpp

```
// adding Rationals
Rational operator+(const Rational &r,
 const Rational &s) {
    return r.Add(s);
}
// multiplying Rationals
Rational operator*(const Rational &r,
 const Rational &s) {
    return r.Multiply(s);
}
```

For example, operator + invokes the addition facilitator `Add()` of its left operand r, using its right operand s as the parameter to the facilitator. The invocation `r.Add(s)` produces the sum of r and s. As such, it is the proper return value for the operation. Thus operator + can accomplish its task with the single statement

```
return r.Add(s);
```

Similarly, operator * can accomplish its task of returning the product of its operands r and s with the single statement

```
return r.Multiply(s);
```

As noted previously, the arithmetic operators are not necessary—we can use the facilitators to directly accomplish the operator tasks rather than invoking the facilitators indirectly via the operators. However, demanding the direct use of the facilitators would conflict with our goal of providing a library that allows client programmers to write clear code that is easily maintainable and reusable. A client's task can be accomplished more readily with the operators—clients are used to manipulating rational values using operators. Therefore, the arithmetic operators are an appropriate and important part of the library.

Programming Tip

> ***Think before overloading***
>
> When overloading an operator, try to imagine how it will be used. Look at the operator in its traditional setting with fundamental objects and make sure that the analogous behavior is present in your overloaded version.

To complete our library implementation discussion, we consider the implementation of the stream operators.

8.4.7 Auxiliary stream operator definitions

The definition of the insertion operator in Listing 8.7 expects two operands. The left operand `sout` is the target output stream for the insertion. The right operand `r` is the `Rational` object to be displayed.

Listing 8.7

Implementation of the stream operators from rational.cpp

```
// inserting a Rational
ostream& operator<<(ostream &sout, const Rational &r) {
    r.Insert(sout);
    return sout;
}
// extracting a Rational
istream& operator>>(istream &sin, Rational &r) {
    r.Extract(sin);
    return sin;
}
```

Like the overloading of the arithmetic operators, the overloading of the insertion operator is straightforward given the existence of an insertion facilitator—the insertion is accomplished using r's public facilitator `Insert()` with output stream `sout` as the parameter to the facilitator.

```
    r.Insert(sout);
```

A reference return to `ostream sout` is then performed to complete the operators's task.

```
    return sout;
```

As discussed in Section 8.3.7, the reference return enables `Rational` insertions to be cascaded with other insertions in a single expression.

The definition of **operator>>**() in Listing 8.7 for overloading extraction is similarly straightforward. After resetting the right operand `r` through the use of its facilitator `Extract()` with the left operand input stream `sin` as the parameter, a reference to `istream sin` is returned. The reference return enables a `Rational` extraction to be cascaded with other extractions in a single expression.

8.5 COPY CONSTRUCTION, MEMBER ASSIGNMENT, AND DESTRUCTION

Our discussion of the `Rational` class has observed that C++ automatically makes available a copy constructor and a member assignment operator. The code segment

```
Rational r(1,2);
Rational s(r);        // s is copy constructed from r
Rational t;
t = r;                // t is member assigned r
```

uses these members in creating `s` and modifying `t` to be duplicates of `r`. The compiler-supplied versions of these members perform a memberwise copying of the source object to the target object. In our example, `r` is the source object for both cases, s is the target for the construction, and t is the target for the assignment. In a memberwise copy, the source's data members are copied bit by bit to the corresponding data members of the target. Memberwise copying is also known as *shallow copying*.

C++ also automatically makes a *destructor* member function available for class-type objects. An object's destructor is invoked automatically as the object goes out of existence. The destructor performs any cleanup processing that is necessary for its object. The compiler-supplied version of the destructor does not perform any actions. Such inaction is appropriate for Rational class objects because when a Rational object goes out of scope, nothing special needs to be done.

Thus destruction is complementary to construction, which performs any processing that is necessary for an object being created. Just as these operations are complementary, so are their naming conventions. The name of the destructor is the concatenation of the tilde operator (~) and the class name. (In other contexts, the ~ is the bit complement operator.) Thus for the Rational class, the destructor is ~Rational().

Programming Tip

Gang of three

A class typically needs to define explicitly a copy constructor, assignment operator, and destructor only if its objects have data members that directly make use of dynamic memory allocations (see Chapter 11). Otherwise, the automatic versions are generally satisfactory. In terms of class design, if you believe there is a need to define one of these three members, you probably need to define all of them.

C++ places two restrictions on destructors—a destructor cannot take a parameter, and a destructor cannot produce a return value. Together these restrictions limit a class to a single destructor.

C++ also places requirements on the form of the copy constructor. A copy constructor has a single formal parameter, which is of the same type as the class. The formal parameter is required to be a **const** reference. The parameter to the assignment operator is expected to meet the same specifications. Unlike the copy constructor and the destructor, the assignment operator has a return type. The return type should be a reference to the class of object being assigned.

If we were to develop explicit definitions for a Rational copy constructor, assignment operator, and destructor for our rational library, we would need to modify the interface in the header file rational.h to include prototypes of these three members:

```
class Rational {
    public:
        //
        // copy constructor
        Rational(const Rational &r);
        // member assignment
        Rational& operator=(const Rational &r);
```

```
                 // destructor
                 ~Rational();
                 //
        }
```

The syntax for the member assignment operator in the preceding class definition is confusing at first glance—an assignment operator should have two operands, yet the declaration specifies only one operand. This syntax is used because the left operand is understood to be the object invoking the assignment operator. Therefore, only the right operand needs to be declared. The reason that the operator returns a value is so that larger expressions can be composed, as in the following code segment:

```
Rational x(1, 2);
Rational y;
Rational z;
z = y = x;
```

By having the assignment operator do a reference return, the operation is more efficient.

Listing 8.8 provides explicit definitions for a `Rational` copy constructor, assignment operator, and destructor. These definitions offer the same functionality as the compiler-supplied versions. We present these definitions to give insight into the basics of copy construction, assignment, and destruction. We will revisit these concepts in Chapter 11, where we develop an ADT that requires these three members be given explicitly.

Listing 8.8

Explicit member definitions for a Rational copy constructor, assignment operator, and destructor

```
// Rational: copy constructor
Rational::Rational(const Rational &r) {
    int a = r.GetNumerator();
    int b = r.GetDenominator();
    SetNumerator(a);
    SetDenominator(b);
}
// Rational: destructor
Rational::~Rational() {
    // no body needed
}
// Rational: assignment operator
Rational& Rational::operator=(const Rational &r) {
    int a = r.GetNumerator();
    int b = r.GetDenominator();
    SetNumerator(a);
    SetDenominator(b);
    return *this;
}
```

Our definition of the `Rational` copy constructor is straightforward. The object being constructed is made a copy of the parameter r to the constructor. To do so, first r's numerator and denominator are used to initialize local objects a and b through invocations of r's member functions `GetNumerator()` and `GetDenominator()`.

```
int a = r.GetNumerator();
int b = r.GetDenominator();
```

Objects a and b are then used by the object being constructed as parameters to its member functions SetNumerator() and SetDenominator().

```
SetNumerator(a);
SetDenominator(b);
```

The definition of the Rational destructor in Listing 8.8 is even more straightforward. Because no action is required, the body of the destructor is empty.

When analyzing the Rational assignment operator in Listing 8.8, remember that if the operator is in use, it is because the target object has invoked the operator to act on the target's data members. Our assignment operator first performs actions similar to the copy constructor. The values of the numerator and denominator of its parameter r are used to set the target's numerator and denominator.

```
int a = r.GetNumerator();
int b = r.GetDenominator();
SetNumerator(a);
SetDenominator(b);
```

The return value for the Rational assignment operator is the expression *this. C++ defines the keyword **this** to be the address of the object whose member function is being invoked. The * in this context is the *dereferencing operator*. The dereferencing operator is a unary operator. The dereferencing operator, when applied to an address, produces the value of the object at that address. The expression *this therefore represents the object whose member function is being invoked, which is the correct value to be returned by the assignment operator.

To illustrate how the copy constructor, assignment operator, and a destructor can come into play in a program, we define and use a small, simple class named C. The definition of class C in Listing 8.9 specifies default and copy con-

Listing 8.9

A simple class C with a default constructor, copy constructor, assignment operator, and destructor

```
class C {
  public:
    C() { // default constructor
      name = s;
      cout << name << ": default constructed" << endl;
    }
    C(const C &c) { // copy constructor
      name = s;
      cout << name << ": copy constructed using "
        << c.name << endl;
    }
    ~C() { // destructor
      cout << name << ": destructed" << endl;
    }
    C& operator=(const C &c) { // assignment
      cout << name << ": assigned using " << c.name
        << endl;
      return *this;
    }
  private:
    string name; // data member
};
```

structors, a destructor, an assignment operator, and a data member `name` of type `string`. Rather than merely prototyping the member functions, the class definition also contains the functions' definitions. This combination is done for simplicity of discussion. You are encouraged in practice to separate interface from implementation.

The class C constructors perform two actions. They assign the data member `name` with the current value of global object `s`, and they use that value to display a message to indicate why they are being invoked. Similarly, the destructor and assignment operator both display messages indicating why they are being invoked.

The class C is used in the following program fragment:

```
string s = "w";
C w;
int main() {
    s = "x";
    C x;
    {
        s = "y";
        C y;
    }
    s = "z";
    C z(w);
    x = w = z;
    return 0;
}
```

By examining the output of the program fragment we can get a sense of how and when the class C member functions come into play. The output associated with this fragment is

```
w: default constructed
x: default constructed
y: default constructed
y: destructed
z: copy constructed using w
w: assigned using z
x: assigned using w
z: destructed
x: destructed
w: destructed
```

This output shows that the first C object defined by the fragment is the global object w. The next two C objects defined are x and y. These objects are local to function `main()`. Object y is defined in an inner block of `main()`. The scope of y is therefore limited to that inner block. The output indicates that fact—y's destructor is invoked automatically when the block is completed. Function `main()` then goes on to copy construct object z from w. Before completing its task, function `main()` makes two assignments:

```
x = w = z;
```

As you should have expected, the output indicates that the assignment operators are evaluated from right to left. Because objects x and z are local to `main()`, they are destroyed with the function's completion. In particular, z is destroyed before x because z was defined after x.

Global objects are destroyed immediately before the program is terminated and control is given back to the operating system. Thus the final program output indicates that w is destroyed. In the exercises, we overload the insertion and addition operators for C objects so that we can observe when the copy constructor comes into play during expression evaluation.

We next turn our attention to developing a library for pseudorandom number sequences. This library is then used in the development of a simple guessing game.

Self-check Questions

14. Consider the following program.

```cpp
#include <iostream>
#include <string>
using namespace std;
int count = 0;
    class obj {
        public:
            obj();
            ~obj();
    };
obj() {
    ++count; cout << count << endl;
}
~obj() {
    --count; cout << count << endl;
}
int main() {
    obj A;
    {
        cout << "begin block" << endl;
        obj B;
        cout << "end block" << endl;
    }
    return 0;
}
```

Give the output of this program.

15. Consider the following program.

```cpp
#include <iostream>
#include <string>
using namespace std;
class thizbin {
    public:
        thizbin();
        thizbin(int a);
        thizbin(int a, int b, int c);
```

```
            print(const string &msg);
        private:
            int i, j, k;
};
thizbin() {
    i = j = k = 0;
}
thizbin(int a) {
    i = j = k = a;
}
thizbin(int a, int b, int c) {
    i = a; j = b; k = c;
};
print(const string &msg) {
    cout << msg << ":" << endl;
    cout << "i = " << i << endl;
    cout << "j = " << j << endl;
    cout << "k = " << k << endl;
}
int main() {
    thizbin A;
    thizbin B(47);
    thizbin C(9, 11, 47);
    A.print("A object");
    B.print("B object");
    C.print("C object");
    return 0;
}
```

Give the output of this program.

16. Consider the following class declaration.

```
class CounterObj {
    public:
        int F1(int x);
        void F2(int x);
        void F3(int x) const;
    private:
        void F4(int x);
        int Count;
};
```

Name the member functions that can modify the data member Count.

17. Consider the following class declaration and function prototype.

```
class Obj {
    public:
        Obj();
        int F1(int x);
        void F2(int x);
```

```
            void F3(int x) const;
        protected:
            void F4(int x);
        private:
            void F5(int x);
            int Count;
    };
    int F6(int y);
```

Can member function F1() call member function F2()? Explain your answer.

Can member function F2() call member function F4()? Explain your answer.

Can member function F4() call member function F2()? Explain your answer.

Can member function F4() call member function F5()? Explain your answer?

Can function F6() call member function F4()? Explain your answer.

Can function F4() call member function F3()? Explain your answer.

Can member function F3() call member function F2()? Explain your answer.

18. Design and implement an ADT for a modulo counter. A modulo counter is a counter that can count up. When counting up, if the counter reaches its maximum value, the counter wraps back around to zero.

19. Design and implement an ADT for a wrap-around counter. A wrap-around counter is a counter that can count up or down. When counting up, if the counter is at its maximum value, the counter wraps back around to zero. When counting down, if the counter is at zero, it wraps around to the maximum value.

20. Design and implement an ADT for scientific notation numbers (i.e., numbers in the form 2.34×10^{-5}). Prototype and implement any auxiliary functions that you feel are appropriate for the ADT.

8.6 ADT FOR PSEUDORANDOM INTEGERS

In Chapter 5, functions Uniform() and InitializeSeed() were developed to assist in the generation of uniform pseudorandom number sequences. As a reminder, the phrase *uniform pseudorandom number sequence* indicates that the produced values appear to be occurring in an equally likely random manner. In this section, we take a more object-oriented view and develop an ADT for uniform pseudorandom number sequences. We will use this ADT in developing a simple guessing game in Section 8.7 of this chapter. The associated library for this ADT will be known as randint; the class defined by the randint library is RandomInt.

Like functions Uniform() and InitializeSeed(), our class Random-Int makes use of both the stdlib library functions rand() and srand() and the time standard library function time(). Therefore, it is worthwhile to review the behavior of these library functions. Each time function rand() is invoked, it returns a uniform pseudorandom number from the inclusive interval 0 through RAND_MAX, where RAND_MAX is defined in the stdlib library header file. Function srand() expects an **unsigned int** as its parameter, which is used to set the seed for generating the next pseudorandom number. Different seed values should cause rand() to produce different sequences of pseudorandom numbers. And by using the current time as the seed, the seed should be different for each run of the program. The current time can be determined using the function time() from the time standard library. Function time() with a parameter of 0 supplies the current time through its return value.

A class for representing uniform random number sequences should allow different kinds of uniform pseudorandom number sequences to be constructed (e.g., sequences from the interval 1 through 6 or from the interval 1 through 32). An object to represent a random number sequence would need to support public methods to

- Generate different pseudorandom number sequences.
- Reproduce the same pseudorandom number sequence.
- Restrict pseudorandom numbers in the sequence to a specified interval.
- Draw (generate) the next number in a sequence.

To support these methods, several other methods would be useful.

- Set the interval from which the numbers are drawn.
- Set the seed for the random number sequence.
- Inspect the low value in the interval from which the numbers are drawn.
- Inspect the high value in the interval from which the numbers are drawn.

In addition, it would be helpful to have an auxiliary function that automatically enables different pseudorandom number sequences to be generated for each program run. EzRandomize() is such a function that is provided as part of the EzWindows library.

The only data our representation requires are the endpoints for the interval from which the pseudorandom numbers are to be drawn. The data members to represent these values should be placed in a private section to support information hiding.

A possible library interface for the preceding analysis is given in Listing 8.10. The class providing the interface is RandomInt.

As indicated in Listing 8.10, class RandomInt has two constructors. The first constructor has two optional parameters a and b, which make it the default constructor. Parameters a and b specify the inclusive interval from which the numbers in the sequence are drawn. The default values for the parameters cause the RandomInt object being constructed to produce the same sequence

Listing 8.10

Header file randint.h
for randint library

```cpp
#ifndef RANDINT_H
#define RANDINT_H

#include <stdlib.h>

class RandomInt {
    public:
        // default constructor
        RandomInt(int a = 0, int b = RAND_MAX);
        // constructor with specified seed
        RandomInt(int a, int b, unsigned int seed);
        // mutators
        int Draw();
        void SetInterval(int a, int b);
        void SetSeed(unsigned int s);
        // inspectors
        int GetLow();
        int GetHigh();
    private:
        // data members
        int Low;
        int High;
};

unsigned int EzRandomize();
#endif
```

of pseudorandom values as through repeated calls to stdlib function `rand()` without using `srand()`. The default interval is 0 through RAND_MAX.

The other `RandomInt` constructor takes three parameters. Its first two parameters are also `a` and `b`, and they again represent the inclusive interval from which the numbers are drawn. The third parameter specifies a seed for generating the initial pseudorandom number in the sequence.

In the following code segment, we define `RandomInt` objects R, S, and T. Object R uses the default parameter settings. Objects S and T both specify the intervals from which the numbers in their sequences are drawn: for object S, it is the inclusive interval 1 through 6; for object T, it is the inclusive interval 1 through 32. For object T, an initial seed value of 88 is also specified. Objects R and S are constructed with the default constructor, while object T is constructed with the other constructor.

```cpp
// sequence with numbers from 0 ... RAND_MAX
RandomInt R;

// sequence with numbers from 1 ... 6
RandomInt S(1, 6);

// sequence with numbers from 1 ... 32 using seed 88
RandomInt T(1, 32, 88);
```

The mutator member function `Draw()` returns the next pseudorandom number in the sequence as its value. For example, the following code segment defines a `RandomInt` object U and then displays the first five numbers in its sequence:

```cpp
RandomInt U;
for (int i = 1; i <= 5; ++i) {
    cout << U.Draw() << endl;
}
```

Because our implementation mimics the behavior of repeated invocations of rand(), the output of the segment is the same as the output of Program 5.4 from Chapter 5.

```
346
130
10982
1090
11656
```

The purpose of auxiliary EzWindows library function EzRandomize() is to set the current seed for the pseudorandom number sequence to an unspecified value that should be different for each invocation of the mutator. For example, suppose the following code segment was run instead of the segment drawing from U. This segment invokes EzRandomize(), defines a Random-Int object V, and then displays the first five numbers in V's sequence.

```
RandomInt V;
EzRandomize();
for (int i = 1; i <= 5; ++i) {
    cout << V.Draw() << endl;
}
```

The invocation EzRandomize() causes a different seed to be in effect for V's pseudorandom number sequence. As the result, the sequence produced by drawing from V is different than the sequence produced by drawing from U.

```
15438
1866
2330
30933
7595
```

Although we did not use it in the preceding code segments, EzRandom-ize() produces a return value. Its return value is the value it passes to srand() to set the seed for rand().

The class RandomInt also has two mutators. Mutator SetInterval() uses its two **int** parameters to set the desired endpoints of the interval from which the pseudorandom numbers are drawn. Mutator SetSeed() uses its single parameter to set the seed value for generating the next pseudorandom number.

The inspectors GetLow() and GetHigh() have analogous roles. They return representations of the low and high endpoints of the interval from which the pseudorandom numbers are drawn.

8.6.1 RandomInt implementation

The implementation file for the randint library member functions is rand-int.cpp. A copy of this implementation file is presented in Listing 8.11. An examination of the listing shows that stdlib functions rand() and srand() establish the RandomInt class functionality.

Listing 8.11

Implementation file randint.cpp for randint library

```cpp
#include <iostream>
#include <string>
#include <stdlib.h>
#include <time.h>
#include "randint.h"

using namespace std;

// RandomInt(): default pseudorandom number sequence
// constructor (both parameters are optional)
RandomInt::RandomInt(int a, int b) {
   SetInterval(a, b);
}

// RandomInt(): pseudorandom number sequence
// constructor with specified seed
RandomInt::RandomInt(int a, int b, unsigned int s) {
   SetInterval(a, b);
   SetSeed(s);
}

// SetInterval(): sets low and high endpoint of interval
void RandomInt::SetInterval(int a, int b) {
   if (a > b) {
      cerr << "Bad random number interval: " << a
       << " ... " << b << endl;
      exit(1);
   }
   else {
      Low = a;
      High = b;
   }
}

// SetSeed(): set seed for sequence
void RandomInt::SetSeed(unsigned int s) {
   srand(s);
}

// Draw(): return next value in sequence
int RandomInt::Draw() {
   int IntervalSize = GetHigh() - GetLow() + 1;
   int RandomOffset = rand() % IntervalSize;
   int Number = GetLow() + RandomOffset;
   return Number;
}

// GetLow(): return low endpoint of interval
int RandomInt::GetLow() {
   return Low;
}

// GetHigh(): return high endpoint of interval
int RandomInt::GetHigh() {
   return High;
}
```

The `RandomInt` default constructor has a straightforward implementation that practices information hiding.

```cpp
RandomInt::RandomInt(int a, int b) {
    SetInterval(a, b);
}
```

The constructor uses mutator `SetInterval()` to specify the endpoints of the interval from which the numbers are to be drawn. Observe that the constructor definition does not indicate that the parameters can have default values. Instead, the class definition specifies the default values.

The other `RandomInt` constructor also has a straightforward implementation that practices information hiding.

```
RandomInt::RandomInt(int a, int b, unsigned int s) {
    SetInterval(a, b);
    SetSeed(s);
}
```

This constructor also uses mutator `SetInterval()` to specify the endpoints of the interval from which the numbers are to be drawn. The constructor then uses mutator `SetSeed()` to specify the seed for the pseudorandom number sequence.

To accomplish its task, mutator `SetInterval()` first examines its parameters to make sure that the requested endpoints are sensible.

```
void RandomInt::SetInterval(int a, int b) {
    if (a > b) {
        cerr << "Bad random number interval: " << a
            << " ... " << b << endl;
        exit(1);
    }
    else {
        Low = a;
        High = b;
    }
}
```

If the endpoints are sensible, data members `Low` and `High` are set using the parameter values.

The mutator member function `SetSeed()` uses its parameter in an invocation of function `srand()`.

```
void RandomInt::SetSeed(unsigned int s) {
    srand(s);
}
```

Because member function `Draw()` uses `rand()` in its generation of pseudorandom numbers, an invocation of `SetSeed()` affects the sequence of numbers that are generated.

The `Draw()` function performs several small steps to produce a uniform pseudorandom number from the desired interval. The steps are similar to function `Uniform()` of Chapter 5.

```
int RandomInt::Draw() {
    int IntervalSize = GetHigh() - GetLow() + 1;
    int RandomOffset = rand() % IntervalSize;
    int Number = GetLow() + RandomOffset;
    return Number;
}
```

Function `Draw()` first calculates the size of the interval in an object `IntervalSize`. To do so it uses inspectors `GetLow()` and `GetHigh()`. Next, a

uniform pseudorandom number produced by `rand()` is taken modulus
`IntervalSize` and assigned to `RandomOffset`

```
int RandomOffset = rand() % IntervalSize;
```

(i.e., `RandomOffset` is assigned a pseudorandom value from the interval 0
through `IntervalSize` − 1).

Suppose `IntervalSize` is 2; the value of the expression `rand()` %
`IntervalSize` will be either 0 or 1. If the value of RAND_MAX is odd, the values 0 and 1 will be assigned to `RandomOffset` in an equally likely pseudorandom manner, because you would expect `rand()` to produce an even number
half the time and an odd number the other half. If the value of RAND_MAX is
instead even, then 0 will have a slightly increased chance of being assigned to
`RandomOffset` because there is one more even number than odd number in
the interval 0 through RAND_MAX.

If the value of RAND_MAX is very large compared to `IntervalSize`, then
the fact that some numbers have an extra $1/(\text{RAND\_MAX} + 1)$ chance of occurring can be ignored. Thus the expression `rand()` % `IntervalSize` produces
pseudorandom numbers in the interval 0 through `IntervalSize` − 1 in a
nearly equal manner.

Because the value of `RandomOffset` is a uniform pseudorandom number
from the interval 0 through `IntervalSize` − 1, the value of the expression
`GetLow()` + `RandomOffSet` is a uniform pseudorandom number from the
interval Low through Low + `IntervalSize` − 1. As `IntervalSize` equals the
value High − Low + 1, the value assigned to `Number` and returned by `Draw()`
is a uniform pseudorandom number from the interval Low through High.

```
int Number = GetLow() + RandomOffset;
```

Program 8.2 demonstrates the use of `EzRandomize()` and `Draw()` to
generate five pseudorandom numbers from the interval 10 through 15.

Program 8.2

*Demonstration of
randint library*

```
// Program 8.2: Display pseudorandom numbers from the
// interval 10 through 15.
#include <iostream>
#include <string>
#include "randint.h"
using namespace std;
int main() {
   EzRandomize();
   RandomInt U(10,15);
   for (int i = 1; i <= 5; i++) {
      cout << U.Draw()<< endl;
   }
   return 0;
}
```

The output of a run of a Program 8.2 follows:

```
15
11
10
14
```

14

The output of another run of the program follows:

12
14
10
13
11

We now use our randint library in the implementation of the ADT for the red-yellow-green game.

History of Computing

Snow White and the seven dwarfs

One of the first companies to achieve prominence with its computer was Remington Rand. Mauchly and Eckert (the designers of ENIAC) produced Remington Rand's successful line of computers that were called the Universal Automatic Computer, or UNIVAC. The UNIVAC caught the public's eye when CBS used it to help predict the outcome of the 1952 presidential election. Because of this television exposure, the term UNIVAC became synonymous with computer.

Although much development of computer technology was done by new companies, some existing companies slowly entered the field. In 1952, after prodding by Thomas J. Watson, Jr., IBM added computer manufacturing to its business. Its first successful machine was the IBM 701. In 1964, with the introduction of the IBM System 360, IBM established its leadership in the industry. During this time period, IBM's dominance of the business-computer market was so great that the computer industry was often referred to as "Snow White and the Seven Dwarfs," with IBM being Snow White. The seven dwarfs were Sperry Rand, Control Data, Honeywell, RCA, NCR, General Electric, and Burroughs, none of which manufacture mainframe computers anymore.

8.7 RED–YELLOW–GREEN GAME

A fun, relatively simple guessing game is the red-yellow-green game. It is normally a two-person game in which one person picks a number between 100 and 999 and the other person tries to guess it. Every time a guess is made, the picker responds to the guesser by telling the number of red digits, yellow digits, and green digits in the guess.

A guess digit is a green digit if the guess digit and the corresponding answer digit are the same. A guess digit is a red digit if it does not correspond to any of the answer digits. A guess digit is a yellow digit if it is neither a red digit nor a green digit. Suppose the answer is 123 and the guess is 422. The reply would be one red, one yellow, and one green. The initial guess digit, 4, is a red digit because it is neither 1, 2, nor 3. The middle guess digit, 2, is a green digit because it matches the corresponding answer digit. The final guess digit,

2, is a yellow digit because it does not match the corresponding answer digit but does match another of the answer digits (the middle answer digit).

When supplying the red-yellow-green information in response to a guess, the reply gives the number of red digits first, the number of yellow digits next, and then the number of green digits. By giving totals only, the game is made harder. Suppose the answer is 653 and the guess is 616; the picker would reply one red, one yellow, and one green. Suppose instead the answer is 492 and the guess is 249; the picker would reply zero red, three yellow, and zero green.

8.7.1 Abstraction and interface

Our goal is to develop an electronic version of the game in which the program plays the role of the number picker.

The initial step in the object-oriented design is to determine the objects that will make up the system. The system in this case is the red-yellow-green game. Overall, there must be a game controller that initiates and runs the game. Also, there must be objects for representing user input and output. So, objects associated with the controller will represent the current three-digit user guess and the three-color response to that guess. Another object associated with the controller will be the three-digit number picked by the program. Notice that all of these controller's objects have three numeric components. Thus it will be advantageous to develop a class to represent an object with three numeric components. Objects of such a class can be used for representing the guess, the response, and the number to be picked.

The next step in object-oriented design is to determine how the objects will interact. For our system, the controller must be able to react to a user guess by producing the red-yellow-green response. The response should then generate another user guess. This interaction continues until the user either guesses the number correctly or quits.

We now turn our attention to a more refined view of the behaviors of our various objects.

Guess object behaviors:

- Getting a guess.
- Assigning a value to a component digit in a guess.
- Inspecting the value of a component digit in a guess.

Response object behaviors:

- Initializing a response in reaction to a guess.
- Assigning the number of reds, greens, and yellows in the response.
- Inspecting the number of reds, greens, or yellows in the response.

Primary game controller object behaviors:

- Randomly choosing a three-digit number from the interval 100 through 999 to start the game.
- Welcoming the user.
- Prompting the user to supply a guess.
- Acquiring the guess.

- Evaluating the guess to produce a response.
- Displaying a response.
- Detecting a winning guess.
- Congratulating a winning guess.
- Permitting the user to quit.
- Coordinating the play of the game.

Supporting game controller behaviors:

- Inspecting the digits in the number to be picked.
- Assigning the digits in the number to be picked.
- Determining the number of reds, yellows, and greens for creating the response.

Object with three numeric components behaviors:

- Inspecting the individual components.
- Setting the individual components.

The name of our class to represent an object with three numeric components (data members) is Element. A copy of the header file for Element is given in Listing 8.12. The class has a constructor that by default initializes its members to 0. To support the behaviors discussed previously, there are three public inspectors and three public mutators. These member functions support information hiding.

Listing 8.12

Header file element.h
for class Element

```
#ifndef ELEMENT_H
#define ELEMENT_H
class Element {
   public:
      // default constructor
      Element(int x = 0, int y = 0, int z = 0);
      // inspectors
      int GetX() const;
      int GetY() const;
      int GetZ() const;
      // mutators
      void SetX(int x);
      void SetY(int y);
      void SetZ(int z);
   private:
      // data members
      int X;
      int Y;
      int Z;
};
#endif
```

The three private data members of Element are named X, Y, and Z. These names were chosen because an Element object resembles a coordinate in three-dimensional space, where the axes are called the *x*-axis, *y*-axis, and the *z*-axis. Given these names for the data members, the names for the associated inspectors and mutators follow immediately.

Listing 8.13

Header file guess.h for
class Guess

```
#ifndef GUESS_H
#define GUESS_H

#include <iostream>
#include <string>
#include "element.h"

using namespace std;

class Guess {
    public:
        // default constructor
        Guess();
        // inspector
        int GetDigit(int i) const;
        // mutator
        bool Update();
    protected:
        // mutator
        void SetDigit(int i, int v);
    private:
        Element Number;
};

// auxiliary operators
ostream& operator<<(ostream &sout, const Guess &G);
#endif
```

The name of our class to represent a user guess object is `Guess`. A copy of the header file for `Guess` is given in Listing 8.13.

The member functions given in the class definition for `Guess` follow from our earlier discussion of object behavior. Public inspector `GetDigit()` gives access to a particular digit in the user's guess. Mutator `Update()` acquires the next user guess. In the implementation given in Section 8.7.2, `Update()` extracts the user's guess from the standard input stream. Other implementations are also possible by simply modifying `Update()`. Protected mutator `SetDigit()` is used to set an individual digit in the representation of the guess. Private data member `Number` stores the three digits in `Element` form. The first digit in the guess will be associated with the X member of `Number`, the second digit in the guess will be associated with the Y member of `Number`, and the third digit in the guess will be associated with the Z member of `Number`. The header file also includes a prototype of an overloaded version of the extraction operator for `Guess` objects.

`Response` is the name of our class for representing a response to a user. The header file for `Response` is given in Listing 8.14. The member functions given in the class definition again follow from our earlier discussion of object behavior. The public inspectors give access to the number of reds, yellows, and greens. The constructor uses protected mutators to set the counts for the number of reds, yellows, and greens in a response. The mutators are in a protected section because once the response is constructed, there is no reason for it to be modified. The color counts are represented using private data member `Counts` of type `Element`. In the implementation, the red count is associated with the X member of `Counts`, the yellow count is associated with the Y member of `Counts`, and the green count is associated with the Z member of `Counts`.

Listing 8.14

*Header file response.h
for class Response*

```cpp
#ifndef RESPONSE_H
#define RESPONSE_H
#include "element.h"
class Response {
   public:
      // constructor
      Response(int r = 0, int y = 0, int g = 0);
      // inspectors
      int GetRed() const;
      int GetYellow() const;
      int GetGreen() const;
   protected:
      // mutators
      void SetRed(int r);
      void SetYellow(int y);
      void SetGreen(int g);
   private:
      Element Counts;
};
#endif;
```

The name of our class to manage the game is RYG. The header file for RYG is given in Listing 8.15. Together with their auxiliary operators, the classes Element, Guess, Response, and RYG form our red-yellow-green game data abstraction.

Listing 8.15

*Header file ryg.h for
class RYG*

```cpp
#ifndef RYG_H
#define RYG_H
#include "guess.h"
#include "response.h"
#include "element.h"
class RYG {
   public:
      // default constructor
      RYG();
      // facilitator
      void Play();
   protected:
      // facilitators
      void Welcome() const;
      void Prompt() const;
      Response Evaluate(const Guess &G) const;
      bool Winner(const Response &R) const;
      void Congratulations() const;
      void Display(const Guess &G, const Response &R)
       const;
      void GoodBye() const;
      int GetRed(const Guess &G) const;
      int GetYellow(const Guess &G) const;
      int GetGreen(const Guess &G) const;
   private:
      // data members
      Element SecretNumber;
      Guess UserInput;
      Response UserFeedback;
};
#endif
```

The header files for `Guess`, `Response`, and `Element` are included in the header file for RYG because of data members `UserInput`, `UserFeedback`, and `SecretNumber`. In addition, there are two public members. One public member is the default constructor that principally initializes `Element` object `SecretNumber`, which represents the number picked by the program. The other public member is `Play()`, which manages the control of the game. To gain insight into the other members of RYG, the implementation of `Play()` is provided in Listing 8.16.

Listing 8.16

RYG member function Play() from ryg.cpp

```cpp
void RYG::Play() {
    Welcome();
    Prompt();
    while (UserInput.Update()) {
        UserFeedback = Evaluate(UserInput);
        Display(UserInput, UserFeedback);
        if (Winner(UserFeedback)) {
            Congratulations();
            return;
        }
        else {
            Prompt();
        }
    }
    GoodBye();
}
```

Member function `Play()` begins by invoking member functions `Welcome()` and `Prompt()`.

```cpp
Welcome();
Prompt();
```

Member function `Welcome()` displays a welcoming message, and `Prompt()` asks the user for an initial guess. Function `Play()` then initiates a **while** loop.

```cpp
while (UserInput.Update()) {
    UserFeedback = Evaluate(UserInput);
    Display(UserInput, UserFeedback);
    if (Winner(UserFeedback)) {
        Congratulations();
        return;
    }
    else {
        Prompt();
    }
}
```

The **while** loop test expression `(UserInput.Update())` updates the user's guess. The loop is iterated once for every guess. If the test expression is false, the user did not supply a value and instead gave up. Under this condition, the loop is exited and an appropriate message is displayed by member `GoodBye()`. (It will be the case that if the user wins the game, the program executes a return statement from within the loop body.)

```cpp
GoodBye();
```

Member function `Evaluate()` examines the user's guess to determine the appropriate response. Member function `Display()` displays the result of the guess in both text and graphical forms. Member function `Winner()` examines the response and determines whether it indicates three greens. If it is the winning response, member function `Congratulations()` indicates this fact and function `Play()` returns. If the response is not the winning response, then `Prompt()` is executed to prepare for the next iteration of the loop. At that point, the **while** loop test expression attempts to update the guess, and if successful, the loop body is executed again. A sample run of the text output of function `Play()` follows.

```
Welcome to the red-yellow-green game.
A number between 0 and 999 has been chosen
for you to guess.

What is your guess? 456
Guess 456 corresponds to 1 red, 1 yellow, and 1 green

What is your guess? 536
Guess 536 corresponds to 1 red, 0 yellow, and 2 green

What is your guess? 526
Guess 526 corresponds to 1 red, 0 yellow, and 2 green

What is your guess? 596
Guess 596 corresponds to 0 red, 0 yellow, and 3 green

Congratulations on your win!
```

A sample display of the graphical output for the guess of 526 follows.

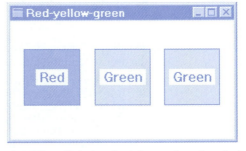

Member function `Play()` is invoked from a function `ApiMain()`. As seen in Listing 8.17, function `ApiMain()` consists of two statements: a definition of an RYG object `Game` to create a game instance and an invocation of `Play()` for the instance.

To assist member function `Evaluate()`, three other member functions are defined for analyzing a guess with respect to a particular color: `GetRed()`, `GetYellow()`, and `GetGreen()`.

Listing 8.17

Red-yellow-green game controller from rygmain.cpp

```cpp
#include <iostream>
#include <string>
#include "ryg.h"
using namespace std;
int ApiMain() {
    RYG Game;
    Game.Play();
    return 0;
}
```

8.7.2 Implementation of classes Element and Guess

We now consider the implementation of the various class member functions and auxiliary operators. We begin with the class Element. Its implementation is given in Listing 8.18. The three inspectors Element and three mutators given there are all straightforward in their implementation. These member functions exist to support information hiding and warrant no further discussion.

Listing 8.18

Implementation of class Element from element.cpp

```cpp
#include "element.h"
// Element(): constructor
Element::Element(int x, int y, int z) {
    SetX(x);
    SetY(y);
    SetZ(z);
}

// GetX(): return X attribute
int Element::GetX() const {
    return X;
}

// GetY(): return Y attribute
int Element::GetY() const {
    return Y;
}

// GetZ(): return Z attribute
int Element::GetZ() const {
    return Z;
}

// SetX(): set X attribute
void Element::SetX(int x) {
    X = x;
}

// SetY(): set Y attribute
void Element::SetY(int y) {
    Y = y;
}

// SetZ(): set Z attribute
void Element::SetZ(int z) {
    Z = z;
}
```

Listing 8.19 contains both the implementation of the class `Guess` and the overloaded insertion operator for `Guess` objects. The `Guess` class constructor initializes its data member `Number` to represent a guess of all zeros.

```
Number.SetX(0);
Number.SetY(0);
Number.SetZ(0);
```

The `Guess` inspector member function `GetDigit()` of Listing 8.19 uses its parameter `i` to determine which digit of the user's guess is to be returned. As discussed previously, the first digit is maintained in the X member of `Number`, the second digit is maintained in the Y member of `Number`, and the third digit is maintained in the Z member of `Number`. The inspector uses a **switch** statement to invoke the proper member function of `Number` to determine the value that the function should return. The value is assigned to object `DigitValue`.

```
switch (i) {
    case 1: DigitValue = Number.GetX(); break;
    case 2: DigitValue = Number.GetY(); break;
    case 3: DigitValue = Number.GetZ(); break;
    default:
        cerr << "Unexpected digit request: " << i << endl;
        exit(1);
}
```

The **default** case in the **switch** statement detects when parameter `i` does not correspond to a valid digit position. In this case, an error message is generated and the program terminates.

After completing the **switch** statement, the function executes the return statement to produce the function value.

```
return DigitValue;
```

The `Guess` mutator member function `SetDigit()` of Listing 8.19 uses its parameters `i` and `v` to set the `i`th digit in a guess to the value `v`. Like `GetDigit()`, `SetDigit()` uses a **switch** statement to determine which mutator member function of `Number` should be invoked. As implemented, the `SetDigit()` does not check that `v` is valid for the specified digit. Such validation of `v` is left to the exercises at the end of the chapter.

The task of `Guess` mutator member function `Update()` of Listing 8.19 is to get the next user input. In our implementation, the user input is extracted as an integer `Value` and then converted to `Element` form.

If there is a successful extraction, a test is made to verify that `Value` is valid (i.e., `Value` falls in the interval 100 through 999). If `Value` is invalid, no updating of the current guess is performed. If `Value` is valid, the following actions are taken:

```
int d1 = Value / 100;
int d2 = (Value - (d1 * 100)) / 10;
int d3 = Value % 10;
```

Object `d1` is the leading digit of `Value`, and it is determined by dividing `Value` by 100. Object d2 is the middle digit of `Value`, and it is determined by

Listing 8.19

Implementation of Guess member functions and auxiliary insertion operator from guess.cpp

```cpp
#include <iostream>
#include <string>
#include <stdlib.h>
#include "guess.h"
using namespace std;
// Guess(): default constructor
Guess::Guess() {
    Number.SetX(0);
    Number.SetY(0);
    Number.SetZ(0);
}

// GetDigit(): get aspect of guess
int Guess::GetDigit(int i) const {
    int DigitValue;
    switch (i) {
        case 1: DigitValue = Number.GetX(); break;
        case 2: DigitValue = Number.GetY(); break;
        case 3: DigitValue = Number.GetZ(); break;
        default:
            cerr << "Bad digit request: " << i << endl;
            exit(1);
    }
    return DigitValue;
}
// SetDigit(): Set aspect of guess
void Guess::SetDigit(int i, int v) {
    switch (i) {
        case 1: Number.SetX(v); break;
        case 2: Number.SetY(v); break;
        case 3: Number.SetZ(v); break;
        default:
            cerr << "Bad digit request: " << i << endl;
            exit(1);
    }
}
// Update(): acquire new guess from player
bool Guess::Update() {
    int Value;
    if (cin >> Value) {
        if ((Value >= 100) && (Value <= 999)) {
            int d1 = Value / 100;
            int d2 = (Value - (d1 * 100)) / 10;
            int d3 = Value % 10;
            SetDigit(1, d1);
            SetDigit(2, d2);
            SetDigit(3, d3);
        }
        else
            cerr << "Illegal guess ignored." << endl;
        return true;
    }
    else
        return false;
}
// operator <<: insert a guess
ostream& operator<<(ostream &sout, const Guess &G) {
    sout << G.GetDigit(1) << G.GetDigit(2) << G.GetDigit(3);
    return sout;
}
```

subtracting `Value` rounded down to the 100s place from `Value` and then by dividing that difference by 10. Object d3 is the trailing digit of `Value`, and it is determined by computing the remainder of `Value` when it is divided by 10; that is, `Value` mod 10.

Once the component digits of the guess are determined, mutator `Set-Digit()` is invoked to set the first, second, and third digits of the guess to their new values.

```
SetDigit(1, d1);
SetDigit(2, d2);
SetDigit(3, d3);
```

After the extraction has been processed, the value **true** is returned. This value indicates that the user has supplied another guess. If no extraction into `Value` was possible (i.e., the expression `(cin >> Value)` evaluated to false), `Update()` returns **false**.

The implementation in Listing 8.19 of the insertion operator << for a `Guess` object consists of two statements. The first statement performs the actual insertion, using G's member function `GetDigit()` to individually display the three digits. The other statement is a reference return of the stream `sout`. As in the overloading of the insertion operator for `Rational` objects, the reference return enables a `Guess` insertion to be part of a larger insertion statement. For example, in the following code segment, `Guess` object `MyGuess` is displayed first, and then a newline character is displayed.

```
Guess MyGuess;
cout << MyGuess << "\n";
```

8.7.3 Implementation of class Response

The implementation of the class `Response` is given in Listing 8.20. The `Response` constructor uses its parameters r, y, and g to initialize the three counts associated with a response. (The parameters have default values of 0.) The counts are maintained in data member `Element` object `Counts`. The initialization is done using mutators `SetRed()`, `SetYellow()`, and `Set-Green()`.

```
SetRed(r);
SetYellow(y);
SetGreen(g);
```

Verification that the values of the three parameters make sense is left to the exercises at the end of the chapter.

As noted previously, the red count is associated with the X member of the `Element` `Counts`, the yellow count is associated with the Y member of `Counts`, and the green count is associated with the Z member of `Counts`. The `Response` inspectors and mutators support information hiding. Their implementation is straightforward.

Listing 8.20

Implementation of
Response member
functions from
response.cpp

```cpp
#include "response.h"
// Response(): default constructor
Response::Response(int r, int y, int g) {
    SetRed(r);
    SetYellow(y);
    SetGreen(g);
}

// GetRed():  get number of reds
int Response::GetRed() const {
    return Counts.GetX();
}

// GetYellow(): get number of yellows
int Response::GetYellow() const {
    return Counts.GetY();
}

// GetGreen(): get number of greens
int Response::GetGreen() const {
    return Counts.GetZ();
}

// SetRed(): set number of reds
void Response::SetRed(int r) {
    Counts.SetX(r);
}

// SetYellow(): set number of yellows
void Response::SetYellow(int y) {
    Counts.SetY(y);
}

// SetGreen(): set number of greens
void Response::SetGreen(int g) {
    Counts.SetZ(g);
}
```

8.7.4 Implementation of class RYG

We will now consider the implementation of the RYG member functions. The implementation spans Listings 8.21 to 8.23, as well as the earlier Listing 8.16 of member function Play().

Listing 8.21 begins with the inclusion of several libraries, one of which is the randint library that was discussed in this chapter. The listing also defines a SimpleWindow object wout. This object is the window in which the EzWindows graphical objects are drawn. The preferred strategy would be to have this object as an RYG data member, rather than as a global object. However, initialization of such a member requires the use of C++'s member initialization list mechanism, which is not considered until the next chapter.

The default constructor is the first member function defined in Listing 8.21. The constructor begins by opening the graphical window wout and invoking EzRandomize() to ensure that the same digits are not picked each

Listing 8.21

*Implementation of RYG
member functions from
ryg.cpp*

```cpp
#include <iostream>
#include <string>
#include <stdlib.h>
#include "randint.h"
#include "rect.h"
#include "label.h"
#include "ryg.h"

using namespace std;

SimpleWindow wout("Red-yellow-green", 10, 4);

// default RYG constructor
RYG::RYG() {
   wout.Open();
   EzRandomize();
   RandomInt x(1, 9);
   RandomInt y(0, 9);
   RandomInt z(0, 9);
   SecretNumber.SetX(x.Draw());
   SecretNumber.SetY(y.Draw());
   SecretNumber.SetZ(z.Draw());
}

// Welcome(): display opening message
void RYG::Welcome() const {
   cout << "Welcome to the red-yellow-green game.\n"
        << "A number between 100 and 999 has been chosen\n"
        << "for you to guess.\n" << endl;
}

// Prompt(): request next guess
void RYG::Prompt() const {
   cout << "What is your guess? ";
}

// Congratulations(): announce their success
void RYG::Congratulations() const {
   Display(UserInput, UserFeedback);
   cout << "Congratulations on your win!" << endl;
}

// GoodBye(): tell player so long
void RYG::GoodBye() const {
   cout << "Better luck next time" << endl;
}
```

time the game is played.

```cpp
wout.Open();
EzRandomize();
```

The constructor then defines `RandomInt` objects x, y, and z. These objects are used to generate the three digits that make up the number picked by the program.

```cpp
RandomInt x(1, 9);
RandomInt y(0, 9);
RandomInt z(0, 9);
```

Object x is used to generate the first digit. Because the number must fall in the interval 100 through 999, the pseudorandom value drawn for the digit must come from the interval 1 through 9. Objects y and z are used to draw pseudorandom values for the second and third digits. These two digits have no restriction on their values, so y and z are associated with the interval 0 through 9.

Next, the RYG constructor sets the three components of its Element data member SecretNumber. As noted previously, the X member of SecretNumber is associated with the first digit of the number picked by the program, the Y member of SecretNumber is associated with the second digit of the number picked by the program, and the Z member of SecretNumber is associated with the third digit of the number picked by the program. The appropriate mutators of SecretNumber are invoked using pseudorandom numbers drawn from the proper intervals as their parameters.

```
SecretNumber.SetX(x.Draw());
SecretNumber.SetY(y.Draw());
SecretNumber.SetZ(z.Draw());
```

The other member functions Welcome(), Prompt(), Congratulations(), and GoodBye() of Listing 8.21 are straightforward and require no analysis.

RYG member function Winner() of Listing 8.22 determines whether its parameter R represents the winning response. Parameter R is the winning response if the number of greens associated with it is three. The member function GetGreen() of R computes the actual number of greens.

The other RYG member function given in Listing 8.22 is Display(). This function has two parameters: a Guess G and a Response R. Function Display() reports the result of the guess. In our implementation, function Display() inserts both a text message to standard output stream cout and a graphical drawing to wout.

The implementation of Display() begins by invoking the inspectors of R to initialize local objects rcount, ycount, and gcount with the counts associated with R.

```
int rcount = R.GetRed();
int ycount = R.GetYellow();
int gcount = R.GetGreen();
```

These counts are used in the insertion statements that produce the textual response and to control the **for** loops that produce the graphical output.

The first insertion statement produces identifying information regarding the guess.

```
cout << "Guess " << G << " corresponds to ";
```

Notice that the insertion statement uses the overloaded version of the << operator for a Guess object to display G. The insertion statement that follows then displays the three counts to the user.

```
cout << rcount << " red, " << ycount << " yellow, and "
     << gcount << " green " << "\n" << endl;
```

The graphical display is then produced. To support this activity, objects cx and cy are defined. They represent the center coordinate of the next color box

Listing 8.22

*Implementation of
other RYG member
functions from ryg.cpp*

```
// Winner(): reports whether response is all greens
bool RYG::Winner(const Response &R) const {
    return R.GetGreen() == 3;
}

// Display(): announce reds, yellows, greens
void RYG::Display(const Guess &G, const Response &R)
 const {
    int rcount = R.GetRed();
    int ycount = R.GetYellow();
    int gcount = R.GetGreen();
    // display textual response
    cout << "Guess " << G << " corresponds to ";
    cout << rcount << " red, " << ycount << " yellow, and "
     << gcount << " green " << "\n" << endl;
    // display graphical response
    float cx = 2;
    float cy = 2;
    for (int r = 0; r < rcount; ++r) {
        RectangleShape Box(wout, cx, cy, Red, 2, 2);
        Box.Draw();
        Label S(wout, cx, cy, "Red");
        S.Draw();
        cx += 3;
    }
    for (int y = 0; y < ycount; ++y) {
        RectangleShape Box(wout, cx, cy, Yellow, 2, 2);
        Box.Draw();
        Label S(wout, cx, cy, "Yellow");
        S.Draw();
        cx += 3;
    }
    for (int g = 0; g < gcount; ++g) {
        RectangleShape Box(wout, cx, cy, Green, 2, 2);
        Box.Draw();
        Label S(wout, cx, cy, "Green");
        S.Draw();
        cx += 3;
    }
}
```

to be displayed. Objects `cx` and `cy` are both initially 2. Inside the loops, `cx` is incremented by 3, which is 1.5 times the length of a side of the box.

```
float cx = 2;
float cy = 2;
```

For each iteration of each of the loops, a `RectangleShape` object is defined and drawn. Similarly, a label identifying the color of the `Rectangle-Shape` object is produced. For example, consider the loop that displays the red boxes (if any).

```
for (int r = 0; r < rcount; ++r) {
    RectangleShape Box(wout, cx, cy, Red, 2, 2);
    Box.Draw();
    Label S(wout, cx, cy, "Red");
    S.Draw();
    cx += 3;
}
```

The loop begins by constructing an object Box of the appropriate color and size positioned at coordinate (cx, cy). After drawing the object, the label that appears in the center of the box is constructed and then drawn. Since the center of the next box is 1.5 units to the right of the current box, cx is incremented by 3. Having done so, we are ready to test whether another red box needs to be drawn. The other two loops operate in an analogous manner.

Listing 8.23 contains the definitions of RYG facilitator functions Get-Green(), GetRed(), GetYellow(), and Evaluate(). All four facilitators have a formal parameter G of type Guess.

| **Listing 8.23**<br><br>*Implementation of some other RYG member functions from ryg.cpp*<br><br> | ```cpp
// GetGreen(): return number of green responses to guess
int RYG::GetGreen(const Guess &G) const {
    int green = 0;
    if (G.GetDigit(1) == SecretNumber.GetX())
        ++green;
    if (G.GetDigit(2) == SecretNumber.GetY())
        ++green;
    if (G.GetDigit(3) == SecretNumber.GetZ())
        ++green;
    return green;
}

// GetRed(): return number of red responses to guess
int RYG::GetRed(const Guess &G) const {
    int sx = SecretNumber.GetX();
    int sy = SecretNumber.GetY();
    int sz = SecretNumber.GetZ();
    int gx = G.GetDigit(1);
    int gy = G.GetDigit(2);
    int gz = G.GetDigit(3);

    int red = 0;
    if ((gx != sx) && (gx != sy) && (gx != sz))
        ++red;
    if ((gy != sx) && (gy != sy) && (gy != sz))
        ++red;
    if ((gz != sx) && (gz != sy) && (gz != sz))
        ++red;
    return red;
}

// GetYellow(): return number of yellow responses to
// guess
int RYG::GetYellow(const Guess &G) const {
    return 3 - GetGreen(G) - GetRed(G);
}

// Evaluate(): determine reds, yellows, and greens
Response RYG::Evaluate(const Guess &G) const {
    return Response(GetRed(G), GetYellow(G),
      GetGreen(G));
}
``` |

Facilitator GetGreen() reports the number of greens associated with G. This value is kept in the local **int** object green, which is initialized to 0. Function GetGreen() then compares the first guess digit with the first digit of the number picked by the program. The value of the first guess digit is obtained through inspector GetDigit() of G. The value of the first digit of the number
```

picked by the program is obtained through the inspector `GetX()` of `Secret-Number`.

```
if (G.GetDigit(1) == SecretNumber.GetX())
    ++green;
```

If the digits test the same, the count of green digits is incremented by 1. If there is a mismatch, no special action is taken. Next, the function compares the second digit of the guess and the second digit of the number picked by the program, and, if they test the same, the count of green digits is incremented by 1. Finally, the inspector compares the third guess digit with the third digit of the number picked by the program, and, if it is appropriate, the inspector increments the count of green digits. Once the comparisons and increments are completed, the count of green digits is returned.

Programmer Alert

Safe input extraction

Professional software normally extracts its input in a character representation. The input is then validated and translated into the desired representation. For example, in the red-yellow-green game, we can extract the guess as three **char** objects. This method provides a safe way of extracting the guess. For example, if an **int** representation is used and a user provides a nondigit, the program terminates with an error message that is incomprehensible to most users. By using the **char** representation, a `Guess` object can do its own validation. In the exercises, this modification to the ADT is considered.

The actions of the `GetRed()` are similar to `GetGreen()`: a count is initialized to 0, the guess digits are compared with the digits of the number picked by the program, the count is incremented for each match, and the count is returned after making the three comparisons. For ease of expression in accomplishing these tasks, function `GetRed()` makes copies of the guess digits and the digits of the number picked by the program.

```
int sx = SecretNumber.GetX();
int sy = SecretNumber.GetY();
int sz = SecretNumber.GetZ();
int gx = G.GetDigit(1);
int gy = G.GetDigit(2);
int gz = G.GetDigit(3);
```

For a guess digit to be red, it cannot match any of the digits in the number picked by the program. Because three mismatches are required, the comparison expression for determining whether a guess digit is a red digit has three terms that are conjuncted together (combined using the && operator). An individual term is true if the guess digit differs from the currently considered digit of the number picked by the program. If all three terms are true, the guess digit is a red digit. For example, the first guess digit `gx` is a red digit if the expression in Figure 8.2 is true.

Figure 8.2

An expression testing whether a guess digit is a red digit

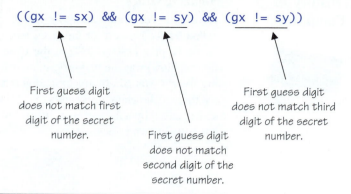

$$((gx \,!=\, sx) \,\&\&\, (gx \,!=\, sy) \,\&\&\, (gx \,!=\, sy))$$

First guess digit does not match first digit of the secret number.

First guess digit does not match second digit of the secret number.

First guess digit does not match third digit of the secret number.

Given the existence of member functions GetRed() and GetGreen(), member function GetYellow() of Listing 8.23 is straightforward. Function GetYellow() simply returns the number of reds and greens subtracted from 3.

```
return 3 - GetGreen(G) - GetRed(G);
```

Function Evaluate() is also given in Listing 8.23. The function constructs and returns the Response object that corresponds with Guess G. The Response object is constructed by using the values of expressions GetRed(G), GetYellow(G), and GetGreen(G) as the actual parameters of the Response constructor.

```
return Response(GetRed(G), GetYellow(G),
   GetGreen(G));
```

This completes our discussion of the RYG ADT and our overall introductions to ADTs.

8.8 POINTS TO REMEMBER

✔ A representation of information and the operations to be performed on it is a data abstraction.

✔ An abstract data type, or ADT, is a well-defined and complete data abstraction that uses the information-hiding principle. An ADT allows the creation and manipulation of objects in a natural manner.

✔ The ADT rule of minimality states: Unless a behavior is generally needed, it should not be part of the ADT.

✔ The class minimality principle states: If a function or operator can be defined such that it is not a member of the class, then do not make it a member. This practice makes a nonmember function or operator generally independent of changes to the class's implementation.

✔ By practicing information hiding in an ADT, client programs are generally immune from changes in the implementation of the ADT.

History of Computing

✔ In C++ an ADT is implemented using classes, functions, and operators.

✔ Constructors initialize objects of the ADT type. It is standard practice to ensure that every ADT object has all of its data members initialized.

✔ A constructor has the same name as its class.

✔ A default constructor is a constructor that requires no parameters.

✔ A copy constructor initializes a new object to be a duplicate of a previously defined source object. If a class does not define a copy constructor, the compiler automatically supplies a version.

✔ A member assignment operator copies a source object to the invoking target object in an assignment statement. If a class does not define a member assignment operator, the compiler automatically supplies a version.

✔ A memberwise copy is a copy where all data members of a source object are copied bit by bit to a target object.

History of Computing

The transistor and the integrated circuit

In 1947 the transistor was invented at AT&T Bell Telephone Laboratories. Transistors essentially function the same as vacuum tubes but are smaller, more reliable, faster, and use less power. Their relative sizes are shown in the following figure.

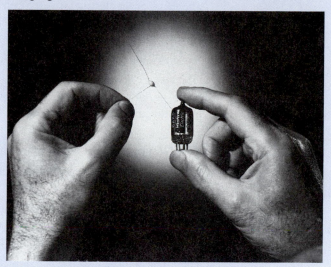

Computers built with transistors began appearing in the late 1950s, ushering in the second generation of computers. Like the transistors from which they were built, these machines were smaller, faster, cheaper, and more reliable than machines built from vacuum tubes.

Prior to transistors, most computers were quite large, often requiring an entire room with special air-conditioning and power to cool the machine and satisfy its enormous energy demands. One company, Digital Equipment Corporation, made its name by specializing in making small computers that came to be known as minicomputers. Digital's first minicomputer, the PDP-8, was introduced in 1963 and was just a little larger than a filing cabinet. Later versions were about the size of a drawer in a filing cabinet. The beauty of minicomputers was that you could put them almost anywhere. Furthermore, they were less expensive than mainframes, which made them a favorite of university scientists who were always trying to get the most out of their research budgets.

Another technological breakthrough came in 1958 with the invention of the integrated circuit by an engineer named Jack Kilby who worked for Texas Instruments. The transistorized computers of the late 1950s and 1960s consisted of many circuit boards that had transistors, resistors, and capacitors soldered to the boards and connected by wires. The integrated circuit allowed these components to be integrated together onto a single block of material, usually silicon. The first computers that used integrated circuits appeared in the middle of the 1960s. However, the true impact of the integrated circuit was not felt until the 1970s.

✔ The versions of the copy constructor and member assignment operator supplied by the compiler perform memberwise copying.

✔ A destructor is a member function that is invoked automatically for a class type object as the object goes out of existence. The destructor performs any cleanup processing that is necessary for the object that is being destroyed. The name of the destructor is the concatenation of the tilde operator (~) and its class's name. A class is permitted to have only one destructor; a destructor does not produce a return value.

✔ Some of the other member functions that commonly exist are called inspectors, mutators, and facilitators.

✔ An inspector member function returns the value of an attribute of an object. Inspector names often begin with get.

✔ A mutator member function provides a method to modify an attribute of an object. Mutator names often begin with set.

✔ A facilitator member function performs a task that depends in part upon the attributes of an object.

✔ The qualifier **const** appended to a function interface indicates that the function does not modify any of the data members. A **const** member function can be used by **const** objects of the class.

✔ The client interface to a class object occurs in the **public** section of the class definition.

✔ Any member defined in any section—whether **public**, **protected**, or **private**—is accessible to all other members of a class.

✔ Members of a **protected** section are intended to be used by other members of the class or by a class derived from the class.

✔ Data members are normally declared in a **private** section. Restricting direct client program access to the data members in an ADT helps ensure the integrity and consistency of their values.

✔ Members of a **private** section are intended to be used only by other members of the class.

✔ An & in the return type for a function or operator indicates that a reference return is being performed. In a reference return, a reference to the actual object in the return expression, rather than a copy, is returned. The scope of the returned object should not be local to the invoked function or operator.

✔ Iostream behavior is extensible. Objects of program-defined types can also have insertion and extraction operations defined for them.

✔ ADT libraries often contain auxiliary functions and operators that are not part of the ADT class, but do provide behavior that is expected with the objects.

✔ Two commonly provided auxiliary operators are insertion and extraction. They are not made member functions in part to give them the same form as insertions and extractions for fundamental type objects.

✔ A pseudorandom number sequence has the appearance and statistical properties of a random number sequence.

8.9   EXERCISES

8.1   Does every class definition define an ADT?

8.2   What properties do you expect in an ADT?

8.3   Why is the information-hiding principle so important to the object-oriented programming paradigm?

8.4   What are the differences between a data member and a member function?

8.5   What are the differences between a mutator and an inspector member function?

8.6   What are the differences between member and auxiliary functions and operators?

8.7   What are the differences in using the various access-specifier labels?

8.8   What is the purpose of the qualifier **const**?

8.9   Why is it unnecessary for constructors to have return types?

8.10   How does a reference return type differ from the standard return type?

8.11   Why are class objects that are not modified in a function or operator typically passed as constant reference parameters rather than as value parameters?

8.12   Member functions that return the value of an attribute of an object are called _____.

8.13   Member functions that set or change the value of an attribute of an object are called _____.

8.14   An _____ is a well-defined and complete data abstraction that uses the information-hiding principle.

8.15   A default constructor requires _____ parameters.

8.16   A _____ constructor initializes a new object to be a duplicate of a previously defined object.

8.17   The client interface to a class object occurs in the _____ section of the class definition.

8.18   Explain how the versions of the copy constructor and member assignment operator automatically supplied by the compiler do their copying.

8.19   How is a reference return indicated? What kind of objects can be used for a reference return? What kind of objects cannot be used for a reference return?

8.20   Why are data members typically defined in a nonpublic section?

8.21   Develop a cloud representation for the class RandomInt. Show an instantiation of the class for a RandomInt object that is associated with the interval 1 through 10.

8.22 Develop a cloud representation for the class RYG. Also show an instantiation of the class.

8.23 Suppose the following definitions are in effect.

```cpp
class Widget {
    public:
        bool Flag;
        Widget();
        Widget(int Value);
        int GetValue() const;
    protected:
        int DataItem;
        void SetValue(int Value);
};
```

a) How many member functions does class Widget have? Explain.

b) How many data members does class Widget have? Explain.

c) Is the function SetValue() defined in the class Widget a constructor? Explain.

d) Is the function SetValue() a public member function of the class Widget? Explain.

e) Can the Widget **public** member functions access the Widget data member DataItem? Explain.

f) Can a client function access the Widget data member Flag? Explain.

g) Does the class Widget support information hiding? Explain.

8.24 Consider the classes A and B and their partial implementation. Identify errors on three different lines and explain them.

```cpp
class A {
    public:
        A();
        A(&int n);
        int A(int n, int m);
        int A3;
    private:
        int A1;
        int A2;
        int A3;
};
class B {
    public:
        B();
        A myA1;
    private:
        A myA2;
};
B::B(int a1, int a2, int a3) {
    myA.A1 = a1;
    myA.A2 = a2;
    myA.A3 = a3;
    myA2 = A(a1+1, a2+1, a3+1);
}
```

8.25   Consider a class `Vehicle` that has two public constructors: one that
        takes no parameters and another that takes a single integer value param-
        eter `x`. `Vehicle` should provide a parameterless member function,
        `evaluate()`, accessible only to `Vehicle` class member code. `Vehi-`
        `cle` should provide a Boolean member function `IsCharged()`, call-
        able by any other function. (This member does not modify any members
        of the class.) `Vehicle` should provide a **void** member function, `set()`,
        that takes a single integer parameter `s`, and is accessible only within
        `Vehicle` class member code. Integer data member `MyTurbo` should be
        accessible only to objects of type `Vehicle`. Complete the class defini-
        tion for the class `Vehicle`.

8.26   Develop a class `Date` for representing a calendar. The class should pro-
        vide a default constructor that initializes the date to September 14,
        1752.[†] Another constructor should initialize a `Date` object to a specific
        value using three integer parameters corresponding to the desired
        month, day, and year. The class should have three public inspectors and
        three public mutators that allow the month, day, and year to be accessed.
        The operators `++` and `--` should be overloaded so that when applied to a
        `Date` object, the object's new value is, respectively, the successive or
        preceding day. The subtraction operator should be overloaded such that
        the difference of two dates is the number of days between them. Also,
        overload the insertion and extraction operators for `Date` objects. Be sure
        that whatever form of insertion is produced, the result is of the correct
        form for an extraction to process. Also define auxiliary functions
        `ToString()`, which returns a `string` version of its `Date` parameter,
        and `DayOfWeek()`, which returns the day of the week on which its
        `Date` parameter falls. The return type for `DayOfWeek()` should be an
        enumerated type whose symbolic constants are `Sunday`, `Monday`,
        `Tuesday`, `Wednesday`, `Thursday`, `Friday`, and `Saturday`.

8.27   Modify the rational library header file to include prototypes for the other
        arithmetic and relational operators.

8.28   Modify the rational library to include implementations of public arith-
        metic `Subtract()` and `Divide()` facilitators for subtraction and
        division.

8.29   Modify the rational library to include an implementation of auxiliary
        relational operators `-` and `/`. The implementation should use the facilita-
        tors developed in the previous exercise.

8.30   Modify the rational library to include an implementation of a public
        mutator `Reduce()` that ensures that the rational number representation
        has a relatively prime numerator and denominator. Hint: Divide the
        numerator and denominator by their greatest common divisor (use
        Euclid's algorithm to determine their greatest common divisor).

---

†.   The current calendar system for most of the world is the Gregorian calendar,
which went into effect on September 14, 1752.

8.31   Modify the rational library to include implementations of public relational facilitators `Equal()` and `LessThan()` for testing equality and less-than relationships.

8.32   Modify the rational library to include an implementation of auxiliary relational operators == and <. The implementation should use the facilitators developed in Exercise 8.31.

8.33   Modify the rational library to include implementations of the relational operators <=, >, and >=. Your implementation should make use of the operators defined in Exercise 8.32.

8.34   Modify the definition of `Rational` member function `Extract()` so that it verifies that a slash was extracted between the numerator and denominator. Discuss whether the function should do its own validation, or should the validation by `SetDenominator()` suffice.

8.35   Place two insertion statements inside each member function defined in `rational.cpp`. The first insertion should be placed at the beginning of the statement body and should display which member has been invoked. The second insertion should be placed at the end of the statement body and should indicate which member has finished executing. Run Program 8.1 and examine the output. Account for each occurrence in the output of these member-identifying statements.

8.36   The `Rational` constructors and the `Rational` member function `Extract()` invoke the mutators `SetNumerator()` and `SetDenominator()` in a similar manner. The two invocation statements in these members can be replaced by the single invocation of a new `Rational` member `SetRational()`, which in turn does the two invocations. This member function would have two **int** value parameters, `numer` and `denom`, that are used to set the numerator and denominator of the invoking object. Add a prototype of the new member to the `Rational` class definition and its implementation to source file `rational.cpp`. Discuss your choice of making the new member **public**, **protected**, or **private**.

8.37   Modify the rational library to include an explicitly defined copy constructor.

8.38   Modify the rational library to include a public member function `FloatingPoint()` that returns a floating-point representation of the object.

8.39   Modify `Rational` member function `Insert()` to have a default parameter value of **cout**. Where should the default value be specified? Why?

8.40   Modify `Rational` member function `Extract()` to have a default parameter value of **cin**. Where should the default value be specified? Why?

8.41   Design an auxiliary function `power()` with two parameters `r` and `n`. Parameter `r` is a `Rational` and `n` is an **int**. The function should return r^n. Discuss your choices for parameter declarations and return type.

Exercises

8.42 Design an ADT library `complex` for complex numbers. Discuss decisions for member functions and operators as well as for auxiliary functions and operators. Also discuss your access restrictions. Compare your decisions to those made in the standard complex library.

8.43 Implement your version of the complex library of Exercise 8.42. Also implement a program that demonstrates the features of your library.

8.44 Suppose the class C of Listing 8.9 is supplemented so that it has the following public inspector and mutator member functions added to it along with the following auxiliary insertion and extraction operators.

```
string C::GetName() const {
    return name;
}
void C::SetName(const string &s) {
    name = s;
}
ostream& operator<<(ostream &sout, const C &c) {
    sout << c.GetName();
    return sout;
}
C operator+(const C &c, const C &d) {
    s = c.GetName() + d.GetName();
    C result;
    return result;
}
```

Explain why the following function `main()`

```
int main() {
    s = "x";
    C x;
    s = "y";
    C y;
    s = "z";
    C z;
    cout << "displaying: " << x << endl;
    cout << "displaying: " << y << endl;
    cout << "displaying: " << z << endl;
    cout << "displaying: " << (x + y) << endl;
    cout << "displaying: " << (z + z + z) <<
endl;
    return 0;
}
```

produces as its output

```
x: default constructed
y: default constructed
z: default constructed
displaying: x
displaying: y
displaying: z
xy: default constructed
xy: copy constructed using xy
xy: destructed
displaying: xy
xy: destructed
```

```
zz: default constructed
zz: copy constructed using zz
zz: destructed
zzz: default constructed
zzz: copy constructed using zzz
zzz: destructed
displaying: zzz
zzz: destructed
zz: destructed
z: destructed
y: destructed
x: destructed
```

8.45   Design and develop an ADT to represent the weekly stock information for the stock-interval problem of Chapter 6. Implement the ADT and a program that uses the ADT to solve the stock-interval problem. Because stock prices are normally kept as rational numbers, your ADT should represent stock information as Rational objects.

8.46   Create a simulation of die rolling. Define two RandomInt objects Dice1 and Dice2 whose pseudorandom number sequences are from the inclusive interval 1 through 6. Simulate 10,000 rolls of the die. For each role, compute the sum of the two numbers. Maintain the number of times each sum occurs. Compare your totals with the expected number of times each sum should occur.

8.47   Does the RandomInt class work properly if the interval from which the numbers are drawn includes negative values? Explain.

8.48   Design and implement an ADT to represent an instance of the game of tic-tac-toe. Your implementation of the ADT should use the EzWindows library to display a graphical view of the game's progress.

8.49   Modify the Guess class so that a user guess is extracted as three **char** objects. If the extracted objects are of the correct form, then convert the character digit representation to numeric digit representations. If the extracted objects are not of the correct form, then generate an error message. What are the advantages of doing the extraction this way?

8.50   Design an ADT for the red-yellow-green game where the ADT object takes on the role of the guesser.

8.51   Modify Guess member function SetDigit() to validate that the new digit value is a proper value.

8.52   Modify the Response constructor to verify that its parameters correspond to valid color counts (i.e., the parameter sum is 3, and the individual parameters are part of the interval 1 through 3).

8.53   Modify the Response mutators SetRed(), SetYellow(), and Set-Green() to verify that the new counts falls in the interval 1 through 3. If these member functions do this testing, is it necessary for the modified constructor of Exercise 8.52 to verify their individual values? Why?

8.54   Overload the output operator for RandomInt. It should do a draw and a display of the value to the stream.

CHAPTER 9

Lists

Introduction

In many problem situations, a programmer needs the ability to define a group of objects as either a one-dimensional or multidimensional list. For such tasks, C++ provides two representation alternatives. One representation is based on arrays; the other representation is based on classes. The array representation is the traditional one and remains important because many legacy libraries work only with this form of list. However, C++ imposes significant restrictions on the use of arrays in an effort to maintain backward compatibility with C. In part because of these restrictions and in part because of software-engineering reasons, arrays are becoming less popular and class representations of lists are becoming the dominant list representation. Several class representations for lists are defined in the Standard Template Library (STL). These classes are known as *container classes* because their objects can hold multiple values, and the most important container class is the `vector` class. Our list examination considers how to define and manipulate both array and `vector` objects.

Key Concepts

- one-dimensional arrays
- array subscripting
- arrays as parameters
- array elements as parameters
- character strings
- Standard Template Library (STL)
- container class
- template class
- vector
- vector subscripting
- vector resizing
- string subscripting
- iterators

- iterator dereferencing
- vector of vectors
- sorting
- function `InsertionSort()`
- function `QuickSort()`
- searching
- function `BinarySearch()`
- algorithm library
- function `find()`
- table
- matrices
- member initialization list
- multidimensional arrays

9.1 NAMED COLLECTIONS

Suppose you need to find the minimum value from a list of five **int** objects
`Value1`, `Value2`, through `Value5`. The following code segment computes
that value.

```
int MinimumSoFar = Value1;
if (Value2 < MinimumSoFar)
    MinimumSoFar = Value2;
if (Value3 < MinimumSoFar)
    MinimumSoFar = Value3;
if (Value4 < MinimumSoFar)
    MinimumSoFar = Value4;
if (Value5 < MinimumSoFar)
    MinimumSoFar = Value5;
```

Notice that a separate **if** statement is needed for each object in the list because,
although the object names are similar, each object is totally independent of the
other objects.

Now suppose that you need the minimum value from a list of 1,000 objects
`Value1` through `Value1000`. Because of object independence, you cannot
simply introduce iteration into the solution as was done for the averaging problem in Chapter 4. And if you proceed as above, with a separate **if** statement
for each object in the group, the resulting very large code segment would be
both clumsy and error prone. Instead, what we need is a list type mechanism
that allows a group of objects of the same type to be created in a single definition. We also require the ability to reference individually the elements of that
list in a concise manner.

Our examination of list types begins with the array, which is the basic C++
list mechanism. After this examination, we consider the class **vector**. The
vector class is known as a *container* class because **vector** objects can hold
multiple elements. The **vector** class is one of several container classes
defined in the STL. We shall see that by using the **vector** class we can overcome some of the programming restrictions associated with arrays. In addition,
we can use vector features to avoid some common programming miscues.

9.2 ONE-DIMENSIONAL ARRAYS

The individual objects that make up an array are known as *elements*. Array elements can be referenced collectively or individually. They can be any fundamental type, pointer type[†], or previously defined derived type. An important
language restriction is that all elements of an array have the same type.

---

† We delay our discussion of pointer object arrays until Chapter 11.

Like other objects, arrays can be defined either with or without initialization. If there is no initialization, then a one-dimensional array definition has the form

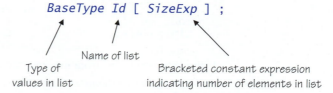

BaseType Id [SizeExp] ;

Type of
values in list

Name of list

Bracketed constant expression
indicating number of elements in list

where *BaseType* is the type of the individual elements in the array; *Id* is an identifier that is the name of the array; and *SizeExp* is a constant, positive expression that uses literals or constants derived from literals to specify the number of objects in the array.

Suppose the following constant definitions are in effect.

```
const int N = 20;
const int M = 40;
const int MaxStringSize = 80;
const int MaxListSize = 1000;
```

Then the following are all correct C++ array definitions.

```
int A[10];                 // array of 10 ints
char B[MaxStringSize];     // array of 80 chars
float C[M*N];              // array of 800 floats
int Values[MaxListSize];   // array of 1000 ints
```

A, B, C, and `Values` are now one-dimensional arrays. Each of these objects is a collection of individual *array elements*. Each array element is itself an object that can be used like any other object.

The act of referring to an individual array element is called *subscripting* or *indexing*. Just as brackets are used in a definition to indicate that an array is being created, so too are brackets used to subscript a particular element of an array. Each element of an array has its own subscript value. The first element of an array has subscript value 0, the second element of an array has subscript value 1, and so on. For array A, the last element has subscript value 9. The following figure shows a representation of A. A dash indicates that the element is uninitialized.

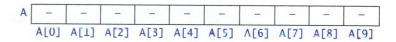

A `|  –  |  –  |  –  |  –  |  –  |  –  |  –  |  –  |  –  |  –  |`

A[0] A[1] A[2] A[3] A[4] A[5] A[6] A[7] A[8] A[9]

In the following code segment, the references to individual array elements of A are all correct.

```
int i = 7;
int j = 2;
int k = 4;
A[0] = 1;              // element 0 of A given value 1
A[i] = 5;              // element i of A given value 5
A[j] = A[i] + 3;       // element j of A given value
```

```
                                    // of element i of A plus 3
    A[j+1] = A[i] + A[0];  // element j+1 of A given value
                                    // of element i of A plus
                                    // value of element 0 of A
    A[A[j]] = 12;                   // element A[j] of A given
                                    // value 12
    cout << A[2];                   // element 2 of A is displayed
    cin >> A[k];                    // element k of A given next
                                    // extracted value
```

If the value extracted from the standard input stream was the value 3, then the effect of executing the preceding code segment is

A	1	–	8	6	3	–	–	5	12	–
	A[0]	A[1]	A[2]	A[3]	A[4]	A[5]	A[6]	A[7]	A[8]	A[9]

Programmer Alert

Bad subscripting

C++ does not provide an automatic way for ensuring that proper array subscripts are used. For example, the following code segment does not generate an error message.

```
int A[10];
int B[5];
B[-5] = 1;
```

Instead of an error message, the likely effect of the preceding assignment is to modify the memory location of object A[5] because most compilers would assign array B immediately after array A in their activation record. Therefore, B[-5] would be referring to the fifth element from the end of A, which is A[5].

The most common subscript error is misreferencing the last element of an array. Both beginning and experienced programmers sometimes forget that the last element of the array has a subscript one less than the size of the array.

In part, because there is no automatic way for ensuring that proper subscripts are used, software developers have turned to the container classes provided in the Standard Template Library. These classes provide iterators and member functions that provide controlled access to the list elements. It is also possible to easily extend these classes so that subscripts are checked automatically.

9.2.1 Array initialization

Individual array element objects are initialized in a manner similar to other objects. In particular, arrays defined in the global scope with fundamental base types have their array elements set to 0 unless there is explicit initialization. Arrays defined in a local scope with fundamental base types have uninitialized array elements unless there is explicit initialization.

The following four array definitions initialize all five of their elements to 0.

```cpp
int Frequency[5] = {0, 0, 0, 0, 0};
int Total[5] = {0};
int Sum[5]({0, 0, 0, 0, 0});
int Count[5]({0});
```

The definition of `Frequency` explicitly sets all of its elements to 0. The definition of `Total` explicitly sets its first array element `Total[0]` to 0 and uses the C++ rule that if only a partial initialization is given, the unspecified elements are set to 0. The definitions of `Sum` and `Count` are analogous using the alternative initialization form.

The following array definitions also do explicit initialization. Because no *SizeExp* is provided, the number of elements in each definition is determined by the number of initialization expressions.

```cpp
int Digits[] = {0, 1, 2, 3, 4, 5, 6, 7, 8, 9};
int Zero[] = {0};
char Alphabet[] = {'a', 'b', 'c', 'd', 'e', 'f', 'g',
    'h', 'i', 'j', 'k', 'l', 'm', 'n', 'o', 'p', 'q',
    'r', 's', 't', 'u', 'v', 'w', 'x', 'y', 'z'};
```

The definition of array `Digits` results in a 10-element array with `Digits[0]` being initialized to 0, `Digits[1]` being initialized to 1, and so on. The definition of `Zero` results in a single-element array with `Zero[0]` being initialized to 0. A single element array is still an array and is treated by C++ consistently in that manner. The definition of `Alphabet` defines a 26-element array with `Alphabet[0]` being initialized to `'a'`, `Alphabet[1]` being initialized to `'b'`, and so on.

When an array is defined with a class base type, initialization is always performed regardless of the scope. The default constructor for the class is automatically applied to each individual array element. Because the default constructor is applied, no explicit initialization is given.

The following example defines an array R of 10 `Rational` objects. Each array element is initialized to represent the default `Rational` value of 0/1.

```cpp
Rational R[10];  // ten rationals initialized to 0/1
```

9.2.2   Constant arrays

As in other object definitions, the modifier **const** can be applied in an array definition. The modifier has the usual effect—after applying the initialization, the object is treated as a constant. In this case the values of the individual array elements cannot be changed. The following example defines and initializes a two-element array B. Afterwards neither of the array elements can be changed.

```cpp
const int B[2] = {10, 100};
```

With the preceding **const** definition in effect, the following statements are invalid.

```
B[0] = 20;        // illegal: a const object cannot be
                  // the target of an assignment
cin >> B[1];      // illegal: a const object cannot be
                  // the target of an extraction
```

A **const** array element is properly used in contexts where only a value is needed.

```
int i = B[1];     // legal: i is a copy of B[1]
cout << B[0];     // legal: B[0] is inserted to the
                  // standard output stream
```

9.2.3   Simple array processing

The following code segment extracts up to `MaxListSize` values from standard input and assigns them in turn to an array `Values`.

```
const int MaxListSize = 10;
int Values[MaxListSize];
int n = 0;
int CurrentInput;
while ((n < MaxListSize) && (cin >> CurrentInput)) {
    Values[n] = CurrentInput;
    ++n;
}
```

The array `Values` can represent up to `MaxListSize` list values. Because the user may not necessarily provide that many values, an object `n` is defined to represent the number of elements in the list that have been assigned values. It will be the case during the processing that the assigned elements (if any) are `Values[0]` through `Values[n-1]`. Thus the place to store a newly extracted value is `Values[n]`. At the beginning of the code segment, none of the array elements has yet been assigned a value, so `n` is initialized to 0.

The preceding code segment also defines an object `CurrentInput` to store the current extracted value from the standard input stream.

A **while** construct is then used to process the extractions. The **while** loop body iterates if the two terms in the test expression are both true.

- The term `(n < ListSize)` when true indicates that there is an unassigned element in `Values` to store a value. Because of the short-circuit evaluation of logical expressions, if this term is false, the second term is not evaluated.

- The term `(cin >> CurrentInput)` when true indicates that there is an extracted value.

If the **while** loop body is executed, the next available array element is used to store the current input value.

```
Values[n] = CurrentInput;
```

After this assignment n is incremented to reflect that another value has been added to the list.

```
++n;
```

The **while** test expression is then reevaluated, and if it is true, the process is repeated.

Suppose the input stream looks like this:

```
4 9 5
```

The first time through the loop, n is 0, so Values[0] is assigned the input value 4. The memory associated with array Values would now look like the following:

Values | 4 | – | – | – | – | – | – | – | – | –

In the next iteration, n will have been incremented to 1, and Values[1] will be assigned the input value 9.

Values | 4 | 9 | – | – | – | – | – | – | – | –

In the following iteration, n will have been incremented to 2, and Values[2] will be assigned 5.

Values | 4 | 9 | 5 | – | – | – | – | – | – | –

Notice by incrementing n after each assignment of an input value to an array element, n represents the number of elements in Values that have been set.

If after n has been incremented it is equal to MaxListSize, the test expression is false and the loop is terminated. The termination is necessary because there are no more unassigned elements in Values for storing additional input values. If the loop is instead terminated because there are no more input values, then n also has the correct value for this case.

If the input stream is initially empty, the loop body is never executed and n remains 0, reflecting the correct value for this case.

Thus no matter how many times the loop body is executed, when the loop is finished, n reflects the number of values assigned to the list.

In the next example, an array List with m elements is searched for a particular value. The object containing the value to be searched is commonly called the *key*.

```
cout << "Enter the search value (number): ";
int Key;
cin >> Key;
int i;
for (i = 0; (i < m) && (List[i] != Key); ++i) {
    continue;
}
if (i == m)
    cout << Key << " is not in the list" << endl;
```

```
else
    cout << Key << " is " << i << "-th element" << endl;
```

Suppose m is the number of array elements in List that have been set so far (it has the role of n for Values). Therefore, only array elements List[0] through List[m-1] must be examined. Because the number m of array elements that have been set is known, a **for** statement easily expresses the subscripts of the array elements that need to be considered—0 through m-1 in increments of 1. We use index variable i to represent the current subscript value. The value of i must be available after the loop, so we cannot declare it in the **for** loop.

The **for** loop test expression processes the current array element List[i]. As in the **while** loop that initialized Values, two terms must be true for the loop to be iterated. The terms for the **for** loop are

- The term (i < m) when true indicates that there is a current element in List for testing whether it matches the key value. Because of short-circuit evaluation, if this term is false, the second term is not evaluated.

- The term (List[i] != Key) when true indicates that the current element is not equal to the key value.

If the test expression is true, we must continue our search for the key value in the next element of List. Because the increment of i in the **for** loop postexpression sets up the next evaluation of the test expression, no actions need to be taken in the **for** loop body itself.

There are several ways to indicate that the loop body requires no action. For example, an empty statement is a legal statement in C++, so the loop could be represented in the following manner:

```
for (i = 0; (i < m) && (List[i] != Key); ++i) {
    ;
}
```

We chose to use the keyword **continue** in a **continue** statement.

```
for (i = 0; (i < m) && (List[i] != Key); ++i) {
    continue;
}
```

A **continue** statement in a loop body indicates that the execution of the body is finished for this iteration. When a **continue** statement is executed in a loop, control is transferred to the end of the loop. In the preceding **for** loop, the effect is that execution continues with the postexpression of the loop (i.e., the ++i expression).

By examining the value of i after the **for** loop has terminated, we can determine whether one of the array elements of List has the same value as Key.

If i has value m, then all array elements were examined and the loop was terminated because there were no more elements to consider. (Remember that List[0] through List[m-1] were the elements to consider.) In this case, the key value is not present, and an appropriate message is inserted to the output stream.

If i does not have the value of m, then it must be that the **for** loop terminated because (List[i] != Key) was false for some i with a value between 0 and m-1. In this case, List[i] is the key value, and the appropriate message is inserted to the standard output stream.

We now trace through the code segment using the following representation for List, m, Key, and i. In terms of execution, we are about to begin the **for** loop.

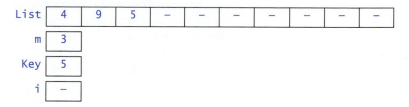

The initialization step of the **for** loop is first executed, and index i is assigned the value 0.

List	4	9	5	–	–	–	–	–	–	–

m | 3

Key | 5

i | 0

The test expression is then evaluated. Based on the values of List, m, key, and i, both terms are true (0 is less than 3, and 4 is not equal to 5). Index i is then incremented to 1 to prepare for the next evaluation.

List	4	9	5	–	–	–	–	–	–	–

m | 3

Key | 5

i | 1

The test expression is then reevaluated. Based on the values of List, m, key, and i, both terms are again true (1 is less than 3, and 9 is not equal to 5). Index i is then incremented to 2 to prepare for the next evaluation.

List	4	9	5	–	–	–	–	–	–	–

m | 3

Key | 5

i | 2

The test expression is again reevaluated. Based on the values of List, m, key, and i, the first term remains true, but the second term is now false (2 is less than 3, but 5 is equal to 5). Because the terms must both be true for the loop to iterate, the **for** loop is terminated.

The **if** statement is then evaluated, and its test expression is found to be false (2 is not equal to 3). As a result, the following output occurs.

```
5 is 2-th element
```

The key value search code segment is typical of array processing. There is initialization to prepare for the processing of the array, a loop to process each array element in turn, and a check to see whether the processing of the list is completed. For example, the following code segment finds the minimum value of a list Values where the list size n is at least 1.

```
int MinimumSoFar = Values[0];
for (int i = 1; i < n; ++i) {
    if (Values[i] < MinimumSoFar) {
        MinimumSoFar = Values[i];
    }
}
```

To find the minimum value in an array requires examining each element in turn. If the code segment keeps track of the minimum array element value seen so far, the lesser of that value and the current element is the minimum value seen so far. If this processing is done for each array element, then after the last array element has been considered, the minimum value seen so far is in fact the minimum. Notice that the above code segment for finding the minimum of an arbitrarily sized list is even smaller than the code segment that was presented at the start of this chapter for finding the minimum of five values!

The following code segment is a commented version of the previous code segment. The numbered comments reflect the preceding discussion. The comments are essentially invariants regarding the value of MinimumSoFar.

```
int MinimumSoFar = Values[0];
// (1): MinimumSoFar is minimum in Values[0] ...
// Values[0]
for (int i = 1; i < m; ++i) {
    // (2): MinimumSoFar is minimum in Values[0]
    // ... Values[i-1]
    if (Values[i] < MinimumSoFar) {
        MinimumSoFar = Values[i];
    }
    // (3): MinimumSoFar is minimum in Values[0]
    // ... Values[i]
}
// (4): MinimumSoFar is minimum in Values[0] ...
// Values[m-1]
```

The first comment is true because MinimumSoFar is initialized to Values[0]. The second comment is true the first time the **for** body is executed because i-1 at that point is 0 and the first comment is true. The third comment is true if the second comment was true because the **if** statement that precedes the third comment updates `MinimumSoFar` if, in fact, `List[i]` is the minimum value in `Values[0]` through `Values[i]`. If the **for** body is repeated, the second comment is again true because the comment at that point is simply a restatement of the third comment from the previous iteration using the incremented value of `i`. The fourth comment is true because it is simply either a restatement of the third comment (if m is greater than 1) or a restatement of the first comment (if m is 1). Because the fourth comment is true, we have correctly determined the minimum value in the list.

9.2.4   Character string arrays

C++ provides another initialization style for **char** arrays to support a representation of character strings. For example, the following definition of `Letters` defines and initializes a *27-element* array.

```
char Letters[] = "abcdefghijklmnopqrstuvwxyz";
```

The first 26 elements of the array—`Letters[0]` through `Letters[25]`—get their initialization character from the corresponding position in the initialization string. That is, the array element `Letters[0]` gets the first character `'a'` in the string, the second array element `Letters[1]` gets the second character in the string `'b'`, and so on through the 26th element `Letters[25]` that gets the 26th character in the string `'z'`.

The last array element `Letters[26]` is initialized to the null character `'\0'`. Array element `Letters[26]` is created because the traditional C++ representation for character strings includes a null character at the end of a string.

The following array definition creates a 13-element array with `Greetings[0]` being initialized to `'H'`, `Greetings[1]` being initialized to `'e'`, and so on through `Greetings[11]` being initialized to `'d'` and `Greetings[12]` being initialized to `'\0'`.

```
char Greetings[] = "Hello, world";
```

The iostream library includes a definition of the insertion operator `<<` for a right operand that is a **char** array. The operation displays all of the characters of the array that precede the first null character in the array. For example, the following insertion causes the phrase `"Hello, world"` to be displayed to the standard output stream.

```
cout << Greetings;
```

The extraction operator is also defined in the iostream library for a right operand that is a **char** array. The extraction by default first skips leading whitespace characters and then extracts the next sequence of nonwhitespace characters from the input stream. A null `'\0'` is automatically stored in the array element that occurs after the element that holds the last extracted character. If the standard input stream contains

```
how   are you   today?  i am fine
```

then the following code segment

```
const int MaxStringSize = 10;
char S[MaxStringSize];
while (cin >> S) {
    cout << S << endl;
}
```

will display the nonwhitespace strings one per line.

```
how
are
you
today?
i
am
fine
```

Upon completion of the code segment, the memory associated with array S would look like the following:

S	'f'	'i'	'n'	'e'	'\0'	'?'	'\0'	–	–	–

The question mark character and the second end-of-string character remain as array values in S because the final extraction involved only four characters.

Although the extraction operator is defined to work with **char** array objects, its use is generally avoided because we cannot be sure that the size of the array will be sufficiently large to hold the next input string. Instead the characters are either explicitly extracted character by character and assigned to an array or one of the overloaded versions of the istream member functions get() or getline() is used.

One version of member function get() has two required parameters and one optional parameter (see Appendix B for a description of other iostream member functions). The required parameters are an array of type **char** and a length. The optional parameter is a **char** whose default value is the newline '\n'. This character is called the *delimiter*. Characters are extracted from the input stream and assigned to the next available array element until one of the following conditions has occurred.

- There are no more characters to extract; that is, end of file is reached.

- The next character to be extracted would be the delimiter.

- The number of extracted characters is one less character than the value of the second parameter.

Regardless of which of the three conditions causes the string extraction process to terminate, a null '\0' is stored in the element following the array element that holds the last extracted value.

The istream member function getline() operates in a similar manner to the preceding member function get() except that if the delimiter is encountered, it is also extracted. However, the delimiter is not assigned to its array parameter.

If the standard input stream contains

```
A
multi-line
  example.
```

then code segment

```cpp
const int MaxStringSize = 10;
char S[MaxStringSize];
while (cin.getline(S, MaxStringSize)) {
    cout << S << endl;
}
```

produces

```
A
multi-lin
e
  example.
```

Upon completion, the memory associated with array S would look like the following:

S	' '	'e'	'x'	'a'	'm'	'p'	'l'	'e'	'.'	'\0'

Programming Tip

Character strings or string class strings?

Prior to this chapter, when we had string processing needs, we used the class `string` from the string library. In subsequent material, we will continue to do so because the `string` class has a more extensive set of capabilities. We will use a character string representation only when we want access to legacy library functions that are based on character strings.

So far our examples have used arrays as local objects. In the next section we develop several useful functions that have arrays as parameters. These functions perform list extraction, list insertion, and list searching.

Self-check Questions

1.   What are the individual objects that make up an array called?

2.   Give the appropriate declarations to define an array named `Scores` that holds 2000 integers.

3.   What is the name of the operation used to access an individual array element?

4.   Write the appropriate statements to define an array named `StackElements` that can hold 50 objects of type `StackObject`.

5.   Write the appropriate declarations to define an array named `Grade-PointAvg` that can hold 500 single-precision floating-point objects.

6.   Assume the following definitions.

```
const int MaxSize = 200;
int Hits[MaxSize];
int i, j, k;
```

Write the C++ statement that adds 6 to element k of `Hits`.

Write the C++ statement that copys element i of `Hits` to element k+1.

Write the C++ statement that sums elements i and k of `Hits` and places the result element j+5 of `Hits`.

7.   Assume the following array definition is given at the global scope.

```
const int MaxSize = 100;
int Points[MaxSize];
```

What are the initial values of the elements of `Points`?

8.   Assume the following array definition is given at the local scope.

```
const int MaxSize = 30;
float TimeStamp[MaxSize];
```

What are the initial values of the elements of `TimeStamp`?

9.   Give an array definition for an array named `Distance` with 10 elements. Each element of `Distance` is to be initialized to the value of its position in the array. For example, `Distance[6]` should be initialized to 6.

10.   Consider the following definitions made at the global scope.

```
const int MaxSize = 6;
int Weights[MaxSize] = {3,4};
```

Give the initial values of the array `Weights`.

11.   Consider the following definition.

```
int Buttons[] = {5, 6, 10, 12, 13};
```

How many elements does array `Button` contain?

12.   Write an array definition for an array `Coefficients` that is initialized with the following values: 23.1, 34.5, 35.6, 28.0, 35.0, 88.2, 91.3.

13. Write an array definition that initializes the character array `Title` to the string `"Madam Bovary"`.

9.3 ARRAYS AS PARAMETERS

The original developers of C, the predecessor language of C++, were concerned with efficiency. For this reason they did not make an array type a *first-class type*. In other words, array objects cannot be used with certain language features that are applicable to objects of other types. This limitation has carried over into the C++ language in three major ways.

- A function return type cannot be an array.
- An array parameter can only be a reference parameter.
- An array cannot be the target of an assignment.

Relaxing these restrictions would require making a copy of individual array elements. This requirement could be quite costly with respect to both memory and processing time if an array is composed of many elements.

The syntax for an array parameter reflects that it can be passed only by reference. No & is required or expected in the definition of an array parameter.

The syntax for an array parameter definition allows the size of a one-dimensional array to be omitted from within the brackets. This flexibility means that the same function can process arrays of different sizes. Although functions do not need the size of the array as part of the parameter declaration, another parameter usually indicates how many elements of the array should be processed.

We now define a **void** function `GetList()` that has three formal parameters. This function will extract values from input stream `cin` and store them in an array.

```
void GetList(int A[], int MaxN, int &n) {
    for (n = 0; (n < MaxN) && (cin >> A[n]); ++n) {
        continue;
    }
}
```

The first parameter is the array A that holds the extracted values. The second parameter MaxN is the maximum number of values to be extracted. The third parameter n upon completion of the function indicates the number of extracted values. It will be the case that MaxN differs from n only if cin does not contain sufficient input values. Both A and n are reference parameters—A because arrays are always passed by reference and n because of the reference parameter syntax.

The body of function `GetList()` consists of a single **for** statement. As in the key-searching code segment, no action is required in the **for** loop body.

The loop test expression has two terms that must be true for the loop to be iterated. The test expression was designed to use short-circuit evaluation. The first term ensures that the number of extracted values so far is less than the maximum number of values to be extracted. Only if this term is true, is the second term evaluated. The evaluation of the second term causes an extraction to be attempted from cin that assigns a value to the next available element of A, which is A[n]. If the extraction is unsuccessful, the value of the operation is 0, which corresponds to false and results in the loop being terminated. If the extraction is successful, the value of the operation is nonzero, which corresponds to true. Thus if a value is assigned to element A[n], the overall test expression is true.

If the test expression is true, n is incremented. The incrementing reflects that another value has been extracted and assigned to the array.

Suppose the standard input stream contained the following values:

```
6 9 82 11 29 85
11 28 91
```

Then code segment

```
const int MaxListSize = 10;
int Scores[MaxListSize];
int NbrScores;
GetList(Scores, MaxListSize, NbrScores);
```

would assign array Scores in the following manner:

Scores	6	9	82	11	29	85	11	28	91	–

Scores is modified because when an element of formal reference parameter array A is set, we in fact change the corresponding element of Scores. The preceding code segment also sets NbrScores to 9.

Note that the invocation of GetList() does not use brackets in passing the actual array parameter Scores. The invoking code segment knows that Scores is an array; therefore, no brackets are needed.

The next function that we consider is PutList().

```
void PutList(const int A[], int n) {
    for (int i = 0; i < n; ++i) {
        cout << A[i] << endl;
    }
}
```

This **void** function has two formal parameters: A and n. The first parameter is the **int** array to be displayed. Because displaying a list does not require any modification to its elements, the modifier **const** is used. The second parameter is a value parameter that represents the number of elements in the array to be displayed. The function uses a **for** statement to iteratively display n array element values one per line to the standard output stream. For example, the following invocation displays our previously defined array Scores.

```
PutList(Scores, NbrScores);
```

The invocation produces as its output

```
6
9
82
11
```

```
29
85
11
28
91
```

We next consider an **int** function Search(), which has three formal parameters. The first parameter is an **int** array List; the second parameter is the number of elements m to be considered, and the third parameter is the key value Key.

```
int Search(const int List[], int m, int Key) {
    for (int i = 0; i < m; ++i) {
        if (List[i] == Key) {
            return i;
        }
    }
    return m;
}
```

Function Search() is similar in purpose to the code segment that searched an array for a key value in Section 9.2.3. However, function Search() does not display a message indicating whether it found the value. If Search() finds the key value in the list, it returns the subscript of the first matching element. If the key value is not among the array element values, Search() returns the number of elements m in the list. Because the list elements occupy subscript positions 0 through m-1 in the array, the value m indicates that the key value is not in the list.

In the following code segment, the previously defined array Scores is searched for two values.

```
int i1 = Search(Scores, NbrScores, 11);
int i2 = Search(Scores, NbrScores, 30);
```

The first invocation initializes i1 to 3 because the first match of the value 11 in the array Scores is with Scores[3]. The second invocation initializes i2 to 9 (the value of NbrScores) because none of the array elements Scores[0] through Scores[8] matches the value 30.

Although subscripts are not used when an array is used as an actual parameter, subscripts are used when an individual array element is passed as an actual parameter. The use of brackets is necessary here because it is the subscript that allows a particular element to be specified. For example, the function main() of Program 9.1 invokes the function Swap()—originally defined in Chapter 6—to interchange the values of a pair of elements from the **int** array Number.

```
Swap(Number[i], Number[n-1-i]);
```

The definition of function Swap() specifies that its two arguments are **int** reference parameters. Because the base type of Number is **int**, passing two Number array elements to Swap() is appropriate.

Program 9.1 initializes the array `Number` using function `GetList()`. After reversing the order of the values in the list, function `PutList()` is used to display the list.

Program 9.1

Display input values in reverse order

```cpp
// Program 9.1: Display inputs in reverse order
#include <iostream>
#include <string>

using namespace std;

void GetList(int A[], int MaxN, int &n);
void Swap(int &Value1, int &Value2);
void PutList(const int A[], int n);

// main(): manage extraction, reversal, and display of list
int main() {
    const int MaxListSize = 100;
    int Number[MaxListSize];
    int n;
    GetList(Number, MaxListSize, n);
    for (int i = 0; i < n/2; ++i) {
        // swap element from front of list with
        // corresponding element from the end of the list
        Swap(Number[i], Number[n-1-i]);
    }
    PutList(Number, n);
    return 0;
}

// GetList(): extract up to MaxN value from input into A
void GetList(int A[], int MaxN, int &n) {
    for (n = 0; (n < MaxN) && (cin >> A[n]);++n) {
        continue;
    }
}

// Swap(): interchange values of parameters
void Swap(int &Value1, int &Value2) {
    int RememberValue1 = Value1;
    Value1 = Value2;
    Value2 = RememberValue1;
}

// PutList(): display n elements of A
void PutList(const int A[], int n) {
    for (int i = 0; i < n; ++i) {
        cout << A[i] << endl;
    }
}
```

9.4 SORTING

Chapter 4 introduced the notion of sorting in Program 4.3, which displayed its three input values in nondecreasing order. We used the term nondecreasing rather than increasing to allow for duplicate values. Here we consider the general sorting problem of arranging the values in a list of arbitrary size into nondecreasing order.

A sort is often an iterative process that rearranges some of the values in the list on each iteration. For example, on iteration `i` the method known as

SelectionSort() finds the ith smallest element of A and exchanges the value of that element with the value of element A[i]. In another example, on iteration i the method known as InsertionSort() correctly places the value of A[i] with respect to the values stored in elements A[0] through A[i-1].

Some sorts are recursive rather than iterative. The recursive methods typically decompose a list into sublists that are then separately sorted. If it is necessary to complete the task, the sorted sublists are merged into a single sorted list.

We consider here the iterative sort InsertionSort(). Later in the chapter we consider the recursive sort QuickSort(). Function Selection-Sort() and another sort are considered in the exercises.

In the discussion that follows, we assume that the list to be sorted is a list of **char** values. The same sorts can be modified easily for other types of values.

9.4.1   The InsertionSort() method

On iteration i, the task of InsertionSort() is to place the value of element A[i] correctly with respect to the previously arranged values of elements A[0] through A[i-1]. For example, suppose the list to be sorted is

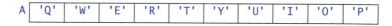

and that we have completed the iterations that placed the first seven values correctly among themselves. The list at that point would look like this:

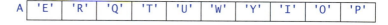

On the next iteration with i being 7, we are to place the value in A[7] correctly with respect to the sorted values in A[0] through A[6]. In this case, the value 'I' in A[7] should come between the value 'E' in A[0] and the value 'R' in A[1]. To do so, we first copy the value of A[7] to a temporary object v and then shift the values in A[1] through A[6]. At that point, the list would look like this:

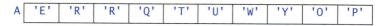

Observe that elements A[1] and A[2] both contain the value 'R'. This is because the elements A[1] through A[6] have been shifted to the right one position.

We then copy the value 'I' from object v to A[1] to complete the iteration.

Although there are several ways to accomplish the shifting process, the preferred method begins by comparing elements A[i] and A[i-1]. If these two elements are in the proper order, then no shifting is necessary for iteration i, as the first i elements of the list are already in sorted order—the sublist composed of the first i-1 elements was previously put in sorted order, and the value of A[i] is no smaller than the largest value in that sublist.

If A[i] is not less than A[i-1], then to make room for the correct value to be placed into A[i], a copy v of A[i] is made. Determining which element values require shifting is straightforward. An index variable j is used to indicate which element in A should be the target of the next shifting. The initial value for j is i, and the first value to be shifted is A[j-1]. Once the shift has been performed, j is decremented. It is decremented because its new value is the index of the location in A now available as a target of shifting, or if appropriate, as the location of value v. A test is then made to determine which case applies. If A[j-1] exists and if v is less than A[j-1], the shifting and comparison process is repeated. Otherwise, the right spot for value v has been found, and the shifting process is terminated.

For example, suppose i is now 8, and A[i], which is 'O', is less than A[i-1], which is 'Y'. A shifting process must be performed. A copy of 'O' is made and placed in v, and the index j is set to 8.

The shifting of A[j-1] and the decrementing of j results in the following situation:

Because 'O' is less than 'W', another shift is performed, copying the 'W' to A[j]. In addition, j is decremented.

Because 'O' is also less than 'U', another shift is performed, copying the 'U' to A[j]. Index j is again decremented.

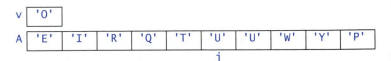

Because 'O' is also less than 'T', another shift is performed, copying the
'T' to A[j]. Index j is again decremented.

Because 'O' is also less than 'Q', another shift is performed, copying the
'Q' to A[j]. Index j is again decremented.

Because 'O' is also less than 'R', another shift is performed, copying the
'R' to A[j]. Index j is again decremented.

Because 'O' is not less than 'I', no shifting is necessary. Instead the 'O'
is copied from v into A[j].

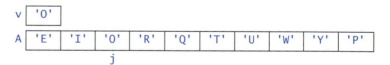

Listing 9.1 defines a **void** function InsertionSort() that implements
the preceding discussion. An outer **for** loop generates the various values for
index variable i, and an inner **do** loop controls the shifting process. Two terms
in the logical expression control whether the **do** loop is iterated again. The first
term determines whether j is greater than 0. If this term is true, element A[j-
1] is available for comparison; if instead j is 0, then the shifting has ended—
element A[j], which is A[0], is the proper location for v. The second term
determines whether A[j-1] is larger than v. If this term is true, additional
shifting is necessary. If instead A[j-1] is not larger than v, no more shifting is
necessary—element A[j] is the location for v. Observe that regardless of
whether the first or second term becomes false, when the loop is completed,
A[j] is the location for v.

Listing 9.1

InsertionSort()

```
// InsertionSort(): sort A using a shifting process
void InsertionSort(char A[], int n) {
    for (int i = 1; i < n; ++i) {
        // find proper spot for A[i]
        if (A[i] < A[i-1]) {
            // some shifting is necessary
            char v = A[i];      // copy A[i] so its spot can
                                // be used for shifting
            int j = i;          // set up index where
                                // available element spot
                                // is located

            do {
                A[j] = A[j-1];  // do the value shift
                --j;            // prepare for next
                                // comparison
            } while ((j > 0) && (A[j-1] > v));
            A[j] = v;           // put v in its spot
        }
    }
}
```

9.4.2   Quality of InsertionSort()

In analyzing a sorting algorithm, we are normally concerned with the total number of element comparisons and the total number of element copies/assignments performed by the sort. For InsertionSort(), the number of element comparisons and copies/assignments is maximized when, for each iteration i, the value of A[i] is the smallest of the first i element values (i.e., A is in reverse-sorted order). Therefore, when i is 1, at most one element comparison and three element copies/assignments are made. When i is 2, at most two element comparisons and four element copies/assignments are made.

In general, on iteration i, at most i element comparisons and i+2 element copies/assignments are made by InsertionSort(). Let n be the number of elements in list A. The total number of element comparisons is therefore at most $1 + 2 + \ldots + n-1$, which is proportional to n^2. The total number of element copies/assignments is at most $3 + 4 + \ldots + n+2$, which is also proportional to n^2. These totals reflect the worst-case performance of InsertionSort(). Because the performance is proportional to the square of the number of elements, we say that the algorithm has *quadratic* worst-case performance.

Suppose InsertionSort() is given a list of values in arbitrary order. For an average iteration, with an arbitrary initial ordering of values, value v is shifted on average into the middle element of the current sublist. Consequently, both the expected number of element comparisons and the expected number of element copies/assignments for an arbitrary list of n elements are proportional to one-half the worst-case performance. Because $n^2/2$ is proportional to n^2, the *arbitrary-case* performance of InsertionSort() is also quadratic.

When InsertionSort() is given a list of elements with the values already in sorted order, only one element comparison is made per iteration and no element copies/assignments are made. Therefore, in an already-sorted list of n elements, $n-1$ comparisons and no element copies/assignments are made.

This behavior represents the *best-case performance* of `InsertionSort()`. Because the performance is proportional to the number of elements, we say that `InsertionSort()` has a *linear* best-case performance.

Many data processing experts believe that the typical list to be sorted has been systematically generated and is already nearly sorted. A nearly sorted list is hard to quantify precisely, but roughly speaking, in a nearly sorted list, the starting position of each value is near its position in the sorted version of the list. Under this scenario, both the average number of element comparisons and the average number of element copies/assignments performed by `Insertion-Sort()` are proportional to *n*. Because of this performance quality, `Insertion-tionSort()` is typically the sorting method of choice when we know that the data was systematically generated.

Self-check Questions

14. Can arrays be passed by value in C++?

15. Write the body of the function `reverse` that takes an array of characters as input and returns them in another array in reverse order. For example given the definitions

```
const int N = 12;
input[N] = "tnedutS doog a m'I";
output[N] = "";
reverse(input, output, N);
cout << output << endl;
```

would output

```
I'm a good Student
```

16. Write an **int** function `LessThan()` with three formal parameters: an **int** array a, an **int** n which is the number of elements in the array, and an **int** value v. The value v is to be optional with a default value of 0. Function `LessThan()` returns the number of elements in list a[0], a[1], ..., a[n-1] that are less than v.

17. Write a function called `Equal` that takes two integer arrays and the size of the array as parameters. Function `Equal()` returns **true** if the two arrays are identical; otherwise it returns **false**. Identical means the arrays contain the same values in the same order.

18. Write a function called `IsSorted` that takes an integer array and the size of the array as parameters. Function `IsSorted()` returns **true** if the array is in ascending sorted order; otherwise it returns **false**.

19. A sorting algorithm that is often used because it is simple is BubbleSort. BubbleSort is so named because the smallest item "bubbles" to the top

of the array when the algorithm is applied. Unfortunately, it is a very inefficient algorithm. The basic idea is to successively compare adjacent elements and swap them if they are out of order. If we are sorting the list into descending order (smallest elements appear first in the array), the smaller elements slowly "bubble" to the top, while the largest elements sink to the bottom. After the first pass, the largest element is at the bottom of the array (i.e., in element a[N-1]). After the second pass the second largest element is in its correct position (i.e., in element a[N-2]), and so on.

Write a program that accepts a number from standard input. This is the size of the array to sort. Using the random number class `RandInt`, fill the array with random values and then sort it using a bubblesort algorithm. Run your program with an array size of 4,000 and then 8,000. Do you notice any significant difference in execution times between the two runs?

20.   Write a program that produces a histogram of the characters used in a textfile. Your program should prompt for and accept a file name that contains ASCII text. Your program reads the file and counts the number of times each alphabetic character is used. Do not distinguish between upper and lowercase characters. After processing the file, the program writes the histogram to stream `cout`.

9.5   CONTAINER CLASSES

As previously discussed, C++ imposes significant restrictions on the use of arrays—a function return type cannot be an array; an array cannot be passed by value, and an array cannot be the target of an assignment. Two other cumbersome restrictions are that the size of the array must be a compile-time constant and that an array cannot be resized—once an array is created we can neither increase nor decrease its number of elements.

For many software projects, the restrictions on arrays have forced developers to use alternative list representations that are often nonportable. The cost of using nonportable representations can be quite high because developers must create and support multiple versions of their software. This expense can now be avoided by using the Standard Template Library (STL) and its container classes as alternatives to arrays.

The container classes of the STL are a set of generic list representations that allow programmers to specify which types of elements their particular lists are to hold. Besides being free of array restrictions, the container classes are extensible. For example, we can derive specialized container classes that automatically perform subscript checking.

Six of eight major container classes view a list primarily as a sequence of elements. The containers supporting this view are `deque`, `list`, `priority_queue`, `queue`, `stack`, and `vector`. The other two container classes `map` and `set` view a list in a more associative manner. Brief descriptions of all eight classes are given in Table 9.1. The classes `priority_queue`, `queue`, and `stack` are sometimes known as *container adapters* or just *adapters*, as these classes are built (adapted) using other containers.

The implementation of container classes in the STL uses the C++ *class template* mechanism. Using formal parameters, known as *template parameters*, as placeholders for particular types and values, a class template describes the general form a class can take. To generate a specific class from a template, the actual types and values of interest are supplied within angled brackets after the name of the template. This use of templates gives the STL its name.[†]

The following code segment defines three lists A, B, and C whose types are classes generated using the container class templates.

```
deque<int> A(10,1);        // A has 10 int elements all
                           // equal to 1
vector<Rational> B(5);     // B has 5 Rational elements
                           // all equal to 0/1
queue<float> C;            // C is an empty list of
                           // floats -- it has no elements
```

List A is of type `deque<int>`; list B is of type `vector<Rational>`; and list C is of type `queue<float>`. The elements of the lists are, respectively, of type `int`, `Rational`, and `float`. As required, the element type for each list is a template parameter contained within the angled brackets after the name of the container template. Observe that constructor parameters are used to specify the initial number of elements and the initial values of those elements. In the next section, we will discuss in detail the different forms the container constructors can take.

Although our three container definitions each supplied one type template parameter, the nonassociative container class templates can generally take either one or two parameters. The first template parameter is always the type of value that the container is to hold (as was the case in the definitions of A, B, and C). If the second parameter is supplied, it is a class that implements a method for allocating memory for the elements of the list.

The associative container class templates can take either one, two, or three template parameters with both the second and third parameters being optional. The first parameter is the type of value the container is to hold. The second parameter is a class that implements a scheme for comparing list elements. The third parameter is a memory allocation parameter.

The `vector` class template is the dominant list representation; therefore, we will use it in subsequent container class examples. The header file for this class is named `vector`. Because the default memory allocation method works in most programming situations, our presentation of class template `vector` ignores the optional allocation parameter.

[†]   We will explore how to develop class and function templates in Chapter 14.

Table 9.1

Major container classes

Container	Description
deque	Supports constant-time random access to individual elements in its sequence. In addition, a deque can insert to or delete from the beginning or end of its sequence in constant time.
list	Supports constant-time sequential access to individual elements in its sequence. In addition, a list can insert or delete an element from anywhere within its sequence in constant time.
priority_queue	Supports priority-based access. A priority_queue provides amortized logarithmic-time access to the element with highest priority. In addition, a priority_queue can insert or delete an element from anywhere within its sequence in amortized logarithmic time.
queue	Supports first-in-first-out element access. A queue provides constant-time access to the beginning or end of its sequence. In addition, a queue can both insert to the end of the sequence and delete from the beginning of the sequence in constant time.
stack	Supports last-in-first-out element access. A stack provides constant-time access to the end of the sequence. In addition, a stack can insert to or delete from the end of its sequence in constant time.
vector	Supports constant-time random access to individual elements in its sequence. In amortized constant time, a vector can insert to or delete from the end of its sequence. An insertion or deletion elsewhere can take time proportional to the size of the sequence.
map	Supports constant-time sequential access to individual elements in the list. A unique key value is associated with each element value. Access to an element based on its key value can be done in time proportional to the log of the number of elements in the list.
set	Supports constant-time sequential access to individual elements in its list. Access to an element based on its value can be done in time proportional to the log of the number of elements in the list.

9.6 CLASS VECTOR

The `vector` class template provides four constructors for defining a list of elements.

- A default constructor to define an empty list.
- A copy constructor to make a copy of an existing list.
- A constructor with a parameter that specifies the initial size of the list. The elements are initialized using the default constructor of the list element type.
- A constructor with two parameters. The first parameter specifies the initial size of the list; the second parameter specifies the initial value of each list element.

Suppose the following code segment giving values to objects N, M, and length has been executed.

```
const int N = 20;
const int M = 40;
cout << "Size of list to produce: ";
int length;
cin >> length;
```

The values of these objects are used in the construction of `vector` objects A, B, C, D, and E.

```
vector<int> A(10);        // vector of 10 ints
vector<char> B(M);        // vector of 40 chars
vector<float> C(M*N);     // vector of 800 floats
vector<int> D(length);    // vector of length ints
vector<Rational> E(N);    // vector of 20 Rationals
                          // with elements set to 0/1
```

Each of the five `vector` objects is a list of individual elements. The initial sizes of the lists come from parameters to the constructors. In particular, the initial size of list D comes from the object whose value is not known until run time!

Each list element is itself an object that can be used like any other object. Because the fundamental types do not have constructors that automatically initialize objects of their types to particular values, the elements of lists A, B, C, and D are uninitialized. However, the elements of E are initialized because the `Rational` class has a default constructor that produces the representation 0/1.

Suppose the following definition is also in effect.

```
Rational r(1,2);
```

We use r in the definition of a vector F. This definition and the definitions of G, H, I, and J each specify a particular initial value for their list elements.

```
vector<Rational> F(N,r);  // vector of 20 Rationals
                          // with elements set to 1/2
vector<int> G(10,1);      // vector of 10 ints
                          // with elements set to 1
vector<char> H(M,'h');    // vector of 40 chars
                          // with elements set to 'h'
vector<float> I(M*N,0);   // vector of 800 floats
```

```
                                    // with elements set to 0
    vector<int> J(length,2);        // vector of length ints
                                    // with elements set to 2
```

The `vector` copy constructor enables us to make a duplicate of a list. For example, given the following code segment, R is a list of 20 `Rational` elements with each element initialized to 1/2; S is a list of 10 `int` elements with each element initialized to 1; and T is a list of length `int` elements with each element initialized to 2.

```
    vector<Rational> R(F);     // vector of length 20
                               // duplicating F
    vector<int> S(G);          // vector of length 10
                               // duplicating G
    vector<int> T(J);          // vector of length length
                               // duplicating J
```

Two `vector` objects with the same element types can be assigned to each other. For example, suppose the following three definitions are in effect.

```
    vector<int> U(10,4);       // vector of 10 ints
                               // with elements set to 0
    vector<int> V(5,1);        // vector of 5 ints
                               // with elements set to 1
    vector<char> W(10,'a');    // vector of 5 chars
                               // with elements set to 'a'
```

These vectors can be represented pictorially as

U	4	4	4	4	4	4	4	4	4	4
V	1	1	1	1	1					
W	'a'	'a'	'a'	'a'	'a'	'a'	'a'	'a'	'a'	'a'

Given these definitions, the following assignment is valid and makes V a duplicate of U.

```
    V = U;                     // V is a duplicate of U
```

The assignment operator = is a member operator of the `vector` class. The assignment operator is defined whenever the source and target objects represent lists of the same type, even if the lists are not the same size. If it is necessary, the assignment operator will resize the assignment target so that it has the same number of elements as the assignment source. Thus after the assignment to V, the three vectors have the following representation.

U	4	4	4	4	4	4	4	4	4	4
V	4	4	4	4	4	4	4	4	4	4
W	'a'	'a'	'a'	'a'	'a'	'a'	'a'	'a'	'a'	'a'

Although U and W have the same number of elements, the following assignment does not compile.

```
W = U;                          // invalid
```

The assignment does not compile because U and W are of different types—U is of type vector<**int**> and W is of type vector<**char**>.

Programmer Alert

> ***Use the right delimiter***
>
> Consider the following code segment. What type of object is A?
>
> ```
> vector<int> A[10];
> ```
>
> Object A is not a vector<**int**> object with 10 elements of type **int**. The reason follows from the use of the 10 in the definition. The 10 is contained within brackets and not parentheses. Thus object A is in fact an array of size 10 whose elements are of type vector<**int**>. Remember it is always prudent to examine your definitions carefully.

The default constructor of the vector class template creates an *empty list*, that is, a list with no elements.

```
vector<int> X;              // empty int vector
vector<char> Y;             // empty char vector
```

Empty lists can acquire elements either through vector assignment or through use of the vector member functions insert() and push_back(). These and other vector member functions are described in Tables 9.2 and 9.3. In both tables, size_type is an unsigned integral type; reference is a type that is convertible to T&; const_reference is a type that is convertible to **const** T&; and const_iterator, const_reverse_iterator, iterator, and reverse_iterator are implementation-dependent pointerlike types to a T object. These types are declared in the class template definition for vector.

9.6.1   Randomly accessing a vector's elements

The vector template class provides several member functions and operators for accessing the elements that make up the vector. These member methods can be grouped into two categories: random access and sequential access methods. A *random access method* puts no restrictions on which element can be referenced in any given access. For example, when using a random access method on a vector<**int**> object A with 10 elements, in successive operations we can access the *i*th and *j*th elements where *i* and *j* are any values in the range 0 … 9. As indicated in Table 9.1, most of the container classes do not provide random access methods; instead, they provide sequential access methods that require the elements to be accessed in forward or reverse list order.

The principal random access methods are overloadings of the subscript operator []. The subscript operator is overloaded for both **const** and non-**const** vector objects. As a non-**const** subscript operation performs a

Table 9.2

Some member functions of the class template vector

`size_type size() const`
Returns the numbers of elements in the `vector`.

`bool empty() const`
Returns true if there are no vector elements; otherwise, it returns false.

`reference front()`
Returns a reference to the first element of the `vector`.

`const_reference front() const`
Returns a constant reference to the first element of the `vector`.

`reference back()`
Returns a reference to the last element of the `vector`.

`const_reference back() const`
Returns a constant reference to the last element of the `vector`.

`iterator insert(iterator pos, const T &val = T())`
Inserts a copy of `val` at position `pos` of the `vector` and returns the position of the copy into the `vector`.

`iterator erase(iterator pos)`
Removes the element of the `vector` at position `pos`.

`void pop_back()`
Removes the last element of the `vector`

`void push_back(const T &val)`
Inserts a copy of `val` after the last element of the `vector`.

`void resize(size_type s, T val = T())`
Let n be the current number of elements in the `vector`. If s > n, then the number of elements is increased to s with the new elements added after the existing elements. The initial value of the new elements is `val`. If s < n, then the number of elements is decreased to s by erasing elements from the end of the `vector`. If s equals n, then no action is taken.

`void vector::clear()`
Removes all elements from the `vector`.

`void vector::swap(vector<T> &V)`
The current `vector` and `vector` V swap values. This operation is typically much more efficient than an individual swapping of the elements.

`reference at(int i)`
If `i` is a valid index, it returns the `i`th element; otherwise an exception is generated.

`const_reference at(int i)`
If `i` is a valid index, it returns the `i`th element; otherwise an exception is generated. The element that is returned cannot be modified

`iterator begin()`
Returns an iterator pointing to the first element of the `vector`.

`const_iterator begin()`
Returns an iterator pointing to the first element of the `vector`. Elements dereferenced by this iterator cannot be modified.

`iterator end()`
> Returns an iterator pointing immediately beyond the last element.

`const_iterator end()`
> Returns an iterator pointing immediately beyond the last element. Elements dereferenced by this iterator cannot be modified.

`reverse_iterator rbegin()`
> Returns a reverse iterator pointing to the last element of the `vector`.

`const_reverse_iterator rbegin()`
> Returns a reverse iterator pointing to the last element of the `vector`. Elements dereferenced by this iterator cannot be modified.

`iterator rend()`
> Returns a reverse iterator pointing immediately ahead of the first element.

`const_reverse_iterator rend()`
> Returns a reverse iterator pointing immediately ahead of the first element. Elements dereferenced by this iterator cannot be modified.

reference return, the resulting value can be either accessed or modified. For a **const** subscript operation, the resulting value can only be accessed.

The member subscript operator works in a manner similar to array subscripting. Each element of a `vector` has its own subscript value. The first element has subscript value 0, the second element has subscript value 1, and so on.

Program 9.2 demonstrates the use of the subscript operator on a 10-element `vector` A whose elements A[0], A[1], ..., and A[9] are initially all 0. Pictorially, A's initial representation is

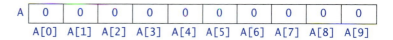

Program 9.2 performs a series of accesses and modifications to the individual elements of A. The last of these modifications is an extraction into element A[k]. If the value extracted from the standard input stream is 88, then the final representation of A would be

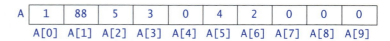

9.6.2   Sequential access methods

For compatibility with other container classes, `vector` also provides sequential access methods. As noted, a sequential access method puts restrictions on which elements can be referenced in a given access. The restrictions are based on whether the sequential access method is *bidirectional* or *unidirectional*. If the sequential access method is bidirectional, the elements accessed in consecutive references must be adjacent to each other in the list. If the sequential

Program 9.2

Demonstrate vector subscript operations

```cpp
// Program 9.2: Demonstrate use of vector
#include <iostream>
#include <string>
#include <vector>

using namespace std;

int main() {
    vector<int> A(10, 0);    // 10 elements all set to 0
    int i = 6;
    int j = 2;
    int k = 1;
    A[0] = 1;                // element 0 of A given value 1
    A[i] = 2;                // element i of A given value 2
    A[j] = A[i] + 3;         // element j of A given value
                             // of element i of A plus 2
    A[j+1] = A[i] + A[0];    // element j+1 of A given value
                             // of element i of A plus
                             // value of element 0 of A
    A[A[j]] = 4;             // element A[j] of A given
                             // value 4
    cout << A[2];            // element 2 of A is displayed
    cin >> A[k];             // element k of A given next
                             // extracted value

    return 0;
}
```

access method is unidirectional, then the next element that can be accessed is the element that occurs immediately after the current element being accessed. The sequential access methods provided by vector are all bidirectional.

The vector sequential access methods are implemented using *iterators*. The value of an iterator object is like a pointer. An iterator object, or just iterator for short, points to either an element in the list or to sentinels that conceptually surround the sequence of elements making up the list. This representation is demonstrated in the following figure, where iterator p is associated with a five-element list A of type vector<int>. In particular, p points to the fourth element of A. The shaded boxes in the figure represent sentinels that conceptually surround the elements of the vector.

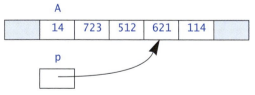

To reference the element at which an iterator points, we use the unary prefix operator *. In this context, the * is called the *dereferencing* operator. When this operator is applied to an iterator, it returns a reference to the value at which the iterator points. Because the dereferencing operation performs a reference return, the resulting value can be either viewed or modified. For example, code segment

```cpp
cout << *p << endl;
*p = 821;
cout << A[3] << endl;
```

produces as its output

    621
    821

This output occurs because p points to the fourth element of A. Thus a modification of the value to which p points, in fact, modifies A. In particular, A[3] is modified.

    A version of the dereferencing operator for **const** objects is also supplied by the vector class. For **const** objects, we can access the value of the element to which an iterator points, but the element cannot be modified.

    The increment operator ++ is defined for iterators. When invoked on an iterator, the increment operator attempts to update the iterator in question to point to the next element in the sequence of elements that make up the list. However, if there are no more elements in the list, the iterator instead points to a trailing sentinel. For our iterator p currently pointing to A[3], the operation ++p causes p to point to the last element of A, which is A[4]. Objects A and p now have the following depiction:

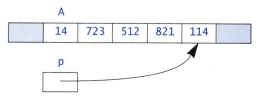

    If the operation ++p is again executed, p would point to a sentinel. The depiction of A and p would be that of the following figure:

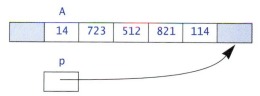

    If the iterator is a bidirectional iterator, the decrement operator -- is also defined. Invoking the decrement operator causes the iterator in question to point to the previous element in the list. For example, the code segment

    --p;
    --p;
    --p;

would cause p to point back three positions. In particular, p would now point to A[2].

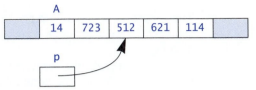

If there are no previous elements in the list, the iterator points to a sentinel.

The iterator p that we have been using is a *forward* iterator. A forward iterator views a list as a sequence that starts with the first element of the list. The STL also provides a reverse iterator view that perceives a list as a sequence that starts with the last element. The vector class supports this view. Suppose q is a reverse iterator pointing to A[3].

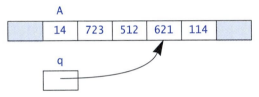

An increment operation

    ++q;

would cause q to point to A[2] because q views our list in reverse order.

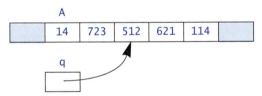

If two decrement operations

    --q;
    --q;

are then performed, q would point to A[4] because a decrement operation brings a reverse iterator toward the rear of the list.

The vector template class provides four methods that return bidirectional iterators: begin(), end(), rbegin(), and rend(). As indicated in Table 9.3, begin() returns an iterator pointing to the first element of the list;

`end()` returns an iterator pointing to a sentinel immediately beyond the last element of the list; `rbegin()` returns an iterator pointing to the last element in the list; and `rend()` returns an iterator pointing to a sentinel immediately ahead of the first element of the list. A depiction of these iterators for vector A is given in the following figure:

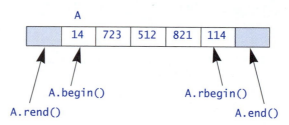

Note that the iterators returned by `rbegin()` and `rend()` view the list in the reverse form. For such iterators, the increment operator ++ moves the iterator toward the front of the list, and the decrement operator -- moves the iterator toward the rear of the list. In a sense, `rbegin()` and `rend()` return iterators facing backwards to the iterators returned by `begin()` and `end()`.

To illustrate these iterator concepts, first suppose `List` is a `vector<int>` object that has been initialized with the following code segment:

```
vector<int> List(5);
for (int i = 0; i < List.size(); ++i) {
    List[i] = 100 + i;
}
```

Thus `List` has the following representation:

	100	101	102	103	104	

The iterator types for `vector` objects are defined in the `vector` class template. When the `vector<int>` class is generated, the iterator types `vector<int>::iterator` and `vector<int>::reverse_iterator` are defined. As these type names are unwieldy, programs using iterators often use the **typedef** statement to produce a more syntactically convenient name. For example, the following **typedef** statements allow us to use `iterator` and `reverse_iterator` rather than `vector<int>::iterator` and `vector<int>::reverse_iterator`.

```
typedef vector<int>::iterator iterator;
typedef vector<int>::reverse_iterator reverse_iterator;
```

With the definitions of `List`, `iterator`, and `reverse_iterator` in effect, the code segment

```
iterator p = List.begin();
cout << *p << " ";
++p;
cout << *p << " ";
++p;
cout << *p << " ";
--p;
cout << *p << endl;
reverse_iterator q = List.rbegin();
cout << *q << " ";
++q;
cout << *q << " ";
++q;
cout << *q << " ";
--q;
cout << *q << endl;
```

produces output

```
100 101 102 101
104 103 102 103
```

Because iterator p starts off pointing to the first element in the list, the initial value displayed on the first output line is the value of `List[0]`. After this insertion, p is twice incremented, and after each increment, an insertion statement displays the element to which p currently points. Because p is a forward iterator advancing toward the end of the list, these operations cause `List[1]` and then `List[2]` to be displayed. Next, iterator p is decremented, and an insertion statement displays the element to which p now points (`List[1]`).

The second output line is produced by manipulating a reverse iterator q that starts off pointing to the last element in `List`. Because q is a reverse iterator, the increment operator advances the iterator toward the front of the list and the decrement operator brings the iterator toward the rear of the list. After displaying the last `List` element `List[4]`, q is twice incremented, and after each increment, an insertion statement displays the element to which q currently points. Thus `List[3]` and then `List[2]` are displayed in succession. Iterator q is then decremented, and an insertion statement displays the element to which q now points (`List[3]`).

The next code segment demonstrates a more typical use of iterators. In this segment, the elements in `List` are totaled using an iterator `li`.

```
int Sum = 0;
for (iterator li = List.begin(); li != List.end();
 ++li) {
    Sum = Sum + *li;
};
```

Like iterator p, iterator `li` starts off pointing to the first element in the `vector` `List`. The loop iterates while `li` is not pointing to the sentinel immediately beyond the end of the list. Each iteration adds the value of the element to which `li` currently points to the running total. To prepare for the next evaluation of the loop test expression, the iterator is incremented.

9.6.3   Passing a vector

By design, `vector` objects can be used like objects of other types; for example, they can be passed by value or by reference, and they can be returned by a function. There is no special notation beyond normal function syntax to pass or return a `vector` object.

Listing 9.2 contains functions `GetList()` and `PutList()`. These functions are the `vector` analogs of the similarly named functions developed for Program 9.1 that manipulated array lists.

```
void GetList(vector<int> &A) {
    int n = 0;
    while ((n < A.size()) && (cin >> A[n])) {
        ++n;
    }
    A.resize(n);
}
void PutList(vector<int> &A) {
    for (int i = 0; i < A.size(); ++i) {
        cout << A[i] << endl;
    }
}
void GetValues(vector<int> &A) {
    A.resize(0);
    int Val;
    while (cin >> Val) {
        A.push_back(Val);
    }
}
```

Function `GetList()` names its formal parameter A. It uses local object n to indicate how many elements have been extracted so far. The loop iterates only while both A has room to store another value and there is, in fact, a value to store. After the loop is completed, the `vector` member function `resize()` is invoked. The parameter to `resize()` specifies the new desired size of the `vector`. For our task, A's size will be either left alone or shrunk. However, `resize()` can also be used to increase the size of a list. The reason we invoke `resize()` is so that subsequent users of the actual parameter can correctly inspect its number of elements through the object's `size()` method.

An alternative to `GetList()` is also given in Listing 9.2. The alternative is `GetValues()`. Function `GetValues()` extracts the remaining input values and makes them elements of the `vector`. Unlike `GetList()`, `GetValues()` is not preconstrained to extract at most a particular number of elements. `GetValues()` accomplishes its task principally through the use of the `vector` member function `push_back()`. Function `GetValues()` begins by resizing its formal parameter A so that the parameter represents an empty list. Alternatively, we could have used the member function `clear()`. Like `resize()`, `clear()` is described in Table 9.3.

The **while** loop of `GetValues()` iterates once for each extracted value for `Val`. The size of the `vector` A is increased with each extraction through the use of `vector` member function `push_back()`. Function `push_back()` increases the size of its invoking `vector` by adding a new element to the end of its list. The value of that new element is the value of `push_back()`'s parameter. Thus by repeatedly executing `A.push_back(Val)`, we ensure that A is correctly set—each extracted value is copied to the current end of the list.

Note that a `push_back()` invocation can be a somewhat expensive operation. Space for a new element might require repositioning the entire vector in memory. If sufficient memory cannot be found, an exception is generated.

Listing 9.3 presents an overloading of the extraction operator for `vector<int>` objects. The form of the overloading is similar to one given for `Rational` objects in Listing 8.7—the left operand of the operator is the `istream` from which the extractions are to be performed, and the right operand is the `vector` object to be updated. Except for the addition of a **return** statement, the body of the operator is similar to that of `GetValues()`. The return of `sin` is done by reference so that the extraction can be part of a larger extraction statement.

Listing 9.3

Vector extraction

```
istream& operator>>(istream& sin, vector<int> &A) {
    A.resize(0);
    int Val;
    while (sin >> Val) {
        A.push_back(Val);
    }
    return sin;

}
```

The following code segment demonstrates the use of our overloaded operator.

```
vector<int> List;
cout << "Enter list of numbers to be processed: ";
cin >> List;
```

If standard input contains the following

```
30 4 54
21 6 54
```

then, after executing the preceding code segment, `List` would have as its representation

List	30	4	54	21	6	54

Function `GetValues()` and the overloading of the extraction operator for `vector<int>` objects demonstrate our claim that the container classes offer greater program flexibility than arrays offer. With this function and operator, we can extract and store a list of arbitrary size. Such extractions would not be possible using arrays, because they must be of fixed size.

We next consider a `vector` function `Search()` that is the analog to the array function `Search()` presented previously in this chapter. The new function has two formal parameters. The first parameter A is of type `vector<int>`,

Programming Tip

> *Generic vector extraction*
>
> In Chapter 14, we consider template functions and classes in detail. As a foretaste of this chapter, consider the following:
>
> ```
> template<class T>
> void GetValues(vector<T> &A) {
>    A.resize(0);
>    T Val;
>    while (cin >> Val) {
>       A.push_back(Val);
>    }
> }
> ```
>
> The syntax **template <class T>** indicates that what follows is a generic form. In this case, the form of a function is given. This function template allows different functions to be instantiated based upon the particular type of **vector** used as the actual parameter. For example, with the following definitions in effect
>
> ```
> vector<int> X;
> vector<Rational> Y;
> ```
>
> the invocations
>
> ```
> GetValues(X);
> GetValues(Y);
> ```
>
> cause functions
>
> ```
> void GetValues(vector<int> &A) {
>    A.resize(0);
>    int Val;
>    while (cin >> Val) {
>       A.push_back(Val);
>    }
> }
> void GetValues(vector<Rational> &A) {
>    A.resize(0);
>    Rational Val;
>    while (cin >> Val) {
>       A.push_back(Val);
>    }
> }
> ```
>
> to be defined and invoked.

and it represents the list to be searched; the second parameter is the **int** key value Key.

```
int Search(const vector<int> &A, int Key) {
   for (int i = 0; i < A.size(); ++i) {
      if (A[i] == Key) {
         return i;
      }
   }
   return A.size();
}
```

The implementation is straightforward. An index i is used to iterate through the list values. If the value is found, the current index is returned. If the value is

Programming Tip

Automatic subscript checking of list elements

As indicated in Table 9.3, the `vector` class template provides a member function `at()` that expects as its parameter an index value `i` into the list. If the index is valid, a reference to the `i`th element of the `vector` is returned. Otherwise, an exception is generated. We can use inheritance (see Chapter 13) to derive a class that overloads the subscript operators so that index checking is automatically performed in conjunction with the subscript operators. A template class `SafeVector` with this behavior is given below. Other methods for developing containers are considered in Chapters 11 and 14.

```
template <class T>
 class SafeVector : public vector<T> {
    public:
        SafeVector() : vector<T>() {}
        SafeVector(int n) : vector<T>(n) {}
        SafeVector(int n, T v) : vector<T>(n,v) {}
        T& operator[](int i) {
            return at(i);
        }
        const T& operator[](int i) const {
            return at(i);
        }
};
```

not found, then the size of the list is returned. Thus this function behaves in a manner comparable to the array version of `Search()`.

One of the advantages of using container classes is that many basic tasks involving containers are defined in the algorithm sublibrary of the STL. These functions typically use iterators to process the elements of the container. For example, the algorithm sublibrary contains a function `find()` that performs a task comparable to `search()`. The header file for this library is `algorithm`.

Function `find()` expects three parameters. The first two parameters are iterators `p` and `q` into a container, the third parameter is a value `v`. Function `find()` determines whether there is an occurrence of `v` among the elements in the list starting at `p` and ending immediately before `q`. If the value `v` is in the list, then `find()` returns an iterator pointing to the first occurrence of `v` in the list. Otherwise, `find()` returns the value `q`. Using the `vector` `List` of our previous example, the invocation

```
find(List.begin(), List.end(), 54)
```

returns an iterator pointing to `List[2]`, and the invocation

```
find(List.begin(), List.end(), 9)
```

returns an iterator equal to `List.end()`. `List.end()` is returned for this invocation because 9 is not one of the values in the list.

A list of some of the functions defined in the algorithm sublibrary is given in Appendix B. Several of those functions can replace functions that we develop in this text. However, the development in the text is worthwhile because the underlying algorithm techniques are useful in other problem situations. It will be our practice to indicate during the discussion when standard algorithm functions are available for the task.

9.7 QUICKSORT

Although the function `InsertionSort()` discussed previously in this chapter has excellent average-case and best-case performances, its worst-case and arbitrary-case performances are substandard. For time-critical client applications that need to sort a list of n elements, `InsertionSort()` can be unacceptable. Instead, such applications often use the `QuickSort()` method. The `Quick-Sort()` method when fully implemented has best-case, arbitrary-case, and average-case performances that are all proportional to the expression $n \log n$. This performance is sometimes known as *linearithmic* performance. We note that the worst-case performance of `QuickSort()` is quadratic and arises when the values in the list are in reverse or nearly reverse sorted order. However, such pathological cases are generally deemed too infrequent to matter.

The `QuickSort()` method begins by choosing a pivot value. The list is then rearranged into three sublists or *partitions*. The middle sublist is composed of an element whose value is the *pivot value*; the values of the elements in the left sublist are no larger than the pivot value, and the values of the elements in the right sublist are no smaller than the pivot value. Because the sublists are partitioned in this manner, the left and right sublists can be sorted independently to produce a totally sorted list. The sublists are sorted by making recursive calls to the `QuickSort()` function. For example, suppose we are to again sort the following list:

B | 'Q' | 'W' | 'E' | 'R' | 'T' | 'Y' | 'U' | 'I' | 'O' | 'P' |

To sort vector B, the invocation of function `QuickSort()` would be

```
QuickSort(B, 0, B.Size() - 1);
```

If `'P'` is the pivot value, partitioning could rearrange A (we will now use the formal parameter name) in the following manner (the shaded portion is the middle sublist):

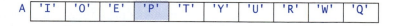

A | 'I' | 'O' | 'E' | 'P' | 'T' | 'Y' | 'U' | 'R' | 'W' | 'Q' |

We can now separately sort the left sublist A[0] through A[2] and the right sublist A[4] through A[9]. Doing so sorts the entire list.

If the pivot element value is chosen well, then the left and right sublists both have approximately $n/2$ elements. It can be shown mathematically that this partitioning method leads to linearithmic performance.

Listing 9.4 provides the header file `qsort.h`. The header file is a collection of prototypes for functions `QuickSort()`, `Pivot()`, `Partition()`, and `Swap()`. Listing 9.5 provides the implementation file `qsort.cpp` for the `QuickSort()` method.

Listing 9.4

Header file for qsort.h
for QuickSort()

```
#ifndef QSORT_H
#define QSORT_H

#include <vector>
using namespace std;

void QuickSort(vector<char> &A, int left, int right);
void Pivot(vector<char> &A, int left, int right);
int Partition(vector<char> &A, int left, int right);
void Swap(char &Value1, char &Value2);

#endif
```

Function `QuickSort()` first makes sure that the list to be sorted requires some processing (that is, at least two elements need to be ordered). Indexes `left` and `right` indicate the left-most and right-most elements of the portion of list A to be sorted in the current invocation of `QuickSort()`. If there are indeed multiple list elements, then function `Pivot()` is invoked first.

The task of `Pivot()` is to rearrange the list so that the pivot value is in `A[left]`. `Pivot()` also ensures that the value of `A[right]` is no smaller than the pivot value. In our basic implementation, `Pivot()` compares elements `A[left]` and `A[right]`. If `A[left]` is greater than `A[right]`, the element values are swapped. (In the exercises, we consider a more intelligent function `Pivot()`.) Suppose the list A to be sorted had the following representation before the invocation of `Pivot()`:

A | 'Q' | 'W' | 'E' | 'R' | 'T' | 'Y' | 'U' | 'I' | 'O' | 'P'

After the invocation of `Pivot()`, A would have the following representation:

A | 'P' | 'W' | 'E' | 'R' | 'T' | 'Y' | 'U' | 'I' | 'O' | 'Q'

`QuickSort()` next partitions the elements of list A that have subscripts in the range `left` through `right`. This task is done by function `Partition()`. When `Partition()` is done constructing the three sublists, it returns the index of the element that now contains the pivot value. `QuickSort()` then performs two recursive calls to sort the elements to the left and right of the pivot element.

The bulk of the sorting is done by the invocations of `Partition()`. This function begins by making a copy `pivot` of the pivot value `A[left]`. Two index variables `i` and `j` are then defined. These indexes are used to index elements from the left and right sides of the list, respectively.

The major loop in `Partition()` is a **do** loop that iterates until the indexes `i` and `j` *cross* (the value of the left-side index `i` is greater than the value of the right-side index `j`).

Listing 9.5

Implementation file for
qsort.cpp for
QuickSort()

```cpp
#include "qsort.h"
// QuickSort(): a recursive partitioning-based sort
void QuickSort(vector<char> &A, int left, int right) {
   if (left < right) {
       Pivot(A, left, right);
       int k = Partition(A, left, right);
       QuickSort(A, left, k-1);
       QuickSort(A, k+1, right);
   }
}

// Pivot(): prepare A for partitioning
void Pivot(vector<char> &A, int left, int right) {
   if (A[left] > A[right])
       Swap(A[left], A[right]);
}

// Partition(): rearrange A into 3 sublists, a sublist
// A[left]    A[j-1] of values at most A[j], a sublist A[j],
// and a sublist A[j+1]    A[right] of values at least A[j]
int Partition(vector<char> &A, int left, int right) {
   char pivot = A[left];
   int i = left;
   int j = right+1;
   do {
       do ++i; while (A[i] < pivot);
       do --j; while (A[j] > pivot);
       if (i < j) {
           Swap(A[i], A[j]);
       }
   } while (i < j);
   Swap(A[j], A[left]);
   return j;
}

// Swap(): interchange elements
void Swap(char &Value1, char &Value2) {
   char RememberValue1 = Value1;
   Value1 = Value2;
   Value2 = RememberValue1;
}
```

For each iteration of the **do** loop, i is incremented in an inner **do** loop until an element is found whose value is at least pivot. Next j is decremented in another inner **do** loop until an element is found whose value is at most pivot. Such elements must exist because Pivot() made A[left] the smaller of A[left] and A[right], and it made A[right] the larger of A[left] and A[right]. We say that A[left] and A[right] act as *sentinels* whose values guarantee that both inner loops of Partition() terminate.

If after the updating of indexes i and j, it is determined that these two indexes have not crossed, then the values of A[i] and A[j] are in the wrong partitions and need to be swapped. For our example, the situation immediately before the first partition swap is the following:

A	'P'	'W'	'E'	'R'	'T'	'Y'	'U'	'I'	'O'	'Q'
	i									j

Programming Tip

How fast can you sort?

In the worst case, both `InsertionSort()` and `QuickSort()` make approximately n^2 element comparisons and element copies/assignments to sort a list with n elements. But we can do better. In the exercises, we consider `MergeSort()`, which for every n-element instance uses on the order of $n \log n$ element comparisons and copies/assignments. No sort that uses comparisons to determine the ordering of the elements can do better. This fact about sorting algorithms can be shown using what is known as an *information-theoretic* argument.

If a list is composed of n distinct values, then there are $n!$ possible orderings of the values. When the first element comparison is made, one-half of the $n!$ orderings are still candidates to be the sorted ordering. For example, if the ith element is smaller than the jth element, then orderings where the value of the ith element precedes the value of the jth element are valid possibilities. After the second comparison, in the worst-case performance at least one-fourth of the $n!$ orderings are still candidates to be the sorted ordering. After the third comparison, in the worst case at least one-eighth of the $n!$ orderings still need to be considered. In a worst-case performance, we need at least $n \log n$ comparisons before only a single candidate ordering might remain to be considered. Therefore, any comparison-based sorting algorithm has a worst-case performance that is at least linearithmic in the number of comparisons.

Programming Tip

QuickSort() comments

The `QuickSort()` algorithm was developed in 1960 by C. A. R. Hoare and is probably the most analyzed computer science algorithm. Our implementation is closest to the version developed by S. Sahni in his text *Data Structures, Algorithms, and Applications in C++*, Burr Ridge: McGraw-Hill, 1998. This text also presents, in part, a wide collection of other sorting and searching algorithms useful to programmers. Because of the importance of `QuickSort()`, implementations of the algorithm are included in the stdlib and standard template libraries.

After swapping, the situation becomes

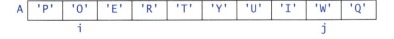

The process is then repeated. Continuing with our example, the situation immediately before the next swap is

and after swapping, the situation becomes

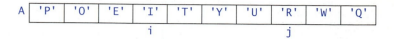

The process continues until the indexes cross each other. For our example, the next iteration of outer **do** loop results in the following situation with crossed indexes:

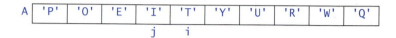

When the indexes cross, the partition has been constructed except for putting the pivot value in the proper spot. At this point in the function's execution, the value of index j represents the subscript of the right-most element belonging to the left partition. If A[j] and A[left] are swapped, then elements A[left] through A[j-1] form the left sublist to be sorted and elements A[j+1] through A[right] form the right sublist to be sorted.

The swapping of A[j] and A[left] results in the following situation:

With the pivot element in place and the left and right sublists formed, the function returns the index j of the pivot element.

QuickSort() makes use of the pivot element index in two recursive calls that separately sort the left and right sublists, which for our example are, respectively, the first four elements and last five elements of list A. Figure 9.1 illustrates all the invocations of QuickSort() to arrange our list correctly. Each entry shows the values of parameters left and right at the start of an invocation.

The arrangement of the values in the list at start of each invocation follows.

```
0 ...  9: QWERTYUIOP
0 ...  2: IOEPTYURWQ
0 ... -1: EOIPTYURWQ
1 ...  2: EOIPTYURWQ
1 ...  0: EIOPTYURWQ
2 ...  2: EIOPTYURWQ
4 ...  9: EIOPTYURWQ
4 ...  3: EIOPQYURWT
5 ...  9: EIOPQYURWT
5 ...  5: EIOPQRTUWY
7 ...  9: EIOPQRTUWY
7 ...  6: EIOPQRTUWY
8 ...  9: EIOPQRTUWY
8 ...  7: EIOPQRTUWY
9 ...  9: EIOPQRTUWY
```

Figure 9.1

*Left and right indexes
into list
Q W E R T Y U I O P
during QuickSort()
invocations*

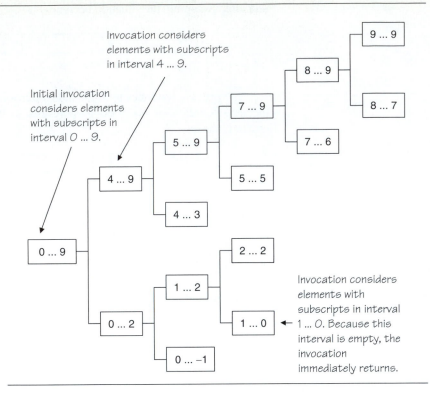

Initial invocation
considers elements
with subscripts in
interval 0 ... 9.

Invocation considers
elements with subscripts
in interval 4 ... 9.

Invocation considers
elements with
subscripts in interval
1 ... 0. Because this
interval is empty, the
invocation
immediately returns.

9.8   BINARY SEARCHING

When the values of a list are in sorted order, there are better searches than function Search() for determining whether a particular value is in the list. For example, when you look up a name in the phone book, you do not start in the beginning and scan through until you find the name—you use the fact that the names are listed in sorted order and use some intelligence to jump quickly to the right page and then start scanning.

The function BinarySearch() given in Listing 9.6 conducts a series of tests that allow it to iteratively reduce the portion of the list A that can possibly contain the value Key. Function BinarySearch() follows the same convention as Search(). If the Key value is present, then BinarySearch() returns the index of a matching element; if the Key value is not present, then Binary-Search() returns A.size().

The portion of the list that could contain the key value is represented by the indexes left and right. Prior to the first **if** test, any list element could contain the Key value. For this reason, left is initialized to 0, and right is

Listing 9.6

BinarySearch()

```
// BinarySearch(): examine sorted list A for Key
int BinarySearch(vector<char> &A, char Key) {
    int left = 0;
    int right = A.size() - 1;
    while (left <= right) {
        int mid = (left + right)/2;
        if (A[mid] == Key)
            return mid;
        else if (A[mid] < Key)
            left = mid + 1;
        else
            right = mid - 1;
    }
    return A.size();
}
```

initialized to `A.size()-1`. Suppose the list and key value have the following representation:

A **while** loop performs the tests that update indexes `left` and `right`. The loop iterates until either the Key value has been found or it has been determined that no portion of the list contains the Key value.

The body of the **while** loop starts by assigning the average of the current values of `left` and `right` to object `mid`. If element `A[mid]` is equal to the Key value, then `mid` is returned.

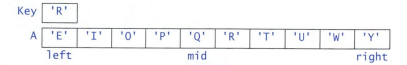

If element `A[mid]` is less than the Key value, then because the list is sorted, all elements to the left of `A[mid]` are also less than the Key value. If the Key value is to be in the list, it must occur to the right of `A[mid]`. Therefore, index `left` is reset to be to the immediate right of `mid`; that is, `left` becomes `right + 1`. For our example, the value of Key, which is `'R'`, is greater than the value of `A[mid]`, which is `'Q'`. After the updating of `mid` at the start of the next iteration, our objects have the following depiction:

If element A[mid] is neither equal to nor less than the Key value, it must be greater than the Key value. As the list is sorted, all elements to the right of A[mid] are also greater than the Key value. If the Key value is in the list, it must occur to the left of A[mid]. Therefore, in this case index right is reset to be to the immediate left of mid; that is, right becomes left - 1. For the previously depicted situation, the value of Key, which is 'R', is less than the value of A[mid], which is 'U'. After the updating of mid at the start of the next iteration, our objects have the following depiction:

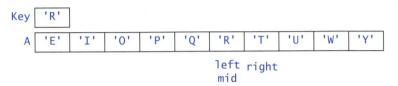

With this situation, the values of Key and A[mid] test equal, so the function returns the value of mid.

It can be shown that in the worst case BinarySearch() performs approximately 2 · log *n* comparisons to process a list of *n* elements. Consequently, for a sorted list of 1,000 elements, 20 comparisons are sufficient for Binary-Search() to determine whether the key value is present. It also means that for a sorted list of 1,000,000 elements, BinarySearch() can determine whether a particular value is present using no more than 40 comparisons!

It can also be shown using an information-theoretic argument that any comparison-based search algorithm requires on the order of log *n* comparisons in the worst case.

The STL algorithm library defines a function binary_search() that is comparable to our BinarySearch(). See Appendix B for a discussion of this function.

9.9 STRING CLASS REVISITED

The following **void** function GetWords() extracts nonwhitespace strings from the standard input stream cin and stores them in a vector<string> object.

```
void GetWords(vector<string> &List) {
    List.resize(0);
    string s;
    while (cin >> s) {
        List.push_back(s);
    }
}
```

Function GetWords() is similar to GetValues() except it extracts character string values rather than **int** values.

If standard input contained

```
a list of words
to be read.
```

then

```
vector<string> A;
GetWords(A);
```

would set A in the following manner:

A[0]	a
A[1]	list
A[2]	of
A[3]	words
A[4]	to
A[5]	be
A[6]	read.

The `string` class can also be viewed as a container class because it holds a sequence of characters. In fact, the subscript operator is overloaded for `string` objects. Suppose t is a `string` object representing "`purple`". Our traditional pictorial representation of t would be

t	purple

However, this alternative representation is also valid.

t	p	u	r	p	l	e

This representation indicates that the individual components, that is, elements, of t can be accessed or modified. For example, the assignments

```
t[1] = 'e';
t[2] = 'o';
```

modifies t so that it now represents the string "`people`".

Let us revisit our `vector` of `string` objects A in recognition of the fact that a `string` is a container.

A[0]	a				
A[1]	l	i	s	t	
A[2]	o	f			
A[3]	w	o	r	d	s
A[4]	t	o			
A[5]	b	e			
A[6]	r	e	a	d	.

Just as the alternative representation of t indicates that its individual characters can be referenced, the preceding representation of A indicates that the individual characters in its list of strings can be accessed and modified. To reference a particular character in a particular string of A, two uses of the subscript operator are necessary—the first subscript selects the particular string to be referenced and the second subscript is applied to that string to select the particular character in that string to be referenced. For example, the expression A[i][j] represents the jth character in the ith string of A. Thus, in a sense, A can be viewed as a two-dimensional list. We shall see a more explicit view of a two-dimensional list in the next section.

In the following code segment, we use a nested loop structure to count the number of occurrences of the character 'o' within A.

```
int ocount = 0;
for (int i = 0; i < A.size(); ++i) {
    for (int j = 0; j < A[i].size(); ++j) {
        if (A[i][j] == 'o') {
            ++ocount;
        }
    }
}
```

Observe that the outer **for** loop iterates once for each string in A. For each string A[i], the inner **for** loop iterates once for each character in A[i]. The processing compares character A[i][j] with 'o'. If the values are the same, the running total in ocount is incremented.

Self-check Questions

21. Write an **int** function LessThan() with three formal parameters: a vector a of integers, an **int** n which is the number of elements in the vector, and an **int** value v. The value v is to be optional with a default value of 0. Function LessThan() returns the number of elements in vector a[0], a[1], ..., a[n-1] that are less than v.

22. Write a function called Equal that takes two vectors of double-precision floating-point values and the size of the vectors as parameters. Function Equal() returns **true** if the two vectors are identical; otherwise it returns **false**. Identical means the vectors contain the same values in the same order.

23. Write a function called IsSorted that takes an integer vector and the size of the vector as parameters. Function IsSorted() returns **true** if the vector is in descending sorted order; otherwise it returns **false**.

24. A sorting algorithm that is often used because it is simple is BubbleSort. BubbleSort is so named because the smallest item "bubbles" to the top of the array when the algorithm is applied. Unfortunately, it is a very inefficient algorithm. The basic idea is to successively compare adjacent

elements and swap them if they are out of order. If are sorting the list into descending order (smallest elements appear first in the array), the smaller elements slowly "bubble" to the top, while the largest elements sink to the bottom. After the first pass, the largest element is at the bottom of the vector (i.e., in element `a[N-1]`). After the second pass the second largest element is in its correct position (i.e., in element `a[N-2]`), and so on.

Write a program that accepts a number from standard input. This is the size of the vector to sort. Using the random number class `RandInt`, fill the vector with random values, and then sort it using a bubblesort algorithm. Run your program with an vector size of 4,000 and then 8,000. Do you notice any significant difference in execution times between the two runs?

25.   Write a program that produces a histogram of the characters used in a textfile. Your program should prompt for and accept a file name that contains ASCII text. Your program reads the file and counts the number of times each alphabetic character is used. Do not distinguish between upper and lowercase characters. After processing the file, the program writes the histogram to stream `cout`.

9.10 FIND THAT WORD—EXPLORING A TWO-DIMENSIONAL LIST

Suppose we want to explicitly represent a two-dimensional list of characters. We can represent such a list as a vector of vectors. Such a list is defined in the following statement.

```
vector< vector<char> > A;
```

The following figure depicts the types of objects associated with A.

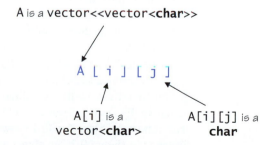

Because we used the default constructor in its definition, A is an empty list. However, through the use of the `resize()` function, we can appropriately set the number of elements in A. For example, suppose we wanted A to contain 13

Multiple angled brackets

One of the steps of translating a program is *lexical analysis*, in which the individual elements of a program are determined. For example, when a double == is found, the compiler classifies these characters as the equality operator, rather than as two assignment operators. Similarly, when a >> is encountered, some compilers will never treat these consecutive angled brackets as two distinct elements, but rather group them as a single element (e.g., insertion operator). This automatic grouping can prevent statements such as the following from successfully compiling.

```
vector<vector<int>> A;
```

If your compiler appears to be generating this type of spurious error messages for container code, try rewriting the statement in the following manner:

```
vector< vector<int> > A;
```

The introduction of whitespace between angled brackets causes the compiler to view the brackets as distinct elements.

vector<**char**> elements. The following statement will reset A so that it represents 13 such elements.

```
A.resize(13);  // A contains 13 vector<char> objects
```

The resize() function in this statement is a member of the vector<vector<**char**>> class. To set the number of characters, represented by each element, we would use the vector<**char**> member function resize(). For example, the following code segment causes each of the 13 elements of A to represent a list of 9 characters.

```
for (int i = 0; i < 13; ++i) {
    A[i].resize(9);
}
```

This vector<vector<**char**>> structure can be used to represent the information to solve a popular word puzzle in which words are hidden in a two-dimensional list of characters. For example, can you find the names Emily, Hannah, Jenna, James, and Zachary among the letters given in Figure 9.2? The names can occur horizontally, vertically, or diagonally in either forward or reverse order.

Listing 9.7 gives a function PuzzleSearch() that controls the search for a given word in a two-dimensional list of characters. To make the search for the hidden word easier, the two-dimensional list of alphabetic characters is surrounded by null characters ('\0'). For example, if a vector<vector<**char**>> object T with 13 rows and 9 columns was to represent the puzzle instance of Figure 9.2, the object would have the form depicted in Figure 9.3.

Recognizing that vector<vector<**char**>> object can be viewed as a two-dimensional list, it is convenient to refer to a list as a *table of characters*. Some other terminology will also prove useful. An element of T is a *row* in the

Figure 9.2

Several names are hidden in this two-dimensional list of letters

```
A  N  N  E  J  Z  E
S  J  A  M  I  J  N
Y  L  Z  I  Q  W  N
E  R  A  L  U  V  A
R  S  C  Y  N  N  O
D  H  H  L  K  F  J
U  J  A  M  E  S  L
A  A  R  N  F  H  I
S  C  Y  D  N  D  O
U  K  T  Z  A  A  R
A  S  D  F  G  Q  H
```

table. T can also be viewed as a series of columns, where the *j*th column is composed of the *j*th elements from the various rows.

Function `PuzzleSearch()` considers each interior character in the table as a possible starting location for the word. The word can proceed in eight directions. The directions differ in how the row and column indexes must be modified to proceed from element to element. For example, to proceed rightward from an element, the row index does not change and the column index increases by 1. Similarly, to proceed diagonally upward and leftward, both the row and column indexes must decrease by 1. For each possible starting element, an **if-else-if** construct is executed with the **if** statements in the construct considering different directions. If the word is found, an appropriate message is displayed and the function returns. If none of the eight directions works out with the current starting element, the process continues with a new starting element. The process terminates either with the word being found or having exhausted all possible starting elements. If the latter occurs, an appropriate message is displayed. The function to check a particular starting location and direction is `CheckWord()`, and it is given in Listing 9.8.

Function `CheckWord()` has six parameters. The first parameter is the table T to be searched. The second and third parameters are, respectively, the row i and column j that form the subscripts for referencing the character in T, which is to be the start of the search. The fourth parameter `Word` is a string that represents the hidden word. The fifth and sixth parameters `RowOffset` and `ColOffset` indicate, respectively, by what amount the current row and column indexes should be incremented to access the next character in T in the search for the hidden word.

The actual check for a given direction is simple. The current row index `row` and column index `col` for subscripting into T are initialized using i and j. Each character in `Word` is considered in turn. If the current character `Word[k]` from `Word` and the current character `T[row][col]` from T mismatch, then our guess for the word's location is wrong and the function returns **false**. If the current characters in `Word` and T match, then the indexes `row` and `col` are incremented by the appropriate offsets so that together they form the subscript of the new character of interest in T. If the **for** loop completes with all the

Listing 9.7

Function
PuzzleSearch() of
puzzle.cpp

```cpp
// PuzzleSearch(): look for Word in T
void PuzzleSearch(const vector< vector<char> > &T,
  const string &Word) {
    for (int i = 1; i < T.size() - 1; ++i) {
      for (int j = 1; j < T[i].size() - 1; ++j) {
        if (CheckWord(T, i, j, Word, 0, 1)) {
            cout << Word << " is at " << i << ", " << j
              << " going horizontally right" << endl;
            return;
        }
        else if (CheckWord(T, i, j, Word, 0, -1)) {
            cout << Word << " is at " << i << ", " << j
              << " going horizontally left" << endl;
            return;
        }
        else if (CheckWord(T, i, j, Word, 1, 0)) {
            cout << Word << " is at " << i << ", " << j
              << " going vertically down" << endl;
            return;
        }
        else if (CheckWord(T, i, j, Word, -1, 0)) {
            cout << Word << " is at " << i << ", " << j
              << " going vertically up" << endl;
            return;
        }
        else if (CheckWord(T, i, j, Word, 1, 1)) {
            cout << Word << " is at " << i << ", " << j
              << " going diagonally right and down"
              << endl;
            return;
        }
        else if (CheckWord(T, i, j, Word, 1, -1)) {
            cout << Word << " is at " << i << ", " << j
              << " going diagonally left and down"
              << endl;
            return;
        }
        else if (CheckWord(T, i, j, Word, -1, 1)) {
            cout << Word << " is at " << i << ", " << j
              << " going diagonally right and up"
              << endl;
            return;
        }
        else if (CheckWord(T, i, j, Word, -1, -1)) {
            cout << Word << " is at " << i << ", " << j
              << " going diagonally left and up"
              << endl;
            return;
        }
      }
    }
    cout << Word << " is not in the Puzzle" << endl;
    return;
}
```

letters matching, then the hidden word has been found and the function
returns **true**.

A simple function `main()` that initializes the puzzle search table and then
allows the user to specify a series of searches is given in Listing 9.9. The func-

Figure 9.3

Representation of puzzle search list

T[0]	'\0'	'\0'	'\0'	'\0'	'\0'	'\0'	'\0'	'\0'	'\0'
T[1]	'\0'	'A'	'N'	'N'	'E'	'J'	'Z'	'E'	'\0'
T[2]	'\0'	'S'	'J'	'A'	'M'	'I'	'J'	'N'	'\0'
T[3]	'\0'	'Y'	'L'	'Z'	'I'	'Q'	'W'	'N'	'\0'
T[4]	'\0'	'E'	'R'	'A'	'L'	'U'	'V'	'A'	'\0'
T[5]	'\0'	'R'	'S'	'C'	'Y'	'N'	'N'	'O'	'\0'
T[6]	'\0'	'D'	'H'	'H'	'L'	'K'	'F'	'J'	'\0'
T[7]	'\0'	'U'	'J'	'A'	'M'	'E'	'S'	'L'	'\0'
T[8]	'\0'	'A'	'A'	'R'	'N'	'F'	'H'	'I'	'\0'
T[9]	'\0'	'S'	'C'	'Y'	'D'	'N'	'D'	'O'	'\0'
T[10]	'\0'	'U'	'K'	'T'	'Z'	'A'	'A'	'R'	'\0'
T[11]	'\0'	'A'	'S'	'D'	'F'	'G'	'Q'	'H'	'\0'
T[12]	'\0'	'\0'	'\0'	'\0'	'\0'	'\0'	'\0'	'\0'	'\0'

Listing 9.8

Function CheckWord() from puzzle.cpp

```cpp
// CheckWord(): look for Word in T starting at [i][j]
// changing row value by RowOffset and column value by
// ColOffset
bool CheckWord(const vector< vector<char> > &T, int i,
 int j, const string &Word, int RowOffset,
 int ColOffset) {
  int row = i;
  int col = j;
  for (int k = 0; k < Word.size(); ++k) {
    if (Word[k] != T[row][col])
      return false;
    else {
      row += RowOffset;
      col += ColOffset;
    }
  }
  return true;
}
```

tion does not perform any validation; an improved version is left as an exercise.

9.11 MAZE RUNNER

Another popular game is traversing a maze by finding a path from the starting point to finishing point. Besides being interesting as a game, the maze traversal problem arises in many important problems such as robot navigation and interconnecting circuit elements on a computer chip.

A sample maze is given in Figure 9.4. In this maze, the starting point is the small square in the upper-left corner. The finishing point is the small square near the lower-right corner. The dark areas represent walls, and the lighter areas between the walls are corridors. The sample maze has no free-standing

Listing 9.9

Function main() from
puzzle.cpp

```cpp
// main(): manage play of puzzle search game
int main() {
   string Filename;
   cout << "Enter puzzle table filename: " ;
   cin >> Filename;
   ifstream fin(Filename.c_str());
   vector< vector<char> > Table(1); // initially 1 row
   string s;
   while (fin >> s) {
      vector<char> v(s.length() + 2);
      v[0] = '\0';
      v[1 + s.length()] = '\0';
      for (int i = 0; i < s.length(); ++i) {
         v[i+1] = s[i];
      }
      Table.push_back(v);
   }
   vector<char> null(Table[1].size() + 2, '\0');
   Table[0] = null;
   Table.push_back(null);
   for (int i = 1; i < Table.size() - 1; ++i) {
      for (int j = 1; j <= Table[i].size(); ++j) {
         cout << Table[i][j];
      }
      cout << endl;
   }
   cout << endl;
   cout << "Enter your puzzle search word: ";
   while (cin >> s) {
      cout << endl;
      PuzzleSearch(Table, s);
      cout << endl;
      cout << "Enter your next search word: ";
   }
   return 0;
}
```

Figure 9.4

Depicts the proper
maze associated with
input file mymaze.dat

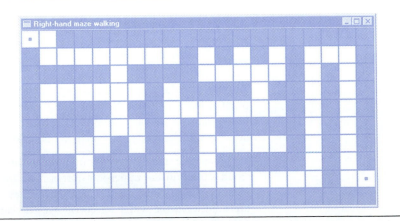

walls (a free-standing wall is one that is not connected to the perimeter). A maze with no free standing walls is called a *proper maze*.

Proper mazes can be solved by using the *right-hand strategy*. The right-hand strategy says to walk along the maze with your right hand constantly sliding along the wall. By doing so, you are guaranteed to reach the finishing point. Note that this strategy does not guarantee your path will be as short as possible. In fact, the strategy may produce a path that doubles back on itself.

We will find it convenient when discussing this problem to have a notion of direction: north heads to the top of the maze, south heads to the bottom of the maze, west heads to the left side of the maze, and east heads to the right side of the maze.

Using the maze in Figure 9.4 with our maze wanderer initially facing east, the first eight steps with the right-hand strategy are one step east, one step south, four steps east, and two steps south. As the most recent step is a southern one, the current direction of the wanderer is south. The progress to this point is shown graphically in Figure 9.5.

Figure 9.5

Depicts the first eight steps of a wanderer through the maze

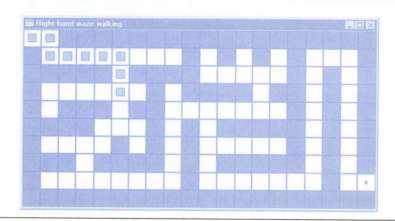

The next steps of our wanderer are four steps west and then one step south. The progress to this point is shown graphically in Figure 9.6. The right-hand strategy now forces a retracing down this dead-end corridor in the opposite direction. However, when the entrance to the corridor is reached the second time, the wanderer is facing east, rather than south. Because the wanderer is facing east, the next step with the right-hand strategy is south. The situation after this step is depicted in Figure 9.7. Observe in the figure that only the outlines of errant steps are depicted for locations that have been retraced by our wanderer.

A complete traversal of the maze using the right-hand strategy is given in Figure 9.8.

A programming solution to the proper maze problem must maintain and manipulate three important objects: a maze, a wanderer through the maze, and the resulting path. These objects will be represented as class-type objects. The names of the corresponding classes will be Maze, Wanderer, and Path.

Figure 9.6

Depicts the first 13 steps of a wanderer through the maze

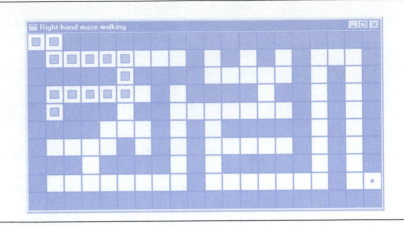

Figure 9.7

Depicts the first 19 steps of a wanderer through the maze

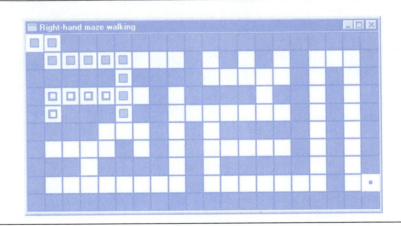

Figure 9.8

Depicts a complete traversal of a wanderer through the maze

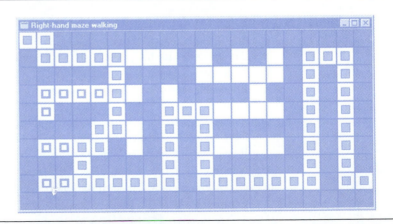

The classes Maze, Wanderer, and Path will make use of a class Location that represents the integer row and column coordinates of a location. The definition of class Location is given in Listing 9.10. The implementation of the class `Location` along with overloadings of the equality operator ==, inequality operator !=, and the extraction operator >> are given in Listing 9.11. The definition and implementation of the `Location` library are straightforward and are not discussed further.

Listing 9.10

*Location class
definition from header
file location.h*

```
class Location {
    public:
        // Constructor
        Location(int r = 0, int c = 0);
        // Inspectors
        int GetRow() const;
        int GetColumn() const;
        // Mutators
        void SetLocation(const Location &p);
        void SetLocation(int r, int c);
        void SetRow(int r);
        void SetColumn(int c);
    private:
        // Data members
        int Row;
        int Column;
};
```

9.11.1   Class maze specification

An important part of the class `Maze` will be a data member `Grid` that represents the layout of the maze as a two-dimensional grid. Member `Grid` will record for each location in the maze whether the location is an obstacle (i.e., part of a wall), available for traversing, the starting point, or the ending point.

It is appropriate to use an enumerated type `Status` to represent the possible location states.

```
enum Status { Free, Obstacle, Start, Finish,
    OutOfBounds };
```

Besides having symbolic constants `Obstacle`, `Free`, `Start`, and `Finish` to represent the possible configurations of a maze location, the type `Status` also has a constant `OutOfBounds`. Constant `OutOfBounds` is associated with locations that are not part of the maze.

Given the type `Status`, we can define `Grid` to be of type `vector<vector<Status>>`. In this representation, `Grid[r][c]` represents the layout of the cth spot in the rth row of the maze.

A design analysis would indicate that the following `Maze` methods are appropriate.

- `Maze(istream &sin = cin)`: default constructor that initializes its representation from a maze specification contained within input stream `sin`.

- `Maze(int r, int c)`: a constructor that creates a pseudorandom maze with dimensions r by c.

- `GetStatus(const Location &p)`: an inspector that returns the state of maze location p. If this location is not part of the maze, the value `OutOfBounds` is returned.

Listing 9.11

*Location class
implementation from
source file location.cpp*

```cpp
#include "location.h"
// Constructor
Location::Location(int r, int c) {
    SetLocation(r,c);
}
// Inspectors
int Location::GetRow() const {
    return Row;
}
int Location::GetColumn() const {
    return Column;
}
// Mutators
void Location::SetLocation(const Location &p) {
    SetRow(p.GetRow());
    SetColumn(p.GetColumn());
}
void Location::SetLocation(int r, int c) {
    SetRow(r);
    SetColumn(c);
}
void Location::SetRow(int r) {
    Row = r;
}
void Location::SetColumn(int c) {
    Column = c;
}
// ==: Location auxiliary operator
bool operator==(const Location &p, const Location &q) {
    return (p.GetRow() == q.GetRow())
    && (p.GetColumn() == q.GetColumn());
}
// !=: Location auxiliary operator
bool operator!=(const Location &p, const Location &q) {
    return ! (p == q);
}
// >>: Location auxiliary operator
istream& operator>>(istream &sin, Location &p) {
    int r;
    int c;
    sin >> r >> c;
    p = Location(r, c);
    return sin;
}
```

- SetStatus(**const** Location &p, Status &s): a mutator that sets the state of maze location p to s.

- GetStart() and GetFinish(): inspectors that, respectively, return the locations of the starting and finishing points for the maze.

- GetNumberRows() and GetNumberColumns(): inspectors that return the dimensions of the maze.

A design analysis would also indicate that the following Maze data members are appropriate.

- StartPos: location of starting point.

- FinishPos: location of finishing point.

These two data `Location` members are in addition to previously discussed data member `Grid`. The complete definition of the `Maze` class is given in Listing 9.12.

Listing 9.12

Maze class definition
from header file maze.h

```
class Maze {
   public:
      // Constructor: extract maze layout from file
      Maze(istream &sin = cin);
      // Constructor: random maze with dimensions r by c
      Maze(int r, int c);
      // Inspectors
      Status GetStatus(const Location &p) const;
      Location GetStart() const;
      Location GetFinish() const;

      int GetNumberRows() const;
      int GetNumberColumns() const;
   protected:
      // Mutator
      void SetStatus(const Location &p,
        const Status &s);
   private:
      // Data members
      vector< vector < Status > > Grid;
      Location StartPos;
      Location FinishPos;
};
```

The definition of `Maze` supports information hiding by making the data members private. The definition makes the member function `SetStatus()` protected. This access restriction on `SetStatus()` reflects our view that the maze, once constructed, does not change. By making this function protected, clients cannot change the maze. However, the protected access restriction allows classes derived from `Maze` to make use of this member.

9.11.2 Class wanderer specification

In developing a specification for the `Wanderer` class, we avoid requiring that a wanderer must interact with a `Maze` object. To do so would affect the reusability of the `Wanderer` class. Rather, what we want is a general-purpose wanderer that we can manipulate to accomplish our goal. An object with the following features would meet our wanderer criteria.

- The ability to receive and process signals that tell it about the layout of its immediate surroundings,

- The ability to carry out commands that tell it to step in a feasible direction.

Given that we are using a look-and-step approach to model the actions of a wanderer, the initialization values needed are simple—just specify the wanderer's initial location and the direction that it initially faces. To represent direction, we will use the enumerated type `Direction`.

```
enum Direction { North, East, South, West } ;
```

Observe that the four directions occur in clockwise order. The type `Direction` is defined in a header file `direction.h`. This header file also prototypes functions `Clockwise()` and `CounterClockwise()`.

```
Direction Clockwise(const Direction &d);
Direction CounterClockwise(const Direction &d);
```

Function `Clockwise()` returns the direction that occurs after its parameter d in a clockwise ordering of the directions. For example, `ClockWise(North)` returns `East`. Function `CounterClockwise()` returns the direction before its parameter d in a clockwise ordering of the directions. For example, `CounterClockwise(West)` returns `South`. The implementations of `Clockwise()` and `CounterClockwise()` are left as exercises.

Our discussion so far suggests the following member methods for a class `Wanderer`:

- `Wanderer(const Location &p = Location(0,0), const Direction &d = East)`: a constructor that builds a wanderer that is at location p facing in direction d.
- `GetDirection()`: an inspector that returns the direction in which the wanderer is currently facing.
- `SetDirection(const Direction &d)`: a mutator that causes the wanderer to face direction d.
- `GetLocation()`: an inspector that returns the location of the wanderer.
- `LookNorth(const Status &s)`: a facilitator that gives the wanderer the message s about the status of the location to the immediate north of the wanderer; that is, the status of the location to the immediate north is s.
- `LookSouth(const Status &s)`: a facilitator that gives the wanderer the message s about the status of the location to the immediate south of the wanderer.
- `LookEast(const Status &s)`: a facilitator that gives the wanderer the message s about the status of the location to the immediate east of the wanderer.
- `LookWest(const Status &s)`: a facilitator that gives the wanderer the message s about the status of the location to the immediate west of the wanderer.
- `MoveNorth()`: a mutator that attempts to move the location of the wanderer to the immediate north of the current location. Prior to the invocation of this member, at least one invocation of `LookNorth()` has been made after the wanderer reached its current location. The move north can be made only if the last such invocation of `LookNorth()` did not receive either the message `Obstacle` or `OutOfBounds`. If the move is made, the wanderer is currently facing `North`. If the move cannot be made, there is no change to the wanderer.
- `MoveSouth()`: a mutator that attempts to move the location of the wanderer to the immediate south of the current location. Prior to the invocation of this member, at least one invocation of `LookSouth()` has

been made after the wanderer reached its current location. The move south can be made only if the last such invocation of `LookSouth()` did not receive either the message `Obstacle` or `OutOfBounds`. If the move is made, the wanderer is currently facing `South`. If the move cannot be made, there is no change to the wanderer.

- `MoveEast()`: a mutator that attempts to move the location of the wanderer to the immediate east of the current location. Prior to the invocation of this member, at least one invocation of `LookEast()` has been made after the wanderer reached its current location. The move east can be made only if the last such invocation of `LookEast()` did not receive either the message `Obstacle` or `OutOfBounds`. If the move is made, the wanderer is currently facing `East`. If the move cannot be made, there is no change to the wanderer.

- `MoveWest()`: a mutator that attempts to move the location of the wanderer to the immediate west of the current location. Prior to the invocation of this member, at least one invocation of `LookWest()` has been made after the wanderer reached its current location. The move west can be made only if the last such invocation of `LookWest()` did not receive either the message `Obstacle` or `OutOfBounds`. If the move is made, the wanderer is currently facing `West`. If the move cannot be made, there is no change to the wanderer.

To implement these methods several data members are necessary. The necessity of two data members is immediately obvious: the current location `CurrPos` and the current direction in which the wanderer is facing `CurrDirection`. To guarantee that the various move member functions are correctly implemented, the results of the last invocations of the corresponding look member functions must be known. These results can be maintained using **bool** objects `OkNorth`, `OkEast`, `OkSouth`, and `OkWest`. An Ok object has the value **true** only if the last invocation of the corresponding Look function did not receive either an `Obstacle` or an `OutOfBounds` message. As a newly constructed wanderer has not received any Look messages, a wanderer's Ok objects are initialized to **false** during construction.

The complete definition of the `Wanderer` class is given in Listing 9.13. The definition of the `Wanderer` class shows that it supports information hiding by making all of the data members private. However, the member functions are all public, because each one is useful to clients.

9.11.3 Maze class implementation

A basic implementation for the `Maze` class is given in Listing 9.14. Our implementation leaves it to the exercises to define a `Maze` constructor that initializes a maze to a random configuration.

The maze constructor defined in our implementation extracts the characteristics of the maze from its input stream parameter `sin`. Stream `sin` should contain the maze characteristics in the following order:

```cpp
class Wanderer {
  public:
    // Constructor
    Wanderer(const Location &p = Location(0,0),
      const Direction &d = East);
    // Inspectors
    Direction GetDirection() const;
    Location GetLocation() const;
    // Facilitators for looking at surroundings
    void LookNorth(const Status &s);
    void LookEast(const Status &s);
    void LookSouth(const Status &s);
    void LookWest(const Status &s);
    // Direction mutator
    void SetDirection(const Direction &d);
    // Movement mutators
    void MoveNorth();
    void MoveEast();
    void MoveSouth();
    void MoveWest();
  private:
    // Data members
    Direction CurrDirection;
    Location CurrPos;
    bool OkNorth;
    bool OkEast;
    bool OkSouth;
    bool OkWest;
};
```

- Number of rows.

- Number of columns.

- Start location.

- Finish location.

- List of locations that contain obstacles.

Each start, finish, and obstacle location supplied in the stream is given as a row and column position.

Given this representation, the actions of the constructor are straightforward. First extract the maze dimensions.

```cpp
int NumberRows;
int NumberColumns;
sin >> NumberRows >> NumberColumns;
```

Then reset `Grid` so that it represents a list of `NumberRow` elements. Each `Grid` element is a `vector<Status>` list with `NumberColumn` elements. The elements of the `vector<Status>` lists are all initialized to the value `Free`.

```cpp
Grid.resize(
  NumberRows, vector<Status>(NumberColumns, Free));
```

The constructor then extracts the maze locations whose `Grid` values should be non-`Free` locations. The first two of these locations are the starting and finish-

Listing 9.14

*Maze class
implementation from
source file maze.cpp*

```
// Constructor: extract maze layout from file
Maze::Maze(istream &sin) {
    // extract dimensions
    int NumberRows;
    int NumberColumns;
    sin >> NumberRows >> NumberColumns;
    // set all grid positions free
    Grid.resize(
      NumberRows, vector<Status>(NumberColumns, Free));
    // extract and set ending points
    sin >> StartPos >> FinishPos;
    SetStatus(StartPos, Start);
    SetStatus(FinishPos, Finish);
    // extract and set obstacles
    Location p;
    while (sin >> p) {
        SetStatus(p, Obstacle);
    }
}
// Inspectors
Location Maze::GetStart() const {
    return StartPos;
}
Location Maze::GetFinish() const {
    return FinishPos;
}
int Maze::GetNumberRows() const {
    return Grid.size();
}
int Maze::GetNumberColumns() const {
    return Grid[0].size();
}
Status Maze::GetStatus(const Location &p) const {
    int r = p.GetRow();
    int c = p.GetColumn();
    if ((r < 0) || (r >= GetNumberRows())) {
        return OutOfBounds;
    }
    else if ((c < 0) || (c >= GetNumberColumns())) {
        return OutOfBounds;
    }
    else {
        return Grid[r][c];
    }
}
// Mutator
void Maze::SetStatus(const Location &p, const Status
 &s) {
    int r = p.GetRow();
    int c = p.GetColumn();
    assert((r >= 0) && (r < GetNumberRows()));
    assert((c >= 0) && (c < GetNumberColumns()));
    Grid[r][c] = s;
}
```

ing points. We use the `Maze` member function `SetStatus()` to reset these
locations to their proper `Status` value.

```
sin >> StartPos >> FinishPos;
SetStatus(StartPos, Start);
SetStatus(FinishPos, Finish);
```

The obstacle locations are extracted iteratively using a **while** loop. These extractions complete the construction.

```
Location p;
while (sin >> p) {
    SetStatus(p, Obstacle);
}
```

Because the implementations of member functions GetStart(), Get-Finish(), GetNumberRows(), and GetNumberColumns() are straightforward, we only discuss the Maze member functions of GetStatus() and SetStatus().

When function GetStatus() of Listing 9.14 is invoked, its Location parameter p may or may not correspond to an actual maze location. For those locations that are not part of the maze, the value OutOfBounds is returned. If its location parameter does correspond to a maze location, the value associated with the maze location is returned.

To determine whether location p is part of the maze, we examine its row position r and its column position c.

```
int r = p.GetRow();
int c = p.GetColumn();
```

Location p is part of the maze if and only if r lies in the interval 0 ... GetNumberRows()-1 and c lies in the interval 0 ... GetNumberColumns()-1. If p is part of the maze, then Grid[r][c] is the value associated with maze location p.

```
if ((r < 0) || (r >= GetNumberRows())) {
    return OutOfBounds;
}
else if ((c < 0) || (c >= GetNumberColumns())) {
    return OutOfBounds;
}
else {
    return Grid[r][c];
}
```

Maze member function SetStatus() of Listing 9.14 is invoked with Location parameter p representing the maze location of interest and parameter set representing the new value associated with that location. Like GetStatus(), SetStatus() first decomposes its parameter p into row and column positions r and c. Our basic implementation then asserts that these values are in the respective intervals 0 ... GetNumberRows()-1 and 0 ... GetNumberColumns()-1. A complete implementation should instead perform error checking and correction.

```
int r = p.GetRow();
int c = p.GetColumn();
assert((r >= 0) && (r < GetNumberRows()));
assert((c >= 0) && (c < GetNumberColumns()));
```

Given that r and c represent a proper maze location, the only action SetSta-tus() must perform is set Grid[r][c] to s.

```
Grid[r][c] = s;
```

9.11.4 Wanderer class implementation

A partial implementation of the Wanderer class is given in Listing 9.15. Our implementation leaves several movement member functions to the exercises.

Listing 9.15

A partial implementation of Wanderer member functions from source file wanderer.cpp

```
// Constructor
Wanderer::Wanderer(const Location &p,
  const Direction &d) {
    CurrPos = Location(p);
    SetDirection(d);
    OkNorth = OkEast = OkSouth = OkWest = false;
}
// Inspectors
Direction Wanderer::GetDirection() const {
    return CurrDirection;
}
Location Wanderer::GetLocation() const {
    return CurrPos;
}
// Direction mutator
void Wanderer::SetDirection(const Direction &d) {
    CurrDirection = d;
}
// Looking facilitators
void Wanderer::LookNorth(const Status &s) {
    OkNorth = (s != Obstacle) && (s != OutOfBounds);
}
void Wanderer::LookEast(const Status &s) {
    OkEast = (s != Obstacle) && (s != OutOfBounds);
}
void Wanderer::LookSouth(const Status &s) {
    OkSouth = (s != Obstacle) && (s != OutOfBounds);
}
void Wanderer::LookWest(const Status &s) {
    OkWest = (s != Obstacle) && (s != OutOfBounds);
}
// A movement mutator
void Wanderer::MoveNorth() {
    if (OkNorth) {
        int r = CurrPos.GetRow();
        CurrPos.SetRow(r-1);
        SetDirection(North);
        OkNorth = OkEast = OkSouth = OkWest = false;
    }
}
```

The Wanderer constructor expects two parameters—a location p and a direction d. Location p is used to set data member CurrPos, which represents the current position of the wanderer. Direction d is used by Wanderer mutator SetDirection() to set the current direction of the wanderer. The data members OkNorth, OkEast, OkSouth, and OkWest represent whether it is safe for the wanderer to proceed in a particular direction. Initially, there is no knowledge of the surroundings, so these members are set to false.

```
CurrPos = Location(p);
SetDirection(d);
OkNorth = OkEast = OkSouth = OkWest = false;
```

To accomplish their tasks, both inspectors `GetLocation()` and `GetDirection()` simply return the value of the data member that maintains the characteristic of interest. For `GetLocation()`, the interesting data member is `CurrPos`; for `GetDirection()`, the interesting data member is `CurrDirection`. Similarly, mutator `SetDirection()` needs only to update data member `CurrDirection` with the value of its parameter d to accomplish its task.

Each of the four Look member functions expects a `Status` value s as a parameter. The value s is a message to the wanderer regarding the nature of the adjacent location in question. For example, when function `LookNorth()` is invoked, it is given the status of the location to the immediate north of the wanderer's current position. If the status of that location is neither `Obstacle` nor `OutOfBounds`, then the wanderer is currently permitted to step north. When this is the case, object `OkNorth` should be set true. If instead, the status of that location is either `Obstacle` or `OutOfBounds`, then the wanderer is not currently permitted to step north. For this case, `OkNorth` should be set false. Thus the assignment

```
OkNorth = (s != Obstacle) && (s != OutOfBounds);
```

correctly updates `OkNorth` with respect to message s. The other Look functions can use the same expression to determine whether it is okay to move in their directions.

With respect to the `Wanderer` Move functions, our implementation defines only the `MoveNorth()` member function. The other Move functions are left to the exercises. The specification of `MoveNorth()` from Section 9.11.2 requires for a northern move that a `LookNorth()` invocation be made after the wanderer arrives at its current position and that the last such invocation of `LookNorth()` receives neither the message `Obstacle` nor the message `OutOfBounds`. If these conditions are met, the wanderer is moved within the same column up one row. If these conditions are not met, the wanderer does not move. In our implementation, these conditions require a move only if the current value of `OkNorth` is true. To move the wanderer up one row:

- Determine the current row position r of the wanderer.

- Set the current row position of the wanderer to r-1.

If the wanderer is moved north, two other actions are necessary to reflect its current state:

- The wanderer's current direction must be updated to north.

- The Ok objects must all be set to false so that the wanderer cannot move until it inspects its new surroundings.

Thus `MoveNorth()` can correctly accomplish its task with the following code segment:

```
if (OkNorth) {
    int r = CurrPos.GetRow();
    CurrPos.SetRow(r-1);
    SetDirection(North);
    OkNorth = OkEast = OkSouth = OkWest = false;
}
```

9.11.5 Path representation

As noted in Section 9.11, the third major object used in modeling a wanderer through a maze is the path that the wanderer travels through the maze. In its simplest form, a path is merely a sequence of locations. However, in practice there are several capabilities for manipulating and inspecting a path that client programmers would find helpful for processing paths in general:

- An append function that allows a path to be extended to a new location.
- A contains function that indicates whether a given location is part of the path.
- An iterator that allows the locations in a path to be iteratively processed.
- A deletion function that allows a segment of the path to be removed.

These capabilities can be obtained by requiring the following public member functions for a `Path` object:

- `Append(const Location &p)`: mutator that appends location p to the end of the representation of the current path.
- `Contains(const Location &p)`: Boolean inspector that determines whether p is currently part of the path.
- `at(int i)`: inspector that returns the ith location in the path.
- `set(int i, const Location &p)`: mutator that sets the ith location in the path to p.
- `begin()`: iterator that returns a pointer to the first location in the sequence of locations that make up the path.
- `end()`: iterator that returns a pointer to a location immediately beyond the final location in the path.
- `size()`: inspector that returns the number of locations in the sequence of locations that make up the path.
- `DeleteLocation(int i)`: mutator that deletes the ith location in the sequence of locations that make up the path.

The `Path` member functions can be implemented using a data member `CurrSeq` of type `vector<Location>`. The `Path` class definition is given in Listing 9.16.

The partial implementation of `Path` given in Listing 9.17 defines only the member functions used by the control program to manage our solution for modeling a wanderer traversing a maze using the right-hand strategy. Implementations of the other `Path` member functions are left to the exercises.

Listing 9.16

Class Path from header file path.h

```
class Path {
    public:
        // Constructor
        Path(const Location &p = Location(0,0));
        // Inspectors
        bool Contains(const Location &p) const;
        Location at(int i) const;
        int size() const;
        // Mutators
        void Append(const Location &p);
        void DeleteLocation(int i);
        void Set(int i, const Location &p);
        // Iterators
        vector<Location>::iterator begin();
        vector<Location>::iterator end();
    private:
        vector<Location> CurrSeq;
};
```

Listing 9.17

Some Path member functions from file path.cpp

```
// Constructor
Path::Path(const Location &p) : CurrSeq(1, p) {
    // no body needed
}
// Inspector
bool Path::Contains(const Location &p) const {
    if (find(CurrSeq.begin(), CurrSeq.end(), p)
    != CurrSeq.end())
        return true;
    else
        return false;
}
// Mutator
void Path::Append(const Location &p) {
    CurrSeq.push_back(p);
}
```

The `Path` constructor in Listing 9.17 uses a *member initialization list* to accomplish its task of initializing `Path` data member `CurrSeq`. A member initialization list is an alternative method for initializing an object's data members. In general, a member initialization list is a series of data members with a specification of their initial values. The data members are separated using commas. The initialization list for a constructor immediately precedes the constructor body. It is separated from the constructor parameter list by a colon. It is important to note that the elements of the initialization list are constructed in the order that they are defined in the class definition rather than their position in the initialization list. For our `Path` constructor, the initialization list makes `CurrSeq` a one-element vector. The value of that element is equal to the constructor's location parameter `p`. This parameter represents the first and currently only location in the path.

The inspector `Contains()` in Listing 9.17 utilizes the previously discussed function `find()` from the STL to determine whether location `p` is part of the current path. If `p` is part of the container element sequence defined by `CurrSeq.begin()` and `CurrSeq.end()`, `find()` returns an iterator pointing to the `CurrSeq` element that contains `p`. Otherwise, `find()` returns `CurrSeq.end()`. By comparing the return value of `find()` with

CurrSeq.end(), we know which Boolean value function Contains()
should return.

The mutator Append() in Listing 9.17 modifies the path representation to
include location p at its end by invoking CurrSeq's member function
push_back(). As previously noted in our vector discussion, function
push_back() appends a copy of its parameter to the end of its sequence.

Thus the member functions of Listing 9.17 have straightforward implementations by using the containers and algorithms of the STL.

Figure 9.9

*An alternative maze
representation*

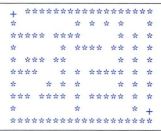

9.11.6   Display representation

Our discussion to this point has deliberately ignored how the maze and the path
of the wanderer are displayed—the rendering of an object is independent of
how it behaves and interacts. For example, the maze represented in Figure 9.4
can also be depicted using characters. Such a representation is given in Figure
9.9. In this figure, an asterisk represents a wall location, a blank represents a
corridor location, and plus signs represent the starting and ending points. A
path through the maze could be represented using hyphens and vertical lines.

To produce a maze-wanderer path rendering comparable to that of Figures
9.4 through 9.8, we suggest a class Display. The definition of Display is
given in Listing 9.18. The class makes use of the enumerated type Display-
Symbol, which is also defined in Listing 9.18.

As indicated in the Display definition, three Display data members
support the actions of its member functions:

- View: a vector of vector<SymbolStatus> elements. This object is
  viewed as two-dimensional grid. View[r][c] indicates how Loca-
  tion(r,c) of the maze-wanderer path is to be rendered.

- DisplayWindow: the SimpleWindow object that contains the graphical
  rendering.

- LocationSide: a floating point value that represents the length in
  centimeters of the side of a square. Each location in the maze-wanderer
  path rendering is displayed in a LocationSide by LocationSide
  section of window DisplayWindow.

The public Display member functions have the following specifications:

- Display(SimpleWindow &W, **const** Maze &M, **float** side = 0.75):
  constructor initializes the display object so that a rendering of the object at
  this point would produce a graphical representation of maze M in window

```
enum DisplaySymbol {
    StartSymbol, FinishSymbol, ErrantSymbol,
    StepSymbol, UnseenSymbol, ObstacleSymbol};
class Display {
    public:
        Display(SimpleWindow &W, const Maze &M,
            float side = 0.75);
        void SetErrant(const Location &p);
        void SetStepped(const Location &p);
        void DisplayAll();
        SimpleWindow& GetDisplayWindow();
        float GetScale() const;
        void DisplayLocation(const Location &p);
    protected:
        void DisplayStart(const Location &p);
        void DisplayFinish(const Location &p);
        void DisplayErrant(const Location &p);
        void DisplayStep(const Location &p);
        void DisplayUnseen(const Location &p);
        void DisplayObstacle(const Location &p);
        void SetScale(float s);
    private:
        vector< vector<DisplaySymbol> > View;
        SimpleWindow &DisplayWindow;
        float LocationSide;
};
```

W. In particular, data member `View` is initialized to be a grid with the same number of rows and columns as `Maze`. For each element `View[r][c]` of that grid, the initial value of `View[r][c]` is determined by the corresponding element in `Maze`. For example, if the corresponding element has `Status` value `Obstacle`, then element `View[r][c]` has `DisplaySymbol` value `ObstacleSymbol`. In the rendering, each location corresponds to a square subsection of `W` where the sides of the subsection are `side` centimeters long. The subsection of `W` associated with `View[r][c]` has its upper-left corner located at window position coordinate `(c*side, r*side)`.

- `SetErrant(const Location &p)`: mutator updates its display object so that location p is associated with `StatusSymbol` value `ErrantSymbol`; that is, `View[p.GetRow()][p.GetColumn()]` is set to `ErrantSymbol`.

- `SetStepped(const Location &p)`: mutator updates its display object so that location p is associated with `StatusSymbol` value `StepSymbol`; that is, `View[p.GetRow()][p.GetColumn()]` is set to `StepSymbol`.

- `DisplayAll()`: facilitator performs a complete graphical rendering to `DisplayWindow` of the maze and wanderer path represented by the display object.

- `DisplayLocation(const Location &p)`: facilitator renders the graphic associated with location p of the maze-wanderer path configuration to the corresponding section of `DisplayWindow`; that is, the graphic associated with `View[p.GetRow()][p.GetColumn()]` is displayed.

- `GetDisplayWindow()`: inspector returns a reference to `DisplayWindow`.
- `GetScale()`: inspector returns the proportionality constant `LocationSide`.

The protected `Display` member functions have the following specifications:

- `DisplayStart(const Location &p)`: facilitator renders a starting-point graphic to the section of `DisplayWindow` associated with location p. In the implementation that produced the depiction in Figure 9.4, the graphic is produced by drawing a small blue `RectangleShape` centered within a white `RectangleShape`.
- `DisplayFinish(const Location &p)`: facilitator renders a finishing-point graphic to the section of `DisplayWindow` associated with location p. In the implementation that produced the depiction in Figure 9.4, the graphic is produced by drawing a small blue `RectangleShape` centered within a white `RectangleShape`.
- `DisplayStep(const Location &p)`: facilitator renders a normal-step graphic to the section of `DisplayWindow` associated with location p. In the implementation that produced the depiction in Figure 9.4, the graphic is produced by drawing a medium blue `RectangleShape` centered within a white `RectangleShape`.
- `DisplayUnwalkedCorridor(const Location &p)`: facilitator renders an empty-corridor graphic to the section of `DisplayWindow` associated with location p. In the implementation that produced the depiction in Figure 9.4, the graphic is produced by drawing a white `RectangleShape`.
- `DisplayObstacle(const Location &p)`: facilitator renders a wall graphic to the section of `DisplayWindow` associated with location p. In the implementation that produced the depiction in Figure 9.4, the graphic is produced by drawing a blue `RectangleShape`.
- `DisplayErrant(const Location &p)`: facilitator renders a retraced-step graphic to the section of `DisplayWindow` associated with location p. In the implementation that produced the depiction in Figure 9.4, the graphic is produced by drawing a small white `RectangleShape` centered within a medium blue `RectangleShape` centered within a white `RectangleShape`.
- `SetScale(float s)`: inspector sets the proportionality constant `LocationSide` to s.

The actual implementation of `Display` is left to the exercises.

9.11.7 Control program

The program that manipulates and displays the wanderer and the maze is `travel.cpp`. The program consists of two functions `ApiMain()` and `MoveOneRightHandedStep()`. Function `ApiMain()` is the actual controller. Function `ApiMain()` uses `MoveOneRightHandedStep()` to repeatedly move the wanderer one step. Function `ApiMain()` is given in Listing 9.19, and function `MoveOneRightHandedStep()` is given in Listing 9.20.

`ApiMain()` implements the following algorithm:

Step 1.   Determine the name of the file `s` that contains maze characteristics.

Step 2.   Define a maze `M` using the file named `s`.

Step 3.   Define a wanderer `W` whose starting location is the starting location of `M`.

Step 4.   Define a path `WP` that consists initially of `W`'s starting location.

Step 5.   Define a display `D` that initially consists of a representation of maze `M`.

Step 6.   Add a representation of the current position of the `W` to `D`.

Step 7.   Render a graphical depiction of `D`.

Step 8.   While `W`'s current location is not the finishing point do

Step 8.1   Move the wanderer using the right-handed strategy one step.

Step 8.2   If `W`'s new location is a previously visited location in `WP`, then modify `D` so that the representation of `W`'s previous location `prev` in `D` is that of an errant step. Also, rerender the current graphical depiction of `prev` in `D`.

Step 8.3   Add a representation of `W`'s current location to `D` and then rerender a graphical depiction of that location.

Step 8.4   Add `W`'s current location to `WP`.

The implementation of the algorithm in function `ApiMain()` begins by prompting and extracting the name of the file that contains the maze instance. The filename is used to initialize an `ifstream` object `sin`. For ease of presentation, we do not verify that the filename represents a valid input stream.

```
string s;
cout << "Enter filename: ";
cin >> s;
ifstream sin(s.c_str());
```

The function continues the algorithm by initializing our maze `M` and wanderer `W`.

```
Maze M(sin);
Wanderer W(M.GetStart(), East);
```

Path `WP` is then initialized using the starting location of the wanderer.

```
Path WP(W.GetLocation());
```

The window `MyWindow` that display our results is then constructed and opened. The dimensions of the window are proportional to the number of rows and columns in the maze. Each location in the maze will correspond to a `unit`-by-`unit` section of window, where `unit` equals 0.75 centimeters.

```
float nr = M.GetNumberRows();
float nc = M.GetNumberColumns();
float unit = 0.75;
SimpleWindow MyWindow("Wandering", nc*unit, nr*unit);
MyWindow.Open();
```

Listing 9.19

Control function
ApiMain() from
travel.cpp

```cpp
int ApiMain() {
    // Open maze data file
    string s;
    cout << "Enter filename: ";
    cin >> s;
    ifstream sin(s.c_str());

    // Initialize maze, wanderer and path
    Maze M(sin);
    Wanderer W(M.GetStart(), East);
    Path WP(W.GetLocation());

    // Initialize and open display windows
    float nr = M.GetNumberRows();
    float nc = M.GetNumberColumns();
    float unit = 0.75;
    SimpleWindow MyWindow("Wandering", nc*unit, nr*unit);
    MyWindow.Open();

    // Define display model
    Display D(MyWindow, M, unit);
    D.SetStepped(W.GetLocation());
    D.DisplayAll();

    // Control wanderer through the maze
    while (W.GetLocation() != M.GetFinish()) {
        // Record current location
        Location prev = W.GetLocation();

        // Make and analyze step
        MoveOneRightHandedStep(W, M);

        if (WP.Contains(W.GetLocation())){
            // Previous location lied in a dead-end corridor
            D.SetErrant(prev);
            D.DisplayLocation(prev);
        }

        // Add step to path and display
        WP.Append(W.GetLocation());
        D.SetStepped(W.GetLocation());
        D.DisplayLocation(W.GetLocation());
    }
    return 0;
}
```

The window MyWindow, the maze M, and the dimension unit are used to construct display object D. Once D is initialized, it is updated to reflect the position of the wanderer. Upon updating, the current maze and wanderer-path configuration is displayed.

```cpp
Display D(MyWindow, M, unit);
D.SetStepped(W.GetLocation());
D.DisplayAll();
```

These actions complete steps 1 to 7 of the algorithm, which are the initialization phase of the control program. The control program then iterates while the wanderer's current location is not the finishing point of the maze. Each iteration begins by recording the current location of the wanderer. The wanderer is then moved a single step.

```cpp
Location prev = W.GetLocation();
MoveOneRightHandedStep(W, M);
```

If the step is to a location that is already part of the path, then location `prev` was part of a dead-end corridor. We test for this situation by invoking WP's member function `Contains()` with the wanderer's current position. If the situation does occur, we modify the representation of location `prev` in display D and then rerender the display of that location.

```
if (WP.Contains(W.GetLocation())){
    D.SetErrant(prev);
    D.DisplayLocation(prev);
}
```

Regardless of whether the new location is already part of the path, the new location represents the current end of the path. To record this fact, the location is appended to the end of the current path WP and the status of the location in display D is set to stepped. The location is then rerendered.

```
WP.Append(W.GetLocation());
D.SetStepped(W.GetLocation());
D.DisplayLocation(W.GetLocation());
```

9.11.8   Implementing the right-hand maze walking strategy

To complete our examination of the maze traversal problem, we develop the function `MoveOneRightHandedStep()`, which determines the next step wanderer W makes in its traversal of maze M.

Suppose a wanderer is proceeding eastward down a corridor and has just reached a corridor intersection as shown in the following figure:

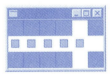

The next step the wanderer takes is south. If the wanderer had entered the intersection from the north, then the step the wanderer takes is west. In general, the preferred next step lies in the direction that is immediately clockwise to the wanderer's current direction.

If the preferred direction cannot be taken, then the secondary preferred step is the wanderer's current direction. An examination of the next figure gives insight into this fact. As the wanderer cannot proceed south, it continues east.

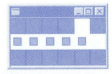

It can be deduced that the secondary direction preference is, in general, counterclockwise to the primary direction preference.

If neither the primary nor secondary direction preference is available, as shown in the next figure, then the tertiary direction preference is the direction counterclockwise to the secondary direction preference. In particular, in the following figure, the wanderer steps north because it cannot go south or east.

If none of the three preferences is available, as shown in the next figure, then the only possibility is to step backward. However, stepping in that direction is equivalent to going counterclockwise in the tertiary preference direction.

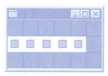

Thus the proper choice of the location for the wanderer's next step can be made in the following manner:

- Let d be the direction that is immediately clockwise to the wanderer's current direction.

- Use a loop that first considers the location adjacent to the wanderer that lies in direction d. If this location is not feasible, then the loop considers, in turn, the other locations adjacent to the wanderer. The other locations are considered in a counterclockwise manner from d.

- The first considered maze location that is not part of a wall maze is the proper one for the right-hand strategy.

Function MoveOneRightHandedStep() of Listing 9.20 correctly implements this process. The function begins by recording the wanderer's current location in object p. The individual row and column coordinates of its location are also recorded, respectively, in r and c.

```
Location p = W.GetLocation();
int r = p.GetRow();
int c = p.GetColumn();
```

The direction d that is clockwise to the wanderer's current direction is then determined.

```
Direction d = Clockwise(W.GetDirection());
```

Function MoveOneRightHandedStep() then begins a **while** loop that iteratively considers the four adjacent locations to the wanderer. Each iteration attempts a move to the neighboring location lying in direction d. To prepare for the next iteration, the value of d is updated to be counterclockwise of its current value. Thus the neighboring locations are considered in the proper order for the right-hand strategy. The loop iterates while the wanderer's current

Listing 9.20

Function
MoveOneRightHanded
Step() from travel.cpp

```
void MoveOneRightHandedStep(Wanderer &W, const Maze &M) {
    // Determine current location
    Location p = W.GetLocation();
    int r = p.GetRow();
    int c = p.GetColumn();

    // Determine preferred direction of movement
    Direction d = Clockwise(W.GetDirection());

    // Process directions in decreasing order of preference
    do {
        // Examine neighbor in direction d and attempt to
        // move there
        Location neighbor;
        switch (d) {
            case North:
                neighbor = Location(r-1,c);
                W.LookNorth(M.GetStatus(neighbor));
                W.MoveNorth();
                break;
            case East:
                neighbor = Location(r, c+1);
                W.LookEast(M.GetStatus(neighbor));
                W.MoveEast();
                break;
            case South:
                neighbor = Location(r+1, c);
                W.LookSouth(M.GetStatus(neighbor));
                W.MoveSouth();
                break;
            case West:
                neighbor = Location(r, c-1);
                W.LookWest(M.GetStatus(neighbor));
                W.MoveWest();
                break;
        }
        // Determine nextmost preferred direction
        d = CounterClockwise(d);

        // test to see if we have not moved
    } while (p == W.GetLocation());
}
```

location is p. In other words, the loop iterates until the wanderer has taken a step away from p.

Suppose the current value of d is South. The neighbor of interest for this case lies in the same column c as the wanderer but the neighbor's row coordinate is 1 greater than the wanderer's row coordinate.

```
neighbor = Location(r+1, c);
```

The wanderer is then directed to look south at the neighboring location.

```
W.LookSouth(M.GetStatus(neighbor));
```

The wanderer next attempts to move south.

```
W.MoveSouth();
```

The move will be made only if the result of looking south had indicated that the neighbor location is part of the maze and not an obstacle. Having attempted a move, d is updated and the loop test is evaluated to determine whether the move was successful.

9.12 MULTIDIMENSIONAL ARRAYS

In addition to defining one-dimensional arrays, it is also possible to define multidimensional arrays. For example, the object M defined below is a two-dimensional array.

```
char M[3][4];
```

Array M can be viewed as consisting of 3 one-dimensional subarrays M[0], M[1], and M[2] with each of these subarrays consisting of four elements. The subarrays are referred to as *rows*. As in our vector of vector examples, to refer to an individual element of a row, an additional subscript is used. For example, M[i][j] is the jth element of the ith row in M.

Arrays with more than two dimensions are also possible. However, in practice, arrays with three dimensions are seldom used, and arrays with more than three dimensions are almost never used.

When memory is reserved in an activation record for a two-dimensional array, the array's elements are assigned memory locations in *row-major* order, which means that row 0 occurs first, row 1 occurs next, and so on.

Within a row, the elements of a two-dimensional array are assigned memory locations in increasing order of subscript. For M, this convention means that M[0][0] is assigned the first unit of the array memory, and M[2][3] is assigned the last unit of the array memory.

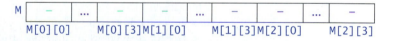

There is a formula for determining which unit of the array memory is assigned to an element. For a two-dimensional array A, with n elements per row, element A[i][j] is assigned the (i*n) + jth unit of array memory. Thus for our array M, element M[i][j] is assigned the (i*4) + jth unit of array memory. For arrays with higher dimension, an analogous scheme is used to assign array elements to memory locations.

The definition of a multidimensional array can include initialization. For a two-dimensional array whose base type is a fundamental type, the array initialization can be a given as a list of values, a collection of initial row values, or a combination of the two. For example, the following definitions of A, B, and C all initialize the corresponding elements to the same value.

```
int A[3][3] = {1, 2, 3, 4, 5, 6, 7, 8, 9};
int B[3][3] ={{1, 2, 3}, {4, 5, 6}, {7, 8, 9}};
int C[3][3] = {1, 2, 3, {4, 5, 6}, 7, 8, 9};
```

As with one-dimensional arrays, if an insufficient number of values is specified, the trailing elements are initialized to 0.

For a multidimensional array whose base type is a class type, no explicit initialization can be given. Instead each array element is initialized using the default constructor for the class.

Functions with parameters that are multidimensional arrays are permitted. Like one-dimensional array parameters, a multidimensional array parameter must be a reference parameter. It is also possible to use a subarray of a multidimensional array as a parameter. For example, we can separately invoke QuickSort() on the three rows of the two-dimensional array M that was defined at the beginning of this section.

```
QuickSort(M[0], 0, 3);
QuickSort(M[1], 0, 3);
QuickSort(M[2], 0, 3);
```

We can make these invocations using rows of M because we are able to consider each row of a two-dimensional array as a one-dimensional array object.

When defining a function with a multidimensional array parameter, the size of each dimension other than the first dimension must be specified. For example, the following function Zero() has a two-dimensional array parameter A with a constant MaxCols that defines the number of elements per row. Parameters rows and columns are used to indicate how many rows and how many elements per row are to be set to 0 by the function.

```
void Zero(int A[][MaxCols], int rows, int columns) {
    for (int r = 0; r < rows; ++r)
        for (int c = 0; c < columns; ++c)
            A[r][c] = 0;
}
```

The following **void** function GetWords() extracts nonwhitespace character strings from the standard input stream cin and stores them in a two-dimensional **char** array. The function has three parameters: the two-dimensional **char** array List to store the strings, the maximum number of strings to be extracted MaxSize, and the count n, which is the number of extracted strings when the function has completed. The maximum length of a string is assumed to be MaxStringSize. This constant, which must be defined elsewhere, is the size of the second dimension in List.

```
void GetWords(char List[][MaxStringSize],
  int MaxSize, int &n) {
    for (n = 0; cin >> List[n]; ++n) {
        continue;
    }
}
```

Function GetWords() is similar to GetList() except it extracts character strings rather than **int** values. In the exercises, an alternative version of Get-Words() is developed that makes use of the cin member function getline().

Suppose standard input contained the following:

```
a list of words
to be read.
```

Then

```
const int MaxStringSize = 10;
const int MaxListSize = 10;
char A[MaxListSize][MaxStringSize];
int n;
GetWords(A, MaxListSize, n);
```

would set A in the following manner:

A[0]	'a'	'\0'	–	–	–	–	–	–	–	–
A[1]	'l'	'i'	's'	't'	'\0'	–	–	–	–	–
A[2]	'o'	'f'	'\0'	–	–	–	–	–	–	–
A[3]	'w'	'o'	'r'	'd'	's'	–	–	–	–	–
A[4]	't'	'o'	'\0'	–	–	–	–	–	–	–
A[5]	'b'	'e'	'\0'	–	–	–	–	–	–	–
A[6]	'r'	'e'	'a'	'd'	'.'	'\0'	–	–	–	–
A[7]	–	–	–	–	–	–	–	–	–	–
A[8]	–	–	–	–	–	–	–	–	–	–
A[9]	–	–	–	–	–	–	–	–	–	–

As you see, the two-dimensional array representation for a list of strings is quite wasteful—most of the array elements are unused. This waste partially explains our preference for the string class representation.

9.12.1 Matrices

A two-dimensional array is sometimes known as a *matrix* because it resembles that mathematical concept. A mathematical matrix A with m rows and n columns is represented in the following manner:

$$\begin{bmatrix} a_{1,1} & a_{1,2} & \cdots & a_{1,n} \\ a_{2,1} & a_{2,2} & \cdots & a_{2,n} \\ \cdots & & & \cdots \\ a_{m,1} & a_{m,2} & \cdots & a_{m,n} \end{bmatrix}$$

Addition is defined for two matrices with the same corresponding number of rows and columns. If A and B are both matrices with m rows and n columns, then their sum C has the following form:

$$\begin{bmatrix} a_{1,1}+b_{1,1} & a_{1,2}+b_{1,2} & \cdots & a_{1,n}+b_{1,n} \\ a_{2,1}+b_{2,1} & a_{2,2}+b_{2,2} & \cdots & a_{2,n}+b_{2,n} \\ \cdots & & & \cdots \\ a_{m,1}+b_{m,1} & a_{m,2}+b_{m,2} & \cdots & a_{m,n}+b_{m,n} \end{bmatrix}$$

Matrix addition is implemented in the following function Add() whose body is a double-nested **for** loop.

```cpp
void Add(const int A[][MaxCols],
  const int B[][MaxCols], int C[][MaxCols],
  int rows, int columns) {
    for (int r = 0; r < rows; ++r) {
        for (int c = 0; c < columns; ++c) {
            C[r][c] = A[r][c] + B[r][c];
        }
    }
}
```

The outer **for** loop of Add() supplies the index variable r to process the current row. The inner **for** loop supplies the index variable c to process the current column in the current row. Together the two indexes enable the sum of a pair of array elements from A and B to be calculated and assigned to the corresponding array element of C.

Container classes are replacing the use of both single-dimension arrays and multidimensional arrays (e.g., a simple vector and a vector of vectors). Unless special conditions exist, we recommend that you use the container classes for your list processing needs. Our recommendation is based partially on the fact that C++ imposes significant restrictions on the use of arrays: A function return type cannot be an array; an array cannot be passed by value; an array cannot be the target of an assignment; the size of the array must be a compile-time constant; and an array cannot be resized. The container classes are free of these restrictions. In addition, the various container classes when coupled with the algorithm library provide extensive capabilities for doing list processing and manipulation.

Programming Tip

Accessing multidimensional arrays

Because multidimensional arrays are stored in row-major order, it is generally more efficient to process array elements row by row rather than column by column. The efficiency comes about in how memory values are brought into the central processing unit. Often contiguous sections of memory called *pages* are brought in with the expectation that values near a desired value are more likely to be referenced than values defined elsewhere in memory. Because a page is contiguous memory, it is more likely to contain a complete row than a complete column.

Self-check Questions

26.   Write a **void** function PrintMatrix() with three formal parameters: an integer matrix with at most MaxCols columns, an integer m that is the actual number of rows in the matrix, and an integer n that is the actual number of columns in the matrix. Function PrintMatrix() prints the values in the matrix row by row.

27.   Write a function that accepts a two-dimensional integer array and flips the array about the diagonal. The example below shows the transformation your function should implement. Your solution should include and use a swap function.

$$
\begin{bmatrix}
5 & 3 & 6 & 4 & 18 \\
12 & 3 & 9 & 22 & 4 \\
4 & 7 & 31 & 4 & 10 \\
34 & 32 & 7 & 11 & 23 \\
24 & 35 & 6 & 8 & 3
\end{bmatrix}
\Rightarrow
\begin{bmatrix}
5 & 12 & 4 & 34 & 24 \\
3 & 3 & 7 & 32 & 35 \\
6 & 9 & 31 & 7 & 6 \\
4 & 22 & 4 & 11 & 8 \\
18 & 4 & 10 & 23 & 3
\end{bmatrix}
$$

28.   Write a function called `Scale()` that accepts a two-dimensional double-precision array and scales the column values using the values in a array called `Weights`. The array `Weights` also holds double-precision values and is also a parameter to **void** function `Scale()`. The number of rows and columns in the arrays also should be parameters to function `Scale()`.

9.13   POINTS TO REMEMBER

✔ Arrays are a C++ type mechanism for defining objects that represent a list of objects.

✔ In defining an array, we must specify the size of the array, that is, the number of elements in the array. The size must be a bracketed expression whose terms represent literal constants.

✔ The typical array is a one-dimensional list. However, multidimensional arrays can also be defined.

✔ By using the subscript operator [], we can reference an individual element of the array.

✔ Each element has its own subscript value: The first element in the array has a subscript of 0, the second element has a subscript of 1, and so on until the last element of the list, which has a subscript that is 1 less than the size of the list.

✔ Once subscripted, an individual array element can be used like any other object—it can be accessed, assigned, displayed, extracted to, passed as a value or reference parameter, and so on.

✔ Arrays are normally processed using iteration. Each time through a loop, a different element is processed.

✔ A **continue** statement indicates that the body of the innermost loop that contains the statement is finished for the current iteration.

The birth of the microprocessor

In the 1970s the number of companies making integrated circuits, or chips as they are now called, was growing rapidly. One area in the United States, about 50 miles south of San Francisco, had so many chip companies that it came to be known as Silicon Valley. Silicon Valley is home to Intel (for Integrated Electronics), then a medium-size company that manufactured memory chips.

In 1969 a Japanese company, Busicom, asked Intel to manufacture chips for a programmable calculator. The company wanted to make a family of calculators that had different features, and so their plans called for the design and manufacture of several different chips with slightly different functions. The job was assigned to an engineer name Ted Hoff. As a good engineer, Hoff analyzed the Busicom design before beginning work on it. He determined that the plan had little hope for success. It would require the costly design of several chips. Attempting to salvage the project, Hoff sought a solution. His solution was to develop a generalized chip that could be programmed—a microprocessor. The features of the different calculators would be supplied by changing the program the microprocessor executed. Thus, only one chip would need to be made. Busicom accepted the changes Hoff suggested, and the first microprocessor, the 4004, was produced in 1971.

Compared to today's microprocessors, the 4004 was quite primitive. It contained only about 2,300 transistors, and it could perform only about 60,000 operations per second. In contrast, today's microprocessors contain 2 to 4 million transistors, and can do 70 to 80 million operations per second. Nonetheless, the introduction of the 4004 marks the beginning of a new era in the computer revolution.

✔ An array is not a first-class object. As such, we cannot use an array as the target of an assignment or as the return value for a function. In addition, when an array is passed as a parameter, it must be passed by reference. These limitations are a carryover from the C language.

✔ When defining a function with an array parameter, the formal parameter definition does not need to include the size of the first dimension. This property makes C++ functions more flexible than their counterparts in languages such as Pascal that require separate functions to process arrays of different sizes.

✔ The elements of an array are always stored in contiguous memory. For a one-dimensional array, the first element is stored at the beginning of its memory, the second element is stored next in memory, and so on. For multidimensional arrays, the array elements are stored in row-major order.

✔ The traditional way to represent a string value is a character string. When an array is used to represent a character string, a null value '\0' is stored in the element that immediately follows the last character in the string.

✔ Elements of a global array whose base type is a fundamental type are initialized to 0 by default.

✔ Elements of a local array whose base type is a fundamental type are not initialized by default.

✔ Elements of an array whose base type is a fundamental type can be set to specific values in their definition using initialization lists. If the initialization list does not specify sufficient values, the unspecified elements are set to 0.

✔ Elements of an array whose base type is a class type are initialized using the default constructor of the base type.

✔ The container classes of the Standard Template Library are a set of generic list representations that allow programmers to specify which types of elements their particular lists hold. Besides being free of array restrictions, the container classes are extensible.

✔ There are eight major container classes. Six of these containers view a list primarily as a sequence of elements. The containers supporting this view are `deque`, `list`, `priority_queue`, `queue`, `stack`, and `vector`. The other two containers classes are `map` and `set`. These two containers view a list in a more associative manner.

✔ The classes `priority_queue`, `queue`, and `stack` are sometimes known as *container adapters* or *adapters*, as these classes are built (adapted) using other containers.

✔ The implementation of container classes in the Standard Template Library uses the C++ class template mechanism.

✔ Using formal parameters, known as template parameters, as placeholders for particular types and values, a class template describes the general form a class can take.

✔ To generate a specific class from a class template, the actual types and values of interest are supplied within angled brackets after the name of the template. This use of templates gave the Standard Template Library its name.

✔ The `vector` class template provides four constructors for defining a list of elements: A default constructor to define an empty list; a copy constructor to make a copy of an existing list; a constructor with a parameter that specifies the initial size of the list, where the elements are initialized using the default constructor of the list element type; and a constructor with two parameters, where the first parameter specifies the initial size of the list and the second parameter specifies the initial value of each list element.

✔ The `vector` template class provides several member functions and operators for accessing the elements that make up the vector. These member methods can be grouped into two categories: random access and sequential access methods.

✔ A random access method puts no restrictions on which element can be referenced in any given access.

✔ The principal random access methods are overloadings of the subscript operator `[]`. The subscript operator is overloaded for both non-**const** and

const vector objects. As a non-**const** subscript operation performs a reference return, the resulting value can be either accessed or modified. For a **const** subscript operation, the resulting value can only be accessed.

✔ The **vector** member subscript operator works in a manner similar to array subscripting. Each element of a **vector** has its own subscript value. The first element has subscript value 0, the second element has subscript value 1, and so on. The member subscript operator does not perform range checking.

✔ The **vector** member function **at()** is similar in behavior to the member subscript operator. However, if the requested element does not exist, an exception is generated.

✔ A sequential access method puts restrictions on which elements can be referenced in a given access. The restrictions vary according to whether the sequential access method is bidirectional or unidirectional.

✔ If the sequential access method is bidirectional, the elements accessed in consecutive references must be adjacent to each other in the list.

✔ If the sequential access method is unidirectional, then the next element that can be accessed is the element that occurs immediately after the current element being accessed.

✔ The sequential access methods provided by **vector** are all bidirectional.

✔ The **vector** sequential access methods are implemented using iterators.

✔ The value of an iterator object can be viewed conceptually as a pointer. An iterator points to either an element in the list or to sentinels that conceptually surround the list.

✔ A forward iterator advances towards the rear of the list; a reverse iterator advances towards the front of the list.

✔ To reference the element to which an iterator points, use the unary dereferencing operator *. The operator returns a reference to the value to which the iterator points. The resulting value can be either viewed or modified.

✔ The iterator increment operator ++ updates the iterator to point to the next element in the sequence. If there are no more elements in the list, the iterator instead points to a trailing sentinel.

✔ The decrement operator -- is defined for bidirectional iterators. The decrement operator updates the iterator to point to the previous element in the list. If there are no previous elements in the sequence, the iterator points to a sentinel.

✔ The **vector** member function **size()** returns the numbers of elements in the vector.

✔ The **vector** member function **insert()** can insert a new element into the list.

✔ The **vector** member function **push_back()** inserts a new element at the end of the **vector**.

✔ The **vector** member function **resize()** can modify the size of the list to a desired length.

- ✔ The `vector` member function `begin()` returns an iterator pointing to the first element of the `vector`.

- ✔ The `vector` member function `end()` returns an iterator pointing immediately beyond the last element of the `vector`.

- ✔ The `vector` member function `rbegin()` returns a reverse iterator pointing to the last element of the `vector`.

- ✔ The `vector` member function `rend()` returns a reverse iterator pointing immediately ahead of the first element of the vector.

- ✔ Two of the major activities performed in conjunction with arrays are sorting and searching.

- ✔ A list is sorted if the values in it are arranged in order by value. The standard ordering is nondecreasing.

- ✔ There are a number of sorting methods whose performance typically varies with the distribution of values in the list.

- ✔ Two of the more important sorting methods are `InsertionSort()` and `QuickSort()`.

- ✔ The task of `InsertionSort()` on its ith iteration is to correctly place the value of the element with subscript i, with respect to the values of list elements, with subscripts 0 through $i-1$. `InsertionSort()` works well in practice.

- ✔ `QuickSort()` is typically implemented as a recursive sort. The method begins by choosing a pivot value. The list is then rearranged into three sublists. The middle sublist is composed of an element whose value is the pivot value; the values of the elements in the left sublist are no larger than the pivot value, and the values of the elements in the right sublist are no smaller than the pivot value. Since the sublists are partitioned in this manner, the left and right sublists can be sorted independently of each other to produce a totally sorted list. The sublists are sorted by making recursive calls to the `QuickSort()` method. `QuickSort()` can be implemented so that it has very good average-case and worst-case performance characteristics.

- ✔ If a list needs to be searched frequently for different key values, consideration should be given to sorting the list first. This preprocessing can be helpful because `BinarySearch()`, which is designed for examining a sorted list, is far more efficient than a standard sequential search through an unsorted list.

- ✔ A member initialization list is a means of specifying the initial values of the data members of a class object. The initialization list is part of the constructor definition, and it immediately precedes the constructor body. The initialization list is separated from the constructor parameter list by a colon. The elements of the initialization list are evaluated in the order in which they are defined in the class definition.

9.14 EXERCISES

9.1   Which operator is used to refer to a particular element of an array?

9.2   Which vector member functions can be used to refer to a particular element of the container?

9.3   Can an array represent more than one type of value? Explain.

9.4   Can a vector represent more than one type of value? Explain.

9.5   Why do we tend to use named constants rather than literals when defining the size of an array or a vector?

9.6   Can an array be a value parameter? Explain.

9.7   Can a vector be a value parameter? Explain.

9.8   Can an object that contains an array as a data member be a value parameter? Explain.

9.9   Can an array element be a value parameter? Can an array element be a reference parameter? Explain.

9.10 Can an element of a vector be a value parameter? Can an element of a vector be a reference parameter? Explain.

9.11 What is a first-class object?

9.12 Are arrays first-class objects?

9.13 Are vectors first-class objects?

9.14 Does a global array with a base type that is a fundamental type have its elements automatically initialized? Explain.

9.15 Does a local array with a base type that is a fundamental type have its elements automatically initialized? Explain.

9.16 Does a local array with a base type that is a class type have its elements automatically initialized? Explain.

9.17 What is row-major order?

9.18 How many objects (including array elements) are defined in the following statements? Explain.

```
int A[100];
float B[25][30];
char C[9][4][4];
Rational D[2];
```

9.19 How many objects (including vector elements) are defined in the following statements? Explain.

```
vector<int> A(100);
vector<float> B;
vector< vector<int> > C(10, A);
Rational D(2);
```

9.20 Write a code segment that does the following:

a) Defines a constant MaxSize equal to 20.

b) Defines an array List whose base type is integer that can represent at most 20 values.

c) Sets the first element of List to the value 19.

d) Sets the last element of List to the value 54.

e) Sets the other elements of List to 0.

f) Displays List.

9.21 Write a code segment that does the following:

a) Defines a constant MaxN equal to 40.

b) Defines an array Scores, whose base type is floating-point, that can represent at most 40 values.

c) Sets the value of each element in Scores so that it matches its subscript value.

d) Displays the values of last five element of Scores.

Answer the following questions regarding Scores.

e) Is the value 3.1415 a legal element value? Explain.

f) Is the value 3.1415 a legal subscript value? Explain.

9.22 Write a code segment that does the following:

a) Defines constants MaxRows equal to 25 and MaxColumns equal to 10.

b) Defines an array Data whose base type is **bool** that can represent a table of values. There are at most 25 rows in the table with at most 10 entries per row.

c) Initializes array Data so that the elements whose row subscript value is odd have the value **true** and initializes the other elements to **false**.

9.23 Examine the following code segment:

```
cin >> A >> B;
cout << A << B << endl;
B = A;
C = A + B;
```

a) Which of the statements are legal if A, B, and C are **int** arrays?

b) Which of the statements are legal if A, B, and C are **char** arrays?

c) Which of the statements are legal if A, B, and C are **float** arrays?

9.24 What would happen during execution if the **for** loop of function main() in Program 9.1 is as follows:

```
for (int i = 0; i < n; ++i)
    Swap(Number[i], Number[n-1-i]);
```

9.25 Design and implement a **void** function Initialize() that has three parameters: A, n, and val. Parameter A is an array of **int** objects; **int** parameter n is the size of array; and **int** parameter val is the value of interest. The function sets each of the n elements of A to val.

9.26 Design and implement a **bool** function Equal() with three parameters: A, B, and n. Parameters A and B are **int** arrays; **int** parameter n is the size of the arrays. The function iteratively compares the elements of the arrays. If each of the n pairs of elements is the same, the function returns **true**; otherwise, the function returns **false**.

9.27   Design and implement an **int** function LessThan() with three formal parameters: an **int** array A, the number of valid elements n, and an **int** value v. The value v is to be optional with a default value of 0. Function LessThan() returns the number of elements in list A[0], …, A[n-1] that are less than v.

9.28   Design and implement the following statistical functions. Each of the functions returns a **float** value and has two parameters: A and n. Parameter A is an array of **float** objects; parameter n is the size of array.

   a) Function Mean(): it returns the average of the n values in the list.

   b) Function Median(): it returns the middle value of the n values in the list if n is odd; it returns the average of the two middle values of the n values in the list if n is even.

9.29   Write a code segment that does the following:

   a) Defines a constant MaxSize equal to 20.

   b) Defines a vector List whose MaxSize elements are integer values equal to 1.

   c) Sets the first element of List to the value 19.

   d) Sets the last element of List to the value 54.

   e) Sets the other elements of List to 0.

   f) Initializes an iterator for the list that points to the trailing list sentinel.

   Answer the following questions regarding List.

   g) Is the value 3.1415 a legal element value? Explain.

   h) Is the value 3.1415 a legal subscript value? Explain.

9.30   Write a code segment that does the following:

   a) Defines constants M equal to 25 and N equal to 10.

   b) Defines a vector BitTable whose elements are vectors of type **bool**. BitTable initially has M elements. Each of these elements initially consists of N undefined Boolean values.

   c) Sets BitTable so that its elements whose index value is odd have all of their elements set to **true**.

   d) Resizes the elements of BitTable whose index value is even to represent empty lists.

9.31   Suppose the following definitions are in effect.

```
int A[10];
int B[10][10];
vector<int> C(10);
vector< vector<int> > D(10);
vector<int> E[10];
vector< vector<int> > F[10];
```

Identify which type of subscripting is occurring in the following code segment:

```
A[1] = 1;
A[A[1]] = 1;
B[1][1] = 1;
C[1] = 1;
C[A[1]] = 1;
D[0] = D[1];
D[1][1] = A[1];
E[1] = E[0];
F[0] = F[1];
F[0][0] = F[1][1];
F[0][0][0] = 1;
E[1][1] = 1;
```

9.32 Suppose the following definitions are in effect.

```
int A[10];
int B[10];
int C[10][10];
vector<int> D(10);
vector<int> E(100);
vector<int> F(10);
```

Identify which of the following assignments are correct and which are not. Explain your answer.

```
A[10] = 1;
A[1] = B[1];
B[1][1] = 1;
C[1][1] = 1;
C[10] = 1;
C[10] = B;
D[0] = D[1];
D[1][1] = 1;
D = E;
D[0] = E[1];
F[0][0] = 1;
F[10] = 1;
E = F;
```

9.33 Modify function Search() to be more like the function find() of the Standard Template algorithm library. The modified function has four parameters: A, lindex, rindex, and key. Parameter A is a vector of **int** objects; **int** parameters lindex and rindex specify a range of elements in A; and **int** parameter key is the value of interest. If the key value is present, the function should return the index of the first element in the subscript range lindex ... rindex whose value is equal to the key value. If the key value is not present, the function should return the value rindex + 1.

9.34 Design and implement a **void** function ListAll() that has three parameters: A, n, and key. Parameter A is a vector of **int** objects; **int** parameter n is the size of array; and **int** parameter key is the value of interest. Function ListAll() displays the indexes of all elements in A that are equal to key. Function ListAll() accomplishes its task through a series of iterative calls to the modified function `Search()` of Exercise 9.33.

9.35   Reimplement function `Pivot()` so that if the sublist to be partitioned has at least three elements, then the pivot value is the median value of the left-most, right-most, and middle elements in the sublist.

9.36   Implement the iterative sorting function `SelectionSort()`. This function on its `i`th iteration finds the `i`th smallest element in the list and interchanges that value with the `i`th element in the array.

9.37   Modify function `InsertionSort()` so rather than specifying the number of elements to be sorted, a range of elements is specified.

9.38   Modify function `QuickSort()` so that it invokes the modified `InsertionSort()` of the previous exercise if the number of elements to be sorted is 20 or less.

9.39   Reimplement function `QuickSort()` so that the elements to be sorted are represented using iterators p and q.

9.40   Implement the recursive sorting function `MergeSort()`. This function conceptually divides the current list of n elements into two sublists of size n/2. If a sublist contains more than one element, the sublist is sorted by a recursive call to `MergeSort()`. After the two sublists of size n/2 are sorted, they are merged together to produce a single sorted list of size n.

9.41   Implement a recursive version of function `BinarySearch()`.

9.42   Design and implement a function `InitializeTable()` that prompts a user for a filename and then extracts a puzzle search table from that file. The extractions are stored in a reference parameter that is suitable for `PuzzleSearch()`. Function `InitializeTable()` also has two other reference parameters m and n, where m is the number of rows extracted and n is the number of columns per row. The function should perform all appropriate validation.

9.43   Given a matrix A with m rows and n columns and a matrix B with n rows and p columns, we can compute the product matrix AB. The product C has m rows and p columns where element C_{ij} has the following definition:

$$C_{ij} = \sum_{k=1}^{n} A_{ik} \cdot B_{kj}$$

Overload the multiplication operator `*` so that it performs matrix multiplication on `vector<vector<int>>` objects. The operator should have the following prototype:

```
vector< vector<int> > Multiply(
  const vector< vector<int> > &A,
  const vector< vector<int> > &B,);
```

9.44   Reimplement function PutList() so that it uses iterators p and q to specify the portion of the list that is to be displayed. Iterator p points to the first element in the list to be displayed; iterator q points to the element beyond the last element that is to be displayed.

9.45   Reimplement function GetWords() so that its list parameter is represented using a multidimensional array of characters. Discuss the relative difference in difficulty in implementing GetWords() this way versus using a list parameter of type vector<string>.

9.46   Overload the insertion operator << for vector<int> objects.

9.47   Overload the extraction operator >> for vector<int> objects.

9.48   Overload the less than operator < for Location objects. Location p is less than Location q if either p's row coordinate is less than q's row coordinate or if the two row coordinates are the same but p's column coordinate is less than q's column coordinate.

9.49   Should location.h include prototypes for auxiliary operators? Why?

9.50   Reimplement function GetList() so that it has an additional reference parameter sin of type istream. Parameter sin is an optional parameter with a default value of cin. GetList() should make its extractions from sin.

9.51   Reimplement function PutList() so that it has an additional reference parameter sin of type ostream. Parameter sout is an optional parameter with a default value of cout. PutList() should make its insertions to sout.

9.52   Overload the insertion operator << for Location objects. Should the form of the values produced be the same as what the extraction operator expects for Location objects? Why?

9.53   Speculate on why we developed and used the class Location rather than the EzWindows library class Position for the maze problem.

9.54   Implement direction library functions Clockwise() and Counter-Clockwise().

9.55   Implement the Wanderer public movement function MoveEast().

9.56   Implement the Wanderer public movement function MoveSouth().

9.57   Implement the Wanderer public movement function MoveWest().

9.58   Reimplement the Wanderer class with the addition of two new public mutator member functions. The new functions are both named SetLocation() and are used to relocate the wanderer. The functions differ in their parameter's representation of the new location of the wanderer; one function expects a Location object as its parameter, and the other function expects to be given the row and column coordinates. What restrictions should be imposed on the new location of the wanderer? For example, must the new location be adjacent to the previous location? Discuss both why and why not. How important are these members to the Wanderer class?

9.59   Implement the constructor for the class Display.

9.60   Implement the public inspectors GetDisplayWindow() and Get-Scale() for the class Display.

9.61   Implement the public mutators SetErrant() and SetStepped() for the class Display.

9.62   Implement the public facilitators DisplayAll() and DisplayLocation() for the class Display.

9.63   Implement the protected facilitators DisplayStart(), DisplayFinish(), DisplayErrant(), DisplayStep(), DisplayUnseen(), and DisplayObstacle().

9.64   Implement the protect mutator SetScale() for the class Display.

9.65   Modify the definition and implementation of the class Display so that the constructor has an additional parameter Origin of type Position from the EzWindows library. The value of this parameter is used in the initialization of a new data member named Offset. Offset represents the location for the upper-left corner of the maze in the display window. The various display functions should use this value as an offset for placing their drawing.

9.66   Implement the public inspectors at() and size() for the class Path.

9.67   Implement the public mutators DeleteLocation() and Set() for the class Path.

9.68   Implement the public iterators begin() and end() for the class Path.

9.69   Can the Path iterators begin() and end() be invoked for constant Path objects? Why? If not, what actions must be taken to implement iterators begin() and end() for constant Path objects?

9.70   Modify the controller ApiMain() of Listing 9.19 so that, after the wanderer reaches its goal, the function displays to the standard output those steps that are not part of the dead-end corridors. This task can be more readily accomplished by deleting from WP the errant steps as they are determined.

CHAPTER 10

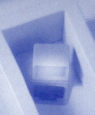

The EzWindows API: a detailed examination

Introduction

At this point, it should be clear that designing and writing good programs is not only fun and interesting, but also intellectually demanding and time-consuming. As we mentioned in Chapter 1, the time-consuming nature of programming is one factor that has led to the software crisis. In this chapter, we introduce the concept of an application programmer interface, or API. Using an API is one way that professional programmers reduce the time and cost of producing software. Essentially, an API provides a set of basic building blocks, or infrastructure, for constructing particular kinds of programs. Rather than building each program from scratch, the programmer uses facilities provided by the API when possible. Properly designed APIs can significantly reduce the effort to construct complicated programs. Indeed, most commercial software is constructed using a variety of APIs. To illustrate the use of an API, we introduce an API for displaying simple graphical objects in a window. The EzWindows API is an object-oriented API that provides facilities for building programs that use a windowing system for input and output. Using the EzWindows API, we will be able to build good programs that look good too!

Key Concepts

- application programmer interface
- graphical user interface
- event-based programming
- callbacks
- mouse events
- graphical programming
- timer events
- bitmaps

10.1 APPLICATION PROGRAMMER INTERFACES

Designing, building, and testing a program is difficult and time-consuming work. To simplify and speed up the development of software, programmers have developed several approaches for shortening the time required to build a program. One of these techniques is to use an *application programmer interface* (API). The basic idea is similar to that of using standard libraries. If a library routine exists for doing a particular job or task, we should use it, rather than write code from scratch, to do the job. Programmers call writing code to do a job when code already exists for doing the job reinventing the wheel. We want to avoid reinventing the wheel whenever possible.

An API is also a set of library routines. What distinguishes an API from a standard library is that an API supports building a specific kind of application or a component of an application with a specific capability. For example, there are numerous APIs for building the graphical user interface (GUI) component of an application. Some popular APIs for developing GUIs include Open Software Foundation's Motif®, Microsoft's Foundation Classes® (MFC), and Borland's ObjectWindows Library® (OWL).

APIs exist for almost every type of application imaginable. For example, there are APIs for building applications that

- Process and produce HTML, the language used to produce documents for distribution via the World Wide Web.
- Use multimedia.
- Employ cryptography.
- Use virtual reality.
- Use the telephone to communicate.
- Access network facilities.
- Control and monitor scientific instruments.
- Produce graphs and plots of data.
- Perform statistical analysis.
- Perform database queries.

Obviously, using an API is a form of software reuse. However, a few ancillary advantages to using an API are worth mentioning. First, APIs usually handle application-specific details that the programmer should not have to worry about. For example, the designers of an API for a GUI have already dealt with major issues, such as consistency of look and behavior, user friendliness, and flexibility, as well as low-level details about how to construct and draw elements on various display devices. Thus the programmer need not worry about these details. In turn, the programmer can concentrate on the application—not on the details having to do with the GUI. Second, use of an API ensures consistency across applications. All applications that use the API have the same look and feel. This consistency makes applications easier to learn and use than applications with a very different look and feel.

Because of the overwhelming benefits of using an API, most applications of any size are developed using one. In this chapter, we introduce and use a simple object-oriented API designed for building programs that use the graphical display capabilities and input devices that are available on most modern desktop machines. The name of the API is EzWindows, for easy windows. We have several reasons for introducing and using EzWindows.

First, it illustrates a style and method of programming that is used in the real world. Most programs are not developed from scratch. They build on an existing infrastructure, such as an API. Second, it allows us to use the input/output paradigm that is common today. Most of today's popular applications use a graphical user interface to communicate with the user. It is rare these days to see an application where the human communicates with the application by typing commands and data on the keyboard. Similarly, the application communicates with the user via graphical displays rather than by printing only text on a screen. Third, EzWindows enables us to develop programs that are much more interesting and fun than we could otherwise create.

10.2 A SIMPLE WINDOW CLASS

EzWindows contains two major classes that are publicly available. In this section, we discuss `SimpleWindow`, a class that encapsulates the creation and control of windows for displaying graphical objects. Section 10.5 discusses `BitMap`, a class that encapsulates the creation and manipulation of bitmapped screen images.

10.2.1 Event-based programming

Previously, our programs contained a function `main()` or a function `ApiMain()`. With the exception of the Kaleidoscope program of Chapter 7, a program began executing when the operating system called either `main()` or `ApiMain()`, and it stopped executing when `main()` or `ApiMain()` returned or the program called `exit()`.

This method works well for conventional programs, but not for programs that use the mouse for input and a graphical display for output. This type of program must respond to events or messages from the operating system. These events include mouse clicks and timer events. For programs that use this paradigm of user interaction, the object-oriented programming model is more appropriate.

With the object-oriented model, we think of the operating system as one object and the program as another. The operating system communicates with the program by sending it messages. Using this approach, it is easy to see that we do not want a program that runs sequentially, starting with a call to function `main()` or `ApiMain()`. In fact, the program needs to be able to receive and send messages. Rather than have an application directly receive from and send messages to the operating system, we will use EzWindows to provide a consistent and simplified set of methods for communicating with the operating system. In effect EzWindows will handle the interaction between the operating system and a user application. With EzWindows the messages or events that a program can receive are start program, mouse click, timer click, refresh, and end program. The interaction between the EzWindows class `SimpleWindow` and a user program is shown in Figure 10.1.

Figure 10.1

Interaction between the EzWindows SimpleWindow class and a user program

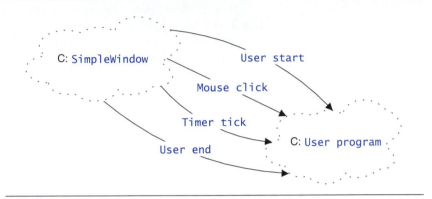

In addition to the messages that EzWindows forwards to the user program, the user program can send messages to the operating system through EzWindows. For example, a user program can tell EzWindows which user routine to call when a mouse click or a timer tick occurs. Telling EzWindows which user routine to invoke when a certain event occurs is called *registering a callback*. In addition to the event services, EzWindows provides facilities for creating windows and displaying various types of objects in a window. For example, a user program can send EzWindows's `SimpleWindow` class a message that directs it to display a text string at a specified location in a particular window. As we proceed through the chapter, we describe some of the capabilities of EzWindows and illustrate their use by writing some simple programs.

10.2.2 SimpleWindow coordinate system

Before exploring the EzWindows API further, we need to revisit the coordinate system for positioning objects as well as a system for specifying the size of objects. EzWindows uses the metric system for specifying both the position of an object and its size. For example, the EzWindows declaration

```
SimpleWindow TestWindow("Hello EzWindows",
    10.0, 5.0, Position(4.0, 4.0));
```

creates a window labeled Hello EzWindows that is 4 centimeters from the left edge of the screen and 4 centimeters from the top edge of the screen. The window is 10 centimeters wide and 5 centimeters high. Figure 10.2 shows the window and its position on the screen.

Figure 10.2

*The EzWindows
coordinate system*

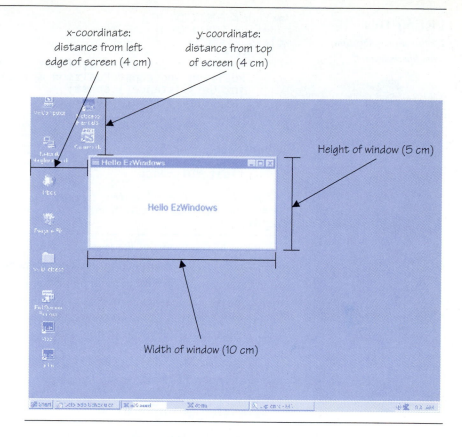

x-coordinate:
distance from left
edge of screen (4 cm)

y-coordinate:
distance from top
of screen (4 cm)

Height of window (5 cm)

Hello EzWindows

Width of window (10 cm)

The prototype of the constructor for the `SimpleWindow` class is

```
SimpleWindow(const string &WindowTitle = "Untitled",
    float Width = 8.0, float Height = 8.0,
    const Position &WindowPosition
    = Position(0.0, 0.0));
```

Notice that the position of the window relative to the upper-left corner of the screen is specified using an object called `Position`. In earlier chapters, the position of a window object was specified by passing both an x- and y-coordinate to any function that dealt with the position of a window object. We used this approach to keep the number of objects we were dealing with to a minimum. Now that we have a better understanding of objects and object-oriented programming, it makes sense to begin to use objects whenever appropriate. It is convenient and natural to encapsulate a window location as a single entity. Consequently, we have created a new class, `Position`, that holds the logical window coordinates of a window object. The class declaration of `Position` is contained in Listing 10.1.

The declaration of `Position` follows our normal convention with a constructor that uses default values of 0 for the x and y distances and inspectors and mutators for the private data. `GetXDistance()` and `GetYDistance()`

Listing 10.1

*Declaration of Position
from file position.h*

```
#ifndef POSITION_H
#define POSITION_H
class Position {
    public:
        Position(float x = 0.0, float y = 0.0);
        Position Add(const Position &p) const;
        int GetXDistance() const;
        int GetYDistance() const;
    protected:
        void SetXDistance(float x);
        void SetYDistance(float y);
    private:
        float XDistance;
        float YDistance;
};
// Auxiliary function for computing new positions
Position operator+(const Position &x, const Position &y);
#endif
```

are public because some of the low-level window manipulation routines need access to the values of the coordinates. The mutators are not public because we do not want clients of `Position` to be able to change the private data. However a derived class created from `Position` might need to change the values of the private data. Making the mutators protected gives the derived class access to the mutators. Listing 10.2 contains the implementation `Position`.

The existence of the class `Position` means that we can conveniently define a location. For example, the definition

```
Position p(2.0, 4.0);
```

Listing 10.2

*Implementation of class
Position from
position.cpp*

```
#include "position.h"
Position::Position(float x, float y) :
 XDistance(x), YDistance(y) {
    // No code needed
}
Position Position::Add(const Position &p) {
    return Position(GetXDistance() + p.GetXDistance(),
     GetYDistance() + p.GetYDistance());
}
float Position::GetXDistance() const {
    return XDistance;
}
float Position::GetYDistance() const {
    return YDistance;
}
void Position::SetXDistance(float x) {
    XDistance = x;
    return;
}
void Position::SetYDistance(float y) {
    YDistance = y;
    return;
}
Position operator+(const Position &a, const Position &b) {
    return x.Add(y);
}
```

instantiates a `Position` object named p whose value is the location that is 2 centimeters from the left edge of the screen and 4 centimeters from the top. Similarly, the definition

```
Position Origin;
```

defines a `Position` object called `Origin` whose value is the upper-left corner of the screen (i.e., location 0, 0).

It will sometimes be convenient to compute a new position given a position and an offset from that position. For this purpose, the + operator has been overloaded so that it operates on two positions. For example, suppose we are given the position

```
Position p1(5.0, 5.0);
```

and we need to compute a new position named p2 that is 2 centimeters to the left and 3 centimeters down from p1. We can compute this new location by adding the proper distance to p1. The code

```
Position p2 = p1 + Position(-2.0, 3.0);
```

creates p2 with the value (3.0, 8.0). As we shall see, the use of the class `Position` simplifies the use of EzWindows objects.

10.2.3 Hello EzWindows

To demonstrate some of the basics of using EzWindows, let's rewrite the hello world program using EzWindows. We want the new program to open a window and display the greeting Hello EzWindows in the center of the window.

To create a window, we need only instantiate a `SimpleWindow` object. The API will handle all of the details. Generally, the definition of a `SimpleWindow` object will be done via a global declaration. Although we normally avoid global declarations, we need to use one in this situation because we want the window to persist during the execution of our program. Recall that an object defined inside a function block is destroyed when the block containing the definition ends. With event-based programming, there is no function that can safely define a window and have it persist throughout the execution of the program.

The global declaration for the window is

```
SimpleWindow HelloWindow("Hello EzWindows", 10.0, 4.0,
    Position(5.0, 6.0));
```

which, when executed, will create a `SimpleWindow` object named `HelloWindow` with the label Hello EzWindows. The window will measure 10 centimeters by 4 centimeters and will be positioned 5 centimeters from the left edge of the screen and 6 centimeters from the top edge of the screen.

When a `SimpleWindow` object is created, it is not immediately displayed. It is up to the programmer to open the window. Our program will open the window and display the text when EzWindows sends the user start message. EzWindows sends this message by calling the function `ApiMain()`, where most of the work is done for our program. The first thing we need to do is to get `HelloWindow` to display itself, so we send an open message to the window. The following call

```
HelloWindow.Open();
```

sends the message. Similar to calls for opening files, we should check to make sure the window indeed opens. The class `SimpleWindow` includes the member function `GetStatus()` that returns the status of the window. The prototype for `GetStatus()` is

```
WindowStatus GetStatus() const;
```

where type `WindowStatus` is

```
enum WindowStatus { WindowClosed, WindowOpen,
  WindowFailure };
```

Thus a better, safer way to open a window is

```
HelloWindow.Open();
assert(HelloWindow.GetStatus() == WindowOpen);
```

If the open fails, the assert macro will print a message for us.

To print our message, we will use two additional `SimpleWindow` public member functions. The first, `GetCenter()`, returns the position of the center of the window. The second, `RenderText()`, displays a text string at a specified location in the window. The following code displays the message in the center of the window.

```
Position Center = HelloWindow.GetCenter();
Position UpperLeft = Center + Position(-1.0, -1.0);
Position LowerRight = Center + Position(1.0,  1.0);
HelloWindow.RenderText(UpperLeft, LowerRight,
  "Hello EzWindows", White);
```

When the location of the center of `HelloWindow` is obtained, a bounding box is computed to position the text. A bounding box is specified by giving the coordinates of the upper-left corner and lower-right corner of an imaginary rectangle. The text is positioned so that its center is the center of the bounding box. The size of the bounding box for `RenderText()` is somewhat irrelevant because `RenderText()` allows the text to extend past the edges of the bounding box (see Figure 10.3). Consequently, we use a box that is 1 centimeter on a side.

The third argument to `RenderText()` is the string to display, and the last argument is the background color to use for the text. Since, by default, a `SimpleWindow` window has a white background, the text is displayed with a white background. The colors supported by EzWindows are defined by the following enumeration:

```
enum color { Black, White, Red, Green, Blue, Yellow,
  Cyan, Magenta };
```

The last piece of our program handles the user end message that the program receives when the operating systems sends a terminate message through EzWindows. Such messages are generated when the controlling window is

Figure 10.3

Text bounding box used by RenderText( )

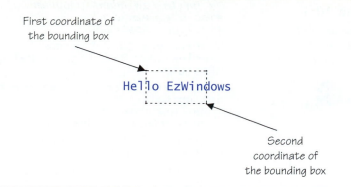

First coordinate of the bounding box

Hello EzWindows

Second coordinate of the bounding box

closed. When EzWindows receives a terminate message, it sends a message to the user application by calling ApiEnd(). For the hello program, the only thing ApiEnd() needs to do is close the window. If the user does not supply an ApiEnd() function, a default ApiEnd(), which performs no actions, is loaded from the EzWindows library. Figure 10.4 shows the window created when our application runs and Listing 10.3 contains the complete code for the program.

Figure 10.4

Window created by hello program

Hello EzWindows

Hello EzWindows

SimpleWindow has additional capabilities, such as handling events from the mouse and a timer and displaying pop-up messages. Before covering these topics, we review the other major class contained in EzWindows—Bitmap.

10.2.4 EzWindows API mechanics

The EzWindows API code and the examples discussed in this chapter are supplied on a CD-ROM that is included with the textbook. The programs are also available via the World Wide Web at

http://www.cs.virginia.edu/c++programdesign

Appendix E contains a reference summary of the EzWindows API. EzWindows is designed so that it can be used on PCs running Windows 98®, Windows

Listing 10.3

*Implementation of
EzWindows hello
program in hello.cpp*

```cpp
// Hello EzWindows program
#include "ezwin.h"
#include <assert.h>
// Create a 10 x 4 window
SimpleWindow HelloWindow("Hello EzWindows", 10.0, 4.0,
  Position(5.0, 6.0));
// ApiMain(): create a window and display greeting
int ApiMain() {
    HelloWindow.Open();
    assert(HelloWindow.GetStatus() == WindowOpen);

    // Get Center of Window
    Position Center = HelloWindow.GetCenter();

    // Create bounding box for text
    Position UpperLeft = Center + Position(-1.0, -1.0);
    Position LowerRight = Center + Position(1.0,  1.0);

    // Display the text
    HelloWindow.RenderText(UpperLeft, LowerRight,
      "Hello EzWindows", White);

    return 0;
}
// ApiEnd(): shutdown the window
int ApiEnd() {
    HelloWindow.Close();

    return 0;
}
```

NT®, and Windows 2000®. It has been tested using the latest versions of both the Borland® C++ and the Microsoft Visual® C++ compilers.

To build and run an EzWindows program requires your program to be compiled and linked with the EzWindows code. Figure 10.5 illustrates this process for the hello program. The dotted box labeled EzWindows API library contains the EzWindows modules that will be linked with the program. The object code for these modules are contained in the library file `ezwin.lib`. The C++ linker is smart, and it pulls from the library only modules that the program being built requires. The dotted box labeled Application module contains the modules written by the programmer.

Figure 10.5

*Building an
EzWindows
application*

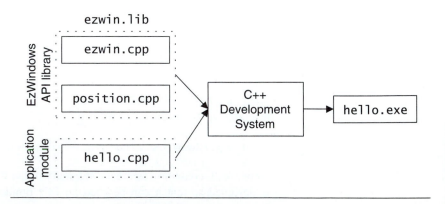

Because most software projects, even those of modest size, consist of more than one module, commercial C++ program development environments provide facilities for specifying the files that need to be compiled in order to produce an executable. Some compilers use what is known as a project file; others use a *Makefile*. In both methods, the programmer specifies the files that need to be compiled, the libraries that should be used, and where to place the executable. Appendix F describes how to set up project files and Makefiles for several of the most popular compilers and platforms.

Once a project file is set up, building the executable usually requires simply clicking on the appropriate button. Indeed, these environments know which files have been modified since the last time the executable was built, and they recompile only the files that have changed in the interim. For large software projects, this selective recompilation can save an enormous amount of time.

Throughout this chapter, most of the projects consist of several modules. To help get the big picture, we will provide a diagram like the one in Figure 10.5 that shows the program modules that go into the application.

Debugging a program that uses the graphical interface is often difficult because there is no easy way to display debugging information. The EzWindows API solves this problem by always opening a window that text can be displayed in by inserting text into the `cout` stream. This window is also used for sending input to a program by extracting from the stream `cin`. We call this window the *control window*.

To illustrate the use of the EzWindows control window to do text input and output, we have modified the hello program to prompt for and read the location to write the hello message. Listing 10.4 contains the code for this program. Its module structure is identical to the previous hello program. Because the program will be using `cin` and `cout`, the file `iostream.h` must be included. When this program is compiled and executed, two windows are created. One is the text window; the second is the window explicitly created by the program. The two windows are shown in Figure 10.6.

Listing 10.4

Program to illustrate stream I/O in an EzWindows program

```cpp
// Program to illustrate mechanics of API program
#include <iostream>
#include <string>
#include <assert.h>
#include "ezwin.h"
using namespace std;

// Create a 10 x 4 window
SimpleWindow HelloWindow("Hello EzWindows",
  10.0, 4.0, Position(5.0, 6.0));

// ApiMain(): demonstrate using cin with EzWindows
int ApiMain() {
  HelloWindow.Open();
  assert(HelloWindow.GetStatus() == WindowOpen);

  cout << "Enter the location in the window\n"
    << "to write the text (e.g., 4 6): ";
  int XCoordinate;
  int YCoordinate;
  cin >> XCoordinate >> YCoordinate;

  Position Location(XCoordinate, YCoordinate);
```

```
        Position UpperLeft = Location + Position(-1.0, -1.0);
        Position LowerRight = Location + Position(1.0, 1.0);
        // Display the text
        HelloWindow.RenderText(UpperLeft, LowerRight,
          "Hello EzWindows", White);
        cout << "Text was rendered at " << XCoordinate << ","
          << YCoordinate << endl;
        return 0;
}

// ApiEnd(): shut down the window
int ApiEnd() {
        HelloWindow.Close();
        return 0;
}
```

Figure 10.6

Windows created by the program in Listing 10.4

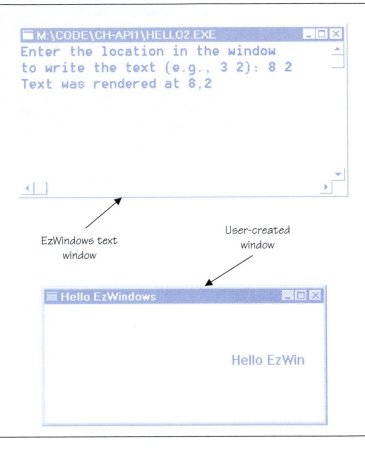

As the figure illustrates, the text that is inserted into stream `cout` is displayed in the text window. Similarly, when the window is active, characters typed on the keyboard are placed in the stream `cin` where they can be extracted.

10.3 THE BITMAP CLASS

Most windowing systems have facilities for displaying graphical images. There are many different formats for storing images. One popular format is called a bitmap. For example, many painting programs save a drawing in the bitmap file format. On many systems, a file containing a bitmap has the extension bmp. EzWindows supports the display of bitmap images.

To illustrate some of the basic EzWindows facilities for displaying a bitmap file, we will write a program that loads and displays a bitmap photograph of the authors of this book. The modules needed for this program are shown in Figure 10.7.

Figure 10.7

Module structure for photo application

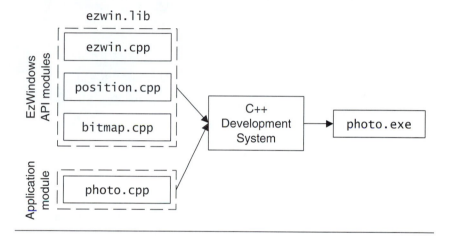

To display bitmaps, in addition to `ezwin.cpp` and `position.cpp`, the module `bitmap.cpp` is also required. This module contains the implementation of the bitmap class. The code we write is contained in the file `photo.cpp`. Figure 10.8 shows the window created and displayed by the program.

Like our hello program in Listing 10.3, we need to instantiate a window. We create a `SimpleWindow` object named `PhotoWindow`. Its global definition is

```
SimpleWindow PhotoWindow("The Authors", 10.0, 7.0,
    Position(5.0, 3.0));
```

Again, all the work is done in `ApiMain()`. `PhotoWindow` is opened, and the location of its center is obtained. We then instantiate a `BitMap` object named `PhotoBmp`. Its definition is

```
BitMap Photo(PhotoWindow);
```

That is, the `BitMap` constructor requires a single argument: the `SimpleWindow` that the `BitMap` should be attached to or associated with. The declarations of `BitMap`'s constructor is

```
BitMap(SimpleWindow &DisplayWindow);
```

Thus a `BitMap` object is constructed by giving a reference to a `SimpleWindow` object.

Figure 10.8

Window created by photo program

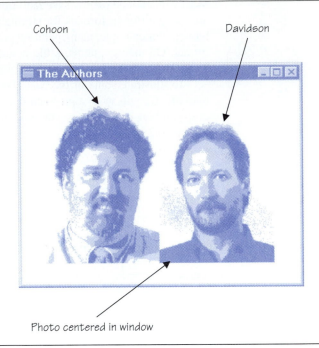

Cohoon

Davidson

Photo centered in window

The next step is to load the image into the `BitMap` object. The code

```
Photo.Load("photo.bmp");
assert(Photo.GetStatus() == BitMapOkay);
```

loads the photo image from the disk into the `BitMap` object. The `BitMap` member function `GetStatus()`, like `GetStatus()` for `SimpleWindow`, returns a status indication. The declaration of `GetStatus()` is

```
BitMapStatus GetStatus() const;
```

and the definition of `BitMapStatus` is

```
enum BitMapStatus {NoBitMap, BitMapOkay, NoWindow};
```

Status `NoBitMap` indicates that the file specified either did not exist or was not a file containing a bitmap, and status `NoWindow` indicates that no window is associated with the `BitMap` object. This situation can happen if the `SimpleWindow` object that was bound to the `BitMap` when it was constructed was closed. In either of these cases, no image is loaded. Status `BitMapOkay` indicates the image was loaded successfully.

The last step is to compute the position within `PhotoWindow` to display the image. Unlike some of the other graphical objects we have used, `BitMap` objects are positioned by specifying the position of the upper-left corner of the image. The following code computes the proper position of the `Photo` bitmap so that it is centered in the window, sets its position, and displays the image in the window.

```
Position PhotoPosition = WindowCenter +
  Position(-.5 * Photo.GetWidth(),
  -.5 * Photo.GetHeight());
Photo.SetPosition(PhotoPosition);
Photo.Draw();
```

The code uses `BitMap` public member functions `GetWidth()` and `Get-Height()` to obtain the width and height in centimeters of the image. Listing 10.5 contains the complete code for the module `photo.cpp`.

Listing 10.5

Program that illustrates loading and displaying a bitmap

```
// Display a bit map image of the authors in the
// center of a window
#include "bitmap.h"
#include <assert.h>

// Open a window to display photograph of the authors
SimpleWindow PhotoWindow("The Authors", 10.0, 7.0,
  Position(5.0, 3.0));

// ApiMain(): display a bitmap photo
int ApiMain() {
  PhotoWindow.Open();
  assert(PhotoWindow.GetStatus() == WindowOpen);

  Position WindowCenter = PhotoWindow.GetCenter();

  // Create a bitmap
  BitMap Photo(PhotoWindow);

  // Load the image
  Photo.Load("photo.bmp");
  assert(Photo.GetStatus() == BitMapOkay);

  // Compute photo position so it s centered in the window
  Position PhotoPosition = WindowCenter +
    Position(-.5 * Photo.GetWidth(),
    -.5 * Photo.GetHeight());

  Photo.SetPosition(PhotoPosition);
  Photo.Draw();

  return 0;
}

// ApiEnd(): shutdown the window
int ApiEnd() {
  PhotoWindow.Close();
  return 0;
}
```

10.4 MOUSE EVENTS

One of the innovations that has made computers much easier to use is the mouse. A mouse enables a user to interact with a program without having to type obscure or hard-to-remember commands. EzWindows provides a simple facility for using the mouse. The basic idea is that the application tells EzWindows what function to call when a mouse click occurs in an EzWindows

`SimpleWindow`. As we mentioned earlier, this procedure is called registering a callback. The `SimpleWindow` declaration of the member function for registering a callback for a mouse event is

```
void SetMouseClickCallback(MouseCallback f);
```

where `MouseCallback` is the **typedef**

```
typedef int (*MouseCallback)(const Position &);
```

This declaration specifies that when an application registers a callback for a mouse-click event, we need to give the name of a function that returns an **int** and accepts a **const** `Position` as its argument. The value of the argument is the position of the mouse sprite when the mouse button was clicked. To illustrate how mouse-click events are handled, let's write an application that opens two windows and displays a different image in each window. When the mouse is positioned in a window and clicked, the bitmap image for that window is redisplayed at that location. Figure 10.9 illustrates what happens when the program runs.

As usual, we define two global `SimpleWindow` objects. We also use global definitions for the two bitmaps because we do not want to keep instantiating them and destroying them when messages are sent to the application from EzWindows. The definitions are

```
SimpleWindow W1("Window One", 15.0, 9.0,
  Position(1.0, 1.0));
SimpleWindow W2("Window Two", 15.0, 9.0,
  Position(8.0, 12.0));
// Define two bitmaps, one for each window
BitMap W1Bmp(W1);
BitMap W2Bmp(W2);
```

Function `ApiMain()` opens the two windows, loads the bitmaps, and displays the bitmaps in each window at a default location. This code is similar to the code we wrote for the previous program. (See Listing 10.5 for the details.) The last action of `ApiMain()` is to register the functions to call back on a mouse click. We need to register a callback function for each window. The code

```
W1.SetMouseClickCallback(W1MouseClick);
W2.SetMouseClickCallback(W2MouseClick);
```

sends a message to `W1` telling `W1` to call function `W1MouseClick` when it receives a mouse-click event. The code sends a similar message to `W2`.

The definition of `W1MouseClick` is

```
int W1MouseClick(const Position &p) {
    // Erase the bitmap
    W1Bmp.Erase();

    // Set its new position and display it
    W1Bmp.SetPosition(p);
    W1Bmp.Draw();

    return 1;
}
```

Figure 10.9

*Window created by
mouse-event program*

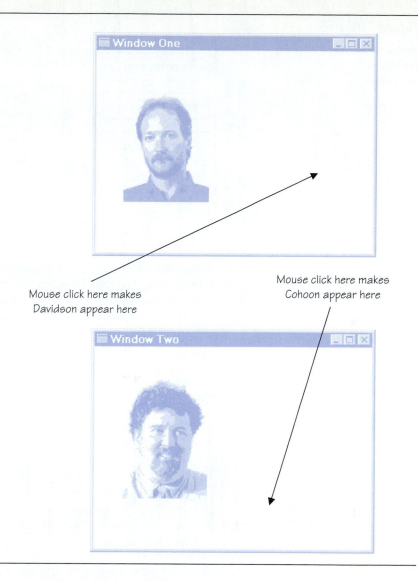

Figure 10.9

*Window created by
mouse-event program*

Mouse click here makes
Davidson appear here

Mouse click here makes
Cohoon appear here

The mouse-event handler for W1 erases its associated bitmap, resets its position using the position passed to it from EzWindows, and draws the bitmap at the new position. Our code is contained in the module `mevent.cpp`. The required module structure is shown in Figure 10.10.

Figure 10.10

Module structure for
mouse-event
application

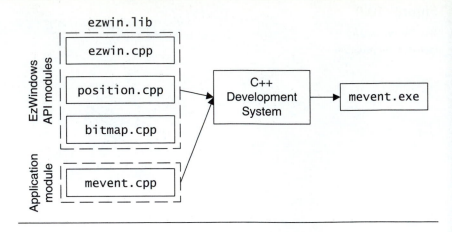

When the modules are compiled and linked, the executable will be placed in the file `mevent.exe`. The code for `W2MouseClick` is similar and is contained in Listing 10.6, which contains the entire program.

Listing 10.6

Program to illustrate
responding to mouse
events

```cpp
// Example showing use of the mouse
// The program displays a bitmap in the window at
// the place where the mouse is clicked
#include "bitmap.h"
#include <assert.h>

// Define two non-overlapping windows
SimpleWindow W1("Window One", 15.0, 9.0,
  Position(1.0, 1.0));

SimpleWindow W2("Window Two", 15.0, 9.0,
  Position(8.0, 12.0));

// Define two bitmaps, one for each window
BitMap W1Bmp(W1);
BitMap W2Bmp(W2);

// W1MouseClick(): callback function for window 1
int W1MouseClick(const Position &p) {

    // Erase the bitmap
    W1Bmp.Erase();

    // Set its new position and display it
    W1Bmp.SetPosition(p);
    W1Bmp.Draw();

    return 1;
}

// W2MouseClick(): callback function for window 2
int W2MouseClick(const Position &p) {

    // Erase the bitmap
    W2Bmp.Erase();

    // Set its new position and display it
    W2Bmp.SetPosition(p);
    W2Bmp.Draw();

    return 1;
```

```
}
int ApiMain() {
    // Open the windows
    W1.Open();
    assert(W1.GetStatus() == WindowOpen);
    W2.Open();
    assert(W2.GetStatus() == WindowOpen);
    // Load the images
    W1Bmp.Load("c1.bmp");
    assert(W1Bmp.GetStatus() == BitMapOkay);
    W2Bmp.Load("c2.bmp");
    assert(W2Bmp.GetStatus() == BitMapOkay);
    // Display the bitmaps at a starting position
    W1Bmp.SetPosition(Position(1.0, 1.0));
    W2Bmp.SetPosition(Position(1.0, 1.0));
    W1Bmp.Draw();
    W2Bmp.Draw();

    // Register the callbacks for each window
    W1.SetMouseClickCallback(W1MouseClick);
    W2.SetMouseClickCallback(W2MouseClick);

    return 0;
}
int ApiEnd() {
    // Close the windows
    W1.Close();
    W2.Close();

    return 0;
}
```

10.5 BITMAPS AND MOUSE EVENTS

A useful feature of a bitmap is the ability to determine whether a location is inside a bitmap. EzWindows BitMaps have this capability built in. The declaration of this member function is

```
bool BitMap::IsInside(const Position &AtPosn);
```

which returns **true** if AtPosn is contained with the bitmap and **false** otherwise. In conjunction with the mouse, this capability provides the facilities for designing simple controls. For example, we can display a BitMap that represents some action to take. We can cause this action to take place by positioning the mouse sprite inside the bitmap and clicking a button. To illustrate this capability, we will write a program that displays the bitmap images of a card. When the mouse is clicked inside the card, the card is flipped over. The application code is contained in the file flip.cpp, and the required modules for this program are shown in Figure 10.11.

Just like the previous EzWindows sample programs, we define a window. We also need two bitmaps: One is the front of the card, and the other is the back. In addition to these global objects, we need an object that remembers

Figure 10.11

Module structure for
flip application

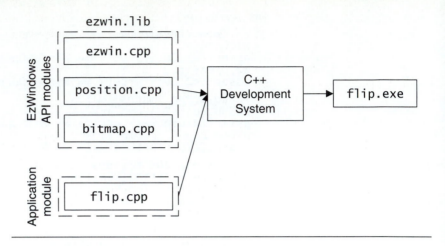

which side of the card is showing. Recall that this object is known as a state variable. The following definitions do the job.

```
// Define a window
SimpleWindow FlipWindow("FlipCard", 15.0, 9.0,
  Position(1.0, 1.0));

// Define bitmaps for the front and back of a card
BitMap CardFront(FlipWindow);
BitMap CardBack(FlipWindow);

// Need a type and object for remembering which side
// of the card is showing
enum Side { Front, Back };
Side SideShowing;
```

The `ApiMain()` function is similar to some of the previous code we have written. What's new here is what happens in our mouse callback function. When the program receives the message, it checks whether the mouse is pointing inside the card. The implementation of the function is

```
int MouseClickEvent(const Position &MousePosition) {
    if (CardFront.IsInside(MousePosition)) {
        // card is selected so flip it
        if (SideShowing == Back) {
            SideShowing = Front;
            CardFront.Draw();
        }
        else if (SideShowing == Front) {
            SideShowing = Back;
            CardBack.Draw();
        }
    }
    return 1;
}
```

If the mouse was clicked inside the card, the code checks the state variable to see which side is showing. If the back side is showing, the code draws the front of the card and changes `SideShowing` to `Front`; if the front side is showing, the code draws the back of the card and changes SideShowing to Back. The effect on the screen is that the card is "flipped" each time the mouse is clicked inside it. The complete code for this demonstration program is contained in Listing 10.7.

Listing 10.7

Program to illustrate checking whether the mouse points at an object

```cpp
// Demonstrate selecting an action by clicking in a bitmap
#include <assert.h>
#include "bitmap.h"

// Define a window
SimpleWindow FlipWindow("FlipCard", 15.0, 9.0,
  Position(1.0, 1.0));

// Define bitmaps for the front and back of a card
BitMap CardFront(FlipWindow);
BitMap CardBack(FlipWindow);

// Need a type and object for remembering which side
// of the card is showing
enum Side { Front, Back };
Side SideShowing;

// MouseClickEvent(): come here when user clicks mouse
int MouseClickEvent(const Position &MousePosition) {
    if (CardFront.IsInside(MousePosition)) {
        // card is selected so flip it
        if (SideShowing == Back) {
            SideShowing = Front;
            CardFront.Draw();
        }
        else if (SideShowing == Front) {
            SideShowing = Back;
            CardBack.Draw();
        }
    }
    return 1;
}
int ApiMain() {
    // Open the window
    FlipWindow.Open();
    assert(FlipWindow.GetStatus() == WindowOpen);

    // Load the images
    CardFront.Load("c1.bmp");
    assert(CardFront.GetStatus() == BitMapOkay);

    CardBack.Load("cardbk1.bmp");
    assert(CardBack.GetStatus() == BitMapOkay);

    // Compute position to display the card
    Position CardPosition = FlipWindow.GetCenter() +
      Position(-.5 * CardFront.GetWidth(),
      -.5 * CardFront.GetHeight());

    CardFront.SetPosition(CardPosition);
    CardBack.SetPosition(CardPosition);

    SideShowing = Front;
    CardFront.Draw();

    // Set up mouse callback
    FlipWindow.SetMouseClickCallback(MouseClickEvent);

    return 0;
}
```

```
int ApiEnd() {
    FlipWindow.Close();
    return 0;
}
```

10.6 TIMER EVENTS

Another feature of EzWindows is the ability to set up a timer. A timer is useful when we want our program to perform some action at a predetermined time or interval. You can think of a timer as an alarm clock managed by EzWindows. When the alarm clock goes off, EzWindows informs the application program by sending it a message through a callback function. The `SimpleWindow` member functions for setting up and managing a timer are `SetTimerCall-back()`, `StartTimer()`, and `StopTimer()`. `SetTimerCallback()` is similar to `SetMouseClickCallback()`. It registers the user's callback function with EzWindows. The callback function will be invoked when a timer event occurs.

The member function `StartTimer()` starts a timer. It takes a single argument, which is how often to generate a timer event. The argument is in milliseconds. For example, the statements

```
SWin.SetTimerCallback(TimerHandler);
SWin.StartTimer(1000);
```

set up a timer for the `SimpleWindow` `SWin`. The timer will go off every 1,000 milliseconds, or once a second. When it goes off, the user routine `TimerHandler()` is called.

When no further timer events are required, a timer is turned off by calling `StopTimer()`. The statement

```
SWin.StopTimer();
```

stops the timer started in the code above.

To illustrate the use of timer events, let's modify `mouse.cpp` from section 10.4 so that the bitmaps are displayed at a random location in the window every half second. Figure 10.12 gives the module structure for this example program.

The new module is called `timer.cpp`, but most of the code is the same as the code in `mouse.cpp`. Instead of setting up two mouse callback functions, we set up two timer-event callback functions. The statements that set up the callback for our two windows are

```
W1.SetTimerCallback(W1TimerEvent);
W2.SetTimerCallback(W2TimerEvent);
bool TimerStatus1 = W1.StartTimer(500);
bool TimerStatus2 = W2.StartTimer(500);
assert(TimerStatus1 && TimerStatus2);
```

and the timer-event callback functions are

```
int W1TimerEvent() {
```

```
        Redisplay(W1, W1Bmp);
        return 1;
    }
    int W2TimerEvent() {
        Redisplay(W2, W2Bmp);
        return 1;
    }
```

Figure 10.12

*Module structure for
timer application*

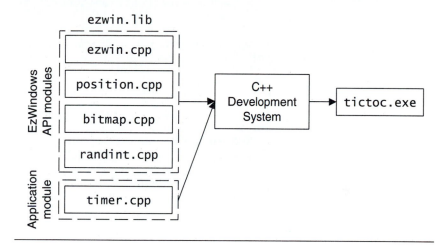

Function ReDisplay() handles the details of generating a random location to
display the bitmap. See Listing 10.8 for its implementation.

Listing 10.8

*Program to
demonstrate use
of a timer*

```cpp
// Example showing use of timer events
// The program displays a bitmap in the window at
// a random location when the timer goes off

#include <assert.h>
#include "bitmap.h"
#include "randint.h"

// Define two nonoverlapping windows
SimpleWindow W1("Window One", 15.0, 9.0,
  Position(1.0, 1.0));

SimpleWindow W2("Window Two", 15.0, 9.0,
  Position(8.0, 12.0));

// Define two bitmaps, one for each window
BitMap W1Bmp(W1);
BitMap W2Bmp(W2);

// Redisplay(): move bitmap to a new location
void Redisplay(SimpleWindow &W, BitMap &B) {
    // Erase the bitmap
    B.Erase();

    // Compute a new position and display the bitmap
    // Make sure the bitmap is completely in the window

    // Initialize random number generator. Then create a
    // random number generator for the X position
    EzRandomize();
```

```
      RandomInt X(1, (int) W.GetWidth());
      int XCoord = X.Draw();
      if (XCoord + B.GetWidth() > W.GetWidth())
         XCoord = XCoord - B.GetWidth();

      // Create RandomInt object the Y position
      RandomInt Y(1, (int) W.GetHeight());
      int YCoord = Y.Draw();
      if (YCoord + B.GetHeight() > W.GetHeight())
         YCoord = YCoord - B.GetHeight();
      B.SetPosition(Position(XCoord, YCoord));
      B.Draw();
   }

// W1TimerEvent(): callback function for window 1
int W1TimerEvent() {
   Redisplay(W1, W1Bmp);

   return 1;
}

// W2TimerEvent(): callback function for window 2
int W2TimerEvent() {
   Redisplay(W2, W2Bmp);

   return 1;
}
// ApiMain(): open the windows and start the timers
int ApiMain() {
   // Open the windows
   W1.Open();
   assert(W1.GetStatus() == WindowOpen);
   W2.Open();
   assert(W2.GetStatus() == WindowOpen);

   // Load the images
   W1Bmp.Load("c1.bmp");
   assert(W1Bmp.GetStatus() == BitMapOkay);
   W2Bmp.Load("c2.bmp");
   assert(W2Bmp.GetStatus() == BitMapOkay);

   // Display the bitmaps at a starting position
   W1Bmp.SetPosition(Position(1.0, 1.0));
   W2Bmp.SetPosition(Position(1.0, 1.0));
   W1Bmp.Draw();
   W2Bmp.Draw();

   // Register the callbacks for each window
   // and start the timers to go off every 500 ms
   W1.SetTimerCallback(W1TimerEvent);
   W2.SetTimerCallback(W2TimerEvent);
   bool TimerStatus1 = W1.StartTimer(500);
   bool TimerStatus2 = W2.StartTimer(500);
   assert(TimerStatus1 && TimerStatus2);

   return 0;
}
int ApiEnd() {
   // Stop the timers and close the windows
   W1.StopTimer();
   W2.StopTimer();
   W1.Close();
   W2.Close();

   return 0;
}
```

10.7 ALERT MESSAGES

It is often handy to pop up a window and display a message that the user cannot ignore. One way to make sure the message is not ignored is to block the user from working in any of the windows that the application has open. Such windows are sometimes called alert windows or modal dialog boxes. The class `SimpleWindow` provides a facility for displaying alert windows. For example, if there is an open `SimpleWindow` called `Jitterbug`, the statement

```
Jitterbug.Message("Nice swatting!");
```

would cause an alert window to appear. Furthermore, the user cannot work in any of the windows belonging to the application until the message box is dismissed. (Program execution is suspended until the message box is dismissed.) To illustrate the behavior of message boxes, let's modify our hello program so that a message box pops up before the text is displayed. The module structure is given in Figure 10.13.

Figure 10.13

Module structure for alert application

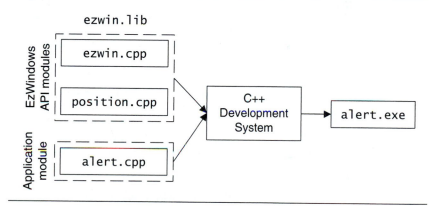

The revised `ApiMain()` is

```
int ApiMain() {
    HelloWindow.Open();
    assert(HelloWindow.GetStatus() == WindowOpen);
    // Get Center of Window
    Position Center = HelloWindow.GetCenter();
    // Create bounding box for text
    Position UpperLeft = Center + Position(-1.0, -1.0);
    Position LowerRight = Center + Position(1.0, 1.0);

    HelloWindow.Message("Click Ok to continue");
    // Display the text
    HelloWindow.RenderText(UpperLeft, LowerRight,
      "Hello EzWindows", White);
    return 0;
}
```

This program creates the windows in Figure 10.14. Notice that the main window does not display any text. Furthermore, if the mouse is clicked inside the main window, a beep warns the user that the program is suspended. When the user clicks on OK, the alert box disappears and the text `Hello EzWindows` is displayed in the window.

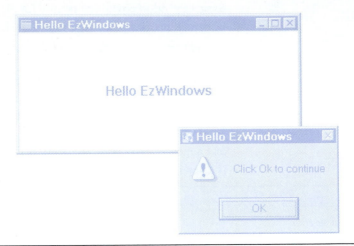

Self-check Questions

1.   What is the process of setting up a routine to call when a certain event occurs?

2.   Write a function called `ReportMousePosition` that displays the coordinates of the cursor when the mouse is clicked within a `SimpleWindow`. Demonstrate the use of the function by writing a driver program that uses function `ReportMousePosition()` to display the coordinates of the cursor.

3.   Write an EzWindows program that prompts for and accepts the name of a file that contains a bitmap. The program should then display the bitmap image in the center of the window.

4.   Write an EzWindows program that displays a bitmap in a `SimpleWindow`. If the mouse is clicked within the bitmap, an alert message is displayed indicating that the bitmap was selected. If the mouse is clicked outside the window, an alert message is displayed indicating that the bitmap was not selected.

5.   Write an EzWindows program that draws a staircase pattern in a window. Your program should produce something that looks like the following.

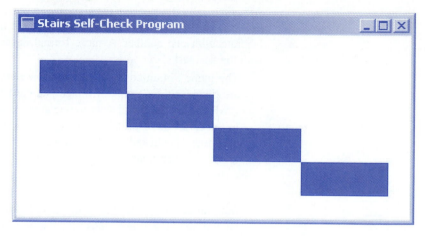

6.   Create a bitmap of a black circle that is about the size of a hole in a piece of notebook paper. You can use any of the widely available drawing programs like Paint or PhotoShop. Write an EzWindows program called `punch` that "punches" holes in a `SimpleWindow` at random locations The rate of the punching program should be controlled by an EzWindow's timer.

7.   Write an EzWindows program that allows you to use the mouse to draw lines in a SimpleWindow. Use the EzWindows class RaySegment from Appendix E.

8.   Write an EzWindows program that prompts for and accepts an integer between 1 and 9. The program then displays a "countdown" in a window. It uses a timer to update the display each second. Use the digit bitmaps found in the EzWindows directory supplied on the CD-ROM that came with your textbook.

10.8   SIMON SAYS

We all remember the childhood game Simon Says. We conclude this chapter on the EzWindows API by developing a computer version of this game. In this game, which we call Simon, a set of cards is displayed in the window. The game starts when the computer flips the cards over momentarily in a random sequence. After the computer has flipped the cards, the player must select the objects in the same order as they were flipped. If the player successfully recalls the order in which the cards were flipped, the computer displays another, longer sequence. The game continues until the player makes a mistake or the player successfully remembers the longest sequence.

Writing the game is actually not too hard when we use the EzWindows API, especially if we design the game using object-oriented principles. First we need to decide which objects we need and how they will communicate or collaborate with one another. A more formal description of the game will help with the first tasks.

The game Simon consists of a window in which several types of images are displayed. One type of image is a card that can be flipped over. Four cards are displayed adjacent to one another across the window. In addition to the cards, there are control images. One image is a restart button. When the mouse is clicked on this button, the game starts over at the beginning level. Another image is a quit button. When it is selected, the game is terminated.

Simon is played as follows: Cards are flipped over momentarily in a random sequence. Initially, three cards are flipped. After a sequence is shown, the player must select the cards in the same order. If the player is successful, a new sequence, one card longer than before, is shown. The player wins the game when a sequence of six cards is recalled successfully.

From the preceding statement, it is clear that we need an object to represent the cards. One behavior of the cards is that they should be able to be flipped. We also need to be able to determine whether the mouse is pointing at a card. We will call this class SimonObject. It should be obvious that the EzWindows BitMap class provides much of the functionality needed by SimonObject. Other, similar objects are the control objects. These are also represented by EzWindows BitMap objects.

Another object that is required is something that controls the play of the game. It will be responsible for generating the sequence, causing the cards to be flipped in the proper order, and then checking to see whether the player recalls the correct sequence. It will also be responsible for setting up the game and determining when the game is over. We will call this class SimonGame.

One other important object is mentioned in our description—the player. Fortunately, we do not need to implement the player because this function is provided by one of us.

The objects in the game provide a natural partitioning of the program into modules, as shown in Figure 10.15. Module simobj.cpp contains the implementation of class SimonObject, and module simon.cpp contains the implementation of class SimonGame. Function ApiMain() and the mouse and timer callback functions are in module simmain.cpp.

SimonGame controls the game, so let's get a rough cut at what it should do and what attributes and objects it should contain. The behaviors or actions provided by SimonGame include setting up the game board in the window, generating a sequence to flip the cards, flipping the cards, and dealing with mouse clicks in the window. A mouse click could be in one of the control bitmaps, which means the player is asking either to restart the game or to quit, or it

Figure 10.15

Module structure of Simon

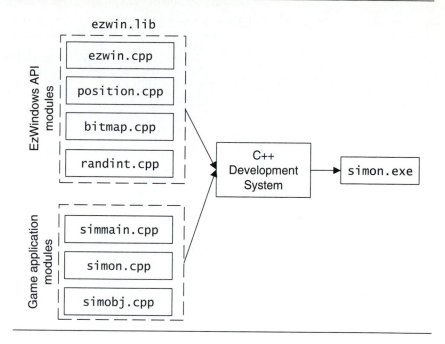

could be inside the card, which means the player is selecting that card as the one that was next flashed in the sequence. The behaviors or responsibilities of SimonGame follow.

- Initialize the game.
- Handle mouse-click events.
- Generate a sequence to flip the cards.
- Manage the play of the game.
- Flip the cards.

Obviously, SimonGame should contain all the attributes of the game. These include the length of the sequence, whose turn it is to go (computer or human), and the sequence to play. In addition to these attributes, SimonGame will contain the SimonObjects, a SimpleWindow to display the SimonObjects, and the bitmaps for controlling the game. The bitmaps for controlling the game will be called Restart and Quit. The attributes of SimonGame follow.

- A SimpleWindow object for the game.
- An array of SimonObjects.
- The restart and quit bitmaps.
- The order to flash the cards.
- A state attribute that contains whose turn it is to go.
- The current sequence length.

Our first version of class `SimonGame` follows.

```
class SimonGame {
    enum Turn { Simon, Player };
    public:
        SimonGame(SimpleWindow &Window);
        void Initialize();
        void Play();
        int MouseClick(const Position &MousePosn);
        int Timer();
        void PickOrder();
    private:
        SimpleWindow &W;
        vector<SimonObject> Posn;
        BitMap Restart;
        BitMap Quit;
        vector<int> Order;
        Turn WhoseTurn;
        int SequenceLength;
};
```

Let's examine the data members first. Like all the objects we have used before that involve a window, `SimonGame` includes a reference to the window that will display the game. `Posn` is a vector of `SimonObjects`. These objects are displayed across the window and flipped in a random sequence. The size of `Posn` will be set when a `SimonGame` object is constructed, and initialized when the game is initialized. `Restart` and `Quit` are the bitmaps for controlling the game. The vector `Order` contains the sequence to flip the `SimonObjects`. The state object `WhoseTurn` contains whose turn it is to go—the computer or the player. Finally, the data member `SequenceLength` contains the length of the sequence to generate. As the game progresses, `SequenceLength` gets larger.

The public member functions include a constructor, which takes as a single argument the window that will display the game. `Initialize()` sets up the game board. `Play()` puts the game into its initial state and starts it. `MouseClick()` and `Timer()` will be called on mouse-click and timer-tick events, respectively. These functions handle much of the logic of the game. `PickOrder()` generates the random sequence to flip the cards.

Now we turn to `SimonObject`. From the description of the game, it is clear that a `SimonObject` should have a flip behavior. We will also need to be able to determine whether the mouse is clicked inside a `SimonObject`. Finally, we will need to be able to draw the `SimonObjects`. As we noted, many of these properties will be supplied by `BitMap`. We can think of a `SimonObject` as packaging a `BitMap` with some additional properties. At this point, the behaviors of a `SimonObject` are

- Flip itself over.
- Determine whether the mouse is clicked inside it.
- Draw itself.

A `SimonObject` contains two bitmaps—one for the front of the object and one for the back. It also has an attribute that indicates which side is currently showing.

The declaration of `SimonObject` follows.

```
enum Side { Front, Back };
class SimonObject {
    public:
        SimonObject();
        void Initialize(SimpleWindow &GameWindow,
          const string &FrontFile, const string
&BackFile,
          const Position &Posn);
        void SetSide(const Side &s);
        Side GetSide() const;
        void Draw();
        void Flip();
        bool IsInside(const Position &MousePosition)
        const;
    private:
        BitMap FrontSide;
        BitMap BackSide;
        Side SideShowing;
};
```

In addition to the behaviors previously listed, a `SimonObject` contains an inspector and mutator for the data member `SideShowing`.

Now that we have a good idea of what our two main objects look like, we can describe how the program will work. The board will consist of some `SimonObjects` and the control buttons. These will be EzWindows `Bitmaps`. We will be able to determine whether the mouse is pointing at a `SimonObject` or control button using `BitMap`'s `IsInside` member function. The flow of the game is controlled by timer events and mouse-click events, which are handled by `SimonGame`. Figure 10.16 shows the classes and the messages that they send one another. As the diagram shows, the `BitMap` class is the key building block for the game.

Essentially, the game has three phases. The initialize phase sets up the board and gets everything ready to play. The second phase flashes the `Simon-Objects`, and in the third phase the player selects the `SimonObjects`. The third phase also checks the player's selection to see whether it is correct.

The first phase is straightforward. We can write it first and then check to see that the board looks like we want it to. The first thing is to write the constructor for `SimonGame`.

```
SimonGame::SimonGame(SimpleWindow &Window) :
  W(Window){
    // Reserve space for the SimonObjects
    // and the sequence for flipping objects
    Posn.reserve(MaxPositions);
    Order.reserve(MaxSequenceLength);
}
```

The preceding code initializes the `W` data member and reserves the needed space in the vectors. All the real work is done in `SimonGame::Initial-`

Figure 10.16

Simon classes and the
messages they send

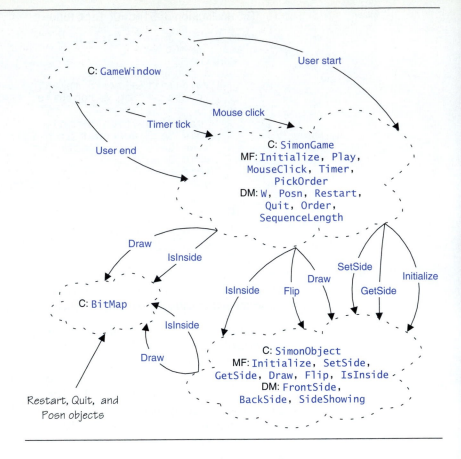

ize(). The first part draws the SimonObjects and loads the BitMap for each position using SimonObject::Initialize(). The code follows.

```
assert(W.GetStatus() == WindowOpen);
SequenceLength = BeginningSequenceLength;
X = InitialPosition.GetXDistance();
Y = InitialPosition.GetYDistance();

// BitMapFile contains the bitmap filenames
vector<string> BitMapFile(MaxPositions);
BitMapFile[0] = "c1.bmp";
BitMapFile[1] = "c2.bmp";
BitMapFile[2] = "c3.bmp";
BitMapFile[3] = "c4.bmp";

for (p = 0; p < MaxPositions; ++p) {
    Posn[p].Initialize(W, BitMapFile[p],
     "cardbk1.bmp", Position(X, Y));
    Posn[p].Draw();
    X += Posn[p].GetWidth() + 0.5;
}
```

BitMapFile contains the filenames of the images to load for each position on the board. We will use bitmaps of cards. The **for** loop initializes each position by calling `SimonObject::Initialize()` and passing it the window, the bitmap for the front side of the `SimonObject`, the bitmap for the back side, and the position of the `SimonObject`. Based on the width of the bitmap, the position of the next `SimonObject` is computed.

The next part of `SimonGame::Initialize()` sets up the control buttons. This code simply loads the bitmaps that contain the images of the buttons and draws them at the proper location. Listing 10.9 shows the complete implementation of `SimonGame::Initialize()`.

Listing 10.9

SimonGame's
Initialize() member
function from
simon.cpp

```cpp
// Initialize(): initialize the game, initializing simon
// game objects
void SimonGame::Initialize() {
    int p;
    float X, Y;
    InitializeSeed();
    assert(W.GetStatus() == WindowOpen);
    SequenceLength = BeginningSequenceLength;

    X = InitialPosition.GetXDistance();
    Y = InitialPosition.GetYDistance();

    // BitMapFile holds the filenames containing the
    // bitmaps
    vector<string> BitMapFile(MaxPositions);
    BitMapFile[0] = "c1.bmp";
    BitMapFile[1] = "c2.bmp";
    BitMapFile[2] = "c3.bmp";
    BitMapFile[3] = "c4.bmp";

    for (p = 0; p < MaxPositions; ++p) {
        Posn[p].Initialize(W, BitMapFile[p],
        "cardbk1.bmp", Position(X, Y));
        Posn[p].Draw();
        X += Posn[p].GetWidth() + 0.5;
    }
    // Set up the control buttons
    Restart.SetWindow(W);
    Restart.Load("rbutton2.bmp");
    assert(Restart.GetStatus() == BitMapOkay);
    X = InitialPosition.GetXDistance();
    Y += Posn[0].GetHeight() + 2.0;
    Restart.SetPosition(Position(X, Y));

    Quit.SetWindow(W);
    Quit.Load("qbutton2.bmp");
    assert(Quit.GetStatus() == BitMapOkay);
    X = Restart.GetWidth() + 2.0;
    Quit.SetPosition(Position(X, Y));

    Restart.Draw();
    Quit.Draw();
}
```

`SimonObject`'s `Initialize()` member function uses `BitMap` member functions to initialize the `FrontSide` and `BackSide`. It also sets the data member `SideShowing` to `Back`. The code for this function is contained in Listing 10.10.

Listing 10.10

*SimonObject's
Initialize() member
function from
simobj.cpp*

```
// Initialize(): load a card face and back for this
// simon object
void SimonObject::Initialize(SimpleWindow &GameWindow,
  const string &FrontFile, const string &BackFile,
  const Position &Posn) {
    FrontSide.SetWindow(GameWindow);
    FrontSide.SetPosition(Posn);
    FrontSide.Load(FrontFile);
    assert(FrontSide.GetStatus() == BitMapOkay);

    BackSide.SetWindow(GameWindow);
    BackSide.SetPosition(Posn);

    BackSide.Load(BackFile);
    assert(BackSide.GetStatus() == BitMapOkay);
    SetSide(Back);
}
```

With these functions implemented, we can write an `ApiMain()` that will display the game window. As usual, we declare a global `SimpleWindow` for the display. We also instantiate a `SimonGame`. The two definitions are

```
SimpleWindow GameWindow("Simon Game", 14.0, 7.0,
  Position(0.25, 0.25));
SimonGame Simon(GameWindow);
```

The preliminary version of `ApiMain()` that displays the game window only is

```
int ApiMain() {
    GameWindow.Open();
    Simon.Initialize();

    return 0;
}
```

Figure 10.17 shows the resulting window.

Figure 10.17

*Window for Simon
before play starts*

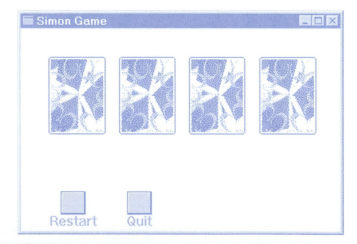

Before going further with the game, let's go ahead and complete the implementation of `SimonObject`. After all, we will need to use its capabilities to implement the game. The inspector `GetSide()` and mutator `SetSide()` are much like all the other inspectors and mutators we have implemented. See Listing 10.11 for their implementations.

Member function `Draw()` is

```
void SimonObject::Draw() {
    if (SideShowing == Back)
        BackSide.Draw();
    else
        FrontSide.Draw();
}
```

which simply decides which `BitMap`, `BackSide` or `FrontSide`, to draw based on the value in `SideShowing`. `Flip()` simply sets `SideShowing` to the opposite of what it currently is and then invokes `Draw()`. Member function `Flip()`'s definition is

```
// Flip(): flip the object and redraw it
void SimonObject::Flip() {
    SetSide(GetSide() == Back ? Front : Back);
    Draw();
}
```

Finally, `SimonObject::IsInside()` simply invokes `BackSide.IsInside()`. It doesn't matter whether we use `BackSide` or `FrontSide`, as they are both at the same position. We note that because EzWindows provides much of the underlying capabilities, all the member functions of `SimonObject` were short and simple.

With the game board set up and `SimonObject` implemented, we can now implement the play. The play of the game is controlled by member function `Play()`, which is called to play a round of the game. A round consists of two phases. In the first phase, the computer flashes the `SimonObjects` in random order. In the second phase, the player must select the objects in the same order. We can think of this as Simon and the player taking turns.

The first step of `Play()` is to mark that it is Simon's turn and to make sure all the objects are flipped over and ready to be flashed. We need this step because some of the objects were undoubtedly flipped over in a previous round. The code follows.

```
WhoseTurn = Simon;
for (int p = 0; p < MaxPositions; ++p) {
    Posn[p].SetSide(Back);
    Posn[p].Draw();
}
```

We can now generate the sequence for flashing the objects, which is accomplished by the member function `PickOrder()`. The random sequence to flash the objects is held in the `SimonGame` data member `Order`. The elements of this array are integers that select a `Posn`. For example, in Figure 10.18 the array `Order` contains the values 1, 0, 2, 3, 3, and 1. This array indicates that

Listing 10.11

Module simobj.cpp

```cpp
#include <iostream>
#include <string>
#include <stdio.h>
#include <stdlib.h>
#include <assert.h>
#include "simobj.h"
using namespace std;

SimonObject::SimonObject() {
};

// Initialize(): load a card face and back for this
// Simon object
void SimonObject::Initialize(SimpleWindow &GameWindow,
 string FrontFile, string BackFile,
 const Position &Posn) {

   FrontSide.SetWindow(GameWindow);
   FrontSide.SetPosition(Posn);
   FrontSide.Load(FrontFile);
   assert(FrontSide.GetStatus() == BitMapOkay);

   BackSide.SetWindow(GameWindow);
   BackSide.SetPosition(Posn);
   BackSide.Load(BackFile);
   assert(BackSide.GetStatus() == BitMapOkay);
   SetSide(Back);
}

// SetSide(): set the current object s side
void SimonObject::SetSide(const Side &s) {
   SideShowing = s;
}

// GetSide(): get the current object s side
Side SimonObject::GetSide() const {
   return SideShowing;
}

// GetHeight(): get the height of the bitmap
float SimonObject::GetHeight() const {
   return FrontSide.GetHeight();
}

// GetWidth(): get the width of the bitmap
float SimonObject::GetWidth() const {
   return FrontSide.GetWidth();
}

// Flip(): flip the object and redraw it
void SimonObject::Flip() {
   SetSide(GetSide() == Back ? Front : Back);
   Draw();
}

// IsInside(): determine if a mouse click is in the image
bool SimonObject::IsInside(const Position &p) const {
   return BackSide.IsInside(p);
}

// Draw(): draw the object to the window
void SimonObject::Draw() {
   if (SideShowing == Back)
      BackSide.Draw();
   else
      FrontSide.Draw();
}
```

the `SimonObject` in `Posn[1]` should be flashed first, then the one in `Posn[0]`, `Posn[2]`, and so on. The idea is to shuffle the values in `Order` to determine the order for flashing the objects held in `Posn`.

Figure 10.18

Selecting an object to flash in a random sequence

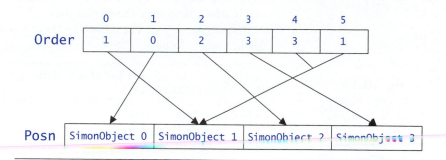

The shuffling of `Order` is done by member function `PickOrder()`. The first step is to initialize `Order`. We need to initialize only the elements of the vector that will be used to generate the sequence. The length of the sequence is held in data member `SequenceLength`. The following code initializes the array.

```
for (i = 0; i < SequenceLength; ++i)
    Order[i] = i % MaxPositions;
```

Notice that because `Order` has more elements than `Posn`, we take the modulus of `i`. This step ensures that the values stored in `Order` are in the range 0 to 3.

After we initialize the array, we can shuffle the values around. For the `i`th element of `Order`, we generate a random number `j`, in the range 0 to `MaxPositions-1`. Then we swap the `j`th element of `Order` with the `i`th element. Listing 10.12 contains the definition of `SimonGame::PickOrder()`.

Listing 10.12

SimonGame's PickOrder() member function from simon.cpp

```
// PickOrder(): generate a random sequence
void SimonGame::PickOrder() {
    for (int i = 0; i < SequenceLength; ++i)
        Order[i] = i % MaxPositions;
    RandomInt R(0, MaxPositions - 1);
    R.Randomize();
    for (int i = 0; i < SequenceLength; ++i) {
        int j = R.Draw();
        int tmp = Order[j];
        Order[j] = Order[i];
        Order[i] = tmp;
    }
}
```

After `Play()` calls `PickOrder()` to produce the sequence, we are ready to flash the cards. Here is where event-based object-oriented programming really comes into its own. In fact, without events, this program would be difficult, if not impossible, to write. The basic idea is that we will use an EzWindows timer to flip the `SimonObjects`. To keep track of the next

SimonObject to be flipped, we add the data member Selection to the private section of SimonGame. Its declaration is

> int Selection;

Selection will also be used in the next phase of the game to keep track of the order in which the player should pick the cards.

So the last step of SimonGame::Play() is to set Selection to 0 and start the timer. Listing 10.13 contains the complete code for Play().

Listing 10.13

SimonGame's Play() member function from simon.cpp

```
// Play(): go play the simon game at the current level
void SimonGame::Play() {
    // it's simon's turn to flash the objects in order
    WhoseTurn = Simon;
    // turn all objects over ready for flashing
    for (int p = 0; p < MaxPositions; ++p) {
        Posn[p].SetSide(Back);
        Posn[p].Draw();
    }

    // pick a random order to flash the simon objects
    PickOrder();
    // Selection keeps track of the number of
    // objects flashed so far
    Selection = 0;

    // Start the timer for flashing the SimonObjects
    W.StartTimer(FlashInterval);
}
```

The timer for the GameWindow is set up in ApiMain(). The call is

> GameWindow.SetTimerCallback(TimerEvent);

and function TimerEvent calls Simon's Timer() member function. The implementation of TimerEvent() is

```
// TimerEvent(): pass timer ticks to the game
// to flip the appropriate card
int TimerEvent() {
    return Simon.Timer();
}
```

The basic idea behind using the timer to flip the SimonObjects is that we set up the timer to generate a callback at twice the speed we want the objects to be flipped. When SimonGame::Timer() receives the first timer-tick message, it flips the first object in the sequence onto its front. When it receives the next tick message, it flips that same object onto its back. When the next timer tick occurs, the next object in the sequence is flipped onto its front, and so on. When the last object in the sequence has been flipped onto its back, we turn off the timer and mark that it is now the player's turn. The data member Selection is used to select the values from the array Order. Listing 10.14 contains the implementation.

The final step in the development of Simon is to handle mouse-click events. The player uses the mouse to select the cards in the order the player remembers them being flipped. The player can also use the mouse to quit the game or to restart the game.

Listing 10.14

Simon's Timer()
member function from
simon.cpp

```
// Timer(): process timer-tick events, flipping
// SimonObjects
int SimonGame::Timer() {
    // see if we are done flashing objects
    if (Selection == SequenceLength) {
        WhoseTurn = Player;
        W.StopTimer();
        Selection = 0;
        return 1;
    }

    // Get the current object
    int p = Order[Selection];
    // flip object to back side if not on that side
    // if on that side, flip it to front and
    // go to next object
    if (Posn[p].GetSide() == Back)
        Posn[p].Flip();
    else {
        Posn[p].Flip();
        ++Selection;
    }

    return 1;
}
```

The setup for handling mouse-click events is similar to the setup for timer events. We send a message to `GameWindow` telling it to call the function `MouseClickEvent()` when a mouse click occurs inside it. The code is

```
GameWindow.SetMouseClickCallback(MouseClickEvent);
```

Function `MouseClickEvent()` forwards the message to Simon's `Mouse-Click()` member function. The code for `MouseClickEvent()` is

```
int MouseClickEvent(const Position &MousePosn) {
    return Simon.MouseClick(MousePosn);
}
```

The first thing `MouseClick()` should do is check whether the control buttons, `Restart` or `Quit`, has been selected. If the `Restart` button was selected, the code should set `SequenceLength` back to the beginning sequence length and call `Play()` to start a new game. If the `Quit` button was selected, we should exit the program.

The initial part of `MouseClick()` is

```
int SimonGame::MouseClick(const Position  &MousePosn) {
    int p;
    // restart button clicked?
    if (Restart.IsInside(MousePosn)) {
        SequenceLength = BeginningSequenceLength;
        Play();
        return 1;
    }
    // quit button clicked?
    else if (Quit.IsInside(MousePosn))
        Terminate();
```

The function `Terminate()` is an EzWindows function that terminates an application. Before EzWindows terminates the application, it sends an `Api-End()` message to the application so any necessary clean up can be done.

If the mouse was not clicked inside one of the control buttons, the next step is to determine whether it's the player's turn, and if so, whether the mouse was clicked inside a card. If the mouse was clicked inside a card, then we need to check whether the card was selected in the correct order. The data member `Selection` is again used to step through the array `Order`. Notice that in `Simon::Timer()`, when all the objects were flipped, `Selection` was set back to 0.

To help determine whether the mouse was clicked while pointing inside a card, we add a member function `Find()` to class `Simon`. `Find()` determines whether the mouse was clicked inside a `SimonObject`. The implementation of this member function follows.

```
// Find(): find the selected simon object
int SimonGame::Find(const Position &MousePosn) const {
    for (int p = 0; p < MaxPositions; ++p)
        if (Posn[p].IsInside(MousePosn))
            return p;
    return -1;
};
```

The code for `Simon::Find()` simply loops over the vector `Posn`, invoking the member function `IsInside()` on each `SimonObject`. If `IsInside()` returns true, the index is returned. If the loop completes, the mouse was not pointing at a `SimonObject` and the value –1 is returned.

With the addition of `Find()`, the development of class `SimonGame` is complete. Listing 10.15 contains the final version of its declaration.

Listing 10.15

Declaration of SimonGame from simon.h

```
#ifndef SIMON_H
#define SIMON_H

#include "simobj.h"

const int MaxPositions = 4;
const int BeginningSequenceLength = 3;
const int MaxSequenceLength = 6;

// Lower this to make the game harder
const int FlashInterval = 800;

// Position of first SimonObject
const Position InitialPosition(1.0, 1.0);

class SimonGame {
    enum Turn { Simon, Player };
  public:
    SimonGame(SimpleWindow &Window);
    void Initialize();
    void Play();
    int Refresh();
    int MouseClick(const Position &MousePosn);
    int Timer();
    int Find(const Position &MousePosn); const
    void PickOrder();
  private:
    SimpleWindow &W;
```

```
                vector<SimonObject> Posn;
                BitMap Restart;
                BitMap Quit;
                vector<int> Order;
                int SequenceLength;
                Turn WhoseTurn;
                int Selection;
        };
        #endif
```

Using `Find()`, we can complete `MouseClick()`. The last part of the function follows.

```
        else if (WhoseTurn == Player) {
            // see if object selected
            if ((p = Find(MousePosn)) >= 0) {
                // flip the object over to show it
                Posn[p].SetSide(Front);
                Posn[p].Draw();
                // check whether the object was selected in
                // the right order
                if (p != Order[Selection]) {
                    WhoseTurn = Simon;
                    W.Message("Wrong Order!");
                }
                // check for successful selection of the
                // entire sequence
                else if (Selection + 1 == SequenceLength) {
                    // reached highest level -- game over
                    if (SequenceLength == MaxSequenceLength) {
                        WhoseTurn = Simon;
                        W.Message("You Win!!!");
                    }
                    // go to the next level
                    else {
                        ++SequenceLength;
                        Play();
                    }
                }
                // next user selection in the order
                else
                    ++Selection;
            }
        }
        return 1;
    }
```

If it's not the player's turn, we just ignore the mouse click. If it is the player's turn, `Find()` is invoked to see whether the mouse is pointing at a `SimonObject`. If it's not, the mouse click is ignored. If the mouse is pointing at one of the `SimonObjects`, we flip it over and check whether it is the next card in the sequence. If the player incorrectly selected the next `SimonObject`, we output a message telling the player that he or she is wrong and reset the game so it is Simon's turn. The player can restart the game by dismissing the alert message and clicking on the restart control button.

If the next `SimonObject` is correctly selected, the code checks whether the end of the sequence has been reached. If the end of the sequence has not been reached, `Selection` is incremented to the next object in the order. If the last object in the sequence was picked, the code determines whether this sequence is the last sequence required to win the game. If it is, a winning message is displayed (see Figure 10.19) and Simon gets another turn. If the longest sequence wasn't reached, the sequence length is increased by 1 and the next round is played.

Figure 10.19

Simon after player wins a game

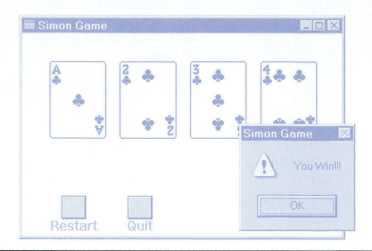

This completes the development of Simon. Listing 10.16 contains the complete code in `simmain.cpp`.

Listing 10.16

Module simmain.cpp

```cpp
#include <iostream>
#include <string>
#include <assert.h>
#include <stdio.h>
#include "simon.h"
using namespace std;

SimpleWindow GameWindow("Simon Game",
 11.5, 7.0, Position(0.25, 0.25));
SimonGame Simon(GameWindow);

// RefreshEvent(): pass window refresh to the game
int RefreshEvent() {
    return Simon.Refresh();
}

// MouseClickEvent(): pass mouse events to player
int MouseClickEvent(const Position &MousePosn) {
    return Simon.MouseClick(MousePosn);
}

// TimerEvent(): pass timer expirations to the game to
// check for card matches
int TimerEvent() {
    return Simon.Timer();
}

// ApiMain(): open the game window, set callbacks, and
// begin play
int ApiMain() {
```

```
    GameWindow.Open();
    GameWindow.SetMouseClickCallback(MouseClickEvent);
    GameWindow.SetRefreshCallback(RefreshEvent);
    GameWindow.SetTimerCallback(TimerEvent);
    Simon.Initialize();
    return 0;
}
// ApiEnd(): shut down the window
int ApiEnd() {
    GameWindow.Close();
    return 0;
}
```

History of Computing

The Apple personal computer

Most of us are familiar with Apple Computer, the makers of the Macintosh computer. Apple was started by two Silicon Valley computer hobbyists, Stephen G. Wozniak and Steven P. Jobs. Wozniak and Jobs had become friends because of their mutual interest in computers and electronics. Wozniak was a member of the Homebrew Computer Club in Silicon Valley, a group of avid computer hobbyists who met to discuss designs, trade parts, and in general discuss anything that had to do with computers. Wozniak, hoping to impress his friends in the club, designed and built a computer that occupied a single circuit board. The computer was a hit at the computer club, and Jobs persuaded a local computer shop to buy 100 of the boards at $500 a piece. With the agreement in hand, Jobs and Wozniak formed the Apple Computer Company, and they went to work. Eventually they sold about 175 of the boards, dubbed the Apple I (see Figure 10.20).

The success of the Apple I convinced them to build another more powerful computer. However, they realized that they would need help and more money. They were quite lucky to meet Mike Markkula, an engineer, who had retired as a millionaire from Intel at the age of 32. He met with Jobs and Wozniak and was impressed with their plans for the Apple II. While Jobs and Wozniak worked on building the Apple II, Markkula rounded up more money to finance the operation and hired additional engineers and managers.

The Apple II was unveiled in 1977 at the West Coast Computer Faire. In its first year, Apple had $700,000 in sales. Four years later that figure had risen to $335,000,000. Apple went public in 1980, and the opening price of a share was $22. By the end of the day, the price had reached $29. Jobs, Wozniak, and Markkula were instantly multimillionaires.

10.9 POINTS TO REMEMBER

✔ Avoid reinventing the wheel. Use library code and APIs to develop applications.

✔ Applications that use graphical interfaces are simpler to use than a text-based interface, but they are harder to develop.

Figure 10.20

Steven Jobs and Stephen Wozniak with the Apple I

✔ Event-based programming involves handling events that are generated outside the program. Typical events include mouse clicks, timer ticks, and messages from the operating system.

✔ A bounding box is a way of specifying the location of an object on the screen. For most window systems, a bounding box is specified by giving the screen coordinates of the upper-left corner and lower-right corner of a rectangle that either encloses the object or that the object is centered within.

10.10 EXERCISES

10.1   Write an EzWindows program that displays a flashing message in a window. The message should be read from `cin`. The message should flash every 2 seconds.

10.2   Search the Internet and create a list of the APIs that are available for building different types of applications. Your list should give the name of the API, the types of applications it was designed to help build, the name of the company that sells the API, and what computing platforms it works on.

10.3   Write an EzWindows program that displays a bitmap that is too large for the window. What happens?

10.4   Write an EzWindows program that opens a window. When the mouse is clicked in this window, the mouse coordinates are displayed in the text control window.

10.5   Write an EzWindows program for displaying bitmaps. The program should prompt the user for the name of the file that contains the bitmap. The program should center the bitmap within the window.

10.6   Write an EzWindows program that reminds someone to do something. The program should prompt for and accept a time specified in minutes. After this specified time has elapsed, the program should remind the user to do whatever he or she needed to do by displaying an appropriate pop-up window.

10.7   Write an EzWindows program that has two windows. The first window contains two buttons. One button is an on switch, and the other is an off switch. The second window is the message window. When the on switch is clicked on, the message in the window flashes every 2 seconds. When the off switch is clicked on, the message does not flash. Be sure to use the object-oriented approach to your design. Determine the objects and develop classes for them.

10.8   The quit and restart buttons used in Simon are not very professional looking. Find two bitmaps that look better and modify the program to use the new bitmaps.

10.9   The supplied version of Simon provides no facility for pausing the game after it starts. Add a pause button to the game.

10.10   A problem with the current version of Simon is that the mechanism for giving a player feedback (i.e., flipping the card over) does not work if a card is duplicated in the sequence. The player receives no feedback to indicate that he or she selected the correct card because it is already flipped over. Devise and implement a method for giving a player feedback that works even when a sequence contains a duplicate card.

10.11   Modify the Simon program so that the game has another level of difficulty. In this version of the game, after the player has completed one round of correctly guessing the sequences, the next round flips the cards faster. The new version of the game should have three levels: slow, medium, and fast.

10.12   Modify the Simon program so that it uses four different bitmaps. You might consider bitmaps that represent related objects like fruit (e.g., orange, apple, cherry, and lemon), shapes (e.g., square, triangle, circle, and ellipse), or musical instruments (e.g., drum, trumpet, violin, and tuba). The bitmaps should be arranged as shown in the following diagram:

10.13 Use the EzWindows API to create a digital timer. It should have three control buttons: start, stop, and reset. The display should consist of minutes and seconds (e.g., mm:ss). To create the display, use the bitmaps for the digits and colon supplied with the EzWindows API code. The timer display should be updated every second.

10.14 Redo the program in Exercise 10.13 so that the display includes a 10th of a second. The timer display should be updated every 10th of a second.

10.15 Write an EzWindows program that displays a poker hand of five cards. Your program should display the cards in a way that minimizes the space taken but still makes the hand visible.

10.16 Write an EzWindows program that simulates a screen saver. The program opens and closes random-size windows at random locations on the screen at a random time interval between 2 and 6 seconds.

10.17 Write an EzWindows program that simulates a screen saver. The program opens a window that is as large as the screen and displays a bitmap of your choice at random locations within the window. It draws the bitmap at a new location at a random time interval between 2 and 6 seconds.

10.18 A card game kids sometimes play is to deal the cards face down in a rectangular pattern. The following diagram shows how the screen should look at the beginning of the game.

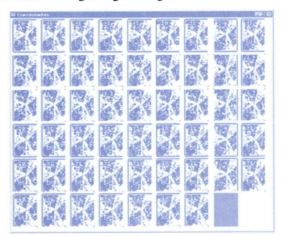

To start the game, a player turns over two cards with the goal of picking two cards of the same face (e.g., two queens or two aces). If the card faces match, the player gets a point; otherwise, the cards are flipped back over. If the player does turn over a matching pair, he or she gets another turn. If the player doesn't pick a match, it's the other player's turn. This game is sometimes called Concentration.

Using the card images supplied on the CD-ROM, write an EzWindows program for practicing Concentration. The program should display the cards as shown in the preceding diagram. A player chooses two cards by clicking on the cards. If the cards match, they are removed from the display; if not, they are flipped back over. The play continues until no cards remain.

10.19 Write an EzWindows program for playing Concentration (see exercise 10.18). One player is the computer. The computer always remembers the cards it turns over, but for some reason, it does not remember the cards the player turns over. Be sure to include a display that shows the current score. A player's score is how many pairs he or she finds. In this implementation, the computer always goes first.

10.20 Implement the game as described in Exercise 10.19 but include buttons that allow the player to choose who should go first—the computer or the player.

10.21 Implement the game as described in Exercise 10.20 but modify the program so that the computer remembers the position of a card that is flipped 60 percent of the time. Can you beat the computer? Modify the program so that the computer has an 80 percent recall of the cards flipped over.

10.22 The Department of Energy (DOE) is in the process of developing a robot that can be used in hazardous environments. The robot, Hazardous Environment Robot Observer (HERO), is controlled by simple commands. HERO understands the following commands:

Command	Action
U or u	Move up
D or d	Move down
L or l	Move left
R or r	Move right
M n or m n	Set movement distance to n 10ths of a centimeter

When HERO executes a movement command (U, D, L, or R), it moves in that direction. It moves a distance that is specified by the last set movement distance command (M) executed. The argument to the movement command is an integer.

To help DOE develop HERO, you have been asked to write a program that displays the actions of HERO. Your program reads a HERO command from the keyboard and displays HERO's action in a display window. Because HERO's intended purpose is to find hazardous materials, the program should indicate when HERO encounters hazardous material. Whenever HERO crosses a region with hazardous material, that region should be highlighted on the screen.

A HERO command file has the following format:

```
20.0 20.0
9.0 9.0
0.0 0.0
M 10
D
D
D
R
D
D
L
L
U
U
```

The first line is the width and height in centimeters of the display window. The second line is the location of the hazardous waste region within the window. The third line is the starting coordinates of HERO. Following these three lines are HERO commands.

Your program should read the first three lines and create a display window of the indicated size, draw the hazardous waste region, and draw HERO at its starting coordinates. After setting up the initial display, your program should read HERO commands and update the display to simulate the movements of HERO. The program should terminate when the last command is executed.

To represent HERO, you should use bitmaps. When HERO is outside the hazardous region, the following bitmap should be displayed.

This bitmap is contained in the file `rbot-r.bmp` in the bitmap directory on the CD-ROM accompanying this textbook.

When HERO enters the hazardous waste region, the bitmap file `trbot-r.bmp` should be displayed. The image contained in this file is

If HERO attempts to move beyond the boundary of the left edge of the display window, HERO should appear at the right edge of the display window. Similarly, if HERO attempts to move beyond the boundary of the right edge of the display window, HERO should appear at the left edge of the display window. When HERO is at the top or bottom edge of the display window, the action is similar. If HERO attempts to move beyond the top edge of the display window, HERO should appear at the bottom of the display window. If HERO attempts to move beyond the bottom edge of the display window, HERO should appear at the top of the display window.

To represent the hazardous waste region use the bitmap contained in the file `hazard.bmp`. This bitmap file contains the following image:

CHAPTER 11

Pointers and dynamic memory

Introduction

Many problem solutions require that a significant amount of information be represented. These tasks can be accomplished with C++ mechanisms that provide for the dynamic creation and management of objects during run time. Such mechanisms allow programs to be flexible and to represent arbitrarily sized data instances. Dynamic objects are created using the **new** operator and are returned to the system using the **delete** operator. Access to a dynamic object is through a pointer, where a pointer is an object whose value is the location of another object. Pointers have similarities to iterators. In fact, an iterator can be viewed as a pointer abstraction. To support pointers, C++ provides two complementary operators—the address operator **&** and the dereferencing operator *. The address operator allows the location of an object to be computed, and the dereferencing operator allows the value stored at a location to be computed. Our discussion begins with pointers.

Key Concepts

- lvalues
- rvalues
- pointer types
- null address
- dereferencing operator *
- indirect member selector operator ->
- address operator **&**
- pointer assignment
- indirect assignment
- pointers as parameters
- pointers to pointers
- constant pointers
- pointers to constants
- arrays and pointers
- command-line parameters

- pointers to function
- dynamic objects
- free store
- operators **new** and **delete**
- exception handling
- `set_new_handler()`
- dangling pointers
- memory leak
- destructors
- copy constructor
- member assignment
- **this** pointer
- qualifier **const**
- pointers to function
- exception handling

11.1 LVALUES AND RVALUES

In C++ there are two kinds of expressions: those that represent objects that can be both evaluated and modified and those that represent objects can only be evaluated. Suppose the following definitions are in effect.

```
int a = 1;
int b;
int c[3];
```

Then the following code segment contains both kinds of expressions.

```
b = 5;
cout << b << endl;
c[0] = 2*a;
```

The expression b represents an object whose value can be evaluated or modified depending on the circumstances. In the first assignment statement, the object represented by expression b is being modified. In the insertion statement, the object represented by expression b is being evaluated. In the second assignment, the expression c[0] represents an object whose value can also be evaluated or modified.

Expressions representing objects that can be both evaluated and modified are *lvalues* (pronounced "el-values"). Thus object names—such as a and b in the preceding code segment—are lvalues, but not all lvalues are object names, as discussed below.

Although the typical assignment statement uses the name of an object as its left operand, the syntax of an assignment statement requires only that the left operand be an lvalue. This flexibility is important because not all objects have names. For example, although an array or a vector has a name, the individual elements do not—individual elements are referenced using lvalue subscript expressions. Thus the assignment to c[0] in the preceding code segment is an example of assignment to an lvalue that corresponds to an object without a name.

The two right operands of our assignment statements, 5 and 2*a, are not lvalues—it would not make sense to allow either 5 or 2*a to be the target of an assignment. These kinds of expressions are *rvalues* (pronounced "are-values"); they cannot be used as the left operand of an assignment. Lvalues do not have such restrictions. Lvalue expressions can be used as either left or right operands of an assignment.

11.2 POINTER BASICS

A pointer is an object whose value represents the location of another object. Pointer objects are defined in conjunction with the unary *indirection* operator * or, as it is more commonly known, the *dereferencing* operator. The following code segment defines three pointer objects: iPtr, s, and rPtr.

```
int *iPtr;
char *s;
Rational *rPtr;
```

Object iPtr is of type pointer to **int**, object s is of type pointer to **char**, and object rPtr is of type pointer to Rational. These pointer types are all different just as **int**, **char**, and Rational are all different types. Because these definitions did not include initialization, the three objects are uninitialized. The following figure depicts the result of these definitions (a dash indicates an uninitialized value).

For explanatory purposes in referring to a pointer type, we use the associated type concatenated with the dereferencing operator; that is, **int*** should be read as "pointer to **int**," and **char*** should be read as "pointer to **char**."

There is one literal value that can be assigned to any pointer object. This literal value is 0, which in this context is known as the *null address*. For example, the following statements all assign the null address.

```
int *iPtr = 0;
char s = 0;
Rational rPtr = 0;
```

A pointer object whose value is the null address is not pointing to an object that can be accessed. In depicting pointer objects whose values are null, we use a filled-in square.

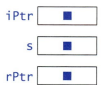

In the next section we discuss operators that allow a pointer to be associated with specific objects. In doing so, we will be able to achieve representations like that shown in Figure 11.1.

The assignment operator is defined for pointer objects. If Ptr1 and Ptr2 have the same pointer type, then the following assignment is legal.

```
Ptr1 = Ptr2;
```

The meaning of the preceding assignment is the same as it is for other objects—the value represented by Ptr1 is modified to hold the value represented by Ptr2. As a result of this assignment, objects Ptr1 and Ptr2 point to the same object. The preceding example uses the name of a pointer object as

Figure 11.1

*Three pointer objects
and the values to
which they point*

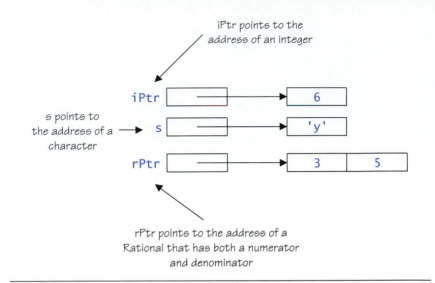

the right operand, but the right operand can, in fact, be any expression that evaluates to the same type as the left operand.

Suppose the following definitions are in effect.

```
int i = 1;
int *iPtr;
char *cPtr;
```

Then none of the following three assignment statements is legal—their right operands do not produce values of the proper type.

```
iPtr = i;    // illegal: i is not an int*
i = iPtr;    // illegal: iPtr is not an int
iPtr = cPtr; // illegal: cPtr is not an int*
```

In the first of these illegal assignment statements, iPtr is the target of the assignment. Therefore, the right operand must evaluate to an **int*** value, but i is an **int**, which makes the assignment illegal. In the second assignment, the right operand must evaluate to an **int**. This evaluation is not possible with iPtr, which is an **int***. In the third assignment, the right operand needs to evaluate to an **int***. However, cPtr evaluates to **char***. Thus none of the assignments met the C++ requirement that the right and left operands of an assignment evaluate to the same type.

11.2.1 Addressing and indirection

C++ provides the unary *address* operator **&** so that the location of an object can be computed and used by a program. When the address operator is applied to

Programmer Alert

Always define one object per statement

When defining a pointer object, some programmers juxtapose the dereferencing operator with the type name rather than the object name as in the following definition:

```
char* Ptr;
```

This form is appealing because it clearly identifies that the type being used is a pointer type. However, it can lead to a misunderstanding. For example, consider the following statement:

```
char* s, t; // really char *s; char t
```

The statement first creates an object s that is a pointer to a **char**. It then creates an object t that is a **char**. The different object types are the result of the right associativity of the dereferencing operator—even though the dereferencing operator is juxtaposed with the type **char**, it is still associated with object s. You should recall our earlier warning that objects should always be defined one per statement. Avoiding this type of error is a principal reason for that warning.

an object in an expression, the value produced by the addressing operation is a pointer to that object. Suppose the following code segment has been executed.

```
int j = 1;
int *Ptr;
Ptr = &j;
```

The first definition initializes j to the value 1; the assignment statement sets Ptr to the address of the memory location for j. The following figure depicts the result of these actions.

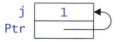

The value of j can now be accessed directly through j *or* indirectly through pointer object Ptr. The indirect method requires the use of the dereferencing operator *.

When the dereferencing operator is used on a pointer object, the dereferencing operation computes the lvalue of the object to which that pointer object points. For example, in the following insertion statement, the value 1 is displayed to the standard output stream.

```
cout << *Ptr << endl; // displaying object j
```

The value 1 is displayed because *Ptr is the object to which Ptr points. Because Ptr points to the memory location where object j is stored, *Ptr evaluates to value 1. Thus when the dereferencing operator acts on a pointer object, the operator's behavior is analogous to when the operator acts on an iterator. In fact, iterators can be viewed as pointer abstractions.

Pointers and dynamic memory

As noted in our initial discussion of lvalues, the left operand of the assignment operator can be any lvalue expression. This flexibility is demonstrated in the following assignment:

```
*Ptr = 0;                    // modifying object j
```

The right operand is the value 0, and the left operand is the expression `*Ptr`. The expression `*Ptr` is an lvalue that refers to `j`. Therefore, this assignment operation indirectly modifies `j` so that it now has the value 0. A picture of memory for objects `j` and `Ptr` is the following:

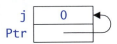

If the following two insertion statements were executed, two zeros would be inserted to the standard output stream.

```
cout << j<< endl;
cout << *Ptr << endl;
```

Like other objects, the definitions of pointer objects can include various initialization expressions, as illustrated in the following code segment:

```
int m = 0;
int n = 1;
int *Ptr1 = &m;
int *Ptr2 = Ptr1;
int *Ptr3 = &n;
```

The first two definitions create and initialize **int** objects m and n. The next three definitions create and initialize **int*** objects Ptr1, Ptr2, and Ptr3.

Pointer `Ptr1` is initialized so that it points to m. Pointer `Ptr2` is initialized so that it is a copy of `Ptr1`'s current value. Therefore, `Ptr2` also points to m. Finally, `Ptr3` is initialized so that it points to n. A picture of the memory for the five objects is the following:

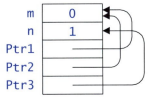

Suppose the following code segment is executed. What would be the changes in the various objects?

```
*Ptr1 = *Ptr3;
Ptr2 = Ptr3;
```

The right operand of the first assignment is the expression `*Ptr3`. Because `Ptr3` is a pointer to the memory location of n, expression `*Ptr3` evaluates to 1. The left operand of the first assignment is the expression `*Ptr1`. Because `Ptr1` is a pointer to the memory location of m, the expression `*Ptr1` is a legal lvalue expression referring to that value of m. Therefore, the first assignment indirectly modifies m so that it is a copy of n. A picture of the memory at this point is the following:

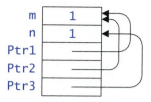

The second assignment in our code segment replaces the value of Ptr2 with the value of Ptr3. Because Ptr3 points to n, Ptr2 now also points to n. The picture of the memory would now be the following:

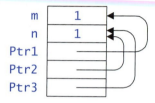

If a pointer object points to class-type objects then, by using the dereferencing and selection operators, individual members can be accessed. Because the selection operator has higher precedence, the dereferencing operator must be nested within parentheses.

```
Rational a(4,3);
Rational *aPtr = &a;
(*aPtr).Insert(cout);  // invokes member Insert() of
                       // object *aPtr. Parentheses
                       // are necessary.
```

Because this syntax is clumsy, C++ includes the indirect member selector operator -> that combines dereferencing with selection. Thus the following statement also displays the Rational object to which aPtr points.

```
aPtr->Insert(cout);
```

The dereferencing and indirect member selector operators are not tools for overcoming class access permissions. A nonpublic data member cannot be accessed by a client using either of these operators. For example, the following statements are illegal.

```
(*aPtr).NumeratorValue = 1;  // illegal: private member
aPtr->DenominatorValue = 2;  // illegal: private member
```

A pointer object whose value is the null address cannot be dereferenced. For example, the following code segment is illegal.

```
int *NullPtr = 0;
*NullPtr = 1;  // illegal: NullPtr is not pointing to
               // a location of an int object
```

11.2.2 Pointers to pointers

C++ allows pointer types whose objects are pointers to pointers. C++ also allows pointer types whose objects are pointers to pointers to pointers, and so on. Although the concept might seem strange, it does have its applications (e.g., dynamic multidimensional lists). The following definition specifies a pointer object `PtrPtr` that points to an **int*** object.

```
int **PtrPtr;
```

Each asterisk in a definition indicates another level of dereferencing. For example, the two asterisks in front of `PtrPtr` indicate a pointer to a pointer, and three asterisks would have indicated a pointer to a pointer to a pointer.

Suppose the following definitions are also in effect.

```
int i = 0;
int *Ptr= &i;
```

Then the following assignment is correct because `Ptr` is an **int***, which makes expression `&Ptr` evaluate to an **int****.

```
PtrPtr = &Ptr;
```

As the result of this assignment, the objects `i`, `Ptr`, and `PtrPtr` have the following relationship:

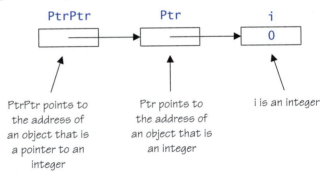

As noted previously, C++ considers two pointer objects to be of different types if the types of values to which they point are different. Therefore, the following assignment is illegal.

```
PtrPtr = Ptr;   // illegal: PtrPtr needs an int**
```

The assignment is illegal because the right operand is of type **int***, but `PtrPtr` expects a value of type **int****.

11.2.3 Pointers as parameters

Up to this point, our examples have been isolated code segments. We now consider a small program, Program 11.1, which invokes a **void** function IndirectSwap(). Function IndirectSwap() has two formal parameters Ptr1 and Ptr2. Both parameters are value parameters of type **char***.

Programming Tip

Pointer power

The ability to access and change the value of an object whose name is not part of the assignment statement is the characteristic that makes pointer objects so powerful but also so confusing. Program errors involving pointers are often subtle and difficult to track down, and so it pays to think carefully about how you are using pointers. A simple technique that helps understand pointers is to draw a picture showing the objects and what points to what. We will use this technique throughout this chapter to help explain how pointers work. The technique of drawing pictures for data structures is so helpful even experienced programmers use this technique when trying to understand or debug code involving pointers.

Program 11.1

Demonstrates that pointers can be used to simulate reference parameters

```cpp
// Program 11.1: Swapping objects using indirection
#include <iostream>
#include <string>
using namespace std;
void IndirectSwap(char *Ptr1, char *Ptr2) {
    // swap the contents of the char objects to which
    // Ptr1 and Ptr2 point
    char c = *Ptr1;
    *Ptr1 = *Ptr2;
    *Ptr2 = c;
}
int main() {
    char a = 'y';
    char b = 'n';
    // pass the lvalues of a and b to IndirectSwap()
    IndirectSwap(&a, &b);
    // display the new values of a and b
    cout << a << b << endl;
    return 0;
}
```

When the program begins, objects a and b are initialized to `'y'` and `'n'`, respectively. The following figure depicts the activation record of `main()` after executing the definitions of a and b.

main()	
a	'y'
b	'n'

The invocation of function `IndirectSwap()` in Program 11.1 is `IndirectSwap(&a, &b)`. The actual parameters for this invocation are the values of the expressions &a and &b. Because expression &a is a pointer to a, value parameter `Ptr1` points to a; and because expression &b is a pointer to b, value parameter Ptr2 points to b. An initial picture of the memory associated with this invocation of IndirectSwap() is the following:

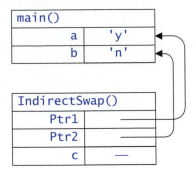

In function IndirectSwap(), local object c is initialized with the value of the expression *Ptr1. In particular, in this invocation of IndirectSwap(), object c is initialized to 'y' because Ptr1 points to object a of main() that has the value 'y'.

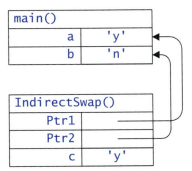

The two assignment statements in IndirectSwap() then modify the objects to which Ptr1 and Ptr2 point.

```
*Ptr1 = *Ptr2;
*Ptr2 = c;
```

Because Ptr1 points to object a of main(), the first assignment in modifying the lvalue *Ptr1 in fact modifies a. Thus the assignment does not alter any of the values in the activation record of IndirectSwap(). The new value of a is the lvalue of *Ptr2. Because Ptr2 points to object b from main(), this assignment in effect gives a the value 'n'.

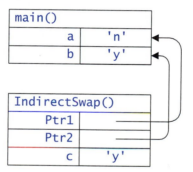

For the second assignment in IndirectSwap(), the left operand is *Ptr2. Because Ptr2 points to object b of main(), this assignment in effect modifies b. Thus this assignment, like the previous assignment, does not alter any of the values in the activation record of IndirectSwap(), but again updates the contents of the activation record for main(). The new value of b is a copy of c, which is a 'y'.

The execution of IndirectSwap() is completed with the second assignment, and the flow of control then returns to main(). Thus the result of the invocation of IndirectSwap() is a swapping of the values of the objects to which the actual parameters point. Function IndirectSwap() is equivalent to function Swap() of Chapter 6.

C++ Language

Importance of reference parameters

Program 11.1 demonstrates that through the use of the dereferencing and address operators and value parameters, we can achieve a side effect that allows us to mimic reference parameters! Since you are now accustomed to C++ programming, this feature may not seem important. However, it is crucial to a C programmer because C does not provide reference parameters. Imagine being a C programmer and every time you need a function with reference parameters, you must instead write a function that performs pointer manipulation while also making sure that the actual parameters to the function are pointers to the objects to be modified. These requirements are both burdensome and error prone. The inclusion of reference parameters in C++ is a critical software-engineering aspect of the language.

Self-check Questions

1.   Give a C++ statement that makes the pointer `IntPtr` point to the integer object `Counter`.

2.   Give a C++ statement that makes the pointer `IntPtr1` point to the same location as the pointer `IntPtr2`.

3.   Give the C++ statement that copies the value pointed to by `Ptr1` to the memory location pointed to by `Ptr2`.

4.   Give a C++ statement that sets the floating-point object pointed to by `FloatPtr1` to 34.5.

5.   Assume that `Ptr1` and `Ptr2` are pointers to two **double** objects. Write the code fragment that swaps `Ptr1` and `Ptr2`. That is, `Ptr2` should point to what `Ptr1` previously pointed to, and `Ptr1` should point to what `Ptr2` previously pointed to.

6.   Assume that `Ptr1` and `Ptr2` are pointers to two **double** objects. Write the code fragment that swaps the values in the memory locations pointed to by `Ptr1` and `Ptr2`.

7.   Give the output of the following program.

```
#include <iostream>
int main() {
    int Value = 10;
    int *ptr = &Value;
    cout << *ptr << endl;
    return 0;
}
```

8. Consider the following declarations and code.

```
int s[10];
int *iptr1;
int *iptr2;
int **iptr3;
for (int i = 0; i < 10; i++)
    s[i] = 9 - i;
iptr1 = s;
iptr2 = &s[3];
iptr3 = &iptr1;
*iptr1 = 5;
*iptr2 = 11;
**iptr3 = 14;
```

In the following picture, write the values (rvalues and lvalues) that are stored in memory after the code is executed. Assume integers and pointers take 4 bytes of memory.

Label	Value	Address
s[0]		1000
s[1]		1004
s[2]		1008
s[3]		1012
s[4]		1016
s[5]		1020
s[6]		1024
s[7]		1028
s[8]		1032
s[9]		1036
iptr1		1040
iptr2		1044
iptr3		1048

9. Give the output of the following program.

```
#include <iostream>
int main() {
    int Value = 10;
    int *ptr = &Value;
    *ptr = 0;
    cout << Value << endl;
    return 0;
}
```

10. Give the output of the following program.

```
#include <iostream>
int main() {
    int Value1 = 10;
    int Value2 = 40;
    int *ptr1 = &Value1;
    int *ptr2 = &Value2;
    ptr1 = ptr2;
    cout << *ptr1 << endl;
    cout << *ptr2 << endl;
    return 0;
}
```

11. Give the output of the following program.

```
#include <iostream>
void Test(int *p, int v) {
    *p = 5;
    return;
}
int main() {
    int Count = 5;
    Test(Count, Count);
    cout << Count << endl;
    return 0;
}
```

12. Give the output of the following program.

```
#include <iostream>
void Swap(int *p1, int *p2) {
    int *temp = p1;
    p1 = p2;
    p2 = temp;
    return;
}
int main() {
    int Value1 = 10;
    int Value2 = 30;
    int *Ptr1 = &Value1;
```

```
            int *Ptr2 = &Value2;
            Swap(Ptr1, Ptr2);
            cout << Value1 << Value2 << endl;
            return 0;
        }
```

11.3 CONSTANT POINTERS AND POINTERS TO CONSTANTS

The modifier **const** can also be applied in pointer definitions. Depending on where the modifier **const** is placed, either the pointer is a constant or the contents of the location to which the pointer points are considered to be constant.

Suppose the following definitions are in effect.

```
char c1 = 'a';
char c2 = 'b';
```

Then the following code segment illustrates the three legal places in a pointer definition where the modifier **const** may be applied.

```
const char *Ptr1 = &c1; // *Ptr1 is considered to
                        // be a constant; Ptr1 is
                        // not a constant
char const *Ptr2 = &c1; // *Ptr2 is considered to
                        // be a constant; Ptr2 is
                        // not constant
char *const Ptr3 = &c1; // Ptr3 is a constant;
                        // *Ptr3 is not constant
```

The modifier **const** can appear immediately before or after the type; the **const** can also appear after the unary operator *. According to the language definition, a type modifier can appear either before or after the type without changing the meaning of the definition. Therefore, the first two definitions in the preceding code segment define pointer objects with similar capabilities.

In the preceding discussion, we used the phrase *considered to be a constant*. For example, the phrase was used with the definition of Ptr1. As a result of that particular pointer definition, the value of the object to which Ptr1 points cannot be changed through an assignment to *Ptr1. However, the value of c1—the object to which Ptr1 points—can still be changed through a direct assignment to c1.

```
*Ptr1 = 'A';  // illegal: *Ptr1 is a constant
c1 = 'A';     // legal: c1 is not a constant
```

A mnemonic that helps remind you what is being defined as constant is reading the definition backwards, substituting *is a pointer to a* for the * in the definition. Thus the definition of Ptr1 reads "Ptr1 is a pointer to a **char** constant," the definition of Ptr2 reads "Ptr2 is a pointer to a constant **char**," and the definition of Ptr3 reads "Ptr3 constant is a pointer to a **char**." Although the last phrase is grammatically poor, this method should help you determine what is constant and what is not. For the preceding definitions, *Ptr1, *Ptr2, and Ptr3 are constants. As a result, the following statements are illegal.

```
*Ptr1 = 'A';   // illegal: *Ptr1 cannot be changed
*Ptr2 = 'B';   // illegal: *Ptr2 cannot be changed
Ptr3 = Ptr2;   // illegal:  Ptr3 cannot be changed
```

Because Ptr1, Ptr2, and *Ptr3 are not constants, the following statements are legal.

```
Ptr1 = Ptr2;   // legal:  Ptr1 can be changed
Ptr2 = Ptr1;   // legal:  Ptr2 can be changed
*Ptr3 = 'C';   // legal: *Ptr3 can be changed
```

In the following definition, we define a constant pointer to a location whose contents are considered to be a constant.

```
const char *const Ptr4 = &c1;
```

As a result, the following assignments are illegal.

```
Ptr4 = &c2;    // illegal:  Ptr cannot be changed
*Ptr4 = 'D';   // illegal: *Ptr cannot be changed
```

The first assignment is illegal because it attempts to modify Ptr4. The second assignment is illegal because it attempts to change the contents to which Ptr4 points.

It is also illegal for a pointer to a constant to be assigned to a pointer that is not pointing to a constant.

```
char *Ptr5 = Ptr4;   // illegal: potentially allows
                     // constant *Ptr4 to be modified
```

C++ Language

Understanding C++ declarations

The syntax of C++ can make understanding declarations difficult. One simple trick is to read the declarations backwards—that is, from right to left. Consider the following declaration

```
char *const Ptr3;
```

Starting from the right we can read as follows "Ptr3 is a constant pointer to a **char**." When we see the keyword **const** we say "constant", and when we see a * we say pointer. Here's another one.

```
char const *Ptr1;
```

So Ptr1 is a pointer to a constant **char**. This little trick really helps when you encounter a really complicated declaration.

11.4 ARRAYS AND POINTERS

In C++ the name of an array is considered to be a constant pointer; that is, the name of an array is associated with a particular memory location, and that association cannot be changed by statements in the program. In fact, the name of an array is associated with the memory location of the first element in the array. For example, consider the following six definitions:

```
int A[5];
int B[10];
int *Ptr1 = A;       // Ptr1 points to A[0]
int *Ptr2 = B;       // Ptr2 points to B[0]
int *Ptr3 = &B[0];   // Ptr3 points to B[0]
int *Ptr4 = &A[4];   // Ptr4 points to A[4]
```

The first two definitions create 5-element and 10-element **int** arrays A and B, respectively. The last four definitions create pointer objects of type **int***. Based on the preceding discussion, the initialization expression A for Ptr1 is equivalent to a pointer to the first element in array A. Similarly, the definition of Ptr2 initializes it to point to the first element of B. The definition of Ptr3 explicitly initializes it to also point to the first element of B. The definition of Ptr4 initializes it to point to the last element in array A.

The equality and relational operators are defined for pointers of the same type; therefore, given the preceding definitions, the comparisons in the following code segment are legal.

```
if (A == B)
    cout << "A and B: same values" << endl;
else
    cout << "A and B: different values" << endl;
if (Ptr1 == A)
    cout << "A and Ptr1: same values" << endl;
else
    cout << "A and Ptr1: different values" << endl;
if (Ptr2 != Ptr3)
    cout << "Ptr2 and Ptr3: different values"
        << endl;
else
    cout << "Ptr2 and Ptr3: same values" << endl;
if (Ptr1 < Ptr4)
    cout << "Ptr1 and Ptr4: Ptr1 is first" << endl;
else
    cout << "Ptr1 and Ptr4: Ptr1 is not first"
        << endl;
```

The output of the code segment is the following:

```
A and B: different values
A and Ptr1: same values
Ptr2 and Ptr3: same values
Ptr1 and Ptr4: Ptr1 is first
```

Note that the relational operators <, <=, >, and >= are defined only for pointers that point to the same array or to the object that occurs in memory immediately after the array.

The increment and decrement operators are defined for pointer objects. The effect of the increment operator ++ on a pointer object is to have the new address to which it points be the starting location of the object immediately after the object to which it previously pointed. Thus the increment operator works on a pointer object in a manner analogous to its operation on an iterator object.

Consider these definitions for A and Ptr.

```
int A[4] = {10, 20, 30, 40};
int *Ptr = A;
```

The following figure depicts the initial values in the memory associated with these definitions.

```
A[0]    10
A[1]    20
A[2]    30
A[3]    40
Ptr
```

If we were to execute the following code segment, it would display the value 20 to output stream cout.

```
++Ptr;
cout << *Ptr << endl;
```

This output occurs because the pointer increment operator updates its operand to point to the object immediately after the object to which its operand previously pointed. As Ptr was pointing to A[0], the increment causes it to now point to the next element in the list, which is A[1]. The memory associated with A and Ptr would have the following depiction:

```
A[0]    10
A[1]    20
A[2]    30
A[3]    40
Ptr
```

Because A[1] is 20, the insertion of *Ptr to cout in the preceding code segment displays the value 20.

The effect of the decrement operator -- on a pointer object is analogous to the behavior of the increment operator. If a pointer object is decremented, the new location to which it points is the object immediately before the object to which it previously pointed. For example, suppose Ptr is now decremented as in the following statement:

```
--Ptr;
```

The new value of Ptr would be the location of A[0].

```
A[0]    10
A[1]    20
A[2]    30
A[3]    40
Ptr
```

Addition and subtraction operators are also defined for pointer objects. For example, the expression Ptr + i would be a pointer to the ith object beyond

Programmer Alert

Inadvertent representation errors

In both a decrement and an increment operation, the system does not check during execution whether the object stored at the resulting address is the same type as the base type of the pointer object. If a type mismatch occurs, then the effect on the program is undefined. For example, consider the following code segment:

```cpp
int A[5];
float x;
int *Ptr = &A[4];   // Ptr points to last element of A
++Ptr;              // undefined: Ptr not pointing to
                    // an int location
```

The initialization of `Ptr` has it point to the last element of **int** array A. In most C++ implementations, **float** object x will occur immediately after A in memory. Therefore, the subsequent increment of `Ptr` has it pointing into the representation of x. As a result, the further use of `Ptr` produces undefined results.

the object to which `Ptr` points. In this expression, `i` is called an *offset*. The contents of that offset address are given by the lvalue expression `*(Ptr + i)`. Similarly, the expression `Ptr - i` is a pointer to the `i`th object prior to the object to which `Ptr` points. The contents of that offset address are given by the lvalue expression `*(Ptr - i)`.

The following example demonstrates the use of the dereferencing and pointer arithmetic operators to display the contents of an array A.

```cpp
int A[4] = {10, 20, 30, 40};
int *Ptr = A;
for (int i = 0; i < 4; ++i) {
    cout << *(Ptr+i) << endl;
}
```

To complete the correspondence between pointers and arrays, we observe that in C++ the expression `*(Ptr+i)` is equivalent to the expression `Ptr[i]`. Therefore, the contents of the array A can also be displayed using `Ptr` in the following manner:

```cpp
for (int i = 0; i < 4; ++i) {
    cout << Ptr[i] << endl;
}
```

11.5 CHARACTER STRING PROCESSING

The iostream library includes definitions for the insertion and extraction operators when the right operands are **char*** objects. The importance of this overloading is diminishing as programmers increasingly use the **string** class for character string representation. However, because many legacy libraries use the **char** array/pointer representation, it is still important to discuss the behavior of these insertion and extraction operators.

The result of inserting a **char** pointer to an output stream is equivalent to displaying a **char** array whose first element is located at the address to which the **char*** object points. An example of this use of the insertion operator is contained in the following code segment:

```
char Text[9] = "Sandrine";
for (char *Ptr = Text; *Ptr != '\0'; ++Ptr) {
    cout << Ptr << endl;
}
```

The output of the code segment is

```
Sandrine
andrine
ndrine
drine
rine
ine
ne
e
```

For each iteration of the **for** statement, the string is displayed that starts at the current location to which Ptr points. Once Ptr points to the address that contains the null character, the test expression evaluates to false and the **for** statement is done.

When the right operand of an extraction operator is a **char*** object, the behavior is the same as that of an extraction target to a **char** array—by default leading white space is skipped and the next nonwhitespace string of characters is extracted. The characters in the extracted string—including a terminating null character—are assigned to memory starting at the location to which the **char*** object points. For example, suppose the following definitions are in effect.

```
char Word[4];
char *WordPtr = Word;
```

If standard input contains

```
ab xyz
```

then the extraction

```
cin >> WordPtr;
```

would have the following effect (the dash again indicates that the object is uninitialized).

Programmer Alert

Make sure the memory is there

When using a **char** pointer with an extraction the pointer must point to a **char** array of sufficient length to store the extracted characters. The pointer is automatically assumed to be pointing to valid and sufficient memory. If it is not, then the effect of the extraction on your program is undefined. What is likely to happen is that the data values stored immediately following the **char** array will be overwritten. If you are lucky, the program will fault near the extraction and the reason for the fault will be obvious. However, the fault can sometimes happen far from the point where the array was over-written. In these cases, determining what went wrong can be challenging.

The interchangeability of pointer and array notation is most obvious in the passing of character strings to functions. The following is a possible implementation of the cstring library function `strlen()`.

```
// strlen() with s passed as a const array
int strlen(const char s[]) {
    int i;
    for (i = 0; s[i] != '\0'; ++i) {
        continue;
    }
    return i;
}
```

The function expects a character string terminated with a null character as its single parameter, and it returns the length of the string (excluding the terminating null character). The length of the string is determined by scanning the array for the terminating null character. The index of the null character is the length of the string (the characters in the string are array elements `s[0]` through `s[i-1]`).

The function `strlen()` can also be implemented in the following manner with the character string being passed via a pointer to its first character.

```
// strlen() with s passed as a pointer to constant
// characters
int strlen(const char *s) {
    int length;
    for (length = 0; *s != '\0'; ++s) {
        ++length;
    }
    return length;
}
```

The **const** declaration of the value parameter `s` indicates that the contents of the location to which `s` points are considered constant; that is, `*s` cannot be the target of an assignment. The length of the string is determined by incrementing a local **int** object `length` once for each nonnull character in the string. A separate increment operation updates `s` so that it points to the next character in the string.

We now consider another implementation of function `strlen()`. This implementation combines the character comparison with a side effect that increments the pointer to the next character.

```
// strlen() with s passed as a pointer to constant
// characters. The incrementing of the pointer is
// done as a side effect of the test expression.
int strlen(const char *s) {
    int length;
    for (length = 0; *s++ != '\0'; ++length) {
        continue;
    }
    return length;
}
```

The test expression has the following interpretation: determine whether the **char** object to which s points is the null character and, as a side effect of that test, increment pointer s. This combination of evaluation and pointer increment is quite common in string-processing code. However, whether the terseness contributes to or detracts from its understanding is debatable.

We next consider an **int** function `strcmp()`. This function expects two strings as parameters, and through its return value indicates whether the two strings are the same or whether the first occurs before or after the second lexicographically (dictionary order).

```
int strcmp(const char *s, const char *t) {
    // look for first difference or until *s is null
    while ((*s == *t) && (*s != '\0')) {
        ++s;
        ++t;
    }
    // return encoding difference
    return *s - *t;
}
```

The string parameters for `strcmp()` are s and t. Function `strcmp()` returns 0 if the strings are the same, returns a negative value if s occurs lexicographically before t, and returns a positive value if s occurs lexicographically after t.

The **while** loop in `strcmp()` iterates while two conditions are true: the current characters to which s and t point are the same, and the current character to which s points is not the null character. (We do not need to explicitly check whether t is null because the existing terms in the **while** expression catch this condition.) When the loop terminates, we examine the current characters to which s and t point to determine the return value of the function. If the characters are the same, the return value, which is the difference *s - *t, will be 0. If the strings are different, then s and t will point to the first difference in the two strings. In this case, the expression *s - *t will be negative if s occurs lexicographically before t and positive if s occurs lexicographically after t.

11.6 PROGRAM COMMAND–LINE PARAMETERS

Many operating systems (e.g., UNIX and Windows) provide command-line interpreters. These interpreters enable a user to type a command or program and then have the operating system execute it. For example, the following instruction uses the command cd to change the current directory to the directory code.

```
cd code
```

In the instruction, the string code is a parameter to the command cd. The command line consists of two strings, cd and code.

As another example, the following instruction runs the program cmd with the strings 123 and ab as its command-line parameters.

```
cmd 123 ab
```

C++ provides a method for creating programs that use command-line parameters. The command-line parameters are communicated to a program via its function main(). To make this communication straightforward, C++ requires that a program view a command line as a sequence of character strings. The first string is the program name, and the remaining strings are its parameters. For our second example, the three strings in order are cmd, 123, and ab.

To access the strings that compose the command line, C++ has an alternative parameter list declaration for main() that specifies two parameters. A prototype of main() using the alternative form is given below.

```
int main(int argc, char *argv[]);
```

The first parameter is an **int** value parameter. By convention, this parameter has the name argc. When the program is run, parameter argc is initialized automatically to be the number of character strings that make up the command line. This number includes the program name in its count, so argc is the number of command-line parameters plus 1 for the program name. For our cmd example, argc is set to 3.

The second parameter in the alternative declaration is an array of **char** pointers. By convention, this array has the name argv. When the program is run, pointer argv[0] is automatically initialized to point to a character string that represents the program name, and pointers argv[1] through argv[argc-1] are automatically initialized to point to character strings that represent the individual command-line parameters to the program. This initialization is depicted for our cmd example in Figure 11.2.

It is important to remember that argc and argv are parameters to main(). As a result, they are not global objects. If other functions require the values of argc and argv during their execution, then argc and argv must be passed to those functions as parameters.

Program 11.2 is a simple program that displays its command-line parameters to the standard output stream. The command-line parameters passed to the

Figure 11.2

Correspondence of command-line parameters and function main() parameters argc and argv

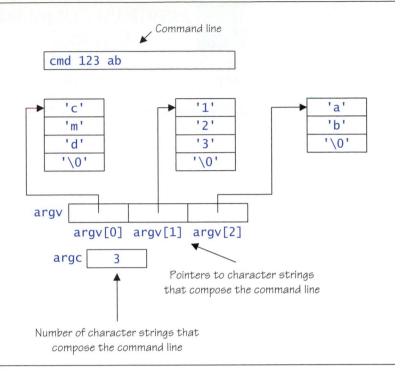

program are iteratively displayed using a **for** loop that iterates once for each command-line parameter. An individual parameter is displayed using the insertion operator. As discussed in Section 11.5, the insertion operator is overloaded for **char*** pointers; that is, the string being pointed to is displayed.

Program 11.2

Mimics operating system command echo

```
// Program 11.2: Mimics operating system command echo.
// The command-line parameters are displayed to the
// standard output stream (separated by spaces).
#include <iostream>
#include <string>
using namespace std;
int main(int argc, char *argv[]) {
   for (int i = 1; i < argc; ++i) {
      // display argv[i]
      cout << argv[i] << " ";
   }
   cout << endl;
   return 0;
}
```

Program 11.3 also uses command-line parameters. This program expects its parameters to be filenames. Each parameter is used, in turn, to open an input file stream. The contents of the file stream are then displayed to the standard output stream. The program makes use of the file stream library **fstream**.

Program 11.3

Mimics operating system command type

```
// Program 11.3: Mimics operating system command type. Each
// command-line parameter is treated as a filename. The
// contents of the associated file are displayed to the
// standard output stream cout.
#include <iostream>
#include <fstream>
#include <string>

using namespace std;

int main(int argc, char *argv[]) {
    ifstream fin;
    for (int i = 1; i < argc; ++i) {
        // open file stream associated with i-th command-line
        // parameter
        fin.open(argv[i]);
        if (fin) {
            // argv[i] is a valid filename, so extract and
            // display the characters in the file
            char c;
            while (fin.get(c)) {
                cout << c;
            }
        }
        else {
            // argv[i] is not a valid filename, so display an
            // error message and terminate
            cerr << argv[0] << ": " << argv[i]
                 << " not a valid file name" << endl;
            return 1;
        }
        fin.close();
    }
    return 0;
}
```

Like Program 11.2, Program 11.3 has a **for** loop that controls the processing of the parameters. If the ifstream object fin successfully opens the file named by argv[i], then the stream extracts the characters in the file character by character. As each character is extracted, it is displayed to the standard output stream. If the file cannot be opened, an error message is displayed. The error message consists of the name of the program being executed along with an indication of which parameter is an invalid filename.

Self-check Questions

13.   Assume the following definition.

```
int GradeList[100];
int *ptr;
```

Give the assignment statement that makes ptr point to the first element of GradeList (i.e., element GradeList[0]).

Give the assignment statement that makes ptr point to the last element of GradeList.

14.   Consider the following C++ code fragment.

```cpp
char *s;
char p[20] = "Happy Holidays";
s = &p[3];
cout << s[4] << endl;
```

What does the code output?

15.   Assume the following definitions.

```cpp
int Weights[100];
int *ptr;
```

Using ptr to access the elements of array Weights, write a loop that
assigns zero to every element of Weights.

16.   Assume the following definition.

```cpp
int A[10] = {0, 1, 2, 3, 4, 5, 6, 7, 8, 9};
```

Give a statement that defines an array of pointers to integers called AR
that is initialized such that the first element of AR points to the last element of A, the second element of AR points to the next to the last element
of A, and so on.

17.   Write a function called WordCopy that copies an array of n integers
starting at address src to a new location starting at address dst. The
prototype of function WordCopy is:

```cpp
void WordCopy(int *dst, int *src, int n);
```

18.   Suppose the prototype of WordCopy was changed to

```cpp
void WordCopy(int *dst, const int *src, int n);
```

Could you still write the copy function? Explain why or why not.

19.   Suppose the prototype of WordCopy was changed to

```cpp
void WordCopy(const int *dst, const int *src, int
n);
```

Could you still write the copy function? Explain why or why not.

20.   Suppose the prototype of WordCopy was changed to

```cpp
void WordCopy(int *dst, int *const src, int n);
```

Could you still write the copy function? Explain why or why not.

21. Write a program called `number`. Program `number` takes a command line of the form

   `number` *filename1* *filename2*

   Program `number` copies *filename1* to *filename2* and it numbers each line. The output of program `number` should look like this:

```
0001:  This is the first line
0002:  This is the second line
....
```

11.7 POINTERS TO FUNCTIONS

In addition to allowing pointers to objects, C++ also allows pointers to functions. The primary use of a pointer to a function is as a parameter to another function. This use enables the function that employs the pointer to perform a variety of actions. Such an ability is important in non-object-oriented languages, but of less use in object-oriented languages like C++, which also have polymorphic mechanisms (see Chapter 14).

Pointer-to-function types are true types. As such, an object that is a pointer to a function can be assigned. Also, the return type of a function can be a pointer to a function, and arrays of pointers to functions can be defined.

The definition of an object that is a pointer to a function must include the return type of the function and the types of the function's parameters (for readability, names of the parameters can also be supplied). The following definition defines an object `FuncPtr` that is a pointer to an **int** function that requires a single **int** value parameter.

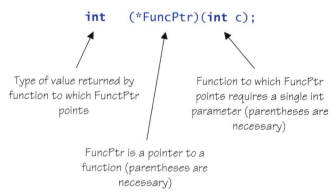

Just as an array name is a pointer to its elements, a function name is a pointer to the code that constitutes its actions. So the following assignment results in `FuncPtr` being a pointer to the **int** function `toupper()`.

   `FuncPtr = toupper;`

Program 11.4 demonstrates the use of pointers to functions. The program first prompts and extracts the name of a file. It then prompts and extracts whether the user wants the contents of the file to be displayed in uppercase or lowercase. A function `Display()` is then invoked. Function `Display()` expects two parameters: the first parameter `fin` is the input file stream; the second parameter `ToFunc` is a pointer to the function that will manipulate the characters in the input stream.

Program 11.4

Demonstrates use of function pointer as a parameter

```cpp
// Program 11.4: Displays a file in either upper- or
// lowercase depending on a user request.
#include <fstream>
#include <ctype.h>
#include <string>

using namespace std;

// Display(): display text stream using ToFunc
// modification
void Display(ifstream &fin, int (*ToFunc)(int c)) {
    // extract and display characters one-at-a-time
    char CurrentChar;
    while (fin.get(CurrentChar)){
        // modify current character using ToFunc
        CurrentChar = (*ToFunc)(CurrentChar);
        cout << CurrentChar;
    }
    return;
}

// main(): manage file stream display
int main() {
    const int MaxFileNameSize = 256;
    // prompt and extract the name of the file
    cout << "Enter name of file: " << flush;
    char FileName[MaxFileNameSize];
    cin >> FileName;
    // make sure a valid filename was provided
    ifstream fin(FileName);
    if (fin) {
        // we have valid file, so determine the action
        cout << "Display file in uppercase or "
            << "lowercase (u, l):" << flush;
        char reply;
        cin >> reply;
        // display file according to request
        if (reply == 'l')
            Display(fin, tolower);
        else if (reply == 'u')
            Display(fin, toupper);
        else {
            cerr << "Bad request" << endl;
            return 1;
        }
    }
    else { // process invalid filename
        cerr << "Invalid file name: " << FileName
            << endl;
        return 1;
    }
    return 0;
}
```

Functions `toupper()` and `tolower()` are used as the text manipulation function parameters in the invocations of `Display()` in `main()`. Functions `toupper()` and `tolower()` are defined in the `ctype` library, and although they are designed for character manipulation, their parameters and return types are defined to be **int**. As the ctype library is a C-based standard library, the include file is `cctype`.

A syntax similar to its parameter declaration is used to invoke `ToFunc` in `Display()`.

```
CurrentChar = (*ToFunc)(CurrentChar);
```

The parameter `CurrentChar` in the invocation contains the currently extracted character from the input stream. `CurrentChar` is modified to get the result of the function invocation. A simpler invocation syntax is permitted—the surrounding parentheses and the dereferencing operator can be omitted as in the following invocation:

```
CurrentChar = ToFunc(CurrentChar);
```

However, the explicit dereferencing syntax is a clear clue to a reader of the code that the actual function being invoked is not `ToFunc`.

History of Computing

The Altair 8800

As chip-fabrication technology improved, Intel produced increasingly powerful chips. In 1974 Intel introduced the 8080 microprocessor. The power of the 8080 rivaled some of the minicomputers being sold at that time. This fact was not lost on a number of inventors and electronics hobbyists. Edward Roberts owned a small company in Albuquerque, New Mexico, that sold hobby kits. With the introduction of the 8080, Roberts saw the opportunity to make and sell a home-computer kit. The kit was the cover story of the January 1975 issue of *Popular Electronics*. The machine was called the Altair 8800. Interestingly, the name Altair was used because a recent episode of the popular TV series *Star Trek* had mentioned the name as the destination of the *Enterprise*. It was also the name of the planet in the classic science fiction movie, *Forbidden Planet*.

It's safe to say that the appearance of the Altair 8800 on the cover of *Popular Electronics* (see Figure 11.3) gave a kick start to the personal computer revolution. The article inspired computer hobbyists all over the United States to begin working on computers and writing software to run on these machines. Several of these hobbyists stand out because they went on to found companies that are shaping the computer industry even today (e.g., Paul Allen and William Gates of Microsoft).

Figure 11.3

The January 1975
cover of Popular
Electronics *featuring*
the Altair 8800

Self-check Questions

22. Consider the following prototype.

    ```
    void (*signal(int sig, void (*func)(int)))(int);
    ```

    Explain what this function does. Hint: Read the pointer to function definitions from right to left.

23. What is the output of the following program?

    ```cpp
    #include <iostream>
    void Func1(int Value) {
        cout << "Func1 says " << Value << endl;
        return;
    }
    void Func2(int Value) {
        cout << "Func2 says " << Value << endl;
        return;
    }
    int main()
    {
    ```

```
            void (*FuncPtr)(int);
            FuncPtr = &Func1;
            (*FuncPtr)(17);
            FuncPtr = &Func2;
            (*FuncPtr)(42);
            return 0;
        }
```

24. Write a function called `Apply`. Function `Apply` takes as parameters an array of integers, the number of elements in the array, and a pointer to a function that returns an integer. Function `Apply` "applies" the function passed to each element of the array.

11.8 DYNAMIC OBJECTS

Based on previous discussions, you should be able to use the dereferencing and address operators to manipulate pointers and the objects to which they point. You should also recognize that pointer notation can be used as alternative notation for manipulating arrays and that pointers are the mechanism by which C++ programs have access to command-line arguments. Although the alternative pointer notation and the access to command-line arguments are both important, these roles are not the main reasons that pointers are part of the C++ language. The major role of pointers is in the creation of dynamic objects, in particular for objects whose memory needs vary during program execution. In fact, it is through the use of dynamic objects that the Standard Template Library (STL) can provide its functionality.

Except for some global stream objects, such as `cout` and `cin`, and some global constants, the objects we have defined in our programs have generally been local objects. A local object comes into existence when its definition is executed, and it is automatically destroyed when its defining scope block has ended. Analogous rules govern the lifetime of a global object—a global object comes into existence when program execution begins (the start of the global scope), and it is automatically destroyed when the program terminates (the end of the global scope).

Dynamic objects are different from local and global objects in that they come into existence as the result of specific memory allocation requests by the program. The dynamic objects continue to exist until the program returns their memory through a specific deallocation request. Thus the lifetime of a dynamic object is independent of its defining scope.

The memory used by a dynamic object is said to come from the free store. Conceptually, the *free store* is memory controlled by the operating system that can be broken up and allocated to a program as needed. The principal C++ method of acquiring free store memory is through the use of the unary operator **new**. When the dynamic objects from a given request are no longer needed, their memory is returned to the free store through the unary operator **delete**.

The operator **new** has three forms. The simplest form is a memory allocation request for a single object that expects the name of a type as the right operand to the **new** operator. If sufficient unallocated free store memory is available, the operation returns a pointer to a memory location of the proper size for that type. This form is used in the following code segment:

```
char *cptr;
cptr = new char;  // cptr points to an uninitialized
                  // char object
```

The code segment first defines a **char*** object `cptr`. If free store memory is available, then the assignment statement in the code segment sets `cptr` to a **char** object memory location that was previously part of the free store. The memory for the **char** object is uninitialized because there are no constructors for fundamental type objects.

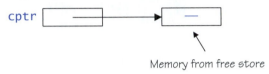

Memory from free store

If the type of object requested from the free store is a class type as in the following example, then the class default constructor is automatically invoked to initialize the newly allocated memory.

```
Rational *rptr;
rptr = new Rational;  // rptr points to a Rational
                      // object representing 0/1
```

The execution of the assignment statement in the preceding code segment causes `Rational` pointer `rptr` to point to a dynamic `Rational` object representing the default value of 0/1.

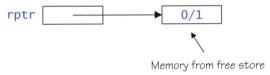

Memory from free store

Once a pointer has been successfully set with a location returned by a **new** request, the object at that location can be used like any other object of that type. In particular, it can be evaluated and manipulated.

In the following statement, the value of the dynamic object to which `cptr` points is set to the value of the next available input character.

```
cin >> *cptr;     // assign next input to the char
                  // object to which cptr points
```

Suppose the next available input is the character `'j'`. After its extraction, memory would have the following depiction:

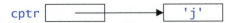

As a result, the following insertion statement displays a `'j'` to `cout`.

```
cout << *cptr;      // display char object to which cptr
                    // points
```

A second form of the **new** operator not only requests a single dynamic object but also provides initialization for that object. The initializer value(s) are specified within parentheses, using commas to separate the initializers. In the following code segment, pointers `ip` and `rp` are defined along with initializers for the values to which they point.

```
int *ip;                // ip points to dynamic
ip = new int(256);      // object representing 256
Rational *rp;           // rp points to dynamic
rp = new Rational (3, 4); // object representing 3/4
```

If sufficient free store memory exists, then `ip` points to a dynamic `int` object that represents 256 and `rp` points to a dynamic `Rational` object that represents 3/4.

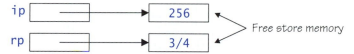

The third form of the **new** operator permits multiple dynamic objects to be requested in a single operation. This form expects the right operand to the **new** operator to be the name of a type along with a subscripted expression indicating the number of requested objects of that type. If sufficient, contiguous, unallocated free store memory is available, the operation returns a pointer to a block of dynamic memory sufficient to hold the requested number of objects. If the type of the requested dynamic objects is a class type, then the class default constructor is invoked automatically to initialize each of the requested objects. This form is used in the following code segment:

```
Rational *rlist;
rlist = new Rational[5];
```

In this assignment statement, if the **new** operation is successful, then `rlist` will point to the first object in a block of memory sufficient to hold five `Rational` objects.

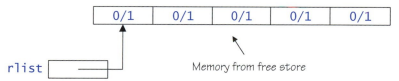

Because the memory is contiguous, pointer `rlist` can be viewed as a `Rational` array with five elements. Each of the dynamic objects is initialized with the `Rational` default constructor; that is, each of the five `Rational` objects initially represents the rational value 0/1.

Although the preceding `rlist` example uses a constant expression in requesting multiple dynamic objects, constant expressions are not a

C++ Language

requirement. For example, the next code segment determines the size of the free store request by extracting a value from `cin`.

```
cout << "Size of list: " << flush;
int ListSize;
cin >> ListSize;
int *values = new int[ListSize];
```

Memory acquired from the free store using either of the single object request forms can be returned to the free store by providing a pointer to that memory as the right operand of a **delete** operation. Such a return is demonstrated in the following code segment that returns the memory to which `cptr` points.

```
delete cptr;
```

A side effect of the **delete** operation is that the value of cptr becomes undefined.

Programmers need to be particularly careful if their code can contain multiple pointers to the same object, because accessing a memory location that has been returned to the free store is illegal. For example, consider the following code segment:

```
char *ptr1 = new char('c');
char *ptr2 = ptr1;
delete ptr1;
cout << *ptr2; // undefined result -- ptr2 points
               // to returned free store memory
```

The segment begins by defining two **char*** pointers ptr1 and ptr2. Pointer ptr1 is initialized via a **new** operation to the location of a dynamic **char** object whose value is 'c'. Pointer ptr2 is initialized to point to that same object.

The **delete** statement that follows the two definitions returns the memory representing the 'c' to the free store. As a result of that deletion, the value of ptr1 becomes undefined. Another side effect of the deletion is that ptr2 has become a *dangling pointer*—ptr2 now points to an invalid memory location.

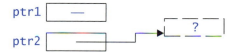

Accessing memory that has been returned to the free store produces undefined results.

Dynamic objects acquired by using the **new** form that specifies the number of objects in the free store request must be returned as a group using a **delete** form that includes a pair of brackets between the keyword **delete** and the pointer to memory being returned. After the deletion, the value of the pointer is undefined.

In the following statement, the **delete** operation returns to the free store the memory of the five Rational dynamic objects to which rlist points.

```
delete [] rlist;
```

If the memory being returned to the free store represents class type objects and if a *destructor* for that class exists, then the destructor is automatically invoked on each of the object(s). A destructor is a member function that performs any necessary processing for the class object that is being destroyed. The classes we defined in previous chapters (e.g., Rational and Maze) have not required such actions, so no destructors were defined for them. Destructors are

If things go wrong

The effect of using a dangling pointer may not be immediately obvious. Therefore, when it is clear that a program using dynamic objects is misbehaving, you should reconsider the impact of each deletion on your data structures. Again, drawing a picture of what is happening can be very helpful in finding programming errors.

normally necessary only for class objects with data members that are pointers to dynamic memory. They are required in such cases because it is the destructor that typically invokes the **delete** operation on those data members.

Consider the following code segment that in successive statements acquires dynamic storage and assigns the location of that storage to pointer **p**.

```
int *p;
p = new int;   // p points to dynamic memory
p = new int;   // p now points to different memory
```

When the first assignment statement is executed, free store memory is acquired and p points to it.

When the second assignment statement is executed, additional free store memory is acquired and p now points to it. The memory acquired in the previous assignment is now lost to the program.

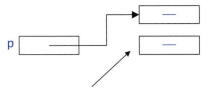

A memory leak has occurred. This location cannot
be accessed by the program.

The loss occurs because there is now no pointer object whose value is the location of the memory acquired in the first **new** operation. This loss is called a *memory leak*. In most C++ implementations, the loss will be in effect for the remainder of program execution. Memory leaks can seriously affect the ability of a program to complete its task—it may be the case that subsequent dynamic memory requests cannot be satisfied because of insufficient free store memory. For this reason, memory leaks should be avoided by keeping careful track of dynamic memory requests.

11.9 A SIMPLE ADT FOR REPRESENTING LISTS OF INTEGER VALUES

We turn our attention to the development of a simple class `IntList` for representing lists of integer values. This class will make use of dynamic memory allocation and deallocation. Our development of the `IntList` class will give insight on how `vector` and other container classes can be implemented. We will revisit the development of container classes in Chapter 14 when we discuss templates and polymorphism.

The primary interface to the `IntList` class resembles an array interface. It uses overloadings of the subscript operator to provide lvalue and rvalue access to individual list elements. (Like an array, the elements of an `IntList` are indexed starting from 0.)

The `IntList` class does not suffer from standard array restrictions. In particular, `IntList` objects can be the source or target of an assignment; `IntList` objects are passable both by reference and by value; `IntList` objects can be the return value for a function; `IntList` objects have a default constructor that allows the number of elements and their initial values to be optionally specified; `IntList` objects can provide access to the number of elements represented by their lists; and the `IntList` overloadings of the subscript operator verify that the index value is in the proper range. To make the `IntList` class even more useful, we also overload the insertion operator for `IntList` objects. In the exercises, we consider an `IntList` extraction operator and iterators.

In the following code segment we use the `IntList` class to define and manipulate some lists.

```
IntList A;              // default list of 10 zeros
cout << "A: " << A << endl;
IntList B(5, 1);        // list of 5 ones
cout << "B: " << B << endl;
cout << "Number of values: ";
int n;
cin >> n;
IntList C(n, 2);        // list of n twos
cout << "C: " << C << endl;
B = A;
for (int i = 0; i < A.size(); ++i) { // modify A
    A[i] = i;
}
cout << "A: " << A << endl;
cout << "B: " << B << endl;
```

If a user entered the value 3 in reaction to the prompt in the preceding code segment, the input/output behavior of the segment would be

```
A: [ 0 0 0 0 0 0 0 0 0 0 ]
B: [ 1 1 1 1 1 ]
Number of values: 3
C: [ 2 2 2]
A: [ 0 1 2 3 4 5 6 7 8 9 ]
B: [ 0 0 0 0 0 0 0 0 0 0 ]
```

As reflected both in the initial code segment comment and in the initial output display, the default constructor creates a list A with 10 elements with the values of those elements all being 0. The segment and output also show that we can construct a list B where we specify both the number of elements (5) and the values of those elements (1). The definition and display of C show that the size of the constructed list can be a value not known until run time. This ability contrasts nicely with arrays whose size must be known at compile time.

The second display of A and B occurs after both the assignment to B using A as the source and the subsequent modification of A's elements. This display shows that shallow copying is not being performed. A and B are distinct mutable objects—modifications can be made to the number of elements and to the values of the elements in either IntList object without affecting the other object.

11.9.1 IntList specification

The class definition for IntList in Listing 11.1 provides a framework for achieving the desired capabilities and behaviors discussed in our introduction to IntList.

Listing 11.1

Definition of class IntList from intlist.h

```
class IntList {
    public:
        // default constructor
        IntList(int n = 10, int val = 0);
        // constructor initializes from a standard array
        IntList(const int A[], int n);
        // copy constructor
        IntList(const IntList &A);
        // destructor
        ~IntList();
        // assignment operator
        IntList& operator=(const IntList &A);
        // inspector for element of a constant list
        int operator[](int i) const;
        // inspector for element of a nonconstant list
        int& operator[](int i);
        // inspector for size of the list
        int size() const { return NumberValues; }
        // resize function
        void resize(int n = 0, int val = 0);
        // append a new element
        void push_back(int val);
    private:
        // data members
        int NumberValues;    // size of list
        int *Values;         // pointer to list elements
};
```

The IntList definition shows three constructors. The first constructor is the default constructor. It has two optional parameters that allow the number of elements and the values of those elements to be specified. The second constructor is the copy constructor. The third constructor is a specialized constructor that creates an `IntList` object from an existing array. The implementation of this constructor is left to the exercises.

The `IntList` constructors are responsible for initializing the two data members `NumberValues` and `Values`. The purpose of `int` data member `NumberValues` is to maintain the size of the list; the purpose of `int*` data member `Values` is to point to the dynamic storage that maintains the values that comprise the list.

As first noted in Chapter 8, C++ specifies that compilers must make versions of the copy constructor and the member assignment operator automatically available to a class. The compiler-supplied versions perform memberwise copying where each source data member is copied in a bit-by-bit manner to the corresponding target data member. Although we used these versions in our previous class development (e.g., `Rational` and `RandomInt`), we do not use them here. For sophisticated classes whose objects can acquire storage dynamically, the straightforward memberwise copying of data members can introduce storage conflicts.

For example, suppose there is no explicitly defined `IntList` copy constructor. Let's consider what happens when the following code segment is executed with the compiler-supplied copy constructor in effect.

```
IntList C(5, 0);
IntList D(C);
```

When `IntList` object C is created, its data members `NumberValues` and `Values` are initialized from scratch. In particular, dynamic space is acquired to hold the various elements in the list. A comparable acquisition is not performed for object D's data member `Values`. Because the compiler-supplied copy constructor is assumed, the two data members of object C are directly copied to object D. Under this scenario, objects C and D share the same dynamic space for their `Values` data members. This scenario is depicted in Figure 11.4.

Under this scenario, any change to C or D affects the other. For example, suppose `C[0]` is set to 1.

```
C[0] = 1;
```

Then a display of object D

```
cout << D << endl;
```

would output

```
[ 1 0 0 0 0 ]
```

rather than its initial representation of five zeros. Such side effects are not what clients would expect in their list manipulations. Therefore, the compiler-supplied copy constructor cannot be used.

For comparable reasons, we cannot use the compiler-supplied member assignment operator. Like the compiler-supplied copy constructor, the compiler-supplied member assignment operator copies directly the data members of a source object to the data members of the target object. Thus this memberwise copying also leads to side effects.

Figure 11.4

Depicts the effect of memberwise copying of one IntList to another

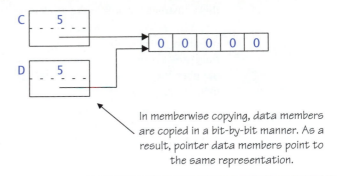

In memberwise copying, data members are copied in a bit-by-bit manner. As a result, pointer data members point to the same representation.

To avoid copying side effects in our ADT, we explicitly develop an IntList copy constructor and a member assignment operator. The two members ensure that the desired copying behaviors occur.

If you are confused by the syntax of the member assignment prototype in Listing 11.1, recall our discussion from Chapter 8—only the right operand of the assignment operator must be specified (the left operand is understood to be the invoking object). In addition, the assignment operation returns a value so that the larger assignment expressions can be composed, as shown in the assignment statement that ends the following code segment:

```
IntList A(11, 28);
IntList B;
IntList C;
C = B = A;
```

The assignment operator performs a reference return for reasons of efficiency—this way no copy needs to be made.

The use of dynamic space by an IntList object requires that we also define a destructor ~IntList() that returns the acquired dynamic space when we are finished with the object. Its definition will ensure that there is no memory leakage when an IntList object is destroyed (e.g., goes out of scope).

The IntList class definition in Listing 11.1 also provides two overloadings of the subscript operator.

```
int operator[](int i) const;
int& operator[](int i);
```

The member subscript operator prototypes differ in their return type and in their use of the member function qualifier **const**. The **const** qualifier is part of a member function's signature. As such, when the compiler translates an invocation of the subscript operator on an IntList object, it will use context to determine which definition applies. The definition of the subscript operator using the qualifier **const** is invoked in situations where a **const** IntList object is inspected.

```
const IntList A(3, 5);
cout << A[2] << endl;
int i = A[1];
```

For such uses, a value return type is appropriate for the operation.

The subscript operator with the reference return type and no function qualifier **const** is used in situations where a non-**const** IntList object is being inspected or mutated.

```
IntList B;
B[0] = 1;
Swap(B[3], B[4]);
cin >> B[5];
```

For such uses, the reference return type is appropriate—the individual element being accessed may be subject to modification.

The purpose of the IntList inspector function size() is to return the number of elements represented by the list (data member NumberValues). The definition of function size() is itself part of the class definition. Although including implementation in a header file is normally discouraged, we do so here to discuss a feature of such functions.

Member functions that have their definitions specified within their class definition have their invocations *inlined*. When an invocation of an inlined function is found during program translation, the compiler effectively textually substitutes the body of the inlined function at the point of invocation. This substitution saves the cost of creating and destroying an activation record for the member function. These savings while not typically important can be extremely critical for time-dependent applications that invoke the inlined function many times. The cost of inlining is often a larger executable unit.

Like size(), member functions resize() and push_back() are IntList analogs of the vector member functions resize() and push_back(). The implementations of resize() and push_back() are left to the exercises.

11.9.2 IntList constructor implementation

Our definitions of the IntList member functions begin in Listing 11.2. This listing provides the definitions of the IntList default and copy constructors and the IntList destructor.

The default IntList constructor has two optional parameters n and val (the defaults for n and val are 10 and 0). Parameter n specifies the initial number of list elements to be represented. Parameter val specifies the initial value of those list elements. For pedagogical simplicity, we use an assert() statement to ensure that the size of the list is sensible. The constructor then sets data member NumberValues to reflect the size of the list to be constructed.

The default constructor makes a dynamic memory allocation request with the **new** operator for n integer values.

```
Values = new int [n];
```

Under the C++ standard, if this request cannot be satisfied, an exception is generated causing the program to terminate if the exception is not caught (i.e., processed). The assert() statement that follows verifies that Values is nonzero. Prestandard C++ compilers use the value 0 to indicate that the request cannot

Listing 11.2

Two IntList constructors and its destructor

```cpp
// constructor initializes elements to given value
IntList::IntList(int n, int val) {
    assert(n > 0);
    NumberValues = n;
    Values = new int [n];
    assert(Values);
    for (int i = 0; i < n; ++i) {
        Values[i] = val;
    }
}
// copy constructor
IntList::IntList(const IntList &A) {
    NumberValues = A.size();
    Values = new int [NumberValues];
    assert(Values);
    for (int i = 0; i < A.size(); ++i)
        Values[i] = A[i];
}
// destructor
IntList::~IntList() {
    delete [] Values;
}
```

be satisfied. Thus regardless of which compiler is being used, if the **for** loop is executed, `Values` points to sufficient storage to represent the elements in the list.

The **for** loop in the default constructor iterates once for each of the n **int** objects that make up the block of dynamic storage to which `Values` points.

```cpp
for (int i = 0; i < n; ++i) {
    Values[i] = val;
}
```

The ith object of the block is associated with the ith element of the list where i varies from 0 to n−1. Array notation is used with pointer `Values` to appropriately set the ith element.

The copy constructor has some similarity with the default constructor. The copy constructor begins by setting data member `NumberValues` using the size of the list represented by the source object A. Because we keep our objects in a coherent state, there is no need to verify that the size of A is sensible. The copy constructor then requests sufficient storage to make a copy of A's list. If the dynamic memory request is satisfied, a **for** loop is executed to initialize that storage.

The **for** loop in the copy constructor iteratively copies the values of the elements represented by A to the appropriate locations in the dynamic storage to which `Values` points.

The assignment statement in the **for** loop body that does the actual copying is interesting in that it contains two different uses of the subscript operator.

```cpp
Values[i] = A[i];
```

The expression `Values[i]` is a use of the array subscript operator and the expression `A[i]` is a use of the `IntList` subscript operator for **const** objects. The context tells the compiler which subscript operation is being performed.

The kind of copying performed by the copy constructor and by the assignment operator is deep copying. In *deep copying* a separate target list is made with each element in the target individually copied from the source list. This form of copying is different from a shallow copy where the copy operation merely duplicates the value of the pointer `Values`. With a deep copy, the source and target lists have identical but distinct representations. The source and target objects' `Values` data members point to different memory locations that contain the same values. In a shallow copy, the two lists share a single representation—the two `Values` data members point to the same memory location.

11.9.3   IntList destructor implementation

As discussed in Chapter 8, the purpose of a destructor is to perform any necessary processing for a class type object going out of existence. For objects with data members that point to dynamic memory, the destructor typically returns that storage to the heap. The `IntList` destructor performs such a task. Its function body consists of a statement that tells the system to reclaim the storage to which `Values` points.

```
delete [] Values;
```

This reclaim is appropriate as `IntList` objects do not share storage. Without this explicit destructor definition, memory leaks would occur whenever an `IntList` object goes out of existence.

11.9.4   Subscript implementation

The two overloadings of the subscript operator for **const** and non-**const** `IntList` objects are given in Listing 11.3. For simplicity of pedagogy, the subscript operators use an `assert()` macro to verify that the index value i is within bounds (i.e., i is in the interval 0 ... `size()`-1). Observe that the two overloadings differ in their return type. The version of the subscript operator for **const** `IntList` objects returns a simple value. A value return prevents the underlying element from being changed. The version of the subscript operator for non-**const** objects does a reference return. By producing an lvalue, the return value can be either accessed or modified.

Listing 11.3

IntList subscript operators from intlist.cpp

```
// inspector of an individual const IntList element
int IntList::operator[](int i) const {
   assert((i >= 0) && (i < size()));
   return Values[i];
}
// inspector/mutator facilitator of individual non-const
element
int& IntList::operator[](int i) {
   assert((i >= 0) && (i < size()));
   return Values[i];
}
```

11.9.5 IntList member assignment and the this pointer

The reassignment of an `IntList` object requires four actions.

- Reset list size.
- Return existing dynamic memory.
- Acquire sufficient new dynamic memory.
- Copy the elements of the source object to the dynamic memory.

You might think it possible to accomplish these actions in the following manner where object A is the `IntList` parameter representing the right operand (i.e., the source object).

```
NumberValues = A.size();
delete [] Values;
Values = new int [NumberValues];
for (int i = 1; i <= A.size(); ++i) {
    Values[i] = A[i];
}
```

But suppose that the preceding code segment is the function body for our member assignment operator. What happens if the following assignment executes when object X is an `IntList` object?

```
X = X;
```

The assignment would make object X undefined! In this case, the left operand and right operand are the same object—formal parameter A of the member assignment operator is an alias for the object whose member assignment operator is being invoked (X). When the **delete** statement performs its release of the dynamic memory controlled by the invoking object, the value of the invoking object's (X's) data member `Values` becomes undefined. Hence A, which is in fact also X, cannot be validly subscripted to access the memory that had previously made up the list.

We cannot dismiss this problem by saying that a programmer never has the need to write such a statement because the problem can also come about in a disguised manner. For example, the object in question can be passed multiple times as a parameter to some function, or the object is both a global object and a parameter.

A simple way to handle this aliasing problem is to perform the assignment only if the two operands represent different objects. C++ provides a pointer to the invoking object that can be used for this purpose. The pointer is referenced using the keyword **this**. We can compare the value of **this** with &A, which is the location of A. If the locations are different, the invoking object needs to be updated. The complete definition of the member assignment operator is given in Listing 11.4.

As suggested, the member assignment operator begins by testing whether the invoking object and A are different objects. If they are different, the invoking object is updated. The assignment operator also tests whether the new representation has a different number of elements. If it does, the current dynamic

```
// assignment
IntList& IntList::operator=(const IntList &A) {
    if (this != &A) {
        if (size() != A.size()) {
            delete [] Values;
            NumberValues = A.size();
            Values = new int [A.size()];
            assert(Values);
        }
        for (int i = 0; i < A.size(); ++i)
            Values[i] = A[i];
    }
    return *this;
}
```

storage is released and new dynamic storage is acquired. If the new representation and the existing representation have the same number of elements, we use the existing dynamic storage to store the new representation.

The new representation is set using a **for** loop to copy the elements of A to Values. The loop is the same as the loop in the copy constructor and warrants no further discussion.

Regardless of whether the invoking object is updated, we must return the current value of the invoking object to complete the operation. By using the indirection operator * in conjunction with **this** (i.e., ***this**), we have an expression that is suitable for the return value of the member assignment operator.

11.9.6 Overloading the insertion operator for IntList objects

The insertion operator is overloaded in Listing 11.5. The auxiliary operator displays the list within a pair of brackets. The individual elements in the list are separated by spaces.

```
// auxiliary insertion operator for IntList
ostream& operator<<(ostream &sout, const IntList &A){
    sout << "[ ";
    // write out the elements
    for (int i = 0; i < A.size(); ++i)
        sout << A[i] << " ";
    sout << "]";
    // all done
    return sout;
}
```

The insertion operator implementation is relatively straightforward. Single insertions of the bracket delimiters occur before and after a **for** loop that displays the individual elements. The overloaded operator does a reference return of type `ostream`. By returning the stream, an `IntList` insertion can be part of a larger insertion expression.

```
IntList A(5, 1);
cout << A << endl;
```

This completes our discussion of the `IntList` class. The exercises provide other extensions to an `IntList` library.

Self-check Questions

25.   Consider the following class declaration.

```
class Node {
    ....
    public:
        int Value;
        Node *Next;
};
```

Consider the following code:

```
Node ANode;
Node *p = new Node(25, NULL); // allocate a node
Node *q;
Node *tp;
Node NodeArray[MaxNodes];
```

Write a line of code that sets `tp` to point to the third element of `Node-Array`.

Write a line of code that makes `q` point to what `p` points to.

Write a line of code that sets the `Value` field of the node that `p` points to to 100.

Write a line of code that sets the next field of `ANode` to NULL.

26.   Write a C++ function called `Copy` that returns a pointer to a copy of an array of `Position` objects. Function `Copy` accepts as parameters the array to copy and the size of the array.

27.   Write a C++ statement that dynamically allocates a floating-point object.

28.   Write a C++ statement that dynamically allocates a 100 element array of integers called `Scores`.

29.   The following is the declaration of class `Stack`. This stack holds `Position` objects. The stack is implemented using a dynamically allocated array.

```
#ifndef STACK_H
#define STACK_H
class Stack {
    public:
        Stack(int StackSize = 20);
        Stack(const Stack &s);
        ~Stack();
```

```
                          // Facilitators
                          // Push a position on the stack
                          void Push(const Position &p);
                          // Pop an element off the stack
                          // returns the element
                          Position Pop();
                          bool Empty() const;
                    private:
                          int MaxStackSize; // Maximum number of
                                            // elements stack can hold
                          int StackTop;
                          Position *Values;
              };
              #endif
```

The declaration

```
    Stack Example(4);
```

creates an initially empty stack that can hold four elements.

Give the implementation of class Stack's constructor.

Give the implementation of class Stack's destructor.

Give the implementation of class Stack's copy constructor.

11.10 POINTS TO REMEMBER

✔ Lvalues are expressions that represent objects that can be evaluated and modified.

✔ Rvalues are expressions that can only be evaluated.

✔ A pointer is an object whose value is the location of another object.

✔ There is a different pointer type for each type of object. There are even pointer types whose objects are pointers to other pointers.

✔ The location of an object can be computed using the address operator &.

✔ The literal 0 can be assigned to any pointer type object. In this context, the literal 0 is known as the null address.

✔ The value of the object at a given location can be computed using the dereferencing operator * on the location.

✔ The dereferencing operator produces an lvalue.

✔ The null address is not a location that can be dereferenced.

✔ The indirect member selector operator -> dereferences a member of an object to which a pointer points.

✔ Pointer operators can be compared using the equality and relational operators.

✔ The increment and decrement operators are defined for pointer objects.

✔ When pointers are passed as value parameters, we can simulate reference parameters by using the dereferencing operator.

History of Computing

The founding of Microsoft

Paul Allen and Bill Gates were computer whizzes who had become friends while attending high school in Seattle. Their deep fascination with computers had drawn them together. Gates, Allen, and a few other students formed a company that did programming. For kids in high school, they did quite well. In fact, they earned about $20,000 from a project that analyzed traffic data for local highway departments.

When the article on Edward Roberts' Altair 8800 appeared in *Popular Electronics* in 1974, Allen was working as a programmer for Honeywell in Boston and Gates was majoring in mathematics at Harvard. When Allen saw the article, he immediately realized its significance. The Altair heralded a new generation of computing—personal computing. Allen rushed over to Harvard and found Gates. He convinced Gates that this was their big opportunity. The Altair would need software to be usable, and Allen proposed that they write a BASIC interpreter for the machine. BASIC was the language used by most hobbyists. Gates called Roberts in Albuquerque and told him that he and Allen had developed a BASIC interpreter that could be adapted for the Altair. Roberts, who had already heard similar claims from several other people, told Gates that he would make a deal with the first person to demonstrate a working BASIC interpreter.

Gates and Allen (see Figure 11.5) then began to write an interpreter for BASIC that would run on the Altair. However, they had one serious problem—they didn't have an Altair. How were they going to develop software for a machine they didn't have? The solution was to write a program for one of the computers at Harvard that could mimic the actions of the 8800, the chip inside the Altair. They could then use this program to test their BASIC. Allen worked on the simulator while Gates worked on BASIC. At the end of February, a little less than eight weeks after they started, they had a BASIC to demonstrate to Roberts. Of course, neither knew whether the code would work at all on the Altair. Allen flew to Albuquerque with the software to do the demonstration. Amazingly, the software worked the first time.

Allen went to work for Ed Roberts, improving the BASIC interpreter to make it more marketable. Gates finished his sophomore year at Harvard, and then he joined Allen in Albuquerque. It was there, in 1975, that they formed a partnership they called Micro-soft. (The hyphen was eventually dropped.) Roberts, Allen, and Gates toured the country in a mobile home to demonstrate Roberts's Altair running Gates and Allen's BASIC.

Microsoft was off to a good start with BASIC, selling versions that ran on other computers to other companies. However, Microsoft's big break came in 1980, when IBM decided to enter the personal computer business. In a departure from typical IBM initiatives, IBM decided to get outside help in developing the software that would run on what is now known as the PC. IBM selected Microsoft to provide both the operating system and the BASIC interpreter that would run on the IBM PC. The operating system came to be known as MS-DOS, for Microsoft Disk Operating System.

The IBM PC became incredibly popular, and Microsoft grew rapidly. In 1985 Microsoft released the very popular Windows operating system, which has sold tens of millions of copies since its introduction. Microsoft is now the undisputed giant of personal computer software, selling popular programs that run both on the PC and Apple's Macintosh computer.

Needless to say, Gates and Allen are extremely wealthy; they are each worth many billions of dollars. (Gates is now the world's richest person.) Allen left Microsoft in 1983 after he was diagnosed as having Hodgkin's disease. He has since recovered and is a major founder/investor in several smaller companies that do advanced software development. Bill Gates is the CEO of Microsoft and continues to be a major player in shaping and defining what computing will be like in the 21st century.

Figure 11.5

Paul Allen and Bill Gates in 1975

✔ An array name is viewed by C++ as constant pointer. This fact gives us flexibility in which notation to use when accessing and modifying the values in a list.

✔ Command-line parameters communicate to programs through the use of pointers.

✔ To access the command-line parameters, function `main()` must be defined to have two formal parameters. The first formal parameter is an **int** whose value is automatically initialized to be one more than the number of actual parameters to the command. The second formal parameter is an array of **char***. Each element of the array is a pointer to a character string. The first element points to the command itself. The other array elements point to the various actual parameters given to the command.

✔ By convention, the first formal parameter of `main()` has the name `argc`, and the second formal parameter of `main()` has the name `argv`.

✔ We can define objects that are pointers to functions. Such objects are typically used as function parameters. This type of parameter gives the function that uses it greater flexibility in accomplishing its task.

✔ Dynamic objects are created during program execution as the result of a specific request for memory.

✔ Dynamic memory is said to come from the free store.

✔ The major C++ memory allocation request mechanism is the **new** operator, which has three forms.

✔ The most basic form of a **new** operation expects a type as the right operand for the operator. If sufficient free store memory is available for an object of that type, the location of a single dynamic object is returned. The dynamic object is initialized only if there is a default constructor for the type of that object.

✔ A second form of a **new** operation supports the initialization of the dynamic object whose location is returned. The initialization is specified as an actual parameter list following the type of object to be allocated.

✔ The third form of a **new** operation has a subscripted expression following the type of object(s) being requested. The expression represents the number of dynamic objects to be returned. If sufficient, contiguous free store memory is available, a pointer to a block that can hold the requested number of objects is returned. The objects in the block are initialized only if their type is a class type with a default constructor.

✔ In the C++ standard, if a **new** operation cannot return the dynamic storage that is requested, an exception is generated. In some current compilers, the null address (0) is returned.

✔ The proposed standard defines the new library that includes a function `set_new_handler()`. This function, when invoked with the null address as its parameter, causes the **new** operator to return 0 for an unsatisfied request.

✔ Unlike local objects, dynamic objects can exist beyond the execution of the function in which they were created. A dynamic object exists until the **delete** operator makes a deallocation request.

✔ The objects acquired in a given **new** operation must be deallocated as a group.

✔ A dangling pointer is a pointer object that points to deallocated memory.

✔ A memory leak is dynamically acquired memory that has not been deallocated, but to which no pointer object points.

✔ A major use of dynamic objects is with ADTs. To implement their representations, many ADTs require data members that point to dynamic objects.

✔ A destructor is a member function that is automatically invoked as an object goes out of existence.

✔ For class types with data members that point to dynamic objects, the destructor normally performs a **delete** operation that returns the dynamic memory to which the data members point.

✔ Class objects that use dynamic memory must generally supply a copy constructor, destructor, and assignment operator. Otherwise, the default versions of the copy constructor and the member assignment operator are used. Such use can lead to unintended side effects.

✔ The keyword **this** can be used in a member function or operator body as a pointer to the object that performed the invocation. The **this** pointer is typically used in the implementations of the assignment operator for an ADT.

✔ Qualifiers are part of member function signatures. A compiler can distinguish in an overloaded function invocation whether the **const** or non-**const** member is being invoked. The **const** member is invoked for **const** objects; the non-**const** member is invoked for non-**const** objects.

✔ To represent numbers of extended precision, classes must be developed. The fundamental types cannot do the job because they have fixed sizes for their representations.

11.11 EXERCISES

11.1 What kind of values do pointer objects represent? Explain.

11.2 What is an lvalue? What is an rvalue?

11.3 Can an rvalue be an lvalue? Can an lvalue be an rvalue? Explain.

11.4 What is the purpose of the address operator? What is the purpose of the dereferencing operator?

11.5 Can pointers of different types be assigned to one another? Explain.

11.6 What happens if a pointer object is incremented by one?

11.7 How are command-line parameters communicated to a program?

11.8 Speculate on why C++ has a different pointer type for each type of object.

11.9 Give definitions that correspond to the following figure:

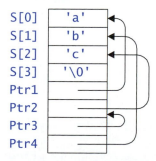

11.10 What is the only literal constant for pointer types? What is its purpose?

11.11 How are array names and pointer objects similar? How are they dissimilar?

11.12 Describe two ways for a function to declare a parameter A that represents a list of **float** values that cannot be modified.

11.13 Suppose Ptr is of type **int*** and i is of type **int**. Identify the problems in the following code segment:

```
Ptr = i;
i = Ptr;
i = &Ptr;
Ptr = Ptr + Ptr;
*i = Ptr;
&i = *Ptr;
```

11.14 Identify the lvalues and rvalues in the following code segment:

```
cin >> k;
i = 0;
A[A[3]] = 2*b;
```

11.15 Define objects for the following situations:
   a) A pointer P that can point to **double** objects.
   b) A pointer Q that can point to pointer objects that point to objects that point to **char** objects.
   c) A pointer R that can point to a **bool** function that has two **int** reference parameters.

11.16 Define a pointer P that is initialized to point to the location of **int** object i. The definition should make it illegal to subsequently modify the value of P.

11.17 Define a pointer P that is initialized to point to the location of **int** object i. The definition should make it illegal to subsequently modify the value of i indirectly through P.

11.18 What is the output of the following code segment? Explain.

```
char A[] = "Patricia";
char *Ptr = A;
++Ptr;
cout << Ptr << endl;
Ptr += 2;
cout << Ptr << endl;
cout << --Ptr << endl;
```

11.19 What is the output of the following code segment? Explain.

```
char A[] = "Rust never sleeps";
char *Ptr;
for (Ptr = &A[16]; Ptr != A; Ptr -= 2) {
    cout << Ptr << endl;
    cout << *Ptr << endl;
}
```

11.20 What is syntactically wrong with the following code segment? Explain.

```
char A[] = "James";
char B[] = "Gertrude";
char *Ptr1 = &A[4];
```

```
char *Ptr2 = &B[5];
if (Ptr1 < Ptr2)
    cout << "Hello" << endl;
else
    cout << "Good bye" << endl;
```

11.21 What is the scope of a dynamic object?

11.22 Describe the three forms of a **new** operation. Give an example of each form.

11.23 Describe the two forms of a **delete** operation. When is their use appropriate?

11.24 What is the free store?

11.25 What is a memory leak?

11.26 Suppose the following command line is to be executed.

```
C:> play A-flat four beats
```

Also suppose that the definition of the function `main()` that implements the `play` command begins as follows:

```
int main(int argc, char *argv[]) { // ...
```

a) What does `argc` represent?

b) What does `argv[0]` represent?

c) What does `argv[1]` represent?

d) What does `argv[argc-1]` represent?

11.27 Suppose the following definitions are in effect.

```
char *cPtr;
char *sPtr[12];
char **cPtrPtr;
```

a) Is `cPtr` of type **char**? Explain.

b) Is `sPtr` a pointer to a **char** array with 12 elements? Explain.

c) Is the following assignment legal? Explain.

```
cPtrPtr = &cPtr;
```

11.28 Suppose the following definitions are in effect.

```
Rational A[10];
Rational B[10];
Rational C;
Rational *D;
```

Which of the following assignments are legal? Explain.

```
B = A;
C = A[1];
D = A;
D = &C;
```

11.29 Consider the following program fragment:

```
void f(int *iPtr) {
    *iPtr = 1;
}
```

```
int main() {
    int i = 0;
    f(&i);
    cout << i << endl;
    return 0;
}
```

a) Is the program syntactically correct? Explain.

b) Is the invocation f(&i) in function main() along with the definition of function f() a simulation of a reference parameter? Explain.

11.30 Under what conditions does the following statement make sense?

```
cout << **Ptr << endl;
```

11.31 Suppose the last parameter to a program is the name of a file to be used
as input. Identify which code fragment(s) below defines and initializes a
stream variable in the function main(), where main() has the following interface: **int** main (**int** argc, char *argv[]). Explain.

a) ifstream myin(argv[argc-1]);

b) ifstream myin(argv[argc]);

c) ifstream myin(argc[argv]);

d) ifstream myin(argv[0]);

11.32 What is the output of the following program?

```
#include <iostream>
#include <string>
using namespace std;
int main() {
    char *s[5] =
        { "BASIC", "IS", "EAT", "NAG", "ENTER" };
    char **sptr[5] =
        { &s[4], &s[3], &s[0], &s[2], &s[1] };
    char ***sptrptr = &sptr[1];
    cout << &s[0][4];
    cout << (*((*sptrptr-2))+1) << endl;
    cout << *(s+1) << endl;
    cout << &s[3][2];
    cout << (**sptr)[4];
    cout << *(s+2) << endl;
    return 0;
}
```

For exercises similar to this one, examine Alan R. Feuer's *The C Puzzle
Book*, Englewood Cliffs, NJ: Prentice-Hall, 1982.

11.33 Define a **void** function Sort() that expects three parameters. The first
parameter is an **int** array A, the second parameter is an integer value n,
and the third parameter LTE is a **bool** function that expects two integer
parameters. Function Sort() sorts list A using LTE to make the comparisons. When invoked, the actual parameter for LTE returns true if,
according to its comparison scheme, the value of first parameter is less
than or equal to the value of the second parameter.

11.34 Define a class Item that has two data members Value and NextItem,
where Value is of type **int** and NextItem is of type Item*. The

default constructor should initialize Value to 0 and NextItem to the null address. Define other constructors, inspectors, and mutators as you see fit.

11.35 What is a dangling pointer?

11.36 What does the keyword **this** represent? What does the expression ***this** represent?

11.37 What is the purpose of the invocation set_new_handler(0)?

11.38 Give a code segment that uses the class Item from Exercise 11.34 to define four Item objects a, b, c, and d. The code segment should also define two Item* objects Front and Rear. The values of these objects should correspond to the following representation:

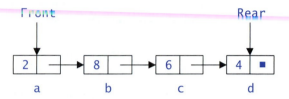

11.39 Identify the mistakes in the following code segment:

```cpp
char *p = new ('a');
char *q = new char('b');
char *r = new char('c');
char *s = new char [100] ('d');
char *t = *q;
char *u = r;
delete q;
*t = 'e';
```

11.40 Write a code segment that sets up a dynamic list of 100 Rational objects. Each of these dynamic objects is to represent 0/1.

11.41 Write a code segment that sets up a dynamic list of 100 Rational objects. Each of these dynamic objects is to represent 3/4.

11.42 Run the following two programs. Speculate on why they perform differently for most C++ implementations.

```cpp
#include <iostream>
#include <string>
using namespace std;
int main() {
    long int counter = 0;
    int *ptr;
    do {
        ptr = new int;
        ++counter;
    } while (ptr);
    cout << counter << endl;
    return 0;
}

#include <iostream>
#include <string>
using namespace std;
```

```
int main() {
    long int counter = 0;
    int *ptr;
    do {
        ptr = new int [1];
        ++counter;
    } while (ptr);
    cout << counter << endl;
    return 0;
}
```

11.43 Perform an experiment that determines the largest block of free store memory that can be allocated on your system. Report your results.

11.44 Does the following code segment represent an infinite loop? Why?

```
while (true) {
    int *p = new int;
    if (p == 0) {
        break;
    }
    delete p;
}
```

11.45 Design a class to represent a table of strings. The class should have at least two constructors. The default constructor creates a table with 10 entries. Another constructor would allow the number of entries in the table to be specified. The basic inspector functions would indicate whether a string is present in the table and what string is represented by a particular entry. The basic mutating functions would be adding and removing strings from the table. Is it necessary for the class to define a copy constructor, destructor, and member assignment? What should be done if the table is full and another string is to be added?

11.46 Define an implementation for the IntList constructor that expects two parameters—an array A and a number of elements n. The constructor creates an IntList instance with n elements. The initial values of those elements are taken from A[0], A[1], ... A[n-1].

11.47 Define an implementation for the IntList member function push_back(). The function has a single parameter val. The function updates the IntList object's representation so that it has an additional element at the end of its current list. The value of the new element is val.

11.48 In the following code segment, identify the various types of subscript operations that are being performed.

```
int A[100];
IntList B(100, 1);
vector<IntList> C(100);
IntList D[100];
A[0] = 1;
B[0] = 2;
C[0] = B;
C[0][1] = 3;
D[0][1] = A[0];
D[0][1] = 4;
```

11.49 Overload the extraction operator for `IntList` objects. The operator should attempt to extract sufficient values to reset the elements of its `IntList` parameter.

11.50 Expand the class definition for the `IntList` library to include iterators `begin()` and `end()`. Implement your iterators such that the return values for the iterators are `int*`, where the value of `Values` is returned by `begin()` and the null address is returned by `end()`.

11.51 Speculate on why the prototype for the `IntList` constructor

```
IntList(const int A[], int n);
```

specifies that its array parameter is passed as a **const**.

11.52 Overload the `InsertionSort()` function of Chapter 9 for `IntList` objects.

11.53 Overload the `QuickSort()` function of Chapter 9 for `IntList` objects.

11.54 Overload the `BinarySearch()` function of Chapter 9 for `IntList` objects.

11.55 Implement a class `Matrix` that has the following class interface:

```
class Matrix {
    public:
        // default constructor
        Matrix(int r = 10, int c = 10, int v = 0);
        // copy constructor
        Matrix(const Matrix &M);
        // destructor
        ~Matrix();
        // assignment operator
        Matrix& operator=(const Matrix &M);
        // inspector for row of constant matrix
        const IntList& operator[](int i) const;
        // inspector for row of nonconstant matrix
        IntList& operator[](int i);
        // inspector for size of a given row
        int RowSize(int i) const;
        // inspector for size of a given column
        int ColumnSize(int i) const;
        // inspector for number of row
        int NumberRows(int i) const;
    private:
        // data members
        int NumRows;          // row size of matrix
        IntList *Values;      // pointer to rows
};
```

The `Matrix` member functions have the following specifications.

- `Matrix(int r = 10, int c = 10, int v = 0)`: initializes object to represent a matrix with r rows and c columns. The initial value of the elements is v.

- `Matrix(const Matrix &M)`: initializes object to be a deep copy of M.

- `~Matrix()`: returns the dynamic storage to which `Values` points.

- **operator=(const** Matrix **&M)**: resets object to be a deep copy of M.
- **operator[](int i) const**: reference returns row i of matrix in constant form.
- **operator[](int i)**: reference returns row i of matrix in nonconstant form.
- RowSize(**int i) const**: returns size of row i.
- ColumnSize(**int i) const**: returns size of column i.
- NumberRows(**int i) const**: returns the number of rows in the matrix.

CHAPTER 12

Testing and debugging

Introduction

Two important aspects of software development are testing and debugging. The purpose of testing is to identify any problems before the software is shipped to customers. Software testing is a major aspect of producing quality software. For large software projects, testing and debugging are 40 to 50 percent of the overall project costs. For major software projects, a large software company might employ as many as one or two testers for every development programmer. Debugging is the process of locating and repairing a problem identified by testing or reported by a user. Debugging is a two step process— you identify the problem; and then you fix it. Like testing, debugging, if not done properly, can consume significant time and resources. In this chapter, we discuss the basics of testing software and strategies for debugging once a problem has been recognized.

Key Concepts

- black-box testing
- white-box testing
- inspections
- unit testing
- integration testing
- system testing
- statement coverage
- equivalence partitioning
- regression test
- boundary conditions
- code reviews
- test harness
- path coverage

12.1 TESTING

We have all encountered bugs or problems in programs we have used. If you have ever had your word processor crash after entering a particularly long passage of text, you know how irritating bugs can be. Some bugs are so costly that they make the newspaper headlines. The crash of the Mars Polar Lander on the surface of Mars in 1999 is a recent example. In this incident, a 165 million dollar mission was lost because of a problem that went undetected despite extensive testing. The story of why the Polar Lander crashed illustrates the difficulties of thorough testing.

The landing was supposed to go like this. As the lander entered the atmosphere of Mars, a parachute would deploy to slow the lander's descent. As it neared the surface, the parachute would be discarded, the lander's three legs would snap into position for landing, and the lander's 12 engines would fire to slow the craft to a speed where it could land safely. Each of the lander's three legs had a sensor that would send a signal to the onboard computer to turn off the spacecraft's landing engines when at least one of the legs touched the surface.

Using a similar lander, investigators determined that when the legs were deployed for landing, vibrations could have caused the leg sensors to send spurious signals. In this scenario, the engines would shut down when the craft was about 130 feet high, and the lander would hit the surface at 50 miles per hour.

So how did this problem go undetected? Various postcrash investigations showed that tests of individual systems would not have exposed the problem. One full-scale system test was conducted that should have revealed the presence of the problem. However, the sensors were improperly wired for that test, and the problem went undetected. After the wiring was corrected, a full-scale test was not repeated because of budgetary constraints and time pressures.

The Mars Polar Lander illustrates why thorough testing is so difficult to do. While all the components work correctly when tested individually (unit testing), the system may not work correctly when tested as a whole (system testing). Thus, one must do both thorough unit testing as well as thorough system testing. Because of budgetary constraints and deadlines, however, all too often we convince ourselves that, even though some aspect of the system has changed, further testing is not warranted. Careful programmers retest before delivering software even after the most trivial changes.

After you have written a program, how do you convince yourself that the program works correctly? The not-so careful programmer runs the program with a few test inputs and then checks to see if the answers are correct. For the simplest programs, this may be enough, but this approach is hardly adequate even for a program of moderate complexity, and it surely will not be sufficient for a complex program of more than a 1,000 lines.

In this chapter we will discuss some strategies for testing the software that you design and implement. Unfortunately, a thorough discussion of testing is beyond the scope of this book. There are many excellent texts devoted just to the theory, science, and art of testing software. Section 12.4 lists a few of the texts that we have found to contain helpful information about testing strategies and procedures.

We should note before proceeding that testing is not a panacea for producing high-quality software. There is a well-known quote by the computer scientist Edgar Dijkstra that gets to the heart of the problem. He observed that "Program testing can be used to show the presence of bugs, but never to show their absence." High-quality software can only be achieved by applying testing along with a number of other software engineering techniques. Informal and formal reviews are necessary. These include formal and informal reviews of the software specification, the proposed design or architecture of the system, as well as the actual code. Indeed, software engineering studies have shown that a disciplined, systematic review process is more effective at avoiding bugs in shipped software than testing. Another important element is the ability to effectively manage and track evolving software. Source-code control systems and software for tracking bugs are commonly used to help automate these tasks. These subjects are typically dealt with in depth in software engineering courses.

12.1.1 Testing—an example

The first thing to realize about bugs and testing is that the earlier problems are found, the better. Software engineering studies have shown that the costs of finding and fixing a problem grow logarithmically with time. For example, a bug found early during the specification phase may cost little or nothing to repair. For the sake of argument, let's say it costs a dollar to fix. That same bug, if discovered during the final testing of the software, may cost hundreds or thousands of dollars to fix.

This means that we should test code as we write it. This approach makes sense from a number of standpoints. Let's say we are designing and coding one particular function that is part of a larger system we are working on. At this point in time, we are enmeshed in the details of the problem. This is a good point to test this module. If a problem is discovered, because of our immediate familiarity of the code, we can most likely fix it quickly. On the other hand, if the problem crops up months later, we will need to refamiliarize ourselves with the code before we can diagnose and fix the problem. Furthermore, it's likely the function or module has grown over time, which again will make finding the bug harder. The process of testing a single module or function is known as *unit testing*.

To illustrate the process of testing, and unit testing in particular, let's begin development of an EzWindow LED timer for displaying elapsed time. LED clocks are used in many consumer electronic devices such as microwave ovens, digital watches, clock radios, and VCRs to display numbers and time (time of day, elapsed time, etc.). An LED timer could be a handy class for building games that have a time limit, developing a computerized scoreboard, and so forth.

Our initial task is to develop the LED class that we will need to build the clock. As we will see, unit testing of our LED class will help us find any problems before we tackle larger problems, but it will also help us refine the interface to the object early: before it is used in a larger project and modification becomes more costly.

Following our object-oriented design approach, we must determine the attributes and behaviors of an LED. Obviously we need to control the value displayed. Since we will be using class LED to construct other objects such as timers and clocks, we need to set an LED object's position in the display window. We also must specify the window in which an LED object will be displayed. Our approach for realizing an LED is to use bitmaps of digits to display a number. For example, the image of the bitmap for the number three looks like this:

The CD-ROM accompanying the book contains bitmaps for the numerals zero through nine.

For our initial cut at designing class LED, we have the following attributes.

- MyDigits—an array of bitmaps to hold the images of the digits 0 through 9.
- MyValue—the symbol to display when the LED is displayed.
- MyPosition—the position of the LED in the window.
- MyWindow—the EzWindow where the LED is displayed.

For the public interface, we will need inspectors and mutators for each attribute. In addition we will need a facilitator that displays the LED. Our initial declaration for class LED is

```
class LED {
   public:
      LED();
      // Inspectors
      Position GetPosition() const;
      int GetValue() const;
      // Mutators
      void SetPosition(const Position &p);
      void SetValue(int d);
      void SetWindow(SimpleWindow *W);
      // Facilitators
      void Show();
   private:
      SimpleWindow *MyWindow;
      BitMap MyDigits[MaxElements];
      Position MyPosition;
      int MyValue;
};
```

Now that we have a preliminary class declaration, we can do an implementation. The implementation is straightforward and is given in Listing 12.1. Now we have a choice. We could continue to develop the code for the clock, or we could stop and test class LED to make sure it works properly by doing unit

Listing 12.1

Implementation of class LED

```
#include "led.h"
const int MaxDigits = 10;
char *DigitNames[MaxDigits] = {
    "digit0.bmp",
    "digit1.bmp",
    "digit2.bmp",
    "digit3.bmp",
    "digit4.bmp",
    "digit5.bmp",
    "digit6.bmp",
    "digit7.bmp",
    "digit8.bmp",
    "digit9.bmp",
};

// LED() -- read the bitmaps for [0-9]
LED::LED() {
    for (int D = 0; D < MaxDigits; ++D)
        MyDigits[D].Load(DigitNames[D]);
}

// GetPosition() -- return current position of the LED
Position LED::GetPosition() const {
    return MyPosition;
}

// GetValue() -- return the current value of the LED
int LED::GetValue() const {
    return MyValue;
}

// SetWindow() -- set the window to display the LED
void LED::SetWindow(SimpleWindow *w) {
    MyWindow = w;
}

// SetPosition() -- set the position of the LED
void LED::SetPosition(const Position &p) {
    MyPosition = p;
}

// SetValue() -- set the value of the LED
void LED::SetValue(int v) {
    MyValue = v;
}

// Show() -- display the LED in the window
void LED::Show() {
    MyDigits[MyValue].SetWindow(*MyWindow);
    MyDigits[MyValue].SetPosition(MyPosition);
    MyDigits[MyValue].Draw();
}
```

testing. As we mentioned earlier, it's much easier to test and find problems now, while we are familiar with the code, rather than waiting for problems to crop up down the road. However, how do we test our object given that we haven't written the program yet? We must provide a *test harness* or *test stub* to exercise our code. A test harness is a small piece of code written to test or exercise the code being developed.

Writing test harnesses is a standard subtask of unit testing. It is tempting to discard these code fragments after testing is completed, but the modest time and effort it takes to save these stubs is an investment that will pay off later when a bug is uncovered. You will already have a set of test harnesses available to help locate the bug and then ensure that the fix did not break something else. We often create a test directory where the various test harnesses we have written for a project are kept.

The following code is our test harness for our LED class.

```cpp
#include "led.h"
SimpleWindow *W;
LED L;
int ApiMain() {
    W = new SimpleWindow("LED Test Window", 4.0f, 4.0f);
    Position p(1.0, 0.5);
    W->Open();
    L.SetWindow(W);
    L.SetValue(1);
    L.SetPosition(p);
    L.Show();
    return 0;
}
```

When we compile and run this code, the following window appears.

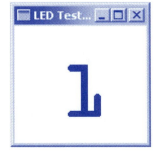

Our code worked! Depending on what we are planning to do, this amount of testing might be enough. However, for code used in a commercial application, we are not even close to being done testing. To thoroughly test this code, we need to think about how the code will be used and what could possibly go wrong. What we need is a systematic approach to unit testing.

First off, we need test cases that demonstrate that the code satisfies its requirements. What are the requirements of class LED? Unfortunately, we did not formally write these down. In a real software project, the first step is to write down formal specifications of what a class is supposed to do. However, we do have an informal idea of the capabilities class LED is supposed to provide since it is to be used to develop clock type objects.

- Class LED should be capable of displaying the digits 0 through 9 in an EzWindow.

- Class LED should be able to be positioned appropriately in an EzWindow.

Using this informal specification, we can design a more comprehensive set of tests. Basically we need to make sure that the class satisfies the stated requirements. Our test cases should make sure that we can display each digit correctly, and we should also include tests to make sure the positioning of the digits works. With a little work, we can write one test harness that does all this in a single run. After some trial and error to get the positions correct, we have the following test harness that displays each digit.

```cpp
#include "led.h"
SimpleWindow *W;
LED L;
int ApiMain() {
    W = new SimpleWindow("LED Test Window", 8.0f, 4.0f);
    W->Open();

    Position p(1.0, 0.5);
    L.SetWindow(W);
    int i;
    for (i = 0; i < 5; ++i) {
        L.SetValue(i);
        L.SetPosition(p);
        L.Show();
        p = p + Position(1.0, 0.0);
    }
    p = Position(1.0, 2.5);
    for (i = 5; i < 10; ++i) {
        L.SetValue(i);
        L.SetPosition(p);
        L.Show();
        p = p +Position(1.0, 0.0);
    }
    return 0;
}
```

Running the test harness produces the following display.

The output shows that class LED can display all the digits and that positioning of the bitmaps works correctly.

The not-so-careful programmer would be done at this point. However, the careful programmer also tests for what happens when the object is used in a way not permitted by the requirements. One of the benefits of this process is that as you think about unit test cases, bugs are often discovered before you even run the test cases. For example, as we think about test cases to ensure the object behaves appropriately when illegal values are passed, we immediately realize we have not handled this case at all. Class LED will crash if a value less than 0 and greater than 9 is passed to it. We had better fix that. Again, it's much easier to fix it now rather than later.

To address this issue, we modify member function SetValue() to assert an error if the value passed to it is not in the valid range. The revised member function is:

```
void LED::SetValue(int v) {
    assert(v >= 0 && v <= 9);
    MyValue = v;
}
```

We generate a couple of test cases to make sure that the error detection code works. One test case passes a value less than 0; the other test case passes a value greater than 9. When we test, we run all the tests to make sure that all the test cases still pass.

So far, so good. However, we are still not done. Class LED will be used to build clocks. To test whether class LED will work in this application, we can do a quick prototype of a clock display. Basically, we will produce a static clock face—the time will not change. This activity makes us realize that class LED is missing some features. To display a clock time like 12:30 P or 11:00 A, class LED needs the ability to display a colon and the letters A and P to denote antimeridian and postmeridian time, respectively.

Again, we revise the implementation of class LED to include these features. As we write the code to prototype a clock face, we discover that it would be convenient in laying out aggregate objects if we could get the length and width of an LED object. This is simple to implement as we can get the length and width of the bitmap used to represent the LED by calling the corresponding BitMap function. This is an example of finding a bug or problem in the interface. Finding these bugs or problems is just as important, if not more important, as finding program errors. Listing 12.2 gives the code for the test harness for the clock prototype.

Listing 12.2

Clock prototype test harness

```
#include "led.h"
SimpleWindow *W;
LED Clock[6];
int ApiMain() {
    W = new SimpleWindow("LED Test Window", 8.0f, 2.5f);
    Position p(0.5, 0.5);
    W->Open();
    int i;
    for (i = 0; i < 6; ++i) {
        Clock[i].SetWindow(W);
        Clock[i].SetPosition(p);
        p = p + Position(Clock[i].GetWidth(), 0.0);
    }

    // Display the time 12:58A
    Clock[0].SetValue(1);
    Clock[1].SetValue(2);
    Clock[2].SetValue(Colon);
    Clock[3].SetValue(5);
    Clock[4].SetValue(8);
```

```
        Clock[5].SetValue(AMIndicator);
        for (i = 0; i < 6; ++i) {
            Clock[i].Show();
        }
        return 0;
    }
```

The display produced by the test harness is shown below.

The prototype unit test process makes us realize we have another problem with class LED. How do we display a time like 1:30 P? We need a way to display a blank (i.e., an unlit LED). Again, adding this new capability is easy at this stage as we are very familiar with class LED (maybe too familiar!). After we add the new capability, we add another test program to our growing suite of programs that test the functioning of the new capability. Our latest addition to our suite of test programs is:

```
    #include "led.h"
    SimpleWindow *W;
    LED Clock[6];
    int ApiMain() {
        W = new SimpleWindow("LED Test Window", 8.0f, 2.5f);
        Position p(0.5, 0.5);
        W->Open();
        int i;
        for (i = 0; i < 6; ++i) {
            Clock[i].SetWindow(W);
            Clock[i].SetPosition(p);
            p = p + Position(Clock[i].GetWidth(), 0.0);
        }
        // Display the time 2:58A
        Clock[0].SetValue(Space);
        Clock[1].SetValue(2);
        Clock[2].SetValue(Colon);
        Clock[3].SetValue(5);
        Clock[4].SetValue(8);
        Clock[5].SetValue(AMIndicator);
        for (i = 0; i < 6; ++i) {
            Clock[i].Show();
        }
        return 0;
    }
```

This test program produces the following display, which verifies that we can produce a blank space.

We should emphasize that each time we make a change to class LED we rerun the entire suite of test programs. This avoids introducing a bug that is discovered only after a series of changes have been made. It is much easier to understand what went wrong when only one set of changes is involved.

After our exercise with testing class LED, you can see why testing is such a time-consuming and expensive part of software development. Running a comprehensive test suite after each change is time-consuming, but there are some things we can do to make it less painful. Programmers typically write "scripts" that automatically run the test suite and report any errors. Using scripts means running the tests is as simple as invoking a command. As new test programs are written, the script is modified so the new test program is included. These scripts are included with the test programs so that in the future other developers know how to run the test programs. Thus, the script serves as documentation for future developers and testers.

Self-check Questions

1.   Typically, what percentage of a project is devoted to testing and debugging?

2.   Explain the difference between testing and debugging.

3.   What is a unit test?

4.   What is a test harness?

5.   Devise a test harness and test cases for function CheckWord() given in Listing 9.8.

6.   Revise the test harness that displayed all the numerals to include the blank, the A, the P, and the colon.

12.1.2 Testing fundamentals

As we mentioned earlier, testing is a serious discipline that is a key to producing high-quality, robust software. Thus it should come as no surprise that testing is a well-studied area with its own terminology and research results. As beginning programmers, devoting some time to understanding the fundamentals of testing will pay handsome dividends in the years to come.

The purpose of testing is to find bugs as early as possible in the development process and to make sure they get fixed before the software is shipped. Exactly what is a bug? Certainly, when a program crashes (e.g., blue-screen of death), that's a bug. However, there are many other types of bugs that are just as serious and not so obvious. For example, suppose the user manual for a document editor says that the way to set a word in boldface type is to underline it and then click the bold button on the toolbar. Suppose you do this, and the selected word remains unchanged. Is this a bug? The program didn't crash, it just did not perform as advertised. This is also a bug.

If we practice sound software engineering techniques, then we will write a complete and detailed specification of what the software is supposed to do, how it will operate, the features it will and will not support, and its performance requirements. In general, a bug is when the program does not meet the specification. However, testers and most programmers classify bugs into the following four broad categories:

- software crashes or data corruption,
- does not meet or satisfy the specification,
- poor or unacceptable performance, and
- hard or difficult to use.

A software crash is when a program fails in a noticeable way. Examples of software crashes include when the program exits unexpectedly or it stops responding to commands and has to be manually killed via operating system commands.

Data corruption occurs when a program writes bad data to a file. Suppose you were editing a file with your favorite word processor or editor, and after you saved the file you discovered the file contained gibberish. This is an example of a data corruption bug. Data corruption bugs are particularly insidious because they can easily go undetected. The error can propagate to other data files, and if the error goes undetected for a long period of time, it can be difficult to restore the corrupted files to a correct state.

An important component of a software specification is the features the system will provide. A list of features helps everybody, including the customer, know when the system is functionally complete. For example, the specification for a calculator program may state that the program should provide operations for converting between various number bases. If this feature gets left out or is incomplete (e.g., you can only convert to binary), then there is a bug.

A performance bug is present when the program fails to meet the performance requirements contained in the specification, or the program performs so poorly that it, in effect, does not satisfy the specification. As an example of a performance bug, suppose your E-mail system includes a feature for searching your archive of saved messages. While the feature works, a search takes so long that you never use the feature. In effect, it is as if the E-mail system did not provide the feature.

Modern user interfaces have made software easier to use than ever. However, we also expect software to do more and more. Designing software that is easy for people of various skill levels to use is a very difficult task. Indeed, the area of user interfaces and usability are subdisciplines of computer science. If the design of a program makes accomplishing a task overly difficult, this too is a bug—a bug in the design of the user interface. As a side note, this kind of bug can be very expensive to fix as a project is nearing completion. Consequently, it is very important to do early testing of the user interface to ensure that the program is easy to use or, as some people like to say, user friendly.

Interestingly, when you are testing a program, crashes and data corruption are the best kind of bugs to encounter. The behavior is clearly an error, and it is often pretty obvious what has gone wrong. On the other hand, bugs where the program has an odd quirk, is slow, or is difficult to use are much more subjective. A developer may argue that the quirk is not a bug, but a feature; that the program is not that slow; or that the program is really not that hard to use.

It is important to understand the limitations of testing. As we mentioned in the introduction, testing cannot show or prove a program is bug free. It can only show or expose bugs. Furthermore, for all but the most trivial programs it is impossible to completely test a program. The problem is that the number of inputs to most programs is very large, and the number of possible paths through the program is also very large. To simplify the problem, let's just talk about the number of paths in a program. Consider the simple program whose controlflow graph is shown in Figure 12.1.

Figure 12.1

Program controlflow graph

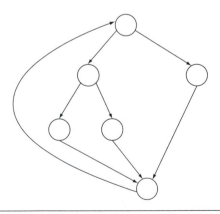

Each circle represents a block of statements. To test this program completely, we must cause the program to execute every possible permutation of statements because any sequence could potentially fail. Disregarding the loop, there are three distinct paths through the program. If the loop executes 20 times, there are 3^{20} different sequences of execution of the statements. That is about 3 billion different test cases! Exhaustively testing all possible executions of a program is impossible.

Clearly we need some good procedures and strategies for testing so that as many bugs as possible are found before the software is delivered, yet testing is done efficiently.

12.1.3 Reviews and inspections

Recall our earlier comment that the sooner you find bugs the better. The goal of design and code reviews is to find bugs even before the code is run. Reviews of a design or code can run the spectrum from an informal meeting where one programmer explains the design or code to another programmer to a rigorous formal process. Whether the review is informal or formal the goal is the same—to identify bugs or problems early in the development process. However, reviews, if done and managed properly, can have other benefits.

A review can be a learning process for all involved. During a review, you may see a particularly elegant or effective design or technique for solving a problem. Similarly, you may see bad design or a poor implementation identified along with an explanation of why it is bad. We can learn from successes as well as mistakes.

Reviews can help entry-level programmers learn the expectations and coding standards of the company. When working on a large project, it is vital that each programmer adheres to the coding standard that has been chosen. A coding standard specifies how the program is to be laid out (i.e., the indentation to use for the various language constructs, expectations for the form and content of comments, constructs that are not permitted, etc.). Uniform use of a coding standard produces code that is more reliable and easier to maintain.

Reviews are also useful for project management. Reviews help managers assess the skills of the project members. These assessments can be used to determine the assignment of tasks to project members and to form effective teams. Reviews can also help management assess the progress of the project. This information can be used to take corrective action such as shifting resources, adding more resources, or allocating more time to certain aspects of the project.

Software engineering studies have shown that reviews are very effective at bug detection—more so than other kinds of testing. A study of a large software organization showed that reviews led to a 14 percent increase in productivity and a 90 percent decrease in defects. Another study found that reviews are at least twice as effective as unit testing.

A review process that has been shown to be very effective is the *inspection*. An inspection is a formal process where the personnel involved are assigned specific roles. Inspections were first employed by IBM in 1976. This pioneering work showed that design and code inspections typically remove 60 percent of the bugs in a product.

One characteristic that distinguishes an inspection from other types of reviews is that an inspection is highly structured. Each person involved in the inspection is assigned one of four roles. Furthermore, each participant receives training on how inspections are carried out and what his or her duties are. A participant in an inspection serves in one of four roles: moderator, inspector, author, or scribe.

Moderator. The moderator is in charge of running the inspection. The moderator's most important job is ensuring that the inspection proceeds at a reasonable pace. The inspection should be thorough so that as many problems as possible are identified, but it should not drag out so as to be unproductive. A very important aspect of being moderator is making sure that the inspection participants treat each other with respect and courtesy. In addition to running the inspection, the moderator is also responsible for distributing the code or design being reviewed to the inspection participants, scheduling the time and place of the inspection, reporting the inspection results, and making sure any action items generated as a result of the inspection are completed.

Inspector. An inspector, or reviewer, is someone other than the author who has some interest in the design or code (e.g., using the code to build a component, implementing the design, testing, etc.). The job of the inspector is to carefully scrutinize the design or code to find any potential problems. The inspection of the code is done prior to the inspection meeting.

Author. The author of the code or the design plays a minor role in the inspection. If the author has done his or her job, the code will be well-documented, easy to understand, and bug free. If the reviewers detect problems or the code is unclear in certain areas, an action item is generated directing the author to remedy the situation. Sometimes what may be perceived as an error by an inspector might not be an error. In this situation, the author can explain why the code is correct.

Scribe. The role of the scribe is to record all the errors that are detected and keep a list of action items generated.

Interestingly, managers are excluded from inspections. Software inspections are technical reviews with the goal of finding as many problems as possible, as early as possible. The presence of management personnel can change the tenor of the inspection. Inspection participants may become more defensive or less likely to speak up if they feel they are being evaluated.

Another characteristic that distinguishes an inspection from other types of reviews is that it consists of five well-defined phases or steps.

Planning. During the planning step, the portion of code to be inspected is chosen, and the moderator assigns tasks to the inspectors. Inspectors may be assigned different parts of the code to review, or they may be asked to review the code from a certain perspective (e.g., testability, extensibility, performance, etc.). Checklists are created to focus the inspectors' attention on certain areas that are known to be critical or that have caused problems in past projects. The moderator also chooses one of the inspectors to be the presenter. During the inspection step, the presenter will walk through the code, presenting it to the inspection team.

Overview. At the overview the author describes any high-level aspects of the project that may have affected the design or code being reviewed. If all of the project participants are familiar with these aspects of the project, the overview can be skipped.

Preparation. Working alone, each inspector carefully reviews the code using the supplied checklists as a guide. The inspectors note any problems or deficiencies in the code and come to the inspection meeting prepared to present their results. The inspector chosen as presenter uses the preparation plans to present the code or design during the inspection meeting. Studies of the inspection process have shown that this phase should last no more than a couple of hours. Reading code is hard work, and after two hours inspectors become tired and errors can go undetected.

Inspection meeting. At the inspection meeting, the presenter walks through the code line by line, explaining what the code does. As the presenter reads and explains the code, any problems for that portion of code are identified and discussed. The scribe records all the errors detected and the action items associated with them. The moderator makes sure that the inspection proceeds at a reasonable pace and the inspection stays focused. For example, it is tempting to discuss how a problem might be fixed. This is not the goal of an inspection. Like the preparation phase, the inspection meeting should not last longer than a couple of hours.

Inspection report. After an inspection meeting, the moderator prepares a written report that identifies the work that needs to be done and who is responsible for each task. Depending on the magnitude of changes, an inspection of the revised code may be scheduled. The inspection report may suggest additions or changes to the checklist based on the results of the inspection. This information can improve the effectiveness of subsequent inspections.

Inspections are effective because they provide a structured environment for having the code read and understood. Left to their own devices, most people find reading code rather boring. As you read code, it is easy to slip into a mode in which you are just skimming the code and not fully understanding what the code is doing. Inspections help people read code in a focused, productive way. Inspections are also effective because they provide feedback about common problems. Integrating this information into checklists for future inspections improves the effectiveness of subsequent inspections.

12.1.4 Black-box and white-box testing

Two other testing strategies for delivering robust, high-quality software are block-box and white-box testing. The testing of class LED at the beginning of this chapter is an example of white-box testing. The term *white-box testing* indicates that we can "see" or examine the code as we devise our test cases. The term *black-box testing* indicates that we cannot examine the code as we devise test cases. The code is hidden in a black-box we cannot see through.

How can you test code when you cannot see it? Why would you want to test code that you cannot see? There are good answers to both these questions. With black-box testing, although you do not know how the code works, the specification tells you what the code is supposed to do. You can create inputs, get output, and check the results for correctness without having access to the source code. The answer to the second question is that white-box testing can bias the testing toward finding errors in the code. If the code does not implement the specification, white-box testing is unlikely to expose that type of bug. The advantage to white-box testing is that knowledge of how the code works can help you test more effectively by avoiding redundant test cases.

Because black-box and white-box testing are complementary, both are used on large software projects. Since this text is about programming, we will focus our discussion on white-box testing. However, the techniques we discuss apply to black-box testing as well.

The key to successful, efficient testing is producing good test cases—test cases that are most likely to expose bugs. This task is hard because the input possibilities accepted by a nontrivial program are, for all practical purposes, infinite. Thus we must find a way to reduce the number of possible test cases into a smaller, more manageable set that is still effective at exposing any potential bugs. The process of weeding out unnecessary or redundant test cases is called *equivalence partitioning*.

The basic idea behind equivalence partitioning is that if two inputs test the same portions of code, you only need one of the inputs in your test set. From a testing standpoint, the two inputs are equivalent. For example, suppose you are developing a calculator program. You have just implemented the addition operation and you are developing test cases to make sure addition works properly before implementing other operations. You try the test cases $1 + 2$, $2 + 1$, $0 + 3$, and $0 + 0$. The calculator produces the correct sums for these test cases. Do you think it will be useful to add the test case $1 + 3$? No, because test case $1 + 3$ is in the same equivalence class as $1 + 2$. If test case $1 + 2$ worked, test case $1 + 3$ will work. A good test case to add would be $-1 + 3$. This test case is in a new equivalence class because the first operand is negative. The self-check exercises ask you to develop additional test cases for the calculator program that are in new equivalence classes.

There are several strategies programmers and testers use to generate effective test cases. One of the most common strategies is boundary testing. The motivation for boundary testing is that program bugs occur most often at boundaries. Furthermore, if the code works properly at the boundaries, it probably works correctly elsewhere. One analogy sometimes used is that if you can walk along an edge of a cliff on a plateau without falling off, you can probably walk in the middle of the plateau. There are several types of boundaries depending on the code. There are loop boundaries—does the loop do the right thing at the beginning and the end; data boundaries—does the code do the right thing when handling data that is at the boundary of allowable values; and capacity boundaries—does the code correctly handle the situation when the array is full and empty.

With white-box testing, we can examine the code to look for boundary conditions. For example, Listing 12.3 contains function `BinarySearch()` introduced in Chapter 9. Initial inspection of this code suggests that the boundary conditions are when the key value being searched for is located at the beginning of the array or at the end of the array. If the code works for those

Listing 12.3

Function
BinarySearch()

```
// BinarySearch(): examine sorted list A for Key
int BinarySearch(vector<char> &A, char Key) {
    int left = 0;
    int right = A.size() - 1;
    while (left <= right) {
        int mid = (left + right)/2;
        if (A[mid] == Key)
            return mid;
        else if (A[mid] < Key)
            left = mid + 1;
        else
            right = mid - 1;
    }
    return A.size();
}
```

situations, it will likely work when the key is located somewhere in the middle of vector A.

An example of a capacity boundary condition is whether the code works when the size of vector A is one or zero. We should include tests for these two cases. Test cases like these are testing degenerate situations. Degenerate situations are ones that would not arise in typical use of the code, but if they occur the program should work. Because the loop is controlled by the size of the vector, these tests also serve as loop boundary tests. If vector A is empty, the loop will not be executed at all. Does this code work when vector A has size one? What about when its size is zero?

As another example of boundary testing, consider the code in Listing 12.4 from the stock charting utility of Chapter 6. Examination of the code shows that the code checks (using function Valid()) that the low stock price is greater than or equal to zero and that the high price is greater than or equal to the low price. This immediately suggests the following data boundary test cases.

Low Stock Price	High Stock Price
0	0
0	10
0	−1
−1	3
10	8

The first test case checks whether a zero stock price is allowed for both the low and the high price. The second test case checks whether the program handles the case where the low stock price is zero and the high stock price is nonzero. The program should produce a graph for these two test cases. The next three test cases should cause the program to produce an error message. The third test case checks whether the program issues an error message when the low stock price is zero and the high stock price is negative. The fourth test case checks the lower boundary of the low stock price. This test should generate an

```
// Valid(): are weekly stock prices sensible
bool Valid(float low, float high) {
    return (0 <= low) && (low <= high);
}
// ReadStockInterval(): read weekly low and high for stock
bool ReadStockInterval(istream &fin,
 const string &FileName, int &Low, int &High, int Week) {
    if (fin == cin)
        cout << "Enter the low and high stock price";
    fin >> Low >> High;
    // if no more data return false
    if (! fin)
        return false;
    // check for valid data
    if (! Valid(Low, High)) {
        cerr << FileName << ": Bad data for week "
            << Week + 1 << endl;
        exit(1);
    }
    return true;
}
```

error. The final test case checks whether the program handles the case where the low stock price is higher than the high stock price.

The test cases can be partitioned into two equivalence classes. The first two test cases are legal input, while the last three are illegal and should cause the program to generate an error message. If the program does not generate an error message, then we have exposed a bug. In general, it is a good idea to classify all test cases as to whether they are valid inputs and the program should produce valid output, or whether they are invalid inputs and the program should generate an error message.

Another approach for generating test cases is to produce a set of test cases that cause each statement in the program to be executed at least once. This is known as *statement* or *code coverage testing*. The basic idea is that unless you have executed every line of code at least once you have not thoroughly tested the code. Of course, statement coverage testing can miss bugs because you may not execute a particular sequence of statements that exposes a bug. Also, for complicated programs, the number of test cases needed to guarantee complete code coverage can be quite high. Nonetheless, code coverage is a technique that is sometimes used. To support code coverage testing, there are software tools available that instrument the code and produce reports that show which program statements have been executed.

There are other techniques for test set generation. One approach is to generate a test set that causes each edge of the program's controlflow graph to be executed. This technique is called *path coverage* or *path testing*. To illustrate path testing, consider the following code fragment.

```
if (x != y)
    y = 5;
else
    z = z - z;
```

```
if (x > 1)
    z = z / x;
else
    z = 0;
```

The controlflow graph of this program is shown in Figure 12.2. A set of tests that cause each edge to be traversed is <x = 0, z = 1> and <x = 3, z = 3>. The first test case causes paths A, B, G, H to be executed. The second test case causes paths E, F, C, D to be executed. The problem with this test set is that an important case has been missed. What happens when test case <x = 0, z = 3> is executed? To address this problem, we would need to test every possible path, which we have seen is infeasible.

Figure 12.2

Controlflow graph of two if-else statements

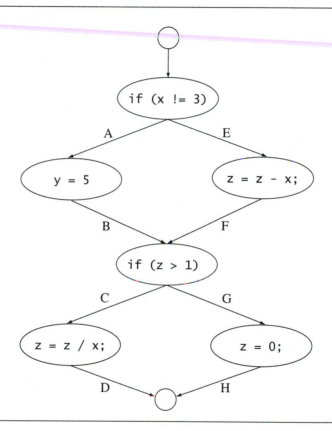

Regardless of the amount of testing and the strategy used to produce the test cases, an important component of testing is automation. As the software is developed, tests will need to be rerun periodically. Thus it is important to set up an automated procedure for running the tests, capturing the output, and comparing the actual output to the expected output. This promotes running *regression tests* periodically. A regression test compares the operation of the new version of the software to the operation of a previous version. The idea is that the behavior of the program should not change in unanticipated ways. If something that once worked no longer works, you have a regression. Regression testing ensures that you do not introduce new bugs or resurrect old ones!

The other reason to automate testing is that the testing procedure will serve to document how to run the tests. This is helpful when a bug is reported and fixed several years after the software is released. Without an automated testing procedure, you would have to remember how to run all the tests and which were supposed to pass and which were supposed to fail.

In summary, testing software is an integral and key component of the software development process. The size, complexity, and importance of today's software systems demand the application of effective testing techniques.

Programming Tip

> ### *Testing tips*
>
> The following are some general tips for effective testing.
>
> **Test early.** The sooner you find bugs, the easier they are to fix. Also, it is easier and more effective to generate tests cases as you develop the code. Unit tests are an effective way to find bugs early in individual components or modules.
>
> **Use inspections.** Inspections are extremely effective at exposing bugs and other deficiencies in the software. Even if a formal inspection process is not practical, sitting down and explaining your code to another programmer can be productive.
>
> **Test boundaries.** Look for boundary conditions in your code and make sure you have test cases that test on the boundary and around the boundary. Off-by-one errors are fairly common, so it pays to test for them specifically.
>
> **Test exceptional conditions.** Try to think of situations that shouldn't happen, and then add tests for them. Typical situations include empty files, no data entered, invalid data, too little data, and too much data. A robust program should handle all these cases.
>
> **Make testing repeatable.** Set up an automated procedure for running your tests and comparing the actual output to the expected output. Scripting languages and shell languages are useful tools for this purpose.

12.1.5 Integration and system testing

Unit testing focuses on a single function, module, or component. Testing done as the pieces of the software are put together is called *integration testing*. *System testing* is testing done when the whole system is put together. Good unit testing simplifies integration and system testing. Since we are confident that the pieces work, we can focus our efforts on testing the interfaces between the pieces or components. Furthermore since we are confident the individual pieces work, when a test fails we can focus our effort to find the problem on the interfaces between the components.

The guidelines for developing good unit tests apply to integration and system testing. The difference is the focus. With integration testing the focus is on testing the interaction between the software components. Thus, the tests inputs you develop should focus on exercising that aspect of the system. Similarly with system testing, the test inputs should look to test overall system behavior, not the behavior of an individual component. That was accomplished by unit testing.

Such a modular approach to testing is necessary because as components are assembled to build larger components and the final system, testing the entire system becomes infeasible.

Self-check Questions

7.   Name the four roles used in an inspection.

8.   With many inspection methodologies, the presenter is someone other than the author of the code. Why is this a good idea?

9.   Explain the difference between black-box testing and white-box testing.

10.   Devise three new equivalence classes of tests for testing the addition operation of the calculator.

11.   What is statement coverage testing?

12.   What is path coverage testing?

13.   Set up a test harness for the binary search function, and test it thoroughly. Report any errors you found.

14.   Devise test cases that cause each statement in the following program to be executed at least once.

```
int Euclid(int x, int y) {
    while (x != y) {
        if (x > y)
            x = x - y;
        else
            x = y - x;
    }
    return 0;
}
```

12.2   DEBUGGING

Testing is the processing of detecting the existence of a bug. *Debugging* is the processing of revealing what the bug is and removing it. Sometimes when a test case exposes a bug, the reason for the bug is obvious. Those are the easy bugs. Other times discovering why a program does not work correctly can be a tedious and time-consuming task—especially if an undisciplined approach is used. In Section 12.2.1, we describe an approach to debugging based on the scientific method. In Section 12.2.2 we give other advice and tips about debugging that experienced programmers use.

12.2.1 The scientific method

Finding that last elusive bug before an assignment is due or the software is shipped can be a frustrating and stressful experience, sometimes so much so that otherwise bright programmers resort to making random changes to their code in hopes that insight into the problem will emerge. This is not a very productive approach. In this section we introduce the notion of applying the scientific method to debugging.

The scientific method is a systematic way of reaching a conclusion based on inductive logic. The scientific method uses the following steps.

Gather data. Observe facts and look for patterns in the data.

Develop a hypothesis. Formulate a plausible explanation that accounts for or explains the observed facts. This is the hypothesis.

Predict new facts. Using the hypothesis, predict new facts or new behaviors that have not yet been observed.

Perform experiments. Design experiments to observe the new facts. Run the experiments and collect data.

Prove or disprove the hypothesis. If the predicted facts are observed, the hypothesis is assumed to be true. If observations do not support the hypothesis, the process is repeated by developing an alternative hypothesis. Additional data may need to be collected to formulate an alternative hypothesis.

Here's a simple example to illustrate the application of the scientific method to debugging. A program is throwing an exception because of a division by zero in an arithmetic statement. You observe that the value used as the divisor in the offending statement is computed by a loop that counts the number of nonzero values in an array. Based on this observation, you hypothesize that the array must not contain any nonzero values. Using this hypothesis, you predict that if you insert code to print the array right before the loop the output will contain all zeros. Running the modified code is the experiment. If the output shows the array contained only zeros, your hypothesis is true. If the output has nonzero values, the result of the experiment did not support the original hypothesis, and you need to formulate another hypothesis to explain why the divisor is zero.

This process sounds time-consuming, but it is really not. Often, the experiment to test the hypothesis can be carried out using a debugger. In the previous example, instead of inserting code and recompiling the program, you could have used the debugger to set a breakpoint before the loop and then print the array.

The important point is that we need to reason about the code and not go willy-nilly changing statements without some clear idea of what we hope to discover.

Here's a real world example to illustrate the power of the scientific method applied to debugging. Sally Code and Chuck Hacker (the names have been changed to protect the innocent) are part of a team of programmers that are creating a computerized mapping program. The program will read a file containing a list of landmarks with positions and generate a map. Sally and Chuck have been assigned an initial task of creating a house icon for representing houses on the map. Figure 12.3 shows a rough sketch of what they plan to draw. They decide to render the house by drawing a red rectangle and placing four white squares inside the rectangle to represent windows. The roof will be a green triangle. It will be implemented using the EzWindows shapes, `RectangleShape`, `SquareShape`, and `TriangleShape`.

Figure 12.3

Sketch of HouseIcon

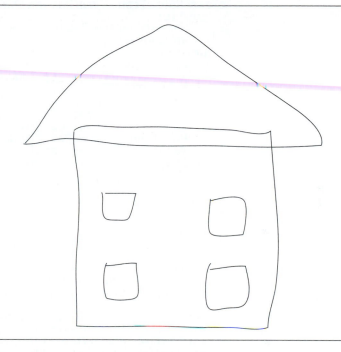

Listing 12.5 contains the `HouseIcon` class declaration and Listing 12.6 contains the partial implementation of `HouseIcon`. The implementation is partial as Sally and Chuck plan to add more features after they get this part working. This is a sign they are good programmers—they develop their code incrementally.

Another indication that Sally and Chuck are good programmers is that after they created and implemented the initial version of `HouseIcon`; they also wrote a test harness to make sure class `HouseIcon` works correctly. If there are any problems with `HouseIcon`, debugging now will be easier than later when the implementation is more complex. Listing 12.7 gives the test harness.

Listing 12.5

Definition of HouseIcon

```
#ifndef HOUSEICON_H
#define HOUSEICON_H

#include "ezwin.h"
#include "position.h"
#include "wobject.h"
#include "square.h"
#include "rect.h"
#include "triangle.h"

class HouseIcon : public WindowObject{
  public:
    HouseIcon(SimpleWindow& w, const Position& p);
    void Draw();
  private:
    RectangleShape HouseBase;
    SquareShape Window1, Window2, Window3, Window4;
    TriangleShape Roof;
    color HouseColor;
    Position HouseBasePosition;
    Position Window1Position;
    Position Window2Position;
    Position Window3Position;
    Position Window4Position;
};

#endif
```

Listing 12.6

*Partial implementation
of HouseIcon*

```
#include "HouseIcon.h"
HouseIcon::HouseIcon(SimpleWindow& w, const Position& p) :
    WindowObject(w, p),
    HouseBasePosition(p), HouseBase(w, p, Red, 3.5, 4.0),
    Roof(w, p + Position(0.0, -2.5), Green, 4.5f),
    Window1Position(p + Position(-0.5, -0.5)),
    Window2Position(p + Position(0.5, -0.5)),
    Window3Position(p + Position(-0.5, 0.5)),
    Window4Position(p + Position(0.5, 0.5)),
    Window1(w, Window1Position, White, 0.5),
    Window2(w, Window2Position, White, 0.5),
    Window3(w, Window3Position, White, 0.5),
    Window4(w, Window4Position, White, 0.5),
    HouseColor(Red) {
    // No code needed!
}

void HouseIcon::Draw(){
    HouseBase.Draw();
    Roof.Draw();
    Window1.Draw();
    Window2.Draw();
    Window3.Draw();
    Window4.Draw();
}
```

<table>
<tr><td>

Listing 12.7

Test harness for
HouseIcon

</td><td>

```cpp
#include "HouseIcon.h"
SimpleWindow *W;
int ApiMain() {
    W = new SimpleWindow("House Icon", 10.0f, 8.0f);
    W->Open();
    Position ButtonPosition(5.0f, 6.0f);

    HouseIcon HomeButton(*W, ButtonPosition);
    HomeButton.Draw();
    return 0;
}
```

</td></tr>
</table>

To their surprise, when Sally and Chuck run their program, they get the following output.

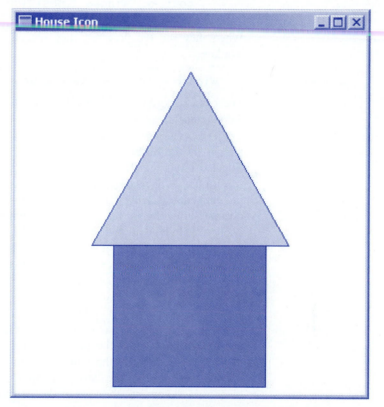

The windows did not appear. It must be a simple error. Indeed, Sally's and Chuck's first thought is that the windows are being drawn behind the red box that is the base of the house. However, inspection of the member function Draw() shows that the windows are being drawn last. Sally and Chuck decide to employ the scientific method to find the bug. Chuck comes up with the following hypothesis. He thinks that the house windows are being drawn, but they not being drawn at the right position. He thinks that the house windows are being drawn elsewhere in the display window and they just cannot be seen. He suggests changing the color of the house windows so they will be visible wherever they are drawn. Sally points out that the EzWindows objects have black borders and that even if the house windows were drawn elsewhere in the display window, they would still be visible. Even though Sally and Chuck did not run the code, they still did an experiment. In this case, Sally and Chuck ran a "thought experiment." Running thought experiments when appropriate is much faster than setting up experiments and running code.

Sally and Chuck need more data to help formulate a plausible hypothesis. Sally suggests printing the locations of the house windows to the console, so they can see where they are supposed to be drawn. They decide to print out the location of just one of the house windows. This should be sufficient since none of the house windows are being displayed. They add the following statement to function `HouseIcon::Draw()`.

```
cout << "Window 1 position is (" << x
     << "," << y << ")" << endl;
```

When they run the program, they get the following output in the console window.

```
Window 1 position is (-1.07374e+008,-1.07374e+008)
```

The *x* and *y* coordinates are out of range. This explains why the house windows did not appear, but now the question is why are the coordinates incorrect.

The positions of the `SquareShapes` used to represent the house windows are set by the `HouseIcon`'s constructor. The code looks correct. Sally and Chuck are stymied. They are out of ideas. This is why debugging can be time-consuming. When you examined the code carefully and still do not see the problem, this usually indicates that your mental model of how the program operates is wrong. In this situation, no amount of looking at the program is likely to help. You are either looking in the wrong place, or you are looking at the right place but just not seeing the problem. There are two things programmers do in this situation. One approach is to explain the problem to someone else. Typically, that person will have a different mindset than you and will quickly point out the error. We often find ourselves saying, "Thanks, I never would have seen that in a million years!"

The other approach is to try and gather more data to expose the flaw in your mental model of the program's operation. In this situation you need detailed data even about that which you think is surely true about the program's operation. To gather this data, programmers use the debugger, or they insert diagnostic statements throughout the program to help them understand the program.

Sally and Chuck insert a `cout` statement in `HouseIcon`'s constructor to display the position of `Window1`. The coordinates are messed up at this point. That's bad news as no other code is being executed between when the coordinates are being set in the data member initialization list and the body of the constructor. At this point inexperienced programmers often jump to the conclusion that something must be wrong with the compiler. This is rarely the case. Furthermore, there's no concrete evidence that something is wrong with the compiler. Sally and Chuck have a real mystery on their hands. As the great detective Sherlock Holmes noted in *The Sign of Four*, "When you have eliminated the impossible, whatever remains, however improbable, must be the truth." The data member initialization list is the only thing left. The problem must be there.

Sally and Chuck use the debugger and set breakpoints in each constructor that involves the house windows—`Position` and `SquareShape`. Perhaps this data will help them see the problem. When the program runs they notice that the constructor for `SquareShape` is called first. That's odd as they had expected the constructor for `Position` to be called first to create the object `Window1Position`. Sally smiles as she realizes what the problem is.

She and Chuck wrote the code based on the assumption that the various constructors were called in the order they appeared on the data member initialization list. In fact, the constructors for the data members are called in the order the objects appear in the class declaration. The object `Window1` is being constructed before `Window1Position` is created and initialized. Hence, the constructor call to create `Window1` is being passed an uninitialized `Position`. The same is true for the `Window2`, `Window3`, and `Window4`.

If Sally's hypothesis is true, one possible fix is to change the order of the private data members in the declaration of class `HouseIcon`. The four house window positions need to appear first. The revised declaration is:

```cpp
class HouseIcon : public WindowObject{
    public:
        HouseIcon(SimpleWindow& w, const Position& p);
        void Draw();
        void MoveAbsolute(const Position& p);
        void MoveRelative(const Position& p);
    private:
        RectangleShape HouseBase;
        color HouseColor;
        TriangleShape Roof;
        Position HouseBasePosition;
        Position Window1Position;
        Position Window2Position;
        Position Window3Position;
        Position Window4Position;
        SquareShape Window1, Window2, Window3, Window4;
};
```

Sally and Chuck run the revised code and the program generates the image shown in Figure 12.4. Finally a house with a view!

This exercise gets Sally and Chuck to thinking about their code. Creating the house should have been simple. What went wrong? Their code depended on an obscure behavior of C++ that is easy to forget or overlook. Chuck wonders what will happen if someone modifies their code down the road. Will the maintainers realize there's a subtle dependency on the order of the data member declarations?

This brings up another important point about debugging. Once you have found a bug, especially one that's been very elusive, it is tempting to go for the quick, easy fix. Good programmers learn from their mistakes. Because they had so much trouble with the code, Sally and Chuck decide to revise `House-Icon` so that it is less likely to break if someone extends or modifies it.

Figure 12.4

*HouseIcon with
windows*

12.2.2 Debugging tips and techniques

The most powerful weapon in your arsenal against bugs is your ability to reason. There are also some handy techniques and tips that can reduce the time spent debugging. Many of these techniques help you apply the scientific method more efficiently.

Simplify the problem. Try to come up with the smallest amount of code that still exhibits the error. You can do this by removing calls to functions that are unnecessary and removing statements that should have no bearing on the problem. Anything you can do to reduce the complexity of the code you are debugging can be helpful. As you are removing code, you probably want to periodically run the code to make sure the bug is still there. If it goes away, you have discovered valuable information that you can use to reason about the cause of the bug. As you remove code, be sure and retain a copy of the original code.

Along these same lines, you should produce the smallest input that still causes the bug. If the program is interactive, try to find the shortest sequence of commands that cause the error to occur. Knowing the precise input that causes the problem is useful information.

Stabilize the error. Bugs that occur sporadically are some of the hardest to track down. If the bug does not happen consistently, work to make the bug appear reliably. If the bug is a hard one to track down, you will probably be running the program over and over again. In this case, you want each run to be productive.

How you make the bug appear reliably depends on the program; you will have to be resourceful. Here are some common techniques programmers use, depending on the situation.

Figure out the exact sequence of inputs or the precise conditions that cause the bug to occur. If you are using a random number generator, make sure the seed is set to the same value on each run.

If the bug only occurs after the program has been running a long time, figure out ways to simulate that behavior. Perhaps there's a memory leak, and the bug only occurs after many dynamic memory allocations. Simulate this behavior by writing a function that allocates lots of memory. Call the function at the beginning of the program to simulate the effect of the program running a long time.

Dump the state of the program periodically. That is, print out key values and data structures. Use this last "state" information you've collected to initialize the program so it fails quickly and reliably.

Locate the error. Try to determine what function or section of code is causing the problem. To do this, print data values and observe at what point in the execution incorrect values are produced. It also helps to try different input values and observe the effect on the code. Sometimes with the right inputs you can "triangulate" the location of the error in the code. Figure 12.5 illustrates the process of triangulating the location of a bug.

Figure 12.5

Triangulating the location of a bug

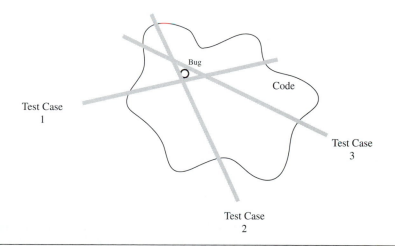

Locating a bug via triangulation often requires running a handful of test cases to narrow the location of the bug down to a region of code small enough to be helpful. The problem is that each test set may identify a large region of code. Consequently, more than two or three test cases are needed to zero in on the location of the bug.

Explain the bug to someone else. In the `HouseIcon` example, explaining the code to someone else could have caught the error. Hopefully, the person you explain the code to has a different mindset or different mental model of what's going on and will immediately see the problem that you were blind to.

If you have worked at a help desk, you have probably experienced the phenomena known as "confessional debugging." A person is explaining the problem and as they do so, it suddenly dawns on them what the problem is. The act of explaining the code to someone makes you think a little more clearly, not skip steps, and so on. Confessional debugging is surprisingly effective.

Recognize common bugs. Some common bugs have specific symptoms. Knowing the symptoms of commonly occurring bugs can help you identify them quickly.

A common bug is *oversubscripting an array*. When this happens the program writes or reads a memory location that it did not intend to access. Any time you see a program in which an object suddenly has an odd value, look at the source code near where that object was declared. Are there any arrays defined either before or after the object that is being trashed? If so, it may be that you are over- or undersubscripting one of these arrays, and it is stomping on the value in the object.

Trashing the stack is another common bug. The problem is also caused by over- or undersubscripting an array, but occurs when a local array (i.e., one that is allocated on the stack). The symptoms are different from the one described in the preceding paragraph. One symptom of stack trashing is when a function return causes a fault, or a function returns to some odd location (e.g., execution continues in some function that did not call the function that was just executing). The error is caused because a local array was over- or undersubscripted and stack locations were overwritten. One of the values stored on the stack is the address of the function to return to when the current function returns. Basically, you are returning to, as some folks like to say, "never-never land."

A debugger can help identify this problem. The procedure is to set a break point right before the function returns. Dump the runtime stack to verify that the return address is correct. If it is not correct, then the stack was trashed by either this function or some function that was called by this function.

Another symptom of stack trashing is that local objects get strange or incorrect values. Here, the stack was trashed, but the return address was not clobbered—local objects of the calling function were trashed. Again, the debugger can be useful in verifying that this is the problem. Set a breakpoint immediately before and after the call to the function that you suspect is trashing the stack. At the first breakpoint, verify that the values of the local objects that you believe are being trashed are correct. Continue execution. At the second breakpoint reexamine the values. Are they incorrect? If so, you probably have a classic case of stack trashing. If the values are still correct, you need to continue your investigation.

Dereferencing a null pointer is another classic bug. Fortunately, most architectures will cause an exception when a null pointer is dereferenced, and you can easily identify the offending source statement. The real issue, however, is why is the pointer null. Sometimes the pointer is legitimately null, and you just forgot to guard the statement dereferencing the pointer with an if-statement. Other times, you have a live bug that you need to remove. In these cases, using the debugger to collect data so you can use the scientific method of debugging is the best course of action.

Recompile everything. Modern IDEs are extremely useful, but sometimes they can get confused. If you have been making lots of changes to the code looking for a bug and the code is not behaving the way you think it should, or changes you have made do not seem to be having an effect, rebuild the entire project from scratch and rerun the code.

Gather more information. If you are stuck and can't seem to understand what's going on, generate more data. Some standard actions taken by experienced programmers include running different test cases, using the debugger to observe the program's flow of execution, printing out intermediate results, and dumping data structures. You need to be selective and only print as much as you can reasonably digest. Sifting through mountains of data can be like searching for a needle in a haystack.

Pay attention to the compiler. Modern compilers are very good at detecting certain types of errors. However, they tend to be conservative and sometimes produce warning messages that end up being spurious. When you are searching for a bug, it's a good time to pay attention to all those warning messages you have been ignoring. If the compiler reports an object is used before being set, then that problem is something work investigating.

Many compilers allow the programmer to control the level at which error and warning messages are issued. Setting the compiler to the strictest level can sometimes yield information that is helpful in searching for a bug.

Fix bugs as you find them. It often happens that when you are looking for a bug, you discover another bug. This bug seems unrelated to the bug you are trying to find. It is tempting to put off doing something about the bug just discovered since you are in the middle of tracking down the original bug. You don't want the trail to go cold.

Generally, it is good practice to fix bugs as you find them. The bug you just found could be related to the one you were originally trying to find. Fixing this bug, could make the other bug go away. This phenomena happens quite often. On the other hand, if you are sure the newly found bug is unrelated to the bug you were originally searching for, then it may be worthwhile to keep hunting.

Take a break. Sometimes you get nowhere with a bug despite spending hours trying different strategies to locate it. While perseverance is a valuable programmer trait, knowing when to take a break and get away from a problem is also valuable. Experienced problem solvers know how important it is to get away and do something that lets the mind wander—jog, listen to music, take a walk, stare out the window, and so on. As you relax, the solution to the problem might just come to you.

Most experienced programmers have war stories about bug hunts. A common story is the "debugger's epiphany." The story goes something like this. Bill Geek has been hunting a particularly nasty bug for days. None of the tried-and-true techniques for finding the bug have worked. Bill decides to take a break and hit the hills for some mountain biking action. When Bill is flying down a hill with trees whizzing by, the last thing he is thinking about is the elusive bug in the web browser. After a great afternoon, Bill heads home for a shower. As he showers, he starts to think about the bug again, and it hits him—the solution to the browser problem suddenly becomes crystal clear. Bill heads to work to run an experiment to validate his hypothesis, but he's confident he's got it.

Stories like Bill's are common. Of course, the best stories always have the programmer doing something unusual when the epiphany occurs!

Think outside the box. It is very easy to get locked into a particular way of looking at or attacking a problem. If you are getting nowhere with a problem, try thinking outside the box. Try something unusual or new that you have not tried before. For example, do the opposite of what you have been doing and see what happens.

Debugging is an important part of the programming process. As you gain experience with programming, you will no doubt develop your own personal style of debugging—favorite techniques, tricks, tools, and so forth. You will also learn to use a source-level debugger. A source-level debugger integrated into a modern IDE is a powerful tool for tracking down bugs. However, the most important point to remember is that the key to effective debugging is to follow a disciplined process. Together, disciplined testing and disciplined debugging ensure that high-quality software is delivered on time and within budget.

Self-check Questions

15.   Describe the steps of the scientific method.

16.   What kind of logic, inductive or deductive, does the scientific method use?

17.   Revise class `HouseIcon` so that it is less likely to break if it is changed.

18.   Write a program that demonstrates the behavior of a program that oversubscripts a global array.

19.   Write a program that demonstrates the behavior of a program that trashes the return address on the stack.

20. Use the Internet to research the Therac-25 accidents. Describe what happened.

12.3 POINTS TO REMEMBER

✔ Testing cannot prove that software has no bugs. It can only show the presence of bugs.

✔ Bugs fall into four broad categories: software crashes or data corruption, failure to meet or satisfy the specification, poor or unacceptable performance, and difficulty of use.

✔ Test early in the development process. It is cheaper and easier to fix bugs when they are identified early.

✔ It is impossible to test a program completely.

✔ Develop prototypes to test functional requirements.

✔ Inspections are an effective way to expose bugs early in the software development process.

✔ Testing without knowledge of how the code works is called *black-box testing*.

✔ Testing with knowledge of how the code works is called *white-box testing*.

✔ Equivalence partitioning helps develop smaller, more effective test suites.

✔ Good test suites include inputs that test the software's boundary conditions.

✔ Statement coverage testing creates test inputs so that every statement in the software is executed at least once.

✔ Path coverage testing creates inputs so that every controlflow edge in the software is executed at least once.

✔ Set up automated procedures for running and checking the results of your tests. This will make testing go faster, and it also serves to document the testing process for future developers and maintainers.

✔ Use the scientific method for debugging.

✔ Take time to fix a bug properly. Resist the temptation to apply a quick fix to get the code running. Time spent fixing a bug properly early in the software development process is an investment that will pay off in the future.

✔ When debugging, try to produce the simplest input that causes the problem. Be sure to add the input to your set of test cases.

✔ Work to make the error consistently repeatable. This will help you understand the bug, and it will speed the debugging process.

✔ Learn to recognize the symptoms of common bugs.

12.4 TO DELVE FURTHER

There are many excellent texts that discuss testing and debugging. The student interested in learning more about testing can begin with the following texts.

- Brian Kernighan and Rob Pike, *The Practice of Programming,* Reading, MA: Addison-Wesley, 1999.

- Steve McConnell, *Code Complete: A Practical Handbook of Software Construction,* Redmond, WA: Microsoft Press, 1993.

- Glenford Myers, *The Art of Software Testing,* New York: Wiley, 1979.

- Ron Patton, *Software Testing,* Indianapolis: Sams Publishing, 2001.

12.5 EXERCISES

12.1 The crash of the Ariane 5 was the result of poor testing practices. Using your library or Internet research facilities, find out about the Ariane 5 crash, and explain how the test procedure was flawed.

12.2 Develop test inputs to test Program 5.1. Your test inputs should achieve full statement coverage of the program. That is, the test inputs should cause every statement in the program to be executed at least once.

12.3 Test data is often partitioned into inputs that test for error conditions and inputs that test that the program works when given valid data. Examine Program 5.3. Develop one set of test inputs for error conditions and a separate set of inputs to demonstrate the program works.

12.4 How many unique paths are there in the following controlflow graph?

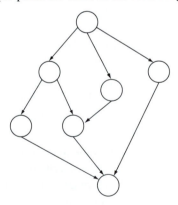

12.5 Develop a test harness, and test input for the class `Display` given in Listing 9.18.

12.6 With four other classmates, perform an inspection of the Red-Yellow-Green game presented in Chapter 8. Prepare an inspection report that describes any problems that the inspection discovered.

12.7 Explain why it is a good idea to have someone other than the programmer responsible for testing a program.

12.8 Another kind of testing is acceptance testing. What is acceptance testing?

CHAPTER 13

Inheritance

Introduction

A key feature of an object-oriented language is inheritance. *Inheritance* is the ability to define new classes using existing classes as a basis. The new class inherits the attributes and behaviors of the classes on which it is based, and it can also have attributes and behaviors that are specific to it. Inheritance is a powerful mechanism that provides a natural framework for producing software that is reliable, understandable, cost-effective, adaptable, and reusable. In this chapter, we introduce C++'s inheritance mechanism by developing a class hierarchy for representing and displaying two-dimensional shapes. The resulting classes are used to refine and expand the kaleidoscope program developed in Chapter 7.

Key Concepts

- is-a relationship
- has-a relationship
- uses-a relationship
- base class
- derived class
- public inheritance
- private inheritance
- single inheritance
- multiple inheritance

13.1 OBJECT–ORIENTED DESIGN USING INHERITANCE

We are all familar with the concept of biological inheritance. All living things inherit characteristics from their ancestors. For example, whether we want to admit it or not, we have all inherited characteristics from our parents. These characteristics may have been unique to our parents, or perhaps our parents inherited the characteristic from their parents. The concept of inheritance can be used to design complex systems. It provides a way of organizing the components of the system into a hierarchical structure that helps us understand the system. In addition, it provides a framework for reusing code.

Typically, inheritance is used to organize abstractions in a top-down fashion from most general to least general. Figure 13.1 contains a hierarchical organization of different types of writing instruments.

Figure 13.1

Writing instrument hierarchy

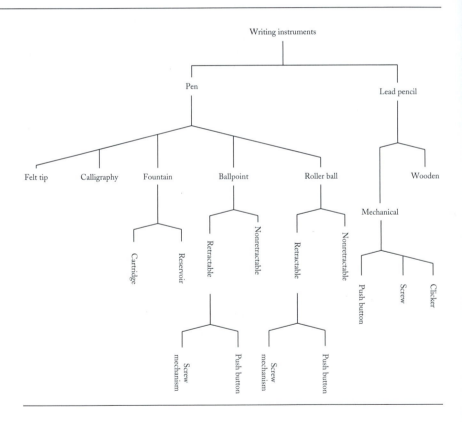

For example, we see different types of pens: ballpoints, roller balls, felt tips, calligraphy pens, and fountain pens. These are all specific types of pens, and they inherit the distinguishing characteristic of a pen—they use ink. However, each type of pen has an attribute that is specific to it and distinguishes it from the other types. At the highest level of hierarchy of pens, the distinguishing characteristic is the mechanism used to put the ink on the paper. Using the notion of inheritance to create a hierarchy of abstractions certainly helps us understand the relationships between the abstractions, but it can also help reduce the effort to create new and useful abstractions.

The relationship that helps us create a hierarchy of abstractions based on inheritance is the *is-a* relationship. The is-a relationship specifies that one abstraction is a specialization of another. For example, a pen *is a* special kind of writing instrument. Similarly, a roller ball is a type of pen, which *is a* type of writing instrument. Notice that the is-a relationship is transitive (that is, a roller ball is a pen, a pen is a writing instrument, therefore a roller ball is a writing instrument), but it is not reflexive (that is, not all writing instruments are pens). Another way of expressing the is-a relationship is to say that a roller ball is a *kind of* pen and that a pen is a *kind of* writing instrument.

In addition to the is-a relationship that represents inheritance between abstractions, two other relationships between abstractions are commonly used in object-oriented design. One, which we have used quite a bit already, is called the *has-a* relationship. The has-a relationship says that some object is part of another. For example, a fountain pen has a nib, and some pencils have an eraser. The has-a relationship implies containment. An automobile contains an engine, a battery, and a horn.

In Chapter 9 we introduced several abstractions that contained the `Location` abstraction. These abstractions used the has-a relationship. A `Maze` has a starting and ending location. Thus `Maze` has a `Location`. Similarly, a `Wanderer` has a location. Therefore, `Wanderer` has a `Location`.

Another relationship between objects is the *uses-a* relationship. The uses-a relationship says that one object uses another object in some way. In object-oriented programming, this relationship is typically realized by one object communicating with another via member functions. For example, suppose the operating system we are using has a clock object that maintains the current date and time. The clock object has member functions that return the current date and time. Other objects that need the date or time use the clock object by calling the appropriate member functions to fetch the current time or date.

13.2 REUSE VIA INHERITANCE

In Chapter 7 we used class `RectangleShape` to develop a program that simulated the images produced by a kaleidoscope. The patterns produced by the program were nice, but most kaleidoscopes use more than one shape of glass to produce the multicolored patterns. Suppose we wanted to enhance the kaleidoscope program so that it used additional shapes such as circles and triangles.

One approach would be to create an additional class to represent a circle. Indeed, if we used the class `RectangleShape` as a model, creating a class `CircleShape` would not be too hard to do.

Listing 13.1 contains the declaration for our original `RectangleShape` class and the declaration for the new `CircleShape` class. Notice that the two

```cpp
class RectangleShape {
    public:
        RectangleShape(SimpleWindow &Window,
            float XCoord, float YCoord, const color &Color,
            float Width, float Height);
        void Draw();
        color GetColor() const;
        void GetSize(float &Width, float &Height) const;
        void GetPosition(float &XCoord, float &YCoord) const;
        float GetWidth() const;
        float GetHeight() const;
        SimpleWindow& GetWindow() const;
        void SetColor(const color &Color);
        void SetPosition(float XCoord, float YCoord);
        void SetSize(float Width, float Height);
    private:
        SimpleWindow &Window;
        float XCenter;
        float YCenter;
        color Color;
        float Width;
        float Height;
};
class CircleShape {
    public:
        CircleShape(SimpleWindow &Window,
            float XCoord, float YCoord,
            const color &Color, float Diameter);
        void Draw();
        color GetColor() const;
        float GetSize() const;
        void GetPosition(float &XCoord, float &YCoord) const;
        SimpleWindow& GetWindow() const;
        void SetColor(const color &Color);
        void SetPosition(float XCoord, float YCoord);
        void SetSize(float Diameter);
    private:
        SimpleWindow &Window;
        float XCenter;
        float YCenter;
        color Color;
        float Diameter;
};
```

definitions are very similiar. The two classes contain exactly the same member functions. Only the member function `SetSize()` differs slightly between the two classes. `RectangleShape` has two `float` parameters to `SetSize()`— `Width` and `Height`, and `CircleShape` has a single float parameter named `Diameter`. Similarly, the private data members of the two classes are identical except that `RectangleShape` stores its size attributes in `Width` and `Height`, whereas `CircleShape` uses `Diameter` to hold its size attribute.

Of course, we would also need to provide implementations of `Circle-Shape`'s member functions. Again, this would not be too hard to do because most of the code would be identical to that developed for `RectangleShape`. Only the member function `Draw()` would be very different. Thus much commonality exists between the two classes

So far, so good, but now suppose we wanted to have other shapes as well. For example, it might be nice to use triangles as well as rectangles and circles. Things start to get complicated and messy. We have a lot of code, some of it similar and some of it not. Furthermore, if we decide to add a new behavior or attribute to our shapes, it becomes harder because we must change all the shapes. We can reduce the complexity of both our design and implementation dramatically if we design our shape abstractions using inheritance. Using inheritance requires us to think about our design in a top-down fashion rather than bottom-up. That is, we need to think about the most general abstraction of a shape and build the more specific abstractions using the general ones as a basis.

Determining the most general abstraction, or base abstraction, for a hierarchy of abstractions is one of the keys to a successful object-oriented design. Unfortunately, designing a flexible hierarchy of abstractions is quite difficult. It is all too easy to make the base abstraction too specific or not specific enough. If the base abstraction is too specific, the is-a relationship may not hold between the abstractions that we wish to create or derive from the base abstraction because a derived abstraction inherits the attributes of its ancestors in the hierarchy. So, for example, if the base abstraction for a hierarchy of passenger vehicle types included an attribute for the number of wheels, all abstractions lower in the hierarchy inherit this attribute. Consequently, this abstraction could not be used to derive abstractions for vehicles without wheels such as ships, sleighs, or all-terrain vehicles that use treads.

If the base abstraction is not specific enough, the problem is that attributes and behaviors will needlessly be duplicated in the derived abstractions. For example, if the base abstraction for a hierarchy of passenger vehicles omits an attribute for the number of passengers, this attribute will have to be added to each kind of vehicle that is derived from that base abstraction.

13.3   A HIERARCHY OF SHAPES

To illustrate the development of a hierarchy of abstractions based on inheritance, we develop a class hierarchy for a set of window objects that consist of two-dimensional shapes and text labels. Using some of the two-dimensional shapes, we design and implement an enhanced kaleidoscope program. The first job is to decide what attributes and behaviors the base class should contain. Because of the way most windowing graphics systems work, the context or window that contains an object must be known in order to display it. Thus an attribute of a window object is the window that contains it. Another attribute of any window object is its location or position in the window. Other attributes such as size, color, or how the object is drawn depend on the type of object and therefore should not be part of the base class. Of course, in addition to the attributes, we will need public member functions that set and manipulate these attributes. Figure 13.2 illustrates the window object abstraction, and Listing 13.2 contains the corresponding class declaration.

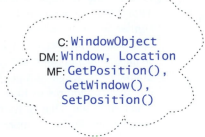

C: WindowObject
DM: Window, Location
MF: GetPosition(),
GetWindow(),
SetPosition()

Listing 13.2

WindowObject class
declaration from
wobject.h

```cpp
#ifndef WINDOWOBJECT_H
#define WINDOWOBJECT_H
#include "ezwin.h"
// WindowObject base class for objects that can be
// displayed in a window
class WindowObject {
    public:
        WindowObject(SimpleWindow &w, const Position &p);
        Position GetPosition() const;
        SimpleWindow& GetWindow() const;
        void SetPosition(const Position &p);
    private:
        SimpleWindow &Window;
        Position Location;
};
#endif
```

The `WindowObject` class contains two private member items: `Location` and `Window` are instances of the classes `Position` and `SimpleWindow`, which were introduced in Chapter 10. The data member `Window` is a reference object. Recall that once reference objects are set to refer to something, what they refer to cannot be changed; therefore once `Window` is set to refer to a particular `SimpleWindow`, it will always refer to that `SimpleWindow`. Once a `WindowObject` is bound to a window, it does not make sense to make it move to or appear in a different `Window`.

The implementation of `WindowObject` is simple and straightforward and is given in Listing 13.3. Notice that the constructor has no body and that the implementations of the member functions are single-line functions.

From this base abstraction, `WindowObject`, we can now derive abstractions for the two-dimensional shapes and text labels. Let's first concentrate on the two-dimensional shapes. The additional attribute that all two-dimensional shapes have is a color. So from the base abstraction `WindowObject`, we derive a new abstraction called `Shape` that has a color. Because `Shape` is derived from `WindowObject`, it inherits the data members (i.e., `Window` and `Location`) and the corresponding member functions (i.e., `GetPosition()`, `GetWindow()`, and `SetPosition()`) from `WindowObject`. Another way to think about the relationship between a base class and a derived class is that the base class provides a set of common services for all the classes derived from it.

```
#include "wobject.h"
WindowObject::WindowObject(SimpleWindow &w,
  const Position &p) : Window(w), Location(p) {
    // No code needed!
}
Position WindowObject::GetPosition() const {
    return Location;
}
SimpleWindow& WindowObject::GetWindow() const {
    return Window;
}
void WindowObject::SetPosition(const Position &p) {
    Location = p;
}
```

Thus `WindowObject` provides the basic services necessary for all objects that will be displayed in a window.

At this point, we have one level of inheritance where `Shape` inherits the behaviors and attributes of `WindowObject`. As our previous discussions of inheritance have illustrated, inheritance can be multilevel. Using another level of inheritance, we can derive specific shape types from the class `Shape`. Three basic shapes that will be useful are rectangles, ellipses, and triangles. Each specific shape will have its own data members for storing the size of the shape because, of course, the size of each shape is specified somewhat differently. Figure 13.3 shows the data members related to size required for each shape type. Similarly, each derived shape will have its own draw member function because how a shape is rendered or drawn on the screen depends on what kind of shape it is.

Thus `EllipseShape` has two data members that are specific to it. They are `Width` and `Height`, which specify the horizontal and vertical diameters of the ellipse. Similarly, `RectangleShape` has two data members, `Width` and `Height`, which are the width and height of the rectangle. For the sake of simplicity, `TriangleShape` is an equilateral triangle where all sides have the same length. Consequently, `TriangleShape` has only one data member— `SideLength`. Figure 13.4 illustrates our hierarchy of window objects thus far.

Figure 13.3

*Shapes and their size
data members*

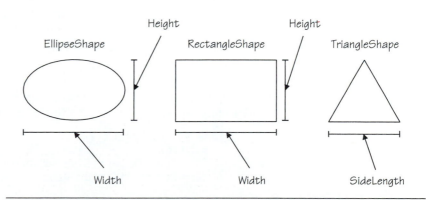

Figure 13.4

Hierarchy of window objects

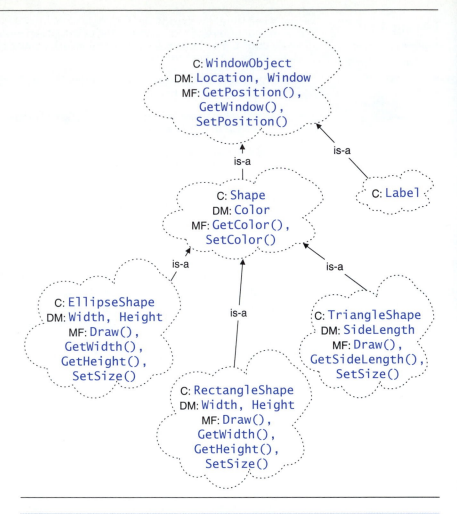

C: WindowObject
DM: Location, Window
MF: GetPosition(),
GetWindow(),
SetPosition()

is-a   is-a

C: Shape
DM: Color
MF: GetColor(),
SetColor()

C: Label

is-a   is-a   is-a

C: EllipseShape
DM: Width, Height
MF: Draw(),
GetWidth(),
GetHeight(),
SetSize()

C: TriangleShape
DM: SideLength
MF: Draw(),
GetSideLength(),
SetSize()

C: RectangleShape
DM: Width, Height
MF: Draw(),
GetWidth(),
GetHeight(),
SetSize()

Programming Tip

Inline member functions

Typically, we have divided a class into two separate components—the interface to the class (`.h` file) and the implementation of the class (`.cpp` file). For example, the interface to class `WindowObject` is contained in `wobject.h`, and the implementation is contained in `wobject.cpp`.

Generally, partitioning a class into an interface (`.h` file) and an implementation (`.cpp` file) is a good rule to follow. However, at times this rule needs to be broken. Sometimes for the sake of efficiency, we need to include the implementation with the interface. In the following code, for example, we include the implementation of `WindowObject` in the `.h` file.

```
class WindowObject {
    public:
        WindowObject(SimpleWindow &w,
          const Position &p);
```

```
            Position GetPosition() const;
            SimpleWindow &GetWindow() const;
            void SetPosition(const Position &p);
        private:
            SimpleWindow &Window;
            Position Location;
    };
    inline WindowObject::WindowObject(SimpleWindow &w,
     const Position &p) : Window(w), Location(p) {
        // No code needed!
    }
    inline Position WindowObject::GetPosition() const {
        return Location;
    }
    inline SimpleWindow& WindowObject::GetWindow()
    const {
        return Window;
    }
    inline void WindowObject::SetPosition(const Position
    &p) {
        Location = p;
    }
```

In addition, the reserved word **inline** has been added to the definitions of constructor and member functions. The **inline** modifier directs the compiler to replace a call to the function with the actual body of the function with the parameters substituted appropriately. This method avoids the overhead of a function call and for heavily used member functions can result in a significantly faster program. Inlining can also be obtained by defining the member functions in the class definition. However, this approach joins the interface and the implementation even more tightly, and we do not recommend it.

13.3.1 Declaring a derived class

To declare a derived class requires a simple addition to the syntax for declaring a class in order to specify the base class. The syntax for declaring a derived class is

Derived class name   Access specifier   Class name of base
                          (usually public)   class

```
    class  DerivedClass : public BaseClass {
    public:
        // public section
        ...
    private:
        // private section
        ...
    };
```

As noted, the access specifier is usually **public**, which says that the public members of the base class are public members of the derived class. This relationship is called *public inheritance*. We can also specify private and protected inheritance; these relationships are rarely used, and we will defer discussing them at this time.

The following code declares class Shape, which is derived from the base class WindowObject.

```
class Shape : public WindowObject {
    public:
        Shape(SimpleWindow &w, const Position &p,
          const color &c = Red);
        color GetColor() const;
        void SetColor(const color &c);
    private:
        color Color;
};
```

C++ programmers often read this as "Shape is a kind of WindowObject."

Other than the change to the first line, Shape's declaration follows our standard technique for declaring a new class. It contains the constructors along with the public member functions. The constructor for a shape has two required parameters—the window that contains the shape and the location to draw the shape. The parameter for color is optional because a default value is provided.

In addition to its constructor, Shape has two public member functions. The inspector GetColor() retrieves the color of the shape, and the mutator SetColor() changes the color. Finally, Shape has one private data member, Color. This data member holds the color of the shape.

From the class shape, we can create the classes for the specific shapes. The following code declares RectangleShape, which is derived from Shape.

```
class RectangleShape : public Shape {
    public:
        RectangleShape(SimpleWindow &Window,
          const Position &Center, const color &c = Red,
          float Width = 1.0, float Height = 2.0);
        float GetWidth() const;
        float GetHeight() const;
        void Draw();
        void SetSize(float Width, float Height);
    private:
        float Width;
        float Height;
};
```

In addition to its constructor, RectangleShape has four public member functions. Two inspectors retrieve the width and height of the rectangle, and SetSize() is a mutator for setting the width and height. Finally, the member function Draw() draws the rectangle. These member functions are specific to RectangleShape because their behavior (i.e., what they do) depends on the particular type of shape. For example, how a rectangle is drawn will be different from how an ellipse or triangle is drawn. Similarly, the parameters necessary to specify the size of a shape depend on the type of shape.

Finally, `RectangleShape` has two private data members, `Width` and `Height`. As in our original version of `RectangleShape`, these members hold the width and height of the rectangle.

Along with `RectangleShape`, we also want to create `EllipseShape` and `TriangleShape` abstractions. Their declarations are very similar to the `RectangleShape`'s declaration. Listing 13.4 contains the declaration for the derived class `EllipseShape`.

Listing 13.4

Declaration of EllipseShape from ellipse.h

```cpp
#ifndef ELLIPSESHAPE_H
#define ELLIPSESHAPE_H
#include "shape.h"
class EllipseShape : public Shape {
    public:
        EllipseShape(SimpleWindow &Window,
          const Position &Center, const color &c = Red,
          float Length = 1.0, float Height = 2.0)
        float GetWidth() const;
        float GetHeight() const;
        void Draw();
        void SetSize(float Width, float Height);
    private:
        float Width;
        float Height;
};
#endif
```

We see that the declaration of `EllipseShape` is nearly identical to `RectangleShape`. In fact, the only differences are the names of the classes and the private member data. Of course, the implementation of the member function `Draw()` will be different.

Listing 13.5 contains the declaration of the class `TriangleShape`. Again, the declaration is similar to the other shapes. The public member section contains a constructor, a draw function, and a set size function. However, for the triangle shape, the private section contains one data member—the length of the sides of the triangle. We need only one side because we have limited ourselves to working with equilateral triangles.

Listing 13.5

Declaration of TriangleShape from triangle.h

```cpp
#ifndef TRIANGLESHAPE_H
#define TRIANGLESHAPE_H
#include "shape.h"
class TriangleShape : public Shape {
    public:
        TriangleShape(SimpleWindow &w, const Position &p,
          const color &c = Red, float SideLength = 1.0);
        float GetSideLength() const;
        void SetSize(float SideLength);
        void Draw();
    private:
        float SideLength;
};
#endif
```

13.3.2 Implementing a derived class

As we have seen, declaring a derived class is not too different from declaring a base class. Similarly, the implementation of a derived class is not very different from the implementation of a base class. The key point to remember is that the derived class constructor essentially adds to a base class object the features needed to make that object into a derived class object; that is, a derived class is a specialization of the base class. Consequently, the constructor for the base class must be called to create a base class object before the constructor for the derived class can do its job. If you think about what inheritance means for a moment, this sequence makes sense. The base class object must exist before it can be turned into a derived class object.

To provide a convenient facility for creating an instance of the base class when an instance of the derived class is being created requires a small extension to how a constructor is specified. The syntax for the constructor of a derived class is

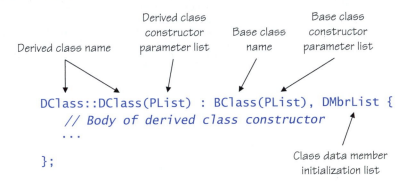

```
DClass::DClass(PList) : BClass(PList), DMbrList {
    // Body of derived class constructor
    ...
};
```

Notice that the first line includes a call to the base class constructor. For example, the implementation of the constructor for **Shape** is

```
Shape::Shape(SimpleWindow &w, const Position &p,
    const color &c) : WindowObject(w, p), Color(c) {
    // no code needed!
}
```

This constructor specifies that when a **Shape** object is defined, the constructor for **WindowObject** should be called and the window and position parameters w and p should be passed to it so a **WindowObject** with those attributes can be created. The constructor for the base class is called before the body of the derived class constructor is executed. This sequence makes sense because the base object forms the basis for the derived object (we need the base object before we turn it into a derived object). After the base object is instantiated and it is turned into a derived object, the constructors for any data members that are on the data member initialization list are invoked. **Shape**'s attribute **Color** is initialized in this way. The last step is to execute the code in the body of the constructor. In **Shape**'s case, everything has been handled by the constructor of the base class and the constructor of the data attribute **Color**. Consequently, no code is needed.

Programming Tip

The constructors for the classes derived from `Shape` are similar. In these, however, the constructors for the specific shapes use the constructor for `Shape`, which in turn uses the constructor for `WindowObject`. For example, the implementation of the constructor for `RectangleShape` is

```
RectangleShape::RectangleShape(SimpleWindow &Window,
  const Position &Center, const color &c, float w,
  float h) : Shape(Window, Center, c),
  Width(w), Height(h) {
     // no code needed!
}
```

This constructor specifies that when a `RectangleShape` object is defined, the constructor for `Shape` should be called and the window, position, and color parameters should be passed to it. The `Shape` constructor will, of course, use the `WindowObject` constructor to initialize the window and position data members.

For example, when the definition

```
RectangleShape Lawn(TWindow, LeftCorner, Green,
  2.5, 3.5);
```

is executed, the first action taken by the compiler is to invoke the `Shape` constructor with the arguments `TWindow`, `LeftCorner`, and `Green`. The implementation of `Shape`'s constructor invokes `WindowObject`'s constructor with the values for `TWindow` and `LeftCorner`. At this point a `WindowObject` is instantiated, the constructors for `Window` and `Location` are invoked, and the empty body of the `WindowObject` constructor is invoked. Then a `Shape` object is instantiated, and the constructor for `Color` is called to initialize it with the value c. Next the body of `Shape`'s constructor is executed, which also requires no code. Finally, a `RectangleShape Lawn` is instantiated, and the `Width` and `Height` constructors are called to initialize them. The last step is to invoke the body of `RectangleShape`'s constructor. Again, no code is needed because the constructor of the parent class and the constructors for the data members have done all the work.

The constructors for the other derived classes are similar. The constructor for the ellipse shape is

```
EllipseShape::EllipseShape(SimpleWindow &Window,
   const Position &Center, const color &c, float w,
   float h) : Shape(Window, Center, c),
   Width(w), Height(h)  {
      // no code needed!
}
```

and the constructor for `TriangleShape` is

```
TriangleShape::TriangleShape(SimpleWindow &Window,
   const Position &p, const color &c, float l)
   : Shape(Window, p, c), SideLength(l) {
      // no code needed!
}
```

The interesting thing to note about these constructors is that they are very short. In fact, we did not need to write any code for the body of the constructors! The reason is that we are able to use the code we developed for the parent class, `Shape`. Although our classes are pretty simple and the savings are not that great, you can imagine that if the classes were even a little bit more complex, the savings would be substantial.

The syntax for defining the implementation of the member functions of a derived class is identical to the syntax for defining the implementation of the member functions of a base class. The syntax is

```
                Derived class    Member     Member function
Return type        name         function    parameter list


    Type CName::MFunction(PList) {
          // Body of derived class member function
          ...

    };
```

For example, the implementation of `RectangleShape`'s `SetSize()` member function is

```
void RectangleShape::SetSize(float w, float h) {
    Width = w;
    Height = h;
    return;
}
```

This mutator function just changes the value of `RectangleShape`'s size attributes, `Width` and `Height`.

Similarly, the implementation of the `Draw()` member function for `RectangleShape` is

```
void RectangleShape::Draw() {
    const Position Center = GetPosition();
    const float Width = GetWidth();
    const float Height = GetHeight();
```

```
    const Position UpperLeft = Center
      + Position(-.5 * Width, -.5 * Height);
    const Position LowerRight = Center
      + Position(.5 * Width, .5 * Height);
    GetWindow().RenderRectangle(UpperLeft,  LowerRight,
      GetColor());
    return;
}
```

`RectangleShape`'s draw member function calls `RenderRectangle()`, which is a member function of the EzWindows class `SimpleWindow`. RenderRectangle paints the rectangle in the window. The parameters to this function are the coordinates of the upper-left and lower-right corners of the rectangle and the color to paint the rectangle. Because our abstraction of a rectangle contained the width and height of the rectangle in centimeters and the location of the center of the rectangle, `Draw()` has to compute coordinates of the upper-left and lower-right corners of the rectangle. This task is simple given the center of the rectangle and its length and width.

Other low-level member functions of the `SimpleWindow` class that we will use are `RenderEllipse()` and `RenderPolygon()`. `RenderEllipse()` is similar to `RenderRectangle()`. The parameters to it are the coordinates of the bounding box of the ellipse and the color of the ellipse. The bounding box is defined to be the rectangle that contains the ellipse. This relationship is illustrated in Figure 13.5.

Figure 13.5

Relationship of an ellipse to its bounding box

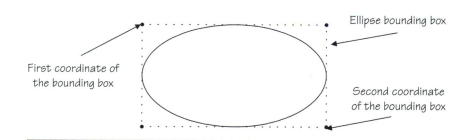

First coordinate of the bounding box

Ellipse bounding box

Second coordinate of the bounding box

The implementation of `EllipseShape`'s `Draw()` function is similar to that of `RectangleShape`'s `Draw()`. The code is

```
void EllipseShape::Draw() {
    const Position Center = GetPosition();
    const float Width = GetWidth();
    const float Height = GetHeight();
    const Position UpperLeft = Center
      + Position(-.5 * Width, -.5 * Height);
    const Position LowerRight = Center
      + Position(.5 * Width, .5 * Height);
    GetWindow().RenderEllipse(UpperLeft, LowerRight,
      GetColor());
    return;
}
```

Construction order

The C++ standard specifies that the constructors for the members of a class are called in the order the members appear in the class declaration—not in the order that the constructors appear on the data member initialization list. Consider the following class declaration for `Obj`.

```
class Obj {
    public:
        Obj(float xCoord, float yCoord,
          const color &c);
        ...
    private:
        Position MyPosition;
        color MyColor;
};
```

The implementation of the constructor for `Obj` is

```
Obj::Obj(float x, float y, const color &c) :
  MyColor(c), MyPosition(x, y) {
    // no code needed!
}
```

When a definition like

```
Obj BlueObj(3.5, 4.6, Blue);
```

is executed, the constructor for `MyPosition` is called before the constructor for `MyColor` because `MyPosition` appears before `MyColor` in the class declaration. To avoid confusion, we recommend putting the data member initializations in the same order as they appear in the class declaration.

In a manner similar to `RectangleShape`'s draw function, the code creates `Position` objects for the coordinates of the bounding box, using the center of the ellipse and the width and height of the ellipse.

The implementation of the `TriangleShape`'s draw member function is a bit more complicated. The low-level routine available for drawing a triangle is called `RenderPolygon`. This function requires three arguments. The first is an array of `Position` objects, or the locations of the vertices of the polygon to draw. The second argument is the number of vertices contained in the array, and the final argument is the color of the polygon. To do its job, `Triangle-Shape`'s draw function must compute the vertices of the triangle. Because we have restricted ourselves to equilateral triangles, the job is not too complicated.

The center of the triangle is located at the intersection of the three lines that bisect the angles at the vertices of the triangle. Figure 13.6 shows an equilateral triangle with the bisecting lines drawn. We assume that the center of the triangle is given by the position (x, y). From this diagram we can see that the position of vertex 1 is $(x, y - r)$, vertex 2 is $(x - b, y + a)$, and vertex 3 is $(x + b, y + a)$. Of course, we know that b is ∫ the length of the side of the triangle. Using the following basic trigonometric functions

$$\tan\theta = \frac{a}{b} \text{ and } \cos\theta = \frac{b}{c}$$

and the fact that θ is 30 degrees, we can compute the length of a and c. The equation for a is

$$a = \tan 30 \cdot b, \text{ and substituting } \frac{l}{2} \text{ for } b \text{ yields } a = \tan 30 \cdot \frac{l}{2}$$

Similarly, the equation for c is

$$c = \frac{b}{\cos 30}, \text{ and substituting } \frac{l}{2} \text{ for } b \text{ yields } c = \frac{l}{2 \cdot \cos 30}$$

Figure 13.6

A triangle, its center, and its vertices

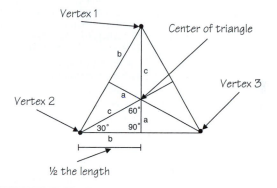

We can now write the code to compute the vertices of an equilateral triangle given its center and the length of its sides. However, one small detail remains. Recall from Chapter 5 that the argument to the trigonometric functions is the angle in radians. One degree is $\pi \div 180$ radians. The code for computing the lengths of the segments c and a is

```
const double Pi = 3.1415;
const float SLength = GetSideLength();
float c = SLength / (2.0 * cos(30 * Pi / 180.0));
float a = tan(30 * Pi / 180.0) * .5 * SLength;
```

With the length of these segments computed, we can create a vector of positions to pass to `RenderPolygon`. Vector elements must be initialized by assigning to each vector element. The code for creating the necessary vector of positions is

```
vector<Position> TrianglePoints(3);
TrianglePoints[0] = Center + Position(0, -c);
TrianglePoints[1] = Center
 + Position(-.5 * SLength, a);
TrianglePoints[2] = Center
 + Position( .5 * SLength, a);
```

and we can now send a message to the window containing the triangle to render the rectangle. The call is

```
GetWindow().RenderPolygon(TrianglePoints, 3,
  GetColor());
```

The complete implementation of `TriangleShape`'s draw function is

```
void TriangleShape::Draw() {
    const float Pi = 3.1415;
    const Position Center = GetPosition();
    const float SLength = GetSideLength();

    // Compute c, the distance from center of the
    // triangle to the top vertex, and a, the
    // distance from the center to the base
    float c = SLength / (2.0 * cos(30 * Pi
    / 180.0));
    float a = tan(30 * Pi / 180.0) * .5 * SLength;

    // Create an array containing the positions of
    // the vertices of the triangle
    vector<Position> TrianglePoints(3);
    TrianglePoints[0] = Center + Position(0, -c);
    TrianglePoints[1] = Center
    + Position(-.5 * SLength, a);
    TrianglePoints[2] = Center
    + Position( .5 * SLength, a);

    // Draw the triangle
    GetWindow().RenderPolygon(TrianglePoints, 3,
    GetColor());
    return;
}
```

To check out our new classes, we should write a program that displays the three shapes in a window to ensure that our code is working properly. The program we will write will display the three shapes centered in a window and aligned along their bottoms. To display the shapes, we will use the EzWindows's `SimpleWindow` class. The global declaration of the window that will contain the shapes is

```
SimpleWindow TestWindow("TestShapes", 17.0, 7.0,
  Position(4.0, 4.0));
```

which will create a window called `TestWindow` with its upper-left corner located 4 centimeters from the left edge of the screen and 4 centimeters from the top of the screen. The window will be 17 centimeters wide and 7 centimeters high. `TestWindow` will be labeled "TestShapes."

Recall that the EzWindows API calls the function `ApiMain()` for any initial processing, and for this simple program, `ApiMain()` will instantiate and draw the shapes. The code to create our shapes is quite simple. The entire routine is

```
int ApiMain() {
    TestWindow.Open();
    TriangleShape T(TestWindow, Position(3.5, 3.5),
    Red, 3.0);
    T.Draw();
    RectangleShape R(TestWindow, Position(8.5, 3.5),
```

```
        Yellow, 3.0, 2.0);
    R.Draw();
    EllipseShape E(TestWindow, Position(13.5, 3.5),
        Green, 3.0, 2.0);
    E.Draw();
    return 0;
}
```

When EzWindows receives a message from the operating system that a window under its control should be closed, it calls `ApiEnd()` to do any cleanup. In our test program, the only cleanup is to close the window as shown in the following code:

```
int ApiEnd() {
    TestWindow.Close();
    return 0;
}
```

Figure 13.7 shows the resulting window. From this output, we can see that the new shapes appear to be implemented correctly. Of course, this simple test by no means constitutes an adequate testing of our shape class hierarchy. Much more thorough testing would be required in practice.

Figure 13.7

Displaying test shapes

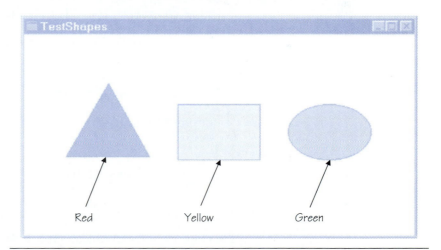

Self-check Questions

1.   What is the relationship that implies containment?

2.   What is the relationship that implies inheritance?

3.   A class that is created from another class via inheritances is called a _____ class.

4.   The class at the top of the inheritance hierarchy is known as the
      _____ class.

5.   What is the output of the following program?

```cpp
#include <iostream>
#include <string>
using namespace std;
class Widget {
    public:
        Widget(int x);
    private:
        int Value;
};
Widget::Widget(int x) : Value(x) {
    cout << "Made Widget: " << Value << endl;
}
class BaseClass {
    public:
        BaseClass(int x);
    private:
        Widget W1;
};
class DerivedClass : public BaseClass {
    public:
        DerivedClass(int y);
    private:
        Widget W2;
};
BaseClass::BaseClass(int x) :  W1(x) {
}
DerivedClass::DerivedClass(int x) : BaseClass(x),
 W2(x+1) {
}
int main() {
    DerivedClass B(10);
    return 0;
}
```

6.   The following is the EzWindow class declaration for `WindowObject`.

```cpp
class WindowObject {
    public:
        WindowObject(SimpleWindow &w,
         const Position &p);
        Position GetPosition() const;
        void GetPosition(float &x, float &y) const;
        SimpleWindow &GetWindow() const;
        void SetPosition(const Position &p);
        void SetPosition(float x, float y);
    private:
        SimpleWindow &Window;
        Position Location;
};
```

Create a new class called `Menu` that will be derived from `WindowObject`. This will allow a menu to be created within a `SimpleWindow`. In addition to the data members inherited from `WindowObject`. Class `Menu` will have the following data members.

- A pointer to a dynamically allocated array of pointers to `BitMaps`. Call this data member `Buttons`. The bitmaps will be the buttons of the menu.

- An integer that indicates the maximum number of buttons in the menu. Call this data member `NumberOfButtons`.

- An integer that is an index into the array `Buttons`. It indicates the next free slot to add a button (see function `AddButton` below). Call this data member `NextFreeSlot`.

In addition to the member functions inherited from `WindowObject`, class `Menu` will have the following public member functions.

- A constructor that accepts three arguments. The first is a reference to a `SimpleWindow`. The menu will be drawn in this window. The second is a constant reference to a `Position`. This will be the location of the menu within the window. The default value should be `Position(0.0, 0.0)`. The third is an integer that indicates the number of buttons in the menu. The default value should be 6.

- A function for adding a button to the menu. Call this function `AddButton`. `AddButton` takes a single parameter: a constant pointer to a `BitMap`. `AddButton` uses `NextFreeSlot` to add the button to the array `Buttons`.

- A function for displaying the menu. Call this function `Display`. It takes no parameters.

Give the implementations of the member functions of class `Menu`.

13.4 PROTECTED MEMBERS AND INHERITANCE

An important feature of C++ is its ability to control access to the members of a class. In our previous examples, we used the keywords **public** and **private** to control access to members of a class. The keyword **protected** signals a third level of access. In terms of a base class, protected members are like private members. They are accessible only by member functions of the class. To illustrate, consider the following code:

```
class SomeClass {
    public:
        void MemberFunction();
        int PublicData;
    protected:
        int ProtectedData;
    private:
        int PrivateData;
};
```

```
void SomeClass::MemberFunction() {
    PublicData = 1;      // access allowed
    ProtectedData = 2;  // access allowed
    PrivateData = 3;     // access allowed
}
void NonMemberFunction() {
    SomeClass C;
    C.PublicData = 1;        // access allowed
    C.ProtectedData = 2;     // illegal
    C.PrivateData = 3;       // illegal
}
```

The member function `MemberFunction()` can access data members in all three sections. However, the nonmember function `NonMemberFunction()` can only access the member data in the public section. The data in the protected and private sections are not accessible.

Based on this example, you might wonder what the difference between protected and private membership is. The difference becomes apparent when a new class is publicly derived from a base class. Consider the following base and derived class declarations:

```
class BaseClass {
    public:
        int PublicData;
    protected:
        int ProtectedData;
    private:
        int PrivateData;
};
class DerivedClass : public BaseClass {
    public:
        void DerivedClassFunction();
    private:
    // Details omitted
};
```

The derived class member functions have access to the public and protected members of the base class, but not to the private members. `DerivedClass-Function()` illustrates a publicly derived member function's access to the members of the base class.

```
void DerivedClass::DerivedClassFunction() {
    PublicData = 1;         // access allowed
    ProtectedData = 2;      // access allowed
    PrivateData = 3;        // illegal
}
```

We should note that although we have used access to data members to illustrate C++'s protection mechanism, the protection mechanism applies to member functions as well.

The question arises as to when one should use protected members in designing a base class. This question has two answers. One answer we can give now; the other must be deferred until we discuss protected and private inheritance in Section 13.5.

In our hierarchy of shapes, we did not use a protected section. The justification is that the derived shapes (e.g., `RectangleShape` or `TriangleShape`) have access to their ancestor data members through inherited public inspector functions. This strategy works well, and it hides the representation of the ancestor class data members from the derived class. However, in some cases accessing inherited class member data through inspectors might be more expensive in terms of run time than accessing them directly. In cases where efficiency outweighs other design considerations, one might be able to justify the use of protected data. In this way, the member functions of the derived class could have direct access to the data held by the base class.

To illustrate, suppose we revised the declaration of the class WindowObject to be

```
class WindowObject {
    public:
        WindowObject(SimpleWindow &Window,
          const Position &p);
        Position GetPosition() const;
        SimpleWindow &GetWindow() const;
        void SetPosition(const Position &p);
    protected:
        Position Center;
        SimpleWindow &Window;
};
```

and Shape to be

```
class Shape : public WindowObject {
    public:
        Shape(SimpleWindow &Window, const Position &p,
          const color &c = Red);
        color GetColor() const;
        void SetColor(const color &c);
    protected:
        color Color;
};
```

That is, the member data are now declared in protected sections. This arrangement allows member functions of a class publicly derived from WindowObject and Shape to directly access this data. For example, with these class declarations RectangleShape's Draw member function could be implemented as

```
void RectangleShape::Draw() {
    const Position UpperLeft = Center
     + Position(-.5 * Width, -.5 * Height);
    const Position LowerRight = Center
     + Position(.5 * Width, .5 * Height);
    GetWindow().RenderRectangle(UpperLeft,
     LowerRight, GetColor());
}
```

Just as in the other implementations of RectangleShape's Draw member function, function GetWindow() is inherited from WindowObject and function GetColor() is inherited from Shape. However, in this version the calls to the public inspector functions have been removed and Shape's relevant data members (i.e., Width and Height) are accessed directly. We generally avoid accessing data members directly. It makes the implementation of the class less flexible because changes to data members will affect all member functions, not just the inspectors.

13.5 CONTROLLING INHERITANCE

The second answer to why one might use a protected section has to do with the kind of inheritance that is used. Let's examine all three types of inheritance: public, private, and protected.

13.5.1 Public inheritance

In our previous examples of inheritance involving the `Shape` class, we used public inheritance. For example, the declaration of the `RectangleShape` was

```
class RectangleShape: public Shape {
    public:
        // details omitted
    private:
        // details omitted
};
```

This declaration specifies that the public members of `Shape` are public members of `RectangleShape` and permits users of `RectangleShape` objects to use `Shape`'s public functions. For example, the following code

```
RectangleShape R(Window, P1);
R.SetColor(Green);    // Use member function of Shape
R.Draw();
```

works because `Shape`'s `SetColor` member function is publicly available to users of `RectangleShape`. With public inheritance, the members of the derived class inherited from the base class have the same protection as they did in the base class. Public inheritance is almost always used in practice because it models the *is-a* relationship.

13.5.2 Private inheritance

To illustrate private inheritance, consider the following revised declaration of `RectangleShape`:

```
class RectangleShape: private Shape {
    public:
        // details omitted
    protected:
        // details omitted
    private:
        // details omitted
};
```

The access specifier has been changed to **private**. With this declaration in effect, the code

```
RectangleShape R(Window, P1);
R.SetColor(Green);
```

R.Draw();

would be illegal. That is, users of RectangleShape are denied access to Shape's public member functions because they are private members of RectangleShape. With private inheritance, the public and protected members of the base class become private members of the derived class. In effect, users of the derived class have no access to the facilities provided by the base class. Interestingly, the private members of the base class are inaccessible to the member functions of the derived class.

Private inheritance is used much less frequently than public inheritance. It is useful when the facilities of the base class are not part of the interface the user will see or the derived class will use. Private inheritance hides the base class from the user, and so it is possible to change the implementation of the base class or remove it all together without requiring any changes to the user of the interface. When an access specifier is not present in the declaration of a derived class, private inheritance is used. Because situations where the use of private inheritance is appropriate are rare and other methods can achieve the same effect, we will defer discussion of its use to more advanced textbooks.

13.5.3 Protected inheritance

With protected inheritance, public and protected members of the base class become protected members of the derived class, and private members of the base class become private members of the derived class. Protected inheritance is appropriate when the facilities or capabilities of the base class are useful in the implementation of the derived class, but are not part of the interface the user of the derived class will see. Protected inheritance is used even less frequently than private inheritance. Table 13.1 summarizes the effects of the three types of inheritance on the accessibility of the members of a derived class. The entry inaccessible indicates that the derived class has no access to the base class member.

Table 13.1

Types of inheritance and the resulting access they permit

Inheritance Type	Base Class Member Access	Derived Class Member Access
public	public	public
	protected	protected
	private	*inaccessible*
protected	public	protected
	protected	protected
	private	*inaccessible*
private	public	private
	protected	private
	private	*inaccessible*

Self-check Questions

7.   Fill in the following table to show how the different inheritance access specifiers affect the ability of the derived class's member functions to access a base class's members.

Inheritance Specifier	Public Members	Protected Members	Private Members
`public`			
`protected`			
`private`			

8.   What is wrong with the following program?

```cpp
#include <iostream>
#include <string>
using namespace std;
class Widget {
    public:
        Widget(int x);
        int GetValue() const;
    private:
        int Value;
};
Widget::Widget(int x) : Value(x) {
    cout << "Made Widget: " << Value << endl;
}
int Widget::GetValue() const {
    return Value;
}
class BaseClass {
    public:
        BaseClass(int x);
        void Print();
    private:
        Widget W1;
};
class DerivedClass : private BaseClass {
    public:
        DerivedClass(int y);
    private:
        Widget W2;
};
BaseClass::BaseClass(int x) :  W1(x) {
}
void BaseClass::Print() {
    cout << W1.GetValue() << endl;
}
```

```
DerivedClass::DerivedClass(int x) : BaseClass(x),
  W2(x+1) {
}
int main() {
    DerivedClass B(10);
    B.Print();
    return 0;
}
```

9.   Is the following a legal program? If so, what does it output?

```
#include <iostream>
#include <string>
using namespace std;
class Widget {
    public:
        Widget(int x);
        int GetValue() const;
    private:
        int Value;
};
Widget::Widget(int x) : Value(x) {
    cout << "Made Widget: " << Value << endl;
}
int Widget::GetValue() const {
    return Value;
}
class BaseClass {
    public:
        BaseClass(int x);
    protected:
        Widget &GetValue();
    private:
        Widget W1;
};
class DerivedClass : protected BaseClass {
    public:
        DerivedClass(int y);
        void Print();
};
BaseClass::BaseClass(int x) :  W1(x) {
}

Widget& BaseClass::GetValue() {
    return W1;
}
DerivedClass::DerivedClass(int x) : BaseClass(x) {
}
void DerivedClass::Print() {
    Widget w1 = GetValue();
    cout << "Value is " << w1.GetValue() << endl;
}

int main() {
    DerivedClass B(10);
    B.Print();
    return 0;
}
```

10.   In the previous question, change `DerivedClass` to use private inheritance. Does the program work? Explain why.

11.   Is the following a legal program? If so, what does it output?

```cpp
#include <iostream>
#include <string>
using namespace std;
class Widget {
    public:
        Widget(int x);
    protected:
        int GetValue() const;
    private:
        int Value;
};
Widget::Widget(int x) : Value(x) {
    cout << "Made Widget: " << Value << endl;
}
int Widget::GetValue() const {
    return Value;
}

class BaseClass {
    public:
        BaseClass(int x);
    protected:
        Widget &GetValue();
    private:
        Widget W1;
};
class DerivedClass : protected BaseClass {
    public:
        DerivedClass(int y);
        void Print();
};
BaseClass::BaseClass(int x) :  W1(x) {
}

Widget& BaseClass::GetValue() {
    return W1;
}
DerivedClass::DerivedClass(int x) : BaseClass(x) {
}
void DerivedClass::Print() {
    Widget w1 = GetValue();
    cout << "Value is " << w1.GetValue() << endl;
}
int main() {
    DerivedClass B(10);
    B.Print();
    return 0;
}
```

13.6 MULTIPLE INHERITANCE

In our shape hierarchy thus far, we used single inheritance. That is, each derived class had a single parent. C++ also supports multiple inheritance. With multiple inheritance, a derived class can inherit from two or more base classes. The derived class inherits the attributes and behaviors of all parents.

To illustrate the concept of multiple inheritance, suppose we have been asked to redesign a bank's computerized accounts system to use object-oriented technology. We first design a base class called **Basic**. This class encapsulates the base set of attributes and actions for any account. Among other capabilities, such a class would certainly maintain a balance, keep a record of transactions, and provide the ability to print the transactions. From **BasicAccount**, we could derive specialized types of accounts. Some candidate account types might be **Loan**, **Interest**, **Checking**, and **Brokerage**. Figure 13.8 shows our inheritance hierarchy thus far.

Figure 13.8

A basic account inheritance hierarchy

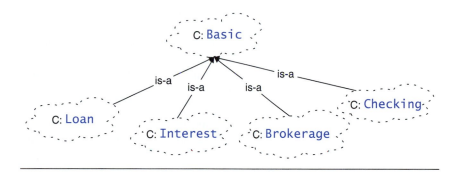

Now we also want to offer other types of accounts such as checking accounts that pay interest or brokerage accounts that allow checks to be written. These new types of accounts can be created using multiple inheritance. An **InterestChecking** account can be created by deriving many of its capabilities and features from the **Checking** and **Interest** account types. Similarly, a **BrokerageChecking** account can be created from **Checking** and **Brokerage** accounts. The new inheritance hierarchy is shown in Figure 13.9.

Multiple inheritance provides a way to create a new class that is the intersection of two existing classes. For example, an **InterestChecking** account can invoke all the public member functions of **Interest** and **Checking** accounts. Thus an **InterestChecking** account is both an **Interest** account and a **Checking** account.

Multiple inheritance provides a powerful capability for creating new abstractions. This power is not without some peril. To illustrate both its power and some of its problems, let's use multiple inheritance to extend our hierarchy of window objects.

In our hierarchy (refer to Figure 13.4), a **Label** class that we have not yet developed was shown. Let's design and implement **Label** so we can use it to

Figure 13.9

*Account hierarchy
with multiple
inheritance*

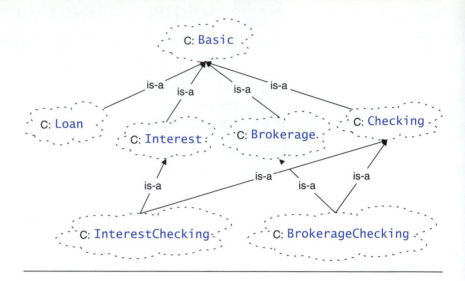

illustrate multiple inheritance. Recall the purpose of the label class was to provide the capability to place text objects in a window. Thus one of the private data members of `Label` should be the text string. In addition, we need a data member that specifies the background color to use when we display the text. We could also include data members that specify the font, the size of the font, and the color of the text, but in the interest of simplicity, we defer these extensions for the exercises. In terms of behaviors, we will need mutators and inspectors for the private data members and a member function that causes the text to be written to the window. Thus the class declaration of `Label` is

```
class Label : public WindowObject {
    public:
        Label(SimpleWindow &w, const Position &p,
          const string &Text,
          const color &Color = White);
        color GetColor() const;
        void SetColor(const color &c);
        void Draw();
    private:
        color Color;
        string Text;
};
```

Listing 13.6 contains the implementation of `Label`. With few exceptions, the code is similar to the various shape classes we have implemented. `Label`'s constructor uses member data constructors to do all the work. Member function `Draw()` is similar to the draw functions for the shape classes. It computes a bounding box required by `SimpleWindow` member function `RenderText` to paint the string in the correct position.

`Label` enables us to label objects on the screen. To illustrate its usefulness, let's modify our test program for displaying shapes so that the shapes are labeled with their class names. With `Label` available, this modification

Listing 13.6

Implementation of class Label from label.cpp

```cpp
#include <assert.h>
#include "label.h"
Label::Label(SimpleWindow &w, const Position &p,
 const string &t, const color &c) : WindowObject(w, p),
 Text(t), Color(c) {
    // No code needed!
}
color Label::GetColor() const {
    return Color;
}
void Label::SetColor(const color &c) {
    Color = c;
}
void Label::Draw() {
    Position Center = GetPosition();
    Position UpperLeft = Center + Position(-2.0, -2.0);
    Position LowerRight = Center + Position(2.0, 2.0);
    GetWindow().RenderText(UpperLeft, LowerRight,
     Text, GetColor());
}
```

requires only a few additions to ApiMain(). After drawing a shape, we just need to instantiate a label object positioned under the shape and display it.

Listing 13.7 contains the revised ApiMain(). In addition to adding the labels, the test program has been parameterized so that it is easy to change the size of the window and have the size of the shapes scale accordingly. The code for ApiEnd() is unchanged. Figure 13.10 shows the window created when the revised program runs.

Listing 13.7

A test program for class Label

```cpp
#include "label.h"
#include "triangle.h"
#include "rect.h"
#include "ellipse.h"
using namespace std;
const float WindowWidth = 14.0;
const float WindowHeight = 3.0;
SimpleWindow TestWindow("TestShapes",
 WindowWidth, WindowHeight, Position(2.0, 2.0));
// ApiMain(): draw shapes and label them
int ApiMain() {
    // Put a 1-centimeter gap between shapes and the
    // edge of the screen
    float ShapeWidth = (WindowWidth - 4.0) / 3.0;
    float ShapeHeight = WindowHeight - 2.0;
    Position ShapeCenter((ShapeWidth / 2.0) + 1.0,
     WindowHeight / 2.0);
    Position LabelCenter((ShapeWidth / 2.0) + 1.0,
     (WindowHeight / 2.0) + ShapeHeight / 2.0 + 0.75);
    TestWindow.Open();

    // Draw a triangle and label it
    TriangleShape T(TestWindow, ShapeCenter, Red,
     ShapeWidth);
    T.Draw();
    Label TLabel(TestWindow, LabelCenter,
     "Triangle", White);
    TLabel.Draw();
```

```
    // Draw a rectangle and label it
    ShapeCenter = ShapeCenter
     + Position(ShapeWidth + 1.0, 0.0);
    RectangleShape R(TestWindow, ShapeCenter, Yellow,
     ShapeWidth, ShapeHeight);
    R.Draw();
    LabelCenter = LabelCenter
     + Position(ShapeWidth + 1.0, 0.0);
    Label RLabel(TestWindow, LabelCenter,
     "Rectangle", White);
    RLabel.Draw();

    // Draw an ellipse and label it
    ShapeCenter = ShapeCenter
     + Position(ShapeWidth + 1.0, 0.0);
    EllipseShape E(TestWindow, ShapeCenter, Green,
     ShapeWidth, ShapeHeight);
    E.Draw();
    LabelCenter = LabelCenter
     + Position(ShapeWidth + 1.0, 0.0);
    Label ELabel(TestWindow, LabelCenter,
     "Ellipse", White);
    ELabel.Draw();

    return 0;
}
```

Figure 13.10

Test shape display

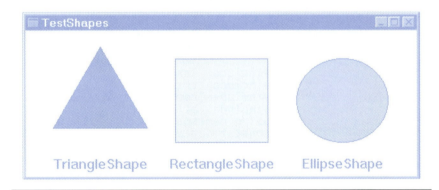

The window object `Label` is quite useful. We can use it to label shapes and print messages in windows. Label will also be useful if we want to create new types of shapes that contain labels. For instance, suppose we need to create a new type of shape for use on black and while monitors. Because the monitor is black and white, we need a way to indicate the color of the shape. We can do this by placing a label in the middle of the shape to indicate its color. Recall that the colors supported by EzWindows are white, red, yellow, green, blue, magenta, and cyan. Therefore, we can use the first letter of the color to label the shape with its color. We want to create new types of shapes that have both the properties of regular shapes and labels. To create these new types of shapes, we make use of multiple inheritance. As you will see, it is the most efficient and simplest way to create these new types of shapes. Indeed, very little new code needs to be written.

To illustrate the multiple inheritance, we will create a new object called `LabeledEllipseShape`, which is derived from `EllipseShape` and `Label`. Figure 13.11 shows the inheritance hierarchy. Labeled versions of the other shapes can be created analogously, and doing so is left as an exercise.

Figure 13.11

The multiple inheritance relationship of LabeledEllipseShape

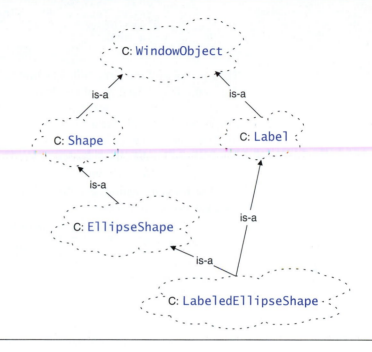

The syntax for declaring a class derived using multiple inheritance is

```
class DClass : public BClass, public BClass {
  public:
        // public section
    ...
  private:
        // private section
    ...

};
```

This syntax is similar to the one specifying a single inheritance. The only difference is that more than one class is being used as a basis for the new class.

The declaration for class `LabeledEllipseShape` is

```
class LabeledEllipseShape : public Label,
 public EllipseShape {
   public:
      LabeledEllipseShape(SimpleWindow &w,
         const Position &Center, const color &c = Red,
         string Text = "R", float Width = 1.0,
         float Height = 2.0);
      void Draw();
};
```

The constructor for a `LabeledEllipseShape` specifies the window, the position of the shape, the color of the shape, the text to label it with, and the size of the ellipse to create. `Draw()` is the only public member function. It will, of course, display the ellipse in the window. The default text to label the ellipse is the first letter of the default color of the ellipse. Labeling the ellipse with its color is useful if the ellipse is used in a program that will be run on a computer with a monochrome monitor.

The implementation of `LabeledEllipseShape` is equally simple. The code for its constructor is

```
LabeledEllipseShape::LabeledEllipseShape(
 SimpleWindow &w, const Position &Center,
 const color c, string t, float Width, float Height)
 : EllipseShape(w, Center, c, Width, Height),
 Label(w, Center, t, c)  {
    // no code needed!
}
```

We see that `LabeledEllipseShape`'s constructor calls the constructors for the two base classes to initialize the data members. They do all the work, and no code is required in the body of the constructor.

The implementation of `LabeledEllipseShape`'s `Draw()` member function brings to light some interesting issues. The code for it is

```
void LabeledEllipseShape::Draw() {
    EllipseShape::Draw();
    Label::Draw();
}
```

Notice the calls to the two `Draw()` member functions. When a new class is created via multiple inheritance, it inherits all the behaviors and capabilities of the base classes. Thus `LabeledEllipseShape` inherits a draw function from both `Label` and `EllipseShape`. This situation is called a *name ambiguity* because when `LabeledEllipseShape` refers to `Draw()`, it is not clear which one should be invoked. We can solve this problem by using the scope resolution operator to specify a member. Thus to draw a `LabeledEllipseShape`, we call `EllipseShape`'s draw function to draw the ellipse and `Label`'s draw function to draw the label.

It is worth noting that because `EllipseShape` and `Label` were derived from the same class, `WindowObject`, and `LabeledEllipseShape` is derived from `EllipseShape` and `Label`, `LabeledEllipseShape` has two instances of everything in a `WindowObject`. It has two `GetWindow()` member func-

Programmer Alert

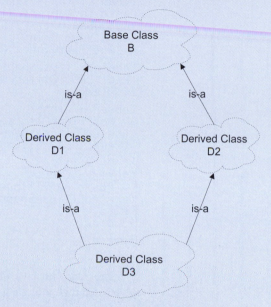

Diamond inheritance hierarchies

Multiple inheritance is a powerful mechanism, but it can create potentially troublesome problems. Consider the following situation. We have two derived classes that are derived from the same base class B. Let's call the derived classes D1 and D2. From these two classes, we create a new class called D3 using multiple inheritance. Remember with inheritance the derived class inherits all the properties and members of the base class. Thus, D1 and D2 inherit the data members of B. Similarly, D3 inherits the data members of D1 and D2. Here's the catch. Both D1 and D2 have the data members of B, so now D3 has two copies of the data members of class B. Pictorially, this looks like the following.

You can see the resemblance of the figure to a diamond. The question is whether you really want two copies of B's data members in D3. Probably not. This situation also causes interesting problems with pointers. Generally one should avoid this type of multiple inheritance hierarchy.

tions, two `GetPosition()` member functions, and two `SetPosition()` member functions. Similarly, it has two instances of the private member data `Center` and `Window`. In general, this duplication causes no problems, and if a particular member function must be invoked, the scope resolution operator can select the appropriate one.

As our `LabeledEllipseShape` example shows, multiple inheritance allows us to create new, powerful classes with a minimum of effort. Without writing very much new code, we created a new class with useful properties. The following code tests `LabeledEllipseShape`.

```cpp
#include <assert.h>
#include "lellipse.h"
const float WindowWidth = 10.0;
const float WindowHeight = 3.0;
SimpleWindow TestWindow("TestShapes",
 WindowWidth, WindowHeight, Position(2.0, 2.0));
// ApiMain(): open the window; create and draw
// the shapes
int ApiMain() {
    // Put a 1-centimeter gap between ellipses
    // and the edge of the screen
    float EllipseWidth = (WindowWidth - 4.0) / 3.0;
    float EllipseHeight = WindowHeight - 2.0;
    Position Center((EllipseWidth / 2.0) + 1.0,
     WindowHeight / 2.0);
    TestWindow.Open();
    assert(TestWindow.GetStatus() == WindowOpen);

    LabeledEllipseShape E1(TestWindow, Center,
     Red, "R", EllipseWidth, EllipseHeight);
    E1.Draw();

    Center = Center
     + Position(EllipseWidth + 1.0, 0.0);
    LabeledEllipseShape E2(TestWindow, Center,
     Green, "G", EllipseWidth, EllipseHeight);
    E2.Draw();

    Center = Center
     + Position(EllipseWidth + 1.0, 0.0);
    LabeledEllipseShape E3(TestWindow, Center,
     Blue, "B", EllipseWidth, EllipseHeight);
    E3.Draw();

    return 0;
}
```

The code creates and displays three ellipses, each of a different color. The ellipses are labeled with a single letter indicating their color as shown in Figure 13.12.

Figure 13.12

Labeled ellipses

Self-check Questions

12. Suppose a class derived using multiple inheritance has member functions with the same name as a member function that is in one of the base classes. Explain how you specify which member function to call.

13. Using multiple inheritance, create a new class called `Bar` that would be suitable for plotting bar graphs using EzWindows. Each bar in the graph has its own legend at the bottom.

14. Consider the following class declarations.

```
class Obj1 {
    public:
        Obj1(int v = 0);
        int GetValue() const;
    private:
        int MyValue;
};
class Obj2 {
    public:
        Obj2(int v = 1.0f);
        float GetValue() const;
    private:
        float MyValue;
};
```

Suppose the class declaration for a derived class was

```
class Obj3 : public Obj1, public Obj2 {
    public:
        Obj3(int v1, float v2);
        void GetValues(const int &v1,
          const float &v2) const;
    private:
        // Nothing
};
```

Give the implementation of `Obj3`'s constructor.

Give the implemention of `Obj3`'s member function `GetValues()`. Member function `GetValues()` returns the values of the two base objects, `Obj1` and `Obj2`.

13.7 A PRETTIER KALEIDOSCOPE

Before moving on, we should put our new shape classes to work. Let's revise our original kaleidoscope program to make use of our new shapes. While we are at it, we should redesign the program to take advantage of the benefits of object-oriented design now that we have a better handle on creating and using classes.

A clear statement of what the program will do always helps in designing a program. From this statement, the abstractions necessary to construct the program can be determined. Here is the statement of what the kaleidoscope program should do.

> The kaleidoscope program displays a kaleidoscope image in a window. The window should be a square 10 centimeters on a side, and it should be labeled Kaleidoscope. The kaleidoscope image consists of the shapes circle, square, and triangle.

> The kaleidoscope should be "turned" once a second so that the image is updated. Each time the kaleidoscope is turned, four new shapes of the same type are added to the image. The centers of the shapes are located on the lines that bisect each quadrant. The shape and its size and color are determined randomly for each turn. Shapes in diagonally opposite quadrants are the same color.

For the above problem statement, we will need abstractions for the window, the kaleidoscope image, and the shapes. For the abstraction for the window, we will use the `SimpleWindow` class introduced previously. We already have one of the shapes—the triangle—and can easily create the other two shapes—the square and circle—using inheritance. Figure 13.13 shows a possible extended hierarchy of shapes.

However, this hierarchy has a serious problem. Recall that a derived class inherits all the attributes and behaviors of its ancestors. Thus `CircleShape` inherits the public member functions `SetSize()` and `Draw()` from `EllipseShape`. Let's assume we have a constructor for `CircleShape` that is similar to the constructors for the other shapes we have implemented. For instance, we could write

```
Circle C(TWindow, Position(4.0, 4.0), Green, 2.0);
```

which instantiates a green circle with a diameter of 2 centimeters contained in `SimpleWindow` TWindow. The position of the circle is 4 centimeters from the top and left edges of the window. Unfortunately, we could then also legally write the code

```
C.SetSize(2.0, 1.0);
C.Draw()
```

which would not draw a circle, but would draw an ellipse with a width of 2 centimeters and a height of 1 centimeter.

The problem is that an `EllipseShape` has a behavior or capability that a `CircleShape` should not have. A `CircleShape` is not an `EllipseShape`, and we should not try to derive a `CircleShape` from an `EllipseShape`, even though it is tempting to do so. The situation with `SquareShape` and `RectangleShape` is analogous. When defining a class hierarchy, we must examine the abstractions carefully to ensure that all the capabilities or behaviors of the ancestor classes are appropriate for the descendant classes.

Figure 13.13

*An extended hierarchy
of shapes*

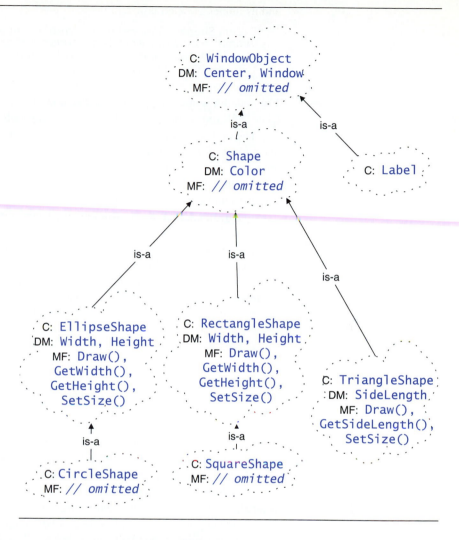

Instead of deriving `CircleShape` and `SquareShape` from `Ellipse-Shape` and `RectangleShape`, we should derive them from `Shape`. The declaration for the class `SquareShape` is

```cpp
class SquareShape : public Shape {
    public:
        SquareShape(SimpleWindow &w,
            const Position &Center, const color &c = Red,
            float SideLength = 1.0);
        float GetSideLength() const;
        void SetSize(float SideLength);
        void Draw();
    private:
        float SideLength;
};
```

and its implementation is

```
SquareShape::SquareShape(SimpleWindow &w,
  const Position &center, const color &c, float s)
  : Shape(w, center, c), SideLength(s) {
  // no code needed!
}
```

The code for a circle is analogous. The complete code for `SquareShape` and `CircleShape` is contained in Listings 13.8 through 13.11.

The only abstraction left to design is the one for a kaleidoscope. The first question is, What attributes and actions should the kaleidoscope abstraction have? An attribute for all objects that are displayed in a window has been the window that the object is associated with. The kaleidoscope class is no different. It should contain a reference to the instance of the `SimpleWindow` that contains it. In addition to the window, the kaleidoscope class needs objects to represent the glass trinkets. We use our newly developed shape classes `CircleShape`, `SquareShape`, and `TriangleShape` to represent the trinkets.

Another obvious attribute of the kaleidoscope is the speed at which it should be turned. According to the problem statement, the kaleidoscope should be updated once a second. We could hard-code this constant into the class, but our class will be more flexible if we make the turning speed one of the kaleidoscope's attributes. In this way, the value can be changed if desired.

Other not so obvious attributes of a kaleidoscope abstraction are the type of shapes it can contain and the number of shapes to draw on each turn of the kaleidoscope. Our goal is to capture all the characteristics of the kaleidoscope within the abstraction. As usual, the data attributes will be private members of the class.

Two attributes that are specifically not part of the abstraction are the size of the largest shape that can be created and the largest offset from the center of the window. The reason we have chosen not to make these attributes part of the class is that they depend on the size of the window that contains the kaleidoscope. If the window is large, then we can use larger shapes, but if the window is small, we certainly do not want to draw a shape that is larger than the window. It is tempting to say that these can be computed once and stored in the class, but remember a window can be resized. In this case, we want the kaleidoscope to adjust what it does too. Consequently, these attributes are computed each time the kaleidoscope is turned, just in case the window is resized.

To summarize, the attributes of a kaleidoscope thus far are

- A `SimpleWindow` for displaying the image.
- The shapes `CircleShape`, `SquareShape`, and `TriangleShape` to represent the glass trinkets.
- The speed to turn the kaleidoscope.

Like the kaleidoscope program we developed in Chapter 7, we need to pick the color for the trinket, the size of the trinket, and the offset from the center of the window to draw the trinket. In addition, we need to pick the type of shape to use for the trinket. We use the `Random` class developed in Chapter 8 to pick these values.

Listing 13.8

Declaration of class SquareShape from square.h

```
#ifndef SQUARESHAPE_H
#define SQUARESHAPE_H
#include "shape.h"
class SquareShape : public Shape {
    public:
        SquareShape(SimpleWindow &w,
          const Position &Center, const color &c = Red,
          float Side = 1.0);
        float GetSideLength() const;
        void SetSize(float SideLength);
        void Draw();
    private:
        float SideLength;
};
#endif
```

Listing 13.9

Implementation of SquareShape from square.cpp

```
#include "square.h"
SquareShape::SquareShape(SimpleWindow &w,
 const Position &center, const color &c, float s) :
 Shape(w, center, c), SideLength(s) {
    // No code needed!
}
float SquareShape::GetSideLength() const {
    return SideLength;
}
void SquareShape::Draw() {
    const Position Center = GetPosition();
    float SideLength = GetSideLength();

    Position UpperLeft = Center
     + Position(-.5 * SideLength, -.5 * SideLength);
    Position LowerRight = Center
     + Position(.5 * SideLength, .5 * SideLength);
    GetWindow().RenderRectangle(UpperLeft, LowerRight,
     GetColor());
}
void SquareShape::SetSize(float s) {
    SideLength = s;
}
```

Listing 13.10

Declaration of class CircleShape from circle.h

```
#ifndef CIRCLESHAPE_H
#define CIRCLESHAPE_H
#include "shape.h"
class CircleShape : public Shape {
    public:
        CircleShape(SimpleWindow &w,
          const Position &Center, const color &c = Red,
          float Diameter = 1.0);
        float GetDiameter() const;
        void SetSize(float Diameter);
        void Draw();
    private:
        float Diameter;
};
#endif
```

To pick the type of shape for the trinket and the color of the trinket, we include in the kaleidoscope abstraction two objects, RandomShape and RandomColor, which are instances of class Random. When a shape type is needed,

Listing 13.11

*Implementation of
CircleShape from
circle.cpp*

```
#include "circle.h"
CircleShape::CircleShape(SimpleWindow &w,
  const Position &center, const color &c, float d)
  : Shape(w, center, c), Diameter(d) {
    // no code needed!
}
float CircleShape::GetDiameter() const {
    return Diameter;
}
void CircleShape::Draw() {
    const Position Center = GetPosition();
    const float Diameter = GetDiameter();

    const Position UpperLeft = Center
     + Position(-.5 * Diameter, -.5 * Diameter);
    const Position LowerRight = Center
     + Position(.5 * Diameter, .5 * Diameter);
    GetWindow().RenderEllipse(UpperLeft, LowerRight,
     GetColor());
    return;
}
void CircleShape::SetSize(float d) {
    Diameter = d;
    return;
}
```

we will ask RandomShape to pick one randomly. Similarly when a color for a
shape is needed, we will ask RandomColor to pick one randomly.

It is tempting to include instances of class Random to pick the size of the
trinket and the offset from the center of the window to place the trinkets, but
because these values depend on the size of the window, different random distri-
butions are required. Consequently, appropriate objects of class Random will
be created each time we need to pick a shape size and an offset.

The actions for the kaleidoscope abstraction are somewhat harder to determine. Like our previous classes, we will want inspectors for the private data.
Thus GetWindow and GetSpeed member functions should be provided.
Another action clearly needed is the turn action. When the kaleidoscope
receives this message, four new shapes are created and added to the display.
Because this message will be sent from the window class that contains the
kaleidoscope, it should be a public member function so that it is accessible to
the window class.

In addition to the constructor and Turn(), class Kaleidoscope will have
one private member function. This utility function will compute the offset from
the center of the window to draw the shapes. Since this capability will be
needed only when Turn() is invoked, it is a private function. Figure 13.14
illustrates how the kaleidoscope objects interact.

Based on our design, we can now create a class declaration for a kaleidoscope abstraction. The declaration of class Kaleidoscope is

```
class Kaleidoscope {
   public:
       Kaleidoscope(SimpleWindow &w, int Speed = 1000);
       int GetSpeed() const;
       SimpleWindow& GetWindow() const;
       int Turn();
```

```
private:
    // types and constants
    enum { ShapesPerTurn = 4,
      NumberOfShapeTypes = 3 };
    enum ShapeType { CircleType, SquareType,
      TriangleType };
    // member function
    float RandomOffset(int Range, float ShapeSize);
    // data members
    SimpleWindow &Window;
    int Speed;    // Speed in uSec to update image
    CircleShape CircleTrinket;
    SquareShape SquareTrinket;
    TriangleShape TriangleTrinket;
    RandomInt RandomShape;
    RandomInt RandomColor;
};
```

Figure 13.14

Interactions between the SimpleWindow and Kaleidoscope hierarchies

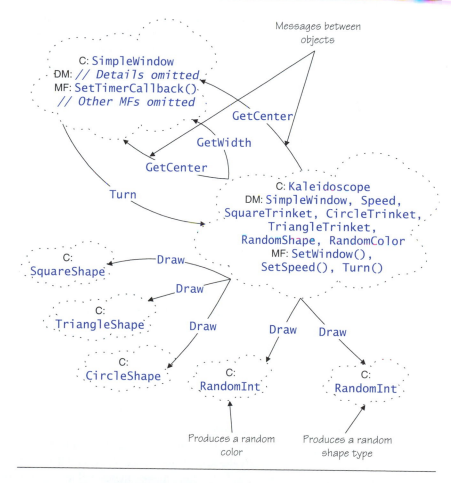

With few exceptions, the declaration is similar to the other classes we have defined. In order to encapsulate the constants ShapesPerTurn and Number-OfShapeTypes in the class declaration, we resort to a trick. We would like to define some private constants in the class declaration, but the current version of C++ does not allow initialized constants to be declared as part of a class. Instead, we can use an anonymous enumeration. The code

```
enum { ShapesPerTurn = 4, NumberOfShapes = 3 };
```

declares an enumeration that does not have a name. However, the members of the enumeration `ShapesPerTurn` and `NumberOfShapes` are defined and given the appropriate values. The member functions of `Kaleidoscope` can refer to these names as if they were constants.

Notice that the window for displaying the kaleidoscope and the shapes for representing the trinkets are data members of class `Kaleidoscope`. This organization models the has-a relationship. A kaleidoscope has a window and it has trinkets. In addition, we have encapsulated within class `Kaleidoscope` the objects for picking a shape color and a shape type.

Now that we have settled on what a kaleidoscope abstraction looks like, we can start on its implementation. Since most of the work is done by member function `Turn()`, let's focus on its implementation. The other member functions are so similar to our previous implementation that we do not discuss them further here. Their implementations are shown in Listing 13.12.

The redesigned kaleidoscope program uses the same method to produce the image as we used in our previous implementation. That is, when a `Kaleidoscope` object receives a turn message, it will draw four shapes—one in each quadrant of the window. Shapes in diagonally opposite quadrants are the same color. The major functional difference between the `Turn()` member function and the kaleidoscope function in Chapter 7 is that each time `Turn()` is invoked, it randomly picks the type of shape to draw.

In addition to the functional difference between the two versions of the program, we have some implementation differences. By using some of the constructs introduced in the preceding chapters, the implementation of the member function `Turn()` can be shortened.

Member function `Turn()` logically starts off like the earlier kaleidoscope function. It obtains the coordinates of the center of the window. However, with the introduction of class `Position` and the `SimpleWindow` class, we obtain the center of the window containing the image by calling `SimpleWindow`'s `GetCenter()` member function, which returns a `Position` object whose value is the center of the window that contains the image. The following code

```
// Get position of the center of the window
const Position CenterOfWindow =
    GetWindow().GetCenter();
```

does the job.

Another improvement to this version is that rather than use `const`s to specify the size of the largest shape and the largest offset from the center of the window, we can make these values a function of the window size. Consequently, the user can resize the window containing the kaleidoscope, and the sizes of the shapes and where they are drawn will be automatically adjusted. To achieve this added flexibility, member function `Turn()` simply

Listing 13.12

Implementation of Kaleidoscope from kaleido.cpp

```cpp
#include <assert.h>
#include <iostream>
#include <vector>
#include <string>
#include "kaleido.h"
using namespace std;
// Kaleidoscope constructor
Kaleidoscope::Kaleidoscope(SimpleWindow &w, int s)
  : Window(w), Speed(s),
  CircleTrinket(w, Position(0,0)),
  SquareTrinket(w, Position(0,0)),
  TriangleTrinket(w, Position(0,0)),
  RandomColor(0, MaxColors - 1),
  RandomShape(0, NumberOfShapeTypes - 1) {
    assert(&w != NULL);
}

// GetSpeed(): return the speed
int Kaleidoscope::GetSpeed() const {
    return Speed;
}

// GetWindow(): return the window that contains the
// kaleidoscope
SimpleWindow& Kaleidoscope::GetWindow() const {
    return Window;
}

// RandomOffset(): generate a random amount to offset a
//   square from the center of the window. Generate a
//   random offset in the
//   interval 0..Range-1 in .1 centimeter increments.
//   The offset generated must take into account
//   the size of the shape so the shapes do not
//   overlap at the center.
float Kaleidoscope::RandomOffset(int Range,
  float ShapeSize) {
    RandomInt R(0, Range * 10);
    float Offset = R.Draw() / 10.0;
    // if Offset is not large enough to keep
    // the shape from overlapping, set the offset
    // to half the shape size
    if (Offset < ShapeSize / 2)
        Offset = ShapeSize / 2;
    return Offset;
}
```

asks `Window` how big it is and uses this value to compute the appropriate values. The corresponding code follows.

```cpp
// The largest shape should be 1 centimeter
// smaller than 1/2 the size of the window
float MaxShapeSize =
  (GetWindow().GetWidth() / 2.0) - 1.0;
// The largest offset should be 1 centimeter
// smaller than 1/2 the size of the window
float MaxOffset
  = (GetWindow().GetWidth() / 2.0) - 1.0;
```

In the first version, the only shape was a square, so the straightforward approach was to instantiate the four squares and draw them. In this version, we can simplify the implementation if we take a different approach. We use data structures to hold the positions and colors of the shapes we will eventually draw. The advantage of this approach is that these attributes need to be created only once, since they are independent of the type of shape that we will draw.

The following code accomplishes the task of initializing the two vectors.

```
vector<color> ShapeColor(2);
ShapeColor[0] = (color) RandomColor.Draw();
ShapeColor[1] = (color) RandomColor.Draw();

// Generate a random size in the interval
// .1 to MaxShapeSize in .1-centimeter increments
// (i.e., 1, 1.1, 1.2, ...)
RandomInt RandomShapeSize(10, MaxShapeSize * 10);
const float ShapeSize = RandomShapeSize.Draw() / 10.0;

// Compute and create the four positions to draw
// the shapes
// Generate an amount to offset the shapes from the
// center point of the window
const float Offset
  = RandomOffset(MaxOffset, ShapeSize);
vector<Position> ShapeLocation(ShapesPerTurn);
ShapeLocation[0] = CenterOfWindow
  + Position( Offset, -Offset);
ShapeLocation[1] = CenterOfWindow
  + Position(-Offset, -Offset);
ShapeLocation[2] = CenterOfWindow
  + Position(-Offset,  Offset);
ShapeLocation[3] = CenterOfWindow
  + Position( Offset,  Offset)};
```

Vector `ShapeColor` holds the two colors that the shapes will be. Vector element `ShapeColor[0]` holds the color of the shape for quadrants 1 and 3, and vector element `ShapeColor[1]` holds the color of the shape that will be drawn in quadrants 2 and 4. The object `RandomColor` of class `Random` produces the random color. Vector `ShapeLocation` holds the positions to draw the four shapes. Vector element `ShapeLocation[0]` is the location in quadrant 1, `ShapeLocation[1]` is the location in quadrant 2, and so on.

The next-to-last step is to pick a shape and to draw the four versions of it. To pick a shape, we use another `Random` object called `RandomShape`. It randomly picks one of the shape types defined in the enumeration `ShapeType` and returns it. The last step is to draw the required four shapes. The code to do this is

```
// Pick a kind of shape to draw
const ShapeType KindOfShape
  = (ShapeType) RandomShape.Draw();
if (KindOfShape == CircleType) {
    for (int i = 0; i < ShapesPerTurn; ++i) {
        CircleTrinket.SetPosition(ShapeLocation[i]);
        CircleTrinket.SetColor(ShapeColor[i % 2]);
        CircleTrinket.SetSize(ShapeSize);
        CircleTrinket.Draw();
    }
}
else if (KindOfShape == SquareType) {
```

```
        for (int i = 0; i < ShapesPerTurn; ++i) {
            SquareTrinket.SetPosition(ShapeLocation[i]);
            SquareTrinket.SetColor(ShapeColor[i % 2]);
            SquareTrinket.SetSize(ShapeSize);
            SquareTrinket.Draw();
        }
    }
    else if (KindOfShape == TriangleType) {
        for (int i = 0; i < ShapesPerTurn; ++i) {
            TriangleTrinket.SetPosition(ShapeLocation[i]);
            TriangleTrinket.SetColor(ShapeColor[i % 2]);
            TriangleTrinket.SetSize(ShapeSize);
            TriangleTrinket.Draw();
        }
    }
```

Essentially, each branch of the if-then-else handles one of the shape types. Each branch loops ShapesPerTurn times, setting the attributes of the trinket drawing it. Listing 13.12 and Listing 13.13 contain the complete code for `kaleido.cpp`.

Listing 13.13

Implementation of Turn member function from kaleido.cpp

```
// Turn(): turn the kaleidoscope
int Kaleidoscope::Turn() {
    // Get logical coordinates of the center of the
    // window
    const Position CenterOfWindow =
      GetWindow().GetCenter();

    // The largest shape should be 1 centimeter
    // smaller than half the size of the window
    const float MaxShapeSize =
      (GetWindow().GetWidth() / 2.0) - 1.0;

    // The largest offset should be 1 centimeter
    // smaller than half the size of the window
    const float MaxOffset =
      (GetWindow().GetWidth() / 2.0) - 1.0;

    // Create four shapes, one in each quadrant. All shapes
    // are the same size. However, size is picked randomly.
    // The colors of the shapes are also chosen randomly.
    // The shapes in diagonally opposite quadrants are
    // the same color.
    vector<color> ShapeColor(2);
    ShapeColor[0] = (color) RandomColor.Draw();
    ShapeColor[1] = (color) RandomColor.Draw();

    // Generate a random size in the interval
    // .1 to MaxShapeSize in .1-centimeter increments
    // (i.e., 1, 1.1, 1.2, ...)
    RandomInt RandomShapeSize(10, MaxShapeSize * 10);
    const float ShapeSize = RandomShapeSize.Draw() / 10.0;
    // Build the four positions to draw the shapes
    // Generate an amount to offset the shapes from the
    // center point of the window
    const float Offset
      = RandomOffset(MaxOffset, ShapeSize);
    vector<Position> ShapeLocation(ShapesPerTurn);
    ShapeLocation[0] = CenterOfWindow
      + Position( Offset, -Offset);
    ShapeLocation[1] = CenterOfWindow
      + Position(-Offset, -Offset);
```

```
    ShapeLocation[2] = CenterOfWindow
      + Position(-Offset,  Offset);
    ShapeLocation[3] = CenterOfWindow
      + Position( Offset,  Offset);
    // Pick a shape to draw
    const ShapeType KindOfShape
      = (ShapeType) RandomShape.Draw();
    if (KindOfShape == CircleType) {
        for (int i = 0; i < ShapesPerTurn; ++i) {
            CircleTrinket.SetPosition(ShapeLocation[i]);
            CircleTrinket.SetColor(ShapeColor[i % 2]);
            CircleTrinket.SetSize(ShapeSize);
            CircleTrinket.Draw();
        }
    }
    else if (KindOfShape == SquareType) {
        for (int i = 0; i < ShapesPerTurn; ++i) {
            SquareTrinket.SetPosition(ShapeLocation[i]);
            SquareTrinket.SetColor(ShapeColor[i % 2]);
            SquareTrinket.SetSize(ShapeSize);
            SquareTrinket.Draw();
        }
    }
    else if (KindOfShape == TriangleType) {
        for (int i = 0; i < ShapesPerTurn; ++i) {
            TriangleTrinket.SetPosition(ShapeLocation[i]);
            TriangleTrinket.SetColor(ShapeColor[i % 2]);
            TriangleTrinket.SetSize(ShapeSize);
            TriangleTrinket.Draw();
        }
    }
    return 1;
}
```

The only remaining part of the program is getting things going. We need to write ApiMain() and ApiEnd(). These functions will be contained in a separate module called kmain.cpp. Figure 13.15 shows the modules required to build the program.

Figure 13.15

Modules needed to build the kaleidoscope program

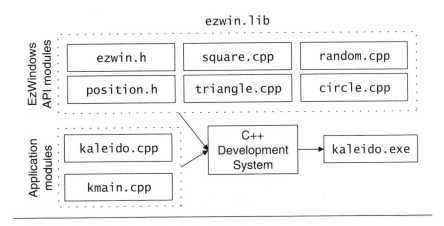

Both the `Kaleidoscope` object and the window where it is displayed are instantiated in the module `kmain.cpp`. Because these objects must persist throughout the execution of the program, they are global objects. The definitions of the objects are

```
SimpleWindow KWindow("Kaleidoscope", 10.0, 10.0,
   Position(2.0, 2.0));
Kaleidoscope KScope(KWindow, 1000);
```

The first creates a window named `KWindow` with the label "Kaleidoscope." The size of the window is 10 centimeters by 10 centimeters. The window is positioned with its upper-left corner 2 centimeters from the left edge of the screen and 2 centimeters down.

The second definition creates a `Kaleidoscope` object called `KScope`. It will be displayed in window `KWindow`. The kaleidoscope will be turned once every 1,000 milliseconds, or once a second.

The order of these definitions is important. The second one refers to the first. Fortunately, C++ executes global definitions in the order in which they appear in the source file.

The job of `ApiMain()` is to initialize the random-number generator, open `KWindow`, make the connection between `KWindow`'s timer, and start the timer. The code follows.

```
int DispatchTimerClick() {
   KScope.Turn();
   return 1;
}
// ApiMain(): begins program execution
int ApiMain() {
   EzRandomize()
   KWindow.Open();
   // Tell KWindow to call function TimerClick
   // when the timer interrupts
   KWindow.SetTimerCallback(DispatchTimerClick);
   // Start the timer and have it interrupt
   // at the requested speed
   KWindow.StartTimer(KScope.GetSpeed());
   return 0;
}
```

For the most part the code is straightforward. The only step that needs explanation is the invocation of `KWindow`'s `SetTimerCallback` member function. We would have liked to set it up so that `KWindow` sent a turn message directly to `KScope`, for example:

```
KWindow.SetTimerCallback(KScope.Turn);
```

Unfortunately, the type-checking rules of C++ prevent us from writing this statement. `SimpleWindow`'s `SetTimerCallback` function expects a pointer to a function that returns an integer. In other words, it expects something with the type `int (*)()`. The type of member function `Turn()` is `int (Kaleidoscope::*)()`. That is, the class that a function is a member of is part of its type. Thus the parameter type expected by `SetTimerCallback` is not what is being passed. To get around this problem, we use a simple indirection. The function KWindow should call on a timer event is set to DispatchTimer-Click, and this function calls KScope's Turn() function.

Just before the program terminates, the routine ApiEnd() is called to do any necessary cleanup. For the kaleidoscope program, the only cleanup is to close Kwindow and return. Listing 13.14 contains the implementation of Api-End() and ApiMain(), as well as the definitions of KWindow and KScope.

Listing 13.14

Implementation of kaleidoscope user interactions from kmain.cpp

```
#include "kaleido.h"
// Instantiate a  window to display the kaleidoscope
SimpleWindow KWindow("Kaleidoscope", 10.0, 10.0,
 Position(2.0, 2.0));
// Instantiate a kaleidoscope named KScope that will
// turn once a second
Kaleidoscope KScope(KWindow, 1000);
// DispatchTimerClick(): call KScope's turn function
int DispatchTimerClick() {
   KScope.Turn();

   return 1;
}
// ApiMain(): open the window, set up the callback,
// and start the timer
int ApiMain() {
   EzRandomize();
   KWindow.Open();
   KWindow.SetTimerCallback(DispatchTimerClick);
   KWindow.StartTimer(KScope.GetSpeed());

   return 0;
}
// ApiEnd(): clean up by closing KWindow
int ApiEnd() {
   KWindow.Close();

   return 0;
}
```

Figure 13.16 shows our new kaleidoscope image after several turns. As you can see, the addition of the new shapes has made the image look much more like a real kaleidoscope image.

13.8 POINTS TO REMEMBER

✔ The is-a relationship indicates inheritance. For example, a car is a kind of vehicle. A border collie is a kind of dog.

✔ The is-a relationship is transitive. A Siamese cat is a type of cat, and a cat is a mammal; therefore, a Siamese cat is a mammal.

✔ The has-a relationship indicates containment. For example, a radio has a tuner. A car has an engine. Aggregate objects are constructed using containment.

✔ Both inheritance and containment are methods for software reuse.

Figure 13.16

*Improved
kaleidoscope image*

✔ A new class that is created from an existing class using inheritance is called a *derived class* or *subclass*. The parent class is called the *base class* or *superclass*.

✔ When an object that is an instance of derived class is instantiated, the constructor for the base class is invoked before the body of the constructor for the derived class is invoked.

✔ When required for efficiency, the implementation of a class can be included with the declaration of the class in the `.h` file. The member functions can be declared inline, and the C++ compiler will replace calls to the member functions with the body of the function. This method avoids the overhead of calling a function and, for heavily used member functions, can significantly reduce the execution time of a program.

✔ Initializing data members of a class using a data member initialization list is more efficient than calling a mutator from the constructor.

✔ Destructors are called in reverse order from the constructor calls. Thus the destructor for a derived class is called before the destructor of the base or superclass.

✔ With public inheritance, the public members of the base class are public members of the derived class. The private members of the base class are not accessible by the member functions of the derived class.

History of Computing

Emerging technologies

The last decade has been characterized by the continued introduction of cheaper and faster computers. Today, a PC costing about $2,000 has 80 to 100 times the computational power of a PC that sold in the middle 1990s for $4,000 or more. Experts agree that this rate of growth will continue. Because of this phenomenal increase in performance and drop in price, computers are being used for a variety of tasks that, even a few years ago, would have been unthinkable. Many cars have computers that control the engine as well as many of the instrument displays. We are beginning to see computers that have enough power to analyze and recognize human speech. Similarly, small "digital assistant" computers that can recognize handwriting are beginning to appear. Although these devices are still limited in their capabilities, it is only a matter of time before we routinely communicate with computers via voice commands.

Today's computers share the common characteristic of using electricity to operate. Some researchers believe that the way to achieve even greater speed is to use light instead of electricity. Indeed, researchers have built an optical replacement for the transistor called the *transphasor*. Some predict that an optical computer, if realized, could easily perform a trillion operations per second. Optical computers would have another advantage. Computers based on optical components could be much smaller than electronic computers because light beams can pass through themselves without interference, whereas computers based on electricity must use wires that cannot cross.

An even wilder and potentially revolutionary approach to building computers involves organic molecules. Currently, computer chips are constructed by placing tiny transistors on a chip of silicon. However, it is possible to build organic molecules that operate much like silicon transistors. Working at this molecular level promises even greater speed and smaller computers. Thus some experts predict that in the future, rather than building a computer from a silicon crystal, we will grow computers from vats of protein.

- ✔ With protected inheritance, public and protected members of the base class become private members of the derived class. The private members of the base class are not accessible to the member functions of the derived class.
- ✔ With multiple inheritance, a derived class inherits the attributes and behaviors of all parent classes.
- ✔ With private inheritance, public and protected members of the base class become private members of the derived class.

13.9 EXERCISES

13.1   Design a hierarchy of toys. The base class is a toy. Examples of possible specialized subclasses are stuffed toy, battery-powered toy, and mechanical toy. Constrain your hierarchy to use only single inheritance. Illustrate your hierarchy by drawing a diagram like the one in Figure 13.1.

13.2   Redo exercise 13.1 to employ multiple inheritance.

13.3   Design an inheritance hierarchy for lights. For example, there are electric lights, combustible lights (kerosene latterns, propane latterns, etc.), and electroluminescent lights. Do not use multiple inheritance. Illustrate your hierarchy by drawing a diagram like the one in Figure 13.1.

13.4   Design an inheritance hierarchy for shoes. Do not use multiple inheritance. The first level of your hierarchy should be men's and women's shoes. Illustrate your hierarchy by drawing a diagram like the one in Figure 13.1.

13.5   Design an inheritance hierarchy of clocks. After you have designed the hierarchy, create classes for each type of clock. Your solution should be a figure like the one in Figure 13.13 and a set of class declarations. Do not implement the member functions of the classes.

13.6   Design an inheritance hierarchy for publications. After you have designed the hierarchy, create classes for each type of publication. Your solution should be a figure like the one in Figure 13.13 and a set of class declarations. Do not implement the member functions of the classes.

13.7   Design a hierarchy of computer printers. Use multiple inheritance in your hierarchy. Illustrate your hierarchy by drawing a diagram like the one in Figure 13.1. Some types of printers to consider in designing your hierarchy are laser, inkjet, impact, and dye sublimation.

13.8   Modify the shape classes so that the shape has a default position. That is, it should be possible to declare a shape by supplying only the window that contains the shape. Before modifying the code, determine a good default position. Justify your answer.

13.9   For the following class hierarchy:

```
class Top {
    public:
        Top ();
        int look();
    protected:
        int peek();
    private:
        int value;
};
class A : public Top {
    // ...
};
```

which of the functions and data members in Top can be accessed from the derived class A?

13.10 Consider the classes Hoo and Wahoo. Identify errors on three different lines and explain them.

```
L1          class Hoo {
L2              public:
L3                  Hoo( );
L4                  Hoo( &int n );
L5                  int Hoo(int n, int m);
L6              protected:
L7                  int HooYear;
L8                  int HooTime;
L9              private:
L10                 int HooDay;
L11         };
L12         class Wahoo : public Hoo {
L13             public:
L14                 Wahoo(int n, int m);
L15         };
L16         Wahoo::Wahoo(int time, int day) {
L17             HooTime = time;
L18             HooDay = day;
L19         }
```

13.11 Assume that class HoundDog is privately derived from class Dog. Indicate whether HoundDog object Blue declared in function main() can access the following members:

a) The private members of HoundDog.

b) The protected members of HoundDog.

c) The public members of HoundDog.

d) The private members of Dog.

e) The protected members of Dog.

f) The private members of Dog.

13.12 The code for the Kaleidoscope's Turn() function used a cascaded if-then-else statement to determine the type of shape to add to the display. A switch statement would be more natural. Modify the code to use a switch statement. Did your code work? What other changes did you have to make to the code to use a switch statement?

13.13 Currently the location of a shape is given by the center of the shape. This method works well for many shapes, but some shapes do not have an easily defined center. Modify the hierarchy of shapes so that the position of a shape is specified by providing the upper-left corner of the bounding box. You must determine the bounding box for an equilateral triangle.

13.14 Design and implement labeled versions of the following existing shape classes:

a) RectangleShape

b) TriangleShape

c) CircleShape

d) SquareShape

13.15 Add the following shapes to the original shapes hierarchy.

    a) Diamond

    b) Pentagon

    c) Hexagon

13.16 Create a class called `CylinderShape` for drawing a cylinder on the screen. Class `CylinderShape` should be derived from the class `Shape`. A cylinder can be rendered by drawing two ellipses and a rectangle. The following picture shows a cylinder that has been drawn using this method.

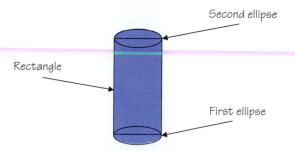

Illustrate the use of your `CylinderShape` by writing a program that accepts the dimensions of a cylinder, renders the cylinder, and adds the volume label. Assume the dimensions of the cylinder are given in centimeters. Make sure you use the appropriate units of measure for the volume.

13.17 Create a class called `StarShape` for drawing stars in a window. Class `StarShape` should be derived from the class `Shape`. A star can be rendered using `SimpleWindow`'s `RenderPolygon` member function. A `StarShape` has the characteristics shown in the following diagram:

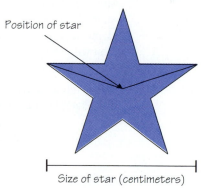

The position of a star is specified by giving the coordinates of its center. The size of a star is specified by giving the length (in centimeters) of the distance across the star. Demonstrate the use of `StarShape` by writing a program that draws six stars in a window. The stars should have the following colors: red, blue, green, yellow, cyan, and magenta.

13.18 Using StarShape and the other shapes we have developed, write a program that creates a SimpleWindow that contains an image of the American flag.

13.19 Modify the kaleidoscope program so that it has a separate control window. The control window contains the following buttons: quit, turn, run, and stop. When the mouse is clicked on the quit button, all windows close and the program terminates. When the turn button is clicked, the kaleidoscope turns. If the kaleidoscope is in automatic mode, the turn button has no effect. When the run button is clicked, the kaleidoscope goes into automatic mode. In this mode, the image is automatically updated every second. If the kaleidoscope is already in automatic mode, this run button has no effect. When the stop button is clicked, the kaleidoscope goes into manual mode. In this mode, the image is updated only when the turn button is clicked. If the kaleidoscope is already in manual mode, the stop button has no effect.

13.20 Use the Kaleidoscope class to write a program that creates four kaleidoscopes. Position the kaleidoscopes in the four quadrants of the screen. Each kaleidoscope should turn at a different rate.

13.21 Redesign the kaleidoscope program so the class Kaleidoscope is derived from class SimpleWindow. Does this approach offer any advantages over the previous design? Explain why or why not. Implement your design.

13.22 The labeled rectangle shape (see Exercise 13.14) can serve as a basis for a button class. Design and implement a button class. The button class has the following properties: When the mouse is clicked inside the button, a user-defined function is called. Thus one of the data members of the button class should be a pointer to a function. Demonstrate your new button class by writing a program that implements a stop watch. The stop watch has two buttons—a start button and a stop button. When the start button is pushed, the current time is recorded. When the stop button is pushed, the elapsed time is displayed in the console window. Hint: You will need to implement a member function IsInside() that works for a rectangular shape.

13.23 Using inheritance, create a new type of shape. These shapes are shaded. For example, the following is a ShadedRectangleShape.

In addition to ShadedRectangleShape, create ShadedEllipse-Shape and ShadedTriangleShape. Your classes should allow the color of the shading to be specified by the client users of the shape. Write a program that demonstrates the use of the new shapes.

13.24 Using multiple inheritance, create a new type of shape. These shapes are shaded and labeled. For example, the following is a `LabeledShaded-RectangleShape`.

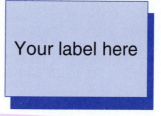

In addition to `LabeledShadedRectangleShape`, create `Labeled-ShadedEllipseShape` and `LabeledShadedTriangleShape`. Write a program that demonstrates the use of the new shapes.

CHAPTER 14

Templates and polymorphism

Introduction

Polymorphism is a language mechanism that permits the same code expression to invoke different functions depending on the type of objects using the code. Name reuse in function overloading is a primitive form of polymorphism. In this chapter we explore the two major C++ mechanisms for providing polymorphic capabilities. The first method is via class and function templates. A template, when invoked with particular types and values, can generate a new function or class. All functions or classes generated from a given template have the same name. The second method is via virtual member functions. In an expression involving a virtual function invocation, the decision on which function to use is delayed until run time. The decision is then based on the type of object being referenced in the invocation. This type of polymorphism is sometimes called pure polymorphism.

Key Concepts

- polymorphism
- pure polymorphism
- function template
- class template
- container class
- sequential list
- linked list
- doubly linked list
- iterator class
- **friend** to a class
- virtual function
- pure virtual function
- abstract base class
- virtually derived class

14.1   GENERIC ACTIONS AND TYPES

If we asked experts to list the necessary features of an object-oriented language, their replies would generally be the same. Their answers would surely state that the most important feature of an object-oriented language is its ability to allow both data and behavior to be encapsulated in a single object. Class and inheritance mechanisms would also appear in all the answers. These three features—objects, classes, and inheritance—are the core of object-oriented programming. If our experts were to agree on one more necessary feature, it would likely be *polymorphism*. A polymorphic function is a generic function that can act upon objects of different types. The actions taken depend on the types of the objects. Analogous behavior is not required but is expected.

A primitive form of polymorphism that we have already seen is function and operator overloading. With overloading we can *repeatedly* define functions or operators with the same name. For example, in previous chapters we overloaded the insertion operator to work with both `Rational` and `IntArray` operands. Another example is when we overload the function `Min()` for the various numeric types so that it returns the lesser value of its two parameters.

Similar to overloading is the C++ *template* mechanism. Templates offer a syntactic convenience that looks like polymorphism. Templates can generate a function or class once the particulars are supplied. This mechanism is not considered true polymorphism because the choice of which function to invoke is made at compile time rather than run time.

The exact nature of some objects is not known during compilation. For such objects, we need to delay until run time the decision on which function to invoke. This technique is considered true polymorphism. It is achieved in C++ using special member functions called *virtual functions*. Templates and virtual functions are the two major topics of this chapter.

14.2   FUNCTION TEMPLATES

C++ has two kinds of templates—*class generators* and *function and operator generators*. The following code segment defines a template that can generate a family of functions, each of which is named `Min()`.

```
template<class T>
  T Min(const T &a, const T &b) {
    if (a < b)
        return a;
    else
        return b;
}
```

A function or operator template definition begins with the keyword **template**. Following this keyword is a template parameter list enclosed within angled brackets. The template parameter declarations are separated from each other by commas. There are two different kinds of template parameters: type and value. A type template parameter specifies a placeholder for a type. A value template parameter specifies a placeholder for a value. Following the template parameter list is a function description that uses the parameters.

The syntax for a value template parameter is the same as a function value parameter—it consists of a known type followed by an identifier name. We note that value template parameters are not typically used in function templates.

The syntax for a type template parameter in a function template consists of the keyword **class** followed by the identifier name of the template parameter.

Each template parameter must be used in the function description. In particular, the template parameters must be used in the signature of the function description. Each function Min() that can be generated from our template example has two constant reference parameters. The type of these two parameters and the return type are the same and are determined by the actual type used for template parameter T. The actual type will be determined by a function invocation using that template name.

Suppose the following code segment appears in the same program as our Min() template definition.

```
int Input1;
int Input2;
cin >> Input1 >> Input2;
cout << Min(Input1, Input2) << endl;
```

A function Min() is then automatically generated and invoked with two constant **int** reference parameters and an **int** return type.

```
int Min(const int &a, const int &b) {
    if (a < b)
        return a;
    else
        return b;
}
```

Similarly, if the code segment

```
Rational x;
Rational y;
cin >> x >> y;
Rational z = Min(x, y);
```

occurs, then the following function Min() with two constant Rational reference parameters and a Rational return type is automatically generated and invoked.

```
Rational Min(const Rational &a, const Rational &b){
    if (a < b)
        return a;
    else
        return b;
}
```

The test expression (a < b) is the interesting part of the Min() template definition because the type of the comparison varies with the template instantiation. The invocation Min(Input1, Input2) causes an **int** comparison to be generated, and the invocation Min(x, y) causes a Rational comparison to be generated. Such comparisons can be generated because the < operator is built in for **int** objects and our definition of the rational library includes an auxiliary < operator.

The following invocation results in a *template instantiation failure*.

```
cout << Min(7, 3.14); // illegal: parameter mismatch
```

Our Min() template does not apply because the values 7 and 3.14 do not have the same type. For a function to be generated using the template, the compiler must be able to form an *exact* match with the template parameter description and the types of the actual parameters in the invocation. Conversions are not automatically tried in an attempt to generate a function.

A template instantiation failure can also result if actions specified within the template are not defined for objects of the type given in the invocation. For example, the invocation of Min() in the following insertion results in an error.

```
cout << Min(cout, cerr);   // illegal: streams cannot
                           // be used in this manner
```

Our template does not apply in part because the < operator is not defined for stream objects.

The usefulness of function templates is especially apparent in sorting. By implementing a sorting algorithm as a template, we can generate sorts for all types of arrays without any additional work on our part. The following code provides a template version of the InsertionSort() defined in Chapter 9.

```
template<class T>
  void InsertionSort(T A[], int n) {
     for (int i = 1; i < n; ++i) {
        if (A[i] < A[i-1]) {
           // some shifting is necessary
           T v = A[i];
           int j = i;
           do {
              A[j] = A[j-1];
              --j;
           } while ((j > 0) && (v < A[j-1]));
           A[j] = v;
        }
     }
  }
```

In the InsertionSort() template definition, the template parameter T is the type of the objects to be sorted. For this template, like the template for determining the minimum value, the < operator must be defined. Observe that the template parameter T is also used in the function body.

The use of a function template does not prevent a program from also having explicitly defined functions with the same name. Program 14.1 demonstrates this point.

Program 14.1

Demonstrates that an explicit function definition can override a template definition

```cpp
#include <iostream>
#include <string>
using namespace std;
template<class T>
 void f(T i) {
    cout << "template f(): " << i << endl;
}
void f(int i) {
    cout << "explicit f(): " << i << endl;
}
int main() {
    f(1.5);
    f(1);
    f('a');
    return 0;
}
```

Program 14.1 defines both a function template f() and an explicitly defined function f() with an **int** parameter. The output of the program is given below.

```
template f(): 1.5
explicit f(): 1
template f(): a
```

This example shows that if there is a choice of functions to invoke, an explicit definition takes precedence over a template definition.

C++ Language

> **Template functions and the standard template library**
> Because the computation of the minimum and maximum for various data types is a frequent program task, the algorithm library component of the STL provides template definitions min() and max() for these tasks and for many other common programming tasks such as searching, sorting, combining, copying, and rearranging lists. For a list of the major elements of the algorithm library refer to Appendix B.

14.3 CLASS TEMPLATES

The template mechanism can also be used for defining a *class template*. For a class template, the keyword **template** and the template parameter declarations precede the class description.

Like function templates, class templates can have type and value template parameters. The type and value template parameters must be used in the declarations of the data members or in the signatures of the member functions.

To generate a class from a class template, you provide actual parameters for the template parameters. The actual parameters are provided after the template name within angled brackets. An actual type parameter must be a known type; an actual value parameter must be a constant whose value can be calculated during compilation.

The following simple example defines and uses a template class named TC. The class has two template parameters X and n. Template parameter X is a type template parameter; n is an **int** value template parameter.

```
template<class X, int n>
 class TC {
    public:
       TC();
       void Assign(X xvalue);
       // ...
    private:
       X ValueArray[n];
};
```

Template class TC<X,n> has a member function Assign() whose parameter xvalue has a type that is determined during class generation from the template. The template class TC<X,n> also has an array data member ValueArray whose type and size are determined during class generation.

The TC<X,n> template is used to generate two classes in the following definitions of objects A and B.

```
TC<char, 80> A;
TC<int, 125> B;
```

Object A is of type TC<**char**,80> and has a member function Assign() with a **char** parameter xvalue. The object also has a data member ValueArray, which is an array of 80 **char** elements. Object B is of type TC<**int**,125> and has a member function Assign() with an **int** parameter xvalue. The object also has a data member ValueArray, which is an array of 125 **int** elements.

In Chapter 11 we developed a simple container class IntArray for the representation of lists of integers. In the next several sections we develop two more general containers. These two containers will have different capabilities. Their development will give insight into the template container classes of the STL.

14.4   A SIMPLE LIST CLASS USING A CLASS TEMPLATE

The choice of which container class to use depends upon your list-processing needs. In choosing a particular container class, a software engineer must examine the information to be represented and determine necessary container characteristics. Some of the questions that the engineer must ask when making the decision are the following:

- Is the maximum number of elements in the list known?

- Do the elements in the list all have the same type?

- Are the elements in the list to be ordered, and if so, how?

- Are the elements in the list to be accessed in a random manner or in a sequential manner?

- What is the required relative efficiency of inspecting, modifying, adding, and removing elements?
- Is the list associative; that is, can we use key values to determine other information regarding the list?

We shall first develop a container class ADT with an arraylike interface similar to `vector`. Afterwards we will develop a container class ADT with a sequential access interface supporting dynamic element insertion and deletion in a manner similar to the STL container class `list`. Both of our ADTs require that all elements in a given collection be of the same type. Thus we will be creating *homogeneous* container classes. We will also develop in this chapter *heterogeneous* lists when we consider polymorphism through virtual functions.

In developing our arraylike container ADT, we have two major choices. We can explicitly develop a class ADT for each individual type for which we want listlike capabilities *à la* `IntArray`, or we can develop a single template class ADT. The latter alternative is clearly preferred.

Because the interface for our first container ADT is to resemble the standard array interface, access to elements will be through a member subscript operator. Its other capabilities include

- Passing one of its objects using any of the parameter-passing styles.
- Using one of its objects as either the source or target of an assignment.
- Passing an element of one of its objects using any of the parameter-passing styles.
- Using an element of one of its objects as either the source or target of an assignment.
- Providing access to the number of elements represented by one of its objects.

The elements represented by one of our arraylike objects will be *type distinguishing* (i.e., a list that represents a collection of **int** elements has a different type than a list that represents a collection of **char** elements). We must also decide whether the number of elements being represented in a list is type distinguishing (e.g., does an object representing 10 **int** elements have a different type than an object representing 20 **int** elements?). If the number of elements being represented is type distinguishing, then the number of elements being represented must be a value template parameter for the list ADT. If the number of elements being represented is not type distinguishing, then the number of elements being represented can be a parameter to the list constructor.

```
template<class T, int n>
  class Bunch {
    public:
        // default constructor
        Bunch();
        // constructor initializes all elements to val
        Bunch(const T &val);
        // constructor initializes from standard array
        Bunch(const T A[n]);
        // inspector for number of elements in list
        int size() const { return NumberValues; } ;
        // inspector for element of constant list
        const T& operator[](int i) const;
        // inspector for element of nonconstant list
        T& operator[](int i);
    private:
        // data members
        T Values[n];       // list elements
        int NumberValues;  // size of list
};
```

14.4.1 Specification

Listing 14.1 defines the interface for a class template named `Bunch<T,n>` where the number of elements being represented is type distinguishing. For example, the objects A and B defined in the following code segment have different types.

```
Bunch<int, 10> A;        // represents 10 ints
Bunch<int, 20> B;        // represents 20 ints
```

This difference means that unless we explicitly overload the assignment operator for each kind of assignment that we want to perform, then the assignment of B to A would be illegal.

```
A = B; // illegal: A and B have different types
```

Listing 14.2 defines a class template named `Array<T>` where the number of elements being represented is not type distinguishing.

Thus the `Array<int>` objects C and D defined in the following code segment have the same type.

```
Array<int> C(10, 1);     // represents 10 1s
Array<int> D(20, 2);     // represents 20 2s
```

Because C and D have the same type, we can assign them to each other (note that the semantics of the assignment have not yet been defined).

```
C = D; // legal: C and D have the same type
```

The definition for template `Array<T>` is more complicated than the definition for `Bunch<T,n>` because the data member `Values` for an `Array<T>` object is a pointer to dynamic space, whereas the data member `Values` for a `Bunch<T,n>` object is an array of n elements. Because an `Array<T>` object acquires dynamic space, the `Array<T>` class needs to define a copy constructor, assignment operator, and destructor. These members are not explicitly

```
template<class T>
  class Array {
    public:
      // default constructor initializes n elements to val
      Array(int n = 10 , const T &val = T());
      // specialized constructor using a standard array
      Array(const T A[], int n);
      // copy constructor
      Array(const Array<T> &A);
      // destructor
      ~Array();
      // inspector for size of the list
      int size() const { return NumberValues; }
      // assignment operator
      Array<T> & operator=(const Array<T> &A);
      // inspector for element of constant list
      const T& operator[](int i) const;
      // inspector/mutator for element of nonconstant list
      T& operator[](int i);
    private:
      // data members
      int NumberValues;  // size of list
      T *Values;         // pointer to list elements
};
```

required for the Bunch<T,n> class because a Bunch<T,n> object does not acquire dynamic space—the compiler-supplied copy constructor, assignment operator, and destructor should suffice.

We believe client programming flexibility should be the basis for deciding which class—Bunch<T,n> or Array<T>—is the basis for our ADT. Therefore, our choice is to develop Array<T> where the number of list elements being represented is not type distinguishing. In the remainder of this section we consider how to implement some of the member functions and operators of the class Array<T>. The class Bunch<T,n> is left to the exercises.

The default Array<T> constructor has two optional parameters n and val that specify the number of elements to be represented and the initial value for those elements. The default value of n is 10, and the default value of val is the value of a T object that has been default constructed. For example, suppose a list R of Rational objects and a list S of string objects are default constructed.

```
Array<Rational> R;        // represents 10 0/1s
Array<string> S;          // represents 10 ""s
```

R then represents a list of 10 elements where each element represents the rational 0/1, and S represents a list of 10 elements where each element represents the empty string "". The elements of R have their 0/1 representation because the default constructor for the Rational class constructs a representation of 0/1. Similarly, the elements of S have their "" representation because the default constructor for the string class constructs a representation of the empty string.

If we need to instantiate a list of *class-type* elements whose class does not have a public default constructor, then values for both n and val must be passed explicitly. For example, the `RectangleShape` class does not have a default constructor. An attempt to default construct an `Array<Rectangle-Shape>` object will generate an error message.

```
Array<RectangleShape> T;    // illegal
```

However, the `Array<RectangleShape>` definition in the following code segment is legal.

```
SimpleWindow W("Drawing Window", 20, 20);
RectangleShape r(W, 2, 2, Blue, 3, 4);
Array<RectangleShape> U(5, r);  // 5 rs
```

The definition of U is legal because we have specified both the number of elements and a legal value for those elements.

Although the fundamental types are not class types and therefore inherently do not have default constructors, we can default construct `Array` lists of such types. We can do so because the compiler automatically supplies the value 0 when a request is made to default construct an object whose type is fundamental. For example, the following definitions are all valid.

```
Array<int> V;         // represents 10 0s
Array<double> X;      // represents 10 0.0s
Array<int> Y(6);      // represents 6 0s
Array<float> Z(21);   // represents 21 0.0s
```

Like the definition of `IntArray` from Chapter 11, the definition of the class `Array<T>` in Listing 14.2 twice overloads the subscript operator. The two member subscript operators differ in their return type and in their use of the qualifier **const**. Because a qualifier is part of a member function signature, a compiler uses context to determine which definition applies when it translates an invocation of the subscript operator on an `Array<T>` object.

The definition of the subscript operator using the qualifier **const** is invoked in situations where a **const** `Array<T>` object is inspected as in the following code segment.

```
const Array<int> A(30, 0);  // represents 30 0s
cout << A[2] << endl;
int i = A[6];
```

The subscript operator with the reference return type is used in situations where a non-**const** `Array<T>` object is being inspected or mutated as in the following code segment.

```
Array<int> B(10, 1);   // represents 10 1s
Array<int> C(20, 2);   // represents 20 2s
B[9] = 17;
Swap(C[3], B[4]);
cin >> B[5];
cout << C[19];
```

The other member functions of the class `Array<T>`—copy constructor, specialized constructor, destructor, assignment operator, and `size()` function—serve a similar purpose to the corresponding member functions of the class `IntArray`. As with the `Array<T>` data members, `NumberValues` maintains the size of the list and `Values` is a pointer to the dynamic memory that maintains the elements of the list.

14.4.2 Implementation

Our definitions of the `Array<T>` member function templates begin in Listing 14.3. In particular, this listing provides the templates for two of the `Array<T>` constructors. The definitions show that the syntax for a template member function defined outside the class definition is quite cumbersome. (The member `size()` defined within the class definition does not suffer in such a manner.)

Note that we define the member function templates in the same file as the class definition itself. Because of current compiler limitations, the definitions cannot be placed in a separate file and linked to the client application. The underlying reason for the compiler limitations is that the `Array<T>` definitions are templates for implementations rather than implementations themselves.

The implementation of the default `Array<T>` constructor with its two optional parameters n and `val` begins with an assertion that the value of n makes sense. We use an `assert()` invocation rather than an **if** statement for pedagogical simplicity. If the value of n makes sense, data member `Number-Values` is set to that value.

```
assert(n > 0);
NumberValues = n;
```

Next space is acquired for maintaining the values that constitute the list.

```
Values = new T [n];
assert(Values);
```

Under the C++ standard, if this request cannot be satisfied, an exception is generated and the program terminates. Previous versions of C++ returned 0 for an unsatisfied request. Thus regardless of which version of C++ your compiler supports, if the **for** statement is reached during program execution, it must be the case that the free store request has been satisfied.

```
for (int i = 0; i < n; ++i) {
    Values[i] = val;
}
```

In the **for** loop, the objects that make up the dynamic space to which `Values` points are set to the value of `val`.

The second `Array<T>` constructor in Listing 14.3 uses a standard C++ array of appropriate type to initialize the `Array<T>` object. The body of this constructor is similar to the body of the default constructor. The only difference is the values used to initialize the dynamic space.

The templates for the `Array<T>` copy constructor, destructor, and assignment operator are given in Listing 14.4. The implementations are all straightforward and closely resemble the corresponding member functions of `IntArray`. The only warranted explanation is that when an `Array<T>` copy is made, whether through construction or assignment, the operation is a deep copy (i.e., a separate list is made with each element individually copied), rather

```cpp
// default constructor initializes n elements to val
template<class T>
 Array<T>::Array(int n, const T &val) {
    assert(n > 0);
    NumberValues = n;
    Values = new T [n];
    assert(Values);
    for (int i = 0; i < n; ++i) {
       Values[i] = val;
    }
}

// constructor initializes from a standard array
template<class T>
 Array<T>::Array(const T A[], int n) {
    assert(n > 0);
    NumberValues = n;
    Values = new T [n];
    assert(Values);
    for (int i = 0; i < n; ++i) {
       Values[i] = A[i];
    }
}
```

than a shallow copy where the copy operation merely duplicates the value of the pointer Values. With a deep copy, the source and target lists have identical but distinct representations. The Values data members point to different memory locations that contain the same values. In a shallow copy, the two lists share a single representation—the Values data members point to the same memory location.

The two straightforward overloadings of the subscript operator for **const** and non-**const** Array<T> objects are also given in Listing 14.4.

```cpp
// copy constructor
template<class T>
 Array<T>::Array(const Array<T> &A) {
    NumberValues = A.size();
    Values = new T [A.size()];
    assert(Values);
    for (int i = 0; i < A.size(); ++i)
       Values[i] = A[i];
}
// destructor
template<class T>
 Array<T>::~Array() {
    delete [] Values;
}
// assignment
template<class T>
 Array<T>& Array<T>::operator=(const Array<T> &A) {
    if (this != &A) {
       if (size() != A.size()) {
          delete [] Values;
          NumberValues = A.size();
          Values = new T [A.size()];
          assert(Values);
       }
       for (int i = 0; i < A.size(); ++i)
          Values[i] = A[i];
```

```
    }
    return *this;
}
// inspector of the value of an individual element
template<class T>
  const T& Array<T>::operator[](int i) const {
    assert((i >= 0) && (i < size()));
    return Values[i];
}

// inspector/mutator facilitator of individual element
template<class T>
  T& Array<T>::operator[](int i) {
    assert((i >= 0) && (i < size()));
    return Values[i];
}
```

The auxiliary insertion operator is twice overloaded in Listing 14.5. The first overloading is a template definition for Array<T> objects in general. The definition requires that the insertion operator be defined for the type of the elements represented in the list. The template version outputs the list within a pair of brackets. The individual elements in a list are separated by spaces. The second overloading of the insertion operator is specifically for Array<**char**> objects. This insertion definition displays the list in "string" style—the individual **char** elements of the list are concatenated together in the output stream.

Listing 14.5

Array auxiliary operators from alist.h

```
// template insertion operator for Array
template<class T>
  ostream& operator<<(ostream &sout, const Array<T> &A){
    sout << "[ ";
    for (int i = 0; i < A.size(); ++i) {
      sout << A[i] << " ";
    }
    sout << "]";
    return sout;
}

// insertion operator for Array<char>
ostream& operator<<(ostream &sout, const Array<char> &A) {
    for (int i = 0; i < A.size(); ++i) {
      sout << A[i];
    }
    return sout;
}
```

Program 14.2 demonstrates some of the capabilities of Array<T>. Its definitions of objects A and B specify both the number of elements and the initial value of those elements. The definition of object C invokes the specialized constructor that uses a standard array and a number of elements to perform the initialization. This constructor is invoked because C++ effectively treats a string as an array of constant **char** objects whose last element is the null character.

The following assignment statement from the test program makes A a distinct copy of B.

```
A = B;
```

Program 14.2

Test program for
Array<T>

```
#include <iostream>
#include <string>
#include "alist.h"

using namespace std;

int main() {
    Array<int> A(5, 0);   // A is five 0's
    const Array<int> B(8, 1); // B is eight 1's
    Array<char> C("hello", 5); // C is h, e, l, l, o
    cout << "A = " << A << endl;
    cout << "B = " << B << endl;
    cout << "C = " << C << endl;
    A = B;
    A[5] = 3;
    A[B[1]] = 2;
    cout << "A = " << A << endl;
    cout << "B = " << B << endl;
    cout << "C = " << C << endl;
    return 0;
}
```

The assignment

```
A[5] = 3;
```

makes use only of the non-**const** version of the member subscript operator. However, the assignment

```
A[B[1]] = 2;
```

makes use of both member subscript operators—the reference to B[1] uses the subscript operator for **const** Array objects, and the result of that operation (the value 3) is used as a parameter to the other subscript operator.

The output of a program run follows.

```
A = [ 0 0 0 0 0 ]
B = [ 1 1 1 1 1 1 1 1 ]
C = hello
A = [ 1 2 1 1 1 3 1 1 ]
B = [ 1 1 1 1 1 1 1 1 ]
C = hello
```

Self-check Questions

1. What is a polymorphic function?

2. Write a templated function that accepts two parameters. The function returns −1 if the value of the first parameter is less than the value of the second parameter; it returns 0 if the values of the two parameters are equal; and it returns 1 if the value of the first parameter is greater than the value of the second parameter.

3. Here is the header file for the Stack class that is implemented using a dynamically allocated array. This data structure holds Position objects.

```
class Stack {
    public:
        Stack(int StackSize = 20);
        ~Stack();
        // Facilitators
        // Push a position on the stack
        void Push(const Position &p);
        // Pop an element off the stack
        // returns the element
        Position Pop();
        bool IsEmpty() const;
    private:
        // Maximum number of elements stack can hold
        int MaxStackSize;
        // Number of elements currently on the stack
        int CurrentStackSize;
        // Top of stack
        int StackTop;
        // Pointer to array of values
        Position *Values;
};
```

It would be nice to have a stack that held any type of object not just `Position` objects. We can do this by making `Stack` a templated class. We could call it `TStack`. Give the declaration of the templated class `TStack`.

4. Why does class `Array<T>` have two overloadings of the subscript operator? Explain your example by giving some code examples that show both overloadings being used.

5. Extend the template class `Array` by adding a `Min` member function that returns the minimum value in the `Array`. Give the modified class declaration as well as the implementation of function `Min()`.

14.5 SEQUENTIAL LISTS

A major problem with arrays is that they cannot grow or shrink in size. In addition, the number of elements is determined at compile time. An `Array<T>` object has more flexibility—its size is determined at run time, and through assignment an `Array<T>` object can represent a list of another size. And by adding member functions such as `push_back()` and `resize()`, we can gain additional flexibility. This addition is considered in the exercises. The approach we consider here is a template list ADT, named `SeqList<T>`, that permits elements to be dynamically inserted or removed anywhere in a list in an *efficient* manner. In terms of the STL container classes, `SeqList<T>` is most similar to `list`.

The name `SeqList<T>` comes from the fact that this ADT offers *sequential* access to the list elements being represented. In such a list, the elements are ordered, and if the program can already access a particular element in the list, then the program can efficiently access the successive element in the list using a forward iterator. Our ADT also provides reverse iterator methods for efficiently accessing the preceding element. An iterator that can access elements in forward or reverse order is a *bidirectional* iterator.

Our implementation of the template `SeqList<T>` ADT uses a data structure known as a *doubly linked list*. A doubly linked list is a collection of elements in which an individual element has three data members: one data member represents an individual list value, and the other two data members are pointers to the next and previous elements in the list. A null pointer value indicates an end of the list.

The following diagram depicts a linked list that represents the values 2, 8, 6, and 4. The arrows in the picture indicate the links from one element to another. The filled-in squares represent null pointers.

14.5.1 SeqItem class template

To implement a linked-list version of `SeqList<T>`, we will define an additional class template, named `SeqItem<T>`, to represent individual elements of the linked list (i.e., a list value and its pointers to elements). The class template definition for `SeqItem<T>` is given in Listing 14.6.

Listing 14.6

Class template SeqItem from slist.h

```
template<class T>
 class SeqItem{
    friend class SeqList<T>;
    friend class SeqIterator<T>;
    friend class ConstSeqIterator<T>;
    protected:
       // default constructor
       SeqItem(const T &val)
         : ItemValue(val), Predecessor(0), Successor(0) {
          // no code needed
       };
    private:
       T ItemValue;            // element value
       SeqItem *Predecessor;   // pointer to previous element
       SeqItem *Successor;     // pointer to next element
};
```

Because client programmers have access to elements in a `SeqList<T>` through other means, the definition of `SeqItem<T>` makes all member functions **protected** and all data members **private**. This qualification means that a client cannot directly define a `SeqItem<T>` object.

A `Seqlist<T>` object requires access to the data members of a `SeqItem<T>` object; therefore, `SeqItem<T>` declares `SeqList<T>` to be a **friend** class. A **friend** of a class has complete access to all class members—regardless of whether they are public, protected, or private. To declare a friend function, operator, or class, the modifier **friend** is applied to the prototype of the function, operator, or class that is to be granted friendship. The actual definition of the **friend** requires no special syntax. The modifier **friend** is examined in detail in Appendix D.

Programmer Alert

Friends—should you trust them?

Although the **friend** mechanism provides some control over what function, operator, or class manipulates the underlying data representation, it still creates a major security hole with respect to information hiding. For this reason, use a **friend** only when absolutely necessary. One situation where using the friend mechanism might be warranted is when we want to define an operator that needs direct access to two different types of objects, and providing low-level access functions to access both objects is impractical. In this case, making the operator a friend of both classes is a viable solution.

The iterator template class SeqIterator<T>, which is presented in Section 14.5.8, is also a **friend** class to SeqItem<T>. The iterator template class ConstSeqIterator<T> is left to the exercises. Its purpose is to provide iterator access to **const** SeqList<T> objects.

As is appropriate for an element of a doubly linked list, a SeqItem<T> object has three data members. The data member ItemValue represents a list value, the data member Predecessor points to the previous element in the linked list, and the data member Successor points to the next element in the linked list.

```
T ItemValue;          // element value
SeqItem *Predecessor;  // pointer to previous element
SeqItem *Successor;    // pointer to next element
```

The definition of the SeqItem<T> class includes the definition of its constructor.

```
SeqItem(const T &val)
 : ItemValue(val), Predecessor(0), Successor(0) {
    // no code needed
};
```

The constructor expects as its parameter a list element value val. Parameter val is used to initialize data member ItemValue in the constructor's member initialization list. The two pointer data members Predecessor and Successor are both initialized to the null address.

The class template definition of SeqList<T> is given in Listing 14.7. The listing shows that the ADT provides the standard member functions such as a default constructor, destructor, copy constructor, and member assignment operator. In addition, the ADT provides the following member functions:

- size(): returns the number of elements in the list.
- front() **const**: returns the first element in the list as an rvalue.
- front(): returns the first element in the list as an lvalue.

Listing 14.7

*Class template SeqList
from slist.h*

```
template<class T>
class SeqList {
    // friends classes
    friend class SeqIterator<T>;
    friend class ConstSeqIterator<T>;
    public:
        // typedef conveniences
        typedef SeqIterator<T> iterator;
        typedef ConstSeqIterator<T> const_iterator;
        // constructor and destructor
        SeqList();
        ~SeqList();
        // inspectors and accessors
        int size() const;
        T& front();
        const T& front() const;
        T& back();
        const T& back() const;
        // iterator facilitators
        iterator begin();
        const_iterator begin() const;
        iterator end();
        const_iterator end() const;
        // convenience functions
        void push_back(const T &val);
        void pop_front();
        // insertion facilitator
        void display(ostream &sout) const;
        // list facilitators
        iterator insert(iterator p, const T &val);
        iterator erase(iterator p);
        void clear();
        // member assignment and copy construction
        SeqList& operator=(const SeqList &S);
        SeqList(const SeqList<T> &S);
    private:
        // data members
        SeqItem<T> *Front;      // pointer to first element
        SeqItem<T> *Back;       // pointer to last element
        int ListLength;         // number of elements
};
```

- `back() const`: returns the last element in the list as an rvalue.

- `back()`: returns the last element in the list as an lvalue.

- `begin() const`: returns a constant iterator pointing to the first element in the list.

- `begin()`: returns an iterator pointing to the first element in the list.

- `end() const`: returns a constant iterator pointing to a sentinel immediately beyond the last element in the list.

- `end()`: returns an iterator pointing to a sentinel immediately beyond the last element in the list.

- `push_back(const T &val)`: convenience function for adding a copy of `val` at the end of the list.

- `pop_front()`: convenience function for removing the first element of the list.

- `display(ostream &sout) const`: displays the list to stream `sout`.
- `insert(iterator p, const T &val)`: inserts a copy of `val` into the list immediately ahead of the element to which iterator `p` points. The function returns an iterator that points to the new element.
- `clear()`: removes all elements from the list.
- `erase(iterator p)`: removes the element from the list to which iterator `p` points. The function returns an iterator that points to the element that had previously followed the removed element.

To support these member functions, `SeqList<T>` specifies three data members. The **int** data member `ListLength` represents the number of elements in the list. Data members `Front` and `Back` respectively point to the `SeqItem<T>` objects representing the first and last elements in the list. The two iterator classes `SeqIterator<I>` and `ConstSeqIterator<T>` are made friends of the `SeqList<T>` class so that they can have access to `SeqList<T>` data members.

14.5.2   SeqList member function basics

The implementations of the `SeqList<T>` member functions are given in Listings 14.8 through 14.12. Listing 14.8 begins with the definition of the default constructor. The constructor uses an initialization list to specify initial values for the data members. The pointers `Front` and `Back` are both initialized to the null address, thus indicating that the list is currently empty. Data member `ListLength` is initialized to 0 to also reflect this list condition.

The `SeqList<T>` destructor uses the member function `clear()` to accomplish its task. Our discussion of `clear()` appears in Section 14.5.6. Inspector `size()` accomplishes its task by simply returning the value of `ListLength`.

The purpose of both `front()` member functions is to provide access to the first element in the list through a reference return. The `front()` functions differ only in how the first element can be manipulated by invoking functions. The `front()` function with the qualifier **const** allows only inspection of the first element in the list; the `front()` function without the qualifier **const** allows inspection and mutation of the first element in the list.

The `front()` functions can accomplish their task only if the list is nonempty. For pedagogical simplicity the functions accomplish this check through an `assert()` statement. Given that there is a first element, its value is maintained by the data member `ItemValue` of the `SeqItem<T>` object to which `Front` points. Thus if there is a first element, `Front->ItemValue` is that element. If `Front`, `Back`, and the linked list have the following depiction, then the functions `front()` return a reference to the location with the value 2 in it.

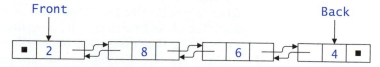

```
// default SeqList constructor
template<class T>
  SeqList<T>::SeqList()
  : ListLength(0), Front(0), Back(0) { // no code needed
}

// SeqList destructor
template<class T>
  SeqList<T>::~SeqList() {
    clear();
}

// size(): return size of list
template<class T>
  int SeqList<T>::size() const {
    return ListLength;
}

// front(): return reference to first element in list
template<class T>
  T& SeqList<T>::front() {
    assert(size() != 0);
    return Front->ItemValue;
}

// front(): return const reference to first element in list
template<class T>
  const T& SeqList<T>::front() const {
    assert(size() != 0);
    return Front->ItemValue;
}

// back(): return reference to last element in list
template<class T>
  T& SeqList<T>::back() {
    assert(size() != 0);
    return Back->ItemValue;
}

// back(): return const reference to last element in list
template<class T>
  const T& SeqList<T>::back() const {
    assert(size() != 0);
    return Back->ItemValue;
}

// begin(): create iterator pointing to first element
template<class T>
  SeqIterator<T> SeqList<T>::begin() {
    return SeqIterator<T>(this, Front);
}

// end(): create iterator pointing to sentinel
template<class T>
  SeqIterator<T> SeqList<T>::end() {
    return SeqIterator<T>(this, 0);
}
```

The two SeqList<T> back() member functions provide access to the last element in the list (if it exists) through their return values. The functions differ only in how the last element can be manipulated by the invoking functions. The back() function with the qualifier **const** allows only inspection of the last element in the list; the back() function without the qualifier **const** allows inspection and mutation of the last element in the list. Given that there is a last element, its value is maintained by the data member ItemValue of the SeqItem<T> object to which Back points. Hence if there is a last element, Back->ItemValue is that element. For our preceding figure, the functions back() return a reference to the location with the value 4 in it.

The next two members defined in Listing 14.8 produce iterators for list manipulation. Function begin() returns an iterator pointing to the first element in the list. The iterator is produced by constructing a SeqIterator<T> object. The SeqIterator<T> constructor that produces the return value takes two parameters—a pointer to the list for which the iterator is associated and a pointer to the particular position within the list. This SeqIterator<T> constructor is a protected member of the SeqIterator<T> class. SeqList<T> member functions can use the constructor because SeqList<T> is a **friend** class of SeqIterator<T>.

Function end() returns an iterator that conceptually points to a sentinel immediately beyond the last element in the list. The SeqIterator<T> class uses the null address to indicate a list sentinel. As such, the object constructed from SeqIterator<T>(**this**, 0) represents an iterator pointing to a sentinel for the current list.

Functions push_back() and pop_front() of Listing 14.9 are convenience functions. They have been implemented because we anticipate that clients will typically want to add elements at the end of the list and remove items from the front of the list. These functions are optional, as their definitions are straightforward invocations of other SeqList<T> member functions. In particular, push_back() can insert a value val at the end of the list by invoking the insert() member function with end() and val as its parameters.

```
insert(end(), val);  // a push_back
```

Function pop_front() can accomplish its task by invoking the erase() member function with begin() as its parameter.

```
erase(begin());       // a pop_front
```

Functions insert() and erase() are discussed in Section 14.5.4.

Listing 14.9

More SeqList member functions from slist.h

```
// push_back(): add value to end of list
template<class T>
 void SeqList<T>::push_back(const T &val) {
   insert(end(), val);
}

// pop_front(): erase value from front of list
template<class T>
 void SeqList<T>::pop_front() {
   erase(begin());
}

// display(): display list
template<class T>
 void SeqList<T>::display(ostream &sout) const {
   sout << "[";
   for (SeqItem<T> *Ptr = Front; Ptr; Ptr = Ptr->Successor)
     sout << " " << Ptr->ItemValue;
   sout << " ]";
}
```

14.5.3 Member function display()

The member function display() of Listing 14.9 allows for the easy overloading of the insertion operator. The list is displayed surrounded by brackets. A **for** loop performs the actual display of the list elements.

```
for (SeqItem<T> *Ptr = Front; Ptr; Ptr = Ptr->Successor)
{
    sout << " " << Ptr->ItemValue;
}
```

The **for** loop initialization statement defines a SeqItem<T> pointer Ptr whose initial value is Front. At this point, the involved objects have the following depiction:

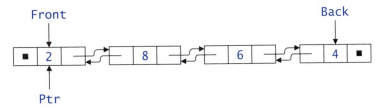

The **for** loop is iterated as long as the value of Ptr is not null. The body of the **for** loop consists of a single insertion statement.

```
sout << " " << Ptr->ItemValue;
```

The ItemValue (2) of the current SeqItem<T> to which Ptr points is inserted to the output stream. Afterwards, Ptr is updated in the post expression (Ptr = Ptr->Successor) of the **for** loop header. Ptr's new value becomes the address of the next element in the linked list. The objects now have the following depiction:

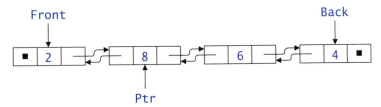

Because Ptr is not null, the loop is iterated again and an 8 is inserted to the output stream. Ptr is again updated. The objects now have the following depiction:

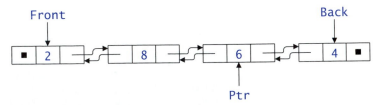

Ptr is still not null and the loop is reiterated causing a 6 to be inserted to the output stream. Ptr is updated once again. The objects now have the following depiction:

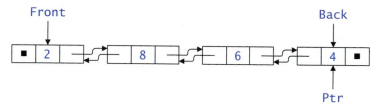

Ptr now points to the last element of the linked list. The loop body is reiterated one last time, and the value 4 is inserted to the output stream. The **for** loop postexpression causes Ptr to now take on the null value. The test expression for the **for** loop then evaluates to 0, and the loop is ended.

To complete the display, the closing right bracket is inserted.

```
sout << " ]";
```

In the exercises we consider an alternative implementation of display() that uses an iterator to advance through the list.

We next define the SeqList<T> insert() and erase() member functions that, respectively, add and remove an element from the list.

14.5.4 Adding an element

The insert() function of Listing 14.10 takes two parameters p and val. Parameter p is an iterator that points to the existing element that is to come immediately after the new element. The value of the new element is val.

The function begins by ensuring that p is associated with our list.

```
assert(p.ThisList == this);
```

A new SeqItem<T> object is then requested from the free store. Pointer curr points to this object. An assertion ensures that the new request was successful.

```
SeqItem<T> *curr = new SeqItem<T>(val);
assert(curr);
```

How the new element is added to the list depends on whether it is to be the last element in the list.

If the new element is not to be the last element (i.e., p.ItemPtr is non-null), then we can define pointers succ and pred to represent the locations that conceptually succeed and precede the new element. (The value of pred may be null if the element to which p points currently is the first element in the list.)

```
SeqItem<T> *succ = p.ItemPtr;
SeqItem<T> *pred = succ->Predecessor;
```

Listing 14.10

*SeqList member
functions from slist.h*

```
// insert(): add an item to the list
template<class T>
 SeqIterator<T> SeqList<T>::
  insert(SeqIterator<T> p, const T &val) {
   // make sure the iterator belongs to this list
   assert(p.ThisList == this);
   // create the item to represent our new element
   SeqItem<T> *curr = new SeqItem<T>(val);
   assert(curr);
   if (p.ItemPtr != 0) { // new item is not the rear
      // determine successor and predecessor of new item
      SeqItem<T> *succ = p.ItemPtr;
      SeqItem<T> *pred = succ->Predecessor;
      // reset links to reflect the changes to the list
      curr->Successor = succ;
      curr->Predecessor = pred;
      succ->Predecessor = curr;
      // determine whether new item is to head the list
      if (succ == Front) { // yes it does
         Front = curr;
      }
      else { // no it does not
         pred->Successor = curr;
      }
   }
   else { // iterator p does not point to a list element
      if (size() == 0) { // curr is the list at this point
         Front = Back = curr;
      }
      else { // curr is to be the end of the list
         curr->Predecessor = Back;
         Back->Successor = curr;
         Back = curr;
      }
   }
   // reflect that the item has been added
   ++ListLength;
   // bring back an iterator to the new item
   return SeqIterator<T>(this, curr);
}
```

This case is depicted in the following figure. In this and subsequent figures, dashed boxes indicate that the associated links are possibly null. Filled-in
circles represent element values.

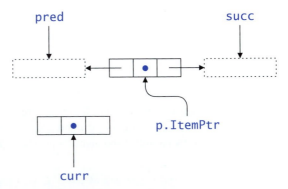

Pointers `succ` and `pred` are then used to correctly set the data members for the new element's successor and predecessor.

```
curr->Successor = succ;
curr->Predecessor = pred;
```

With these assignments the objects of interest now have the following depiction:

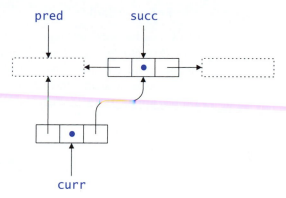

Because we know that for this case an element is following the new element, we set the predecessor of that element (`succ->Predecessor`) to be the new element.

```
succ->Predecessor = curr;
```

With this assignment the objects of interest have the following depiction:

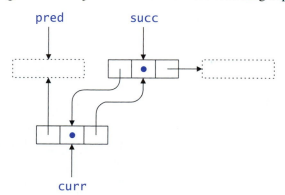

Depending on whether the new element is or is not at the front of the list, we must set either `Front` or the previous predecessor of the new element's successor (`pred->Successor`) to point to the new element.

```
if (succ == Front) {
    Front = curr;
}
else {
    pred->Successor = curr;
}
```

We now consider the case when the new element is to be the last element in the list. Our implementation divides this case into two subcases. These cases depend on whether the list is currently empty (i.e., whether `size()` has the value 0).

If the list is currently empty, then the new element is both the first and last element of the list. As such, data members `Front` and `Back` should both point to the new element.

```
Front = Back = curr;
```

This subcase does not require us to set the new element's `Successor` and `Predecessor` data members to the null address because that is the value given to these members during the new element's construction. The depiction of the objects of interest after this assignment statement would be

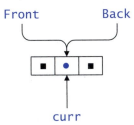

If instead the list is not empty, then the new element's predecessor should be the element that was previously the last element in the list.

```
curr->Predecessor = Back;
```

After the assignment, the objects of interest have as the following depiction:

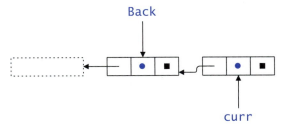

For this subcase, we must also have the new element's predecessor point to the new element.

```
Back->Successor = curr;
```

In addition, we must update `Back` to reflect that the new element is now the end of the list.

```
Back = curr;
```

These assignments would result in the following depiction:

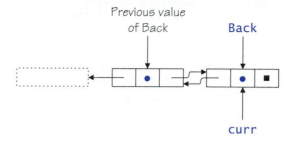

No matter how the insertion is accomplished, we must update data member `ListLength` to reflect the presence of another element in the list.

```
++ListLength;
```

The return value for the function is an iterator that points to the new element.

```
return SeqIterator<T>(this, curr);
```

14.5.5 Removing an element

The `erase()` function of Listing 14.11 begins with two assertions. The first assertion checks that the iterator points to the current list. The second assertion checks that there is in fact an element to remove.

```
assert(p.ThisList == this);
assert(p.ItemPtr);
```

Function `erase()` then defines objects `curr`, `pred`, and `succ`. Object `curr` is a pointer to the element to be removed. Objects `pred` and `succ` are pointers to the same locations to which that element's `Predecessor` and `Successor` data members point.

```
SeqItem<T> *curr = p.ItemPtr;
SeqItem<T> *pred = curr->Predecessor;
SeqItem<T> *succ = curr->Successor;
```

The objects in question have the following depiction:

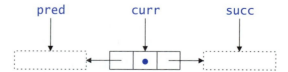

Checks are then made to determine whether `curr` points to either the first or last element in the list.

If `curr` points to the first element in the list, then that element's successor is the new front of the list.

```
Front = succ;
```

Listing 14.11

*SeqList member
functions from slist.h*

```cpp
// erase(): remove an item from list
template<class T>
 SeqIterator<T> SeqList<T>::erase(SeqIterator<T> p) {
    // make sure the iterator belongs to this list
    assert(p.ThisList == this);
    // make sure the iterator points to an item
    assert(p.ItemPtr);
    // identify item and its neighbors (if any)
    SeqItem<T> *curr = p.ItemPtr;
    SeqItem<T> *pred = curr->Predecessor;
    SeqItem<T> *succ = curr->Successor;
    // determine whether item heads list
    if (curr == Front) { // yes it does
        // successor (if any) now heads the list
        Front = succ;
    }
    else { // no it doesn t
        // predecessor should point to its successor (if any)
        pred->Successor = succ;
    }
    // determine whether item ends the list
    if (curr == Back) { // yes it does
        // predecessor (if any) now ends the list
        Back = pred;
    }
    else { // no it doesn t
        // successor should point to its predecessor (if any)
        succ->Predecessor = pred;
    }
    // can delete the item -- its neighborhood is updated
    delete curr;
    // reflect that the item has been removed
    --ListLength;
    // bring back an iterator to the successor (if any)
    return SeqIterator<T>(this, succ);
}
```

If instead `curr` does not point to the first element in the list, then that element's predecessor should point to the element's successor.

```cpp
pred->Successor = succ;
```

If `curr` points to the last element in the list, then that element's predecessor is the new end of the list.

```cpp
Back = pred;
```

If instead `curr` does not point to the last element in the list, then that element's successor should point to the element's predecessor.

```cpp
succ->Predecessor = pred;
```

Having reset the links so that the element in question has been cut out of the list, we can now return its storage to the free store. We also update `ListLength` to reflect that there is one less element.

```cpp
delete curr;
--ListLength;
```

To complete the function, we return an iterator to the element that had previously followed the removed element.

```
return SeqIterator<T>(this, succ);
```

14.5.6 Removing all elements

The task of member function `clear()` of Listing 14.12 is more straightforward than `erase()`, as there are no special cases to consider. The function begins by setting a `SeqItem<T>*` object `Ptr` to the value of `Front`. `Ptr` is used to iterate through the elements in the linked list.

```
SeqItem<T> *Ptr = Front;
```

The loop iterates while `Ptr` points to an actual element in the list (i.e., it is not null). Within the body of the loop, a temporary pointer object `Next` remembers the next element of the linked list (`Ptr->Successor`). Once the current linked list item has been deleted, `Ptr` is reset to `Next` to prepare for the next possible iteration of the loop.

```
while ( Ptr ) {
    SeqItem<T> *Next = Ptr->Successor;
    delete Ptr;
    Ptr = Next;
}
```

When the loop is finished, to complete `clear()`, the three data members of the `SeqList<T>` object are reset so that they reflect the representation of an empty list.

```
Front = Back = 0;
ListLength = 0;
```

The exercises consider an alternative implementation of `clear()` using iterators.

Listing 14.12

SeqList clear() member function from slist.h

```
// clear(): purge list
template<class T>
 void SeqList<T>::clear() {
    SeqItem<T> *Ptr = Front;
    while ( Ptr ) {
        SeqItem<T> *Next = Ptr->Successor;
        delete Ptr;
        Ptr = Next;
    }
    Front = Back = 0;
    ListLength = 0;
}
```

14.5.7 A small program using SeqList template class

Program 14.3 demonstrates some features of our `SeqList<T>` template class. It performs a mixture of additions and deletions to a list of integers. Note that the actual overloading of the insertion operator is straightforward and is left to the exercises. The output of Program 14.3 is given below.

```
List: [ ]
Adding: 1
List: [ 1 ]
Adding: 2
List: [ 1 2 ]
Adding: 3
List: [ 1 2 3 ]
Adding: 4
List: [ 1 2 3 4 ]
Adding: 5
List: [ 1 2 3 4 5 ]
Removing: 1
Removing: 2
List: [ 3 4 5 ]
Removing all
List: [ ]
Adding: 62154
List: [ 62154 ]
```

Program 14.3

A limited test program for the SeqList<T> template class

```cpp
// Program 14.3: demonstrate some SeqList<T> capabilities
#include<iostream>
#include<string>

using namespace std;

#include "slist.h"

int main() {
    SeqList<int> A;
    cout << "List: " << A << endl;
    for (int i = 1; i <= 5; ++i) {
        cout << "Adding: " << i << endl;;
        A.push_back(i);
        cout << "List: " << A << endl;
    }
    cout << "Removing: " << A.front() << endl;
    A.pop_front();
    cout << "Removing: " << A.front() << endl;
    A.pop_front();
    cout << "List: " << A << endl;
    cout << "Removing all" << endl;
    A.clear();
    cout << "List: " << A << endl;
    cout << "Adding: " << 62154 << endl;
    A.push_back(62154);
    cout << "List: " << A << endl;
    return 0;
}
```

14.5.8 A SeqList iterator class

An important list processing operation that is conspicuously absent in Program 14.3 is the individual referencing of list elements. This capability is provided by the template class `SeqIterator<T>` that works with `SeqList<T>`. In general, an iterator class provides the means for individually accessing the elements of an associated container class. Depending on the associated class, an iterator class may also provide the means to modify a referenced element. Our template class `SeqIterator<T>` provides both the ability to access and modify the elements of a list. The definition of the `SeqIterator<T>` class template is given in Listing 14.13.

Listing 14.13

SeqIterator class template definition from slist.h

```cpp
template<class T>
  class SeqIterator {
    friend class SeqList<T>;
    public:
      // default constructor
      SeqIterator();
      // specific constructor
      SeqIterator(SeqList<T> &L);
      // mutate to next element in list
      SeqIterator<T>& operator++();        // prefix version
      SeqIterator<T> operator++(int);      // postfix version
      // mutate to previous element in list
      SeqIterator<T>& operator--();        // prefix version
      SeqIterator<T> operator--(int);      // postfix version
      // inspector for a constant iterator
      const T& operator*() const;
      // inspector/mutator for a nonconstant iterator
      T& operator*();
      // test for equality
      bool operator==(const SeqIterator<T> &p) const;
      // test for inequality
      bool operator!=(const SeqIterator<T> &p) const;
      // bool cast
      operator bool() const;
    protected:
      // specific constructor for SeqList use
      SeqIterator(SeqList<T> *P, SeqItem<T> *q);
    private:
      SeqList<T> *ThisList;    // pointer to iterated list
      SeqItem<T> *ItemPtr;     // pointer to current element
};
```

The default constructor for the class `SeqIterator<T>` associates the iterator with the null list. The other public constructor associates the iterator with the list represented by its parameter L. In particular, if the list is nonempty, the iterator is associated with the first element in L; otherwise, the iterator is associated with the list sentinel.

The protected constructor for the class `SeqIterator<T>` has two parameters: P and q. Parameter P is a pointer to the list with which the iterator is to be associated; parameter q is a pointer to a particular location in that list. This constructor is used by `SeqItem<T>` to construct iterators to particular elements.

At the end of the following code segment, iterators a, b, and c are defined. The a definition uses the default constructor. Therefore a is not associated with any particular list. The b definition uses the other class-defined public constructor to associate b with the first element of a `SeqList<char>` A. The c definition uses the compiler-supplied copy constructor to associate c with that same element of A.

```
SeqList<char> A;
A.push_back('x');
A.push_back('y');
A.push_back('z');
SeqIterator<char> a;
SeqIterator<char> b(A);
SeqIterator<char> c = A.begin();
```

The SeqIterator<T> iterator class provides a rich set of capabilities. Some of the member capabilities are provided by overloading the increment operator ++, the decrement operator --, and the dereferencing operator *. The discussion of the decrement operator is deferred to the exercises.

The increment operator is twice overloaded. These overloadings allow the operator to be used in prefix and postfix form. To distinguish which definition is which, C++ associates the definition with the empty parameter list with the prefix form. The postfix form is associated with the definition with the dummy **int** parameter.

C++ Language

Prefix or Postfix?

The increment (++) and decrement (--) operators can be either prefix or postfix. To distinguish between the prefix and postfix overloadings of the ++ and -- operators, an **int** argument is used to indicate that the function is to be used for postfix application of the operator. The argument is never used, it is purely a syntactic device to allow the compiler to distinguish between the prefix and postfix declarations of the overloadings of the operator. Stroustrup suggests that the way to remember which overloading is prefix and which is postfix is to note that prefix takes no argument like all the other prefix operators (*, !, etc.) and that the dummy argument is only used for the "odd" postfix ++ and --.

If an iterator is associated with an element that is not the last element in its list, then the ++ operator associates the iterator with the next element in the list. If instead the iterator is associated with the last element in the list, then the ++ operator associates the iterator with the trailing sentinel. The prefix version does a reference return of the iterator after it has been updated. The postfix version does a value return of the value of the iterator before it has been updated.

The dereferencing operator * is also twice overloaded. Both versions provide access to the element currently associated with the iterator. Overloading with the member function modifier **const** allows rvalue access to the element by **const** SeqIterator<T> objects. Overloading without the member function modifier **const** allows lvalue access to the element by SeqIterator<T> objects.

The following code segment uses the increment and dereferencing operators to help display the first two elements of the previously defined list A.

```
cout << *b << endl;
```

```
++b;
cout <<*b << endl;
```

The output of the segment is

```
x
y
```

Because the dereferencing operator for a nonconstant iterator returns an lvalue, by assigning to *b, we can modify the associated list.

```
*b = 'w';
cout << "List: " << A << endl;
```

The output of the segment is

```
List: [ x w z ]
```

The equality operator == and the inequality operator != are overloaded for iterator objects. The equality operator returns true if the iterators are associated with the same element and returns false otherwise. The inequality operator acts in the opposite manner—it returns true if the iterators are associated with different elements and returns false otherwise.

A cast member operator **bool** is also defined. The cast returns a true value if the iterator is associated with an actual element in the list; the cast returns a false value if the iterator is not currently associated with any element in the list. The existence of the cast permits an iterator to be used where a logical expression is expected. (The conversion will be automatically attempted by the compiler.) An example of an automatic conversion appears in the test expression of the **for** statement in the following code segment:

```
for (SeqIterator<char> p = A.begin(); p ; ++p) {
    cout << "Element: " << *p;
    if (p == A.begin()) {
        cout << " front";
    }
    cout << endl;
}
```

A **for** test expression must evaluate to a logical value for successful compilation. If the test expression is not a logical expression (as is the case with our test expression p, which is SeqIterator<**char**>), the compiler applies a **bool** conversion if there is one. Because the **bool** conversion we have defined for SeqIterator<T> objects evaluates to true when the iterator points to a list element, expression p evaluates to true and the **for** loop body is executed.

Because p points in particular to the first element in the list, the first iteration of the loop produces the following output:

```
Element: x front
```

The postexpression ++p for the loop causes the iterator to point to the element representing 'w'. The loop is reiterated to produce as its output

```
Element: w
```

The evaluation of the postexpression causes iterator p to point to the element representing the ízí. The loop is reiterated to produce as its output

```
Element: z
```

The evaluation of the postexpression causes the iterator to be associated with the trailing sentinel. When the test expression is evaluated this time, based upon the behavior we described for the conversion, the test expression evaluates to false.

14.5.9 Implementation of the SeqIterator iterator class

The implementations of the SeqIterator<T> member functions and operators are given in Listings 14.14 and 14.15. The definitions of all of the members are relatively straightforward.

The SeqIterator<T> default constructor associates the iterator being constructed with the null list. To do so, data members ThisList and ItemPtr are set to the null address using an initialization list. In general, ThisList maintains a pointer to the list in question and ItemPtr points to the current position of interest within the list. (A nonnull address is associated with the list sentinel.)

The other SeqIterator<T> public constructor associates the iterator being constructed with the list represented by L. The data members are set using an initialization list. The initial value of data member ThisList is the address of the list represented by parameter L. The initial value of data member ItemPtr is L.Front. Thus if L is a nonempty list, the iterator is associated with the first element of L; otherwise, the iterator is associated with the list sentinel for L. (A null value for data member ItemPtr indicates that the iterator is associated with the list sentinel.)

The protected SeqIterator<T> constructor also sets both of its data members using an initialization list. With this constructor, the initial value of data member ThisList is a pointer to the list in question (parameter P), and the initial value of ItemPtr is a pointer to a list position (parameter q). Because the constructor definition does not examine q to see that it is sensible, it is possible to erroneously pass a pointer value that is not associated with list L. A more secure version of the constructor is considered in the exercises. This constructor is used by SeqList<T>'s iterator-producing member functions. These member functions can use the protected constructor because SeqList<T> is a **friend** class to SeqIterator<T>.

The prefix increment operator ++ for a SeqIterator<T> iterator accomplishes its task by first ensuring that the iterator is nonnull. (For pedagogical purposes, we use an assert statement.) If the iterator is nonnull, it is possible to evaluate the expression ItemPtr->Successor. The value of the expression is either the address of the next element in the list (if there is another element) or it is the null address (if the iterator is currently associated with the last element

Listing 14.14

*SeqIterator member
from slist.h*

```
// SeqIterator(): default constructor
template<class T>
 SeqIterator<T>::SeqIterator() : ThisList(0), ItemPtr(0) {
   // no code needed
}

// SeqIterator(): specific public constructor
template<class T>
 SeqIterator<T>::SeqIterator(SeqList<T> &L)
   : ThisList(&L), ItemPtr(L.Front) {
   // no code needed
}

// SeqIterator(): specific protected constructor
template<class T>
 SeqIterator<T>::SeqIterator(SeqList<T> *P, SeqItem<T> *q)
   : ThisList(P), ItemPtr(q) {
   // no code needed
}

// ++: produce successor (prefix version)
template<class T>
 SeqIterator<T>& SeqIterator<T>::operator++() {
   assert(ItemPtr != 0);
   ItemPtr = ItemPtr->Successor;
   return *this;
}

// ++: produce successor (postfix version)
template<class T>
 SeqIterator<T> SeqIterator<T>::operator++(int) {
   assert(ItemPtr != 0);
   SeqIterator<T> remember(*this);
   ItemPtr = ItemPtr->Successor;
   return remember;
}

// *: inspector for a constant iterator
template<class T>
 const T& SeqIterator<T>::operator*() const {
   assert(ItemPtr != 0);
   return ItemPtr->ItemValue;
}

// *: inspector/mutator for a nonconstant iterator
template<class T> T& SeqIterator<T>::operator*() {
   assert(ItemPtr != 0);
   return ItemPtr->ItemValue;
}
```

in the list). Either way the value of expression `ItemPtr->Successor` is now the correct value for `ItemPtr`.

```
ItemPtr = ItemPtr->Successor;
```

Note that the private data member of the `SeqItem<T>` class can be accessed because the `SeqIterator<T>` class is a **friend** class to the `SeqItem<T>` class. To complete the operation, a reference to the iterator is returned.

```
return *this;
```

The postfix increment operator `++` for a `SeqIterator<T>` iterator accomplishes its task by first ensuring that the iterator is nonnull. (For pedagogical purposes, we again use an assert statement.) The iterator then makes a copy of the invoking object and stores it in the object `remember`. Object `remember` is to be the return value of the operation.

```
SeqIterator<T> remember(*this);
```

`ItemPtr` is then updated to point to its successor.

```
ItemPtr = ItemPtr->Successor;
```

To complete the operation, iterator `remember` is returned.

```
return remember;
```

Like the increment operators, the dereferencing member operators * first determine whether there is an associated element. If so, the return value of both dereferencing operators is the value of the associated element, which is simply `ItemPtr->ItemValue`. The two dereferencing operators differ only in whether they return that element as an rvalue or lvalue.

The equality, inequality, and insertion operators and the **bool** cast are overloaded in Listing 14.15 for `SeqIterator<T>` objects.

Listing 14.15

SeqIterator member functions and auxiliary operator from slist.h

```
// ==: do the iterators refer to the same element
template<class T>
  bool SeqIterator<T>::operator==(const SeqIterator<T> &p)
  const {
    return ItemPtr == p.ItemPtr;
}
// !=: do the iterators refer to different elements
template<class T>
  bool SeqIterator<T>::operator!=(const SeqIterator<T> &p)
  const {
    return ! (*this == p);
}
// bool: cast indicates whether the iterator points to an
// element
template<class T>
  SeqIterator<T>::operator bool () const {
    return *this != this->ThisList->end();
}
// <<: overload insertion operator for list iterator
template<class T>
  ostream& operator<<(ostream &sout,
    const SeqIterator<T> &a) {
    return sout << *a;
}
```

The equality operator == tests whether the `ItemPtr` data members of the invoking object and that of the right operand p point to the same location. If the pointer values are the same, the operator returns true; if the pointer values are different, the operator returns false.

```
return ItemPtr == p.ItemPtr;
```

The inequality operator != tests whether the `ItemPtr` data members of the invoking object and that of the right operand p point to different locations.

The operator is implemented by taking the complement of an equality operation.

```
return ! (*this == p);
```

In general, defining a class operator in terms of another class operator is preferred to a definition that performs the operation directly. This implementation strategy is preferred because it reuses existing features.

The **bool** cast operator is also defined in Listing 14.15. The cast converts an iterator value into a **bool** value. Our cast works by testing whether the iterator is pointing to a sentinel. If the iterator is pointing to a sentinel, the cast returns false; otherwise, the cast returns true. In particular, the cast is implemented using the inequality operator. The operator compares the invoking iterator with an iterator that is explicitly pointing to a sentinel.

```
return *this != this->ThisList->end();
```

For client convenience, the auxiliary insertion operator is overloaded for a SeqIterator<T> iterator object. Its task is accomplished by simply inserting the value associated with the current element to its output stream operand sout.

This completes our discussion of a sequential list ADT and template polymorphism. We next consider true polymorphism.

Self-check Questions

6.   How does one distinguish between the postfix and prefix overloading of the increment operator?

7.   Using class SeqList<T> write a program that reads a list of character strings from a file. The program writes the strings with any duplicate strings deleted.

8.   Using class SeqList<T> write a program that reads a list of screen coordinates and stores them in the list as Position objects. The program then draws small CircleShapes at each position.

14.6 POLYMORPHISM

Suppose you want to develop a client program that manipulates figures using the various shapes designed in Chapter 13. You would probably like to have a collection of figure objects in which each figure object is viewed as a list of the various shapes composing the figure being represented. In general, such a list would be a heterogeneous list, containing, for example, circles, rectangles, and triangles. To process a heterogeneous list, we need polymorphic capabilities.

What type of object can represent a collection of disparate shapes? Your first guess might be a simple Shape array because Shape is the base class for our various shapes. After all, a CircleShape is a Shape, a RectangleShape is a Shape, a TriangleShape is a Shape, and so on.

Suppose a window W and a position P have been previously defined as well as the objects S, R, T, and C that are given below.

```
SquareShape S(W, P, Blue, 1);
TriangleShape T(W, P, Red, 1);
RectangleShape R(W, P, Yellow, 3, 2);
CircleShape C(W, P, Yellow, 4);
```

Also suppose that an array A of Shape objects has been defined in the following manner:

```
Shape A[4] = {S, T, R, C};   // figure A is composed of
                             // four shapes
```

Can we display our figure A using the following loop?

```
for (int i = 0; i < 4; ++i) {
    A[i].Draw();
}
```

The answer is no because A is an array of Shape objects and there is no Shape::Draw() member function to invoke iteratively.

A next attempt might be to add a Draw() member function to the Shape class, as shown in Listing 14.16, to act as a placeholder. Because a Shape object does not have a full specification, the only characteristic of the object that a Draw() function can express is an indication of the object's color. However, the **for** loop still does not work as desired. Each time through the loop, it is the Shape::Draw() function that is invoked, which just displays the invoking object's color. In particular, although S represents a SquareShape, A[0] is only a Shape. The initialization of A[0] using S did not assign all Square-Shape properties to A[0]; only the members that are Shape members are copied.

Listing 14.16

Shape definition with a placeholder Draw() function

```
class Shape : public WindowObject {
    public:
        Shape(SimpleWindow &w, const Position &p,
          const color c = Red);
        color GetColor() const;
        void SetColor(const color c);
        void Draw() { cout << GetColor(); };
    private:
        color Color;
};
```

Your next attempt in representing a figure might be to have A be an array of Shape pointers

```
Shape *A[4] = {&S, &T, &R, &C};
```

where, for example, based on the preceding definition, A[0] is a pointer to a SquareShape, A[1] is a pointer to a TriangleShape, and so on. The earlier **for** loop cannot be used, because the elements of A are no longer Shape objects, but pointers to Shape objects. Now consider the following **for** loop.

Does this loop perform the desired actions of drawing the various Shape objects?

```
for (int i = 0; i < 4; ++i)
    A[i]->Draw();
```

The answer depends on how base class Shape is defined. If the base class Shape for our derived shape classes is defined as in Listing 14.17, where the member function Draw() has the modifier **virtual** applied to it, then the new loop does work in the desired manner.

Listing 14.17

Shape class definition with a virtual Draw() function

```
class Shape : public WindowObject {
    public:
        Shape(SimpleWindow &w, const Position &p,
         const color c = Red);
        color GetColor() const;
        void SetColor(const color c);
        virtual void Draw();            // virtual function!
    private:
        color Color;
};
```

In the new loop, when i equals 0, member function Square-Shape::Draw() is invoked to process A[0]; when i equals 1, member function TriangleShape::Draw() is invoked to process A[1]; and so on. *It is not the type of pointer that determines the invocation, but the type of object at the location to which the pointer refers!* The reason this implementation works is that the Draw() member function for base class Shape is a *virtual function.*

If a virtual function is invoked via either a dereferenced pointer or a reference object, then the actual function to be run is determined from the type of object that is stored at the memory location being accessed rather than the type of the pointer or reference object. The definition of the derived function *overrides* the definition of the base class version. In general, the determination of which virtual function to use cannot be made at compile time and must instead be made during run time. As a result, slightly more overhead is associated with the invocation of a virtual function than with a nonvirtual function.

Programming Tip

Flexibility for future enhancements

Because the decision on which function to call in a virtual function invocation is delayed until run time, it is possible to compile a function that performs a virtual function invocation in its body even though the derived class that will eventually supply the function has not yet been implemented or even defined! This capability is important for software vendors who design libraries where the source is to be kept proprietary. A library client can develop derived classes and have them make use of the vendor library functions without the client needing access to vendor implementation files.

14.7 VIRTUAL FUNCTION NUANCES

The invocation A[i]->Draw() in the **for** loop of the previous section represents our first true use of polymorphism—the invocation performs different actions depending on the type of object being accessed. This polymorphic capability in dealing with its individual elements effectively makes A a heterogeneous collection. To see some of the subtleties involving virtual functions, suppose that the definitions of Listing 14.18 are in effect for the next several examples.

As a first example, try to determine the output of the following code segment:

```
A.Display();
B.Display();
C.Display();
Ptr = &A;
Ptr->Display();
Ptr = &B;
Ptr->Display();
Ptr = &C;
Ptr->Display();
```

The first three lines of output produced by the segment are

```
BaseClass Display
DerivedClass1 Display
DerivedClass2 Display
```

These output lines occur because objects A, B, and C are of type BaseClass, DerivedClass1, and DerivedClass2, respectively, and therefore invoke the Display() functions BaseClass::Display(), DerivedClass1::Display(), and DerivedClass2::Display().

The next three lines of output produced by the segment are

```
BaseClass Display
DerivedClass1 Display
DerivedClass2 Display
```

This output occurs because Ptr is a pointer to a BaseClass object that invokes the virtual member function Display() through dereferencing. The decision on which virtual function to invoke is made at run time when it is determined that Ptr in successive displays is pointing to memory where BaseClass, DerivedClass1, and DerivedClass2 objects are stored.

Now suppose the following code segment is executed:

```
A = B;
A.Display();
A = C;
A.Display();
```

The output produced by this segment is

```
BaseClass Display
BaseClass Display
```

Listing 14.18

Some definitions for illustrating virtual function basics

```cpp
class BaseClass {
    public:
        BaseClass() { return; };
        virtual void Display() {
            cout << "BaseClass Display" << endl;
        };
        void Print() {
            cout << "BaseClass Print" << endl;
        };
};
class DerivedClass1 : public BaseClass {
    public:
        DerivedClass1() { return; };
        virtual void Display() {
            cout << "DerivedClass1 Display" << endl;
        };
        void Print() {
            cout << "DerivedClass1 Print" << endl;
        };
};
class DerivedClass2 : public BaseClass {
    public:
        DerivedClass2() { return; };
        virtual void Display() {
            cout << "DerivedClass2 Display" << endl;
        };
        void Print() {
            cout << "DerivedClass2 Print" << endl;
        };
};
class DerivedClass3 : public BaseClass {
    public:
        DerivedClass3() { return; };
        virtual void Display(int i) {
            cout << "DerivedClass3 Display " << i << endl;
        };
        void Print() {
            cout << "DerivedClass3 Print" << endl;
        };
};
void Output(BaseClass &R) {
    R.Display();
}

BaseClass A;
DerivedClass1 B;
DerivedClass2 C;
DerivedClass3 D;
BaseClass *Ptr;
```

This output occurs because A is a `BaseClass`. Therefore, the two assignments to A copy over only the `BaseClass` data members, which means that the `Display()` function that is invoked is the one from `BaseClass`.

If function `Output()` of Listing 14.18 is invoked as below

```cpp
Output(A);
Output(B);
Output(C);
```

then the output produced by the segment is

```
BaseClass Display
DerivedClass1 Display
DerivedClass2 Display
```

This output occurs because the parameter to `Output()` is a reference parameter. Thus the type of object at the memory location being referenced determines which virtual member function is invoked.

In still another use of the objects from Listing 14.18, consider the following code segment:

```
Ptr = &A;
Ptr->Print();
Ptr = &B;
Ptr->Print();
Ptr = &C;
Ptr->Print();
```

The output produced by the segment is

```
BaseClass Print
BaseClass Print
BaseClass Print
```

This output is produced because member function `Print()` is not virtual. Therefore, the decision on which member function to invoke is determined at compile time, which in turn causes the base class member function to be used.

Note that the `Display()` functions for the derived classes `Derived-Class1` and `DerivedClass2` would remain virtual even if they were not explicitly given the modifier **virtual** as the `Display()` function for `Base-Class` was given. The modifier is unnecessary because a member function of a derived class is automatically virtual if it has the same name and signature as a virtual base class member function. Although the modifier **virtual** is syntactically unnecessary in such cases, it is generally added to provide supporting information to a reader of the derived class definition.

Listing 14.18 also derives the class `DerivedClass3` from `BaseClass`. `DerivedClass3` defines a member function `Display()` with a signature different from the `Display()` of `BaseClass`. As such, the following statement would be illegal because the `BaseClass` member function `Display()` is hidden.

```
D.Display(); // illegal: Display() is hidden
```

However, the invocations of `Display()` in the following code segment are legal

```
D.Display(3);
D.BaseClass::Display();
Ptr = &D;
Ptr->Display();
```

and produce the following output:

```
DerivedClass3 Display 3
BaseClass Display
BaseClass Display
```

The first of the preceding invocations of `Display()` for obvious reasons calls the `Display()` of `DerivedClass3`. The second invocation uses the scope operator to explicitly call the `Display()` of `BaseClass`. Because a `DerivedClass3` object does not have a `Display()` member function with an empty parameter list and because a `DerivedClass3` object is a `BaseClass` object, the expression `Ptr->Display()` in its dereferencing of `BaseClass` pointer `Ptr` invokes the `Display()` of `BaseClass`.

Note that when overriding a base class member function, the derived class function cannot differ only in return type. For the overloading to occur, the signatures of the two functions must be different.

Programming Tip

> ***Assume reuse***
>
> When defining a class, unless you know it can never serve as a base class for a derived class, give the class a virtual destructor. For example, a `Shape` class could have a destructor with an empty function body. By making the destructor virtual, all derived destructors will also be virtual and then, whenever an object is deleted, the correct destructor will be invoked regardless of the context.

14.8   ABSTRACT BASE CLASSES

A virtual member function is a *pure virtual function* if it has no implementation. A pure virtual function is defined by assigning that function the null address within its class definition. For example, the class definition of `Shape` in Listing 14.19 makes its member function `Draw()` a pure virtual function. A class with a pure virtual function is known as an *abstract base class*.

Listing 14.19

Shape class definition with a pure virtual Draw() function from

```
class Shape : public WindowObject {
  public:
    Shape(SimpleWindow &w, const Position &p,
      const color c = Red);
    color GetColor() const;
    void SetColor(const color c);
    virtual void Draw() = 0; // pure virtual function!
  private:
    color Color;
};
```

Because an abstract base class does not have a complete implementation, attempting to define an object of an abstract base class type through construction is illegal. In particular, there can be no construction of an object of an abstract base class type in a definition, or as a return value, or as a value parameter. Thus the declaration and prototypes below are illegal.

```
Shape S;              // illegal: no Shape definition
Shape f();            // illegal: no Shape return value
void f(Shape S);      // illegal: no Shape value
                      // parameter
```

Because no construction is needed, you may use an abstract base class as a reference. Therefore, the following declarations and prototypes using Shape are legal.

```
TriangleShape T(W, P, Red, 1);
Shape &R = T;          // T is a TriangleShape that is
                       // a Shape
Shape& F();            // can return a reference to an
                       // existing Shape
void G(Shape &S);      // can pass an existing Shape as
                       // a reference
```

The main use of an abstract base class is to provide a standard interface for derived classes. An abstract base class describes the interface that derived classes must support. However, when appropriate, the abstract base class leaves the implementation of that functionality to the derived classes. For this reason, Draw() was made a pure virtual function in Listing 14.19—the drawing activities for specific shapes are left to the derived shape classes.

In the following example, we use the functionality of the abstract base class Shape to create and display a simple drawing of a house. The two functions that implement this activity are given in Program 14.4. The output of the program is given in Figure 14.1. The functions are named BuildHouse() and DrawFigure(). Both functions manipulate a sequential list object of type SeqList<Shape*>. A sequential list allows us to add as many shapes as needed to represent the house.

Figure 14.1

Dream house drawing using BuildHouse() and DrawFigure()

Program 14.4

House building and displaying from house.cpp

```cpp
// Program 14.4: Display a dream house
#include "shape.h"
#include "triangle.h"
#include "circle.h"
#include "rect.h"
#include "square.h"
#include "slist.h"

// prototypes
SeqList<Shape*>* BuildHouse(SimpleWindow &W);
void DrawFigure(SeqList<Shape*> *F);

// ApiMain(); manage building and display of house
int ApiMain() {
    SimpleWindow Window("House", 10, 10);
    Window.Open();
    SeqList<Shape*> *DreamHouse = BuildHouse(Window);
    DrawFigure(DreamHouse);
    return 0;
}

// BuildHouse(): use basic shapes to make a house
SeqList<Shape*>* BuildHouse(SimpleWindow &W) {
    // House composed of a list of parts
    SeqList<Shape*> *House = new SeqList<Shape*>;

    House->push_back( // house has a square frame
        new SquareShape(W, Position(5, 7), Blue, 5)
    );

    House->push_back( // house has a triangular roof
        new TriangleShape(W, Position(5, 3), Red, 5)
    );

    House->push_back( // house has a skylight
        new CircleShape(W, Position(5, 7.75), Yellow, 1.5)
    );

    House->push_back( // house has a door
        new RectangleShape(W, Position(5, 8.5), Yellow,
            1.5, 2)
    );

    House->push_back( // house a left window
        new SquareShape(W, Position(4,6), Yellow, 1.5)
    );

    House->push_back( // house has a right window
        new SquareShape(W, Position(6,6), Yellow, 1.5)
    );

    return House;
}

// DrawFigure(): draw shapes in list F
void DrawFigure(SeqList<Shape*> *F) {
    for (SeqIterator<Shape*> P = F->begin(); P; ++P) {
        (*(*P)).Draw();
    }
}
```

Function `BuildHouse()` returns a pointer to a sequential list of type `SeqList<Shape*>`. Each element of that list is a pointer to a component shape of the drawing. Because both the shapes that compose the figure and the sequential list whose elements point to those shapes must exist after the completion of `BuildHouse()`, these objects are constructed by `Build-House()` using free store memory.

The house representation is quite simple—the elements in the sequential list point to only six shapes. The shapes are a frame for the house, a roof, a door, a skylight over the door, and two upstairs windows. The frame and windows are `SquareShape` objects; the roof is a `TriangleShape` object; the door is a `RectangleShape` object; and the skylight is a `CircleShape` object. The figure is composed in a manner that the door is drawn after the skylight. Because the upper part of the door overlaps the skylight, the skylight appears to be a semicircle.

The purpose of function `DrawFigure()` is to iteratively invoke the `Draw()` functions of the shapes pointed to by the list to which F points. Function `DrawFigure()` uses an iterator P of type `SeqIterator<Shape*>` to accomplish this task. The body of the **for** loop that processes the various elements of list is

```
(*(*P)).Draw();
```

The subexpression `(*P)` dereferences iterator P to produce a pointer to a shape. This value is a pointer to one of the shapes in the figure. `(*(*P))` dereferences pointer `(*P)` to produce the current shape of interest. The selection operator is then applied so that the `Draw()` member function can be invoked. Because `Shape` has a virtual `Draw()` function, the `Draw()` function of the derived class is invoked.

Functions `BuildHouse()` and `DrawFigure()` are used by `ApiMain()` in Program 14.4 to produce and display the object to which `DreamHouse` points.

```
SeqList<Shape*> *DreamHouse = BuildHouse(Window);
DrawFigure(DreamHouse);
```

14.9 VIRTUAL MULTIPLE INHERITANCE

The modifier **virtual** can also be used with class derivation and is particularly useful when a derived class inherits from the same base class multiple times. If the modifier is applied, then only one copy of each base class data member is inherited. To illustrate this behavior, we first define a class `Base-Class` with a data member `DataValue` of type **int** and two derived classes `DerivedClass1` and `DerivedClass2` from `BaseClass`.

```
class BaseClass {
    protected:
        int DataValue;
};
class DerivedClass1 : public BaseClass {
    // ...
};
class DerivedClass2 : public BaseClass {
    // ...
};
```

If a class `MultipleClass1` is derived from both `DerivedClass1` and `DerivedClass2` without using the modifier **virtual**, then objects of type `MultipleClass1` would have two distinct data members named `DataValue`.

```
class MultipleClass1
  : public DerivedClass1, public DerivedClass2 {
      // ...
};
```

A `MultipleClass1` member function needs to use the resolution operator to distinguish between the two data members. The following insertion and extraction are legal because they are unambiguous references to specific `DataValue` objects.

```
// inside a MultipleClass1 member function
cout << DerivedClass1::DataValue,      // unambiguous
cin >> DerivedClass2::DataValue;       // unambiguous
```

The following assignment statement is not legal in a `MultipleClass1` member function, because there is no context to distinguish which `DataValue` is being referenced.

```
// inside a MultipleClass1 member function
DataValue = 1024;                      // ambiguous
```

To see the effect of the modifier **virtual** in a class derivation, suppose we define a class `MultipleClass2`, which is virtually derived from both `DerivedClass3` and `DerivedClass4` which are in turn virtually derived from `BaseClass`.

```
class DerivedClass3 : virtual public BaseClass {
      // ...
};
class DerivedClass4 : virtual public BaseClass {
      // ...
};
class MultipleClass2
  : virtual public DerivedClass3,
    virtual public DerivedClass4 {
      // ...
};
```

Inside a member function of `MultipleClass2`, we do not need to use the resolution operator to distinguish which `DataValue` is being referenced—the modifier **virtual** ensures that we have only one data member `DataValue`. The data member can be referenced directly or by using the resolution operator with the base classes. Thus the following insertion statements display the same value.

```
// inside a MultipleClass2 member function
cout << DataValue << endl;
cout << BaseClass::DataValue << endl;
cout << DerivedClass3::DataValue << endl;
cout << DerivedClass4::DataValue << endl;
```

History of Computing

The information superhighway

While advances in computing yield more computational power, advances in computer networking bring that power into more and more homes. Vast amounts of information are accessible via computer networks. For example, at our university, many of the works of Thomas Jefferson have been made available via the Internet. This electronic availability means that scholars all over the world can have access to this work without ever leaving their offices. In the courses at our university that use this text, students have e-mail, access to a bulletin board or newsgroup devoted to the class, and access to the class Web site (e.g., `http://www.cs.virginia.edu/cs101`). If students have questions, they can send e-mail to the instructor rather than telephone or attempt to see the instructor in person. Usually, they receive a prompt answer to their question. In addition, as questions are answered, both the question and the answer are posted as appropriate to a newsgroup or to the Web site. Thus a student can benefit from questions asked by other students, much as if everyone were in the classroom. Inexpensive and fast communication is changing the way we interact. How broad, inexpensive, high-speed access to information changes society is a matter of intense interest to computer and social scientists. We definitely live in interesting times.

Self-check Questions

9.   Consider the following code.

```cpp
#include <iostream>
using namespace std;
class BaseClass {
    public:
        BaseClass(int i = 3);
        virtual void Print() const;
        int GetValue() const;
    private:
        int MyValue;
};
BaseClass::BaseClass(int v) : MyValue(v) {
}
void BaseClass::Print() const {
    cout << "BaseClass Print " << GetValue() << endl;
    return;
}
int BaseClass::GetValue() const {
    return MyValue;
}
class DerivedClass : public BaseClass {
    public:
        DerivedClass(int i = 12);
        virtual void Print() const;
        int GetValue() const;
    private:
        int MyValue;
```

```
};
DerivedClass::DerivedClass(int v) : MyValue(v) {
}

void DerivedClass::Print() const {
    cout << "DerivedClass Print " << GetValue()
      << endl;
    return;
}

int DerivedClass::GetValue() const {
    return MyValue;
}
int main() {
    BaseClass B(1);
    DerivedClass D(10);
    BaseClass *Bptr1 = new BaseClass(3);
    BaseClass *Bptr2 = new DerivedClass(5);
    DerivedClass *Dptr1 = new DerivedClass(10);

    B.Print();
    Bptr2->Print();
    Bptr2 = Dptr1;
    Bptr2->Print();
    return 0;
}
```

Give the output of this program.

10.   Consider the following code.

```
#include <iostream>
using namespace std;
class BaseClass {
    public:
        BaseClass(int i = 3);
        virtual void Print() const;
        int GetValue() const;
    private:
        int MyValue;
};
BaseClass::BaseClass(int v) : MyValue(v) {
}

void BaseClass::Print() const {
    cout << "BaseClass Print " << GetValue() << endl;
    return;
}

int BaseClass::GetValue() const {
    return MyValue;
}
class DerivedClass : public BaseClass {
    public:
        DerivedClass(int i = 12);
        virtual void Print() const;
        int GetValue() const;
    private:
        int MyValue;
};
DerivedClass::DerivedClass(int v) : MyValue(v) {
```

```
        }
        void DerivedClass::Print() const {
            cout << "DerivedClass Print " << GetValue()
              << endl;
            return;
        }

        int DerivedClass::GetValue() const {
            return MyValue;
        }
        void f(BaseClass &B) {
            B.Print();
            return;
        }

        int main() {
            BaseClass B(1);
            DerivedClass D(10);

            f(B);
            f(D);
            return 0;
        }
```

What is the output of the above program?

11. Find out what happens when you assign a derived-class object into a base-class object. Using the declarations from the code given in Question 9, the statement

```
    B = D;
```

is an example of such an assignment.

12. Using your answer from Question 11, give the output of the following program.

```
        #include <iostream>
        using namespace std;
        class BaseClass {
            public:
                BaseClass(int i = 3);
                virtual void Print() const;
                int GetValue() const;
            private:
                int MyValue;
        };
        BaseClass::BaseClass(int v) : MyValue(v) {
        }
        void BaseClass::Print() const {
            cout << "BaseClass Print " << GetValue() << endl;
            return;
        }
        int BaseClass::GetValue() const {
            return MyValue;
        }
        class DerivedClass : public BaseClass {
            public:
```

```
            DerivedClass(int i = 12);
            virtual void Print() const;
            int GetValue() const;
        private:
            int MyValue;
    };
    DerivedClass::DerivedClass(int v) : MyValue(v) {
    }

    void DerivedClass::Print() const {
        cout << "DerivedClass Print " << GetValue()
          << endl;
        return;
    }

    int DerivedClass::GetValue() const {
        return MyValue;
    }
    int main() {
        BaseClass B(1);
        DerivedClass D(10);

        B.Print();
        D.Print();
        B = D;
        B.Print()
        return 0;
    }
```

13.   It is illegal to copy a base-class object into a derived class object. Using
       the declarations from the code given in Question 12 and the statement

       ```
       D = B;
       ```

       explain why such assignments are illegal.

14.10 POINTS TO REMEMBER

✔ Polymorphism is a language mechanism that permits the same interface to
  invoke different functions or operators depending upon the type of objects
  using the interface.

✔ Name reuse in function overloading is a primitive form of polymorphism.
  Another method of achieving syntactic polymorphism is the use of
  function and class templates.

✔ A function template is a mechanism for generating a new function.

✔ A class template is a mechanism for generating a new class.

✔ A template parameter can be either a type or a value.

✔ The type template parameters in a function template definition can be used
  to specify the return type and parameter types of the generated function.

✔ All template parameters in a function template definition must be used in
  the function interface. The template parameters can also be used in the
  function body.

✔ The C++ standard describes a standard template library that in part includes template versions of common computing tasks such as searching and sorting.

✔ All template parameters in a class template must be used in the definition of the class interface.

✔ Class templates are particularly useful in the development of container class ADTs. A container ADT represents a list of objects.

✔ One major way of classifying container ADTs is by whether they efficiently support random access or only sequential access to the elements in the list.

✔ Through the use of class templates, we can develop a container class that represents lists in an arraylike manner. A major reason that such a container class is preferred to standard arrays is that the container class does not suffer array use limitations (e.g., a container class can be the return type of a function or be a value parameter).

✔ A linked list is a method for implementing a dynamic list of values. A linked list represents the collection using a group of objects that have two components. One component maintains the list value being represented; the other component is one or more pointers to other objects in the list representation. One pointer that is normally present is a successor pointer that points to the next object in the representation. In doubly linked lists, the other pointer that is normally present is a predecessor pointer.

✔ A **friend** of a class can be a function, operator, or another class. A **friend** of a class can access all of that class's data members. Such access violates the information hiding principle.

✔ The standard template library defines a collection of common container classes for list representation. The representations differ in how the elements of the list can be accessed. Various container classes support random access of the elements, sequential access of the elements, and associative access of the elements.

✔ Often a container class will have an iterator class associated with it. The iterator class provides the means for iteratively accessing the various elements of the list.

✔ Conversion operators can be overloaded. A standard conversion operator to overload is **bool**. When the conversion is applied to the object of the specified type, the conversion can produce a value that indicates whether the object has a desired value. For example, in the **SeqIterator** iterator class, the **bool** operator was overloaded to indicate whether the iterator object currently represented a valid element in the list.

✔ The C++ method of achieving true polymorphism is through virtual functions.

✔ A virtual function is required to be a member function.

✔ If a function of a derived class has the same name and type as a virtual function of its base class, then the member function of the derived class overrides the base class function.

✔ With a virtual function, the decision on which actual function is being invoked in an interface is delayed until run time. The decision will be based on the type of object being accessed by a pointer or reference object, rather than by the type of the pointer or reference object.

✔ By declaring an array of pointers for a common base type, the array can be used to represent a heterogeneous list—the individual elements can point to objects of the different derived types from that base class.

✔ When a virtual function is invoked by dereferencing one of the elements in a heterogeneous list, the action to be taken can be specific to the derived type of the object to which the pointer refers. Such code will continue to work properly even if a new derived type is defined and one of its objects is added to the list.

✔ Destructors for a base class are typically virtual. That way, regardless of the context of the destruction, the appropriate destructor is invoked.

✔ A pure virtual function is a virtual function to which the pure specifier has been applied, that is, it has been assigned the null address.

✔ A pure virtual function has no implementation.

✔ It is not possible to construct an object from a class with a pure virtual function, because the construction cannot be completed.

✔ A class with a pure virtual function is an abstract base class.

✔ An abstract base class is used to describe the common interface of its derived classes. For example, because a common activity of shape manipulation is drawing the shape to the display, a virtual member function Draw() should be part of the shape common interface. Because only a derived shape has sufficient characteristics to be rendered to a display, the Draw() member should be a pure virtual function.

✔ The modifier **virtual** can be used in conjunction with class derivation.

✔ The modifier **virtual** is useful when a derived class inherits from the same base class multiple times. The modifier indicates that there should be only one copy of each data member from that base class. If the modifier is not present, then the normal rules of multiple inheritance apply, which means that each inherited class supplies a copy of the data member.

14.11 EXERCISES

14.1   Speculate on why templates are not considered as important as virtual functions in terms of the object-oriented paradigm.

14.2   Discuss why templates as a language mechanism are considered to be closer to name reuse in function overloading than to pure polymorphism.

14.3 Why is the decision on which virtual function to invoke made at run time rather than at compile time?

14.4 Implement a template version of a search function for determining whether an array contains a particular value. Will your template function work if you use the template container class Array as the template parameter type? Why?

14.5 Implement a template version of QuickSort().

14.6 Design and implement template functions Min() and Max() for finding the minimum and maximum values in a list represented by a SeqList<T> object.

14.7 Identify and correct the error(s) in the following definition so that it is a valid template.

```
template<type S, type T>
  int S f(S A[n]) {
    S x;
    cin >> x;
    A[x] = x;
}
```

14.8 Design and implement a template function Search() for determining whether a given value appears in a list represented by a SeqList<T> object. If the given value is in the list, function Search() should return a SeqIterator<T> iterator that is associated with an element with that value. If the given value is not in the list, function Search() should return a SeqIterator<T> iterator associated with a trailing sentinel.

14.9 Design and implement a template function Sort() that sorts a list represented by a SeqList<T> object.

14.10 What is a **friend**? What access rights does it have?

14.11 Redo the Rational class so that the type of the data members comes from a template type representing an integral value type. Test your implementation by trying the various standard integral types.

14.12 Implement the template class Bunch<T,n>.

14.13 Design and implement an Array<T> member function resize() with two parameters n and val. Parameter n is an integer parameter representing the new desired size of the list. It has a default value of 0. Parameter val is a reference to a constant T object representing the value of any objects to be added to the list as the result of the resize operation. Its default value is equal to a T object that has been default constructed. An element from the old list being represented should remain represented if its index remains valid. What is the run time of this operation?

14.14 Design and implement an Array<T> member function push_back() member function analogous to the vector push_back() function. What is the run time of this operation?

14.15 Design and implement an `Array<T>` member function `clear()` member function analogous to the `vector clear()` function. What is the run time of this operation?

14.16 Design and implement an `Array<T>` member function `insert()` member function analogous to the `vector insert()` function. What is the run time of this operation?

14.17 Design and implement an `Array<T>` member function `erase()` member function analogous to the `vector insert()` function. What is the run time of this operation?

14.18 Redesign and reimplement the `Array<T>` ADT so that a client can specify a desired subscript interval. For example, the definition

```
Array<int> Month(1, 12, 0);
```

represents an array of 12 elements. The first element has an index of 1; the last element has an index of 12. The elements are all initialized to 0.

14.19 What changes to `Array<T>` and `SeqList<T>` need to be made to make them appropriate base classes for inheritance?

14.20 No implementation of a copy constructor or a member assignment is specified for `SeqList<T>` ADT. What type of operations (if any) are performed by default? Why? Explicitly implement deep copy versions of the two member operations.

14.21 Modify the `SeqList<T>` ADT by including a member subscript operator `[]` whose integer operand `i` is an index into the list. The operator returns a reference to the `i`th element in the list being represented. Compare the relative efficiencies of the `Array<T>` and `SeqList<T>` subscript operators.

14.22 What is the output of the following code segment? Why?

```
SeqList<int> P;
P.push_back(1);
P.push_back(2);
P.push_back(3);
SeqIterator<int> a = P.begin();
SeqIterator<int> b = P.begin();
++a;
++a;
*a = *b;
P.display(cout);
```

14.23 Why is the `SeqIterator<T>` iterator functionality developed in a separate class rather than being part of the `SeqList<T>` class?

14.24 Redesign the `SeqList<T>` iterator ADT so that a member function `insert_after()` is defined. The function expects two parameters: an iterator p and a value `val`. A copy of the value `val` is added after the element to which iterator p points.

14.25 Reimplement `SeqList<T>` member function `display()` to make use of the iterator class `SeqIterator<T>`.

14.26 Reimplement SeqList<T> member function clear() to make use of the iterator class SeqIterator<T>.

14.27 Design and implement a member addition operator for SeqList<T> objects. The result should append a copy of the elements represented by the right operand SeqList<T> to the end of the list of the invoking SeqList object.

14.28 Design and implement a member subtraction operator for SeqList<T> objects. The result should remove all occurrences of the elements represented by the right operand SeqList<T> from the list of the invoking SeqList<T> object.

14.29 Overload the insertion operator for SeqList<T> objects by using the SeqList<T> member function display().

14.30 Design and implement a convenience **bool** member function empty() for SeqList<T> objects that returns true if the associated list has no elements. Otherwise, the function returns false.

14.31 Reimplement the SeqList<T> without having the data member ListLength. No functionality is to be lost. Which members have their run time affected and how?

14.32 Why is no check needed in the overloading of the insertion operator for a SeqIterator<T> to make sure that the iterator is associated with an actual element?

14.33 Implement the prefix version of the SeqIterator<T> operator --.

14.34 Implement the postfix version of the SeqIterator<T> operator --.

14.35 Design and implement a **bool** SeqIterator<T> member function isfront() that returns true if the iterator is associated with the first element in the list. Otherwise, the iterator returns false.

14.36 Design and implement a **bool** SeqIterator<T> member function isback() that returns true if the iterator is associated with the last element in the list. Otherwise, the iterator returns false.

14.37 Redesign and reimplement the SeqIterator<T> class so that its default constructor takes two optional parameters L and pos. Parameter L is a pointer to the list to be associated with the iterator. The default value for L is the null address. Parameter pos is of type IterStatus, where the definition of IterStatus is as follows:

```
enum IterStatus
  {frontposition, backposition, sentinelposi-
tion};
```

The default value for pos is sentinelposition. If the value of pos is frontposition, then the iterator is initially associated with the first element in the list. If the value of pos is backposition, then the iterator is initially associated with the last element in the list. If the value of pos is sentinelposition, then the iterator is initially associated with a sentinel for the list. Note that checks need to be made to ensure that the association with a particular element makes sense (i.e., the element must exist). Modify the `SeqList<T>` code to make use of this constructor. Explain why we go to this effort.

14.38 Design and implement the `ConstSeqIterator<T>` class so that constant `SeqList<T>` objects can be accessed. Your implementation should add as many as the features of the `SeqIterator<T>` class as possible. Your implementation should also contain a constructor that constructs a `ConstSeqIterator<T>` object from a `SeqIterator<T>` object. Should a complementary constructor be added to the `SeqIterator<T>` class that constructs a `SeqIterator<T>` object from a `ConstSeqIterator<T>` object? Why or why not?

14.39 Use the `ConstSeqIterator<T>` class of Exercise 14.38 to help implement `SeqList<T>::begin()` **const** and `SeqList<T>::end()` **const** member functions.

14.40 Design and implement a base container class template `bucket`. The classes `Array<T>` and `SeqList<T>` should be redesigned and derived from `bucket<T>`. The class `SeqIterator<T>` should be redesigned and renamed so that it works with both the `Array<T>` and `SeqList<T>` classes.

14.41 Write a function `BuildPerson()` similar to `BuildHouse()` that uses the abstract base class `Shape` and the various derived classes to construct a picture of a person. An example person is given below.

14.42 Speculate on why pure virtual functions are used rather than virtual functions that simply do an immediate return. Consider what would happen if a derived class did not have an overriding definition.

14.43 Which of the following activities are appropriate actions for inclusion as virtual functions in the abstract base class Shape? Why?

a) Rotating.

b) Repositioning.

c) Scaling.

d) Flipping.

e) Setting a stipple pattern.

14.44 Which activities in the preceding list are appropriate actions for inclusion as pure virtual functions in the abstract base class Shape? Why?

14.45 Design an abstract base class for the writing instrument hierarchy discussed in Chapter 13. Design derived classes for various types of writing instruments. Use insertion statements in your implementation to indicate the particular instrument property associated with the various member functions.

14.46 Design a hierarchy for vehicles. From the base class, derive classes that organize vehicles by energy source—fossil fuel, solar, chemical, steam, electric, or nuclear; by use—commercial, individual, agricultural, or governmental; and by whether the vehicle is wheeled or nonwheeled. Further develop the hierarchy for classes for snowmobiles, school buses, and station wagons. Justify which functions are virtual or pure virtual.

14.47 Design a hierarchy for representing trees. Justify which functions are virtual or pure virtual.

14.48 Design a hierarchy for representing birds. Justify which functions are virtual or pure virtual.

14.49 Design a class Segment that uses the EzWindows class Position to specify the endpoints of a line. Redefine the shape hierarchy to describe the polygonal shapes using a list of Segment objects.

CHAPTER 15

Software project – Bug Hunt!

Introduction

We are now ready to put some of the object-oriented skills we have learned to use. In this chapter we design and implement a program called Bug Hunt. The object of the game is to eliminate bugs that scurry around inside a window. The bugs are eliminated by swatting them with the mouse. The implementation of the game requires the use of most of the object-oriented features of C++ that we have covered, including inheritance, virtual functions, and polymorphism. The implementation of the game makes heavy use of the EzWindows API.

Key Concepts

- encapsulation
- inheritance
- derived class
- virtual functions
- polymorphism
- object-oriented design

15.1 BUG HUNT

Bug Hunt is simple to play. A bug is scurrying around in a window. The object of the game is to get rid of the bug. A bug is eliminated by clicking the mouse when the sprite is positioned over a bug. Like bugs in programs, Bug Hunt bugs are hard to get rid of. The player has to click on a bug several times before it is eliminated. Once the player gets rid of a bug, another trickier bug appears. The game ends when there are no more bugs to get rid of. If the player misses a bug, the game starts over from the beginning.

Sounds simple enough, so let's begin with the high-level design of the game. The game consists of several objects. From the description above, it is obvious that a key object is a bug. In fact, this version of the game has two types of bugs—a slow bug that's easy to get rid of and a fast bug that's hard to eliminate. Inheritance will prove useful in realizing an implementation of the bugs. Another object is the window that contains the bugs. We will use the EzWindows class `SimpleWindow` to implement the window. Finally, we need an object that controls the play of the game, a game controller. It sets up the game, maintains the state of the game, and controls the game as it progresses. Figure 15.1 illustrates some aspects of the high-level design of the program.

Using EzWindows, the game controller receives both mouse-click events and timer-tick events from the window. On a mouse-click event, the game controller sends a message to the bug to see if it is pointed at. If so, the bug records the hit. If the bug has been hit enough times, it dies. When a bug dies, the game controller removes the bug and advances the game to the next stage. If the mouse click is not pointing at the bug, then the game controller starts the game over from the beginning.

On timer-tick events, the game controller tells the bug to move. If the timer-tick events occur fast enough, the bug appears to scurry around within the window. Of course, how the bug moves is part of the implementation of the bug, and the game controller need not know or understand how that is done.

Our program consists of three modules. The module `bug.cpp` contains the code that relates to the implementation of the bugs. The module `control.cpp` contains the implementation of the game controller, and `bughunt.cpp` contains the start-up and cleanup code for the program (i.e., `ApiMain()` and `ApiEnd()`). In addition, each module will have a corresponding `.h` file that contains the interface to the module. Of course, the program will be linked with the EzWindows API library code.

Since Bug Hunt centers around the behavior of the bug, let's begin with it.

15.2 BASE CLASS BUG

Because the game requires different types of bugs, it makes sense to use inheritance. The basic idea is to have a base class with all the common behaviors required by a bug and to create specialized versions of bugs (i.e., with different

Figure 15.1

High-level design of Bug Hunt

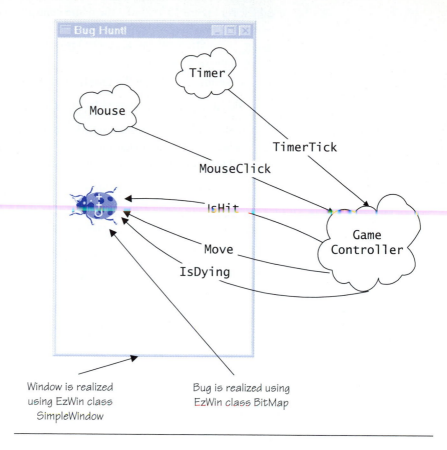

Window is realized
using EzWin class
SimpleWindow

Bug is realized using
EzWin class BitMap

behaviors) via inheritance. As shown in Figure 15.2, two types of bugs will be derived from the base class Bug—SlowBug and FastBug. The difference between a SlowBug and a FastBug is how they move.

Figure 15.2

FastBug and SlowBug are derived from Bug

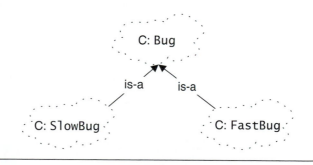

From the perspective of the game controller, the interface to the two types of bugs should be the same. So let's begin our design by considering the behaviors or methods that a bug needs from the perspective of the game controller. As Figure 15.1 shows, the game controller needs to be able to ask a bug whether it was hit, to make a bug move, and to find out whether the bug is dying. In addition, the game controller needs to be able to create and kill bugs as the game progresses.

To summarize, the public interface for Bug should include

- Move—Bug moves to next location in the window.

- IsHit—Bug determines whether the supplied window coordinates are within it. If so, it updates the count of hits it has taken and returns true; otherwise, it returns false.

- IsDying—Bug returns true if the number of hits taken is equal to or greater than the number of hits required to kill it.

- Create—Bug is created and drawn in the window.

- Kill—Bug is removed from the window.

What attributes should Bug have? Because a Bug is displayed in an EzWindows SimpleWindow, it should contain a reference to the window that contains it to facilitate its display. In addition, it should have a position within the window. A Bug will also contain an EzWindows BitMap so that an image for a bug can be displayed. To simulate a bug moving in a window, we will use four bitmap images. Each image corresponds to the direction the bug is moving (Figure 15.3). Because we want to simulate the erratic movements of a bug, Bug has an attribute that is the probability that the bug will change direction. Other attributes are the direction the bug is currently moving, the number of mouse hits the bug has taken so far, and the number of mouse hits required to kill the bug.

Figure 15.3

Bitmaps used to simulate moving bug

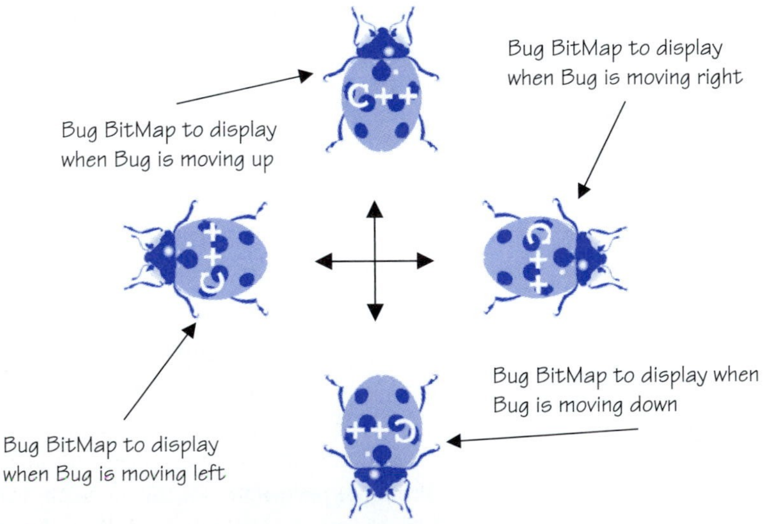

Bug BitMap to display when Bug is moving up

Bug BitMap to display when Bug is moving right

Bug BitMap to display when Bug is moving left

Bug BitMap to display when Bug is moving down

To summarize, the attributes of `Bug` should include

- `Window`—the window that contains the bug.
- `Bmp`—an array of four bitmaps that correspond to the direction the bug is moving.
- `HitsTaken`—the number of mouse-click hits the bug has taken so far.
- `HitsRequired`—the number of mouse-click hits the bug can take before it is killed.
- `DirectionChangeProbability`—the likelihood that the bug will change direction.
- `CurrentDirection`—the direction (up, down, left, or right) that the bug is moving.
- `CurrentPosition`—the current location of the bug.

An important implementation question is how to make the bug appear to move in the window. A simple technique for making a screen object appear to move is to erase the bitmap image of the object and then redraw it at its new position. Figure 15.4 illustrates the technique. If the erase/redraw operations are done frequently enough and the new position is not too far from the original position, the image will appear to move. This technique works reasonably well if there are not too many objects and they are not moving too fast. If smoother, faster motion is required, other slightly more complicated techniques can be used. For Bug Hunt, however, the simple technique just outlined is acceptable.

Figure 15.4

Simulating motion by erasing and redrawing

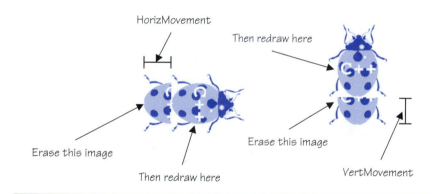

Class `Bug` will also contain two data members, `HorizMovement` and `VertMovement`. These will hold, respectively, the amount to move the bitmap image horizontally and vertically to simulate motion.

Of course, in addition to the public member functions, class `Bug` needs inspectors and mutators. Because these will be used only by class `Bug` and the classes derived from `Bug`, they are not part of the public interface for `Bug`. To make these member functions inaccessible to users of `Bug`, yet make them accessible to classes derived from `Bug`, these methods are declared in the protected section. Thus `Bug` has a public interface and a protected one. The data members of Bug are still in a private section, and the derived classes must use the inspectors and mutators provided in the protected section to access them. Listing 15.1 contains the declaration for Bug.

Listing 15.1

Declaration of class
Bug from bug.h

```
#ifndef BUG_H
#define BUG_H
#include "bitmap.h"
#include "randint.h"

// class for a simple bug
enum Direction {Up, Down, Left, Right };
const int BugBitMaps = 4; // One bitmap for each direction
class Bug {
   public:
      Bug(SimpleWindow &w, int HitsNeeded = 3,
        int DirectionChangeProbability = 50);
      bool IsHit(const Position &MousePosition);
      bool IsDying();
      void Create();
      void Kill();
      virtual void Move() = 0;
   protected:
      // Bug inspectors
      SimpleWindow& GetWindow() const;
      Position GetPosition() const;
      Direction GetDirection() const;
      float GetHorizMovement() const;
      float GetVertMovement() const;
      int GetDirectionChangeProbability() const;
      BitMap &GetBmp(const Direction &d);
      const BitMap &GetBmp(const Direction &d) const;
      // Bug mutators
      void SetWindow(SimpleWindow &w);
      void SetDirection(const Direction &d);
      void SetHorizMovement(float h);
      void SetVertMovement(float v);
      void Draw();
      void Erase();
      void SetPosition(const Position &p);
      void ChangeDirection();
      Position NewPosition() const;
      RandomInt GeneratePercentage;
   private:
      // Data members
      SimpleWindow &Window;
      vector<BitMap> Bmp;
      float HorizMovement;
      float VertMovement;
      int HitsRequired;
      int HitsTaken;
      int DirectionChangeProbability;
      Direction CurrentDirection;
      Position CurrentPosition;
};
#endif
```

Preceding the declaration of Bug in Listing 15.1 is the declaration of an **enum** that gives symbolic names to the four directions. Using an enumeration instead of numbers to encode the direction of a bug helps make the program more readable and understandable.

Bug is an abstract base class because public member function Move() is a pure virtual function. We made it a pure virtual function because it's only use will be to realize implementations of "real" bugs. These bugs will differ in how they move. Making Bug a pure virtual function ensures that an object of type Bug can never be instantiated.

Most of the member functions of Bug are short and simple. Listing 15.2 contains the implementation of the member functions of class Bug.

Listing 15.2

Constructor and member functions of class Bug from bug.cpp

```cpp
// Bug(): constructor for a bug
Bug::Bug(SimpleWindow &w, int h, int p) : Window(w),
  HitsRequired(h), HitsTaken(0),
  GeneratePercentage(1, 100),
  DirectionChangeProbability(p) {
    Bmp.reserve(BugBitMaps);
    GeneratePercentage.Randomize();
    return;
}
void Bug::Create() {
    HitsTaken = 0;
    Draw();
    return;
}
void Bug::Kill() {
    Erase();
    return;
}
// Hit(): return true if mouse is inside bug
// and update hit taken count
bool Bug::IsHit(const Position &MousePosn) {
    if (GetBmp(GetDirection()).IsInside(MousePosn)) {
        ++HitsTaken;
        return true;
    }
    else
        return false;
}
// IsDying: is the bug dying
bool Bug::IsDying() {
    return HitsTaken >= HitsRequired;
}

// inspectors
SimpleWindow& Bug::GetWindow() const {
    return Window;
}
Position Bug::GetPosition() const {
    return CurrentPosition;
}
Direction Bug::GetDirection() const {
    return CurrentDirection;
};
float Bug::GetHorizMovement() const {
    return HorizMovement;
};
float Bug::GetVertMovement() const {
    return VertMovement;
}
```

```
int Bug::GetDirectionChangeProbability() const {
   return DirectionChangeProbability;
}
BitMap &Bug::GetBmp(const Direction &d) {
   return Bmp[d];
}
const BitMap &Bug::GetBmp(const Direction &d) const {
   return Bmp[d];
}
// mutators
void Bug::SetWindow(SimpleWindow &w) {
   Window = w;
   return;
}
void Bug::SetDirection(const Direction &d) {
   CurrentDirection = d;
};
void Bug::SetHorizMovement(float h) {
   HorizMovement = h;
   return;
}
void Bug::SetVertMovement(float v) {
   VertMovement = v;
   return;
}
// facilitators
void Bug::Draw() {
   GetBmp(GetDirection()).Draw();
   return;
}
void Bug::Erase() {
   GetBmp(GetDirection()).Erase();
   return;
}
void Bug::ChangeDirection() {
   RandomInt R(Up, Right);
   SetDirection((Direction ) R.Draw());
   return;
}
// SetPosition(): set position for all bug bitmaps
void Bug::SetPosition(const Position &p) {
   for (Direction d = Up; d <= Right;
    d = (Direction) (d + 1))
      Bmp[d].SetPosition(p);
   CurrentPosition = p;
   return;
}
// NewPosition(): compute a new position for a bug
Position Bug::NewPosition() const {
   const Position OldPosition = GetPosition();
   if (GetDirection() == Left)
      return OldPosition + Position(-GetHorizMovement(),0);
   else if (GetDirection() == Right)
      return OldPosition + Position(GetHorizMovement(),0);
   else if (GetDirection() == Up)
      return OldPosition + Position(0, -GetVertMovement());
   else
      return OldPosition + Position(0, GetVertMovement());
}
```

The implementation of Bug's constructor is

```
Bug::Bug(SimpleWindow &w, int h, int p) :
  Window(w), HitsRequired(h), HitsTaken(0),
  GeneratePercentage(1, 100),
  DirectionChangeProbability(p) {
    Bmp.reserve(BugBitMaps);
    return;
}
```

The constructor initializes several of Bug's data members. It initializes the Window data member with the reference to the SimpleWindow that will contain the bug. It initializes HitsRequired to the number of hits the bug can take before being killed, and it initializes HitsTaken to 0. The data member initialization list also sets up object GeneratePercentage so that it will produce a uniform distribution of integers between 1 and 100. This sequence of pseudorandom integers will be used to randomly change the direction in which a bug is moving. Finally, the data member DirectionChangeProbability is initialized. This attribute controls how often a bug changes directions.

The data member initialization list does most of the work required by the constructor. The only job left to do in the body of the function is to reserve BugBitMaps elements in the vector Bmp. This vector will hold the bitmap images of the bug.

The public member functions Create() and Kill() call the protected member functions Draw() and Erase(). In addition, Create() sets the data member HitsTaken to 0 so that a new bug starts with zero hits. The implementations of these public member functions are

```
void Bug::Create() {
    HitsTaken = 0;
    Draw();
    return;
}
void Bug::Kill() {
    Erase();
    return;
};
```

The implementation of Bug's protected member function Draw() gets the current direction the bug is moving and invokes the BitMap::Draw() function for the appropriate bitmap. Its implementation is

```
void Bug::Draw() {
    GetBmp(GetDirection()).Draw();
    return;
};
```

The code for Bug::Erase() is similar except that the function Bit-Map::Erase() is called instead.

```
void Bug::Erase() {
    GetBmp(GetDirection()).Erase();
    return;
};
```

The member function `SetPosition()` sets a bug's position, but it also sets the position of the four bitmaps that contain the images of the bug going in each of the four directions. Updating the bitmap positions whenever `Bug::MyPosition` is updated ensures that all the bitmaps are positioned consistently. The code for `SetPosition()` is

```
void Bug::SetPosition(const Position &p) {
    for (Direction d = Up; d <= Right;
    d = (Direction) (d + 1))
        Bmp[d].SetPosition(p);
    CurrentPosition = p
    return;
}
```

The code calls `BitMap::SetPosition()` for each of the four bitmap images and then updates `Bug::CurrentPosition`.

The member function `NewPosition()` computes and returns the next position for the bug. The function looks at the direction in which the bug is moving and computes a new position by adding the proper movement distance to the current x-coordinate or the current y-coordinate of the bug, depending on the bug's direction. Its implementation is

```
Position Bug::NewPosition() const {
    const Position OldPosition = GetPosition();
    if (GetDirection() == Left)
        return OldPosition
            + Position(-GetHorizMovement(), 0);
    else if (GetDirection() == Right)
        return OldPosition
            + Position(GetHorizMovement(), 0);
    else if (GetDirection() == Up)
        return OldPosition
            + Position(0, -GetVertMovement());
    else
        return OldPosition
            + Position(0, GetVertMovement());
}
```

The function uses the protected inspectors `GetHorizMovement()` and `GetVertMovement()` to obtain the proper distance to move the bug in either the x or the y direction.

15.2.1 Derived class SlowBug

From **Bug**, we can create different types of bugs, that is, bugs that move differently. They may also look different, but that's not essential. The Bug Hunt game starts with a light blue, big, slow bug that doesn't change directions very often (see Figure 15.5). The class declaration of `SlowBug` is

```
class SlowBug : public Bug {
    public:
        SlowBug(SimpleWindow &w, int HitsNeeded = 4,
        int DirectionChange = 10);
        void Move();
};
```

That is, SlowBug is a kind of Bug, and it inherits all the properties and behaviors of Bug. SlowBug's constructor, by default, sets the number of hits necessary to kill a slow bug to 4. SlowBug has its own move function. This function will define the behavior of a slow bug. The declaration of class SlowBug follows declaration of class Bug in file bug.h.

Figure 15.5

Slow and fast bugs and the corresponding bitmap files

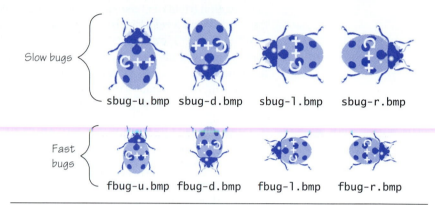

Slow bugs

sbug-u.bmp   sbug-d.bmp   sbug-l.bmp   sbug-r.bmp

Fast bugs

fbug-u.bmp   fbug-d.bmp   fbug-l.bmp   fbug-r.bmp

The implementation of SlowBug's constructor, unlike that of Bug, does quite a bit of work. In particular, it loads the bitmaps that will be used to display the bug in the game window. Listing 15.3 contains the implementation of SlowBug's constructor.

Listing 15.3

Implementation of SlowBug constructor from bug.cpp

```cpp
SlowBug::SlowBug(SimpleWindow &w, int h, int p) :
Bug(w, h, p) {
    // Load the bitmaps for the bug going in the
    // four directions
    vector<string> BitMapFiles(BugBitMaps);
    BitMapFiles[0] = "sbug-u.bmp";
    BitMapFiles[1] = "sbug-d.bmp";
    BitMapFiles[2] = "sbug-l.bmp";
    BitMapFiles[3] = "sbug-r.bmp";

    for (Direction d = Up; d <= Right;
    d = (Direction) (d + 1)) {
        GetBmp(d).SetWindow(GetWindow());
        GetBmp(d).Load(BitMapFiles[d]);
        assert(GetBmp(d).GetStatus() == BitMapOkay);
    }
    // Set the distance to move the bug in the
    // horizontal and vertical direction
    // The distance is based on the size of the bitmap.
    SetHorizMovement(GetBmp(Right).GetWidth() / 10.0);
    SetVertMovement(GetBmp(Up).GetHeight() / 10.0);
    // Initially make it go right
    SetDirection(Right);
    SetPosition(Position(3.0, 3.0));
    return;
}
```

The first part of the code loads the bitmaps that depict the bug moving in each of the four directions (see Figure 15.5). The second section of the code computes how much to move the bug on each timer tick. Both a horizontal and vertical distance to move are computed. The distance to move is based on the size of the bitmap. Here, a `SlowBug` will move 1/10 the size of the bitmap that is being rendered each interval. The last two lines of the constructor set the initial direction (right) and the initial position (3 centimeters from the left edge of the window and 3 centimeters from the top edge of the window).

The job of `SlowBug::Move()` is to make the bug move in a particular way. A slow bug has the following behavior. When a slow bug hits the side of the window, it turns and goes in the opposite direction. A slow bug randomly changes direction about 10 percent of the time.

The beginning of `SlowBug::Move()` is

```
Erase();
// Randomly change directions
if (GeneratePercentage.Draw()
  < GetDirectionChangeProbability())
    ChangeDirection();
SetPosition(NewPosition());
Draw();
```

The first step is to erase the currently displayed bitmap. The next step is to determine whether the direction should be changed. Using the `GeneratePercentage` object, a random number between 1 and 100 is drawn. If the number drawn is less than `DirectionChangeProbability`, then `ChangeDirection()` is called to randomly pick a new direction, and the bug is set to go in that direction. (See Listing 15.2 for the implementation of member function `ChangeDirection()`.) Otherwise, the bug continues in its current direction. Once the direction is determined, a new position is computed, and the bug is redrawn at its new location.

The next step of `Move()` is to determine whether the bug, on its next move, is going to go through the side of the window. If it will, the bug is turned to go in the opposite direction. The code for accomplishing this is

```
Direction BugDirection = GetDirection();
float BugX = GetPosition().GetXDistance();
float BugXSize = GetBmp(GetDirection()).GetWidth();
float BugY = GetPosition().GetYDistance();
float BugYSize = GetBmp(GetDirection()).GetHeight();
// Decide if it needs to turn around
if (BugDirection == Right
  && BugX + BugXSize + GetHorizMovement()
  >= GetWindow().GetWidth())
    SetDirection(Left);
else if (BugDirection == Left
  && BugX - GetHorizMovement() <= 0.0)
    SetDirection(Right);
else if (BugDirection == Down
  && BugY + BugYSize + GetVertMovement()
  >= GetWindow().GetHeight())
    SetDirection(Up);
else if (BugDirection == Up
  && BugY - GetVertMovement() <= 0.0)
    SetDirection(Down);
```

The first block of code obtains some needed information about the bug. It obtains the current direction of the bug, the *x*-coordinate and the *y*-coordinate of the position of the bug, and the height and width of the bitmap being displayed.

Using this information, the code determines whether the bug is about to hit a window edge. For example, if the bug is moving to the right, and the right edge of the bitmap plus the amount it can move horizontally extends past the right edge of the window, the bug is turned to the left. (Recall that all coordinates as well as the size of the window are in centimeters.) Figure 15.6 illustrates the calculation. Similar calculations are performed for the three other directions.

Figure 15.6

Determining whether a bug is about to go through the side of the window

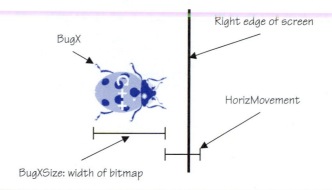

BugX

Right edge of screen

HorizMovement

BugXSize: width of bitmap

15.2.2 Derived class FastBug

Using base class `Bug`, we also want to create a fast bug whose behavior is different from `SlowBug`'s behavior. The declaration of class `FastBug` is very similar to that of `SlowBug`.

```
class FastBug : public Bug {
    public:
        FastBug(SimpleWindow &w, int HitsNeeded = 3,
          int DirectionChangeProbability = 20);
        void Move();
};
```

A `FastBug` is smaller than a `SlowBug` and is killed with only three hits. However, compared to a `SlowBug`, a `FastBug` changes directions more often. The constructor for `FastBug` is similar to `SlowBug`'s constructor. Listing 15.4 contains the implementation of `FastBug::FastBug()`.

The differences between `FastBug`'s constructor and `SlowBug`'s constructor are that a different set of images are loaded, `HorizMovement` and `Vert-Movement` are computed differently, and the initial direction and position are set differently. The key difference, however, is that `HorizMovement` and `VertMovement` are larger in `FastBug`, relative to the size of the bitmap, than

Listing 15.4

*Implementation of
FastBug constructor
from bug.cpp*

```cpp
FastBug::FastBug(SimpleWindow &w, int h, int p) :
  Bug(w, h, p) {
    // Load the four bitmaps for the bug to go in
    // four directions
    vector<string> BitMapFiles(BugBitMaps);
    BitMapFiles[0] = "fbug-u.bmp";
    BitMapFiles[1] = "fbug-d.bmp";
    BitMapFiles[2] = "fbug-l.bmp";
    BitMapFiles[3] = "fbug-r.bmp";

    for (Direction d = Up; d <= Right;
     d = (Direction) (d + 1)) {
       GetBmp(d).SetWindow(GetWindow());
       GetBmp(d).Load(BitMapFiles[d]);
       assert(GetBmp(d).GetStatus() == BitMapOkay);
    }
    // Set the distance to move the bug in the horizontal
    // and vertical directions. The distance is based
    // on the size of the bitmap. This should be a larger
    // distance than for a SlowBug, so it moves faster
    SetHorizMovement(GetBmp(Right).GetWidth() / 5.0);
    SetVertMovement(GetBmp(Up).GetHeight() / 5.0);
    // Initially make it go down
    SetDirection(Down);
    SetPosition(Position(6.0, 2.0));
}
```

they were in `SlowBug`. Consequently, a `FastBug` appears to move faster than a `SlowBug`.

The implementation of `FastBug::Move()` is very different from the implementation of `SlowBug::Move()`. This is, of course, because we want `FastBug` to behave differently. We want it to move faster and be able to move through the window walls to the other side. Some computer scientists might call this a Heisenbug. In fact, if the only difference between a `FastBug` and a `SlowBug` had been the speed at which they move, we would not have needed a new class. This one difference could have been handled by setting the attributes of a generic bug to the proper values (i.e., loading the proper bitmaps and setting `HorizMovement` and `VertMovement` appropriately).

The first part of the implementation of `FastBug::Move()` is similar to that of `SlowBug`. The code is

```cpp
void FastBug::Move() {
    Erase();

    // Change directions randomly
    if (GeneratePercentage.Draw()
     < GetDirectionChangeProbability())
       ChangeDirection();
    SetPosition(NewPosition());
    Draw();
```

The second part of the implementation determines what the bug should do when the side of the window is hit. Unlike a `SlowBug`, which just reverses direction when it hits the edge of the window, a `FastBug` "tunnels" through

and appears on the other side of the window moving in the same direction. The
code that implements this behavior follows.

```cpp
// Get bug position and its size
Direction BugDirection = GetDirection();
float BugX = GetPosition().GetXDistance();
float BugXSize = GetBmp(GetDirection()).GetWidth();
float BugY = GetPosition().GetYDistance();
float BugYSize = GetBmp(GetDirection()).GetHeight();
// Decide whether bug pops through at the opposite side
if (BugDirection == Right
   && BugX + BugXSize + GetHorizMovement()
   >= GetWindow().GetWidth()) {
     Erase();
     SetPosition(Position(1,
       GetPosition().GetYDistance()));
     Draw();
}
else if (BugDirection == Left
   && BugX - GetHorizMovement() <= 0.0) {
     Erase();
     SetPosition(
       Position(GetWindow().GetWidth() - BugXSize,
       GetPosition().GetYDistance()));
     Draw();
}
else if (BugDirection == Down
   && BugY + BugYSize >= GetWindow().GetHeight()) {
     Erase();
     SetPosition(
       Position(GetPosition().GetXDistance(), 0.0));
     Draw();
}
else if (BugDirection == Up
   && BugY - GetVertMovement() <= 0.0) {
     Erase();
     SetPosition(
       Position(GetPosition().GetXDistance(),
       GetWindow().GetHeight() - BugYSize));
     Draw();
}
```

The logic for determining whether the bug is at one of the four edges of the
window is exactly the same as the code in `SlowBug::Move()`. The difference
is what happens. For a `FastBug`, the current image is erased, and the bug is
drawn at the opposite screen edge. The direction in which it is moving remains
the same.

The similarity of the logic in the move functions of `SlowBug` and `Fast-Bug` suggests that we can simplify the code by writing utility functions for
determining whether a bug is at one of the window edges. To be usable by both
classes, these functions should be members of the base class `Bug`. The following four member functions are added to the protected section of class `Bug`:
`AtRightEdge()`, `AtLeftEdge()`, `AtBottomEdge()`, and `AtTopEdge()`.
These functions return true if the bug is at the corresponding edge and false
otherwise.

The implementations of these protected member functions are

```cpp
// AtRightEdge(): determine whether bug is at right
// edge of the window
bool Bug::AtRightEdge() const {
    return (GetPosition().GetXDistance()
      + GetBmp(GetDirection()).GetWidth()
      + GetHorizMovement() >= GetWindow().GetWidth());
}
// AtLeftEdge(): determine whether bug is at left
// edge of the window
bool Bug::AtLeftEdge() const {
    return (GetPosition().GetXDistance()
      - GetHorizMovement() <= 0.0);
}
// AtBottomEdge(): determine whether bug is at bottom
// edge of the window
bool Bug::AtBottomEdge() const {
    return (GetPosition().GetYDistance()
      + GetBmp(GetDirection()).GetHeight()
      + GetVertMovement() >= GetWindow().GetHeight());
}
// AtTopEdge(): determine whether bug is at top
// edge of the window
bool Bug::AtTopEdge() const {
    return (GetPosition().GetYDistance() -
      GetVertMovement() <= 0.0);
}
```

Using these functions for `FastBug::Move()`, the revised code for determining whether a bug should "tunnel" through the edge of the window is

```cpp
if (BugDirection == Right && AtRightEdge()) {
    Erase();
    SetPosition(Position(0.0,
      GetPosition().GetYDistance()));
    Draw();
}
else if (BugDirection == Left && AtLeftEdge()) {
    Erase();
    SetPosition(
      Position(GetWindow().GetWidth() - BugXSize,
      GetPosition().GetYDistance()));
    Draw();
}
else if (BugDirection == Down && AtBottomEdge()) {
    Erase();
    SetPosition(Position(GetPosition().GetXDistance(),
      0.0));
    Draw();
}
else if (BugDirection == Up && AtTopEdge()) {
    Erase();
    SetPosition(Position(GetPosition().GetXDistance(),
      GetWindow().GetHeight() - BugYSize));
    Draw();
}
```

The analogous code for `SlowBug::Move()` would also be shorter and cleaner.

Now that we have our bugs implemented, we can begin the design and implementation of the game controller.

15.3 CLASS GAMECONTROLLER

The job of the game controller is to control the play of the game. It needs to maintain the state of the game as it progresses and handle both mouse-click events and timer-tick events. The public interface to the game controller should include

- Reset—put the game back in its initial state.
- Play—start the game.
- MouseClick—handle a mouse-click event.
- TimerTick—handle a timer tick.

In addition to these public member functions, the game controller includes the following private data members:

- GameWindow—a pointer to the SimpleWindow for the game.
- Level—the current level of the game.
- Status—the status of the game.
- KindOfBug—a vector that points to the different bug types used in the game.

Listing 15.5 contains the declaration of the class GameController. The code contains two enumerations. The first enumeration defines the levels of play. This version of Bug Hunt has two levels of play. At the first level a slow bug is hunted, and in the second level a fast bug is hunted. The second enumeration defines the various stages or status of the game. For example, the enumeration member SettingUp indicates that the game is being initialized and is not ready for play. Similarly, the status Playing indicates a game is in progress and that mouse-click events and timer-tick events should be handled appropriately. The constant NumberOfBugTypes defines how many different types of bugs the game supports. As the comment notes, this constant should correspond to the number of levels of the game.

Listing 15.5

Declaration of class GameController in bughunt.h

```
#ifndef BWINDOW_H
#define BWINDOW_H
#include "bug.h"

enum GameLevel { Slow, Fast, Done };
enum GameStatus {GameWon, Playing, GameLost,
 SettingUp };

// Speed of game (i.e., timer interval)
const int GameSpeed = 100;

class GameController {
  public:
    GameController(const string &Title = "Bug Hunt!",
      const Position &WinPosition = Position(3.0, 3.0),
      const float WindLength = 14.0,
      const float WinHeight = 10.0),
    ~GameController();
    SimpleWindow *GetWindow();
    void Reset();
    void Play(const GameLevel Level);
    int MouseClick(const Position &MousePosition);
```

```
      int TimerTick();
   private:
      void BugHit();
      GameLevel CurrentLevel() const;
      Bug *CurrentBug() const ;
      SimpleWindow *GameWindow;
      GameLevel Level;
      GameStatus Status;
      vector<Bug*> KindOfBug;
};
#endif
```

The `GameController` constructor allocates all the game objects, including the window and the bugs. In addition, the `GameController` initializes the data members `Level` and `Status`. Its implementation is

```
GameController::GameController(const string &Title,
  const Position &WinPosition, float WinLength,
  float WinHeight) : Level(Slow), Status(SettingUp) {
    // Create a window and open it
    GameWindow = new SimpleWindow(Title,
     WinLength, WinHeight, WinPosition);
    GetWindow()->Open();

    // Create the bugs. Note this must
    // be done AFTER the window is opened
    // because initialization of the bugs depends on
    // having a window.
    KindOfBug.reserve(NumberOfBugTypes);
    KindOfBug[Slow] = new SlowBug(*GetWindow());
    // Create a fast bug
    KindOfBug[Fast] = new FastBug(*GetWindow());
}
```

Notice that the code contains an important comment—the bugs must be constructed after the window is opened. This sequence is required because when a `Bug` is constructed, its bitmaps are initialized, which requires knowing the `SimpleWindow` object that will contain it.

Class `GameController` has a destructor whose function is to deallocate the objects that have been dynamically allocated. These objects include the window and the bugs. Thus `GameController::~GameController()` simply deletes these objects. Its implementation is

```
GameController::~GameController() {
    // Get rid of the bugs and the window
    delete KindOfBug[Slow];
    delete KindOfBug[Fast];
    delete GameWindow;
}
```

The public member function `Reset()` simply sets the game back to the beginning level and is used when a player misses a bug. The game starts over from the beginning. The code for `Reset()` is

```
void GameController::Reset() {
    Status = SettingUp;
    Level = Slow;
    CurrentBug()->Create();
}
```

Member function `Play()` is equally simple. Its implementation is

```cpp
void GameController::Play(const GameLevel l) {
    Level = l;
    Status = Playing;
    GetWindow()->StartTimer(GameSpeed);
}
```

`Play()` sets the level, changes the status to playing, and starts the timer so that the current bug can be moved.

Most of the control of the game centers on handling mouse-click events and timer-tick events. On a mouse click, we must check to see whether the game is in progress, and if so, whether the current bug is hit. If it is hit, the member function `BugHit()` is called to update the status of the game. The status of the game is checked to see whether the game has been won. If so, a Sim-pleWindow alert box pops up with a winning message.

If the game is in progress, but the player missed the bug, the timer is stopped, a message is displayed, the current bug is killed, and the game starts over. Listing 15.6 contains the code for `GameController::MouseClick()`.

Listing 15.6

Implementation of MouseClick and TimerTick from file control.cpp

```cpp
// MouseClick(): check to see whether they hit the bug
// If so, update the status of the game
int GameController::MouseClick(const Position
&MousePosition) {
    // Only pay attention to the mouse if game
    // is in progress
    if (Status == Playing
      && CurrentBug()->IsHit(MousePosition)) {
        BugHit();
        // They won the game!
        // Let them know and start over
        if (Status == GameWon) {
            GetWindow()->StopTimer();
            GetWindow()->Message("You Won!");
            Reset();
            Play(Slow);
        }
    }
    else {
        // They missed the bug
        // Let them know and start over
        GetWindow()->StopTimer();
        GetWindow()->Message("You Missed!");
        CurrentBug()->Kill();
        Reset();
        Play(Slow);
    }
    return 1;
}
// TimerTick(): move the bug
int GameController::TimerTick() {
    CurrentBug()->Move();
    return 1;
}
```

The code for `GameController::TimerTick()` is also contained in Listing 15.6. It sends a message to the current bug telling it to move. Notice that C++ support of polymorphism makes this code both natural and simple. The appropriate Move() is automatically called depending on the current type of bug.

The final GameController member function to discuss is the private member function BugHit(). Its implementation is

```
// BugHit(): player hit the bug
void GameController::BugHit() {
    // Determine if bug is dying. If so, kill it
    // and determine if the game is over.
    // If the game is not over advance to
    // the next level of play
    if (CurrentBug()->IsDying()) {
        CurrentBug()->Kill();
        Level = (GameLevel) (Level + 1);
        if (Level == Done)
            Status = GameWon;
        else
            // Create the new faster bug
            CurrentBug()->Create();
    }
}
```

The code determines whether the current bug is dying. If so, the bug is killed, the current hit count is reset, and the game advances to the next level. If there is no next level, the status of the game is set to GameWon; otherwise, the next kind of bug is created.

15.4 BUG HUNT

The only remaining piece of the program is the code that creates a game and sets up the callbacks. This code is contained in Listing 15.7. Function Api-Main() initializes the EzWindow pseudorandom-number generator and then creates a game called BugHunt. Both the mouse and timer callbacks are set up, and play starts at level Slow. ApiEnd(), which is called when the program is sent a terminating message, deletes the game. This action, of course, invokes the destructor for GameController, which deletes the bugs and the window.

This completes the design and implementation of Bug Hunt. As we mentioned at the beginning of the chapter, the implementation of Bug Hunt consists of three modules (bug.cpp, control.cpp, and bughunt.cpp); their interfaces (bug.h, control.h, and bughunt.h); and the EzWindows API library. The CD-ROM contains the complete and final code. The design of Bug Hunt exemplifies the design of many games. The controller coordinates the play of the game and is responsible for keeping up with the state of the game. The start-up code sets up the interface between the player and the game by arranging for the appropriate parts of the program to handle the mouse clicks. This model can be used to develop many fun and interesting games. Some possibilities are described in the exercises.

Listing 15.7

Functions to set up callbacks and start and terminate the game from bughunt.cpp

```cpp
#include "bughunt.h"
GameController *BugHunt;
// TimerCallback(): on a timer tick call BugHunt s
// timer-tick handler
int TimerCallback(void) {
   BugHunt->TimerTick();

   return 1;
}

// MouseCallback -- on a mouse click call BugHunt s
// mouse-click handler
int MouseCallback(const Position &MousePosition) {
   BugHunt->MouseClick(MousePosition);

   return 1;
}

// ApiMain(): allocate the game controller, set up
// the callbacks, and start the game
int ApiMain() {
   EzRandomize();
   BugHunt = new GameController();
   (BugHunt->GetWindow())->
    SetTimerCallback(TimerCallback);
   (BugHunt->GetWindow())->
    SetMouseClickCallback(MouseCallback);
   BugHunt->Play(Slow);

   return 0;
}

// ApiEnd(): destroy the game
int ApiEnd() {
   delete BugHunt;

   return 0;
}
```

<h1 style="text-align:center">Self-check Questions</h1>

1. Class Bug uses a vector to hold the bitmap images of the bugs. Change class Bug to use an array for the bitmaps. Compare your modified implementation of Bug Hunt to the existing implementation. How is it better? How is it worse?

2. Implement an EzWindows version of a Fifteen puzzle. The original Fifteen puzzle consisted of a square tray containing 15 numbered square pieces and one open space in a 4-by-4 arrangement. One person scrambles the pieces by sliding them so that the numbers were out of order. To solve the puzzle, one had to slide the pieces around to get them back in order.

   When the Fifteen puzzle was developed in 1865, the plastic pieces had numbers. Today you can still find Fifteen puzzles, but typically they have a picture instead of numbers. Our EzWindows Fifteen puzzle implementation also uses a picture. Figure 15.7 shows a sample screenshot of a EzWindows Fifteen puzzle.

Figure 15.7

*Screenshot of Fifteen
puzzle game*

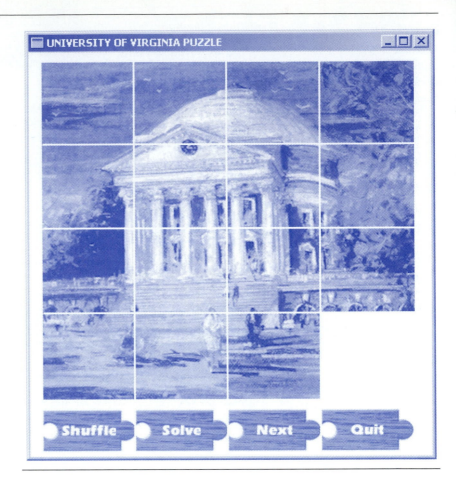

3.   A calculator is a handy utility that is included with most operating sys-
      tems. Try out the calculator application on your computer system. Most
      of these applications present a user-interface that models a physical cal-
      culator. Implement an EzWindows application for a calculator applica-
      tion. Figure 15.8 shows a screenshot of a EzWindows calculator
      application.

15.5 POINTS TO REMEMBER

✔ Do not hesitate to rewrite code to make it shorter and more
   understandable. The time spent redesigning code will pay for itself later.

✔ Inheritance provides a natural way to reuse code. In Bug Hunt, the code
   for the base class Bug is used by the derived classes SlowBug and
   FastBug. If new bugs are added to the game, they too can use the code
   developed for the base class.

Figure 15.8

Screenshot of calculator application

✔ Containment is a way to build complex objects out of other objects. In Bug Hunt, the GameController class is built using containment. A game contains a window (i.e., a SimpleWindow) and different kinds of bugs (i.e., array KindOfBug).

✔ Encapsulation is a way of building software where details about an object are hidden from the users of the object. The game controller in Bug Hunt uses the class Bug. How a bug is represented and how it moves is encapsulated in the class Bug. The game controller does not know how a bug is represented or how it moves, but it can ask a Bug to move by calling its public member function Move().

✔ Polymorphism enables us to write code that manipulates objects related by inheritance without regard to the specific kind of object being manipulated. In Bug Hunt, the game controller can manipulate a bug without regard to whether it is a FastBug or a SlowBug. For example, the

History of Computing

Parallel computing and the grand challenges

The standard model of computing is to do things in a serial fashion. Each computation is done in sequence, with one computation being completed before the next one is started. In parallel computing, the idea is to do as many computations in parallel as possible. Of course, to do so requires several computer chips that can work together. Just as five people can clean a house quicker than one person working alone, many computers working together on a single problem can reach a solution faster than a single computer can.

Of course, the problem with parallel computing is that when the number of computers working on a problem becomes very large, it becomes difficult to partition and coordinate the work to be done. Imagine the difficulties you might have if 100 people showed up to help you clean your house! You would have a hard time keeping them busy and out of each other's way.

As with any new technology, problems are to be expected. Researchers are making great strides in parallel computing. As a way of focusing the efforts to develop usable parallel systems, scientists and engineers have identified a list of important problems, dubbed the "Grand Challenge" problems. These are fundamental problems in science and engineering, with broad economic and scientific impact, whose solutions can be advanced by applying high-performance computing techniques and resources. Many of these problems involve using the computer to model a complex system. Examples include modeling the weather so that accurate, long-term weather forecasting becomes a reality, modeling geological activity so that forecasting earthquakes is possible, and modeling environmental effects on ecosystems so that any negative impact can be predicted and avoided or minimized.

Other Grand Challenge problems involve what is popularly called virtual reality. *Virtual reality* is using the computer to create an artificial environment that is indistinguishable from reality. If this concept makes you think of the HoloDeck in the television series *Star Trek: The Next Generation*, you've got exactly the right idea. Primitive virtual reality systems are already in use. Most airplane pilots learn to fly a new aircraft by flying a simulator of the aircraft. This type of simulator is very realistic, and it is much cheaper and safer to learn to fly a new plane by starting in a simulator, rather than starting out in the real plane. Work is underway to develop similar techniques so that surgeons can be trained in delicate procedures. Although these systems are primitive in comparison to the Enterprise's HoloDeck, advances in computing, display and sensor technology, and computer graphics will no doubt expand the uses of virtual reality systems.

member function `Move()` is a polymorphic function. Through the magic of polymorphism, when the game controller tells a bug to move, the

`Move()` function appropriate for the type of bug being manipulated is called.

15.6 EXERCISES

15.1   In Bug Hunt, two enumerations, `GameLevel` and `GameStatus`, are defined in `control.h`. These should really be encapsulated in class `GameController`. Modify the Bug Hunt code so that these enumerations are encapsulated in class `GameController`. Document the changes you make by including comments at the beginning of each module that outline the change, who made them, and when they were changed.

15.2   Modify Bug Hunt so that it includes a new type of bug called `WarpBug`. This bug occasionally goes into hyperspace, disappears for an interval, and returns at a random location in the window. A `WarpBug` requires two hits to be killed. The new Bug Hunt will have three levels of play.

15.3   One of the deficiencies of Bug Hunt is that players get no feedback when the mouse is clicked unless they miss the bug or the bug is finally killed. Think of a scheme for providing feedback when the player hits a bug. Modify Bug Hunt to implement your scheme.

15.4   Most bugs run faster when you hit them. Modify Bug Hunt so that when a bug is swatted, it moves faster.

15.5   Modify Bug Hunt so that if the player misses a bug, another bug appears. The number of bugs in a window should not exceed three. Observe what happens when several bugs are in the window. Explain why this happens.

15.6   Modify Bug Hunt to include a timer. If all the bugs are not killed in a set time period, the player loses the game.

15.7   Modify Bug Hunt to include a timer. When a player kills all the bugs, record the time (in seconds) it took that player to kill all the bugs. Store the scores in a file and display them at the end of the game.

15.8   Design and implement a new game called Balloons. In this game, a balloon appears at the bottom of the window and begins floating to the top. The player must "pop" the balloon before it reaches the top of the window. If the balloon reaches the top, the player loses and the game starts from the beginning. As play progresses, balloons that move differently appear. At each level, the balloons behave in a way that makes them harder to pop than the balloons at the previous level.

15.9   Design and implement a new game called Terminator. In this game, the player controls a robot (use the bitmaps from Chapter 10). The object of the game is to chase the bugs with the robot and "terminate" them. A bug is terminated when the robot catches the bug by touching it. Like Bug Hunt, there are two types of bugs—a slow bug and a fast bug.

To control the movement of the robot, you should create a separate window that has control arrows in it. By clicking on an arrow, the player causes the robot to move one step in that direction. To make the game challenging, design the bugs so that they can travel through walls. That is, when a bug hits the edge of the window, it should reappear at the opposite window edge. A robot cannot travel through walls.

Be sure to design your game so that it is easy to add different types and numbers of bugs. You should initially allow for three slow bugs and two fast bugs.

APPENDIX A

Tables

Table A.1 lists the ASCII character set. Table A.2 describes the C++ operator precedence rules.

A.1　ASCII CHARACTER SET

Code	Char.	Name	Code	Char.	Code	Char.	Code	Char.
0	^@	NUL	32	SP	64	@	96	`
1	^A	SOH	33	!	65	A	97	a
2	^B	STX	34	"	66	B	98	b
3	^C	ETX	35	#	67	C	99	c
4	^D	^EOT	36	$	68	D	100	d
5	^E	ENQ	37	%	69	E	101	e
6	^F	ACK	38	&	70	F	102	f
7	^G	BEL	39	'	71	G	103	g
8	^H	BS	40	(	72	H	104	h
9	^I	TAB	41	)	73	I	105	i
10	^J	LF	42	*	74	J	106	j
11	^K	VT	43	+	75	K	107	k
12	^L	FF	44	,	76	L	108	l
13	^M	CR	45	-	77	M	109	m
14	^N	SO	46	.	78	N	110	n
15	^O	SI	47	/	79	O	111	o
16	^P	DLE	48	0	80	P	112	p
17	^Q	DC1	49	1	81	Q	113	q
18	^R	DC2	50	2	82	R	114	r
19	^S	DC3	51	3	83	S	115	s
20	^T	DC4	52	4	84	T	116	t
21	^U	NAK	53	5	85	U	117	u
22	^V	SYN	54	6	86	V	118	v
23	^W	ETB	55	7	87	W	119	w
24	^X	CAN	56	8	88	X	120	x
25	^Y	EM	57	9	89	Y	121	y
26	^Z	SUB	58	:	90	Z	122	z
27	^[	ESC	59	;	91	[	123	{
28	^\	FS	60	<	92	\	124		
29	^]	GS	61	=	93	]	125	}
30	^^	RS	62	>	94	^	126	~
31	^_	US	63	?	95	_	127	DEL

A.2　OPERATOR PRECEDENCE

The following table summarizes the precedence of the major C++ operators. Operators with equal precedence are separated from operators of lesser precedence by horizontal lines.

Operator	Description	Category	Association
()	function call	postfix	left
[]	subscript	postfix	left
. ->	selection, indirect selection	postfix	left
::	scope resolution	postfix	left
++ --	increment, decrement	postfix	right
! ~	logical not, bitwise not	unary	right
+ -	arithmetic plus, negation	unary	right
++ --	increment, decrement	prefix	right
& *	address, indirection	unary	right
sizeof	size	unary	right
()	cast	unary	right
new delete	allocate, free	unary	right
.*	member selection	postfix	left
->*	member pointer selection	postfix	left
* / %	multiplicative	binary	left
+ -	additive	binary	left
<< >>	shift	binary	left
< <= > >=	ordering	binary	left
== !=	equality	binary	left
&	bitwise and	binary	left
^	bitwise xor	binary	left
|	bitwise or	binary	left
&&	logical and	binary	left
||	logical or	binary	left
? :	conditional	ternary	right
= *= /= %= += -= <<= >>= &= ^= |=	assignment	binary	right
throw	exception	unary	right
,	sequential evaluation	binary	left

APPENDIX B

Standard libraries

The C++ standard includes an extensive collection of libraries. Some of the libraries were originally C libraries: assert, ctype, errno, float, limits, locale, math, setjmp, signal, stdarg, stddef, stdio, stdlib, string, and time. Other libraries are specifically for C++. These libraries include algorithm, deque, exception, fstream, iomanip, iostream, iterator, limits, list, locale, map, new, numerics, queue, set, stack, string, stringstream, utility, and vector. For a complete specification of these libraries, please refer to a language reference manual, your compiler documentation, or one of the following sources.

- B. Stroustrup, *The C++ Programming Language, 3rd ed.*, Reading, MA: Addison-Wesley, 1998.

- International Standard for Information Systems—Programming Language C++, ISO/IEC FDIS 14882, Washington, DC: American National Standards Institute, 1998.

- P. J. Plauger, *The Standard C Library*, Englewood Cliffs, NJ: Prentice-Hall, 1992.

- P. J. Plauger (editor), A. A. Stepanov, M. Lee, and D. R. Musser, *The C++ Standard Template Library*, Englewood Cliffs, NJ: Prentice-Hall, 2000.

B.1 LIBRARY NAMING AND ACCESS

In the C++ standard, access to a standard library does not require use of a header suffix. For example, the following statement includes the iostream library.

```
#include <iostream>
```

Similarly, access to a C-derived standard library does not require the use of a header suffix. However, a C library name should be preceded by a c to indicate its origin. For example, the following statement includes the C assert macro library.

```
#include <cassert>
```

It is expected that for a reasonable time most compilers will allow the libraries to be included with or without the header suffix. In fact, several compilers at this point require some use of the header suffix. For such compilers, the iostream and assert libraries would be accessed in the following manner:

```
#include <iostream.h>
#include <assert.h>
```

The versions that use the header suffix most likely add their declarations to the global scope, whereas the versions without the suffix add their definitions to the `std` namespace. (See Appendix D for a namespace discussion.)

The discussion in the next sections presents a limited selection of functions, types, macros, and objects from some of the C and C++ libraries. Other important standard libraries have been introduced throughout the text (e.g., Chapter 3 introduces the string library; Chapter 5 discusses the ctype, assert, and iomanip libraries; and Chapter 9 considers vector and other container classes from the Standard Template Library). In addition, in Appendix C we give further coverage to the string class and some of the other container classes.

B.2 IOSTREAM LIBRARY

The iostream library and hierarchy has been discussed and used throughout the text. Besides defining the insertion and extraction operators and manipulators, and the global stream objects `cin`, `cout`, `cerr`, and `clog`, the library also provides access to `ios`, `istream`, and `ostream` member functions. The `istream` member functions include

`int istream::get()`

   If the input stream contains additional data, the function extracts and returns the next character; otherwise, it returns EOF.

`istream& istream::get(char &c)`

   If the input stream contains additional data, the function extracts and assigns the next character to `c`; otherwise, the effect on `c` is undefined. A reference to `*this` (the invoking object) is returned.

```
istream& istream::get(char s[], int n,
  char delim = '\n')
```

> Extracts characters from the input stream and assigns them to s until one of the following conditions occurs: n-1 characters have been extracted, there are no more characters to extract, or the next character to be extracted has the value delim. If the last condition occurs, the delimiter is not extracted. A null terminating character is placed after the last extracted value copied to s. A reference to *this is returned.

```
istream& istream::getline(char s[], int n,
  char delim = '\n')
```

> Extracts characters from the input stream and assigns them to s until one of the following conditions occurs: n-1 characters have been extracted, there are no more characters to extract, or the next character to be extracted is the delimiter character. If the last condition occurs, the delimiter is also extracted but not assigned to s. A null terminating character is placed after the last extracted value copied to s. A reference to *this is returned.

```
int istream::peek()
```

> If the input stream contains additional data, the function returns the next character to be extracted; otherwise, it returns EOF.

```
istream& istream::unget(char c)
```

> Character c is pushed back to the input stream. It will be the next character to be extracted. A reference to *this is returned.

The iostream library also provides access to an ios member function that some programmers use to detect end of file on an input stream.

```
bool ios::eof()
```

> Returns true if end of file has been reached on the stream; otherwise, the function returns false.

The iostream library also provides two ostream member functions that are analogous to get() and getline().

```
ostream& ostream::put(char c)
```

> Inserts the character c to the output stream. A reference to *this is returned.

```
ostream& ostream::write(const char s[], int n)
```

> Inserts n characters from s to the output stream. Null characters are considered valid. A reference to *this is returned.

The iostream library also provides another ostream member function that is sometimes useful.

```
ostream& ostream::flush()
```

> Forces any insertion operators that have not yet completed to be completed. A reference to *this is returned.

B.3   STDLIB LIBRARY

The C-based stdlib library is a miscellaneous collection of types, functions, and macro definitions. The major type declared in this library is the integral type `size_t`. Some of the more commonly used functions in this library are

int `abs(`**int** `n)`
> Returns the absolute value of n.

double `atof(`**const char** `s[])`
> Returns a **double** representation of the number represented by string s. If the string is nonnumeric, the value of the function is undefined.

int `atoi(`**const char** `s[]`
> Returns an **int** representation of the number represented by string s. If the string is nonnumeric, the value of the function is undefined.

long int `atol(`**const char** `s[])`
> Returns a **long int** representation of the number represented by string s. If the string is nonnumeric, the value of the function is undefined.

void `exit(`**int** `status)`
> The program terminates with a return value of `status`.

void `free(`**void** `*ptr)`
> Gives the memory to which `ptr` points back to the free store.

void* `malloc(size_t size)`
> Returns a pointer to size bytes of now-allocated free store memory. If there is insufficient free store memory, 0 is returned.

int `rand()`
> Returns a pseudorandom integer in the range 0 to RAND_MAX. The default seed value to generate the sequence is 1.

void `srand(`**unsigned int** `val)`
> Sets the seed for the pseudorandom number generator to `val`.

int `system(`**const char** `s[])`
> Passes the string s to the operating system to be run by its command processor. A system-dependent integer value is returned.

B.4   MATH LIBRARY

A significant amount of software development is concerned with scientific programming. The term *scientific programming* is a catch-all phrase for programming that makes extensive use of mathematical formulations and models. Such programs often make use of trigonometric, exponential, and logarithmic functions. For software portability purposes, the C-based math library has been developed with many common math functions.

Unlike the other standard libraries discussed in this appendix, the actual math function definitions are not necessarily automatically linked to the program being translated. For compilers that are invoked from a command-line prompt, the linking is typically requested via a parameter to the compilation command. For compilers that are part of larger programming environments, the linking is sometimes requested by setting an appropriate library option. The math library is treated differently because, depending on the circumstances, programmers may prefer to link to different library implementations. Possible library trade-offs can be floating-point accuracy and efficiency. The implementations of other standard libraries are more straightforward than the math library and do not normally require considering such trade-offs.

Some of the more commonly used functions in this library are

`acos(x)`
Returns the angle whose cosine is x.

`asin(x)`
Returns the angle whose sine is x.

`atan(x)`
Returns the angle whose tangent is x.

`ceil(x)`
Returns the smallest whole number greater than or equal to x.

`cos(x)`
Returns the cosine of angle x.

`cosh(x)`
Returns the hyperbolic cosine of angle x.

`exp(x)`
Returns e^x.

`fabs(x)`
Returns the absolute value of x.

`floor(x)`
Returns the largest whole number less than or equal to x

`log(x)`
Returns the natural log of x.

`log10(x)`
Retiurns log base 10 of x.

`pow(x, y)`
Returns x^y.

`sin(x)`
Returns the sine of angle x.

`sinh(x)`
Returns the hyperbolic sine of angle x

`sqrt(x)`
Returns the square root of x.

`tan(x)`
Returns the tangent of angle x

`tanh(x)`
Returns the hyperbolic tangent of angle x.

B.5 TIME LIBRARY

The C-based time library is a collection of types, functions, and macro definitions for manipulating calendar and program time. The major types declared in this library are `clock_t`, `time_t`, and `tm`. Types `clock_t` and `time_t` are integral types. Type `tm` is a **struct** type with the following definition:

```
struct tm {
    int tm_sec;     // seconds after the current minute
    int tm_min;     // minutes after the current hour
    int tm_mday;    // day of month
    int tm_mon;     // month of year
    int tm_year;    // years since 1900
    int tm_wday;    // days since Sunday
    int tm_yday;    // days since January 1
    int tm_isdst;   // flag indicating if daylight savings
                    // time is in effect: positive value
                    // means in effect, zero value means
                    // not in effect, negative value means
                    // unknown
};
```

The functions in this library deal with *calendar time*, which represents the current date and date using the Gregorian calendar, and *local time*, which is a calendar time for an implementation-dependent specific time zone. Some of the functions included in this library are

`char* asctime(const tm *tptr)`
> Returns a pointer to a character string that is a representation of the `tm` object `*tptr`.

`clock_t clock()`
> Returns a `clock_t` value that when divided by CLOCKS_PER_SEC is an approximation of the number of seconds of processor time used by the program so far.

`double difftime(time_t t1, time_t t2)`
> Returns a **double** value that is the difference between times `t1` and `t2`.

`tm* localtime(const time_t *tptr)`
> Returns a pointer to a local-time `tm` representation of the calendar time represented by `*tptr`.

`time_t mktime(tm *tptr)`
> Returns a `time_t` representation of the calendar time of the local time represented by object `*tptr`. Object `*tptr` is also modified to represent a calendar time.

`time_t time(time_t *tptr)`
> Returns a `time_t` representation of the current calendar time. If `tptr` is nonnull, then `*tptr` is also set to the current calendar time.

B.6   CSTRING LIBRARY

The C-based cstring library provides string handling functions. It also defines the integral type `size_t` and the NULL macro. Some of the functions are

`char* strcat(char *t, char *s)`
> Appends a copy of string `s` including its terminating null character at the end of the target string `s`. The copying begins by replacing the null character that terminates `t`. The function returns `t`.

`char* strchr(const char *t, int c)`

If character c is not a character in string t, then the function returns NULL; otherwise, the function returns a pointer to the first occurrence of the character c in string t.

`int strcmp(char *t, char *s)`

Makes a lexicographical comparison of string s to string t. If the strings are equal, then the function returns 0; if s occurs before t lexicographically, the function returns a negative value; otherwise, the function returns a positive value.

`int strcmp(char *t, char *s, size_t n)`

Makes a lexicographical comparison of the first n characters of string s to string t (if either of strings is less than n characters long, the comparison is based on the length of the shorter string). If the characters of s and t being compared are equal, then the function returns 0; if the characters of s occur lexicographically before the characters of t, then the function returns a negative value; otherwise, the function returns a positive value.

`char* strcpy(char *t, char *s)`

Copies the source string s to the destination string t, including the null character that terminates s. The function returns t.

`size_t strlen(const char *s)`

Returns the number of characters that precede the null character which terminate s.

`char* strncat(char *t, char *s, size_t n)`

Appends a copy of the first n characters of string at the end of the target string t. If the length of the string s is less than n, the appending ends with a copy of the null character that terminates s. The copy begins by replacing the null character that terminates t. The function returns t.

`char* strncpy(char *t, char *s, size_t n)`

Copies the first n characters of source string s to the destination string t. If the length of s is less than n, null characters are used for padding. The function returns t.

`char* strrchr(const char *t, int c)`

If character c is not a character in string t, then the function returns NULL; otherwise, the function returns a pointer to the last occurrence of the character c in string t.

`char* strstr(const char *t, const char *s)`

If string s has 0 length, then the function returns t; if string s is not a substring of string t, then the function returns NULL; otherwise, the function returns a pointer to the first occurrence of a copy of string s in string t.

B.7 ALGORITHM LIBRARY

The Standard Template Library provides an algorithm library that offers more than 50 methods for manipulating arrays, containers, and other objects. The header file for these methods is `<algorithm>`. In this section, we describe some of major methods in this library.

In using these methods different conditions are sometimes placed on the iterators, sequences, and return types used by the algorithms. These requirements can be summarized as follows:

- A difference type `diff_type` is integral.

- The iterator increment operator ++ associates all forward, input, output, and bidirectional iterators with the next element in the sequence. If there is no next element, the iterator is associated with a sentinel.

- An input or output iterator should be passed through only once (i.e., algorithms using input or output iterators should be single pass).

- All iterators must be capable of dereferencing via the * operator.

- A dereferenced output iterator must be assignable (a dereferenced input iterator need not be assignable).

- The increment operator `--` associates all bidirectional iterators with the previous element in the sequence (if there is one). If there is no next element, the result is not necessarily defined.

- The subscript operator [] needs to be defined for a random access iterator. If `a` is a random access iterator and `i` is integral, then `a[i]` is a reference to the `i`th element in the sequence starting from `a`.

- A predicate is a function that returns a logical value. It takes as its parameter a dereferenced iterator.

- A sequence is defined by its starting and ending iterators `s` and `e`. A starting iterator `s` points to the first element in the sequence; an ending iterator `e` points to a sentinel for the sequence.

Two important algorithm library template functions are `for_each()` and `sort()`. These function have the following specifications:

```
template<class Iter, class Func>
  Func for_each(Iter s, Iter s, Func f)
```

> Applies function `f` to each element in the sequence defined by input iterators `s` and `e`. Parameter `f` is used as the return value.

```
template <class Iter>
  void sort(Iter s, Iter e)
```

> Sorts the sequence of elements defined by random access iterators `s` and `e`.

We use these functions in the following program.

```cpp
#include <iostream>
#include <vector>
#include <algorithm>
using namespace std;
#include "randint.h"
void set(int &val) {
    RandomInt u(1,100);
    val = u.Draw();
}
void display(int val) {
    cout << " " << val;
}
int main() {
    EzRandomize();
    vector<int> A(5);
    for_each(A.begin(), A.end(), set);
    for_each(A.begin(), A.end(), display);
    cout << endl;
    sort(A.begin(), A.end());
    for_each(A.begin(), A.end(), display);
    cout << endl;
    return 0;
}
```

Besides using algorithm library functions `for_each()` and `sort()`, the program uses functions `set()` and `display()` that we have defined as part of the program.

Function `main()` begins by invoking `EzRandomize()` to set the pseudo-random number generator to an arbitrary value. Function `main()` then defines a vector A with five integer elements (the elements are initialized to a default value of 0). The `for_each()` function is then invoked. Each of the `for_each()` invocations has its function parameter process the entire sequence of elements in A. In the initial `for_each()` invocation, function `set()` is invoked iteratively on each element of A. Function `set()` modifies its given element by assigning the element a pseudorandom value from the interval 1 ... 100. The `for_each()` function is then invoked a second time to iteratively display the elements of A using function `display()`. The elements are then rearranged using function `sort()`. Afterward, `for_each()` is invoked a third time to redisplay the elements. A sample run of the program follows.

```
47 31 83 91 57
31 47 57 83 91
```

The other major algorithms supplied by the library are

```cpp
template <class Iter, class T>
  bool binary_search(Iter s, Iter e, const T &v)
```

The sequence of sorted values defined by forward iterators s and e is examined for the value v. If v is in the sequence, true is returned; otherwise, false is returned.

```
template <class In, class Out>
  Iter copy(In s1, In e1, Out s2)
```

The sequence of values defined by input iterators s1 and e1 are copied to the sequence starting at the location to which output iterator s2 points. The return value of the function is an iterator to the sentinel of the new copy.

```
template<class Iter, class T>
  diff_type count(Iter s, Iter s, const T &v)
```

Returns the number of occurrences of value v in the sequence defined by input iterators and e.

```
template<class Iter, class Pred>
  diff_type count_if(Iter s, Iter s, Pred p)
```

Counts the number of occurrences where the predicate p is true in the sequence defined by input iterators s and e.

```
template<class Iter, class Pred>
  bool equal(Iter s1, Iter e1, Iter s2)
```

Returns true if the elements in the sequence defined by input iterators s1 and e1 are equal to the corresponding elements in the sequence starting at s2. Otherwise, the function returns false.

```
template<class Iter, class T>
  Iter find(Iter s, Iter s, const T &v)
```

Returns an iterator to the first occurrence of value v in the sequence defined by input iterators s and e. If there is no occurrence of v in the sequence, sentinel e is returned.

```
template<class Iter, class Pred>
  Iter find_if(Iter s, Iter s, Pred p)
```

Returns an iterator to the first occurrence where the predicate p is true in the sequence defined by input iterators s and e. If there is no occurrence in the sequence, sentinel e is returned.

```
template <class Iter class T>
  Iter lower_bound(Iter s, Iter e, const T &v)
```

Returns an iterator pointing to the first occurrence of the value v in the sorted sequence defined by forward iterators s and e. If there is no occurrence of v in the sequence, then an iterator pointing to the first element greater than v is returned (if there is no such element, a pointer to a sentinel is returned).

```
template<class T>
  const T& max(const T &a, const T &b)
```

Returns the maximum of a and b.

```
template <class In1, class In2, class Out>
  Out merge(In1 s1, In1 e1, In2 s2, In2 e2, Out s3)
```

The sequence of sorted values defined by input iterators s1 and e1 are merged with the sequence of sorted values defined by input iterators s2 and e2 to produce a combined sequence of sorted values. The combined sequence is stored at the location to which output iterator s3 points. The return value of the function is an iterator to the sentinel of the combined sequence.

```
template<class T>
  const T& min(const T &a, const T &b)
```
Returns the minimum of a and b.
```
template <class Iter>
  void random_shuffle(Iter s, Iter e)
```
The sequence of elements defined by random access iterators s and e is shuffled (rearranged) in a pseudorandom manner.
```
template <class Iter, class T>
  Iter remove(Iter s, Iter e, const T &v)
```
Removes occurrences of the value v in the sequence defined by forward iterators s and e. The function returns an iterator pointing to the sentinel of the compacted sequence.
```
template <class Iter, class T>
  void replace(Iter s, Iter e, const T &v, const T &w)
```
Replaces occurrences of the value v with the value w in the sequence defined by forward iterators s and e.
```
template <class Iter>
  void reverse(Iter s, Iter e)
```
The sequence of elements defined by bidirectional iterators s and e is reversed.
```
template <class T>
  void swap(T &a, T &b)
```
Swaps the values of objects a and b.
```
template <class Iter, class T>
  Iter unique(Iter s, iter e)
```
Removes all but the first element from every group of consecutive equal-valued elements from the sequence defined by forward iterators s and e. The return value of the function is an iterator to the sentinel of the compacted sequence.
```
template <class Iter class T>
  Iter upper_bound(Iter s, Iter e, const T &v)
```
Returns an iterator pointing to the last occurrence of the value v in the sorted sequence defined by forward iterators s and e. If there is no occurrence of v in the sequence, then an iterator pointing to the first element greater than v is returned (if there is no such element, a pointer to a sentinel is returned).

APPENDIX C

Standard classes

The proposed C++ standard defines more than 100 standard classes and structs. The discussion in this appendix is limited to a partial coverage of the Standard Template Library container and string classes. For further information regarding the standard classes consider the following reference materials:

- B. Stroustrup, *The C++ Programming Language, 3rd ed.*, Reading, MA: Addison-Wesley, 1998.

- X3 Secretariat, Draft Standard—The C++ Language, X3J16/97-14882, Washington, DC: Information Technology Council (NSITC), 1997.

- P. J. Plauger (editor), A. A. Stepanov, M. Lee, and D. R. Musser, *The C++ Standard Template Library*, Englewood Cliffs, NJ: Prentice-Hall, 2000.

C.1 CONTAINER CLASSES

The container classes of the Standard Template Library are a set of generic list representations that allow programmers to specify which types of elements their particular lists are to hold. Besides being free of array restrictions, the container classes are extensible. For example, we can derive specialized containers classes that automatically perform subscript checking.

There are eight major container classes. Five of these containers view a list primarily as a sequence of elements. The containers supporting this view are `deque`, `list`, `priority_queue`, `queue`, `stack`, and `vector`. The other two containers classes are `map` and `set`. These two containers view a list in a more associative manner. A brief description of the eight classes follows. The classes `priority_queue`, `queue`, and `stack` and are sometimes known as *container adapters* or just *adapters*, as these classes are built (adapted) using other containers.

deque

Supports constant-time random access to individual elements in its sequence. In addition, a `deque` can insert to or delete from the beginning or end of its sequence in constant time.

list

Supports constant-time sequential access to individual elements in its sequence. In addition, a `list` can insert or delete an element from anywhere within its sequence in constant time.

priority_queue

Supports priority-based access. A `priority_queue` provides amortized logarithmic-time access to the element with highest priority. In addition, a `priority_queue` can insert or delete an element from anywhere within its sequence in amortized logarithmic time.

queue

Supports first-in-first-out element access. A `queue` provides constant-time access to the beginning or end of its sequence. In addition, a `queue` can both insert to the end of the sequence and delete from the beginning of the sequence in constant time.

stack

Supports last-in-first-out element access. A stack provides constant-time access to the end of the sequence. In addition, a `stack` can insert to or delete from the end of its sequence in constant time.

vector

Supports constant-time random access to individual elements in its sequence. In amortized constant time, a `vector` can insert to or delete from the end of its sequence. An insertion or deletion elsewhere can take time proportional to the size of the sequence.

map

Supports constant-time sequential access to individual elements in the list. A unique key value is associated with each element value. Access to an element based on its key value can be done in logarithmic time.

set

>Supports constant-time sequential access to individual elements in its list. Access to an element based on its value can be done in logarithmic time.

The nonassociative container class templates can generally take either one or two parameters. The first template parameter is always the type of value that the container is to hold. If the second parameter is supplied, it is a class that implements a method for allocating memory for the elements of the list. Because the default memory allocation method works in most programming situations, our presentation ignores the optional allocation parameter.

The associative container class templates can take either one, two, or three template parameters with both the second and third parameters being optional. The first parameter is the type of value the container is to hold. The second parameter is a class that implements a scheme for comparing list elements. The third parameter is a memory allocation parameter.

Our discussion of the containers deals primarily with the `vector` class. We do so because it is the dominant list representation. Our discussion of the other classes highlights the differences and similarities to `vector`.

C.1.1   Container vector

The template abstract data type `vector<T>` supports objects that can represent a list of elements using an arraylike notation. Objects of this class and the `string` class of the following section will eventually replace most uses of conventional arrays and character strings. Our presentation of class template `vector` is simplified in that an optional template parameter regarding memory allocation is ignored.

The following list describes selected `vector<T>` member functions and operators. In the description, `size_type` is an integral unsigned type, `iterator` is a random access iterator, `reference` is a type that is convertible to `T&`, and `const_reference` is a type that is convertible to `const T&`. These types are declared in the class definition for `vector<T>`.

`vector::vector()`

>The default constructor creates a vector of 0 length.

`vector::vector(const T &V)`

>The copy constructor creates a vector that is a duplicate of vector `V`.

`vector::vector(size_type n, const T &val = T())`

>Explicit constructor creates a vector of length `n` with each element initialized to `val`.

`vector::~vector()`

>The destructor releases any dynamic memory for the vector.

`reference vector::at(int i)`

>If `i` is a valid index, it returns the `i`th element; otherwise, an exception is generated.

`const_reference vector::at(int i)`

>If `i` is a valid index, it returns the `i`th element; otherwise, an exception is generated. The element that is returned cannot be modified.

`reference vector::back()`
> Returns a reference to the last element of the vector.

`const_reference vector::back() const`
> Returns a constant reference to the last element of the vector.

`iterator vector::begin()`
> Returns an iterator that points to the first element of the vector.

`const_iterator vector::begin()`
> Returns an iterator pointing to the first element of the `vector`. Elements dereferenced by this iterator cannot be modified.

`void vector::clear()`
> Removes all elements from the vector.

`bool vector::empty() const`
> Returns true if there are no elements in the vector; otherwise, it returns false.

`iterator vector::end()`
> Returns an iterator that points immediately beyond the last element of the vector.

`const_iterator vector::end()`
> Returns an iterator that points immediately beyond the last element. Elements dereferenced by this iterator cannot be modified.

`iterator vector::erase(iterator pos)`
> Removes the element of the vector at position `pos`. Returns the position of the copy into the vector.

`reference vector::front()`
> Returns a reference to the first element of the vector.

`const_reference vector::front() const`
> Returns a constant reference to the first element of the vector.

`iterator vector::insert(iterator pos, const T &val = T())`
> Inserts a copy of `val` at position `pos` of the vector. Returns the position of the copy into the vector.

`vector<T>& vector::operator =(const vector<T> &V)`
> The member assignment operator makes the vector a duplicate of vector V. The modified vector is returned.

`reference vector::operator [](size_type i)`
> Returns a reference to element `i` of the vector.

`const_reference vector::operator [](size_type i) const`
> Returns a constant reference to element `i` of the vector.

`void vector::pop_back()`
> Removes the last element of the object

`void vector::push_back(const T &val)`
> Inserts a copy of `val` after the last element of the object.

`reverse_iterator vector::rbegin()`
> Returns a reverse iterator that points to the last element of the vector.

`const_reverse_iterator vector::rbegin()`
> Returns a reverse iterator that points to the last element of the vector. Elements dereferenced by this iterator cannot be modified.

`iterator vector::rend()`
> Returns a reverse iterator that points immediately ahead of the first element.

`const_reverse_iterator vector::rend()`
> Returns a reverse iterator that points immediately ahead of the first element. Elements dereferenced by this iterator cannot be modified.

`void vector::resize(size_type s, T val = T())`
> Let n be the current number of elements in the vector. If s > n, then the number of elements is increased to amount s with the new elements added after the existing elements and the initial value of the new elements being val. If s < n, then the number of elements is decreased to s by erasing elements from the end of the vector. If s equals n, then no action is taken.

`size_type vector::size() const`
> Returns the numbers of elements in the vector.

`void vector::swap(vector<T> &V)`
> The current vector and vector V swap values. This operation is typically much more efficient than an individual swapping of the elements.

The vector library also overloads the equality and relational operators.

`bool operator ==(const vector<T> &U, const vector<T> &V)`
> Returns true if vectors U and V have the same size and the corresponding elements are equal; otherwise, it returns false.

`bool operator !=(const vector<T> &U, const vector<T> &V)`
> Returns !(U == V).

`bool operator <(const vector<T> &U, const vector<T> &V)`
> The operator returns true if the sequence of elements in U is a proper initial subsequence of the elements in V (i.e., U[i] equals V[i] for i in the interval 0 ... U.size() - 1 and U.size() < V.size()). The operator also returns true if there exists an i in the interval 0 ... U.size() - 1 such that U[i] is less than V[i] and the subsequences U[1], U[2], ... U[i-1] and V[1], V[2], ... V[i-1] are equal. Otherwise, the operator returns false.

`bool operator <=(const vector<T> &U, const vector<T> &V)`
> Returns !(V < U).

`bool operator >(const vector<T> &U, const vector<T> &V)`
> Returns (V < U).

`bool operator >=(const vector<T> &U, const vector<T> &V)`
> Returns !((U < V).

C.1.2 Container list

The list container provides all of the functionality described for the vector container except subscripting and the at() member functions. These behaviors are not supplied because the list iterators do not support random access. The list container also provides member functions splice() and merge() for combining lists and member function sort() for rearranging a list. In addition, member functions `push_front()` and `pop_front()` add and remove the initial element of the list.

C.1.3   Container deque

The deque container resembles an amalgam of the `vector` and `list` classes. It supports the same behaviors as `vector` and also supports the `list` behaviors `push_front()` and `pop_front()` for adding and removing the initial element of the list.

C.1.4   Container map

The container `map` provides efficient retrieval of (key, value) pairs based on the key. (The keys are required to be unique.) Efficient retrieval is possible because the elements of a `map` are maintained in sorted order based on the keys. A map container provides the standard iterator member functions `begin()`, `end()`, `rbegin()`, and `rend()`. The subscript operator is overloaded to perform key-based retrieval and insertion. Member functions `find()`, `count()`, `lower_bound()`, and `upper_bound()` allow the finding and counting of elements based on their key value. In addition, there are traditional container member functions `insert()`, `erase()`, `empty()`, `size()`, and `swap()`.

C.1.5   Container set

The container `set` is like `map` except there are no keys. Because there are no keys, there is no member subscript operator. Other than this member operator, the interfaces of `map` and `set` are comparable.

C.1.6   Adapter container queue

A `queue` is an adapter class that provides first-in-first-out access of its elements. In particular, there are member functions `front()` and `back()` for accessing the first and last element, `push()` for inserting a new last element, and `pop()` for removing the first element. In addition, there are traditional container member functions `empty()` and `size()`. The default implementation for `queue` uses `deque`.

C.1.7   Adapter container priority_queue

A `priority_queue` is an adapter class that supports priority-based removal of elements, where the priority of an element is proportional to its value. In particular, there are member functions `top()` for accessing the element with highest priority, `push()` for inserting a new element, and `pop()` for removing the element with highest priority. In addition, there are traditional container member functions `empty()` and `size()`. The default implementation for `priority_queue` uses `vector`.

C.1.8   Adapter container stack

A `stack` is an adapter class that provides last-in-first-out access of its elements. In particular, there are member functions `top()` for accessing the last element, `push()` for inserting a new last element, and `pop()` for removing the last element. In addition, there are traditional container member functions `empty()` and `size()`. The default implementation for `stack` uses `deque`.

C.2   CLASS STRING

In the standard, the class `string` is an instantiated version of the template class `basic_string`.

> **typedef** basic_string<**char**> string;

This abstract data type supports objects that can represent a sequence of characters (the sequences may be of arbitrary length). During program execution, a `string` object can represent different sequences of varying length.

C.2.1   String member functions

The following list describes selected `string` member functions and operators. In the description, `size_type` is an integral unsigned type, `iterator` is a random-access iterator, `reference` is a type that is convertible to T&, and `const_reference` is a type that is convertible to **const** T&. These types are declared in the class definition for `string`. Some of the member functions use an integral constant `npos` that is also defined in the class. The constant has a value that lies outside of the interval $0 \ldots n-1$, where n is the number of characters in the string being represented.

   `string::string()`
        Default constructor initializes to represent empty string.
   `string::string(const char s[])`
        Initializes an object to represent a copy of the null-terminated **char** array s representation of a string sequence.
   `string& string::append(const char s[])`
        Adds a copy of the null-terminated array s to the end of the current string. The modified current string is returned (`*this`).
   `string& string::append(const string &s)`
        Adds a copy of string s at the end of the current string. The modified current string is returned (`*this`).
   `const_reference string::back() const`
        Returns a constant reference to the last element of the string.
   `reference string::back()`
        Returns a reference to the last element of the string.

`iterator string::begin()`

Returns an iterator that points to the first element of the string.

`const char* string::c_str() const`

Returns a pointer to the initial element of a **char** array whose elements are a copy of the string being represented. A null character terminates the copy.

`int string::compare(const string &s, size_type n) const`

Compares the current string starting at its position n with string s. If the compared portions are the same, then the function returns 0; if the current string-compared portion occurs first lexicographically, then a negative value is returned; otherwise, a positive value is returned.

`const char* string::data() const`

Returns a pointer to the initial element of a **char** array whose elements are a copy of the string being represented.

`bool string::empty() const`

Returns true if the string represents the empty string; otherwise, it returns false.

`iterator string::end()`

Returns an iterator that points immediately beyond the last element of the string.

`string& string::erase(size_type n, size_type m)`

Characters from position n through m are removed from the string. A reference to the modified string is returned (*`this`).

`size_type string::find(const string &s,`
`  size_type n = 0) const`

Searches rightward in the current string for the substring s, with the search beginning at position n. If substring is found, the function returns the starting position of the first-found occurrence of the substring. If the substring is not found, the constant npos is returned.

`const_reference string::front() const`

Returns a constant reference to the first element of the string.

`reference string::front()`

Returns a reference to the first element of the string.

`string& string::insert(size_type n, const string &s)`

Inserts a copy of string s between positions n and n+1 of the current string. The modified current string is returned (*`this`).

`const_reference string::operator [](size_type i) const`

If i is less than `size()`, the function returns a copy to ith character being represented by the string; if i equals `size()`, 0 is returned; otherwise, the behavior is **undefined**.

`reference string::operator [](size_type i)`

If i is less than `size()`, the function returns a reference to ith character being represented; otherwise, the behavior is undefined.

`size_type string::rfind(const string &s,`
`  size_type n = npos) const`

Searches leftward in the current string for the substring s with the search beginning at position n. If substring is found, the function returns the starting position of the first-found occurrence of the sub-string. If the substring is not found, the constant `npos` is returned.

`size_type string::size() const`

Returns the length of the string.

C.2.2   String auxiliary functions

The library also overloads the insertion, extraction, plus, and relational opera-tors.

`istream& operator >>(istream &sin, string &s)`

Extracts the next nonwhitespace string from input stream `sin` and assigns it to `s`. It returns a reference to `sin`.

`ostream& operator <<(ostream &sout, string &s)`

Inserts string `s` to the output stream `sout`. It returns a reference to `sout`.

`string operator +(const string &s, const string &t)`

Returns a string is the concatenation of strings `s` and `t`.

`string operator +(const string &s, char c)`

Returns a string that is the concatenation of string `s` and the character `c`.

`string operator +(char c, const string &s)`

Returns a string that is the concatenation of character `c` and the string `s`.

`string operator +(const string &s, const char t[])`

Returns a string that is the concatenation of string `s` and the null-ter-minated character array `t`.

`string operator +(const char s[], const string &t)`

Returns a string that is the concatenation of the null-terminated char-acter array `s` and the string `t`.

`bool operator ==(const string &s, const string &t)`

Returns `s.compare(t) == 0`.

`bool operator !=(const string &s, const string &t)`

Returns `s.compare(t) != 0`.

`bool operator <(const string &s, const string &t)`

Returns `s.compare(t) < 0`.

`bool operator <=(const string &s, const string &t)`

Returns `s.compare(t) <= 0`.

`bool operator >(const string &s, const string &t)`

Returns `s.compare(t) > 0`.

`bool operator >=(const string &s, const string &t)`

Returns `s.compare(t) >= 0`.

APPENDIX D

Advanced topics

In this appendix, we consider three advanced topics—namespaces, exceptions, and friends. A *namespace* is a named collection of classes, functions, objects, types, and other namespaces. Namespaces are particularly useful for client applications that must be able to distinguish between various overloaded classes and functions. An *exception* is a program error that occurs during execution. If an exception occurs and an exception-handler code segment is in effect for the exception, then flow of control is transferred to the handler. Software developers often provide exception detection and handling for events such as unsatisfied dynamic allocation requests, arithmetic errors (e.g., division by 0), unexpected input, and improper array subscripting. Lastly we consider C++'s **friend** attribute. The **friend** attribute is for those limited situations where access to data members by selected nonmember functions or classes is appropriate.

D.1   NAMESPACES

C++ recognizes several different scopes or, more properly, *namespaces*. For example, there is a local namespace whose elements (e.g., classes, functions, objects) are limited to the block in which they are declared. The other primary namespaces are the global namespace and the `std` namespace. We have used the `std` namespace throughout our examples, for it is the namespace in which the standard library classes and functions reside.

Within a given namespace, and subject to the rules of overloading, the names of the elements are unique. The C++ standard includes the **namespace** and **using** mechanisms that allow other namespaces to be defined and referenced. Inside a namespace, a collection of classes, functions, objects, types, and other namespaces can be declared.

D.1.1   Definitions

Multiple libraries are frequently required in developing an application. Because these libraries may come from different sources, they may define classes or functions with the same name. Suppose there is a library lib1 with header file `lib1.h` containing the following:

```
#ifndef LIB1_H
#define LIB1_H
class SimpleWindow {
    // EzWindows window representation ...
};
#endif
```

Similarly, suppose there is a library lib2 with a header file `lib2.h` containing the following:

```
#ifndef LIB2_H
#define LIB2_H
class SimpleWindow {
    // basic house window representation ...
};
#endif
```

Both lib1 and lib2 define `SimpleWindow` classes. What happens if a client application attempts to use both classes in the same program file, as in the following code segment?

```
#include "lib1.h"
#include "lib2.h"
void BuildHouse() {
    SimpleWindow FigureWindow; // lib1 or lib2?
    SimpleWindow StormWindow;  // lib1 or lib2?
    // process objects ...
}
```

Function `BuildHouse()` will not compile because of the ambiguity of which `SimpleWindow` class to use in the definitions of `FigureWindow` and `Storm-Window`. If libraries lib1 and lib2 had instead been developed using the namespace mechanism, we could individually specify which `SimpleWindow` class to use as in the following code segment that redefines `BuildHouse()`.

```
#include "lib1.h"
#include "lib2.h"
void BuildHouse() {
    lib2::SimpleWindow FigureWindow;    // lib1
    lib1::SimpleWindow StormWindow;     // lib2
    // process objects ...
}
```

Thus namespaces create virtual packages whose elements can be fully specified to prevent name ambiguity.

The basic syntax for defining a namespace is quite simple.

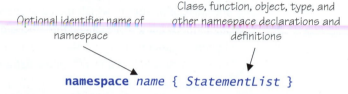

```
namespace name { StatementList }
```

To enable the modified version of function `BuildHouse()` to use both `SimpleWindow` classes, we redefine the header file for library lib1 using a namespace `lib1`.

```
#ifndef LIB1_H
#define LIB1_H
namespace lib1 {
    class SimpleWindow {
        // EzWindows window representation ...
    };
}
#endif
```

And we redefine similarly the header file for library lib2 so that it uses a namespace `lib2`.

```
#ifndef LIB2_H
#define LIB2_H
namespace lib2 {
    class SimpleWindow {
        // basic house window representation ...
    };
}
#endif
```

The name of a namespace is typically a variation on its header file name. To ensure namespace name uniqueness, software suppliers of a library sometimes include their name as part of the namespace name.

```
namespace FantasticFunctionsClassyClassesLib {
    // namespace definition
}
```

A client can avoid using an unwieldy name by using a namespace alias.

```
namespace Lib = FantasticFunctionsClassyClassesLib;
```

As the example suggests, a namespace alias has the following syntax:

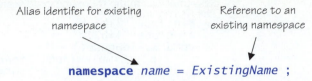

Alias identifer for existing namespace

Reference to an existing namespace

```
namespace name = ExistingName ;
```

A namespace is not required to have a name. Such a namespace is an *anonymous namespace*. When an anonymous namespace is used, it is defined typically at the beginning of the translation unit (program file). The elements in an anonymous namespace can be referenced only in that same translation unit. The elements of an anonymous namespace are part of the global namespace for the translation unit in which the namespace occurs. Therefore, elements of an anonymous namespace can be referenced by using only their names. In the following example, an object MaxSize is defined in the anonymous space and then used within function f() in the definition of an array s.

```
namespace {
    const int MaxSize = 256;
}
void f() {
    int s[MaxSize];
    // process s ...
}
```

A namespace can have additional definitions and declarations appended to it. Also, namespace definitions can be nested. For example, the following code segment first defines namespace A, which contains function f(). Function g() is then defined. Namespace B is then defined; it contains function h() and namespace C, which contains a function i(). Namespace A is then modified to also include function j().

```
namespace A {
    void f();
}
void g() {
    // can use namespace A's f(); cannot use namespace
    // B at all; cannot use namespace A's g()
}
namespace B {
    void h();
    namespace C {
        void i();
    }
}
namespace A {
    void j();
}
```

Function g() in the preceding example cannot use the components of namespace B because they are not declared when g() is translated. For a similar reason, g() cannot use function j() of namespace A.

D.1.2 Using namespaces

The **using** statement is often used with namespaces. This statement is a mechanism for indicating which declaration is to be in effect. There are two forms of the **using** statement.

Namespace whose elements are to be
part of current namespace

↓

using namespace *name* **;**

Namespace being   Element of namespace to be
referenced   part of current namespace

↙   ↓

using *name::element* **;**

Suppose the following definitions are in effect.

```cpp
namespace A {
    void f() {
        cout << "f(): from namespace A" << endl;
    }
    void g() {
        cout << "g(): from namespace A" << endl;
    }
}
namespace B {
    void f() {
        cout << "f(): from namespace B" << endl;
    }
    namespace C {
        void f() {
            cout << "f(): from namespace C" << endl;
        }
    }
}
void g() {
    cout << "g(): from global namespace" << endl;
}
```

What happens if the following example code segment is executed?

```cpp
g();
A::f();
B::f();
B::C::f();
using namespace A;
f();
```

The result is the following output:

```
g(): from global namespace
f(): from namespace A
f(): from namespace B
f(): from namespace C
f(): from namespace A
```

There is no ambiguity regarding function g() in the example because non-namespace definitions take precedence. The invocation A::f() in the example is unambiguous because it is fully qualified using the scope resolution operator. The invocation B::f() is also unambiguous because the other function f() declared within the inner namespace C requires additional qualification to be referenced. The invocation B::C::f() is similarly unambiguous because it is fully qualified using the scope resolution operator.

The **using** statement in the example indicates that the definitions in namespace A are to be part of the current namespace.

```
using namespace A;
```

As there is no ambiguity with existing functions in the namespace, no qualification is needed in the invocation of f() following the **using** statement. However, the statement below would not compile.

```
g();
```

An ambiguity would exist here because there are two functions named g() with the same signature in the current namespace. We can use the scope resolution operator to distinguish between these two functions.

```
::g();    // g() from global namespace
A::g();   // g() from namespace A
```

If in the example we had used the component namespace C of namespace B rather than namespace A as in the following code segment:

```
g();
A::f();
B::f();
B::C::f();
using namespace B::C;
f();
```

then the final invocation in this segment produces as its output:

```
f(): from namespace C
```

This output occurs because the definitions in C now take equal precedence with other names in the current namespace.

In the next code segment, we define a namespace **constants** that contains several object definitions.

```
namespace constants {
    const double pi = 3.141592;
    const double e  = 2.718281;
    const double c  = 299792.4;
}
```

The **using** statement in this next segment provides access only to pi from namespace **constants**.

```
using constants::pi;
double r;
cout << "Circle radius: " << flush;
cin >> r;
double c = 2 * pi * r;
```

```
    cout << "Circumference of circle with radius
        << ": " << c << endl;
```

As a result, the definition of object c does not introduce any syntactic
ity.

D.2 EXCEPTION HANDLING

An exception is a program error that occurs during execution. If an exception
occurs and an *exception-handler* code segment is in effect for the exception,
then flow of control is transferred to the handler. If instead an exception occurs
and there is no handler for it, the program terminates.

D.2.1 Basics

In Chapter 8 we developed the Rational ADT. In particular, we developed a
mutator member function SetRational() whose integer parameter denom is
supposed to be the new value of the denominator. The function definition is
repeated below.

```
void Rational::SetDenominator(int denom) {
    if (denom != 0) {
        DenominatorValue = denom;
    }
    else {
        cerr << "Illegal denominator: " << denom
            << "using 1" << endl;
        DenominatorValue = 1;
    }
}
```

Function SetRational() examines the value of denom. If denom is not
0, data member DenominatorValue is set to denom; otherwise, an error
message is displayed and DenominatorValue is set to 1.

An alternative implementation of SetDenominator() is presented in
Listing D.1. This version *throws an exception* if there is an attempt to set the
denominator to 0.

Listing D.1
 	
Catching and
processing an illegal
denominator mutation
	<pre>void Rational::SetDenominator(int denom) {
	  try {
	    if (denom != 0) {
	      DenominatorValue = denom;
	    }
	    else {
	      throw(denom);
	    }
	  }
	  catch (int d) {
	    cerr << "Illegal denominator: " << denom
	      << " using 1" << endl;
	    DenominatorValue = 1;
	  }
	}</pre>

Exception handling has three components: *trying*, *throwing*, and *catching*. Code that deals with situations in which exceptions can arise either directly or indirectly through function invocations is put in a **try** *block*. A **try** block is a statement block with the keyword **try** preceding it.

One of the statements in a **try** block can be a **throw** statement. A **throw** statement resembles a function invocation; for example, **throw**(denom). If an errant situation is detected, the **throw** statement is invoked with information regarding the detected error wrapped within parentheses. A *copy* of the information is passed via the **throw** statement to an exception handler.

Following the **try** block are the **catch**-exception handlers. There is typically a **catch** handler for each type of exception that can occur within the **try** block.

A **catch** handler specification resembles a function definition.

Type of exception to be processed

Name of the information passed to the handler

```
catch ( ParameterType ParameterName ) {
      HandlerBody
}
```

Statement list to process the exception

A **catch** handler begins with the keyword **catch** and a single-parameter parameter list. The type of the parameter should match a type of exception that can be thrown from the **try** block. Following the parameter list is a statement block. The statement block is executed if the **catch** handler is invoked to process an exception.

In the SetDenominator() function body of Listing D.1, a **try** block tests the value of denom.

```
try {
    if (denom != 0) {
        DenominatorValue = denom;
    }
    else {
        throw(denom);
    }
}
```

If the value of denom is 0, an exception is thrown,

```
throw(denom);
```

where the value of the exception is 0 (the value of denom).

Because we have defined a **catch** handler that processes the throwing of an **int**, there is an exception handler for a bad denominator.

```
catch (int d) {
    cerr << "Illegal denominator: " << d
        << " using 1" << endl;
    DenominatorValue = 1;
}
```

The denominator handler displays the value of the exception in an error message and sets the denominator value to 1. Thus in practice, the `SetDenominator()` of Listing D.1 is effectively the same as the `SetDenominator()` of Chapter 8.

Although the exception-handling mechanism appears excessive for the task at hand, the mechanism is needed if programs in general are to follow the object-oriented programming paradigm. For example, suppose an error occurred within a function `f()` that was invoked by a function `g()` that was invoked by a function `h()`. Suppose further that to correct the error, function `h()` that initiated this invocation sequence must regain the flow of control. The exception-handling mechanism has this flexibility—it can *unwind* the function invocations and allow corrective action to take place at the problem source. After the correction is completed, flow of control continues with the statement that follows the **catch**-handler list that handled the exception.

Let's expand our rational example. In the `Rational` implementation of Chapter 8, `SetDenominator()` is invoked only by the `Rational` constructors and by mutator `Extract()`. Instead of having `SetDenominator()` catch the exception as in Listing D.1, we can have these member functions catch the exception so that function-specific processing is performed. An example of such processing is given in Listing D.2.

The revised definition of function `SetDenominator()` in Listing D.2 throws an exception if the denominator value is 0, but it does not catch the exception. If an exception does occur, flow of control is immediately transferred from function `SetDenominator()` to the invoking function. If the invoking function does not catch the exception, flow of control is immediately transferred to that function's invoking function. This unwinding process continues until either one of the functions in the chain of invocations catches the exception or until the function invocations are completely unwound. If the latter situation occurs, the program is terminated. For our example, if either the Listing D.2 `Rational` constructor or `Extract()` member function is invoked, the exception is caught.

If the constructor catches the exception, an error message is displayed and `SetDenominator()` is reinvoked with a legal denominator value.

```
catch (int d) {
    cerr << "Illegal denominator: " << d
    << " using 1" << endl;
    SetDenominator(1);
}
```

If the `Extract()` member function catches the exception, an error message is displayed and `Extract()` is recursively invoked to extract a legal rational value.

```
catch (int d) {
    cerr << "Illegal denominator: " << d << endl;
    cerr << "Reenter rational value: ";
    Extract(sin);
}
```

```cpp
void Rational::SetDenominator(int denom) {
   if (denom != 0) {
      DenominatorValue = denom;
   }
   else {
      throw(denom);
   }
}
Rational::Rational(int numer, int denom) {
   SetNumerator(numer);
   try {
      SetDenominator(denom);
   }
   catch (int d) {
      cerr << "Illegal denominator: " << d
         << " using 1" << endl;
      SetDenominator(1);
   }
}
void Rational::Extract(istream &sin) {
   int numer;
   int denom;
   char slash;
   sin >> numer >> slash >> denom;
   SetNumerator(numer);
   try {
      SetDenominator(denom);
   }
   catch (int d) {
      cerr << "Illegal denominator: " << d << endl;
      cerr << "Reenter rational value: ";
      Extract(sin);
   }
   return;
}
```

D.2.2 Generic exception catching

C++ allows a special **catch** handler to be defined that can catch any type of exception. Consider the following example:

```cpp
try {
   cout << "Enter number: ";
   double d;
   cin >> d;
   if (d < 0) {
      throw(d);
   }
   char *p = new char;
   cout << "Enter character: ";
   char c;
   cin >> c;
   if (isupper(c)) {
      throw(c);
   }
}
catch(bad_alloc b) {
   cout << "Cannot satisfy new request" << endl;
}
```

```
catch (...) {
    cout << "Exception was thrown" << endl;
    throw;
}
```

The preceding code segment consists of a **try** block and a **catch** handler list consisting of two **catch** handlers.

The second of the two **catch** handlers has an ellipsis . . . for its parameter list. The ellipsis indicates that this **catch** handler is to catch exceptions not caught by the handlers that preceded it in the **catch** handler list. Note that the order in which the **catch** handlers are defined is important. When processing an exception, the exception is given to the first handler whose parameter list satisfies the generated exception. Therefore, the ellipsis **catch** handler should always be the last **catch** handler in the handler list.

Our definition of the ellipsis **catch** handler is interesting in itself in that it contains a **throw** statement. When an exception handler throws an exception without any parameter list, it effectively rethrows the same exception that it received. This rethrowing is a not a recursive invocation. Rather it indicates that additional handling is necessary and that the current handler is not the handler to do that processing. The additional processing is found by unwinding the function invocation chain in a search for another exception handler for the generated exception.

D.2.3   Specifying possible exceptions

As part of a function's interface, we can specify which type of exceptions it can throw back to the invoking function. This specification follows the parameter list. The specification consists of the keyword **throw** followed by a parenthetical expression that lists the types of objects that can be thrown. In the prototype for the following function f(), we indicate that **int** and **double** are the exception types that might require handling if f() is invoked.

```
void f(char c) throw(int, double);
```

If function f() attempts to generate an exception other than types **int** or **double** (or in general, types derived from the types in the **throw** list), then this exception is mapped to an invocation of std namespace function unexpected(), which by default terminates the program. For example, suppose function f() has the following definition:

```
void f(char c) throw(int, double) {
    if (isupper(c))
        throw(1);
    else if (islower(c))
        throw(1.0);
    else if (c == '.')
        throw(c);
}
```

If the invocation

```
f('a')
```

is executed, then a **double**-type exception is generated to the function that invoked f(). If instead, the invocation

```
f('A')
```

is executed, then an **int**-type exception is generated to the function that invoked f(). If instead, the invocation

```
f('.')
```

is executed, then the program is terminated. It is terminated because a **char**-type exception is thrown, where the **char** type is neither one of the types **int** or **double** nor is it derived from either the types **int** or **double**.

D.2.4   Catching dynamic allocation exceptions

We discussed in Chapter 11 that prior to the adoption of the C++ standard, if a free store request could not be satisfied, the **new** operation was defined to return the null address (0). We also discussed how under the C++ standard, if a **new** request cannot be satisfied, an exception is generated. The switch to exception handling allows programs to take different actions depending on the type of free store memory request that cannot be satisfied.

The type of exception thrown by an unsatisfied **new** request is bad_alloc. The type bad_alloc is part of the std namespace and is defined in the new library, which is one of the standard libraries. (Draft versions of the standard used the type xalloc, which is part of the except library.)

The following program determines the approximate size of the free store. It does so by counting the number of **new** requests that can be made. The counting is completed when a bad_alloc exception is generated.

```cpp
#include <iostream>
#include <string>
#include <new>
using namespace std;
int main() {
    long int size = 0;
    try {
        while (true) {
            char *p = new char;
            ++size;
        }
    }
    catch(bad_alloc b) {
        // no body needed
    }
    cout << "Free store size: " << size << endl;
    return 0;
}
```

The program begins by defining local object size, which represents the number of satisfied **new** requests. Object size is initialized to 0.

A **try** block is then initiated. The **try** block consists of a **while** loop that iterates until an exception is generated.

```
try {
    while (true) {
        char *p = new char;
        ++size;
    }
}
```

A **new** request is made in each iteration of the **while** loop. If no exception is generated, size is incremented. If an exception is generated, it is a bad_alloc exception from the **new** operation.

The exception is caught by the catch(bad_alloc b) handler. As no processing is necessary, the handler body is empty.

```
catch(bad_alloc b) {
    // no body needed
}
```

Control is transferred from the handler to the insertion statement that follows the catch handler. The insertion displays the initial size of the free store.

```
cout << "Free store size: " << size << endl;
```

D.2.5   Legacy code

So that legacy code can remain viable, C++ compilers typically provide a straightforward method to specify that the null address be returned as the result of an unsatisfied **new** operation. The method uses **void** function set_new_handler(). Function set_new_handler() is part of the new library. The function expects as its parameter, a pointer to an exception handler for the **new** operator. If the null address is used as the actual parameter, then the traditional behavior of returning the null address for an unsatisfied **new** operation is generally put in effect.

The standard does define a variant of the **new** operation that returns a null pointer for an unsatisfied **new** request. This variant is demonstrated in the following code segment:

```
char *p = new(nothrow) char;
if (p) {
    cout << "New request was satisfied" << endl;
}
else {
    cout << "New request was not satisfied" << endl;
}
```

Object nothrow is a constant defined in the new library. This constant, when passed to a **new** operation, indicates that the operation is not to generate an exception if the **new** request cannot be satisfied. Instead, the null address is to be returned for an unsatisfied **new** request.

D.3 FRIENDS

Almost every rule has an exception, including the information hiding rule. For situations where access to data members by selected nonmember functions or classes is appropriate, C++ offers the **friend** attribute. We used the **friend** attribute in Chapter 14 in our development of a sequential list container ADT. However, because many introductory courses will not cover that material, we also briefly discuss the **friend** attribute in this appendix. We do so in the context of the Rational ADT of Chapter 8, which offers a simple, convenient example of how the **friend** attribute can be used.

D.3.1 An alternative Rational implementation

As you recall Rational arithmetic and stream operators were accomplished through auxiliary operators. The operators were made auxiliary for consistency of use. For example, if u is a Rational object, then our implementation correctly handles both of the following statements:

```
cout << (u + 2) << endl;
cout << (2 + u) << endl;
```

If instead the operators had been made Rational members, then the second insertion would not compile under C++ promotion rules.

The auxiliary operators of Chapter 8 achieved their functionality by invoking the appropriate public Rational member facilitators. For example, the addition and multiplication operators had the following definitions:

```
Rational operator+(const Rational &r,
 const Rational &s) {
    return r.Add(s);
}
Rational operator*(const Rational &r,
 const Rational &s) {
    return r.Multiply(s);
}
```

We now consider an alternative implementation that makes the operators friends of the Rational class. A friend of a class has complete access to all class members—regardless of whether they are public, protected, or private. To grant friendship to another function, operator, or class, apply the C++ modifier **friend** to a prototype of that function, operator, or class within the definition of the class granting friendship.

A revised definition of the Rational class using friends is given in Listing D.3. Observe that the prototypes of the arithmetic and stream operators are now in the class definition with the **friend** attribute as the initial component of their declaration. Also observe that the facilitators are gone. They are not necessary, as the operators can be defined to explicitly perform the operations.

Listing D.3

Rational class definition with friend arithmetic and stream operators

```
class Rational {
    // friend operators
    friend Rational operator+(const Rational &r,
      const Rational &s);
    friend Rational operator*(const Rational &r,
      const Rational &s);
    friend ostream& operator<<(ostream &sout,
      const Rational &s);
    friend istream& operator>>(istream &sin, Rational &r);
    public: // member functions
        // default constructor
        Rational();
        // a second constructor
        Rational(int numer, int denom = 1);
    protected:
        // inspectors
        int GetNumerator() const;
        int GetDenominator() const;
        // mutators
        void SetNumerator(int numer);
        void SetDenominator(int denom);
    private:
        // data members
        int NumeratorValue;
        int DenominatorValue;
};
```

The definition of a **friend** function or class requires no special syntax. (The compiler is suitably informed by the definition of the class granting friendship.) In Listing D.4 we give operator definitions for Rational addition and multiplication that make use of nonpublic members.

Listing D.4

Implementation of auxiliary operators using Rational friendship capabilities

```
// adding Rationals
Rational operator+(const Rational &r, const Rational &s) {
    int a = r.GetNumerator();
    int b = r.GetDenominator();
    int c = s.GetNumerator();
    int d = s.GetDenominator();
    return Rational(a*d + b*c, b*d);
}

// multiplying Rationals
Rational operator*(const Rational &r, const Rational &s) {
    int a = r.GetNumerator();
    int b = r.GetDenominator();
    int c = s.GetNumerator();
    int d = s.GetDenominator();
    return Rational(a*c, b*d);
}
```

The two operator definitions in Listing D.4 are similar. Both begin by constructing local objects a, b, c, and d to represent the numerator and denominator components of operands r and s. Because the operators are friends of the Rational class, the operators can access protected member functions GetNumerator() and GetDenominator(). The objects a, b, c, and d are then used to produce the `Rational` objects that act as the return values for the operations.

Although the **friend** mechanism provides some control over what function, operator, or class manipulates the underlying data representation of a class, it can create a major security hole with respect to information hiding. For example, the friend does not necessarily follow safe programming practices and may directly manipulate data members rather than using inspectors and mutators. For this reason, use the **friend** mechanism cautiously.

APPENDIX E

EzWindows API reference manual

This appendix summarizes the EzWindows API types, classes, and capabilities.

E.1   ENUMERATED TYPES

The EzWindows API defines three enumerated types: `color`, `WindowStatus`, and `BitMapStatus`.

Enumerated type `color` provides symbolic names for the possible colors that can be displayed in a `SimpleWindow`.

```
enum color { Black, White, Red, Green, Blue, Yellow,
  Cyan, Magenta};
```

Enumeration type `WindowStatus` defines the possible states for a `SimpleWindow` object

```
enum WindowStatus {WindowClosed, WindowOpen,
  WindowFailure};
```

where

- `WindowClosed` indicates an unopened window. Objects cannot be displayed in a window with this status.
- `WindowOpen` indicates an opened window. Objects can be displayed in a window with this status.
- `WindowFailure` indicates a failure state. Objects cannot be displayed in a window with this status.

Enumeration type `BitMapStatus` defines the possible states of a `BitMap` object

```
enum BitMapStatus {NoBitMap, BitMapOkay, NoWindow};
```

where

- `NoBitMap` indicates there is no bitmap to be displayed.
- `BitMapOkay` indicates there is a bitmap to display and an associated window.
- `NoWindow` indicates there is no associated window with the bitmap.

E.2   COORDINATE SYSTEM

Figure E.1 illustrates the EzWindows coordinate system. The origin is the upper-left corner of the screen. All coordinates are expressed as centimeters from the origin. The unit of measure for the size of EzWindows objects is also centimeters.

Figure E.1

*The EzWindows
coordinate system*

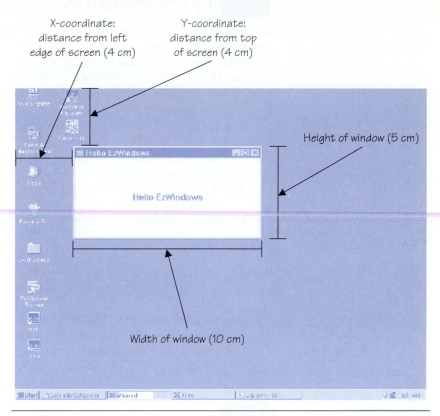

X-coordinate:
distance from left
edge of screen (4 cm)

Y-coordinate:
distance from top
of screen (4 cm)

Height of window (5 cm)

Hello EzWindows

Width of window (10 cm)

Some EzWindows API functions use a bounding box to specify the size of an object. For example, the following diagram illustrates the bounding box for an ellipse.

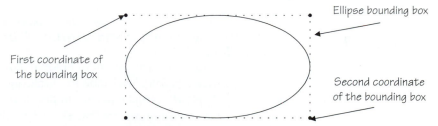

Ellipse bounding box

First coordinate of
the bounding box

Second coordinate
of the bounding box

A bounding box is specified by giving the EzWindows coordinates of the upper-left and lower-right corners of a rectangle that bounds the shape.

E.3   CLASS POSITION

The class `Position` allows objects that represent the logical window coordinates of a window object to be defined and manipulated. The class provides two public constructors that are described below.

    Position::Position(float x = 0.0, float y = 0.0)

> Creates a `Position` object that associates the value of x with its x-coordinate and the value of y with its y-coordinate.

The `Position` class also provides two public members functions that are described below.

    int Position::GetXDistance() const

> Returns the x-coordinate of the position.

    int Position::GetYDistance() const

> Returns the y-coordinate of the position.

In addition, the + operator is overloaded to use `Position` objects as operands.

    Position operator+(const Position &a, const Position &b)

> Returns a position whose x-coordinate and y-coordinate are respectively the sum of a's and b's x-coordinates and a's and b's y-coordinates.

    Position operator-(const Position &a, const Position &b)

> Returns a position whose x-coordinate and y-coordinate are respectively the difference of a's and b's x-coordinates and a's and b's y-coordinates.

E.4   CLASS SIMPLEWINDOW

The class `SimpleWindow` allows objects that represent simple window displays to be defined and manipulated. The class provides several public constructors that are described below.

    SimpleWindow::SimpleWindow(const char *WindowTitle
      = "Untitled", float Width = 8.0f,
      float Height = 8.0f,
      const Position &WindowPosn = Position(3.0f, 3.0f));

> Creates a `SimpleWindow` for displaying graphical objects. Parameter `WindowTitle` is a pointer to the character string to be displayed in the title bar of the window. The default title is `"Untitled"`. Parameter `Width` is the width of the window in centimeters. The default width is 8 centimeters. Parameter `Height` is the height of the window in centimeters. The default height is 8 centimeters. Parameter `WindowPosition` is the position of the window. The first coordinate is the distance in centimeters from the left edge of the screen. The second coordinate is the distance in centimeters from the top edge of the screen. The default position is (3.0, 3.0), which positions the upper-left corner of the window 3 centimeters from the left edge of the screen and 3 centimeters from the top edge of the screen.

```
SimpleWindow::SimpleWindow(const string &WindowTitle,
  float Width = 8.0f, float Height = 8.0f,
  const Position &WindowPosn = Position(3.0f, 3.0f));
```
Creates a `SimpleWindow` for displaying graphical objects. Parameter `WindowTitle` is a string to be displayed in the title bar of the window. Parameter `Width` is the width of the window in centimeters. The default width is 8 centimeters. Parameter `Height` is the height of the window in centimeters. The default height is 8 centimeters. Parameter `WindowPosn` is the position of the window. The first coordinate is the distance in centimeters from the left edge of the screen. The second coordinate is the distance in centimeters from the top edge of the screen. The default position is (3.0, 3.0), which positions the upper-left corner of the window 3 centimeters from the left edge of the screen and 3 centimeters from the top edge of the screen.

The `SimpleWindow` class also provides several public members functions that are described below.

```
WindowStatus SimpleWindow::Close();
```
Closes the window and makes it disappear. The return value is `WindowClosed`.

```
void SimpleWindow::Erase(const Position &UpperLeft,
  float Width, float Height);
```
Erases a rectangular region. The upper-left corner of the rectangle is specified by the `Position UpperLeft`. A rectangle `Width` centimeters wide and `Height` centimeters high is erased.

```
Position SimpleWindow::GetCenter() const;
```
Gets the location of the center of the window. The function returns a `Position` value that represents the logical coordinates of the center of the window, which are measured in centimeters from the left and top edges of the window.

```
float SimpleWindow::GetHeight() const;
```
Returns the height of the window in centimeters.

```
WindowStatus SimpleWindow::GetStatus() const;
```
Returns a `WindowStatus` value that represents the state of the window.

```
float SimpleWindow::GetWidth() const;
```
Returns the width of the window in centimeters.

```
float SimpleWindow::GetXPosition() const;
```
Returns the x-coordinate of the position of the window.

```
float SimpleWindow::GetYPosition() const;
```
Returns the y-coordinate of the position of the window.

```
void SimpleWindow::Message(
  const string &Msg = Message );
```
Pops up an alert window with a message. The parameter `Msg` is the character string to display in the alert window.

```
WindowStatus SimpleWindow::Open();
```
Makes window appear on the display and be enabled for displaying objects. The function returns a `WindowStatus` value that represents the state of the window.

```
void SimpleWindow::RenderEllipse(
  const Position &UpperLeft,
  const Position &LowerRight, const color &c,
  const bool Border = false);
```
Draws an ellipse. The bounding box is specified by the parameters UpperLeft and LowerRight. The ellipse is filled with color c. If Border is false, draw the ellipse without a border; otherwise, draw it with a black border.

```
void SimpleWindow::RenderPolygon(
  const vector<Position> &PolyPoints, int NPoints,
  const color &c, const bool Border = false);
```
Draws a closed polygon. The points of the polygon are held in the vector PolyPoints. The parameter NPoints is the number of points in the polygon. The polygon is filled with color c. If Border is false, draw the polygon without a border; otherwise, draw it with a black border.

```
void SimpleWindow::RenderPolygon(
  const Position PolyPoints[], int NPoints,
  const color &c, const bool Border = false););
```
Draws a closed polygon. The points of the polygon are held in the array PolyPoints. The parameter NPoints is the number of points in the polygon. The polygon is filled with color c. If Border is false, draw the polygon without a border; otherwise, draw it with a black border.

```
void SimpleWindow::RenderRectangle(
  const Position &UpperLeft,
  const Position &LowerRight, const color &c,
  const bool Border = false);
```
Draws a rectangle. The bounding box is specified by the coordinates UpperLeft and LowerRight. The rectangle is filled with color c. If Border is false, draw the rectangle without a border; otherwise, draw it with a black border.

```
void SimpleWindow::RenderText(
  const Position &UpperLeft,
  const Position &LowerRight,
  const string &Msg = "Message",
  const color &TextColor = Black,
  const color &BackGroundColor = White);
```
Displays a text string in a window. Parameter UpperLeft is the position of the upper-left corner of the bounding box for the text message. Parameter LowerRight is the position of the lower-right corner of the bounding box for the text message. Parameter Msg is the string to be displayed in the window. The default message is "Message". Parameter TextColor is the color of the text message. The default text color is black. Parameter BackGroundColor is the background color for the text. The default background color is white.

```
void SimpleWindow::RenderText(
  const Position &UpperLeft,
```

```
const Position &LowerRight,
const char *Msg = "Message",
const color &TextColor = Black,
const color &BackGroundColor = White);
```

Displays a text string in a window. Parameter `UpperLeft` is the position of the upper-left corner of the bounding box for the text message. Parameter `LowerRight` is the position of the lower-right corner of the bounding box for the text message. Parameter `Msg` is a pointer to a character string to be displayed in the window. The default message is `"Message"`. Parameter `TextColor` is the color of the text message. The default text color is black. Parameter `BackGroundColor` is the background color for the text. The default background color is white.

```
void SimpleWindow::SetMouseClickCallback(
  MouseClickCallbackFunction f);
```

Registers a callback for a mouse click. Function `f()` will be called when a mouse click occurs in the window. Function `f()` must be declared to take a single parameter of type **const** `Position &`, and it must return an **int**. The return value of `f()` indicates whether the event was handled successfully. A value of 1 indicates success, and a value of 0 indicates that an error occurred.

```
void SimpleWindow::SetRefreshCallback(
  RefreshCallbackFunction f);
```

Registers a callback for a refresh message. Function `f()` is called when the window receives a refresh event. The function `f()` must be declared to take no parameters, and it must return an **int**. The return value of `f()` indicates whether the event was handled successfully. A value of 1 indicates success, and a value of 0 indicates that an error occurred.

```
void SimpleWindow::SetQuitCallback(
  QuitCallbackFunction f);
```

Registers a callback for a quit message. Function `f()` is called when the window receives a quit event. The function `f()` must be declared to take no parameters, and it must return an **int**. The return value of `f()` indicates whether the event was handled successfully. A value of 1 indicates success, and a value of 0 indicates that an error occurred.

```
bool SimpleWindow::StartTimer(int Interval);
```

Starts timer running. Parameter `Interval` is the number of milliseconds between timer events. The return value indicates whether the timer was successfully started. A return value of true indicates success, and a return value of false indicates that the timer could not be set up.

```
void SimpleWindow::StopTimer();
```

Turns off the timer.

```
void SimpleWindow::SetTimerCallback(
  TimerTickCallbackFunction f);
```

Registers a callback for a timer tick. Function `f()` will be called when a timer tick occurs. The function `f()` must be declared to take no parameters, and it should return an `int`. The return value of `f()` indicates whether the event was handled successfully. A value of 1 indicates success, and a value of 0 indicates that an error occurred.

E.5   CLASS WINDOWOBJECT

Class `WindowObject` is the base class for class `Shape`. The class provides one public constructor.

```
WindowObject::WindowObject(SimpleWindow &w,
   const Position &p);
```

Creates a `WindowObject` that is centered at position `p` in window `w`.

The `WindowObject` class also provides several public members functions that are described below.

```
Position WindowObject::GetPosition() const;
```

Returns the position of the window object.

```
void WindowObject::GetPosition(float &XCoord,
   float &YCoord) const;
```

Returns the position of the window object. The x-coordinate is returned in `XCoord`, and the y-coordinate is returned in `YCoord`.

```
SimpleWindow& WindowObject::GetWindow() const;
```

Returns the window containing the `WindowObject`.

```
void WindowObject::SetPosition(const Position &p);
```

Sets the position of the `WindowObject` to `p`.

```
void WindowObject::SetPosition(float XCoord,
   float Ycoord);
```

Sets the coordinates of the `WindowObject` to `Position(XCoord, YCoord)`.

E.6   CLASS RAYSEGMENT

Class `RaySegment` represents rays in the `SimpleWindow` graphics system. Class `RaySegment` is derived from class `WindowObject`. A ray has a starting point that is a `Position`. This data member is inherited from `WindowObject`. Figure E.2 shows a `RaySegment`.

The `RaySegment` class provides two public constructors that are described below.

```
RaySegment::RaySegment(SimpleWindow &w,
   const Position &StartPoint, const Position &EndPoint,
   const color &c = Black, float Thickness = 0.1f,
   bool Arrowhead = false);
```

Creates a RaySegment object to represent a ray. The ray is contained in `SimpleWindow` w. Its starting position is `StartPoint`, and its ending position is `EndPoint`. The ray has color c, which defaults to black. The ray is `Thickness` centimeters thick. The default thickness is 0.1 centimeters. If `Arrowhead` is true, the ray is drawn with an

Figure E.2

*An EzWindows
RaySegment*

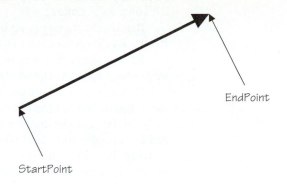

EndPoint

StartPoint

arrowhead at its ending point; otherwise, the ray has no arrowhead. The default is no arrowhead.

```
RaySegment::RaySegment(SimpleWindow &w, float StartX,
  float StartY, float EndX, float EndY,
  const color &c = Black, float Thickness = 0.1f,
  bool Arrowhead = false);
```

Creates a RaySegment object to represent a ray. The ray is contained in SimpleWindow w. Its starting point is Position(StartX, StartY), and its ending point is Position(EndX, EndY). The ray has color c, which defaults to black. The ray is Thickness centimeters thick. The default thickness is 0.1 centimeters. If Arrowhead is true, the ray is drawn with an arrowhead at its ending point; otherwise, the ray has no arrowhead. The default is no arrowhead.

The RaySegment class provides several public member functions that are described below.

```
void RaySegment::ClearArrowhead();
```

Sets the ray to be drawn without an arrowhead.

```
void RaySegment::Draw();
```

Draws the ray in its associated window.

```
void RaySegment::Erase();
```

Erases the ray.

```
color RaySegment::GetColor() const;
```

Returns the color of the ray.

```
Position RaySegment::GetEndPoint() const;
```

Returns the ending point of the ray.

```
void RaySegment::GetEndPoint(float &x, float &y) const;
```

Returns the ending point of the ray in x and y.

```
float RaySegment::GetLength() const;
```

Returns the length of the ray in centimeters.

```
void RaySegment::GetPoints(Position &Start,
  Position &End) const;
```

Returns the starting and ending points of the ray.

```
Position RaySegment::GetStartPoint() const;
```

Returns the starting point of the ray.

void RaySegment::GetStartPoint(**float** &x,
  float &y) **const**;
> Returns the starting point of the ray in x and y.

float RaySegment::GetThickness() **const**;
> Returns the thickness of the ray.

bool RaySegment::HasArrow() **const**;
> Returns true if the ray has an arrow; otherwise, it returns false.

void RaySegment::SetArrowhead();
> Sets the ray to be drawn with an arrowhead.

void RaySegment::SetColor(**const** color &c);
> Sets the color of the ray to c.

void RaySegment::SetEndPoint(**const** Position &p);
> Sets the ending point of the ray to p.

void RaySegment::SetEndPoint(**float** x, **float** y);
> Sets the ending point of the ray to Position(x, y).

void RaySegment::SetPoints(**const** Position &StartPoint,
  const Position &EndPoint);
> Sets the ray's starting point to StartPoint and its ending point to EndPoint.

void RaySegment::SetStartPoint(**const** Position &p);
> Sets the starting point of the ray to p.

void RaySegment::SetStartPoint(**float** x, **float** y);
> Sets the starting point of the ray to Position(x, y).

void RaySegment::SetThickness(float t);
> Sets the thickness of the ray to t. The units of thickness is centimeters.

E.7   CLASS SHAPE

Class Shape is the base class for classes CircleShape, EllipseShape, RectangleShape, TriangleShape, and SquareShape. The class provides a public constructor that is described below.

Shape::Shape(SimpleWindow &w, **const** Position &p,
  const color &c = Red);
> Creates a Shape object that is centered at position p in window w. The color of the object is c, which by default is the value Red.

The Shape class provides several public member functions that are described below.

void Shape::ClearBorder();
> Set the shape to not have a border.

virtual void Shape::Draw() = 0;
> Member function Draw() is a pure virtual function.

color Shape::GetColor() **const**;
> Returns the color of the object.

bool Shape::HasBorder() **const**;
> Returns true if the shape has a border; otherwise, it returns false.

```
void Shape::SetBorder();
```
Sets the shape to have a border.
```
void Shape::SetColor(const color &c);
```
Sets the color of the object to c.

E.8 CLASS ELLIPSESHAPE

Class EllipseShape is derived publicly from class Shape. An EzWindows EllipseShape is shown below.

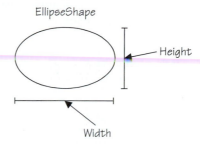

The class EllipseShape has the following public constructor:
```
EllipseShape::EllipseShape(SimpleWindow &w,
  const Position &p, const color &c = Red,
  float Width = 1.0f, float Height = 2.0f);
```
Creates an EllipseShape object to represent an ellipse. The ellipse is centered at position p in window w. The ellipse has color c, which by default is the value Red. The ellipse has width Width and height Height. The default values of parameters Width and Height are 1.0 and 2.0, respectively. Parameters Width and Height are centimeters.

The class EllipseShape also has the following public member functions:
```
void EllipseShape::Draw();
```
Draws the ellipse in its associated window.
```
void EllipseShape::Erase();
```
Erases the ellipse from its associated window.
```
float EllipseShape::GetHeight() const;
```
Returns the height of the object in centimeters.
```
void EllipseShape::GetSize(float &Width,
  float &Height) const;
```
Returns the width and height of the object in centimeters.
```
float EllipseShape::GetWidth() const;
```
Returns the length of the object in centimeters.
```
void EllipseShape::SetSize(float Width, float Height);
```
Sets the width of the ellipse to Width and the height of the ellipse to Height. Parameters Width and Height are centimeters.

E.9 CLASS CIRCLESHAPE

Class `CircleShape` is derived publicly from class `Shape`. An EzWindows `CircleShape` is shown below.

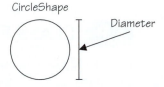

CircleShape

Diameter

Class `CircleShape` has the following public constructor:

```
CircleShape::CircleShape(SimpleWindow &w,
   const Position &p, const color &c = Red,
   float Diameter = 1.0f);
```

> Creates a `CircleShape` object to represent a circle. The circle is centered at position `p` in window `w`. The circle has color `c`, which by default is the value `Red`. The circle has diameter `Diameter`. The default value of `Diameter` is 1.0. Parameter `Diameter` is centimeters.

The class `CircleShape` also has the following public member functions:

```
void CircleShape::Draw();
```

> Draws the circle in its associated window.

```
void CircleShape::Erase();
```

> Erases the circle from its associated window.

```
float CircleShape::GetDiameter() const;
```

> Returns the diameter of the circle in centimeters.

```
void CircleShape::SetSize(float Diameter);
```

> Sets the diameter of the circle to `Diameter`. Parameter `Diameter` is centimeters.

E.10 CLASS RECTANGLESHAPE

Class `RectangleShape` is derived publicly from class `Shape`. An EzWindows `RectangleShape` is shown below.

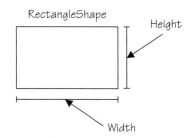

RectangleShape

Height

Width

Class `RectangleShape` has the following public constructors:

```
RectangleShape::RectangleShape(SimpleWindow &w,
  const Position &p, const color &c = Red,
  float Width = 1.0f, float Height = 2.0f);
```

Creates a RectangleShape object to represent a rectangle. The rectangle is centered at position p in window w. The rectangle has color c, which by default is the value Red. The width of the rectangle is Width. The height of the rectangle is Height. The default values of Width and Height are 1.0 and 2.0, respectively. Parameters Width and Height are centimeters.

```
RectangleShape::RectangleShape(SimpleWindow &w,
  float XCoord, float YCoord, const color &c = Red,
  float Width = 1.0f, float Height = 2.0f);
```

Creates a RectangleShape object to represent a rectangle. The rectangle is centered at Position(XCoord, YCoord) in window w. The rectangle has color c, which by default is the value Red. The width of the rectangle is Width. The height of the rectangle is Height. The default values of Width and Height are 1.0 and 2.0, respectively. Parameters Width and Height are centimeters.

The class RectangleShape also has the following public member functions:

```
void RectangleShape::Draw();
```

Draws the rectangle in its associated window.

```
void RectangleShape::Erase();
```

Erases the rectangle from its associated window.

```
float RectangleShape::GetHeight() const;
```

Returns the height of the rectangle in centimeters.

```
void RectangleShape::GetSize(float &Width,
  float &Height) const;
```

Returns the width and height of the rectangle in centimeters.

```
float RectangleShape::GetWidth() const;
```

Returns the width of the rectangle in centimeters.

```
void RectangleShape::SetSize(float Width,
  float Height);
```

Sets the width of the rectangle to width and the height of the rectangle to Height. Parameters Width and Height are centimeters.

E.11 CLASS TRIANGLESHAPE

Class `TriangleShape` is derived publicly from class **Shape**. An EzWindows `TriangleShape` is shown below.

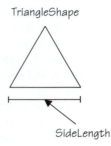

TriangleShape

SideLength

Class `TriangleShape` has the following public constructor:

```
TriangleShape::TriangleShape(SimpleWindow &w,
  const Position &p, const color &c = Red,
  float SideLength = 1.0f);
```
> Creates a `TriangleShape` object to represent an equilateral triangle. The triangle is centered at position **p** in window **w**. The triangle has color **c**, which by default is the value **Red**. The length of a side of the triangle is `SideLength`. The default value of `SideLength` is 1.0. Parameter `SideLength` is centimeters.

The class `TriangleShape` also has the following public member functions:

```
void TriangleShape::Draw();
```
> Draws the triangle in its associated window.

```
void TriangleShape::Erase();
```
> Erases the triangle from its associated window.

```
float TriangleShape::GetSideLength() const;
```
> Returns the side length of the triangle in centimeters.

```
void TriangleShape::SetSize(float SideLength);
```
> Sets the side length of the triangle to `SideLength`. Parameter `Side-Length` is centimeters.

E.12 CLASS SQUARESHAPE

Class `SquareShape` is derived publicly from class **Shape**. An EzWindows `SquareShape` is shown below.

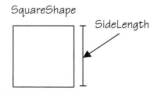

SquareShape

SideLength

Class SquareShape has the following public member functions.

```
SquareShape::SquareShape(SimpleWindow &Window,
  const Position &Center, const color &c = Red,
  float Side = 1.0f);
```
> Creates a `SquareShape` object to represent a square. The square is centered at position p in window w. The square has color c, which by default is the value `Red`. The length of the side of the square is `SideLength`. The default value of `SideLength` is 1.0. Parameter `SideLength` is centimeters.

The class `SquareShape` also has the following public member functions:

```
void SquareShape::Draw();
```
> Draws the square in its associated window.

```
void SquareShape::Erase();
```
> Erases the square from its associated window.

```
float SquareShape::GetSideLength() const;
```
> Returns the side length of the square in centimeters.

```
void SquareShape::SetSize(float SideLength);
```
> Sets the side length of the square to `SideLength`. Parameter `SideLength` is centimeters.

E.13 CLASS LABEL

Class `Label` is publicly derived from `WindowObject`. An EzWindows `Label` is shown below.

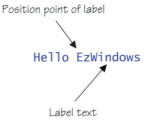

Position point of label

Hello EzWindows

Label text

Class `Label` has the following public constructors:

```
Label::Label(SimpleWindow &w, const Position &p,
  const string &Text, const color &TextColor = Black,
  const color &BackGroundColor = White);
```
> Creates a `Label` object to represent a text message. The message is contained in the `string` object `Text`. The message is centered at position p in window w. The color of the message text is `TextColor`. The default color of the message text is black. The message has background color `BackGroundColor`, which by default is white.

```
Label::Label(SimpleWindow &w, float XCoord,
  float YCoord, const string &Text,
  const color &TextColor = Black,
  const color &BackGroundColor = White);
```
> Creates a `Label` object to represent a text message. The message is contained in the `string` object `Text`. The message is centered at

position (XCoord, YCoord) in window w. The color of the message text is TextColor. The default color of the message text is black. The message has background color BackGroundColor, which by default is white.

```
Label::Label(SimpleWindow &w, const Position &p,
  const char *Text, const color &TextColor = Black,
  const color &BackGroundColor = White);
```

Creates a Label object to represent a text message. The char pointer Text is a pointer to the text message to display. The message is centered at position p in window w. The color of the message text is TextColor. The default color of the message text is black. The message has background color BackGroundColor, which by default is white.

```
Label::Label(SimpleWindow &w, float XCoord,
  float YCoord, const char *Text,
  const color &TextColor = Black,
  const color &BackGroundColor = White);
```

Creates a Label object to represent a text message. The char pointer Text is a pointer to the text message to display. The message is centered at position (XCoord, YCoord) in window w. The color of the message text is TextColor. The default color of the message text is black. The message has background color BackGroundColor, which by default is white.

The class Label also has the following public member functions:

```
void Label::Draw();
```

Draws the label in its associated window.

```
void Label::Erase();
```

Erase the label from its associated window.

```
color Label::GetColor() const;
```

Returns the background color of the label.

```
void Label::SetColor(const color &c);
```

Sets the background color of the label to c.

CLASS BITMAP

Unlike the window shape objects (i.e., `RectangleShape`, `EllipseShape`, `CircleShape`, etc.), a bitmap is positioned using the upper-left corner of its bounding box. An EzWindows `BitMap` is shown below.

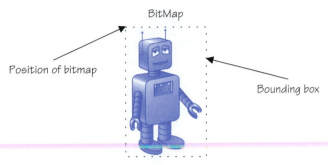

Class `BitMap` has the following public constructors:

`BitMap::BitMap();`

Creates a `BitMap` object with `BitMapStatus` `NoBitMap`. The object is not associated with any window.

`BitMap::BitMap(SimpleWindow &w);`

Creates a `BitMap` object with `BitMapStatus` `NoBitMap`. The object is associated with window w.

`BitMap::BitMap(SimpleWindow *w);`

Creates a `BitMap` object with `BitMapStatus` `NoBitMap`. The object is associated with the window pointed to by w.

The class `BitMap` also has the following public member functions:

bool `BitMap::Draw();`

Attempts to display the bitmap object to the associated window. The `BitMapStatus` of the object must be `BitMapOkay` for the display to be successful. If the bitmap is displayed, the function returns true; otherwise, the function returns false.

bool `BitMap::Erase();`

Overwrites the bitmap on the display by drawing a white rectangle of the same size. If the bitmap is successfully erased, the function returns true; otherwise, the function returns false.

bool `BitMap::IsInside(`**const** `Position &p)` **const;**

Returns true if position p lies within the bitmap; otherwise, the function returns false.

float `BitMap::GetHeight()` **const;**

Returns the height of the bitmap in centimeters.

`Position BitMap::GetPosition()` **const;**

Returns the position of the bitmap.

void `BitMap::GetSize(`**float** `&Width,`
  float `&Height)` **const;**

Returns both the width and height of the bitmap in centimeters.

`BitMapStatus BitMap::GetStatus()` **const;**

Returns the current `BitMapStatus` value associated with the object.

`float BitMap::GetWidth() const;`
> Returns the width of the bitmap in centimeters.

`float BitMap::GetXPosition() const;`
> Returns the distance from the upper-left corner of the bitmap to the left edge of the associated window. The distance is in centimeters.

`float BitMap::GetYPosition() const;`
> Returns the distance from the upper-left corner of the bitmap to the top edge of the associated window. The distance is in centimeters.

`BitMapStatus BitMap::Load(const string &Filename);`
> Uses the file whose name is `Filename` to set the bitmap. If the file contains a valid bitmap, the status of the object is set to `BitMapOkay`; otherwise, the status of the object is set to `NoBitMap`.

`BitMapStatus BitMap::Load(const char *Filename);`
> Uses the file whose name is pointed to by character string `Filename` to set the bitmap. If the file contains a valid bitmap, the status of the object is set to `BitMapOkay`; otherwise, the status of the object is set to `NoBitMap`.

`void BitMap::SetPosition(const Position &p);`
> Sets the position of the bitmap to p.

`void BitMap::SetWindow(SimpleWindow &w);`
> Associates the bitmap with window w. The `BitMapStatus` of the bitmap is set to `NoBitMap`.

E.15   CLASS RANDOMINT

Class `RandomInt` provides the ability to produce uniform random numbers in a specified interval. The class has the following public constructors:

`RandomInt::RandomInt(int a = 0, int b = RAND_MAX);`
> Creates a `RandomInt` object that generates pseudorandom numbers in the inclusive interval (a, b). The default interval is (0, RAND_MAX). The value RAND_MAX is defined in `stdlib.h`.

`RandomInt::RandomInt(int a, int b, unsigned int Seed);`
> Creates a `RandomInt` object that generates pseudorandom numbers in the inclusive interval (a, b). The pseudorandom-number generator is initialized with the value in `Seed`.

The class `RandomInt` also has the following public member functions:

`int RandomInt::Draw();`
> Returns the next pseudorandom number.

`unsigned int EzRandomize();`
> Generates a new seed value for the pseudorandom-number generator. Returns the new seed.

`int RandomInt::GetLow() const;`
> Returns the low endpoint of the interval.

`int RandomInt::GetHigh() const;`
> Returns the high endpoint of the interval.

`void RandomInt::SetInterval(int a, int b);`
> Sets the inclusive interval for `RandomInt` object to (a, b).

```
void RandomInt::SetSeed(unsigned int Seed);
```
Sets the pseudorandom-number generator seed to Seed.

E.16 MISCELLANEOUS FUNCTIONS

```
long GetMilliseconds()
```
Returns the value of a timer that is ticking continuously. The resolution of the timer is milliseconds.

```
void Terminate()
```
Sends a terminate message to the EzWindows window manager.

APPENDIX F

Projects and makefiles

Building software that uses application programmer interface (API) libraries and other run-time libraries places a significant administrative burden on the programmer. The programmer must locate the correct include files so that program modules can be compiled. In addition, the programmer must locate the required library files so that they can be linked with the application binaries to create an executable file. Even small programs may have several libraries that must be linked with the application code to produce an executable file. To simplify the software construction process, personal computer compilation systems, such as Borland C++ and Microsoft Visual C++, provide an integrated development environment (IDE) that supports creating, editing, compiling, linking, and debugging programs. On UNIX platforms, rather than provide an integrated development environment, special software supports each software development task—an editor for creating and editing programs, a compiler for compiling, a linker for linking programs, and a debugger for debugging. To manage the compilation and linking task, UNIX systems provide a program called make. In this appendix, we describe how to use two popular IDEs and the UNIX make utility to create EzWindows applications.

F.1 PROJECT AND MAKEFILE FUNDAMENTALS

A project or makefile stores the information that specifies how to compile and link an application. The project or makefile contains the location of the source files for the application, the location of the include files (both system and user include files) required to compile the application, the location of the libraries to link with the application, and any necessary compiler options that must be enabled or disabled to compile and link the application.

To show you how to create a project for building an EzWindows application, we create project files using Borland C++ and Microsoft Visual C++ IDEs. The same steps can be applied to an existing project to modify it to match your computer's configuration. For the UNIX makefile facility, we dissect an existing makefile and describe the changes to make so it can be used to build another application. Thus the presented makefile can be used as a model for creating a makefile for different applications.

When describing the steps to create a project using one of the IDEs, we use the following notation to specify which menu item to select. The instruction File→New specifies the following action: Select the File menu and then select the command New on the submenu that appears from the File menu. Such instructions may be cascaded arbitrarily to specify several levels of submenus. For example, the instruction File→New→Project specifies that the command Project should be selected when the New submenu appears.

As a working example in the following sections, we use the Simon program of Chapter 10. Recall that the Simon program comprises several source modules. Figure F.1 shows the application modules that must be compiled and the libraries that must be linked with application modules to create the Simon executable. Section F.2 describes how to create a project for Borland C++ 5.0. Section F.3 describes how to create a project for Microsoft Visual C++ 5.0. These descriptions should be helpful to users of earlier versions of these compilers. Section F.4 concludes this appendix by describing a typical UNIX makefile, how to modify it to conform to a different computer configuration, and how to change it to build a new application.

F.2 BORLAND C++ IDE

The Borland C++ IDE stores the information about how to build an application in a project file. Borland project files have the extension .ide. The main window for the Borland IDE is shown in Figure F.2. Across the top of the window are various commands such as File, Edit, and Search. Clicking on a com-

Figure F.1

Module structure of Simon

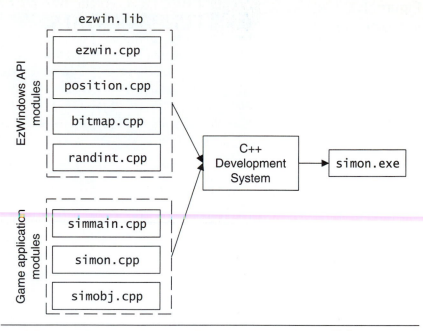

mand item causes a menu to appear. For example, clicking on `Help` causes the following submenu to appear.

Below the menu items are various buttons. This area is call the toolbar. The toolbar contains shortcuts to many of the frequently used commands. For example, the first button on the left executes the command to open a file. This command can also be executed by performing the following action:

`File→Open`

After you become familiar the basics of the Borland C++ IDE, you can explore the use of the some of the advanced features of the environment. You can obtain help about any of the features of the IDE by clicking on the help toolbar button [icon] and then clicking on the item of interest. A help file that explains the feature is displayed.

Figure F.2

Borland C++ IDE

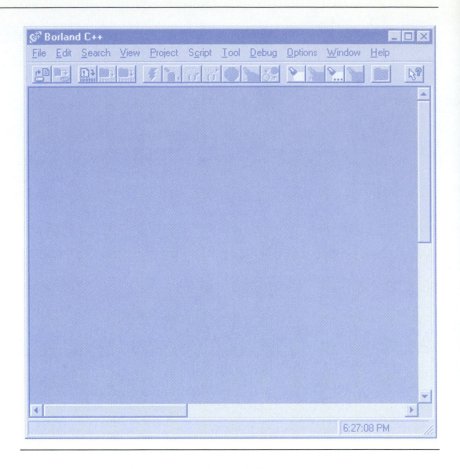

F.2.1   Creating a project file

The first step towards creating a project for an EzWindows application is to create a project file. To do so, perform the following actions:

> File→New→Project

This set of menu selections opens the dialog box shown in Figure F.3. We need to fill in the appropriate fields. The `Project Path and Name` field contains the location to save the project file and the name of the project file. The location would typically be path to the directory that contains the source files for the application. For our example, we want to store the project file in the directory `d:\jwd\simon`. The project name is the name of the file in which to store the project information. For our example, we want to store the project information in the file `simon.ide`. Thus in the name field we would enter `d:\jwd\simon\simon.ide`.

Next, we must specify the name of the file we want to build. The `Target Name` field contains the name of the file to store the executable. By default, the IDE puts the name `proj0000` in the field. We want the executable we build to

Figure F.3

*Borland C++
New Target dialog box*

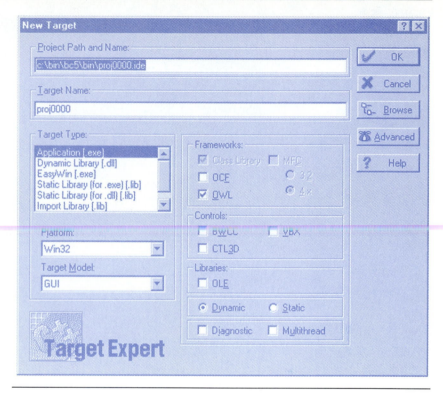

be called `simon`, so we click at the end of the field, erase `proj0000` by back-spacing over it, and enter `simon`.

The target type for an EzWindows application is `Application [.exe]`. By default, this entry is usually the application type that is selected in the `Target Type` scroll-down list. However, if target type `Application [.exe]` is not selected, you should select it.

The appropriate entry for `Platform` is `Win32`. For the `Target Model` field, the choice depends on whether the application requires a console. Any EzWindows application that accepts keyboard input from the user via the iostream object `cin` or writes to the display via the iostream object `cout` requires a console. For this type of EzWindows application, the proper selection is `Console`. If the application does not use the iostream library, the appropriate selection is `GUI`. The Simon program does not use the iostream library; therefore, we select `GUI`.

Within the `Frameworks` section of the dialog box, the only item that should be selected is `Static`. This completes the configuration of the New Target dialog box. Our completed dialog box is shown in Figure F.4. To save the project file, click on the `OK` button.

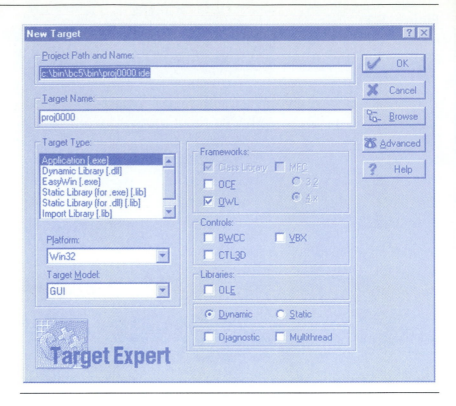

F.2.2   Adding source files to the project

After saving the project file, the IDE creates a project window shown in Figure
F.5. This window lists the files that make up the project. By default, the IDE
always adds three files to the project: `target.cpp`, `target.def`, and `tar-
get.rc`, where `target` is the name entered in the `Target Name` field. For an
EzWindows application, the `.def` and `.rc` files must be removed. To remove a
file from a project, select the file with the mouse and then click on the right
mouse button. This action brings up a menu with several selections. To remove
the file from the project, select the `Delete node` action. Do these steps for
both the `.def` and `.rc` files.

Figure F.5

*Borland C++ Project
window*

```
Project : d:\jwd\simon.ide                    _ □ X
 •  ⊟ □ ❀ ✔ simon.exe [.exe]
 •          ─┐ simon.cpp [.cpp]
 •          ─┐ simon.def [.def]
 •          ─┐ simon.rc [.rc]
```

After deleting the unnecessary files, we need to add the files that make up the project. As shown in Figure F.1, the project comprises the application source files `simon.cpp`, `simmain.cpp`, and `simobj.cpp` and the EzWindows library. Thus we need to add application files `simmain.cpp` and `simobj.cpp`, and the EzWindows library `ezwin.lib` to the project. To add a file to the project, in the project window select the root file of the project. In our example, the root file is `simon.exe`. After selecting the root file, we right-click the mouse to bring up the menu of commands and select `Add node`. This brings up a standard file selection dialog box. Navigate to the location of the source files and select each one to add to the project by holding down the control key and clicking on the files. Click the `Open` button after you have selected the files to finish adding them to the project. Note that you should not add the header files. Figure F.6 shows the file selection dialog boxes after the application source files have been selected.

We also must add the EzWindows library `ezwin.lib` to the project. Again, we select the `Add node` command. Before navigating to the location of the EzWindows library files, we need to change the `Files of type` field (see Figure F.6) so that it displays library files. To do this, select the entry `Librar-ies (*.lib)`. Next, navigate to the location of the EzWindows library and select `ezwin.lib`. To add the library to the project, click the `Open` button.

Figure F.6

File selection dialog box

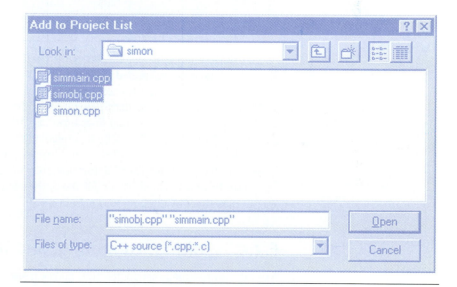

F.2.3 Setting project options

The last step in setting up a project file is to make sure that the project options are set correctly. We must make sure that the paths for finding the system include files as well as the EzWindows include files are set. To bring up the dialog box for changing the project options, execute the following command:

```
Options→Project
```

This brings up the dialog box shown in Figure F.7.

Figure F.7

Borland C++
Project Options
dialog box

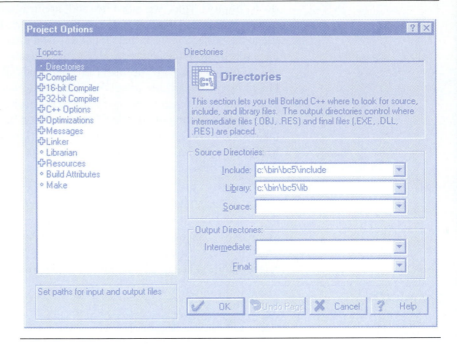

By default, the IDE sets the `Include:` field to contain the path where the system include files are located and sets the `Library:` field to contain the path where the system library files are located. To successfully compile an EzWindows application, we must add the location of the EzWindows include files to the `Include:` entry. Additional directories are added by inserting them in the field and separating the entries by a semicolon. For our example, the location of the EzWindows include files is `d:\book\ezwin\include`. Figure F.8 shows the `Project Options` dialog box after the EzWindows include directory entry has been added. When all the entries have been made, the changes are put into effect by clicking the OK button.

F.2.4   Editing, compiling, and linking

After the project file is set up, the IDE makes it easy to edit, compile, and link a program. To edit a program module, simply double click on the file in the `Project` window. This action will open the file in an editor window. You may then make changes to the file by using the integrated editor. To save the modified file to disk, click on the save file button:

To compile and link the application, perform the following action:

Figure F.8

*Borland C++
Project Options
dialog box after
adding the
EzWindows include
directory*

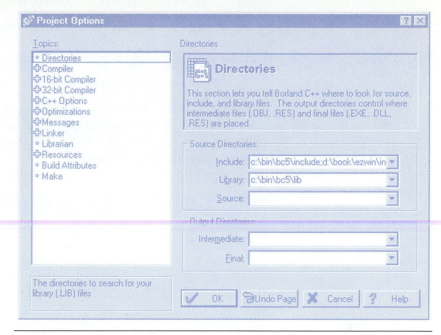

Project→Make all

This command directs the IDE to compile all the modules that have changed since the last compilation and then to link all the object files and required libraries into an executable unit. The executable is written to the file `simon.exe` because that was the name we specified when we set up the project file.

F.2.5   Saving a project file

To save a project file, make sure the `Project` window is the active window. The window can be made the active window by clicking in the `Project` window. The window with the colored title bar has the mouse focus. Once the project window has the focus, the project file can be saved by executing the following command:

File→Save

If any open editing windows have unsaved files, all active files can be saved by executing the following command:

File→Save All

F.2.6   Executing an EzWindows application

To execute an EzWindows application using Borland C++, you should switch to a console window. A console window can be created from the `Start` menu by executing the following command:

> Start→Programs→Command Prompt

At the command prompt in the console window, change directories to the location of the application executable. From the command prompt, execute the application by typing its name. Figure F.9 shows the console immediately before executing the Simon application.

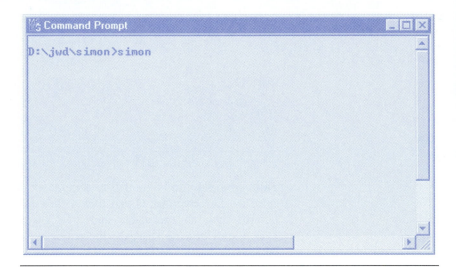

F.3   MICROSOFT VISUAL C++ IDE

The Microsoft Visual C++ IDE stores the information about how to build an application in a project file. Visual C++ project files have the extension `.dsp`. The main window for the Microsoft IDE is shown in Figure F.10. Across the top of the window are various commands such as `File`, `Edit`, and `View`. Clicking on a command item causes a menu to appear. For example, clicking on `Help` causes the submenu in Figure F.11 to appear.

Below the menu items are various buttons. This area is called the toolbar. The toolbar contains shortcuts to many of the frequently used commands. For example, the second button on the left executes the command to open a file. Another way to open a files is to execute the following command:

> File→Open

After you become familiar the basics of the Microsoft Visual C++ IDE, you can explore the use of the some of the advanced features of the environment. You

Figure F.10

*Microsoft Visual C++
IDE*

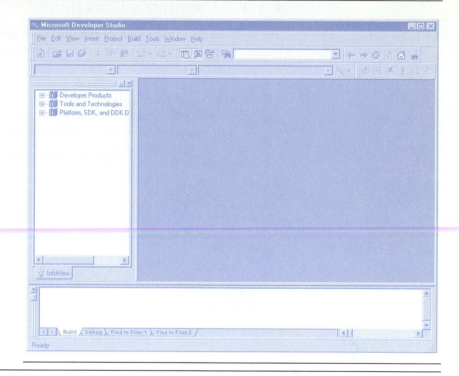

Figure F.11

*Microsoft Visual C++
help menu*

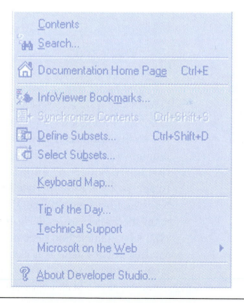

can obtain help about any of the features of the IDE by executing the Help
command.

F.3.1   Creating a workspace

The first step towards create a project file for an EzWindows application is to create a project. To do this, perform the following actions:

File→New

The dialog box shown in Figure F.12 should appear. This dialog box is for creating a new Visual C++ project.

Figure F.12

Microsoft Visual C++
New dialog box

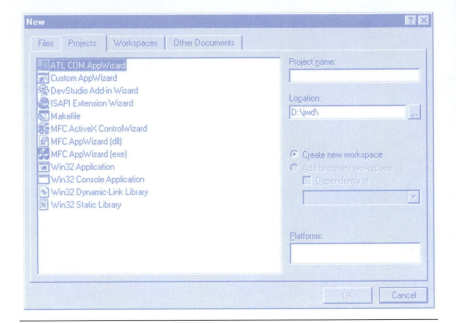

Within the New dialog box, the type of application you are building must be set. The correct choice depends on whether the application requires a console. Any EzWindows application that accepts keyboard input from the user via the iostream object cin or writes to the display via iostream object cout requires a console. For this type of EzWindows application, the correct selection is Win32 Console Application. If the application does not use the iostream library, the appropriate selection is Win32 Application.

The final step is to specify the location of the project. In our example, we want the project to reside in d:\jwd\simon, so we navigate to d:\jwd and type simon in the Project name: field. As we type in the name of the project, the Location: field is updated automatically to become d:\jwd\simon. To create the project, click on the OK button.

F.3.2   Adding source files to the project

After creating the project file, the IDE fills in the ClassView and FileView window that shows the name of the project and the classes and files that constitute the project (see Figure F.13). To view the files that constitute the project, click on the FileView tab. Initially, the project is empty, and we need to add the source files to the project.

Figure F.13

*Microsoft Visual C++
ClassView and
FileView window*

To bring up the dialog box for adding files to the project, we execute the command:

Project→Add to Project→Files

This step brings up the dialog box shown in Figure F.14. We can add the source files to the project by holding the control key and clicking on the source files. After all the files have been selected, click on the OK button.

We also must add the EzWindows library ezwin.lib to the project. Again, we execute the Project→Add to Project→Files command. Before navigating to the location of the EzWindows library files, we need to change the Files of type field (see Figure F.14) so that it displays library files. To do so, select the entry Library Files (.lib). Next navigate to the location of the EzWindows library and select ezwin.lib. To add the library to the project, click on the OK button.

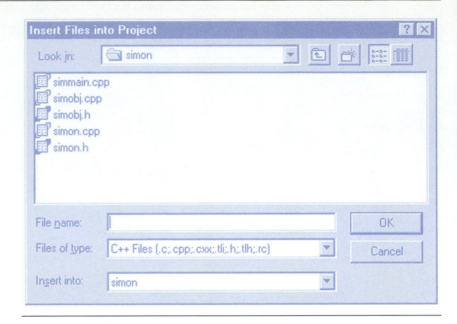

F.3.3   Setting project options

The last step in setting up a project file is to make sure that the project options are set correctly. We must make sure that the paths for finding the system include files and the EzWindows include files are correctly set. To bring up the dialog box for changing the project options, perform the following action:

> Tools→Options

This step brings up the dialog box shown in Figure F.15.

By default, the IDE sets the Directories entry to contain the path where the system include files are located. To successfully compile an EzWindows application, we must add the location of the EzWindows include files to the set of directories to search for include files. Additional directories are added by clicking on a blank field and typing the path. For our example, the location of the EzWindows include files is d:\book\ezwin\include. Figure F.16 shows the Options dialog box after the EzWindows include directory entry has been added.

It is also possible to add the path for the EzWindows include files by double-clicking on the blank entry. This step brings up an Open File dialog box. When all the entries have been made, the changes are put into effect by clicking on the OK button.

Figure F.15

*Microsoft Visual C++
Options dialog box*

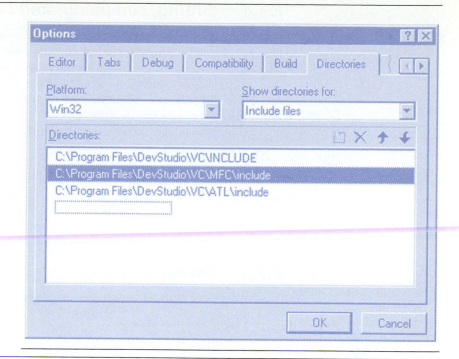

Figure F.16

*Microsoft Visual C++
Options dialog box
after adding the
EzWindows include
directory*

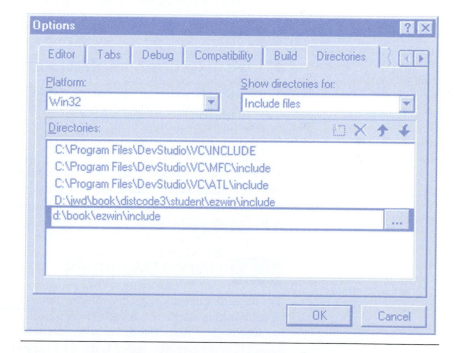

F.3.4   Editing, compiling, and linking

After the project file is set up, the IDE makes it easy to edit, compile, and link a program. To edit a program module, simply double-click on the file in the `ClassView/FileView` window to open the file in an editor window. You may then make changes to the file by using the integrated editor. To save the modified file to disk, click on the disk button on the toolbar. To save all modified files, click on the disks button on the toolbar.

To compile and link the application, execute the following command:

> `Build→Build simon.exe`

This command directs the IDE to compile all the modules that have changed since the last compilation and then to link all the object files and required libraries into an executable unit. The executable is written to the file `simon.exe` because that is the name of the project.

F.3.5   Saving a project file

To save a project file, perform the following action:

> `File→Save Workspace`

If any open editing windows have unsaved files, all active files can be saved by executing the following command:

> `File→Save All`

F.3.6   Executing an EzWindows application

To execute an EzWindows application using Microsoft C++, you should switch to a console window. A console window can be created from the `Start` menu by executing the following command:

> `Start→Programs→Command Prompt`

At the command prompt in the console window, change directories to the location of the application executable. From the command prompt, execute the application by typing its name. Figure F.17 shows the console immediately before executing the Simon application.

F.4   UNIX MAKEFILES

For the UNIX operating system, information about how to build an application is contained in a makefile. A *makefile* describes which application files depend on which other files. The `make` program uses this information to determine which files must be recompiled and linked to produce the application's executable unit. The basic idea is that the `make` program compiles only the files that have changed or depend on a file that has changed. This approach reduces the

Figure F.17

*Executing an
EzWindows
application in a
console window*

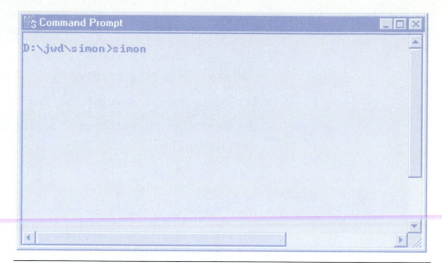

time to build the application during the software development phase of a project.

For example, suppose we have a header file `simon.h` that is included by the files `simon.cpp` and `simobj.cpp`, but is not included by the file `simmain.cpp`. If we modify `simon.h`, the files `simon.cpp` and `simobj.cpp` must be recompiled, but not the file `simmain.cpp`.

The make facility of UNIX is quite powerful. In this appendix, we give only a brief overview of its features so that you may adapt an existing makefile to your needs. For a more complete introduction to makefiles, check *Managing Projects with make, 2nd edition,* by Andrew Oram and Steve Talbott and published by O'Reilly and Associates.

Listing F.1 contains the makefile for the Simon program. It specifies how to build the executable `simon`. By convention, a makefile specification is typically stored in a file named `Makefile` or `makefile`. To run the make program and build an application, you just type the command `make` at a shell prompt. The `make` program looks in the current directory for a file named `Makefile` or `makefile` and processes it.

In a makefile, a comment begins with the # character. As with C++ programs, comments help readers understand the specification.

The following lines of the makefile tell the `make` program that C++ files have the extension `.cpp`.

```
.SUFFIXES:
.SUFFIXES: .cpp $(SUFFIXES)
```

Some C++ systems expect C++ files to have the extension `.cc`. If this is the case on your system, you should change the `.cpp` in the second line to `.cc`. All the C++ files provided with this textbook have the extension `.cpp`.

```
#
# The following lines specify that the C++ files will
# have a cpp extension. Do not change these lines!
#

.SUFFIXES:
.SUFFIXES: .cpp $(SUFFIXES)

# Set CC to be the name of the your C++ compiler.
# Set EZWINDIR to point to the directory that contains
# the EzWindows directories (include and lib).
#
CC       = g++
EZWINDIR = ../../EzWindows
X11DIR   = /X11.6


#
# The CPPFLAGS variable specifies where to find
# the X11 include files and the EzWindows include files.
# This line should not need to be changed.

CPPFLAGS=-I$(X11DIR)/include -I$(EZWINDIR)/include


#
# The LDFLAGS variable specifies where to find the library
# files. This line should not need to be changed.

LDFLAGS=-L$(X11DIR)/lib -lX11 -lsocket \
   -L$(EZWINDIR)/lib -lezwin -lXpm


#
# The OBJS variable tells the compiler which object files
# need to be created to build the application.
#

OBJS=simmain.o simobj.o simon.o


#
# The following rule specifies how to build the
# the program executable.
#

simon: $(OBJS)
   $(CC) -o simon $(OBJS) $(LDFLAGS)

simmain.o: simon.h

simon.o: simon.h

simobj.o: simobj.h
#
# The target below indicates to the make program how to
# process a file with a cpp extension.
# Normally this is necessary but the cpp extension
# isn t defined for make.

.cpp.o:
   $(CC) $(CPPFLAGS) -c $<


#
# As a standard practice, a clean target is included in
```

```
# most makefiles.
# Executing  make clean , deletes all object files and the
# executable.

clean:
    rm -f *.o simon
```

The following group of lines set variables that will be used throughout the makefile specification.

```
CC        = g++
EZWINDIR = ../../EzWindows
X11DIR    = /X11.6
```

For example, the first line sets the make variable CC to the command name of the C++ compiler to compile the source code. In this fragment, it is set to g++, the C++ compiler distributed by the Free Software Foundation. Appropriate use of make variables offers the same advantages as C++ constants. They make the specification easier to modify. For example, on Sun Microsystems computers running the Solaris operating system, the command to invoke Sun's C++ compiler is CC. This compiler can be used by setting the variable CC to CC.

The second line sets the make variable EZWINDIR to the path that contains the EzWindows include and library directories. The third line sets X11DIR to the location of the X11 software. These variables may need to be changed to reflect the location of the corresponding software on your particular system.

The line

```
CPPFLAGS=-I$(X11DIR)/include -I$(EZWINDIR)/include
```

sets a variable that tells the C++ compiler where to look for the X11 and EzWindows include files. This line should not need to be modified.

Similarly, the assignment

```
LDFLAGS=-L$(X11DIR)/lib -lX11 -lsocket \
    -L$(EZWINDIR)/lib -lezwin -lXpm
```

sets a variable that tells the UNIX loader, ld, where to find the necessary library files. Again, in most circumstances this line should not require modification.

The assignment

```
OBJS=simmain.o simobj.o simon.o
```

sets the variable OBJS to the names of the object files that make up the application. The Simon application has three application object modules: simmain.o, simobj.o, and simon.o. For a different application, this line would be modified to set OBJS to the object modules that make up that application.

The next set of lines is the heart of the makefile. These lines are *dependency rules* that specify how to build the application. A dependency rule has the following general form:

```
Dependency line
    command line
```

A dependency line specifies the files a target depends on. A target depends on a file if the file is used in some way by the target. One common kind of dependency is when a source file includes a header file. The source file depends on the header file. Similarly, an executable unit depends on an object file if the object file is needed to build the executable unit.

The most commonly used form of dependency line is

```
target: dependents
```

The target is the name and extension of the file to be built. A target must begin a line in the makefile. The target name cannot be preceded with spaces or tabs. The dependents are the file (or files) whose modification date and time `make` checks to see whether it is newer than target. Each dependent file must be preceded by a space.

The command line specifies how to build the target. The command must be indented by at least one space or tab; otherwise, it will be interpreted as a target. So, for example, the lines

```
simon: $(OBJS)
    $(CC) -o simon $(OBJS) $(LDFLAGS)
```

from the Simon makefile specify that the target `simon` depends on `OBJS`, which has the value `simmain.o`, `simobj.o`, and `simon.o`. If any of these object files is newer than the target `simon`, make executes the command line. The command line produces a new `simon`, which is newer than the object files. If the object files are older than `simon`, then `simon` is up-to-date and no action is necessary.

The `make` program handles transitive dependencies. That is, if a dependent appears elsewhere in the makefile as a target, `make` updates or creates that target before using the dependent in the original target. For example, the line

```
simmain.o: simon.h
```

specifies that `simmain.o` depends on the header file `simon.h`. So, if we edit `simon.h` and save the changes, its time and date stamp will be later than `simmain.o`. If we issue a `make` command to build `simon`, make sees that `simon` depends on `simmain.o`, which in turn depends on `simon.h`. Since `simon.h` is newer than `simmain.o`, make first attempts to build `simmain.o`. It may appear that the makefile does not have a command line that specifies how to build `simmain.o`. However, it does. The lines

```
.cpp.o:
    $(CC) $(CPPFLAGS) -c $<
```

are an *implicit dependency rule*. An implicit dependency rule specifies that one type of file is constructed from another type of file and describes how to perform the construction. The above lines specify that `.o` files are constructed from `.cpp` files and that the `.o` files are constructed by running the C++ compiler. Thus `make` knows to compile `simmain.cpp` to build `simmain.o`. Similarly, it builds `simon.o` and `simobj.o` by compiling `simon.cpp` and `simobj.cpp`, respectively. After all the necessary object files have been built, their time and date stamps will be later than `simon`, so the command to build `simon` is executed.

The first target in a makefile is special. If the command `make` with no arguments is entered at a shell prompt, `make` attempts to build the target specified in the first dependency rule. Wcan also specify a particular target to build. The command

```
make simmain.o
```

causes `simmain.o` and all its dependents to be built. This use of `make` is handy for forcing the compilation of a single module.

The `make` program has many options. One useful option is `-n`. The command

```
make -n
```

prints the `make` commands, but does not perform them. This option is useful for debugging a makefile. The command

```
make -B
```

builds all targets regardless of time and date stamps. This option is useful for forcing `make` to rebuild everything from scratch. The complete list of options can be viewed by typing the following command at a shell prompt:

```
man make
```

F.4.1   Executing an EzWindows application

To execute an EzWindows application under UNIX with the X11 window system, you should create a terminal window (`xterm`) running a shell. Creating a terminal shell depends on the window manager you are using. For most window managers, moving the mouse to a blank area of the screen and right-clicking brings up a menu that allows an `xterm` to be started. Figure F.18 shows a typical `xterm` window. From the shell prompt, execute the EzWindows application by typing its name.

Figure F.18

*An X11 xterm on
UNIX*

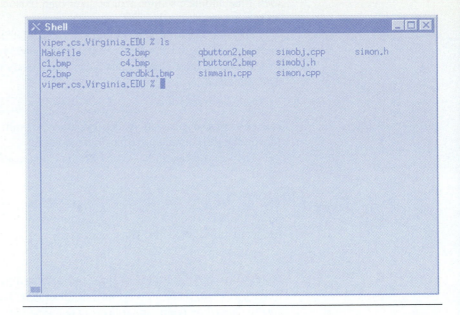

Index